BUILT FROM SCRATCH

The Energy Companies of Tenneco

A Memoir by Some Who Were There

BUILT FROM SCRATCH
The Energy Companies of Tenneco

A Memoir by Some Who Were There

Joe B. Foster
Executive Vice President, Tenneco Inc.

Clifford W. Rackley
Senior Vice President & Group Executive, Tenneco Inc.

Bob Thomas
Chairman & CEO, Tenneco Gas

Harry J. Briscoe
Vice President Exploration, Tenneco Oil Exploration & Production

Gary Cheatham
Vice President, Tennessee Gas Pipeline

Dick Hines
Pipeline & Compressor Superintendent, Tennessee Gas Pipeline

Larry Augsburger
Vice President Administration,
Tenneco Oil Exploration & Production

STORYARTSMEDIA

BUILT FROM SCRATCH
The Energy Companies of Tenneco
Copyright © 2013 Tenneco Energy History Group LLC
All rights reserved.

Published by Story Arts Media
PO Box 1230, Boulder, CO 80306
www.storyartsmedia.com

ISBN: 978-0-9889754-6-0 (hardcover)
ISBN: 978-0-9889754-7-7 (softcover)
Library of Congress Control Number: 2013950505
www.tennecohistorybook.com

Cover and Interior Design by Joseph Daniel

NOTE ON PHOTOGRAPHS: Sadly, much of Tenneco's photographic record has been accidently lost or destroyed since the company was sold in 1988. Hence, many of the images reproduced in this book have been re-scanned from photos printed in Tenneco company publications and, as a result, are of lesser quality than desired. However, the authors believe these images are still of great historical significance and have opted for their use.

Excerpts from material created by The History Factory
for Tenneco's 50th Anniversary used with permission.

Printed in the United States

Culture eats Strategy for breakfast.
~ Peter Drucker

Look back over the past, with its changing empires that rose and fell,
and you can foresee the future, too.
~ Marcus Aurelius

"An executive cannot gradually dismiss details., Business is made up
of details ….. Success is the sum of detail."
~ Harvey Firestone

Big companies are like marching bands. Even if half the band is playing
random notes, it still sounds kind of like music. The concealment
of failure is built into them.
~ Doug Coupland

Do not kill the goose that lays the golden egg.
~ English Proverb

COMMONLY USED TERMS

Company Names Used – The three "energy" companies of Tenneco were most commonly known as Tennessee Gas Transmission Company (TGT), Tenneco Oil Exploration and Production Company (TOE&P), and Tenneco Oil Processing and Marketing Company (TOP&M). Through the 53-year history of the combined companies, a variety of official names existed for the companies and their own affiliates and subsidiaries. For purposes of simplicity, the names and acronyms used throughout the book may or may not have been the "official" ones for that exact point in time. "Tenneco", "TGT", "TGP", "Tenneco Oil", "E&P" and "P&M" will appear regularly throughout the book, referring in general to the respective pipeline, exploration and production, or refining and marketing entity being discussed. Tenneco Inc. was the corporate parent company holding most of the businesses discussed here at the times of their respective sales.

Job Titles – In the TGT and P&M sections of the book, titles attributed to sidebar quotes or stories will generally be the titles of the referred at the times being discussed. In the E&P section of the book, titles will most generally be the title held at the time of the sale in 1988, unless otherwise noted.

GLOSSARY

Throughout the book a variety of common abbreviations used in the energy industry, and acronyms used within Tenneco will be utilized.

Oil & Gas Values
MCF, MMCF, BCF, TCF - Thousand, million, billion, trillion cubic feet (of gas)
MCFGD - Thousand cubic feet of gas per day
MBO, MMBO, BBO - Thousand, million, billion barrels (of oil)
BOPD - Barrels of oil per day
BOE - Equivalent Barrels of oil (converting gas to oil equivalent)
NEB - Net equivalent barrels
$$MM - Millions of dollars
$$B - Billions of dollars

Companies
TGT - Tennessee Gas Transmission Co.
TGP - Tennessee Gas Pipeline Co.
NGT - Northeastern Gas Transmission
Viking - Viking Gas Transmission
MGT - Midwestern Gas Transmission
ETNG - East Tennessee Natural Gas
CIG - Channel Industries Gas
E&P, or TOE&P - Tenneco Oil Exploration & Production Co.
P&M, or TOP&M -Tenneco Oil Processing & Marketing Co.
TOC - Tenneco Oil Co.
TPC - Tennessee Production Co.
TGO - Tennessee Gas and Oil
Tenn Inc, or Tenneco Inc.

E&P Operating Divisions
PCD - Pacific Coast Division
MCD - Mid Continent Division
RMD, (ERMD, WRMD) - Rocky Mountain Division (Eastern, Western)
GCD, (TGD) - Gulf Coast Division (Texas Gulf Coast Division)
SWD - Southwestern Division
LOD - Lafayette Offshore Division
WGD - Western Gulf Division
CGD - Central Gulf Division

EGD - Eastern Gulf Division
INT - International Division
SAD - South America Division

TGP Divisions
A – Houston
B - Monroe, Lafayette, LA
C - Middleton, TN
D - Winchester, KY
E - Hamburg, NY
F - Agawam, MA
G- Lafayette, LA

E&P Titles
Pres, EVP, SVP, VP - President, Executive Vice President, Senior Vice President, Vice President
DGM or GM - Division General Manager
Prod Mgr or PM - Division Production Manager
Expl Mgr or EM - Division Exploration Manager

Offshore Geography (Blocks)
GOM - Gulf of Mexico
CS - Chandeleur
EC - East Cameron
GC - Green Canyon
HI - High Island
MI - Mustang Island
MO - Mobile Bay
MP - Main Pass
SMI - South Marsh Island
SS - Ship Shoal
V - Vermilion
WC - West Cameron

Other
LDC - Local Distribution Company
KCL - Kern County Land Company
HOM or HO&M - Houston Oil & Minerals
SJB - San Juan Basin
FPC - Federal Power Commission
FERC - Federal Energy Regulatory Commission

TABLE OF CONTENTS

FOREWORD

I first became of aware of Tenneco in 1966, when I entered Rice University as a 17-year old freshman. The Tenneco Building, which had opened only three years earlier, dominated the north end of the downtown skyline, and it quickly became my favorite building. I learned that Tenneco had cut its teeth during World War II building a pipeline system to supply much needed natural gas to factories vital to the war effort. After the war, Tenneco had achieved national prominence as one of the major companies whose trunk lines first connected the vast supplies of natural gas in the southwestern United States to the vast potential demand in the urban-industrial centers of the northeast. At the time I arrived in Houston, the company was still primarily a natural gas pipeline company.

I graduated from Rice in 1970 and left the region for more than a decade. When I returned in the early 1980s, the Tenneco Building had almost vanished from the Houston skyline, lost among the taller new skyscrapers that had shot up all over Houston during the go-go years of high oil prices in the 1970s. At the same time, Tenneco's pipeline system also had become somewhat obscured by an array of other businesses that had grown within the company. Some, such as oil and gas exploration, production, and processing had close ties to the pipeline business; others shared little with the original business of the company—except for the capital generated by the pipelines that had helped acquire, build, and sustain them.

The company had developed into a prototype of the conglomerate, a thoroughly diversified concern held together by financial and management ties instead of historical and technical ones. Conglomeration had become the norm for large oil and gas companies in the 1970s and early 1980s, and Tenneco had become one of the most highly diversified concerns in the industry.

For a time after I joined the faculty at the University of Houston, I talked with Tenneco officials about writing a history about the process by which their pipeline company had evolved into a conglomerate. But changes within the company in the early 1990s ended such plans, and in subsequent years the company sold off most of its holdings. It then gradually faded into the mist of history, where it joined many other companies that did not survive the chaotic conditions of the boom and bust in oil and gas of the 1970s and 1980s. Several of my graduate students worked on aspects of Tenneco's history, and one of them—David Raley—completed a partial history of the company in 2011. "Built from Scratch" draws on the academic work of David and other historians who have written about the natural gas industry.

The heart of the book, however, is personal, not academic. Former Tenneco employees provide most of the memories used to reconstruct the rise and fall of Tenneco. The insights of those who built the company literally from the ground up infuse the narrative with a personal dimension often slighted in more academic works, including my own. The book was put together by men who took great pride in their years at Tenneco; they generally came away from the experience with memories of important events and people in a company that was a good place to work. It treated its workers well and remained a good corporate citizen while also making major contributions to the development of the natural gas and oil industries. At its best, this book puts the reader's thumb on the pulse of Tenneco as it faces the challenges of regulation and competition in this vital sector of the American economy.

As I grow older, I become increasingly dissatisfied with the detached tone and general lack of human perspectives in corporate histories. "Built from Scratch" is a welcome change. Yet a certain sadness lies just beneath the surface of the narrative. The writers and those they interviewed know only too well how the story ends: a once proud energy company built around the sturdy backbone of its pipeline system proved unable to adjust to the economic turmoil of the late 20th century. Rising tensions between its energy businesses and its diversified businesses in other unrelated industries marked the end of the road for Tenneco.

Despite the passing of the company several decades ago, my brain still tells my mouth to say "the Tenneco Building" when I refer to the company's former headquarters. On occasion I still refer to Tenneco as "the best Houston-based company;" if this comment is made in one on my undergraduate classes, I then have to stop and identify the company to my students, most of whom were born after the company had ceased to exist.

My work with the former company employees who compiled this book reminded me why I still hold Tenneco in such high esteem. You have in your hands the work of a group of men whose life's blood helped build a successful company. These men came away from their careers both proud and loyal—so much so that they devoted three or four years of their retirements working together as a team (as had been the norm in Tenneco) to produce a volume of personal recollections about the evolution of the company. In their hearts, they know that Tenneco was too good to be forgotten. They are right. Enjoy the book. Tenneco deserves to be remembered.

Joe Pratt
Cullen Professor of History and Business
University of Houston
August 2013

INTRODUCTION

ACKNOWLEDGEMENTS

Joe Foster, the retired Senior Executive for all of the Tenneco Energy companies when Tenneco Oil was sold in 1988, was the primary coordinator of the project. Dick Hines and Gary Cheatham, long-time pipeline employees, who had initiated a project to write the Tenneco story as early as 2003, were the primary contributors to the story of the early years of Tennessee Gas Transmission Co. Bob Thomas, retired President of Tennessee Gas, wrote the TGT history for the time period from 1970 forward through the eventual sale of TGT in 1996. Foster asked Harry Briscoe to function as the primary author and compiler of the stories of Tenneco Oil E&P. Harry enlisted the help of Larry Augsburger, former Vice President of Administration. Foster put out a request to Cliff Rackley, retired President of Tenneco Oil P&M, who responded quickly and ably to produce the section on Processing and Marketing. Ralph Cunningham, who succeeded Cliff as President of TOP&M, provided additional material.

Joseph Daniel, Founder of Story Arts Media, undertook the considerable challenge of coordinating the work of this diverse group, serving as publisher, editor and designer to move the project to completion. Foster provided memories, lots of data, an office and a helpful executive assistant named Shirley Vaughn whose assistance was invaluable. Three other ladies, Jeanette Dansereau, Betty Donahoe, and Johanna Gonzalez provided invaluable assistance to the TGT authors in transcribing of taped interviews and typing the manuscripts, respectively. In typical "Tenneco Fashion", this project has truly been a "team" effort.

In 2004 David Raley, a Ph.D. candidate in business history at the University of Houston, was seeking a topic to use as the basis of his dissertation. Through Joe Foster, Raley worked with Hines and Cheatham and used much of the work they had produced. Raley's work was very helpful in the production of this book and his permission to use it is gratefully acknowledged.

A primary resource for the book came from a number of personal archives. Mr. Foster's suite in Houston contains a spare office that is filled with company newsletters,

On Halloween Day in 1944, H. B. McDowell turned the valve to allow natural gas to flow from the Aqua Dulce field in South Texas into a brand new pipeline, headed for markets in the Mid-Atlantic States. The building of the original pipeline by Tenneco Gas and Transmission Company was a remarkable feat of vision, persistence, engineering, construction, management, and public relations – something that could not be duplicated today. Tennessee Gas was literally built from nothing but an idea, built "from scratch" in the terminology of the day.

In fact though, the laying of that first long pipeline just set the stage for what would become one of the most amazing stories of business success in the second-half of the twentieth century. The predecessor of Tenneco Oil Company evolved quickly in the late 1940s as a strategy within Tennessee Gas, and within just a few more years, Tenneco Oil itself would grow to include separate companies in both the "E&P" (exploration and production) and "P&M" (processing and marketing) segments of the energy industry. Later, the businesses would grow to become "Tenneco Inc", a major conglomerate with interests in many businesses well beyond the foundations in energy.

This book tells the story of the "Energy" companies of Tenneco – Tennessee Gas Transmission, Tenneco Oil Exploration & Production, and Tenneco Oil Processing & Marketing, as they were known at the ends of their days. It is a remarkable story of building successful businesses from "the ground up". The evolution of "Tenneco Energy" occurred during two general segments of time. The first, from 1943 through roughly the mid-1960s, was one of focus on ventures entirely within the energy realm. From the mid-1960s, until their eventual demise on the auction blocks, the three "energy siblings" continued to grow and evolve, but they operated as subsidiaries under the umbrella of a large and diverse corporate parent. The story of the second segment of time is one of coexistence, and to some degree of competition, with disparate manufacturing businesses that had themselves become parts of the corporate family.

Most of the employees of the "energy companies" of Tenneco spent the majority of their careers during that second segment of time. These dedicated employees were intent on building the best "energy outfit" out there, and they did just that. Regardless of the ultimate analysis of Tenneco, Inc., the story of the Energy Companies of Tenneco is a story of success, a story built from the hard work of dedicated employees. The intent of this book is to describe and celebrate the work of the employees of "Tenneco Energy".

During the 50-plus years covered by the saga you are about to read, three related, but distinct and separate, companies grew to positions of prominence within their own sectors of the energy world. As a result, the story, which starts simply enough, evolves into three separate tales. The book is arranged to accommodate – and to celebrate – the three independent organizations, but also to note the significant partnerships and synergies that occurred amongst the three, as sister companies. The three separate sections of the book will tell the stories of those three organizations. This book was composed "by committee". Seven principal author-editors have combined to produce what you will be reading ahead. As such, you will find some difference in narrative style, and to a degree, in content. The authors would like to think those differences reflect the personalities of the entities themselves. Typically, a single author, on completion of a major project like this, might proclaim pride in "my" book. In a case such as this, we rather might claim the same for "our" book. This is a book designed to recognize the many accomplishments of the employees who worked in these Tenneco companies. The "committee" (photo below), would prefer to think of this as "their" book, as it was truly the employees who 'wrote the story'.

A comment of "regret"—The compilation of the stories for this book involved accessing many resources, some in the form of a printed records, and many as personal contributions and remembrances, either our own, or as submittals from others. We appreciate greatly the many stories we received from former employees. Despite that, it is painfully evident that the book is in many ways incomplete. There are a number of events that deserved inclusion or more space than they received. There are a great many more Tenneco stories out there. There are things we know to have happened for which we just did not have information. Too much time has passed; too many stories have been lost. We apologize for these shortcomings — there are some holes.

Joe B. Foster

magazines, memos, internal reports, correspondence, speeches, scrapbooks and notepads; probably most of the printed material that Tenneco ever produced. In their early work, Dick Hines and Gary Cheatham had assembled a considerable similar resource of printed materials and conducted a series of personal interviews with key players in the history of Tenneco Energy. The various members of the writing group added their own stacks, with many pieces dating well back into the 1940s. As the project developed, numerous other past executives and employees from the companies sent in materials from their own files, and from their own memories. We are grateful for those submittals.

In particular, the "library" contains a historical record in the form of many of the items produced by the outstanding internal communications staffs that worked at the three companies through the years. Starting with The Line, TGT's original monthly magazine (Premier Issue from 1946 shown above), and then progressing through the entire gamut of name changes, the Prologs, E&P Updates, Timelines, Tenneco Magazine, Tenneco Topics, the Tenneco Inc. Annual Reports, the recruiting and advertising materials, the contributions from the internal company press, all were a critical resource of exceptional quality and value.

The photographs included in the book have come from several sources, including the personal collections of the contributors, and significantly, from the many publications mentioned above, produced by Buddy Nixon, long-time Tenneco corporate photographer. All sources are gratefully acknowledged.

Photo by: Joseph Daniel

The Built From Scratch *author team, left to right, titles at time of the sale of respective entities. Harry Briscoe, Vice President Exploration, Tenneco Oil E&P; Cliff Rackley, Senior Vice President and Group Executive, Tenneco Inc.; Bob Thomas, Chairman and CEO, Tenneco Gas; Larry Augsburger, Vice President Administration, Tenneco Oil E&P; Gary Cheatham, Vice President, Tennessee Gas Pipeline; Dick Hines, Pipeline & Compressor Superintendent, Tennessee Gas Pipeline; Joe B. Foster, Executive Vice President, Tenneco Inc.*

buried a million years
...now serving the nation

A new titan is at your beck and call!

Natural gas, the giant imprisoned in the earth until
the pipeline unleashed its mighty power.

Now a billion and a half cubic feet of the world's finest
fuel flow daily through the 2200-mile pipeline
of Tennessee Gas. The nation's longest, this great artery
brings natural gas from the Southwest where most
of it is to the fuel-hungry East where it's needed most.

And does it by the simplest, most direct means of transportation
known . . . delivers it dependably, economically to homes
and industry round the calendar and clock . . . by pipeline.

HOME HEATING

COOKING

HEATING WATER

DRYING CLOTHES

TENNESSEE GAS
TRANSMISSION COMPANY
HOUSTON, TEXAS

AMERICA'S LEADING TRANSPORTER OF NATURAL GAS

I

TENNESSEE GAS
TRANSMISSION COMPANY

1943 ~ 1996

By Gary Cheatham & Bob Thomas

Palls of black coal smoke were common in most American cities during the 1930s.

TGT IN THE BEGINNING

The Promoters

The gas pipeline company which grew into a multinational conglomerate had its origins in the 1930s as a modest project to supply natural gas to Nashville, Tennessee. While longtime Tennessee Gas CEO and president Gardiner Symonds was responsible for the creation and subsequent prodigious growth of the Tenneco conglomerate, the original concept for the business had its roots more than a decade earlier. The story of that preliminary decade is an interesting complex of persistence in the face of continual challenge and seemingly never-ending bad luck. An entrepreneur and salesman named Wade Thompson, along with a small group of promoters and investors founded what eventually became Tenneco before World War II. Thompson had a vision for a gas pipeline company which would supply the needs of Nashville and alleviate the choking pollution created by the burning of coal. Thompson's vision later evolved into an effort to bring gas from Louisiana to war industries in Tennessee during the opening days of the Second World War. Eventually, the promoters and their gas suppliers proposed building a pipeline stretching from the gas fields of south Texas to the Appalachian region. This vision, under new ownership, became a reality during the height of World War II.

Wade Thompson was a natural promoter and salesman. Born in eastern Kentucky in 1895, his upbringing and early life were colorful. He left school at 12, married at 16, sold merchandise from horseback, taught school, joined the army, operated a store, and made a fortune building houses for mill workers. At one point he was worth an estimated $200,000 before the Stock Market Crash of 1929 and the Great Depression wiped out his fortune. Hoping for a new start, Thompson and his family moved to Nashville in 1930. Fresh from the coal and oil fields of eastern Kentucky, Thompson was already familiar with a little used by-product of oil drilling and coal mining known as natural gas. He envisioned piping natural gas from Kentucky or eastern Tennessee to replace the coal upon which Nashville was dependent. He believed clean-burning natural gas would improve the city and provide him a chance to re-coup his fortunes.

Only a handful of cities had natural gas service in the 1930s. It was more common in the 1920s and 1930s to flare or vent natural gas than to pipe it to consumers. In addition to these concerns, Thompson had no experience in gas and no money to construct a pipeline. Thompson's reputation as a smooth-talker and a bad risk preceded him; he was known in some circles as "Fly-by-Night Thompson". His gas project seemed doomed before it ever began.

Natural Gas Corporation of Tennessee

In 1933, a wildcat oil prospector discovered natural gas in Macon County, Tennessee, some sixty-five miles from Nashville. The wildcatter, Charlie West, came to Nashville looking for financial backing, and coincidentally, approached Glendon B. Fisher, Wade Thompson's employer. Fisher and a partner formed the Natural Gas Syndicate of Tennessee and hoped to bring this gas to Nashville. They hired Wade Thompson to sell stock in the new company. Thompson's raised $20,000, but through bad luck and the inexperience of those involved, the syndicate soon ran short of funds. After buying the Macon County well, the company drilled several expensive dry holes in the area. Discouraged, the investors sold out to Thompson and Thomas Shriver, a Nashville attorney. Thompson and Shriver then conceived a pipeline stretching from the proven gas fields of northern Louisiana to Tennessee, a distance of several hundred miles. Recent improvements in metallurgy and welding during the 1920s had made long-distance pipelines possible. A recently-completed Chicago pipeline extended 980 miles from the mid-continent region to Chicago. New pipelines also served Houston, Denver, Omaha, Kansas City, St. Louis, and Atlanta, but few were planned for the 1930s. Even though the project was technically feasible, it faced major obstacles, not the least of which was financing. Thompson's credit was bad, but he refused to give up, sank all the funds he had into the venture, and spent the next several years trying to interest new investors in his company.

In 1938 Shriver introduced Thompson to John Edgerton, a wealthy retired president of the National Association of Manufacturers. Thompson and Shriver convinced Edgerton that the pipeline idea was sound, and dependent

Thompson found few willing to listen to his scheme as he supported his family by selling cemetery lots. Palls of black smoke were common in most American towns and cities during the 1930s; many people even regarded smoke as a symbol of progress or as an inevitability of urban life. Coal powered the electrical plants, most locomotives and employed tens of thousands of miners across the country. While many municipalities used manufactured or "town" gas for lighting or cooking, even this was sometimes made from coal.

only on sufficient financing. Edgerton agreed to become president of the company, which had been renamed Natural Gas Corporation of Tennessee in 1936. Edgerton used his contacts and business reputation to quickly get pledges for $100,000 from his friends. One of the crucial backers Edgerton interested in the pipeline was Victor Johnson, Sr., the founder of Mantle Lamp (now Aladdin Industries).

Johnson was by far the most influential person Thompson and his associates had attracted to their shoestring operation. Johnson invested a modest $5,000, probably on the strength of Edgerton's reputation and their friendship. In 1938, Edgerton, now President, made plans to visit Louisiana to arrange contracts with gas producers, but during a conversation with Thompson about the upcoming trip, Edgerton had a massive heart attack and died on the spot. Edgerton's death left Thompson and Shriver in a difficult position. None of the $100,000 pledged by Edgerton's friends was forthcoming, and other investors began to back out. Johnson also wanted out, but Thompson used all his skill to prevent him from getting away. Thompson followed Johnson around the country by bus, talking to him at every opportunity and, surprisingly enough, extracting further funding from him. Even with Johnson's support, Natural Gas Corporation of Tennessee was a company in name only. While Thompson and Shriver had signed up potential customers along the proposed pipeline route from Louisiana to Nashville (with extensions to Knoxville and Chattanooga), the company had no gas reserves, no operations, no cash flow, no employees, and no pipeline. Johnson's confidence in Thompson was limited, and he refused to allow his name to be used to promote the company. Thompson needed someone with a solid reputation to obtain the financing to build the pipeline.

Promoting Tennessee Gas

One of the key personalities attracted to the company was Curtis Dall, a former son-in-law of President Franklin D. Roosevelt. Although his marriage to Anna Roosevelt had ended in 1935, Dall's association with FDR lent him a certain respect and provided important contacts in both business and government. Dall, a former stockbroker with Lehman Brothers, had extensive connections in New York and Washington, D.C. Dall became interested in Thompson's company by chance "on a trip to Nashville, Tennessee, early in 1940, …. I ran into a project which greatly interested me." Dall's connections made him attractive, and Thompson and his associates were eager to bring him aboard. Dall's connections in Washington and his association with the Roosevelt family made him a natural promoter for Natural Gas Corporation of Tennessee. He agreed to become the new president of the company, although he worked almost exclusively as a promoter rather than an executive. His duties initially involved interesting new investors in the pipeline, but later his connections would make him company point man in Washington to deal with the Federal Power Commission (FPC). He traveled throughout Tennessee, making speeches to potential investors and attracting considerable attention from the press. Dall's efforts brought in a further $100,000 in stock sales.

Tennessee Gas and Transmission Company

In early 1940, Victor Johnson suggested forming a new company, Tennessee Gas and Transmission Company (TGT) to replace the earlier Natural Gas Corporation of Tennessee. The new company was formed specifically to promote and build a Louisiana-to-Tennessee pipeline. Curtis Dall continued as president, Wade Thompson, Shriver, and several others made up the board of directors. The corporate charter also provided for the issuance of preferred and common stock to raise capital. A few days after the incorporation, the board of directors voted to buy out Natural Gas Corporation of Tennessee for $125,000, with most of the money going to satisfy creditors. The TGT board also authorized the purchase of Victor Johnson's Eastern Tennessee Oil and Gas Co., which owned an inactive franchise to provide gas to Knoxville and several commercial gas wells in Kentucky and Tennessee. The terms were $180,000 in cash and $200,000 in securities. The board also voted an additional 30,000 shares of common Tennessee Gas stock to Johnson for his service and contributions to the company. This amounted to two-thirds of all outstanding Tennessee Gas common stock.

Tennessee Gas and the Federal Power Commission

Tennessee Gas's first case before the regulators was on the state level. Southern Natural Gas had recently applied for a certificate to serve the Chattanooga market, which Tennessee Gas saw as a vital part of its future service area. The company's attorneys (led by Shriver) intervened in the case before the Tennessee Railroad and Public Utilities Commission, fearing that the loss of the Chattanooga market would make the new company unattractive to investors. Two days after Tennessee Gas was formed, the commission convened a hearing, and after some debate, the commission granted Tennessee Gas's request for a thirty day continuance.

The proposed Louisiana-to-Tennessee pipeline would require approval from the Federal Power Commission since it would cross several State boundaries. Dall filed an application with the FPC to build a pipeline from Louisiana to Nashville, with extensions to Knoxville and Chattanooga. With Dall's action, the regulatory process shifted from Tennessee to Washington. Southern Natural Gas stridently opposed Tennessee Gas's plans to bring gas into "its" market of Chattanooga at FPC hearings in Washington. Southern questioned the competence and integrity of Wade Thompson, labeling him a "fly-by-night" promoter. In his defense, Thompson produced several mayors

One of the earliest pipeline investors was Victor Johnson, Sr.

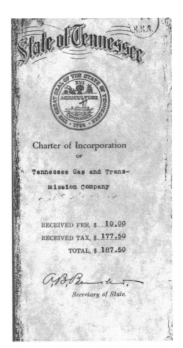

The original charter of the Tennessee Gas and Transmission Company, which was founded on April 1, 1940 by a group of speculators led by Kentucky native Wade Thompson.

Curtis Dall (top right) with father-in-law, President Franklin D. Roosevelt (lower left).

and other officials from towns in Alabama and Tennessee who testified about his long-term efforts to bring natural gas into the upper South. While attorneys for Southern Natural Gas and Tennessee Gas argued before the FPC in Washington, Curtis Dall was making further efforts to secure gas supplies and financing for Tennessee Gas. By August 1940, cost estimates for the pipeline had ballooned from $12 million to $20 million. Dall approached Phillips Petroleum about purchasing natural gas, and discovered that Phillips was also interested in helping obtain some or all of the $20 million needed to build the pipeline. On August 15, 1940, Phillips agreed to finance the pipeline, in return for thirty percent of Tennessee Gas's common stock. The board of directors quickly authorized this arrangement, and even congratulated Dall on a job well done.

Dall spent much of the rest of 1940 trying to secure gas reserves to satisfy the FPC requirement of a 20-year supply. Throughout the early process, the FPC was remarkably patient with Tennessee Gas and allowed a postponement to provide TGT additional time to secure sufficient gas reserves, pushing the hearings into early 1941. Contracts with Union Sulfur Company and Continental Oil were signed, covering 70% of TGT's requirements. Dall was negotiating with Stanolind for 25%, and promised the board that the final five percent would come from individuals and smaller companies. While Tennessee Gas's gas supplies were seemingly secure, its efforts to obtain financing were in serious jeopardy. The pending contract with Phillips fell through and Tennessee Gas's position before the FPC became untenable. TGT had hired an engineering firm to draw up plans for the pipeline and seemed to have secured its gas supply, but without financing the FPC was certain to deny a certificate to Tennessee Gas. Then, following more delays, the FPC did something rather remarkable. In July 1941, it dismissed Tennessee Gas's application, not due to lack of financing, but because it had no jurisdiction over the pipeline.

Tennessee Gas had filed its application for a certificate under section 7(c) of the Natural Gas Act, which only gave the FPC regulatory authority over interstate transportation of natural gas into existing markets. In effect, the FPC stated that since Tennessee Gas was seeking to introduce gas into new markets, the FPC could not grant a certificate. As originally written, the Natural Gas Act of 1938 contained this curious provision to protect the politically powerful coal and railroad industries from competition with natural gas.

If

Dall could secure both gas and financing from Phillips, two of Tennessee Gas's major problems would be solved, given that the FPC required financing, engineering plans, and a 20-year gas supply before any certificate would be granted.

The FPC was empowered to grant certificates in markets with existing natural gas service, but could not intervene in untapped markets, effectively barring natural gas from many areas of the country, especially in states with no major natural gas reserves.

Back to the Drawing Board

The loss of the Phillips deal and the dismissal of the case before the FPC were major setbacks for Tennessee Gas, but the directors of Tennessee Gas seemed to have an unlimited supply of optimism. Dall went back to the state public utility commission in Tennessee and filed new requests to service various areas of the state. Tennessee Gas was supported in its new application by a number of Tennessee industries, including steel and chemical companies and several public utilities. Testimony showed that the upper South faced an electricity shortage due to increased demand from defense-related industries. The two largest aluminum plants in the nation were located in the area Tennessee Gas intended to serve with its pipeline, and a new plant was planned for Muscle Shoals, Alabama, in the northwestern corner of the state. Large supplies of natural gas would find ready markets in Tennessee and the surrounding region.

By September 1941, the state commission had given Tennessee Gas tentative approval to serve twenty-six counties, contingent on securing the necessary financing within 120 days. A further provision stipulated that Tennessee Gas could not enter markets already served by manufactured gas interests, unless those proved inadequate to meet demand. Before financing could be arranged, yet another crisis emerged, this one making international headlines! On December 7, 1941, the Japanese attacked Pearl Harbor, bringing the United States into World War II. Within days, the government halted all major construction projects not yet commenced. Once again it seemed as if Tennessee Gas's efforts would fail. Refusing to give up, Thompson and Dall formulated a new strategy. Dall decided to petition the government to declare Tennessee Gas's proposed pipeline "a national defense project," since some of its customers would be the large aluminum smelters at Alcoa and Muscle Shoals. Aluminum was a critical war materiel. Ideally, if this were approved, the Reconstruction Finance Corporation (RFC) or some other agency would arrange the financing of the pipeline and the War Production Board (WPB) would provide the steel priorities to build the pipeline. In February 1942, Tennessee Gas won a major victory when Congress amended the Natural Gas Act, stripping the language that referred to "markets." The revised law now required all interstate pipelines to obtain a certificate of public convenience and necessity, regardless of market. In effect, the newly revised Natural Gas Act opened all markets to natural gas. New pipelines would be subject to regulatory oversight by the FPC. With this good news, Curtis Dall returned to Washington and filed a new application with the FPC two days after the amendment became law.

Dall's new application reflected Tennessee Gas's latest strategy in having the pipeline declared "a national defense project." The new plan differed significantly from TGT's original proposal, which had specified a Louisiana-to-Nashville route. The newly proposed pipeline would be a 24-inch diameter line originating in the gas fields of northern Louisiana, crossing Mississippi to a point near Muscle Shoals, Alabama, where gas would be sold to a new aluminum plant under construction there.

From Muscle Shoals the line would go northward to Brace, Tennessee, where it would fork. One branch would run to Nashville, the other to Alcoa, Tennessee (the site of another large aluminum smelter) and then to Knoxville. The cost for line, with some modifications and extensions, was estimated between $29.5 million and $35.7 million.

Tennessee Gas soon amended its FPC application, this time adding an extension to Ashland, Kentucky and a proposal to sell gas only to defense industries there. Both Dall and Thompson made frequent trips to Washington during the early months of 1942, visiting members of Congress, WPB officials, and others. Curtis Dall even used his personal connections to "grease the skids;" FDR wrote a "high-sounding" letter, which Dall showed liberally around Washington.

By the summer of 1943 the FPC was close to ruling on Tennessee Gas's latest application. Critical shortages of natural gas in the Appalachian region were expected in the near future, perhaps up to 300 MMcf (million cubic feet) on peak days and up to 15 Bcf (billion cubic feet) a year due to declining production from the rapidly-depleting Appalachian gas fields. Cities in the region such as Pittsburgh, Cleveland, and Youngstown had hundreds of defense plants relying on natural gas. As growing shortages curtailed gas deliveries, vital defense plants stood idle, threatening the Allied war effort. The federal government was keen to remedy this situation. While local production waned, other parts of the United States had plenty of natural gas. In the Southwest, large fields were virtually untapped, since gas was nearly worthless and was normally only produced as a by-product of oil drilling. In south Texas, natural gas was more likely to be flared or re-injected into the ground, than sold.

Just when the situation for Tennessee Gas was looking up, a new problem arose - competition. Hope Natural Gas, a subsidiary of Standard Oil (New Jersey), applied for a certificate to build a pipeline to link the mid-continent gas fields with its northeastern distribution system. Hope had initially been supportive of Tennessee Gas's pipeline efforts, even testifying years earlier on Tennessee Gas's behalf before the FPC. But, as setback after setback delayed the pipeline, Hope's management decided to build its own pipeline. The proven Hugoton field in the mid-continent would supply the gas.

Since shortages were expected in the near term, and with two competing pipelines on the table, the FPC would choose one or the other, and would do it quickly. Hope was an established natural gas company with a distribution network in the Northeast and a proven record before the FPC. As a Standard Oil subsidiary, Hope could draw on the considerable financial resources of the parent company, both in credit and in direct aid. In addition, Hope had already conducted feasibility studies and acquired a partial right-of-way for a proposed Texas-to-Appalachia pipeline, but not from the Hugoton field. Tennessee Gas was a new company without financing, no operations, no track record, and its gas supplies were problematic. It appeared that the FPC would favor Hope's application over that of Tennessee Gas.

The FPC stepped up the pressure on Tennessee Gas; on July 5, 1943 the commission gave Tennessee Gas sixty days to arrange firm financing and gas supply commitments. The company had neither of those elements in hand. On August 28 the FPC designated the proposed pipeline "a vital war program," and indicated that the necessary steel priorities would be forthcoming to whichever company received a certificate to build the pipeline. The RFC would provide some financing as well, but the pipeline builders would have to come up with approximately $12 million (equity). The commission also indicated that steel orders for the new pipeline must be placed no later than October 1, and the WPB expected a finished and operating pipeline by the winter of 1944-45.

The Chicago Corporation

Fortuitously, during the summer of 1943, Tennessee Gas had found a new supply of natural gas in south Texas. The Chicago Corporation, a Chicago-based investment trust, owned several gas extraction plants as well as trillions of cubic feet of gas reserves in the Stratton-Agua Dulce field near Corpus Christi, Texas. Chicago's extraction plants removed liquid hydrocarbons such as butane and propane from natural gas, which were then sold. The dry gas (methane) was re-injected into the ground since no ready market existed for it at the time in Texas. Texas had few industries, a relatively small population, and an oversupply of gas. Chicago was interested in marketing this processed gas for a decent price, but the real markets for it were the defense industries and cities in the Northeast, thousands of miles away .

In early August 1943, Victor Johnson flew to Chicago to negotiate with the Chicago Corporation for gas supplies. Chicago was willing to sell Tennessee Gas the gas on easy terms, providing that the pipeline be extended to the Corpus Christi area. Both sides agreed to a tentative deal, and on August 23 Tennessee Gas filed an amended application with the FPC, stating that "[the] applicant has agreed upon the terms on a contract with the Chicago Corporation…for a supply of natural gas." The cost of the proposed line had increased to $47.5 million, which reflected a pipeline that was 40% longer (1265 miles) and had 33% more capacity (200 million cubic feet) than previously. Tennessee Gas also indicated that "[TGT] intends to offer evidence at the further hearing herein in respect to firm commitments for the necessary financing of its proposed pipeline system." The final business plan of the Tennessee pipeline was gradually taking shape. All that was needed was to find a way to pay for it.

With gas supplies assured, Victor Johnson now had the task of raising the $12 million cash needed to secure the RFC loan. Before any commitments

A SMALL WORLD

Chicago Corporation's interest in Tennessee Gas's planned pipeline partly stemmed from its own foray into the pipeline business. During the late 1930s, Chicago's subsidiary, Reserve Gas Pipeline Company, had spent more than $100,000 on feasibility studies and an application for a certificate to build a pipeline to the New York area. Chicago shelved these plans at the onset of World War II, believing that steel pipe would be impossible to obtain for the duration of the war.

Some initial design work on Reserve's pipeline was done by Ray Fish who was then an engineer with Stearns-Roger Manufacturing, an engineering, design, manufacturing and construction company. Fish had been brought into the project by Clyde Alexander, a Corpus Christi promoter who later met with Curtis Dall about possible collaboration between Reserve and Tennessee Gas. While these plans came to naught, it was probably through Alexander that Dall and Tennessee Gas learned about the Chicago Corporation's gas reserves and Reserve's general plan to sell south Texas gas in the Northeast.

Both Fish and Alexander would later serve on the Tennessee Gas board of directors.

could be made, fate had one more surprise for Tennessee Gas. On August 29, Johnson failed to show up for a meeting with Wade Thompson at the Willard Hotel in Washington. Thompson knocked on Johnson's door, and receiving no answer, he found a maid to open the room. Johnson lay dead in his bed of a heart attack.

Johnson's death doomed the original Tennessee Gas and Transmission Company. Tennessee had an agreement for gas supplies, but without Johnson's involvement, no financing could be secured within the short time remaining before the final hearing on September 7, barely a week away. With all other efforts at obtaining financing having failed, Tennessee Gas now had only one option. Tennessee Gas informed the FPC they were negotiating with Chicago Corporation about a financing arrangement.

Chicago Takes Over – The Founding of TGT

Tennessee's last stroke of bad luck provided a windfall for the Chicago Corporation. On September 18, 1943 the Chicago Corporation offered a financing plan to Tennessee Gas under which: 1) Chicago would lend Tennessee Gas $500,000 to buy the outstanding preferred stock and to settle any liabilities against the company. 2) Chicago would arrange for the financing and construction of the pipeline in return for 90% ownership in Tennessee Gas; 3) all serving directors and officers of Tennessee Gas were to resign September 20, to be replaced by nominees of Chicago's choosing. A fourth condition stipulated that Tennessee Gas had until 1:30 p.m. on September 20 to accept the offer, or Chicago reserved the right to withdraw it.

Chicago's move was brilliantly conceived and executed. The Tennessee Gas directors had little choice in the matter as FPC hearings on Hope Natural Gas's pipeline application were scheduled for the following day . If the directors refused Chicago's offer, the FPC would almost certainly approve Hope's certificate, leaving Tennessee Gas with nothing to show for their 13+ years of effort. Thompson and Dall had little choice but to sell to Chicago and accept the 10% equity position.

The Tennessee Gas board convened on September 20 to consider Chicago's offer. After some debate, the board voted unanimously to accept it. Chicago immediately nominated a new president and a board of directors who took charge of TGT. That same afternoon the FPC announced that Chicago's commitment to provide financing for the pipeline met the commission's requirements, and it had decided to issue Tennessee Gas a certificate of public convenience and necessity for the Tennessee Pipeline.

Following the Chicago Corporation's takeover Tennessee Gas's new board consisted of Clyde H. Alexander, Arthur D. Chilgren, Ray C. Fish, Charles F. Glore (Chairman of the Chicago Corporation), Paul Kayser (President of El Paso Natural Gas and Gulf States Petroleum), Richard Wagner (President of the Chicago Corporation), and Henry Gardiner Symonds, the new Presi-

In the view of Gardiner Symonds, longtime president of Tenneco Gas, Johnson's death left Wade Thompson with a "dead horse" on his hands.

dent of Tennessee Gas. The board members were all experienced hands in the natural gas industry, and several of them played important roles in building Tennessee Gas's pipeline.

Symonds Takes the Reins

The new president of Tennessee Gas was forty-year-old Gardiner Symonds, a vice-president and director of Chicago Corporation. Symonds was born in Pittsburgh in 1903 to Amy Irene (Millberry) and Nathaniel G. Symonds, a Westinghouse vice president and a member of the city's business elite. Symonds was raised in Chicago, where he proved to be a gifted leader and organizer from a young age. He served as high school class president and graduated as valedictorian at age sixteen.

After high school, Symonds earned a scholarship to Stanford University, but was uncertain as to what he wanted to study in the university. He eventually selected geology, receiving his undergraduate degree in 1924. The following year, Symonds entered Harvard Business School. According to Symonds, he "had nothing more specific in mind than to try to get a broad business education. The business world and I were barely nodding acquaintances, if that." Symonds excelled at Harvard, earning an MBA with distinction in 1927.

Symonds had joined the Chicago Corporation in 1930 as assistant treasurer. Chicago Corporation, an investment trust, had been organized in 1929 and capitalized at $60 million; its directors included businessmen from Swift & Co., Marshall Fields, Pullman, International Harvester, and several other large corporations. Symonds gained the notice of his superiors quickly, and was promoted to vice president after two years, at the age of 29. By 1940, Symonds was a senior executive and had been named to the board of directors of the Chicago Corporation. He was thirty-seven.

In 1938, Symonds and his family moved to Corpus Christi, Texas to manage Chicago Corporation's oil and gas interests in south Texas. The oversupply of natural gas rendered it practically worthless in much of Texas. Symonds received a few offers to purchase gas at one to one and one-half cents per mcf, prices so low that Symonds was not interested. Nonetheless; there were eager markets for natural gas in other parts of the country. It would fall to Symonds to market the trillions of cubic feet of gas owned by the Chicago Corporation.

Symonds looked to the growing cities and factories of the northeast where demand for gas was increasing. Symonds had worked closely with Clyde Alexander on the Reserve Gas Pipeline Project before World War II and became familiar with many of the issues involving establishing a long-distance natural gas pipeline. While the Chicago Corporation invested more than $100,000 the project went nowhere when Northern utilities would not pay the prices Reserve wanted, offering only $.16 to $.18 per mcf, while Reserve wanted a few cents more. Even at the lower rates, however, it was clear that natural gas was worth at least sixteen times in New York what it traded for in Texas. Sy-

In his high school annual Symonds was listed as: Manager of the Football Team, Manager of the Basketball Team, Manager of the Baseball Team, and Manager of the Debate Team. And under his photo the class prophet added: "This is the smallest High School I have ever managed."

GARDINER SYMONDS
The Quintessential Workaholic

Aside from his leadership and organizational abilities, Symonds also had a strong work ethic which soon became apparent. After completing his MBA, Symonds took a job with the Continental Illinois Bank and Trust Company of Chicago, serving as a statistician, prospectus writer and clerk. His duties at first included moving furniture and running errands for his bosses in addition to his clerical work. Symonds excelled at the job, and he considered it to be a valuable experience even as his superiors recognized his potential and promoted him into management. He later counseled young businessmen not to think themselves as too good to do manual labor. His advice also included humility and a willingness to do anything moral and legal asked of them. This work ethic was part of Symonds' successful personal philosophy, and it became a part of the corporate culture of Tennessee Gas.

Symonds was also a quintessential workaholic who rarely took time off work. Symonds was always working, even when ostensibly on vacation or away from his office. He had few hobbies, mostly playing cards and golf on rare occasions. In a 1968 interview with Nation's Business, Symonds was unapologetic in his views on work, stating openly that "basically, I don't enjoy relaxing."

Despite his obsession with work, Symonds was a devoted husband and father. He married his childhood sweetheart, Margaret Clover, in 1928 and they had five children. Symonds worked long hours, sometimes sixteen-hour days, but always took time to spend with his children.

monds was already familiar with the concept of a south Texas pipeline when he became president of Tennessee Gas a few years later.

Establishing Tennessee Gas An Impossible Task

Following Chicago Corporation's buyout of Tennessee Gas, the FPC issued a certificate of public convenience and necessity authorizing the construction of Tennessee Gas's pipeline on September 24, 1943. The FPC instructed Tennessee Gas to commence construction on the pipeline no later than February 1, 1944, and specified that the pipeline was to be in service for the winter of 1944-45. This mandate allowed barely 10 months to build a 1,265-mile pipeline, with nothing in hand but a plan. The Chicago Corporation and its new subsidiary were now faced with the task of establishing an organization for Tennessee Gas, hiring competent personnel, securing materials for the pipeline, planning and engineering the pipeline, mapping, surveying, and obtaining rights-of-way along the route. Doing this during peacetime would have been daunting; doing it amid the shortages and uncertainties of World War II seemed impossible.

Symonds was fortunate in that he already had some experience and a number of important contacts due to his involvement with the Reserve project a few years previously. Not coincidentally, Tennessee Gas's second employee (after Gardiner Symonds) was Ray Fish. Fish was hired to oversee the engineering work on the Tennessee Gas pipeline. Fish and Symonds were already acquainted since Fish had done the basic design work on the proposed Reserve gas pipeline and he had worked on the designs for Chicago's south Texas recycling plants. He was named vice president in charge of engineering and construction with Tennessee Gas, and served on the Tennessee Gas board.

A number of Chicago Corporation personnel were transferred to the new Tennessee Gas. W.E. Mueller from Chicago's Oil and Gas Division became Vice President and Treasurer. Harold Burrow was hired from Chicago Corporation as Purchasing Agent (he later served as president of Tenneco), W.C. Norman became Assistant Secretary and Assistant Treasurer. Charles S. Coates became District Superintendent and later, Senior Vice President. In addition to these early employees, Binford Arney and C.C. Small, headed up the legal, land, and right of way department. With the initial management in place, Tennessee Gas began operations by late September, 1943, only a few days after the FPC had issued its ruling.

First Things First - Preliminary Activities

Symonds and Tennessee Gas's managers moved quickly to new offices in Houston in late September and continued the efforts of organizing the company. By October 1, 1943, a week after receiving their FPC certificate, orders for major equipment had been placed with manufacturers, including compressors, valves, and steel pipe. Stearns-Roger Manufacturing Co. received a turn-key contract to build the seven self-contained compressor stations, several gas metering stations, as well as a dehydration plant near Corpus Christi to remove water and other impurities from the gas. Dozens of smaller contractors supplied a myriad of other needs. Tennessee Gas placed many of these orders even before it had established its offices in Houston.

By November 5, 1943, Tennessee Gas had signed contracts for the river crossings and main construction areas. Nine construction companies received contracts to build the pipeline, with more than half the mileage going to two major groups: Williams Brothers and Bechtel-Dempsey-Price. Construction was divided into fourteen sections in order to maximize speed and efficiency; work on all sections was to begin simultaneously and "proceed with utmost speed" in order to meet the stringent deadlines imposed by the FPC. Due to heavy rain and equipment shortages during the initial phases of the project, the construction spreads were later increased to twenty-three and the workforce expanded.

After letting contracts for material and construction, Tennessee Gas faced further challenges. One of the most pressing was the necessity of obtaining right-of-way from more than 12,000 individual landowners along the pipeline route. Tennessee Gas's pipeline would cross more than seventy counties in seven states, making land titles a potential source of delay. Some good fortune did exist as parts of the right-of-way had already been acquired and surveyed. An appropriate right-of-way from the Monroe, Louisiana area to the pipeline terminus at Cornwell Station, West Virginia, was already available. Hope Natural Gas, Tennessee Gas's former rival in obtaining the certificate for the Texas-to-West Virginia pipeline, had already surveyed and purchased a right-of-way for their proposed pipeline in the early 1940s. With more than half the right-of-way secured, Tennessee Gas's contractors were able to immediately begin construction on the eastern portions of the pipeline. Surveyors and agents obtained much of the remaining right-of-way in western Louisiana and Texas by late 1943.

Hiram Moore and John Talbot left Houston in mid-November 1943 and commenced selecting six compressor station sites from Station 4 at Jasper, Texas to Station 14 at Burnaugh, Kentucky. Apparently, the Station 2 site near East Bernard, Texas, had already been selected from the Chicago Corporation's Reserve Gas Pipeline design. From Monroe, Louisiana, eastward they relied on the original survey of the Hope Natural Gas right of way. They usually selected sites on all-weather roads with a spacing of about 170 miles apart. Hope's right of way also included a number of station sites which were acquired in fee, but were too small for TGT's compressor stations. The compressor stations were re-numbered years later to reflect the main line valve number at the location.

Pipeline Overview

The Tennessee Pipeline was a remarkable feat of logistics, engineering, financing, and construction. Some of the basic engineering for the pipeline had been completed prior to the issuance of the certificate of public convenience and necessity, however, Tennessee Gas engineers led by Ray Fish continued working on the design even as the pipeline was under construction. Tennessee Gas's pipeline was among the first all-welded long distance pipeline to use continuous welds which proved durable and cost-effective, and became the standard in the post-war era.

The original design capacity of the pipeline was 207,000 mcf per day. When finished, the pipeline spanned 1,265 miles; 1,180 miles were 24-inch diameter pipe, and the final 85 miles were 20-inch diameter pipe. The pipeline began near Driscoll, Texas, at Tennessee Gas's large dehydration plant and proceeded northeasterly, skirting the Houston area, and passing south of Shreveport and to the north of Monroe, Louisiana. The line crossed the Mississippi River on the Greenville, Mississippi, toll bridge and thence northeast across Mississippi and into Tennessee, where it passed north of Nashville and into Kentucky. Near Danville, Kentucky, the pipeline took a more easterly course into West Virginia. The pipeline originally terminated at Cornwell Station (near Kenova), West Virginia, where up to 165,000 mcf of gas was delivered to Hope Natural Gas. A smaller tie-in with United Natural Gas at Clendenin, West Virginia provided that company with up to 45,000 mcf. The ultimate destination of the South Texas gas were the factories, homes, and power stations of the northern Appalachian region.

The pipeline drew its gas supplies primarily from the Stratton-Agua Dulce field near Corpus Christi, but also from Chicago Corporation's Wardner, Coastal, and Gulf Plains Recycling Plants via a feeder system of small-diameter pipelines. Ten percent of its supplies came from reserves owned by Paul Kayser, who was president of El Paso Natural Gas and Gulf States Petroleum and owned extensive gas reserves in south Texas. Kayser also served on the Tennessee Gas board of directors. Estimates of the total reserves available to the pipeline in the Stratton-Agua Dulce field were approximately three trillion cubic feet. A later pipeline extension to the San Salvador field (owned by Kayser) in South Texas added an additional trillion cubic feet of reserves. Raw gas from the wells and recycling plants went first to the dehydration plant near Driscoll, Texas where the gas was processed, dehydrated and stripped of impurities before entering the Tennessee pipeline.

The initial design of the pipeline provided for seven compressor stations positioned at approximately 170-mile intervals along the line. The compressor stations were self-contained, with electrical generators supplying power and pipeline gas powering the compressors and generators. On-site crews living in company housing operated and maintained the compressor stations.

In addition to the compressor stations, the company constructed three types of gas-meter stations: purchase meters, sales meters, and check meter stations. The purchase gas meter stations measured gas taken into the line from outside suppliers; all were initially located in Nueces County, Texas where most of the gas supplies originated. The three sales meter stations operated at points where Tennessee Gas's pipeline intersected the pipeline systems of other companies; two sold gas to United Fuel Gas Company and the other served Hope Natural Gas at the pipeline terminus, all in West Virginia. The check meter stations were located at various points along the pipeline and measured the gas passing through the system, which helped to isolate leaks (or theft). All of the metering and compressor stations were designed and built for Tennessee Gas by Stearns-Roger.

The Tennessee pipeline had block valves at approximately ten-mile intervals along the pipeline and, just like Roman roads, TGT had mile post markers at each mile along the line. These main line valves could be used to isolate any compromised section of the pipeline, allowing for easy repair and maintenance. Among the innovations on the Tennessee Gas pipeline was the use of welds to install the block valves; prior pipelines had used bolted-flanges with gaskets to secure the valves. Tennessee Gas welded in the valves to reduce cost and time, both crucial issues during construction.

Opposition to the Pipeline

Despite the support of the Federal Power Commission, the War Industries Board, the War Department, and many large corporations, Tennessee Gas faced considerable resistance to its plans to build the pipeline. Most of the opposition came from two camps; industries which would suffer from increased energy competition, and those who feared that Texas was being unfairly stripped of its natural resources. The opposition mounted an ineffectual campaign to stop or delay the pipeline, but proved a troubling element in Tennessee Gas's efforts to finish the pipeline on time.

During Tennessee Gas's hearings before the FPC, several coal companies, unions, and railroads expressed opposition to the pipeline, fearing increased competition from the new fuel. The declining coal industry was eager to keep Tennessee Gas out of the Appalachian region, which was a major coal-mining area. During the twentieth century, coal continually lost market share to oil and natural gas throughout the country. In 1920, coal had accounted for more than 78% of the total energy used in the United States, while natural gas accounted for less than five percent of the energy used that year, and oil accounting for just over thirteen percent. However, by 1940, coal's dominance had eroded to a bare majority of energy consumed in the United States—52.4%—while the market share of natural gas had jumped to more than twelve percent and oil to more than thirty-one percent. Facing huge losses, the coal industry petitioned the FPC to keep Tennessee Gas out of the Appalachian region, traditionally a strong market for coal. The coal industry

was seconded in this approach by the railroads, who profited from hauling bulky coal to end-users, as well as by the unions, whose members labored in the mines, on the railroads, and in the factories powered by coal. The unions feared that the rise of the natural gas industry in the Northeast would lessen their influence, since natural gas needed far fewer workers to extract, transport, and market than did coal. The unions were also cognizant of the fact that Tennessee Gas and many of its competitors were headquartered in the South and Southwest, areas traditionally hostile to labor unions and unionization.

The FPC rejected the arguments of the coal industry and their allies, despite investigating several alternatives to the use of natural gas in the Northeast. The FPC quoted the Solid Fuels Administrator for War in its decision, who had stated on September 18, 1943 that "coal production has been unable to keep pace with the expansion of war requirements... there is a far better chance that the situation will grow worse before it grows better, because the coal industry faces strict limitations despite any efforts which can be made to raise production levels." Undeterred, the coal industry and its allies approached the seven states crossed by the proposed pipeline, attempting to halt Tennessee Gas at the state level. Here its potential for success was greater, since seven different utility commissions regulated gas across the pipeline route. Success in any of the seven could seriously delay Tennessee Gas. However, the state commissions concurred with the decisions of the FPC, ruling that the Tennessee Gas pipeline was vital to the war effort, and construction should proceed. By early 1944 the coal industry had given up their efforts to halt the pipeline.

Another threat to the pipeline came from organizations and individuals who feared that Tennessee Gas was stripping Texas of its natural resources. These included several Chambers of Commerce and manufacturing associations who played on Texans' fears and prejudices, as well as prominent politicians such as Texas governor Coke Stevenson, Texas senator W. Lee "Pappy" O'Daniel, Railroad Commission members Beauford Jester, and Olin Culberson, who tapped into popular apprehension over the export of natural gas. Several Texas newspapers, notably the Dallas Morning News, also opposed the pipeline. In general, opponents of the pipeline argued that industry would have no incentive to relocate to Texas if cheap natural gas was available in the Northeast, thus "robbing" Texas of its industrial future for temporary gains. Opponents played upon regional tensions, pointing out that Tennessee Gas was owned by the Chicago Corporation, a "Yankee" corporation from the North, not owned or controlled by Texans. Opponents insinuated that out-of-state businessmen might not have the best interests of the state at heart.

Refuting such arguments fell upon the shoulders of Gardiner Symonds, and to a lesser extent upon Brown Booth, whom Symonds hired to head a public relations effort to convince Texans that the Tennessee Gas pipeline was good for the nation, good for the war effort and good for Texas. Symonds was a vigorous advocate for Tennessee Gas and its pipeline, confronting reporters and politicians alike about their attempts to keep the gas in Texas. Symonds noted that the Chicago Corporation was a good corporate citizen, having invested millions in Texas and creating hundreds (later thousands) of jobs in the state and paying substantial taxes. In a letter to Coke Stevenson, Symonds pointed out that natural gas was a practically worthless commodity in Texas prior to Tennessee Gas's efforts to build its pipeline; Texas producers could get no more than 1½ cents per mcf for their gas before 1943, and there were few markets for the gas in Texas in any case. Tennessee Gas wanted to pay Texans nearly five times more than the going rate for their gas ($.05 per mcf), which would give landowners substantial royalties, employ thousands of people, and result in nearly $2 million a year in taxes to the state. Aside from the direct benefits to Texas, the pipeline would also aid the war effort in providing defense plants with a continuous and reliable source of fuel.

Symonds argued that higher prices meant that less gas would be wasted through flaring or venting, since producers and landowners would now have an incentive to conserve and market their gas to Tennessee Gas. Increased prices would have the further effect of stimulating exploration and extraction, likely increasing the Texas gas reserves through new discoveries. Furthermore, argued Symonds, Tennessee Gas Pipeline would only increase exports by 10%, in no way endangering Texas' huge proven reserves of natural gas. Gas from fields in the Permian Basin and the Texas Panhandle already left the state for Arizona, Colorado, Minnesota, Ohio, Iowa, Illinois, Michigan, and Mexico. Symonds and Tennessee Gas thus pointed out the obvious; the pipeline would be a boon to Texas' economy in terms of royalties, taxes, jobs, and economic growth. Noting that gas delivered to end-users in the Northeast was priced at between $.30 and $.40 per mcf, Symonds argued that business would still come to Texas, given that gas in Texas could be had for as little as $.05 per mcf in practically unlimited quantities.

Symonds skillfully rebutted Tennessee Gas's critics in the media, writing not only to Coke Stevenson but also replying to editorials calling for a halt to pipeline construction. In a letter to the Dallas Morning News, Symonds responded to an editorial calling for the curtailment of gas deliveries to out-of-state customers. The article, *Fuel will be Required for Industrial Future* also insinuated that no public input on the pipeline had been taken into consideration and Tennessee Gas would collect excess profits at the expense of the future of Texas, His letter carefully refuted each and every contested point, noting that open hearings on the pipeline were conducted in Washington over a period of several years, profits were strictly limited by the FPC to 6.5% of capital investment, as well as reiterating his stance that Tennessee Gas was effectively quintupling the price of natural gas paid to producers and landowners in Texas. In light of staunch support for the pipeline on the Federal level, as well as from Gardiner Symonds and many others, the opposition to the pipeline failed to make any headway and construction began in late 1943.

In rebuttal to a negative editorial Symonds wrote the Dallas Morning News, stating that "the text of the article is so full of inaccuracies and misleading information as to make me wonder whether the Dallas Morning News is departing from its acknowledged high standard of journalistic reporting."

Building the Wartime Pipeline

Tennessee Gas and its contractors proceeded with construction as quickly as possible. With contractors signed up, materials ordered, and financing in place, a brief groundbreaking ceremony was held at a site on the Cumberland River in Tennessee (the state where the company originated) on December 4, 1943. Gardiner Symonds officially inaugurated the pipeline, and some work was done before the first pipe was officially welded on January 10, 1944.

Tennessee Gas and its contractors operated on a "stop-loss" basis; the contractors were compensated for equipment rental and were paid a set fee per foot of pipeline completed. Several of the contractors also agreed to a

The only known photo of Wade Thompson (squatting, third from left) at the groundbreaking ceremony for the original pipeline in 1943. Gardiner Symonds is standing directly behind him.

The

Oil Weekly captured the moment writing, "Over and above all, the line(s) is more than a metal conduit for moving oil; it is a symbol of American spirit, an expression of determined people whose purpose is freedom." Similarly, the construction of the TGT pipeline the following year, with its more complex compressor stations, dehydration plant, metering stations and housing also captured that same American "can-do spirit" in a time of crisis.

share of cost-savings to Tennessee Gas. However, the contractors had to overcome a number of problems to get the line built in time including right-of-way issues, lack of equipment, labor problems, and especially bad weather.

An early problem that developed was the lack of heavy equipment. With the construction demands of World War II, equipment was exceedingly scarce. New equipment was difficult or impossible to come by. Contractors such as Bechtel-Dempsey-Price had been given priorities for heavy equipment, but these did not guarantee that necessary equipment could be rented, purchased, or even located. According to the late Oscar Dempsey of Bechtel-

"We *were prohibited from hiring anybody good . . . all of the good people, bear in mind, were on jobs and . . . we were very lucky to get anybody. And we needed people."*

Ray Fish

Chain saws were not yet common equipment in 1944 as pipeline crews cleared right-of-way.

Dempsey-Price, equipment priorities were nothing more than "a hunting license." With most heavy equipment devoted to the war effort, Tennessee Gas's contractors were forced to scour the country for equipment to lease, borrow, or buy. In some cases, contractors were forced to improvise or to rely on mule teams to complete their spreads.

Another problem the contractors faced was the width of the right-of-way in the eastern portions of the line. When Hope Natural Gas had purchased the original right-of-way during the 1930s, they counted on building the pipeline partly with animal power, and purchased a relatively narrow 30-foot right-of-way along most of the route. Hope apparently intended to use mule teams to pull the welding equipment and wrapping machines, relying on trucks or tractors only to move the heavier sections of pipe. Tennessee Gas's contractors found it difficult to stay on the narrow right-of-way they had. Tennessee Gas was forced to pay damages when its contractors deviated from the right-of-way, as well as to restore farmland to good condition after the pipeline was built.

Obtaining skilled and experienced labor was a serious problem for Tennessee Gas. Because of wartime employment restrictions, the company could not easily hire workers away from other jobs. They were forced to hire people who were between jobs, no easy feat considering the labor shortages caused by World War II. Tennessee Gas relied on word-of-mouth and informal contacts to recruit workers. TGT made it known they were paying higher-than-average salaries, and this helped to fill the ranks.

Labor issues also plagued the contractors. With many able-bodied men away in the military, Tennessee Gas's contractors hired practically anyone who applied. Experienced workers of all types were in short supply. Skilled welders were particularly hard to find, and most of the poorly-trained liberty-ship welders who applied had to be turned away. Even so, problems with welds were common; during the testing phase after construction, one Tennessee Gas employee remarked that welds routinely broke when put under load. Damaged welds would be repaired or cut out and replaced with a new piece of pipe, resulting in delays. Leaks also plagued the Tennessee pipeline. Repair crews routinely worked twenty-hour days fixing leaks. The crews found the leaks by listening for escaping gas as well as through the use of fire baskets--pieces of burning charcoal wrapped in wire mesh tied to the end of a long cane fishing pole. The leaking gas would catch fire, and the spot would be marked and repaired.

Contractors also faced hostile unions, violence, and sabotage. While some areas of the pipeline proceeded with relatively few labor problems, the contractors building the line through Kentucky and Mississippi dealt with labor hooliganism. Union members in Kentucky picketed Bechtel-Dempsey-Price's employees, and the situation escalated when the company refused to allow union organizers access to the workers. AFL agents were accused of harassing Bechtel-Dempsey-Price's employees; at one point,

"The contractors used anybody that could operate a piece of equipment, drive a truck, or what-not, and they didn't care, they'd tear down gates and tear down private phone lines... so the landowners got quite riled up. It was not uncommon for landowners to deny access to their land by locking gates or even by blocking the right-of-way with tractors or trucks."

Pipeline tester B.J. Whitley, Sr.

Laying pipe through a rocky section of Kentucky. Dynamite was used to blast open such areas.

During the height of World War II all able bodied personnel, both men and women, were either in some branch of military service or in wartime-related jobs.

Dick Freeman, who later became CEO, was Tennessee's first Personnel Manager after being hired away from the Lummus Company where he was Personnel and Safety Manager. Word spread quickly that Tennessee Gas was paying top dollar to staff their Houston head-quarters with experienced people.

For example, Kenny Bradbury was working at Ellington Field as a material clerk for a construction company when he dropped by the Tennessee offices in late-December, 1943. Freeman hired him on the spot, but only on the condition he start work immediately and not take his customary Christmas time off.

Bradbury said, "A few years later when my wife and I got married, Freeman loaned me his wife's car to use on our honeymoon around town prior to our flying to Mexico. In fact, World War II ended when we in Monterrey."

According to Harold Burrow, who later became President of Tennessee Gas, "We hired everyone who came in the front door those first few months, evaluated them after their first week on the job and either kept them, or ran them off." At the end of 1943 TG&T had 80 employees, of which 8 had transferred from the Chicago Corporation. Staffing the seven new compressor stations and pipeline locations was a big challenge. Upon commencement of construction, any experienced people were fair game for Tennessee Gas.

The original experienced field personnel were hired away from Lone Star Gas, Mississippi River Fuel, Northern Natural, Panhandle

seventeen AFL members were in jail for damaging equipment, harassing workers, and for assaulting one the contractor's superintendents. Faced with sabotage of its equipment, Bechtel-Dempsey-Price hired armed guards and appealed to the state of Kentucky for assistance, which agreed to supply state police to protect the workers. On several occasions Bechtel-Dempsey-Price equipment was targeted at night by vandals who poured sand or sugar into gas tanks, ruining hard-to-replace machinery.

Problems with landowners were common along the line. In some case, eminent domain had to be used to claim right-of-way from recalcitrant landowners who wanted nothing to do with the pipeline. Occasionally, landowners threatened violence to keep contractors off their land, though no major bloodshed erupted. Inexperienced contract workers contributed to the problems with landowners. The greatest of the challenges the contractors faced was the weather. 1944 was an unusually wet year; the rain began in January and continued along portions of the pipeline well into April. Heavy rains churned the soil into deep mud, entrapping equipment and workers alike. Trenches filled with water and collapsed, further delaying construction. The

weather was so poor that by the end of April, 1944, only 76 miles of pipeline had been finished—just 6% of the total. Desperate to finish the line before the end of the year, Tennessee Gas increased the number of construction spreads to twenty-three, bringing in smaller contractors to make up for lost time. The workforce increased to levels between 9,000 and 11,000.

Wooden slats were placed on the pipe to prevent damage when laying the line underwater to cross a lake or river.

Construction continued throughout the summer and fall of 1944. With improving weather and a looming deadline, the contractors made up for lost time, eventually reaching a pace of more than seven miles a day. Bechtel-Dempsey-Price laid the final sections of the pipeline in Kentucky, having been delayed by bad weather, extremely rough terrain and labor problems. The final tie-in was on Halloween day, 1944, with gas reaching Tennessee Gas's customers less than twenty-four hours later. The Tennessee Gas pipeline had been completed in less than eleven months after the groundbreaking, with 94% of the pipeline built in just six months, between May 1, 1944 and October 31, 1944. The new pipeline

A party to celebrate the completion of the line was held in Houston on November 14, 1944.

would prove to be of immense value to the war effort, and played a crucial role in keeping Appalachian defense plants in operation during the final months of World War II. The completion of the Tennessee Gas pipeline during World War II was a remarkable achievement and example of the benefits of the public-private partnership between the FPC and Tennessee Gas. Led by Gardiner Symonds, the new Tennessee Gas had hired managers and engineers, hired contractors, contended with landowners and suppliers, answered critics, and overcome incredible challenges to finish the pipeline on schedule. With gas flowing to defense plants and other customers, a resource which would have been useless or wasted in Texas proved vital to the United States' victory in the Second World War. Tennessee Gas augmented the rapidly dwindling reserves of the Appalachian gas fields, delivering more than ten billion cubic feet of gas into the Appalachian area in the final two months of 1944. By the end of 1945, Tennessee Gas had delivered more than seventy-three billion cubic feet of gas to its customers, employed more than six hundred employees, and earned a profit of $3.5 million.

TGT's First Rate Case

After just six weeks of gas sales through the newly-completed Tennessee Pipeline in 1944, the FPC ordered an investigation into TGT's rates, marking a turning point in the public private partnership which had hitherto existed. The investigation was triggered by rate increases from Warfield Natural Gas and Cincinnati Gas Transportation Company, two local distribution companies who indirectly received gas from TGT. The FPC sought to determine whether rates charged by Tennessee Gas, were "unjust, unreasonable, unduly discriminatory or preferential." In addition to the rates, the FPC investigation also sought to determine if the Chicago Corporation, then the largest stockholder in TGT (81% of its voting stock and 90% of common stock), should

Eastern, United Gas and other pipeline and construction companies. Many joined the company during construction and quickly became the nucleus of TGT's field management.

This first generation of field managers was a hard-drinking, hard-driving group of people. However, they knew the business and served Tennessee well during the wartime years and beyond. Many of these managers learned their skills at the "school of hard knocks" where the smartest and sometimes the toughest guy on the crew was "boss." The compressor station and pipeline field crews were selected from the local talent pool, many of whom were "4-F" or had military deferments for other reasons. In addition, many were older farmers who had the technical skills to train as operators, oilers, repairmen and other maintenance positions. The 1944 vintage equipment was not that complicated from the perspective of a farmer or a mechanic who had maintained his own equipment for years. Even the small contingent of older employees who came from the pool halls and domino parlors found positions in the wartime pipeline field organization where they could contribute and earn very attractive wages compared to local rates.

Dick Freeman, who had also been a Ford dealer earlier in his career, played a major role in helping procure cars and trucks during the war, since civilian car and truck production stopped at the start of WWII. Freeman became Assistant to the TGT President in the fall of 1947 and was replaced by Curtis M. Smith as Manager of the Personnel Department.

Smith came from Shell Oil in November, 1944, where he worked in personnel and industrial relations. Curtis Smith was a man of many talents. While at the University of Oklahoma he formed a

college band whose bookings helped finance his education and survive the depression.

At Tennessee Gas Smith maintained that "A company is judged by the employees it keeps. Many office managers are very fussy about having handsome and harmonious office furnishings and then ruin the effect by untidy, carelessly dressed and dowdy looking personnel." Curtis Smith had the reputation of hiring the most attractive group of secretaries, clerical personnel, receptionists, elevator operators and telephone switchboard operators in downtown Houston. This was confirmed by the fact that many of the surrounding office workers took their lunch smoke breaks outside the Commerce Building, and later the Tenneco Building, to watch the TGT women file past on the way to lunch and shopping. Tenneco gained its reputation based upon Curtis Smith's hiring practices, which closely parallel those of former Texas Congressman Charlie Wilson who was featured in the 2007 movie, "Charlie Wilson's War."

Jerry West, a former Amoco Landman, said, "I always came a few minutes early every evening to pick up my wife, who worked for Superior Oil, in order to watch the parade of beautiful women coming out of the Tenneco Building." In fact, the Superior Oil Industrial Relations Manager married one of Curtis Smith's clerks.

Curtis Smith continued to advance into positions of increasing responsibility during his career and became President of Tennessee Life Insurance Company, a subsidiary of TGT.

The post-war Houston office workforce demographics reflected a significant percentage of single men and women. One bachelor Navy veteran was quoted to have said "Man, this is like swimming in a sea of matrimony."

fall under FPC regulation as a natural gas company under the NGA. Not only did the Chicago Corporation own a controlling interest in Tennessee Gas, but Tennessee purchased virtually all of its gas supplies from the Chicago Corporation. Rather than risk coming under the regulatory authority of the FPC, and thus public scrutiny of its operations, the Chicago Corporation divested itself of Tennessee Gas and Transmission in short order. On September 10, 1945, Chicago sold its entire interest to a group of securities underwriters headed by Stone & Webster of New York. The same day, the Chicago nominated board of directors resigned with the exception of Gardiner Symonds, who severed his ties with Chicago Corporation and remained president of Tennessee Gas. In early 1946, Stone & Webster placed the Tennessee Gas stock up for sale, and Tennessee Gas became a publicly-traded corporation. The divestiture did not end the FPC rate case. The investigation dragged on for two and a half more years as the FPC probed both the Chicago Corporation and TGT's rates. Chicago was not removed from the investigation until May 1947, since

A certificate for TG&T's original Class A stock. Common stock was sold to sharholders in 1945.

they continued to sell gas to the newly-independent TGT and the FPC sought to determine the exact relationship between the two companies. Eventually, the FPC found that Chicago Corporation was not subject to their jurisdiction and removed them from the investigation. However, the rate investigation sans the Chicago Corporation continued as the FPC probed TGT's records and subpoenaed TGT executives. After more than two and half years of hearings and investigation, the FPC found that TGT had overcharged its customers by $850,000 and exceeded the "allowable" rate of return on investment.

TGT accepted the commission's ruling and agreed to reduce its future rates to compensate. The FPC accepted the new rate schedule and finally dismissed its investigation in July 1947. The Natural Gas Act of 1938 required that Tennessee obtain permission for each new addition to its pipeline network. This process was lengthy, expensive, and very public, making any plans for future growth well known to Tennessee's competitors. Even though regulation initially allowed a comfortable return on investment, the possibilities for future growth were constrained in this environment—regulation was both a help and a hindrance to Tennessee Gas. Symonds concluded that unlimited possibilities for growth lay outside of gas transmission. With a steady stream of income derived from its pipeline, diversification seemed to be an avenue to future growth. Tennessee would branch out beginning in 1945 into oil and gas production and in the 1950s into refining and overseas operations. This trend accelerated, and by the mid-1960s, Tennessee Gas (renamed 'Tenneco' in 1966) was a pioneer in the nascent conglomeration movement.

The Inch Lines

When German U-boats commenced to sink American oil tankers off the East Coast in February, 1942, and a total of twelve had gone down by month end, the oil supply on the Eastern Seaboard began to suffer. By August, a 24" diameter pipeline designed to carry crude oil was under construction from Longview, Texas to southern Illinois with a 20" diameter extension to Phoenixville, Pennsylvania. The War Emergency Pipelines (WEP), under contract with Defense Plants Corporation (DPC), constructed what became known as the Big Inch, the nation's largest diameter oil pipeline which was completed in September 1943.

Meanwhile, pipeline crews also begin laying a 20" diameter products pipeline in April 1943 from Beaumont, Texas and the Houston Ship Channel to Little Rock and then on to Linden, New Jersey. This line was named the Little Big Inch and commenced operation in March 1944. About fifteen thousand workers were involved in this massive project which shared a common right of way from Little Rock to Linden.

Attempts to dispose of the Inch Lines began in the summer of 1945, before the end of the war. The owner of the lines, the Reconstruction Finance Corporation (RFC), which had provided financing, solicited bids from 135 potential purchasers of the lines and all of their associated "war surplus property." Public hearings and the debate over who should buy the lines dragged on and the pipelines remained unsold and unused through the end of 1946.

In the meantime, a major gas shortage, compounded by a coal strike, developed in the Appalachian area where Tennessee Gas had not been able to complete its first expansion prior to the onset of winter. In late October 1946, TGT proposed to lease the Inch Lines, convert them to gas use in six days and alleviate the upcoming winter gas shortage. TGT's strategy was not only

The gas pipeline construction boom was ongoing in the late 1940's when large numbers of World War II veterans were graduating from colleges across the pipeline system. Former Chief Engineer "Jumping Joe" King is credited with originating the strategy of hiring scores of college graduates for manual labor jobs at field locations and on pipeline survey parties. Many started off as "stob drivers" on survey parties where the pace and physical demand of the work quickly separated the men from the boys. As pipeline construction tapered off in the 1950s, the demand for survey parties dropped dramatically. Many of those now-surplus college graduates were transferred to Houston office engineering positions and soon began to replace the first generation pipeline managers in both Houston office and field locations. Tennessee Gas found that its second generation managers were better educated and applied more sophisticated management techniques. Surprisingly, the Houston area retired "stob drivers" continue to meet for lunch periodically, although their numbers are dwindling.

Tennessee Gas commenced to design all of its compressor stations and pipelines in-house after the first pipeline was completed in 1944. It organized a highly acclaimed engineering department with an array of disciplines which continued in-house design and construction supervision of Tennessee's facilities until the downturn in the mid-1980s.

Meanwhile, the Federal Power Commission had very detailed and tedious accounting procedures for regulated interstate pipeline companies which required scores of clerks and accountants to provide the periodic reports necessary to justify the pipeline's allowed rate of return.

Ronald L. McVey was one of the first CPAs hired in early 1945 and he went on to become President

of Tennessee Gas before he retired. McVey had a degree in chemical engineering from Iowa State prior to becoming an accountant and working some 19 years for the Public Service Company of Colorado in Denver. He moved to Arthur Anderson & Co. where he audited several client firms, including Tennessee Gas and Transmission Company in Houston. Ron McVey said "I was looking for a young and ambitious company, and was doubly glad to find one that believes in playing the game according to the rules."

Howard Gray was the Superintendent of Measurement in 1960 when he proposed that the Company recruit a group of graduate engineers who, upon completion of an 18 month training program, could provide a reservoir of talent for replacing TGT's second generation of managers and technical staff. Seven engineers were recruited in 1961 from the three most prestigious engineering schools in Texas and two other recent hires were placed into the program. After about six months the program was expanded to two years duration with participants spending three months in each department of the Company. The "Gas Cadets", as they became known, were rotated through a variety of assignments in both Houston office and field locations. Almost every day involved a new experience and some provided an opportunity for leadership training. Upon completing the training program, most of the "Cadets" moved into desirable assignments. Ironically, only two of the original nine finished their careers at Tenneco, while about one-half of the "Gas Cadets" early departures was attributed to Tenneco's downturn in the 1980s. Joe Parrish served as executive coordinator of the training program.

Gardiner Symonds was notorious for his fifteen goals for

to alleviate the crisis, but to gain the inside track on purchasing the lines for permanent transport of natural gas. The new owner, the War Assets Administration (WAA), conducted brief hearings and issued TGT a five month lease which became effective on December 2, 1946. In addition, the FPC issued TGT a temporary certificate for the lease operation and gas sales.

Tennessee Gas began a frantic effort, working around the clock, to connect both lines to gas supplies on the South ends and markets in the Appalachian region. Within three days gas was flowing into the Little Big Inch from Tennessee's pipeline. The Big Inch was more complicated, since field lines had

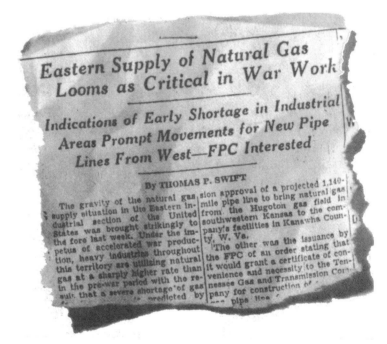

Accelerated war production of heavy industry resulted in increased demands for natural gas.

to be fabricated from several East Texas gas fields to near Longview, Texas where the Big Inch originated. Nevertheless, TGT had gas flowing into the Big Inch on December 9 and reaching Ohio customers two days later. TGT had never been able to entirely purge the Big Inch, since it had partially filled with water during its down-time. Water caused a continuing problem of freeze-offs which required de-icing of sections with alcohol and glycerin to keep gas flowing. Tennessee estimated the lines only operated at 75% of capacity due to the presence of water. The Inch Lines' electric pumping stations were by-passed and, without compression, the system relied only on wellhead pressure for gas movement through the lines.

Despite the numerous problems, the lease was a short-lived success which netted TGT a profit of more than $800,000. During the five month lease period TGT made upgrades and improvements to the Inch Lines totaling $250,000 and demonstrated that conversion to natural gas transport was practical.

In testimony before Congress, former Secretary of Interior Harold Ickes urged the WAA to sell the Inch Lines, since they were depreciating in value by more than $10,000 per day and requiring about $60,000 per month in maintenance costs. Ickes quoted from a Ford, Bacon & Davis engineering report, which "recommended that the only economic and sensible use of the lines was and is for the transportation of natural gas." Furthermore, Ickes opposed the continued lease or sale to Tennessee Gas on the premise that the company was seeking to create a monopoly by buying or leasing its only competition. Ickes never explained how TGT could create and maintain a monopoly under the regulatory scrutiny of the FPC.

The WAA opened bids for the Inch Lines on February 10, 1947. The winning bid of $143,127,000 was offered by a new company formed by George and Herman Brown of Houston called Texas Eastern Transmission Company (TETCO). Their bid was slightly less than the original construction price of $146 million and about thirty million above WAA's estimated value of the lines. Transcontinental Gas Pipe Line placed second with a bid of $131 million, while TGT was third with a bid of $123,700,000. J. W. Crotty's bid of one dollar-sixty cents for the Big Inch and forty cents for the Little Big Inch was fourth in the bidding. The Brown brothers' construction company, Brown & Root, was well connected in Washington, especially with their friend, Texas Congressman Lyndon B. Johnson.

Tennessee Gas which he shared with field employees during the late 1940's. His first four were: 1) To make money, 2) That every Tennessee location be the place where everyone wants to work, 3) That he expected TG&T employees to be the highest paid in the natural gas pipeline business at one point in time during each calendar year, and 4) That Tennessee Gas employees have the best benefits in the industry, in fact, equal to Lincoln Electric and Sears Roebuck, the known leaders in industry at that time.

When the first issue of THE LINE magazine rolled off the presses in February, 1946, Gardiner Symonds described its purpose with the following statement: "We think that every TGT employee has something in common with his fellow employees, and it is our intention to develop and emphasize this fraternity." And so the Tenneco "family culture" was born in the regulated gas business and it continued to propagate in the oil company as it grew and earned its reputation in the industry.

In the late 1950s, one of the most visible TGT personalities about town was Vice President Stone "Red" Wells. He was elected to the Houston Independent School District Board of Trustees whose meetings were televised. Stone Wells was the most loquacious member of the Board and seldom failed to entertain the TV audience.

As diversification efforts commenced in the late 1960s, Tenneco acquired several manufacturing enterprises with large employee workforces. It became apparent that Tenneco's "family culture" was nontransferable and could not replace the existing, longstanding manufacturing plant cultures, some of which were unionized.

Great trainloads of big-inch pipe rolled to construction site in new markets across Ohio, New York, Pennsylvania and into New England. W.C. McGee (center) would become President of Tennessee Gas Pipeline Company in 1959.

TGT EXPANSION

Postwar Pipeline

On a trip to New York in 1947, Symonds sat up on his bed after a brief catnap and shouted to his attorney Malcolm Lovett: "Malcolm, we're going to New England!"

In January 1945, barely two months after the completion of the wartime pipeline, the War Production Board (WPB) requested that Tennessee Gas "give consideration to the feasibility of installing additional compressor stations, compressors, and auxiliary apparatus" on the Tennessee pipeline in order to prevent an anticipated shortage of natural gas in the Appalachian region during the winter of 1945-1946. The WPB anticipated a shortfall of approximately 60,000 mcf by the end of the year. In response to this, and eager to increase its capacity and market presence, Tennessee Gas applied for a certificate to operate four additional compressor stations, install two additional compressors and cooling equipment in existing compressor stations, and build a 95-mile long 16-inch extension of the Tennessee pipeline from the Stratton-Agua Dulce field (the southern terminus of the pipeline) to the San Salvador gas field in Hidalgo County, Texas. The four additional compressor stations had been anticipated during the original construction of the Tennessee pipeline. The FPC ruled on June 8, 1945 that the looming shortage of 60,000 mcf justified the construction of the four new compressor stations, as well as the upgrades to existing stations. However, this came with a caveat; FPC approval would last only as long as the war emergency. The FPC concluded that "there is no warrant in the record extending such authorization beyond the war period. Applicant's witnesses submitted no estimates of post-war requirements in the Appalachian area." The FPC also questioned Tennessee's rates, ruling that the proposed 21.75-cent rate would bring more than the allowable 6.5% return plus depreciation and investment. The commission ordered that in the interest of the public good, Tennessee Gas could charge no more than 18.25 cents per mcf to its customers in the Appalachian region. With FPC approval and federal backing, the four additional compressor stations were built during the latter half of 1945, coming online in January 1946. The new stations increased the capacity of the Tennessee pipeline to approximately 260,000 mcf daily. Due to improving finances, Tennessee Gas was able to purchase the four stations from the Reconstruction Finance Corporation (successor to the Defense Plant Corporation) in early 1946. The slow progress by contractors in constructing these four compressor stations resulted in TGT dismissing the contractors, taking over the jobs in late 1945 and completing the work with Company forces. For several years thereafter, Tennessee constructed all of its compressor stations with Company labor.

Starting in 1946, TGT designed most of its facilities and pipelines in house. Its Engineering Department was staffed with experts representing all of the disciplines needed for design of compressor stations, pipelines, meter stations, dehydration facilities, shops, utility systems, power generation facilities, houses and offices. As Tenneco began to participate in several joint ventures in the early 1970s, it became apparent that its Engineering Department ranked amongst the best in the interstate pipeline industry. When the downturn commenced in the mid-1980s, layoffs and early retirements compelled TGT to use outside engineering firms to design facilities.

A snowy valve-turning ceremony for a new pipeline system in Buffalo, New York in 1950.

The Battle for Boston & New England

The loss of the Inch Lines was a major setback to Tennessee Gas, since their acquisition would have given TGT access to the New York and Philadelphia metropolitan areas, which were still served by town gas. With these markets out of reach, Gardiner Symonds set his sights on Pittsburgh, Buffalo, Boston and

TGT CULTURE
Communications

Once the Chicago Corporation assumed control of Tennessee Gas and Transmission Company in late September, 1943, the drumbeat of opposition to exporting natural gas out of Texas commenced. Two of the most vocal opponents were Texas Governor Coke Stevenson and Texas Railroad Commissioner Olin Culbertson, although neither had any regulatory control over the TGT line. In addition, the Corpus Christi Chamber of Commerce and the South Texas Chamber of Commerce opposed the line and this may have contributed to moving the TGT headquarters from Corpus Christi to Houston. The Dallas Morning News along with San Antonia Manufacturers Association also opposed TGT's export plan. And later, the Houston Press and the Houston City Council expressed opposition after the pipeline was in operation.

Brown Booth was hired as TGT's first director of public relations in 1944 to help curtail the tide of opposition to this new pipeline. Booth had been the editor of the Austin Statesman and knew his way around the political landscape in Austin. In addition to polishing TGT's public relations image with these opponents, Booth published the first issue of the Line magazine in February 1946 and it quickly became a popular item with Tennessee Gas employees and their families. The Line typically included a message from management, the current safety record, developments related to system expansion, featured stories and local reports from all field locations and each Houston Department. Three times each year the Line included quarterly Financial Reports and in the March issue, it included the previous year's Annual Report.

New England, areas which still relied on coal and inferior manufactured gas.

Symonds reasoned that TGT could do an end run around both Transco and Texas Eastern by building a line across upper New York State which could easily be extended to Massachusetts where gas could be sold to an affiliate or LDCs. Tennessee announced plans for its entry into the New England market as early as 1947, when it applied for a certificate of public convenience and necessity to build a 400-mile extension of its pipeline from eastern Kentucky to Buffalo, New York. A 33-mile lateral would connect to the Pittsburgh market and a 44-mile connection would cross upper New York State potentially supplying communities along the route such as Rochester, Syracuse, and Albany and terminating near Pittsfield, Massachusetts, where Tennessee would sell gas to either LDCs or a subsidiary company of Tennessee. This Buffalo extension could put TGT into the Boston market ahead of its two rivals. Meanwhile, Transcontinental Gas, which had placed second in the bidding for the Inch Lines, was granted permission by the FPC to build an entirely new pipeline from south Texas to New York City in May 1949, to an area already served by TETCO. This action presented New York City with two suppliers and it was unlikely a third would be allowed. The FPC temporarily put a halt to Gardiner Symonds' plans. In its ruling of July 29, 1949, the FPC noted that the proposed expansion of Tennessee's pipeline to Buffalo would be in the public interest, and agreed that Tennessee had sufficient gas supplies to service Buffalo and Pittsburgh. However, the FPC balked at extending the line further to the east, noting in its decision that Tennessee's reserves were not sufficient to justify the Boston expansion. The FPC dismissed Tennessee's application for the Boston expansion without prejudice, which sent Gardiner Symonds and Tennessee Gas back to the drawing board and encouraged Tennessee's competition.

Texas Eastern faced local resistance to its expansion plans. Texas Eastern had been on the verge of getting to New England as early as 1947, well ahead of Tennessee Gas. Texas Eastern had sought partners to create a regional gas company to distribute Texas Eastern's gas in New England. Called Minute Man Gas Company, the new local gas company was organized by E. Holley Poe, a founder and former president of Texas Eastern. Plans called for Minute Man to be jointly owned by three large New England utilities and Texas Eastern, with Texas Eastern holding the majority stake. Texas Eastern would also be the major gas supplier to Minute Man. The venture failed at the last moment when Poe was unable to secure financing for the company.

Undaunted by the failure of Minute Man, Texas Eastern proposed a new partnership with the same utilities that Poe had dealt with on the Minute Man deal. The major difference was that Texas Eastern would now own a minority stake in the new company, no more than twenty-eight percent, while the local utilities would control the rest. In exchange, Texas Eastern would be the sole gas supplier to the proposed company. The new company, called Algonquin Gas Transmission Company, would be locally-controlled but would sell only

Texas Eastern gas in New England, shutting out arch-rival Tennessee Gas except for a few areas of Vermont, New Hampshire, and Maine that Algonquin did not plan to serve. While TETCO was putting Algonquin together, Gardiner Symonds formulated a remarkably similar plan to get Tennessee Gas into New England. A few weeks before the incorporation of Algonquin, Symonds organized a New England subsidiary of Tennessee Gas, the Northeastern Gas Transmission Company. Symonds served as president and directed the new company to begin working for FPC approval for a single New England gas distribution system controlled by Northeastern. Just days after its formation, Tennessee applied for a certificate to serve the major cities and communities of New England. Symonds was not eager to accept the presence of Texas Eastern in New England, and resolved to fight Algonquin's application before the FPC.

Tennessee was quickly building the infrastructure needed to support these ambitious expansion plans. In addition to adding significant mainline capacity, Tennessee also signed new purchase contracts with dozens of gas producers in Texas and Louisiana. FPC hearings into both Algonquin's as well as Northeastern's petitions to serve New England began in July 1950. In papers filed with the FPC, Northeastern proposed to serve New England with gas purchased from both Tennessee Gas as well as Transco, which had received permission in April 1950 to increase its system capacity in anticipation of such an arrangement. This proposed arrangement ensured that Transco would not enter the New England market on its own, eliminating another potential competitor from the market. Tennessee Gas would supply 120,000 Mcf to Northeastern, while Transco would provide the remainder, some 65,000 Mcf. Algonquin planned to purchase its entire gas supply from Texas Eastern. In an initial ruling in October 1950, the FPC found both proposals to serve New England unsatisfactory. Both companies had indeed sought to "cherry-pick" New England by only including the major cities and towns in their systems. In the view of the FPC, this was not in the public interest and therefore unacceptable. The FPC chastised both companies for putting their interests ahead of those of New Englanders, and refused to certify either project. Algonquin approached Northeastern on October 5, 1950, and proposed that the two companies craft a plan to divide the entire New England market between them. The Algonquin proposal was dead on arrival at Northeastern. Symonds and Northeastern's management were not interested in cooperation, given the poor feelings toward Texas Eastern which had developed after the loss of the Inch Lines. A few days after receiving Algonquin's proposal, Northeastern ignored it entirely and applied for a certificate to serve all of New England with the FPC. Gardiner Symonds responded by denying that the FPC had authorized any division of the New England market. He asserted that it was the position of Northeastern that Algonquin was under the control of the coal interests, who had repeatedly tried to block the expansion of natural gas into New England. The coal industry, Symonds reasoned, did not have the public interest of New England at

had a thoroughbred horse farm. Later the men toured a well being drilled by Humble Oil on the ranch. Humble drilling experts explained the process. The tour group was bussed back to Kingsville, flew to Brownsville and drove into Mexico for a game dinner at Matamoros that evening.

The Company underwent a name change and the TENNECO magazine was created in the spring of 1967 to communicate quarterly with employees and other key people outside the Company. Al Smith, who had edited the Line for about 12 years, was chosen to edit the TENNECO magazine. It was designed to be of a medium of information covering the entire Tenneco industrial complex published in a slick magazine format. This publication was discontinued in 1987 as the Company's downturn worsened.

The Line's companion publication, COMMUNIQUE, was created in tabloid format in 1984 to communicate fast-breaking news and issues affecting the TGT Companies and industry. David Cunningham, the Line editor, also served as editor of COMMUNIQUE. By the end of 1986, the Fall/Winter issue of the Line was one of only two issues that year. This "Special Issue" was "A Tribute To Our Retirees" and contained 23 pages of photos and write-ups of retirees representing some 7,691 years of dedicated service to TGP. The layoffs and retirements of large numbers of experienced people, which actually commenced in 1984, had a detrimental effect on the "family culture" that Gardiner Symonds worked so hard to develop. In the early 1990s a condensed version of the Line magazine printed on recycled paper was introduced titled, "On The Line".

A "management newsletter" was introduced in 1972 and a new publication was created for Tenneco Oil Company. Later, Tenneco Topics was designed as a monthly tabloid newsletter for all Houston-based employees in 1978. Tenneco Oil P&M published it final commemorative issue of Tenneco Times in December, 1988, after the sale of both Oil Companies had been finalized. It recapped the history of P&M and featured photos of 23 members of the "Tenneco Retail Hall of Fame". Tenneco Oil E&P published a similar commemorative issue and included a roster of all E&P employees. TOC issued a number of special publications over the years, but one of the more attention-grabbing was a two-page brochure printed on yellow construction paper in the late 1960s titled, downtown Tenneco Oil. It was designed to attract secretaries and clerical personnel with Sandra Slay as the Company contact.

Tenneco's first two 16 mm movies were photographed and produced by Bob Bailey, a veteran Houston photographer. The first movie, "Gas", was presented in 1946 and told the story of TGT's first war-time pipeline being constructed. It was so popular that a second 30 minute film titled, "Gas Goes to Market", was produced. It told the dramatic story of natural gas from its formation millions of years ago to its delivery as a clean, efficient fuel for the present day markets on the Eastern seaboard. Both films were tremendous successes among the field personnel and their families. Houston employees could check out a 16mm projector and the film and show it to their families or various community groups. Over the years Tenneco produced numerous training and promotional films for its various divisions.

After the sale of the oil companies a new publication titled, Symposium, was introduced in the Spring, 1989. It was edited by

heart in seeking to deny natural gas to the area. While Symonds may not have wanted to work with Algonquin, the FPC had other plans.

Just a month after Northeastern rejected Algonquin's proposal to divide New England, the FPC ruled on Northeastern's request to serve the entire region. On November 8, 1950, the FPC granted Northeastern a certificate to serve a portion of New England, but held back large areas, including Boston, from Tennessee's service area. In all, Northeastern received 54% of the market, with the remainder reserved for Algonquin. The bulk of Northeastern's customers were to be in western and central Massachusetts, along with important communities in western Connecticut such as Stamford, Bridgeport, and Norwalk, among others. The FPC also granted Northeastern service to areas of Massachusetts north of Boston and in three communities in New Hampshire (Nashua, Manchester, and Concord). When finalized, Algonquin would serve eastern Connecticut, Rhode Island, Boston, and the Cape Cod region. Ironically, the FPC plan excluded largely rural Vermont, northern New Hampshire, and Maine from both companies' plans; the exclusion of these areas had been criticized by the FPC just a month before. While this ruling potentially settled the matter of gas service in New England, Symonds was not satisfied with the outcome. Nevertheless, Northeastern accepted the FPC ruling in the short term. Tennessee Gas moved quickly to complete its New England extension and enter the market areas given to it by the FPC ruling. The new pipeline, approximately 300 miles long, delivered southwestern gas to utilities in upstate New York and New England when it was completed on September 28, 1951. The new line was a milestone for Tennessee Gas, since they had indeed reached New England ahead of Texas Eastern. Algonquin lagged behind, beginning construction on its pipeline only in May 1951, even as Tennessee Gas was nearly completed. By December of the following year, Algonquin's 254-mile pipeline from Lambertville, New Jersey to Boston was still unfinished—partly because of continuing interference by Gardiner Symonds and Northeastern. Despite the seemingly final division of New England, Northeastern filed a petition before the FPC in March 1951, requested permission to increase the diameter of its main line from 20- to 24-inch pipe, arguing that this increase was necessary due to a shortage of 20-inch pipe and that general market conditions also warranted it. The shortage of 20-inch pipe was contrived, as Symonds himself ordered Northeastern's pipe supplier to roll 24-inch pipe instead of the 20-inch that Northeastern had originally requested. Despite misgivings, the FPC ruled in favor of Northeastern's request, granting permission for the larger diameter pipeline on the basis of projected market demand.

With a more robust pipeline system in the works, Northeastern moved in on Algonquin's market area. In June 1951, just a month after Algonquin had begun construction of its pipeline, Northeastern applied for a certificate to serve two additional distribution companies, as well as all of the communities in Algonquin's service area. He later explained his actions in a *Time* article in 1952, stating "They [Algonquin] delayed us for two years . . . and made all the trouble they could. I'm just vindictive enough to want to do the same thing to them." And so it proved. The FPC granted Tennessee's request to serve the additional distribution companies, but denied Northeastern's request to serve Algonquin's market area, prompting Gardiner Symonds to request a rehearing before the commission which was denied. By 1950, the FPC had permitted the Company to increase its delivery capacity to 1,310,000 MCF per day, compared to its initial capacity of 200,000 MCF per day. The TGT workforce had grown from 634 to 1,993 employees in the five years of operation. Two additional pipeline loops using larger diameter pipe had been installed along most of the pipeline route and, in some instances, a fourth parallel line was laid to accommodate the capacity increase of over six times the original volume. TGT had installed 15 compressor stations by the end of the decade, totaling 241,600 horsepower.

The 1950s

The decade of the 1950s witnessed the completion of major natural gas supply lines into the remaining metropolitan areas across the United States. These included the Northeastern project which commenced in the late 1940s. Tennessee Gas had relied on growth through the annual expansion of its pipeline system for increased year-over-year earnings. With the prospect of fewer major opportunities for growth in the interstate pipeline business, TGT redirected its investments into non-regulated businesses, many of which were not energy related. Despite this change of strategy, Tennessee Gas continued to pursue the expansion of its basic business. The 1950s brought new challenges and a fascinating array of projects.

Mississippi River Bridge

During the summer months of 1950 the Company was engaged in substituting four 26-inch lines for the original two 18-inch lines on the Mississippi River Bridge near Greenville, Mississippi. In connection with this operation, TGT arranged with the City of Greenville to retire the bonded debt on the bridge through rental payments, thereby rendering the bridge toll free to all traffic.

Gabe Plant

Stone & Webster Engineering Corporation constructed a $10.5 million liquid hydrocarbon recovery plant beside TGT's pipelines near Gabe, Kentucky in 1951. It had the capability of removing 350,000 gallons daily of ethane, propane, butane and natural gasoline from the main line gas stream. Its entire output had been contracted for a 20-year period. The hydrocarbon liquids were piped about 65 miles to a new Mathieson Chemical plant on the Ohio River near Brandenburg, Kentucky. Tennessee Gas employees operated the "stripping plant." This new hydrocarbon venture presented another phase in TGT's market diversification and benefitial to the Company's shareholders.

Alice H. Brink and was published quarterly for management and professional employees of Tenneco around the world. By then, Tenneco had become a manufacturing company with a pipeline subsidiary.

The parent company established Tenneco Business Services (TBS) based in The Woodlands, Texas in 1995. Its goal was to consolidate the administrative functions of all Tenneco companies into one entity through a shared services concept. These activities included Employee Benefits, Human Resources and Payroll, Finance and Accounting, Supplier Development, Environmental, Health and Safety, Information Technology and Communications. TBS saved approximately $7 million in operating income in 1995 and anticipated saving about $100 million over the 1996-1997 rollout period. With restructuring in all divisions, TBS would result in the net loss of about 650 professional and clerical positions throughout Tenneco. TBS issued a quarterly publication titled, ServiceLine, to keep employees informed of its progress. With the sale of the last energy division, Tenneco Gas employees only received two issues of ServiceLine.

Communications
1. Line Magazines
2. Quarterly Reports
3. Annual Reports
4. Leased Phone Lines
5. FM Radios
6. Press Releases
7. Advertising Programs
8. Shareholder Information
9. On-The-Line
10. Tenneco Magazine
11. Communique
12. Facts About Tenneco
13. Tenneco Topics
14. Special Publications

Trans-Canada Pipe Line, Ltd.

In 1954 TGT Senior Vice President Charles S. Coates resigned from the Company he helped found and moved to Canada to become the Executive Vice President of Trans-Canada Pipe Line, Ltd. with Gardiner Symonds' blessing.

Symonds and Clint Murchinson were instrumental in launching Trans-Canada and obtaining FPC approval for its imports to the United States. TGT took a 5.6% interest in the Canadian line in 1955 and assisted it in obtaining line pipe and with the financing process. Coates became President during the construction phase and stayed with Trans-Canada through December 1958. Coates was joined by Joe Parrish and several dozen other TGT-ers during the construction phase of establishing Trans-Canada. Several stayed with the new firm, but Joe Parrish, George Montroy and others returned to enjoy very productive careers with Tennessee Gas.

A-K Line

Tennessee Gas constructed a 370-mile long 30" pipeline from Agua Dulce, Texas to Kinder, Louisiana, in 1955. It was originally designed as a Texas coastal gathering line that was positioned to make industrial gas sales along its route. It was later capped at the Texas/Louisiana State line and the Texas portion of the line became the main intrastate pipeline for Channel Industries Gas.

The Muskrat Line

Perhaps the most challenging construction project during the 1950s was the 355-mile long Muskrat Line crossing the Mississippi Delta marshlands from Southeast Louisiana to the mouth of the Mississippi River. The project was billed as the largest project ever seen in Southeast Louisiana. It provided the first outlet for gas being produced with oil in many major fields in the area.

Some 18 dredges cut a canal 40 feet wide and 8 feet deep. TGT "bulk-headed and plugged" the canal at each intersecting bay or waterway to prevent salt-water intrusion into the marshes. Following the dredges was a barge mounted ditching machine to cut a narrow trench in the canal for the pipeline. A traditional long pipe-laying barge with its welding, coating, wrapping and cementing stations laid the line. Following this lay barge was another dredge to cover the pipe in the trench. A total of seven spreads constructed the line. The work was further complicated by the numerous gathering laterals which connected to the 24" and 20" line and their respective side valves and main line valves. Each of these was mounted on a piling–supported platform.

The Muskrat Line was unique in that it crossed 130 navigable streams, lakes, bays, and canals along with numerous smaller bayous and ponds along it 355 mile route, but only four roads and two railroads. The Muskrat Line was truly a challenging pipeline to construct.

He was "the ablest and toughest operator in the whole business."

– a description of Gardiner Symonds in PipeLine: The History of Canada Pipe Lines.

Contruction of the "Muskrat Line" through the Louisiana marshland and offshore waters.

Midwestern Gas Transmission Company

Midwestern Gas's Southern system was placed in service October 7, 1959. It was a 30-inch pipeline commencing at TGT's Portland, Tennessee, compressor station and following a direct path to Joliet, Illinois, where it delivered gas to three large Chicago area utilities. Its capital cost was $51 million.

Midwestern's original application to the FPC reflected a single line from Portland to the Canadian border near Emerson, Manitoba. This route was strenuously opposed by the Chicago LDCs and their other pipeline suppliers. Midwestern re-designed the system into two components with the Northern System taking an altogether different track and terminating near Marshfield, Wisconsin, where it delivered gas into the Michigan-Wisconsin Gas system. The Northern system was awaiting National Energy Board approval for the export of gas from Canada at the end of the decade The three northernmost compressor stations on the Northern system in Minnesota were eventually built behind dikes to protect them from flood waters from the nearby Red River of the North.

Investments & Financials

Tennessee Gas was listed on the New York Stock Exchange for the first time on March 17, 1958. Its original trading symbol was "TGT." East Tennessee Natural Gas became a subsidiary of Tennessee Gas Transmission Company on November 17, 1959 when 94% of its common stock was exchanged for TGT stock. Each ETNG shareholder received one share of TGT stock for each 2¾ East Tennessee shares.

Houston-based Aviation staff posing with Tenneco's Bolkow Bo-105 helicopter on the left, a British Aircraft Corporation BAC 1-11 in the center and a Lockheed Jetstar on the right.

Tenneco Takes to the Air

In the beginning the newly constructed 1,265 mile long gas pipeline was in need of periodic patrols across its entire length. Typically, a pre-war pipeline used pipeline walkers to walk the pipelines looking for dead vegetation or vapor clouds indicating leaks, for erosion of cover over the pipe and instances where landholders had built structures which encroached on the right of way. TGT's line was so lengthy that a combination of windshield and pipeline walker surveys did not appear practical. There were many stretches along the pipeline right of way where pedestrian surveys were very time consuming and were miles from the nearest access road.

Aerial Patrols

The first aerial patrol operation commenced in the spring of 1945 with Henry Hinkle flying a single engine Stinson based in Monroe, Louisiana. Initially, pipeline superintendents and foremen flew the entire route in their district to acquaint themselves and the pilot with the exact location of the pipeline. The route was easy to follow in the heavily forested areas, but very difficult in open cultivated fields and pasture land. Hinkle had no radio contact with the ground crews in those early years, since FM radio systems were not installed until 1947. He devised a warning system of problems by dropping red cloth bags which contained advisory information for the pipeline crews. Compressor station personnel monitored the pilot's progress when he circled the plant twice and flew on to the next station which was alerted by a private leased telephone line of Hinkle's anticipated arrival time at their location. By 1952, Tennessee Gas had expanded into New England and was using four fixed wing planes to patrol its system. Each pilot flew over 100,000 miles each year. TGT continued to use fixed wing aircraft for pipeline patrols flying at about four hundred feet above the ground until 1964.

Corporate Aircraft

Meanwhile, back in the Houston office the increased demand for travel between the home office and the far flung rural compressor stations became apparent during the first year of operations. TGT acquired a new twin engine Beechcraft which was equipped to accommodate five passengers and a crew of two and hired Anthony Zuma as chief pilot. Tony had 11 years of flying experience and had flown airways in the United States, Canada and Central and South America. Assisting Zuma was flight engineer, Kenneth D. Moore, who joined the Company in November, 1945.

The TGT Aviation Department was created in early 1947 with Chief Pilot Tony Zuma reporting to Personnel Director Dick Freeman. TGT's new Beechcraft was hangared at the La Porte, Texas, Municipal Airport where it eventually shared space with fixed wing patrol planes and other TGT aircraft. Tony Zuma was instrumental in organizing a highly acclaimed corporate aviation department during his long career with Tenneco.

A Douglas DC-3 was added to the fleet in early 1947. It was equipped to carry 16 passengers and had a range of about 1,400 miles, whereas the Beechcraft only had a range of approximately 700 miles. In 1948, a Stinson Voyager was added to the fleet for pipeline patrol use and based in Monroe, Louisiana. In early 1951, TGT was one of three companies that purchased Martin B-26 Marauder aircraft for civilian conversion. A second B-26 was purchased from a Michigan salvage company and underwent a similar civilian conversion. These planes were configured to carry 14 passengers and a crew of two and provided fast comfortable transportation for TGT executives. Jack Hamel, Les Briggs, Bill Schmidt, Russ Weatherson, Walt Burgett, Lynn Perry, Harvey Crumm, Lee Armstrong, Leo New, Jim Ruble, Charles Walling, Oscar Dudley, Sidney Pourchott and Zuma were among the many TGT pilots who flew the B-26s. They were flown for about eight years and became obsolete

Douglas DC-3

Cessna 170

Martin B-26

Sikorsky S-76

Cessna Citation V

Tenneco Aviation enjoyed a "golden era" until the economic downturn of 1984. During that time they were the envy of the corporate aircraft industry and their fixed wing safety record was unblemished since its inception in 1945.

49

WYLIE LOONEY

Wylie Looney was the only person to manage three pipeline field divisions and, in doing so, he ran about one-half of the field organization over his 34-year career. He was also the only Division Manager (originally titled Division Superintendent) to bridge the first and second generations of field personnel. Wylie ran Division "E" for 17 years and it became known as the "Looney Gas Company."

He had a reputation as a down-to-earth, matter-of-fact and somewhat philosophical person and was well known for his "Looneyisms." His most famous dictum was: "A fact is a fact and you can't deny that." But he was also a good judge of people and an effective manager. In the early 1970s, a compressor engineer noticed a policy paper on the bulletin board of a Division "D" compressor station. The engineer took the multi-page paper back to the Houston-based Compressor Department where the policy was analyzed for its justification. While Looney was chastised for not seeking Houston's approval and thought he was going to be fired, the Compressor Department made minor modifications, re-titled the policy and adopted a "Normal Progression Policy" for all hourly field operations employees. Looney had originally devised his "Route of Progression Policy" after encountering several maintenance men in Division "D" who had been in the same entry-level job, without a promotion, for some 10-12 years. According to TGP Senior Vice President Harry Long, Looney "built his field organization on pride and made people feel good about themselves."

when the turbo-prop and turbo-jets came on the scene. During its day, the B-26 was the Queen of TGT's fleet of fifteen aircraft.

A large, modern hangar was constructed in 1954 on the South side of Houston Municipal Airport, which is now known as William P. Hobby Airport. All of TGT's Aviation operations were moved from their previous location at La Porte.

Qualitron Aero, Inc.

Qualitron was acquired by Tenneco Inc. in late 1969 as an adjunct to its own corporate aircraft servicing operations. Qualitron Aero was a full-service aeronautics firm engaged in all phases of aircraft support, modification and engineering. Tenneco moved its entire corporate aircraft operation from Hobby Airport to the Qualitron Fixed Base of Operations (FBO) facility at Bush Intercontinental.

Rotor Wing Operations

The first helicopter purchased by the Company in 1964 was a Bell 47J2A based at the TGP District 524 hangar at the Houma, Louisiana, Airport. Phil Fillingham was hired to pilot the machine. Meanwhile, the TGP Division F patrol pilot, Don Gaunt, based in Agawam, Massachusetts, pointed out to Vice President Tony Zuma that flying fixed wing aircraft over densely populated areas was in violation of the Federal flight waiver TGP had been granted. Since helicopters would be in compliance with the waiver, Zuma made the decision to purchase another Bell helicopter for the required pipeline patrols in Division F.

Following the purchase of the first two helicopters in 1964, there were two significant phases in the growth of rotor wing operations. First, Don Gaunt made a flight with Mr. Symonds in a new leased Bell Jet Ranger at a time when his helicopter was in the shop for normal maintenance. Symonds was so impressed with the helicopter that he was quoted as saying "Every pipeline division should have one." Upon his return to Houston, Mr. Symonds instructed Tony Zuma to start placing orders for the TGP helicopters.

This explosive growth in the late 1960s led to many changes, since Tenneco Aviation had very little "hands on" helicopter maintenance experience. With the large number of helicopters coming on line, it was imperative that the Aviation Department expand to maintain the quality that was needed to assure a high standard of safety. Dale Benton was named to head this department and set about to hire some of the most talented helicopter pilots in the country. Meanwhile, Glen Everett was instrumental in establishing the policies and procedures to comply with the Federal regulations.

Al Hopson had been the Chief Pilot over the patrol aircraft for several years. Lynn Clough replaced Hopson as Rotor Wing Flight Operations Manager when Al's health failed in 1971.

The second growth phase occurred in 1973 when the decision was made to move into twin engine helicopter operations. This decision was prompted when a Tenneco Chemicals 206A Bell Jet Ranger based at TGP Station 329 near Mahwah, New Jersey, suffered an unexplained engine failure and was forced to make an emergency landing at a ski resort, injuring several skiers. This incident made the Company acutely aware of the risk of flying single engine aircraft over densely populated areas. Tenneco management made the decision to purchase a twin engine Bolkow Bo-105 helicopter for flying in the New York area. This same concern for safety resulted in the purchase of additional Bo-105 helicopters for the Houston area, offshore, Massachusetts and Kentucky.

The Golden Years

As the Tenneco Aviation Department continued to grow when Tenneco diversified into non-energy related businesses, it was evident that the Company needed its own hangar facility at the new Bush Intercontinental Airport. With each large manufacturing business acquisition came aircraft, one or more pilots and a support staff which was rolled into the Tenneco Aviation Department. A large, state-of-the-art hangar and office facility was constructed in 1980 south of Qualitron's FBO to accommodate Tenneco's Houston-based jet fleet and helicopters.

In addition to the previously mentioned fixed wing aircraft, the Company owned or leased at various times during the golden years: two Vickers Viscount 800 Series, two Fairchild F-27s, one Fairchild Hiller F-227, and later, three British Aircraft Corporation BAC 1-11s, four Lockheed Jetstars, three Gulfstream G-IIs, one Boeing 727 and several small corporate jets based around the country. The Company also owned 23 helicopters based at thirteen pipeline and corporate locations with 33 rotor-wing pilots.

It is fair to say that, both inside and outside of Tenneco, there were differing opinions about Tenneco's "air force". The aircraft devoted to the operations side of the business were clearly justified. Using helicopters to transfer personnel in the Gulf of Mexico; using small aircraft and helicopters to fly the pipeline rights of way checking for leaks and evidence of trespassing or tampering with the surface facilities; or for getting key people and materiel to remote locations in tough situations, made sense. It was the use of Tenneco's "executive aircraft" which was questioned from time to time. This occurred after Tenneco became a "conglomerate" when executive company plane ownership and usage expanded and seemed to become susceptible to abuse.

When the business downturn began in 1984, the first layoffs commenced at Tenneco Aviation, signaling the end of "the golden years." However, the Tenneco Aviation department was the envy of the corporate aircraft industry and their fixed wing safety record was unblemished since its inception in 1945.

Wylie Looney joined TGT in July, 1944 after nine years with Lone Star Gas Company. He was hired as a utility inspector during the original pipeline construction. After several promotions, he ran TGP Divisions "E", "D" and "A" before retiring in 1978.

DICK HINES

Shortly after he was discharged from the US Navy at the close of WWII, Dick Hines received a job offer from Tennessee Gas for a clerical position at Station 96, Campbellsville, Kentucky. From that start in January, 1947, Dick became a construction clerk and had responsibilities from Greenville, Mississippi, to the end of the pipeline at Clendenin, West Virginia. He reported to the Division Superintendent, Cecil Porter. This was a mobile job which exposed him to a variety of construction activities and enabled him to establish positive relationships with a number of talented TGT-ers. As TGP's major construction wound down, Hines was promoted to Pipeline Foreman at a new district in Mercer, Pennsylvania. There he distinguished himself as an innovator while devising new crew truck cabins and modifying commercial trucks for oil field-type service. He advanced to Pipeline Superintendent in mid-1955, became the first District Superintendent on the system in 1959 with responsibilities for both pipeline and compressor operations. Dick was the first TGP Assistant Division Manager when the job was created in 1965. Two years later he replaced Wylie Looney as Division Manager in Division E. Hines transferred to Houston in early 1981 and completed his 43 years with TGP as Pipeline and Compressor Superintendent.

The '60s were defined as "A decade of solid even-paced and outstanding growth for Tenneco Inc."

TGT GAME CHANGER, NAME CHANGER YEARS

Regulation

The decade of the 1960s was both a game changer and a name changer for Tennessee Gas. The Company came out of the starting blocks, picked up speed and with the acquisition of Kern County Land Company in 1967, hit passing gear in the race to become a diversified business enterprise. This decade marked the first time in history the Company earnings exceeded $500 million in a single year. Its newest pipeline, Midwestern Gas Transmission, put its Northern Division in service in October, 1960, and commenced importing its entire gas supply from Canada.

Later in 1960, TGT filed an application with the FPC and the California Public Utilities Commission (CPUC) to construct a pipeline from south Texas across Mexico and terminating near Los Angeles. The 1,600-mile Tex-Mex Pipeline would deliver gas to Southern California Edison and the Los Angeles Department of Water and Power for power generation and to help alleviate the air pollution problem in the Los Angeles Basin. Humble Oil & Refining Company had contracted to supply a major portion of the gas with Petroleos Mexicanos (Pemex) supplying a small amount.

Meanwhile, TGT had a stack of rate cases pending at the FPC, all seeking an "adequate and just" rate of return. The three cases were stacked upon one another and subject to future refunds, if the regulatory body failed to approve TGT's version of rate of return. The rate of return in these cases was not a guaranteed return, but one that had to be earned with economical financing of expansions and prudent operation of facilities. In late 1962, TGT settled all rate cases with the FPC and agreed to refund $134 million, part of which was to be compensated by tax rebates of approximately $70 million, since a 52% tax rate had been paid on the earnings over the previous five years.

The Company proceeded to apply for annual capacity increases over the remainder of the decade while the FPC continued to conduct hearings into 1965 on the Tex-Mex Pipeline which had been modified and shortened to an all-US pipeline and re-named Gulf Pacific. In the meantime, the FPC adopted new accounting procedures with respect to the 7% Investment Tax Credit recently enacted by Congress to stimulate investment in new plant and equipment. This change resulted in an increase in 1964 earnings.

Organizational Changes

W. C. McGee, Jr., President of Tennessee Gas Pipeline, was elected to the Tennessee Gas Board of Directors in 1960. "Maggie," as he was known to all, was a very popular executive with his employees and effectively bridged the gap between TGT's first generation employees and those in the second.

In early 1961, TGT formed Tenneco Corporation as its subsidiary to own all non-pipeline properties. In addition, TGT formed Tenneco Oil Company as a subsidiary of Tenneco Corporation to own and operate its far flung integrated oil operations. The intent of the TGT Board was to more clearly separate the government-regulated business from its oil and other non-utility businesses.

George R. Perrine, former Chairman of the Illinois Commerce Commission, was named President of Midwestern Gas Transmission Company (MGT), a Chicago-based subsidiary of TGT in 1963. MGT had record high deliveries and earnings the following year and applied for its first Northern System expansion.

Tennessee Gas Transmission's name changed to Tenneco Inc. in April, 1966 to more accurately describe its broad scope of businesses. The TGT name was maintained as a subsidiary to administer and control its pipeline businesses while Tennessee Gas Pipeline, operated as a division of the parent and the other three pipelines functioned as subsidiaries.

The following year resulted in Omar H. Simonds, Jr., formerly Senior Vice President of TGT, becoming President of TGT. Ron McVey, who had served as TGT President, was moved to Chairman of the Board of TGT. At his request, W. C. "Maggie" McGee became chairman of the Operating Policy Committee of TGP in early 1969. He had been President of TGP since 1959. He was succeeded by L. W. A. "Bud" Campbell as President of Tennessee Gas Pipeline Company.

HARRY LONG

Harry Long went from his first job as a "stob driver" on a survey party in November, 1949 to become the President of Tennessee Gas Pipeline from April, 1979 through April, 1984. One of Harry's proudest accomplishments was the 1964 promotion of the International Correspondence School (ICS) courses offered to all Operating and Compressor field employees. Initially, over 90% of the eligible employees enrolled in the courses. They had a choice of three out of 15 total courses offered and could continue the coursework for up to two years at the Company's expense. This technical training program was the outgrowth of system-wide training offered in 1954 and 1955 by the Petroleum Extension Service of the University of Texas.

Gardiner Symonds' welcome to Houston was less than enthusiastic when he and the four original Chicago Corporation transfers drove to Houston in his Buick in late September, 1943. Their mission was clear: to lease office space and establish a headquarters in downtown Houston. Unfortunately, Symonds drove past the Rice Hotel upon their arrival about 1 o'clock in the morning and proceeded to do a "U" turn, since Texas Avenue was a two-way street then and practically deserted at that hour of the morning. However, he was given a traffic ticket by an observant Houston policeman. This was TG&T's welcome to Houston.

Gardiner Symonds and his Corpus Christi team leased two offices and a reception room in the Second National Bank Building on Main Street, which is now the South Coast Life Building, and opened offices for business in Houston. Then on October 1, TGT signed a lease for two floors in the National Standard Building and, when these quarters were ready, they moved in on October 12. Neither of these office buildings were air conditioned. Employee #5, Lowell Alden, said "I moved everything I had in the drafting room in a wastebasket and walked over to the National Standard Building." Alden had been the first person hired in the Engineering Department by Charlie Coates. He was a draftsman who eventually headed up Tenneco's Graphic Arts Department.

Later, TGT leased space on two additional floors of the National Standard Building. As the Houston workforce expanded during pipeline construction and into the first year of operations TGT leased space in the 22-story

Technical & Other Milestones

The Tennessee Gas Engineering Department had designed all compressor stations and pipelines since 1944. TGT had relied upon relatively slow speed reciprocating engine driven compressors, except at the Moorhead, Kentucky electric station which burned after a lightning strike and was replaced by industrial grade gas turbines driving centrifugal compressors. Other exceptions were the three similar gas turbine stations on its 800 Line in the mid 1950s. When the 500 Line was built to transport offshore Gulf of Mexico gas from Bay Saint Louis, Mississippi, to Centerville, Tennessee, it was powered initially by three pairs of reciprocating engine compressor stations, plus the first onshore station at Bay Saint Louis. The three pairs were master and slave stations where each slave was controlled from its master station relying on early computer technology. The masters were built in 1959 and the companion slave stations, designed for unattended operation, were built in the early 1960s as the volumes of offshore gas increased dramatically, requiring more pipeline capacity.

In late 1964, TGP installed its first barge-mounted, remotely-controlled compressor station 526A, south of Port Sulphur, Louisiana. Tennessee Gas then automated Station 249 in 1968 and Station 538 at Heidelberg, Mississippi, in 1969; its first large master reciprocating engine-powered station with computer controls monitored and operated from a remote location. The continued improvements in specific fuel consumption of the large gas turbine driven centrifugal units, along with their less complicated automation systems, led to their increased use in the following decade.

Tennessee Gas dedicated its first Liquefied Natural Gas (LNG) storage/peak shaving plant near Hopkinton, Massachusetts, in 1967. While the liquefaction plant performed to specs, its two underground storage caverns failed to function as designed and the project was abandoned.

Houston Offices

As Bud Campbell was about to depart for Church early one Sunday morning in 1961 he received a phone call from Gardiner Symonds who invited him over to his home to discuss a proposition. Symonds had an artist's rendition of a 33-story office building which occupied an entire block of downtown Houston adjacent to the Ten Ten Garage. He told Bud that he wanted him to build the building. Campbell, who had a very impressive portfolio of successful construction projects and an aggressive management style, vacated his job as Vice President of Pipeline Operations to head up a Tennessee Gas Building Corporation team to supervise the construction of the building by the general contractor, W. S. Bellows Construction Corporation. Bud reported to Charlie Lingo who was President of Tennessee Gas Building Corporation at the time.

In mid-March, 1963, TGT departments began to occupy the new Ten-

The new 33-story Tenneco Gas Building provided more than a million square feet of office space.

Commerce Building and eventually purchased both the Commerce Building and its 12-story Annex in 1951. The Commerce Building was a modern, state of the art office facility and featured beautiful marble walls in the restrooms and elevator lobbies. Tennessee's optimum employee growth projections indicated the need to consolidate its employees in a single building which was not possible with existing long term tenant commitments in the Commerce Building. At the time, TGT's 1,600 employees were scattered across nine additional locations in the city.

TGT's Houston office staff began to move into the newly constructed Tennessee Building in early 1963. It was outfitted with several unique features including the new Centrex telephone system bypassing switchboard operators and permitting callers to ring their desired parties directly. The system, called "Direct Inward Dialing", was only the second installation in the Southwest. The new office sported another unique feature – a US Post Office in the basement, the only one in downtown Houston.

A NEAR CATASTROPHE

In 1961, the U. S. Army Corps of Engineers built the Greenup Locks and Dam on the Ohio River some 2,000-feet upstream of TGP's submerged pipeline crossings. During construction, the flow of the river changed dramatically and commenced to erode the river bank and expose TGP's high pressure pipelines. The swift current directed against the bank literally sucked the bank, trees and all, into the river. Harry Long was chosen to devise a plan to prevent further bank erosion before it ruptured one or all of Tennessee's three main pipelines going to the Northeast. The loss of these pipelines would have been a major disaster for the Company and may have resulted in bankruptcy.

Harry purchased a rock quarry and hired drivers to haul some 200,000 tons of rock to stabilize the bank and cover the pipelines. They hauled rocks, mostly in one ton slabs and one rock to a truck, for four months until the bank was stabilized. When spring came, TGP commenced construction of a double line aerial crossing about 2,000-feet further downstream of the submerged crossings. The

two 30-inch diameter lines were suspended by cables from two 268-foot tall towers on the river banks. The two inverted "Y" towers were positioned 2,285 feet apart and were raised along with the upper

nessee Building, although the grand opening in late 1963 was scheduled to coincide with the twentieth anniversary of the Company. Gardiner Symonds personally welcomed employees and their families in his office during the Sunday open house tours which preceded the formal dedication ceremonies on Monday, September 30, 1963. The construction of the new building and completion of the move-in took place in less than 23 months after ground breaking. TGT occupied approximately 65% of the building initially with Superior Oil, U. S. Steel, Anderson Clayton & Company and several individual lawyers leasing about five floors.

The building won numerous architectural awards for its architect, Skidmore, Owings & Merrill. One article was titled "The Glass Box Goes 3-D" and depicted the building as one of the two largest office buildings in downtown Houston with approximately one million square feet of usable office space. The building rose some 500 feet above street level and was about 195 feet square. It is positioned in the center of a 250-foot square downtown Houston block. At the time it was the only downtown office building with a 600-gallon-per-minute water well in its sub-basement. The sub-basement was also the home of a massive Supply Room equipped with a state of the art vertical conveyor system which could deliver items to any floor of the building within 14 minutes.

The architect incorporated a unique feature in the building corridors, lower floor wall panels, elevator walls and cabinetry in various parts of the structure. The builders searched the world over for a massive white oak capable of yielding from one trunk the amount of paneling needed. They located a tree in Germany's famed Black Forest of Bavaria whose growth rings indicated an age of over 500 years. It was carefully felled and skillfully peeled to produce over 400,000 square feet of white oak veneer.`

The Tennessee Building's exterior was clad in amber-gray anodized aluminum, which was originally thought to be too drab, but gives the surface a bronze appearance in sunlight. Its outside walls were recessed five feet to gain the benefit of shading and are fitted with glare-proof gray glass. Additional shading is provided by horizontal, aluminum sun deflectors.

The office areas, which surround a vertical core containing the elevators and other service facilities, are free of interior obstructions like columns. This clear-span design allows the use of floor-to-ceiling partitions which are movable, but give the appearance of permanence. Consequently, individual offices can be quickly sized to any multiple of five-foot six-inch modular units, each with its ceiling fixture that supplies lighting and air conditioning.

The Tennessee Building was also home to the Tennessee Bank and Trust Company which was originally located at 306 Main Street. The Bank was suspended a full story above street level and featured drive-in banking and night depository facilities on Louisiana Street. When the corporate name change occurred in 1966 the building was renamed the Tenneco Building.

In 1968 a group of picketing union protesters were featured on the ten o'clock Houston TV news in what the reporter described as at the entry to the "Anderson Clayton Building." Gardiner Symonds was livid, since Anderson Clayton & Co. occupied only a small percentage of the Tenneco Building. He immediately commissioned the building manager, Phil Godshalk, to install illuminated signs on all four sides of the upper floor of the building as illustrated on the cover of this publication. The seven-letter TENNECO signs fit nicely between the columns which ran from top to bottom of the building. Though the architect complained, the signs were not removed until several years later when it became less popular to display corporate signage on the top of Houston office buildings.

In 1978 Tenneco announced it was planning to move all of its 700 pipeline employees to a West Houston campus-like facility. Charles Falkenhagen was appointed as the lead person to coordinate this effort. After re-evaluating Tenneco's real estate holdings in the downtown area, the idea was scrapped. Tenneco not only owned the Tenneco building and Ten Ten Garage, but a 50% interest in the 1100 Milam building, the Hyatt Regency Hotel and its parking garage. This financial stake in downtown Houston real estate evidentially "trumped" any move to the suburbs.

Decade Ends With a Flourish

N. W. "Dick" Freeman returned to the Company from an extended medical leave and was elected President of Tenneco Inc. Many Tenneco observers believe the Company made its most successful acquisition when it acquired Kern County Land Company (KCL) in late 1967. Its assets included six ranches with cattle and horses, 17,000 acres of Company-operated irrigated farmland and another 100,000 acres leased to others in the San Joaquin Valley, two feedlots, oil and gas production, various precious metals and hard mineral rights, 54% of J. I. Case Company, 50% of Watkins-Johnson Company, Walker Manufacturing Company, 1,000 miles of irrigation canals in and around Bakersfield and several large real estate investments. KCL's senior water rights on the Kern River dated back to the 1860s when Kern County was first settled. The lands totaled 1.8 million acres owned and 794,000 acres of long term leases in three states. The following year a new slogan appeared in Tenneco Inc.'s national advertising; "Building Businesses is our Business." (The KCL acquisition is described in detail in the E&P section of this book.)

By the end of the decade TGT was now selling gas in 25 states with consolidated revenues of $561 million in 1969. The 1960s were characterized as "A decade of solid even-paced and outstanding growth for Tenneco Inc."

pipeline from barges lined across the river. The second line was then capped and floated across the river without the need for barges. It was raised by cables and secured into brackets under the first pipeline. This aerial river crossing is the largest on the TGP system.

APPLICATION DENIED FOR GULF PACIFIC

In July, 1966, the FPC reversed an earlier Trial Examiner's decision and denied the Gulf Pacific application. This came as a major disappointment to many in the company who had devoted seven years to the project. The Company's official statement reads "Under current economic conditions and... with the overall return limited to 6% per annum, the project would have been a burden to Tenneco Inc. for many years. The current high cost of capital would have made it next to impossible to have financed the project economically, and therefore would have precluded any contribution by Gulf Pacific to net earnings until after 1970 at the earliest. We believe that the same amount of capital and manpower can be invested more profitably in our non-pipeline businesses, resulting in a much better return to stockholders."

The most surprising reaction to the decision was the resignation of Tenneco President Harold Burrow, who had been with the Company since day one and had been a strong proponent of expanding TGT's pipeline business. Insiders speculate that Burrow was not Symond's choice to lead Tenneco into a diversification program and was forced out. However, Burrow denies that and says he was just "burned out" and wanted to do something different. Gardiner Symonds gave Mr. Burrow and his wife an all-expense paid trip around the world as a retirement gift from the Company.

The clean and polished look of a typical MGT compressor room (Portland, Tennessee) in the '70s.

TGT THE SEVENTIES

Setting the Stage

Overcoming obstacles and responding to change had always been a constant process throughout the earlier history of Tenneco. Despite this background, the advent of the 1970s with its dramatic domestic and international turmoil put major stresses on the industry, the Company and its people. The area pricing approach established by the Federal Power Commission (FPC) in the 1960s began to take a toll on new natural gas reserve generation. The trend of production exceeding reserve generation that had begun in 1968 continued with a vengeance into the 1970s with the market clamoring for more gas and producers reluctant to drill because of poor economics.

Leaders in Tennessee Gas Transmission and the industry had been issuing warnings for many years about the potential for a shortage of natural gas. In the 1970 summer issue of The Line magazine, O.H. Simonds, Jr., President of TGT wrote: "You may recently have heard a great deal about the natural gas industry's concern over the shortage of gas supply. It is true that the nation's proved recoverable reserves have declined markedly in the past two years and that unless greater incentives for exploration and development of new reserves are provided there will be a more serious shortage in the future."

Tenneco Executive Vice President Wilton E. Scott later continued on this subject with expressed concerns about the natural gas policies being pursued by the Regulatory agencies. Messages by Simonds and Scott supported the same ones that Gardiner Symonds had been making for several years only now it had critical impact and needed immediate attention.

NATURAL GAS PRICES AND DEMAND, 1950-1971

Year	Total Marketed Production (Trillions of Cubic Feet)	Average Wellhead Price (Cents per MCF)
1950	6,280	6.5
1951	7,457	7.3
1952	8,013	7.8
1953	8,397	9.2
1954	8,743	10.1
1955	9,405	10.4
1956	10,082	10.8
1957	10,680	11.3
1958	11,030	11.9
1959	12,046	12.9
1960	12,771	14.0
1961	13,254	15.1
1962	13,877	15.5
1963	14,747	15.8
1964	15,462	15.4
1965	16,040	15.6
1966	17,207	15.7
1967	18,171	16.0
1968	19,322	16.4
1969	20,698	16.7
1970	20,921	17.1
1971	22,493	18.2

The major portion of the production was sold into the interstate market where wellhead prices were fixed by the Federal Power Commission under their area pricing regulations. The average price increases were due to the impact of the growing intrastate market.

Source: American Gas Association, Gas Facts, 1974

OMAR H. SIMONDS, JR

Omar graduated from Yale University with a degree in Applied Economics Science in 1942. A year later he finished his Naval air cadet training, received his commission and was married. Omar spent much of WWII as a Naval flight instructor at Corpus Christi, Texas, prior to joining Tennessee Gas as a right-of-way agent in 1947. He moved into the Gas Sales Department a year later and began a rapid progression up the ranks to Vice President in 1958. Many Tenneco observers believe he had a special knack for dealing with TGT's eastern LDC customers because of his upbringing in New Jersey and collegiate experience at Yale.

Simonds was elected President of TGT in October, 1967, following Ron McVey. He held the position until July, 1974 when he was named President of Tenneco Realty, Inc.

The competition for contracting the reduced level of new reserves became even more intense. It quickly became clear that the increased demand was going to rapidly outstrip interstate gas supply due to the dramatic wellhead price differential between price-controlled gas committed to the interstate market and reserves that could be sold into the more attractive intrastate market which was not subject to regulated pricing control. By 1971 some eighty percent of new natural gas reserve additions were being committed to the intrastate market. An immediate result was that several of TGT's interstate pipeline competitors initiated pipeline curtailment that year. The resulting outcry from customers, regulators and the general public was immediate with forceful messages conveyed to "do whatever is required to assure adequate supply."

INTERSTATE RESERVE ADDITIONS (TCF)

Year	AGA Reserve Additions Excluding Revisions	Reserve Committed to Interstate Market	Percentage
1968	9.8	6.4	65
1969	9.6	6.2	64
1970	11.3	3.5	31
1971	11.1	2.2	20

Source: FPC

The specter of the lack of access to new reserves was quite ominous to the Company because by this time TGT had grown to an annual delivery of 1.87 Trillion Cubic Feet (TCF) to its industrial and regional distribution company customers. Long-term contracts were in place to not only continue to provide this supply but to actively work to increase deliverability to meet the growing demand. The fact that the total nationwide interstate new supply was

L. W. A. "BUD" CAMPBELL

After obtaining his degree in Civil Engineering from Iowa State, Bud worked for the Austin Company, building Dow's magnesium plant at Freeport, Texas. He joined the Army infantry in 1944 and found himself in the Battle of the Bulge and just a few miles from Berlin as WWII ended. He returned to the Austin Company and, after two projects joined TGT in 1947 as an engineer on several construction projects. Bud advanced to District Superintendent, Construction Superintendent, Assistant Chief Engineer and Chief Engineer before his election to Vice President in 1958. Gardiner Symonds hand-picked Bud to supervise the construction of the new Tennessee Building in 1961. Upon its completion, he returned to TGP as VP of Operations.

Bud succeeded Maggie McGee as President of Tennessee Gas Pipeline in 1969 and he held that position for three years. In 1972, he and Joe Parrish traded jobs and Bud became Executive Vice President of Operating Services for TGT. Bud was a high-energy guy who had been very active in numerous community activities, including his Church. Insiders say Bud was bored with the Operating Services job and, after 27 years with Tennessee Gas, he resigned in late 1973 to serve in an administrative capacity for $1 per year with the Brazos Presbytery, an organization of 120 Presbyterian Churches in the Houston area.

only 2.2 TCF that year indicated the magnitude of the challenge. Underlying these contractual requirements was the recognition that the product being delivered was essential to the physical and economic survival of a major portion of the nation. Alternative supplies or suppliers capable of offsetting the loss of TGT system deliveries were simply not available in the short term and certainly not during the depth of winter. Even the weather patterns were not helpful during these early 1970s and the continuing cold winters had already raised the prediction of global cooling. Pressure on the Company to provide new supplies to customers was becoming intense.

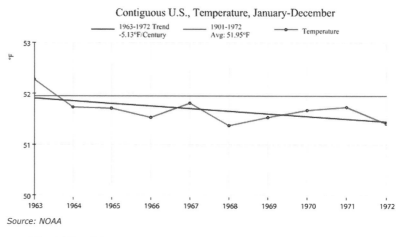

Contiguous U.S., Temperature, January-December

Source: NOAA

The TGT delivery commitments were clear and the obstacles to meeting these commitments were also rapidly coming into focus. Until federal pricing regulations could be changed, demand would grow, reserve generation would decline and what reserves were generated would be committed to the intrastate market wherever possible. Major efforts were initiated by the industry in the political and regulatory arena to deregulate natural gas pricing but it was recognized that the wheels of national policy would turn slowly.

In the 1971 Tenneco Annual Report, N.W. Freeman cited the shortages of natural gas and oil to the nation and noted that energy considerations would affect how many businesses planned for the future. He discussed how Tenneco was adapting to the crisis by trying to develop alternative fuel sources such as Liquefied Natural Gas (LNG) and Synthetic Natural Gas (SNG) in addition to fortifying the Company's reserves through exploration and expanding and upgrading facilities in the Gulf of Mexico. It was clear that Tenneco and TGT recognized the critical state of the energy industry and were preparing to meet the challenge.

Critical Areas of Focus

The actions taken by TGT to meet the growing challenges fell primarily in three different areas. These actions would provide the guidelines for TGT's efforts during the 1970s and to some extent the remainder of its corporate life. The first and most significant from the standpoint of the impact on management, organizational structure and economic decisions was to commit to the securing of non-traditional supplies which required a global outlook. The dearth of available domestic gas supplies committed to the interstate market required an international search for any energy form that could be economically acquired and moved to the United States for use by Tenneco's pipelines and their customers. Looking beyond North America for pipeline supplies was a new objective for TGT and required the development and acquisition of new talents. As had been their history and character, the employees stepped up to help meet this challenge.

The second area of focus by TGT was the expansion of pipelines in the Gulf of Mexico to facilitate the entry of additional gas into its system. Additional pipeline gas through existing and new connections on both the Canadian and Mexican borders were also pursued. Innovative methods of securing gas reserve commitments such as providing advance production payments in the offshore areas were encouraged and pursued. The significance of these objectives was based on the recognition that not all gas supply areas were created equal. Areas where reserves were committed to the interstate market merited primary attention. At the parent company level, these supply concerns were a major factor in Tenneco Inc. increasing its budget allocation to Tenneco Oil E&P to allow it to acquire leases with attractive gas reserve potential in the blockbuster Gulf of Mexico lease sale in 1970.

The third area was to ensure that the fundamental requirement of the organization to provide a safe, efficient and profitable delivery system was met regardless of the source, form or location of the supply. While this had always been a primary objective of the Company, the possibility of differing forms and qualities of pipeline supplies mandated extraordinary care. With over 15,290 miles of pipeline, 78 compressor stations and transporting about 16% percent of the interstate natural gas consumed in the U.S., this challenge had to be met on a daily basis. Without success in this area, progress in the other areas would not be meaningful and the Company would fail.

These three areas of focus had to be addressed simultaneously and continuously which required innovative and aggressive action. In the heavily regulated world that existed, change requiring governmental approval would come very slowly. As a result, innovative actions to secure future supply for customers were often undertaken without knowledge that the costs incurred would be approved by regulators or allowed to be recovered in rates by the Company. In addition, supplemental projects involved years of lengthy negotiations, major construction operations and expected project lives of at least 20 years after being placed in service. This required projections of available long term financing, final product cost, future natural gas pricing and demand with all being subjected to the risk of securing the necessary governmental approvals. Despite these uncertainties, TGT realized that the value

JOSEPH L. PARRISH, JR.

Joe was Executive Vice President and Chief Operations Officer for Tennessee Gas Transmission Company when he retired in November, 1984. After graduating from high school in Nashville, Tennessee he earned a B. S. in Chemical Engineering from the Virginia Military Institute in 1941. After a year with Remington Arms Company, he served as an Army field artillery officer in the Pacific theater for about four years during World War II. Joe was awarded the Bronze Star and several other medals during the Pacific campaign and left the Army having attained the rank of Major.

Following the War he attended Harvard University and earned an MBA in September, 1947. Parrish was interviewed on campus by Gardiner Symonds and accepted a job with a new company, Tennessee Gas Transmission Company. He was assigned as Construction Engineer at Station 87, Portland, Tennessee. Joe then spent his second year in Gas Sales in Houston before being transferred as Chief Engineer of Northeastern Gas Transmission in New England through 1954. In 1955 through 1958 he was Chief Engineer of Trans-Canada Pipe Line Company before returning to Tennessee Gas as Vice President of construction. Parrish was elected President of Tennessee Gas Pipeline in 1972 and served in that capacity until 1979 when he moved to his final job with TGT.

He served as Director and Committee Chairs in numerous industry associations: Southern Gas Association, American Gas Association, Independent Natural Gas Association

of a natural gas pipeline system without supply rapidly approached zero and therefore these risks had to be taken.

As diversification progressed within the Company, the name of the parent organization was changed to Tenneco Inc. in 1966 and a new corporate office was established. At that point, TGT became simply one of the operating divisions of Tenneco with responsibility for providing overall management and administrative services for all of Tenneco's natural gas pipelines. By the beginning of 1970, TGT consisted of four separate operating pipeline companies and when combined with TGT management and supporting departments employed a total of 3,231 people. Within the Houston headquarters, the individual operating pipelines (except for East Tennessee Natural Gas headquartered in Knoxville, Tennessee) also had managerial, technical and professional staff. The combined workforce in Houston under the TGT umbrella numbered 1855 people or 57% of the entire Pipeline organization.

1971 TENNESSEE GAS TRANSMISSION CORPORATE STRUCTURE

President – O. H. Simonds, Jr.

Senior Vice President	Vice President	
J. L. Parrish, Jr.	J. M. Johnson	H. E. Long
J. S. Brogdon, Jr.	B. L. Reynolds	J. F. Shivers

Tennessee Gas Pipeline	Midwest Gas Transmission	East Tennessee Natural Gas	Channel Industries
President	President	President	President
L.W.A. Campbell	George Perrine	T. K. Davis	H. E. Rowe

Vice President		Vice President	Vice President
Fred Clarke E. U. Cochrane		John M. Robertson, Jr.	Thomas R. Bell
Howard Gray W. M. Rogers			
Roger Stark William Such			
George White			

Division Managers	Division Managers	General Superintendent	General Superintendent
A – Frank Ballard	Northern – Gaines Murray	Ben Simpson	Ned Thomas
B – Hugh Fisher	Southern – N. J. Smith		
C – Otis Korn			
D – Wylie Looney			
E – Dick Hines			
F – Bob Swords			

While the headquarters and most support staff was located in Houston, the other 43% of Company employees were involved in field operations all along the 15,290 miles of pipeline. The key leaders directing the daily activities of these 1376 employees were the Division Managers or General Superintendents in each of these four pipelines. Prior to early 1970, the TGP Division Managers reported directly to the President of TGP but later reported to another Pipeline officer.

The simplified organizational chart above shows only the officers at the individual Company levels and the leaders in field operations. Obviously, there were many other key leaders at the departmental levels that were instrumental in the success of the Company. TGT believed that every employee had the capability of being a key leader in his or her area of responsibility

The Global Search

By 1971, TGT had grown tremendously from the building of the original pipeline in the 1940s to one transporting 16 percent of the interstate natural gas consumed in the United States. Wylie Looney was the only one of the six Division Managers along the pipeline that was a veteran of the original line construction. The remaining five had been involved in the continued expansion that had followed. Managers such as Dick Hines and Bill Hancock knew how to build pipelines and compressor stations to deliver excess gas from the fields in Texas to the hungry markets in the Northeast. The hiring of returning World War II veterans and the resulting new college graduates in the late 1940s and early 1950s had resulted in a stable of highly competent executives leading an excellent engineering, marketing and administrative organization. Among this group were leaders such as J. L. Parrish, Jr., L.W.A. Campbell, James S. Brogdon and O.H. Simonds to name only a few. The dramatic change from excess gas supply to one of shortage began the era of searching for non-traditional, supplemental gas and required additional expertise in a new energy world.

The initial step in augmenting the TGT organization to address global supply was taken in 1971 by Tenneco Inc. Executive Vice President Wilton Scott who had just been named Board Chairman of both TOC and TGT. Scott placed Jack Ray, a TOC Vice President, on special assignment to investigate new sources of supply without regard to their form or geographic location so long as they could economically supplement the supplies available to the TGT system. Ray had previously had extensive involvement in international activities and operations with TOC. Ray immediately established an International Energy Contracts Group within TGT staffed by selected employees from TGT, TOC and Tenneco Inc. to address the problem. While this group was to identify potential targets, the technical support required for design, construction and integration would come from departments within TGT.

Early studies indicated major gas reserves in excess of the countries' domestic requirements were located in the Siberian region of the USSR, the Canadian Arctic Islands, Algeria, Trinidad and Tobago and Nigeria. The development of the Liquefied Natural Gas (LNG) technology which allowed gas to be super-cooled to a liquid form and transported by insulated tankers opened these previously unavailable areas of the world for gas acquisition. Worldwide supplies to supplement domestic U.S. reserves were now an option for TGT and its pipeline competitors. The competition for these supplemental supplies became as intense as it was for domestic supplies.

North Star

The first supplemental gas supply project utilizing LNG technology was initiated in late 1971. A consultant, Wally Zimmerman, approached Jack Ray and an official with Texas Eastern Transmission Company about a potential Soviet gas export project. The target was the Urengoiske field located in the Central Siberian area of the USSR. Since the field had in excess of 200 TCF of proven natural gas and the USSR was eager to monetize some of their excess reserves, it appeared the venture had benefits for both buyer and seller. The

of America as well as two private companies. Joe was well liked and highly respected throughout TGT and the gas industry.

initial meeting in Moscow by TGT and Texas Eastern went well and after returning to Houston, the Houston construction company, Brown and Root, accepted an invitation to join the group as the construction advisor.

The venture, named "The North Star Project," was gigantic in scale. The project would involve building a 1,430-mile pipeline system (including 205 miles of gathering facilities) from the Urengoiske gas field in Siberia to an LNG plant to be located near Murmansk which provided an ice-free port with a minimum depth of 40 feet. Fourteen compressor stations would be required and both the pipeline and the compressor stations were to be constructed and operated under Arctic conditions. The issues to be confronted and resolved included construction equipment working in extremely low temperatures, pipeline metallurgy, coatings and winter welding techniques. Compressor stations constructed in the permafrost areas had to include "gas discharge cooling" to protect both the permafrost and the integrity of the pipeline. The estimated cost of the pipeline system was $5.8 billion.

The LNG and port design, estimated to cost $3.3 billion, was based on facilities to liquefy and store 2.4 Billion Cubic Feet of gas per day in the form of LNG. The facilities included four dual LNG liquefaction trains, four natural gas pre-treating trains, four 800,000-barrel LNG storage tanks, a refrigerant makeup system and two LNG tanker berths. These facilities would liquefy and store unloaded LNG volumes equivalent to 1.6 Billion Cubic Feet of gas per day (1.6 BCFD) to be delivered to Saint John, New Brunswick, Canada and 620 Million Cubic Feet of gas per day (620 MMCFD) to Le Havre, France.

Fifteen LNG tankers, costing $7.8 billion, would be required to deliver the U.S. portion of the gas. As a bonus, the tankers would be built by Newport News Shipbuilding which was owned by Tenneco Inc. The re-gasification facility in Saint John, estimated to cost $1.5 billion, would deliver the gas into a pipeline which would move the gas to the TGT and Texas Eastern pipeline systems in the Northeastern portion of the U.S.

In January, 1972, each partner set forth members of the initial team that would participate in a meeting to be held in Moscow. The following areas of expertise were included: pipeline engineering and design; reservoir engineering; geology; LNG ship design and operation; LNG plant design and operation; finance and the three company leaders. The Tenneco team consisted of Jack Ray (team leader), Ewell Muse (economics and finance), Steve Chesebro' (reservoir engineering), Joe Parrish, Harry Long and Newsom Caraway (pipeline engineering and design), Vic Staffa and Bill Penn (LNG specialists) and Tom Spurlock (geology). It is important to recognize that in the designing and negotiating of the North Star Project and in every other major project pursued by TGT, the people physically meeting with potential suppliers were supported by the expertise of a multitude of people throughout the organization. Each of these was an integral part of the project and it is unfortunate that space does not allow every person in each project to be named. Upon arrival in Moscow in a wintery

Dinner on the KGB

The North Star team learned during the first trip that it was being watched very closely by the KGB and by the end of the trip began to recognize some of the agents. At dinner one night, they realized the KGB was seated at the table next to them. When the check for the dinner was brought to the table, the team found they did not have enough rubles among them to pay the bill so the KGB paid the bill for them. The office of the team's consultant reimbursed the KGB the next day.

- Ewell Muse

January, the team had two days to prepare for the first meeting to lay out the size and scope of the project for the Soviets. Four other meetings occurred over the next 2-3 weeks and detailed questions about the project were answered.

Several other meetings took place later in 1972 and in early 1973 and by mid-1973 a Letter of Intent (LOI) was signed with Soyouis Gas Export. The LOI did not have a final negotiated price in it but the team was offering $.60/MMBTU fob Murmansk and the Soviets were countering with $.90/MMBTU. A meeting to finalize the negotiations was set for October, 1973 in Houston.

The Russians arrived in Houston on October 3rd. After a brief meeting on October 4th, the meeting was adjourned and moved to Tenneco's Columbia Lakes facilities to complete the negotiations. Negotiations continued until October 8th when the Soviets were called back to Moscow due to the beginning of the Arab-Israeli war which created skyrocketing oil and gas prices. Another meeting was held in Moscow in 1974 in an effort to find a way to make the project work economically but the price the Soviets were currently demanding was no longer acceptable. Additional meetings were held over the next several years without success and in 1982 the project was abandoned due to governmental opposition and cold war politics.

Arctic Islands Gas Development Partnership

Another of the Company's early supplemental projects to enhance its future supply picture involved natural gas located in the high Arctic Islands of Canada. Panarctic Oils, Limited had discovered gas in 1968 while drilling wells on King Christian and Melville Islands both located above 75 degrees North latitude. The indicated presence of large reserves of natural gas encouraged Jack Ray to enter negotiations with Charles Hetherington, president of Panarctic, for access to this potential supply. These negotiations led to an announcement on July 12, 1971, by Jack O. O'Brien, president of Tenneco Oil & Minerals, Tenneco's Canadian subsidiary, that Tenneco had elected to participate in a $75 million natural gas exploration and development program in the Arctic Islands. Joining Tenneco as partners in the exploration venture were Texas Eastern Transmission Company, Columbia Gas System, Inc. and Northern Natural Gas Company. The Arctic Islands Gas Development Partnership was formed and signed a Letter Agreement with Panarctic Oils Limited of Calgary committing to make funds available for operations over a five-year period ending August 31, 1976 on 55 million acres of Panarctic's land. Panarctic agreed to sell the partnership all gas volumes that would become available after Canada's domestic needs were met. Tenneco's share of the gas to be made available was 50% based upon the Company's commitment to spend up to $25 million for exploratory drilling and up to $12.5 million for development drilling.

Work began immediately after the initial letter agreement was signed. To facilitate the effort, the Partnership established an office in Calgary led by

PIPELINE SAFETY

The building of the domestic interstate pipeline system had grown rapidly from the 1940's This growth was slowed when in March, 1965 an explosion occurred on a TGP pipeline on the discharge side of its Natchitoches, Louisiana, compressor station (station 40). Unfortunately, several people were killed, five houses in a nearby subdivision were destroyed and extensive damage was sustained by vehicles and other structures. The TGP Operating Research Department played a key role in determining the rupture had been caused by stress corrosion cracking. This was a new phenomenon and required the development of new testing and safety standards for the pipeline industry.

Primarily as a result of this new development, the Pipeline Safety Act of 1967 was passed which required the review of existing test procedures and the development of new codes and standards which were to become effective in 1970. Within TGP, Chief Engineer George White established a Codes and Standards group lead by Bob Dean and assisted by Joe Whitley, Jr. and Al Richardson to work closely with the Government's Office of Pipeline Safety (OPS). White and this group played a major role in developing the American Society of Mechanical Engineers (ASME) Gas Transmission and Distribution Piping Systems Code to ensure the future safety of the interstate pipeline network. The result of these joint efforts was the creation of a set of standards for pipeline safety that is used worldwide and continuously updated and improved.

- *Gary Cheatham*
& Dick Scroggin

JACK H. RAY

A dramatic change occurred in the management of TGT in May, 1972 when Jack Ray was transferred from Tenneco Oil, where he was Vice President in charge of international gas acquisitions, to TGT as Executive Vice President with overall responsibility for energy supplies. This transfer marked the first time a TOC officer was moved from the oil division into gas, since the forerunner of TOC was created as the Production Department within TGT in late 1945. Ray's transfer reflected Tenneco's awareness of the need to bolster its gas supplies from sources beyond the lower 48 states.

Jack Ray had graduated from the U. S. Military Academy where he played football on the Army team which posted a near-perfect win record over his three years with one tie, a 0-0 game with Notre Dame. His Army career was cut short by a knee injury which forced him to resign his commission. He enrolled at the University of Texas and earned a B. S. degree in Petroleum Engineering. Jack began his career in the oil business with a 10-year stint with Magnolia Petroleum Company, now a part of ExxonMobil. In 1959, Ray joined Tenneco Oil and held a number of challenging field positions before TOC Chairman Wilton Scott put him on special assignment to investigate new supply sources in 1970. Jack organized a unique department in TGT, International Energy Contracts, which eventually developed 21 supplemental gas supply projects during the 1970s.

Ray was elected President of TGT in July, 1974 and served in that position for nine years. He had an exceptional, effective ability to

Tenneco Oil & Minerals vice president Robert C. Thomas and staffed by other Tenneco Oil & Minerals employees to complete negotiations on the contractual documents and supervise the exploration and drilling operations being funded by the four pipeline companies. By the summer of 1972, three natural gas discoveries had been made and work was progressing on five other wells. At the conclusion of 1973, all contracts had been executed and it was estimated that over 14 trillion cubic feet of gas had been discovered. At this point, Bob Thomas was moved to TGT in Houston as vice president of International Energy Contracts reporting to Jack Ray who had been named Executive Vice President of TGT.

Arctic Challenges

A map of the world centered on the North Pole looks totally different than the ones normally seen. Geographically, the Partnership drilling activities were closer to Murmansk, USSR, than to the Calgary headquarters presenting logistical difficulties. Working conditions varied from the extremes of 24 hours of daylight to 24 hours of darkness with each creating its issues. Wintertime temperatures were in the minus 30 degrees or lower range with chill factors exceeding a minus 100 degrees at times testing both men and materials. Polar Bears were king and to be avoided since no guns were allowed in the drilling camps. Despite these challenges, the potential prize of major gas reserves warranted the effort.

The Polar Gas Project

The reserve generation in the Arctic Islands was very encouraging but the next challenge was to determine the most economical method of moving the natural gas to the U.S. for benefit of the Company and its partners. While many esoteric methods were proposed and considered, the more traditional methods of movement by ice-breaking LNG tankers or through pipelines built into Southern Canada where connection could be made with existing natural gas infrastructure already exporting into the U.S. were the two receiving detailed consideration. The pipeline method was selected due to the uncertainty of winter delivery by ice-breaking LNG tankers and this led to the formation of the Polar Gas Group. This Canadian-American organization consisting of Tenneco Oil & Minerals, Trans-Canada Pipelines, Canadian Pacific Investments Limited, Panarctic Oils Limited and Texas Eastern Transmission Corporation agreed to a cooperative effort to pursue constructing a 3,200-mile, large diameter pipeline extending from above the 75th parallel through Canada and ending at the U.S. border. There was strong political interest in Canada concerning the routes to be taken by the pipeline. Political leaders in Quebec could see major benefits should the pipeline be routed around the east side of Hudson's Bay while the Province of Ontario strongly preferred a route on the west side of the bay. As a result, both of the routes were evaluated. Ultimately, economics won out and neither of these two routes was selected.

To prepare for the building of a pipeline, the Polar Gas Project's 1973 studies consisted of summer bathymetry studies of channels between the islands, photography, environmental studies and ice research. The studies were managed by Montreal Engineering Company, Ltd. and Bannister Pipelines Ltd., but several Tennessee Gas Pipeline engineers including Newsom Caraway and H. E. Degrennia took part in the study. The magnitude of the project insured the attention of TGT officials and during the cold winter of 1974 Harry E. Long, vice president of TGP and Jack Ray, executive vice president of TGT visited the work site and reviewed the progress of the research. By winter's end, the feasibility studies related to water currents under the ice, the stability of the ice and other tide and ice related research issues were in midstride. Polar Gas cut trenches through nearly 30 miles of ice across the Byam and Austin channels during the two-month ice research program to determine potential ice movement and the capability of the sea ice to bear the load of pipe and pipeline construction equipment. As the winter ended, additional studies on the environment and ice were nearing completion.

Some TGT employees were more fortunate and were able to conduct Arctic feasibility studies in more comfortable surroundings. One such employee was Earl Sturgeon, manager of TGP's research laboratory in Houston, Texas. According to Sturgeon: "When the Company became interested in the search for natural gas in the Arctic, our primary responsibility of examining products and methods used in our system became more apparent. We are using our technical ability to learn about some of the unique problems associated with construction and maintenance of an Arctic system."

In his Houston lab, Sturgeon simulated conditions found in the Arctic Islands in order to test pipe, coatings and other pipeline materials. An "Icebox Committee" was set up in 1974 to guide the project. A "cold room" was built the following year in which studies were conducted in 80 degrees below zero temperatures. Arising from this research was important information related to external pipe coating and cathodic protection. Leonard Choate, who was placed in charge of the experimental phase of the project noted: "There is a definite need to find out how materials and coatings will react under hostile Arctic conditions. We are taking known products and seeing whether they can withstand the ice and cold or if further development is necessary." Of special importance was determining if pipe could withstand being exposed to alternating freezing and thawing temperatures and the impact on the existing permafrost. Other experiments included testing coatings for field bending in cold temperatures and evaluating the use of instruments, insulation, lubrication and other devices under extremely cold temperatures. The program was a great success and provided the Company with the information necessary to construct and operate pipelines in extremely cold climates.

The fact that Tenneco and TGT were prepared in the early 1970s to par-

operate on the international scene, much like a diplomat. Jack Ray was one of the most colorful and dynamic individuals to hold the office of TGT President. Here are three fun stories that exemplify his personality...

DRESS CODES

In December, 1973, TGT provided to employees a dress code that attempted to clarify the accepted standards of work attire. In January, 1976, President Jack Ray felt it necessary to issue a reminder concerning the code and other workplace issues. The paragraph concerning the code and written in his inimitable style read "I call your attention to the dress code put out in December, 1973 which permitted the wearing of pant suits by women. I suggest you reread and circulate that document. I do not recall that it approved or even mentioned pajamas, yard clothes or eccentric dress of any kind by men or women. Personally, I think the pretty women we have here look great in dresses." Jack would not be politically correct in today's world either.

AN EARLY WARNING

New or current employees that had never traveled with Jack Ray were often given an important warning about departure times. They were advised that if Jack asks if an early departure was acceptable, he doesn't mean an hour ahead of the normal daily starting time but more likely 4:00 to 5:00 AM. Be careful of the departure time you are accepting – if you think you really have a choice.

COST OF SERVICE

Jack Ray once commented that the only place he had seen the phrase "cost of service" advertised was at the horse barn in the rural town where he was raised. He added, "All I know about 'cost of service' is that somebody is usually getting screwed!"

TRINIDAD & CHOCOLATE

Many countries, when considering a company as a partner in a major energy project, required support by the prospective partner in developing other sectors of their economy. The stable of companies under the Tenneco umbrella offered TGT access to a wide variety of expertise in evaluating industrial and other opportunities in Trinidad and Tobago. As an example, Trinidad had once been a major grower of Cacao trees providing cacao beans for the World chocolate market but disease and farming practices had greatly reduced the planting and production of cacao trees. Through Tenneco West, a major supplier of almonds for the Hershey Company, we learned that Hershey was conducting an experimental project on growing Cacao trees in Costa Rica. Through that relationship, a Hershey representative joined the TGT team on several trips to share information beneficial to the Trinidadian agricultural sector. This type of capability was of major benefit to Tenneco Energy companies in other countries around the world and was later termed the "Tenneco Model."

- Bob Thomas

ticipate in another multi-billion dollar global gas project involving hostile climatic conditions underlined the bleak outlook for the Company's pipeline system and its ability to continue funding other Tenneco endeavors if the decline in available gas reserves could not be arrested. While the investment in the exploration phase of the Arctic Islands Gas Development Project was completed by the mid 1970s, the Polar Gas Project remained in the Company's plans for an additional twenty years. During this time, the pipeline length had been reduced to approximately 1300 miles in length by planning to build the line to connect Canadian gas fields discovered in the Beaufort Sea, the Mackenzie River Delta area and potentially the Alaskan North Slope production fields with existing facilities in the Province of Alberta. The Company was well aware that success would depend upon the cost of building the line, the attitudes of both the Canadian and United States governments concerning the project and the state of the U.S. natural gas reserve base. The continuing interest in the project was based upon the realization that the major reserves already discovered were sufficient to support 20 years of gas delivery through the pipeline if the price to the U.S. consumer were economically attractive. Unfortunately, the economics remained unfavorable over the years and the reserves are still in place awaiting changed economic conditions.

The Flexibility of LNG

The North Star Project was simply the first LNG supply project pursued by TGT and many others were pursued during the 1970s. Advances in LNG technology covering liquefaction, storage and transportation had made natural gas a global commodity rather than simply a regional resource. Economic studies indicated that any major natural gas resource surplus to the host country's needs and located within 5000 miles of the U.S. East coast or the TGP system along the Gulf coast should be evaluated for potential purchase. The ultimate key was the requirement that the landed price must be competitive in the U.S. market. Because of the continuing need for new gas reserves, the Company continued its search for LNG supplies throughout the 1970s and into the early 1980s.

One of the earlier TGT interests in the LNG technology was not for acquiring supply but in developing the storage capability for natural gas for use in meeting peak day delivery requirements of the Company's domestic system. Despite an earlier failure in attempting to store LNG in an underground granite cavern in Hopkinton, Massachusetts, East Tennessee Natural Gas (ETNG) requested regulatory approval in 1972 for an above ground LNG storage facility in Fordtown, Tennessee. That the project was approved by the federal government in 1973 reflected the fact that not only was the petition well organized, but even more importantly, was well timed. The energy crises had reached the point that even adverse public opinion regarding LNG could not stop the project. When FPC approval was granted, Thomas R. Bell, president of ETNG, stated that "a positive step toward easing the energy problems of homeowners served by natural gas distribution companies in Tennessee and Southwestern Virginia had been made." The facility itself was capable of liquefying 5.5 million cubic feet of gas per day when demand was low by chilling it to 260 degrees below zero and returning it to the pipeline in a gaseous state at a rate of 100 million cubic feet per day during high demand periods. The plant was always managed by ETNG staff and is still operating efficiently today.

Trinidad and Tobago

The Arab oil embargo initiated in late 1973 placed yet another obstacle in the path of securing international LNG supplies. Existing LNG projects such as the El Paso – Algerian arrangement destined for the U.S. market and several other European projects were placed in jeopardy due to host country demands for higher prices. This placed a premium on LNG supplies from non-OPEC countries. As a result, the country of Trinidad and Tobago immediately caught the eye of TGT. This small Caribbean country had seen new gas discoveries far in excess of their limited domestic demand for natural gas and they were looking for a way to monetize this asset.

Geographically, Trinidad was well placed for future TGT LNG supply because the shipping distance to potential Company receiving terminals on the U.S. East Coast was less than to the Gulf Coast providing significant transportation savings. Tenneco Oil E&P was also interested in the offshore oil and gas potential in Trinidad and with their partners drilled several successful wells off the North Coast of the islands. Having two Tenneco companies with interests in the economic future of the country was a real benefit during negotiations with government officials. TOC maintained a country manager living in Port-of-Spain and the TGT negotiating team maintained close contact with managers Earl Knott and later Ken Watts during their many trips to Trinidad.

Negotiations began for an LNG project in late 1974 and continued through much of the 1970s until Tenneco Trinidad LNG reached an agreement with the Government of Trinidad and Tobago to purchase and ship LNG to the U.S. market. Because governmental approvals by both governments were required before construction could begin, first deliveries were not expected until 1983. By that date, the U.S. energy crises had faded and gas prices were changing rapidly. The project no longer appeared economically feasible for the U.S. market and was ultimately abandoned. The Trinidadians continued to pursue LNG and by the 1990s had completed a facility selling LNG into the European market.

Alaskan Gas

The discovery of the Alaskan Prudhoe Bay field in 1968 had focused world-wide attention on that tremendous oil and gas resource. Initially, the plan by the producers was to re-inject the gas back into the reservoir to main-

partment in Shreveport where he was previously employed. Findley, who was never at a loss for diplomatic words, said "This just shows what a cheap outfit you guys are working for". TGT's Christmas bonuses were discontinued by the Board of Directors after 1964 and were replaced by an equivalent salary increase and other benefit changes. Over the years Tenneco was consistent in never taking away a benefit without an equivalent offset.

TGT hired its first nurse, Mrs. Dorothy W. Schaefer, in mid-1952 to care for the minor medical needs of the Houston office staff. Then later in 1953 the Company hired its first Company doctor, Bobby Moers. Dr. Moers had been a two-time All-American Basketball player at the University of Texas in 1939 and 1940, a three-time All Southwest Conference third baseman and had roomed with Dr. Denton A. Cooley, who was also a basketball star at UT. Dr. Moers worked part time for TGT and routinely gave physical exams to all newly hired employees in the Houston office.

When the Tenneco Employee Center opened in 1982 an expanded Health, Environmental Medicine and Safety Department was formed and Dr. Edward J. Bernacki, vice president and corporate medical director, was recruited to organize and manage the Health and Fitness portion of the new Employee Center and to look after the overall health of Tenneco's Houston-based employees. According to Dr. Bernacki, "Our primary goal is to insure that Tenneco employees get the best possible medical care and reach the highest level of health possible. I feel that we can achieve part of this goal by providing on-site medical care."

Dr. Bernacki also implemented several very unique programs

tain maximum oil deliverability but at some future date the gas would need to be moved to a major market outlet. The vision of some thirty trillion cubic feet (TCF) of gas becoming available led to intense competition for the gas which would require a method for moving the gas to the lower 48-market. By March, 1974, the Arctic Gas Pipeline Company formed by a consortium of sixteen U.S. and Canadian firms filed for a certificate to transport this gas to the U.S. market. The plan was to build a 48-inch gas pipeline Eastward through the Arctic National Wildlife Range and then south following the Mackenzie River into Southern Canada and the U.S. Other competing applications for moving the gas were quickly made even though the producer owners were reluctant to commit to gas contracts.

Rather than joining any of the proposed transportation projects, TGT elected to first begin discussions with the State of Alaska that held a 12.5 % royalty interest in any gas sold from the Prudhoe Bay field. By 1975, a contract was signed with the State whereby TGT would have the right to purchase approximately 1.3 TCF of their royalty gas whenever a transportation system was completed. The contract was contingent upon TGT supporting the State-favored Trans-Alaska project and securing the necessary federal permits for the project. The Trans-Alaska project would involve building a pipeline across Alaska to tidewater generally following the oil pipeline route. Once at the coast, the gas would be liquefied and shipped to the west coast U.S. market. Being contractually required to support this project was not a problem since TGT firmly believed this was the only transportation project that could be built in any reasonable time frame. It was a totally U.S. project not requiring export or import permits, would not cross Canada which was facing significant native claims problems along all pipeline routes and would land gas in a major U.S. market at the lowest cost. Based upon these factors, TGT joined with El Paso and Southern Natural Gas to compete for a certificate to move Prudhoe Bay gas to market by this method. Both the project and the contract were terminated in 1978 when the U.S. government favored a Canadian pipeline route following the route of the existing Alaskan highway. Such a pipeline is yet to be built.

Algerian LNG

Nigeria and Algeria remained on the TGT radar screen as potential LNG suppliers. Both had tremendous reserves and transportation distances to TGT markets placed the supply within economic reach. Algeria was already selling LNG to European countries, had negotiated an agreement with El Paso to supply the U.S. market and Panhandle Eastern had signed a contract in 1972 for additional Algerian supply. TGT opened negotiations with the Algerian government and on October 4, 1976, Tenneco LNG, Inc. signed a 20-year contract with Societe Nationale Sonatrach calling for the importation of one billion cubic feet (BCF) of LNG per day. The gas was to be delivered to a receiving terminal to be built in Saint John, New Brunswick, Canada where it would be re-gasified and delivered into a Canadian pipeline for delivery to the Maine border. The terminal at Saint John was not without its own challenges since it experienced a 40-foot tidal variation. From that point, Tenneco Atlantic Pipeline had filed to build a 498-mile pipeline to move the gas through New England and into TGP's main lines in New York and Pennsylvania. In 1977, Canadian approval was received and initial acceptance was granted by a Federal Power Commission (FPC) administrative law judge. A year passed with no final regulatory decision but in late 1978, the Federal Energy Regulatory Commission (FERC – successor to the FPC) through David J. Bardin stated "we cannot conclude that a long term commitment to an LNG project is now needed." With this rejection, the Algerian contract was terminated.

Nigerian LNG

Nigeria had substantial natural gas reserves and opened negotiations with both European and U.S. companies. TGT pursued this potential supply and negotiated with them over a period of several years. It was interesting that the Nigerian team favored the Bahamas as a location for negotiating sessions rather than Lagos, Nigeria. This choice also met favor with the TGT team for a great many reasons. After concluding that the price being demanded for delivered Nigerian LNG was well above competitive prices on the East Coast of the U.S., TGT broke off further negotiations. Ultimately, the Nigerian LNG volumes were committed to the European market because of their more favorable pricing.

Norwegian LNG

In 1976, TGT made contact with Statoil, the National Oil Company of Norway. Substantial gas reserves had been discovered in the Norwegian sector of the North Sea and additional exploratory interest was high. Norway appeared to be an ideal project for future gas supply since they had growing gas reserves, a limited domestic market for natural gas and was geographically close to the TGT system in the Northeastern U.S. Import facilities designed for receiving North Star gas from Russia would also be ideally located for Norwegian gas. While Statoil had no gas for sale at the time, TGT wanted to get an early oar in the water.

Tenneco Oil Company also had high interest in Norway and considered it to be the top area of potential for the International Division of Tenneco Oil Company. From 1977 on, several of the companies within Tenneco Inc. joined together to assist Tenneco Oil Company in their effort to secure an interest in offshore blocks controlled by Norway. Since Norway required all applicants for drilling interests to establish efforts to cooperate with Norwegian industry, Tenneco's stable of companies were perfectly situated to respond to this requirement. The Norwegians began to label this as the "Tenneco Model." The potential for additional discoveries of gas also fit TGT's need for future sup-

that were precedent setting in the Houston business community. Not only did he conduct the required physical exams for all employees desiring to participate in the Fitness Center, but he negotiated contracts with several Medical Center institutions to provide first class care for employees and their families needing their services. The contracts with Dr. Denton A. Cooley at the Texas Heart Institute for cardiac surgery and care, with Dr. Robert G. Grossman at Methodist Hospital for Neurosurgical procedures and with the University of Texas' M. D. Anderson Cancer Center for treatment of cancer saved the lives of many employees and their family members. In addition, specialists from these institutions conducted health seminars aimed at upgrading employee health care, preventing disease and promoting well-being.

Bernacki's Medical Center contracts were highly acclaimed by several larger companies, both foreign and domestic-based, who came to inspect the Health and Fitness facilities and to determine if they could replicate the medical contracts program. Dr. Bernacki ran the program for over a dozen years and at one time had 35 employees in his Department. After the departure of CEO Jim Ketelsen in late 1991, the program was reduced in scope and Dr. Kenneth D. Wells replaced Dr. Bernacki as head of Tenneco's Corporate Medical Department.

In 1983 the Great Plains Gasification Associates, where Tenneco Synfuels was a 30% owner of the plant, directed their Finance Committee and benefits representatives to evaluate the benefit plans of the five partners and develop a package which could be adopted for its 822 employees in North Dakota. The evaluation concluded that the Tenneco benefits program was slightly better than the other four partners after a typical employee had been on the job for 20 years.

Meanwhile, Tenneco Oil Company had been experiencing something different. During the mid-1970s the market place for oil and gas technical professionals had become very volatile. As the price of oil shot up after the oil embargo of the early 1970s to a peak of $38 per barrel by the end of the decade, the number of independent oil companies also escalated. These small companies needed technical professions and were willing to go to any extremes to attract experienced geologists and engineers. Tenneco Oil's technical workforce suffered during that period with turnover rates reaching double digits. The company's ability to reach its objective of annually replacing production with new reserves was being restricted by the shortage of experienced professional oil finders. Every angle was being pursued to attract and retain key personnel.

One of the biggest advantages available to independent oil companies was over-rides or a piece of the action for the technical professionals who were assigned to specific projects. This type of sharing ownership with employees was not available to employees in publicly owned companies like Tenneco. At Tenneco, a different approach was needed to attack the problem and retain its personnel. Special compensation programs were put into place for retention purposes. But there was a feeling that having one of the better benefit programs in the industry wasn't receiving the respect it deserved. Tenneco needed to do a better job of presenting the advantages of what was being offered. It needed more than good pay and job security. Everyone knew the company offered a retirement plan and a Thrift Plan that created significant asset values down the road, but what did that

ply. Over the next several years, TGT personnel worked closely with Statoil in pipeline and natural gas plant construction and operations. Statoil personnel spent time at TGT plant operations along the Gulf Coast to prepare them for operating their anticipated onshore gas plants. When surplus gas became available in Norway, the ready market in Europe was very attractive and the LNG export plan failed to materialize. As a result, TGT's activities in Norway were unsuccessful in terms of LNG supply but were beneficial to TOC in the expansion of their Norwegian exploration activities.

Coal Gasification

While Tenneco consistently pursued LNG as a method to help alleviate the energy crunch, this was not the only type of supplemental supply project receiving company attention. In 1972, N.W. Freeman noted that "we believe that large coal gasification plants can be developed to provide substantial quantities of pipeline gas to serve the growing needs of our customers. Development of this technology can provide gas for many, many years in the future." To investigate this future, the Company joined the COGAS project in 1973 with FMC Corporation, Panhandle Eastern Pipe Line Company, Consolidated Natural Gas Company, Republic Steel Corporation and Rocky Mountain Energy Company with the intent of exploring the conversion of coal into synthetic gas and crude oil. The potential benefit of coal gasification as a domestic supply appeared attractive to TGT and a decision was made to pursue this approach. Since the COGAS process was designed for production of both oil and synthetic natural gas (SNG), it was not utilized in the Company's future SNG efforts, but it established technical expertise within the Company.

TGT formed several organizations to acquire coal reserves, water supplies and additional technical expertise to support the construction of coal gasification plants in three separate geographic areas of the country. Over a six-year period during the 1970s, Tenneco Coal Company acquired over two billion tons of surface minable lignite for the production of SNG. The most prolific deposits straddled the Montana-North Dakota border near the communities of Beach, North Dakota and Wibaux, Montana. The Beach-Wibaux lignite areas contained enough low ratio strippable lignite to supply four or more coal gasification plants for their proposed thirty-year lives. Several drum-sized samples of the Beach-Wibaux lignite were shipped to Frankfurt, Germany for testing by Lurgi Mineraloeltechnik GmbH. The results indicated the lignite was quite suitable for feedstock in Lurgi's proprietary gasifiers.

The second resource necessary for SNG production was substantial quantities of water. Former Kern County Land (KCL) employee, Jack Tindall, was the strategist behind TGT's water acquisition efforts. Jack had been the Vice President and General Manager of Kern Island Canal and Water Company, KCL's public utility. He had also served as Water Master of the

Kern River in California's San Joaquin Valley prior to his transfer to Tenneco Oil in Oklahoma City. TGT's water subsidiary, Intake Water Company, perfected an appropriative water right on the Yellowstone River for 80,650-acre-feet per year which could be used for a variety of beneficial uses. The water would be diverted during the spring season high water period and stored in an adjacent reservoir for later use. The state of Montana challenged the 1973 Water Right filing in State District Court and lost on all counts. Intake also prevailed in the appeal process and ended up with a Montana Supreme Court decreed water right.

Lignite was also found and leased in five Texas counties but not in sufficient quantities to support a commercial coal gasification plant. Mississippi lease areas were similarly small and of slightly lower quality lignite for gasification feedstock because of higher moisture content. In 1974, Tenneco Coal Company sold 50% of its interest in the Texas and Mississippi lignite reserves in an effort to share the risks of developing and marketing lignite for power generation uses. Most of the Texas deposits were later sold to two operating companies for power generation fuel in the early 1990s.

Great Plains

As TGT continued to move forward with its Beach-Wibaux SNG project, it was invited to join the Great Plains Gasification Associates (GPGA) project in mid-1978 as a 25% partner. When it became apparent that the gas industry could not simultaneously finance more than one of these large SNG plants, the Company scaled back its efforts at Beach-Wibaux and focused on maximizing its participation in the country's first commercial coal gasification plant. TGT assigned people to almost every department of the new enterprise to assist in construction and gain expertise for potential future coal gasification efforts.

When the Great Plains partnership began arranging its permanent financing, several participants were surprised to learn they could not finance their share of the plant's $2.1 billion capital cost, even with a Department of Energy Loan Guarantee. The four original partners were compelled to bring a fifth partner into the group and to reallocate their shares according to each company's financial capability. The new lineup had Tenneco SNG Inc. at 30%, ANR Gasification Properties at 25%, MCN Coal Gasification at 20%, Transco Coal Gas Company at 15% and Pacific Synthetic Fuel Company at 10% ownership. When Tenneco became the lead partner, Bob Thomas assumed chairmanship of the GPGA Board. Within a few months however, Thomas was named President of TGT replacing Jack Ray who had been moved to Tenneco Inc. As a result, Tenneco Inc. formed a new subsidiary, Tenneco Synfuels, headed by Clifford W. Rackley to manage its Great Plains team together with its team involved in the Cathedral Bluffs shale oil project in western Colorado. Rackley, a former TOC President, was a seasoned executive with expertise in business development, refining and process plant operations and was also

really mean and how significant were these assets?

In a Tenneco Oil Company management meeting in 1977, the facts about asset accumulation were laid out before the management group by TOC's Vice President, Larry Augsburger. The presentation illustrated the asset values that could be accumulated during a working career by employees of Tenneco. Three different cases were presented that represented almost everyone in attendance. Attendees were instructed to select the case that most closely represented their age, salary and years of service to retirement. A graphic illustration projected the salaries of each case over a working career. The projections included merit increases and promotional advancements that were considered reasonable and realistic. The cash asset value of the retirement plan benefit was calculated based on the present value worth of the earned age 65 benefit. Also, contributions to the Thrift Plan and the corresponding company's matching contributions were based on the salary levels of the projection. In addition, internal earnings growths were determined based on reasonable assumptions.

To insure that all the assumptions used in the presentation were reasonable and appropriate, a respected international benefits consulting firm in Chicago was contracted to review and adjust the assumptions and estimates as they deemed necessary. The presentation became known as the "Three Million Dollar Man", which was the total value accumulated over a working career at Tenneco. It was stated after the management meeting presentation, "Now, I only need three million dollars and Farrah Fawcett and I'm The Six Million Dollar Man". This referred to a TV series in the late 1970s by that name starring Lee Majors, the husband of movie star, Farrah Fawcett. The presentation was well received and was later presented at most of the Tenneco Oil locations outside of Houston. In many cases the spouses were encouraged to attend.

In the final analysis, Tenneco employees had been encouraged to diversify their holdings in the Tenneco Thrift Plan and were advised not to invest exclusively in Tenneco Common Stock. Bankruptcies of several Houston-based energy companies confirmed the wisdom of this advice. As TOC employees departed the Tenneco building in 1988 and Tenneco Gas employees "followed suit" about eight years later, they could be confident that their Thrift Plan values were well preserved and their retiree income had not gone into the tank.

the most qualified among the GPGA partners to manage the new venture. Rackley became Chairman of the Great Plains Gasification Associates Management Committee.

Construction of Great Plains occurred year-round over a four-year period and was completed on time and on budget despite the winter of 1981-1982 when wind chill factor temperatures dropped to a bone-chilling 109 degrees below zero. Its first synthetic gas was produced for delivery into the Northern Border Pipeline on July 28, 1984. Pipeline affiliates of the four original GPGA partners had executed 25-year gas purchase agreements with pricing set at $6.75 per dekatherm subject to a cap such that the price could not exceed the price of No. 2 fuel oil. During the first year of operation, both oil and natural gas prices began to drop dramatically and Great Plains was forecasting an operating loss of $1.3 billion during the first ten years of the plant's operation. GPGA requested 10 years of price guarantees from the Synthetic Fuels Corporation (SFC), a Carter Administration creation. When the SFC's financial aid package was rejected by President Reagan as a budget cutting measure, the GPGA partners bailed out on August 1, 1985, and turned the keys to the plant over to the Department of Energy which had guaranteed the loan from the Federal Financing Bank. DOE, under political pressure from North Dakota, continued to operate the plant with GPGA's original workforce. DOE formally acquired the plant and related assets at a sheriff's auction on the steps of the Mercer County Courthouse on June 30, 1986 with a bid of $1.0 billion.

The Great Plains plant continued to operate and was a technical success. However, DOE concluded it was not appropriate for them to compete in the natural gas marketplace. DOE then solicited bids from 15 potential buyers, including two original GPGA partners, and on August 5, 1988, selected Basin Electric Power Cooperative on behalf of its two subsidiaries as the successful bidder. Dakota Gasification Company (DGC) and Dakota Coal submitted a check to DOE for $85 million cash and an array of future profit sharing, a waiver of future production tax credits, $70 million for mining rights and equipment, $15 million for the pipeline connecting the plant to the Northern Border pipeline and a $30 million line of credit. Some 778 employees of the 822 in GPGA's operating subsidiary were offered positions in the new company.

The pricing mechanism for Great Plains was troublesome from the start of production because of the gas "bubble" that had developed and the FERC's plan for gas price deregulation. Litigation initiated by pipeline purchasers and other affected consumer groups occurred several times and the SNG price and mandatory gas purchase volumes were reestablished in an agreed settlement with FERC on December 18, 1996. The original gas purchase contracts expired in 2009.

Dakota Gasification made numerous improvements in this first of a kind plant which boosted SNG production from its design rate of 137.5 million standard cubic feet of gas per day (MMCSFD) to a routine rate of 160 MMSCFD. In addition, they began to recover the planned by-products of anhydrous ammonia, sulfur, ammonium sulfate, krypton, phenol, cresylic acid and carbon dioxide which added to plant revenue. Ironically, Great Plains was the only one of TGT's 21 different potential supplemental LNG and SNG projects to complete the contractual process, secure all necessary approvals and begin production. The Company recovered its Great Plains cost of some $165 million from investment tax credits and tax credits from production prior to the plant's sale by DOE.

Domestic, Canadian and Mexican Pipeline Expansion

While the search for supplemental supplies from global sources was a major area of focus by TGT during the early 1970s, the search for domestic supply and pipeline gas from Canada and Mexico also became intensified. Several of TGT's competitors had already begun curtailing their customers in 1971 and the forthcoming supply shortfall was becoming apparent. By 1972, curtailment by other interstate pipelines reached nearly 650 BCF per year. Tenneco Inc. had in 1970 taken several steps to meet the future challenges by accelerating funding for lease acquisition by TOC in the Gulf of Mexico which was soon followed by drilling operations resulting in several major discoveries. The significant factors were that the federal waters in the Gulf were already dedicated to the interstate market and TOC was the largest single supplier of natural gas to TGP. This was a powerful combination and a great benefit to all the customers of the TGT system. To take maximum advantage of the situation required TGP to accelerate construction of new pipeline facilities.

The following year, TGP began construction of major pipeline facilities to access discoveries in several blocks including West Cameron 180F, West Delta 68U and 94V. Between 1972 and 1973, additional offshore additions were made in West Cameron 135 and 173, East Cameron blocks 273, 255, 254, West Delta 64, Eugene Island blocks 215, 257, 338, Ship Shoal 94 and 168 and in South Pass. While completion of these facilities was very important, additional offshore pipelines were required to connect these platforms to the onshore gas transmission facilities. A major pipeline construction project that became known as the "Blue Water System" received Federal Power Commission (FPC) approval in 1971. This order authorized Tennessee Gas Pipeline and Columbia Gulf Transmission Company to construct a $44.2 million facility to transport gas from the offshore Louisiana area. Under the plan, both companies interconnected some of their existing lines and proposed new facilities onshore in Southern Louisiana and Offshore Western Louisiana. This new system consisted of large diameter gas gathering header pipeline approximately 70 miles long with onshore connections on both ends of the system. This line extended from Columbia's existing 30-inch pipeline near Pecan Island in Block 245, where a new platform was constructed. TGP connected to the line by building and operating a short 30-inch line from its

PEMEX PROJECT

In mid-1976, Mario Gonzales, a Tenneco civil engineer, was contacted by his brother-in-law, a manager of procurement at Pemex asking for assistance in finding a vendor for field compressor units to be installed in south Mexico. He also referred to Pemex's intentions to lay a new gas pipeline from the Villahermosa area to Reynosa for export of natural gas to the United States.

Jack Ray, President of Tennessee Gas Transmission, and Harry Long, Vice President of Tennessee Gas Pipeline, put together a team from the departments of engineering, procurement, planning, and materials to provide technical assistance to Pemex. During numerous trips to Mexico City, Pemex requested hydraulic studies, pipe and gas turbine specifications, and construction equipment availability and techniques.

In early 1977, Bill Hancock, Manager of Civil Engineering, flew the entire proposed pipeline route to assess the route, right-of-way, river crossings, distance, and pipe classification requirements for Pemex. In June of 1977, Jack Ray and representatives of other gas pipeline companies were called to a Pemex meeting in Mexico City where Pemex allocated the largest percentage of the gas volume to Tennessee Gas Pipeline with Texas Eastern Pipeline receiving the next largest volume. Jack Ray suggested a TGP engineer work within the Mexico City Pemex office to coordinate and provide technical support for the project. Within two weeks, Don Johnson was transferred from the TGP Engineering Department to Mexico City and installed in a Pemex office.

Pipeline construction began in 1977 and large numbers of TGP personnel assisted in the areas of automatic welding, pipe inspection, pipe testing, and compressor

existing header in Block 245. The Blue Water System was completed in 1972 and was a major factor in moving additional supplies from federal offshore waters. The Pipelines' capacity was significant with capacity at 500 MMCF per day per company. TGP's share amounted to approximately 10 percent of their total daily sales.

The industry exploration and pipeline connection efforts also required new efforts to build, improve and expand existing major transmission systems moving gas to the major U.S. markets. While the major focus was on the offshore areas dedicated to the interstate markets, TGT was also alert to gas discoveries throughout Texas. An important onshore project was the Company's participation in the construction of a 508-mile pipeline to move natural gas from west Texas to the Texas gulf coast. Channel Industries, a Tenneco subsidiary responsible for intrastate operations, acquired a 20% interest in the Oasis Pipe Line Company, the owner of the new line. Construction was completed in August, 1972 and gas began flowing into the eastern terminus near Houston shortly thereafter. The investments by Tenneco in both the onshore and offshore areas in Texas and Louisiana proved to be some of the better investments of the 1970s.

Continued Reserve and Deliverability Decline

Despite the maximum effort to secure domestic supply in the early 1970s, the interstate market with its low regulated prices could not compete with the unregulated intrastate market. While the search for global and domestic supplemental gas supply also continued with intensity, the recognition of the lengthy gestation period between original project agreements and final governmental approvals provided little promise of an early sheltering of TGT from declining reserves at home. As a result, TGP was forced in 1974 to join other interstate pipelines and embark on an extended curtailment program. The industry-wide natural gas shortages had reduced TGT's annual consolidated gas deliveries to 1.794 TCF, a substantial reduction from the previous year. Curtailment by TGP directly affected East Tennessee Natural Gas (ETNG) and the Midwestern Gas Transmission (MGT) Southern system forcing them to reduce deliveries by 13%. Mother Nature was not helpful either and a cold winter created demands for increased deliveries to residential and commercial customers at the expense of restricting supply to industrial customers. While industrial customers had interruptible contracts, their service had never been interrupted and the sudden change was a shock. Adding to the dilemma that year was the impact of Hurricane Carmen creating delays in attaching offshore facilities, repairing damaged pipelines and generally reducing gas available for either supplying customers or refilling gas storage for additional deliverability during the coming winter's peak demands. Connected reserves were also being produced at maximum capacity resulting in steeper deliverability declines than originally anticipated. It was reported that by the winter of 1976 –1977, curtailment by interstate pipelines totaled over 3.7 Trillion Cubic Feet (TCF) or 16% of the domestic natural gas market. The average annual curtailment by TGP during the year 1974 through 1979 was 204 BCF.

TOTAL INTERSTATE PIPELINE CURTAILMENTS
BCF

Year	Total
1970	17
1971	286
1972	649
1972-1973	1031
1973-1974	1191
1974-1975	2418
1975-1976	2975
1976-1977	3790

Source: FPC

Since pipelines were paid for transporting gas, the impact of curtailment was going to have a future impact on income unless additional supplies became available. TGP began investigating every innovative approach to contracting and connecting new supplies to minimize or eliminate curtailment. One such method was the advanced payments program which involved advancing funds to producers either prior to or during their drilling operations in return for their committing the reserves discovered to TGP. Advanced payments by TGP totaled $95 million in 1977. This program served the purpose of encouraging accelerated drilling and securing gas contract commitments. Since this was essentially a low or no cost loan to producers, it was subjected to strong criticism from regulators and other parties and was later terminated.

The extension of TGP pipelines into ever deeper Gulf waters was a favored method of securing access to new reserves. An example of this approach was the 32-mile, large diameter pipeline laid from Ship Shoal 198 to a new producing facility further offshore in the Eugene Island 349 area. When completed, the line would transport up to 374 MMCFD and the gas would ultimately end up in the east leg of the Blue Water system and destined for the TGP facility onshore at Cocodrie, Louisiana.

Gas From Mexico

In addition to looking into the deeper water of the Gulf of Mexico, TGT took steps even further South into Mexico. The importation of gas from Mexico was looked upon very favorably not only because of the need for supply but because of its proximity to the U.S. and the mainline system of TGP. For pipeliners, the geographic proximity translated into lower transmission costs and in turn to lower prices for consumers. Major gas discoveries by Petroleos Mexicanos (PEMEX) in their Chiapas and Tabasco areas in Southeastern Mexico had triggered great interest by TGT because of the possibility of some of their gas being made available for export. When TGT learned in 1976 that Pemex was planning to build an 800-mile pipeline from the discovery areas to deliver gas to Central and Northern Mexico, TGT President Jack Ray quickly offered design and construction assistance for the Pemex project. TGP Vice

station horsepower and design. In mid-1978, our involvement in the project ended abruptly when President Carter denied the import license for the gas. Don Johnson returned to the Houston TGP Engineering Department; however, TGP continued to advise Pemex for several months.

- Don B. Johnson

President Harry Long was given the task of assembling a TGP team to provide technical assistance for the project and Bill Hancock and Don Johnson were early members of the team.

While Company engineers were assisting Pemex in pipeline design and construction, other TGT officials were holding negotiating sessions with Pemex in an effort to contract for gas to be delivered to TGP facilities at the U.S.-Mexican border. In August, 1977, Jack Ray and Harold Longworthy were invited to meet with Pemex in Mexico City to discuss a potential gas contract. When they arrived, they found five other U.S. pipeline companies also present. It was reported that a Pemex official told the group that each company had been chosen to receive some of their surplus gas because Mexico wanted their gas to go into all parts of the U.S. The six companies agreed to form Border Gas, Inc. and the consortium signed a letter of intent at the meeting. Border Gas was to receive two billion cubic feet of gas per day at the border with the price to be based on the heating value of No. 2 fuel oil in New York harbor. The contract with Pemex required approval by both the U.S. and Mexican governments and a problem quickly arose covering the import price. The price parity with fuel oil required by Pemex resulted in a gas price of about $2.65/MCF which was substantially higher than the $1.75/MCF ceiling price previously set by the U.S. government. As a result, Mexican officials terminated the negotiations.

Jack Ray, as head of the Border Gas consortium, persuaded the group to hold together in the hopes the U.S. government would reconsider its position. Another cold winter in 1978 combined with continued curtailment in the U.S. did result in talks being resumed in early 1979. These negotiations were successful and resulted in the final contract being accepted. There were, however, important changes in the contract terms. The parties of the Border Gas Group were to remain Texas Eastern Transmission Company, El Paso Natural Gas, Transcontinental Gas Pipeline, Southern Natural Gas, Florida Gas Transmission and TGT with its assigned volume equal to 37-1/2 percent of the total contract quantity. However, the export volumes were to be reduced to only 300 MMCF per day rather than the original two billion cubic feet per day. The gas was still to be based upon an energy-equivalency basis but on an average cost of a basket of five international crude oils rather than the price of the higher-priced fuel oil originally required. This contract received all the necessary governmental approvals and TGT was scheduled to receive 112.5 MMCF per day. The valve opening ceremony took place on January 15, 1980 and was attended by TGT President Jack Ray and Executive Vice President Joe Parrish, Jr. TGP Vice President William Such later expressed the feeling that the importation of Mexican gas was "a tremendously important agreement."

Canadian gas continued to be received at MGT's Minnesota border connection and TGP's import point at Niagara Falls, New York. While the price of imported gas changed according to market factors, gas continued to flow under the existing long term contracts. The Company also continued every effort to increase Canadian volumes with limited success until the late 1970s.

Maintaining the companies' profitability was quite difficult while pursuing the global energy search and maintaining and expanding the pipeline systems and changes resulting from external events further complicated the effort. The extremely cold weather of 1976 and 1977 not only required continued curtailment of deliveries but forced TGP to go from seasonal to daily cutbacks. It was estimated that U.S. interstate pipelines were able to deliver only 75-80% of their firm contractual demand during this period. Not only did this pressure Company profitability but irate consumer demands began to force government action.

Regulatory Changes

The incoming Carter Administration proposed the creation of a Department of Energy and took additional steps to make more gas available to the interstate market. An Emergency Natural Gas Act was passed in early 1977 which allowed purchase of gas at higher than FPC regulated pricing levels to alleviate shortages in Northeastern U.S. markets. This allowed interstate pipelines to compete with intrastate pipelines for supply but the increased cost had to be justified in future rate cases.

The Emergency Natural Gas Act was helpful in the short term but it led to the passage of the Natural Gas Policy Act of 1978 (NGPA). This far-reaching act created some 26 different pricing categories of natural gas based upon vintage, location and well depth. Suddenly, Gas Contracting, Accounting and Marketing Departments were subjected to major changes in the way their business was conducted. The NGPA also set 1985 as the year when the price for all new gas produced, whether for intrastate or interstate markets would be deregulated. While Tenneco and the pipeline industry had long been pushing for deregulation, the delay until 1985 and the interim pricing complications were not exactly what they had in mind. Unfortunately, the Administration also passed the Power Plant and Industrial Fuel Use Act along with the NGPA. The Fuel Use Act discouraged the use of natural gas by electrical utilities and large industrial users. This was based upon the rationale that natural gas was too valuable to be burned under industrial boilers and in power plants and should instead be reserved for residential and commercial consumers. Since there were many more residential and commercial consumers than industrial boiler and power plant operators, the political logic was pretty clear. Fortunately, the Fuel Use Act was rescinded within a relatively short time as available supply began to increase. Despite its complexity, the NGPA was helpful during the close of the 1970s because it allowed interstate pipelines like the TGT system to compete for gas that had been previously consumed only within the producing

THE RATE DEPARTMENT

Shortly after I was hired by the TGP Rate Department, we filed the TGP 1976 rate case while we continued efforts to settle the 1973 rate case and two 1975 cases. We continued to file rate cases every year from 1976 through 1983. The major issues between TGP and its customers were related to supply curtailment and the costs related to finding replacement supplies. Tenneco Oil Company was TGP's largest supplier and, therefore, received a larger portion of the costs related to contracting for increased domestic supply. For that reason, it was at the center of controversy in most of these rate cases. Filing and working to settle these rate cases required major time and effort by personnel in the Rate, Legal, Marketing and Accounting Departments.

- Tom Norris

states. The fact that this competition would soon begin to increase the average cost of gas supply did not appear to be a major problem to pipelines in curtailment or their customers crying for additional gas.

With freedom to search throughout existing reserve areas in the U.S., TGT took immediate steps to become competitive in previous intrastate reserve strongholds. The NGPA also created the Federal Energy Regulatory Commission (FERC) to replace the old Federal Power Commission.

Onshore drilling activity in the Arkoma Basin in Oklahoma and Arkansas led the Company and three partners to form Ozark Gas Transmission Company. This company filed with the FERC to build a 265-mile pipeline to transport gas out of this promising producing area into the nation's interstate pipeline grid. This was the first opportunity for the Company to access reserves from an area where TOC had been active for many years. The regulatory approval for new pipeline projects under the new FERC continued at a slow pace and gas only began to flow some four years later in 1982.

The increases in the purchase price for new gas under the NGPA also opened up opportunities for increased Canadian supply. A Canadian border import connection in Minnesota by MGT's Northern System and at Niagara Falls by TGP placed the company in good position to secure additional gas contracts. In the late 1970s, the Canadian National Energy Board (NEB) granted an export license to Sulpetro, Ltd. for 300 MMCFD of which 75 MMCFD was contracted to TGP. Canadian approval was also obtained to ship an additional 200 MMCFD to MGT under an existing contract.

While competing for pipeline gas from Canada, Mexico and previously intrastate domestic areas, the offshore Gulf of Mexico continued to receive heavy company activity. In 1978, TGT built the Company's first offshore compression platform at East Cameron 49 B. The platform was located 25 miles south of Grand Chenier, Louisiana in 50 feet of water. As described by Terry Manuel, East Cameron 49 B was the first fully operational offshore compression and liquid separation platform designed and built by TGP. TGP Engineer, Bill Bailey was the chief design engineer for the facility. It had to be designed to do a great many things efficiently. It had to generate electrical power, receive produced natural gas laden with liquid hydrocarbons and water and then remove these liquids from the gas stream. Fuel gas for the generators and turbines was diverted and then the remaining gas stream was compressed to a higher pressure. The liquid hydrocarbons were then re-injected into the gas stream as it entered the pipeline destined for the onshore Grand Chenier gas stripping facility and the process water returned to the ocean. This was a unique and unusual design that utilized platform space that was always limited.

The same year, TGT and Southern Natural Gas Company filed to develop a large underground storage facility in Louisiana. The facility used a nearly

Inching its way across the Gulf, a pipeline barge lowers an ever-lengthening line of welded pipe.

depleted gas reservoir in the Bear Creek field to add 65 BCF of additional gas storage capacity. This facility was critical in helping smooth out pipeline deliverabilities during both peak and slack demand periods.

As the decade of the 1970s neared its conclusion, it appeared the Company had made significant commitments to address two of their critical areas of focus. These were the securing of non-traditional supply requiring a global outlook and the expansion of pipeline capabilities in the Gulf of Mexico including the securing additional pipeline gas from Mexico and Canada. These efforts by the Company to secure supply from all possible sources began to satisfy the market demand by the end of the 1970s. As a result, the curtailment of customer deliveries imposed since 1974 was finally ended in 1980. So successful was the gas industry in adapting to the shortage, there was beginning a discussion about a possible, short-term gas bubble. For an industry and a Company that had been pushed by customers and regulators for the past 10 years to make every effort to secure additional supply, an excess supply of gas seemed more like a gift than a threat.

Ensuring Profitability

The company's third critical area of focus was to continue to ensure a safe, efficient and profitable delivery system regardless of the form, source or location of the available supply. The combined effects of reduced pipeline thruput, the cost of the global gas search which might not be recoverable in rates and the ongoing pipeline construction, maintenance and safety programs had the potential of creating a major impact on the company's financial position. To counter the impact of these increasing costs, the Rate Department under Vice President Jolly Johnson would file a rate case with the Federal Power Commission requesting an increase in transportation rates. The Commission would often suspend the requested rate for a year or more to allow negotiations between the Company, its customers and the Commission staff to be concluded. After these negotiations, a final decision by the Commissioners still might not be forthcoming for an additional year. Any funds collected by the Company under the proposed new rates following the initial filing were always subject to refund to customers when a final Commission decision was rendered. For this reason, there was always a high degree of uncertainty related to recovery of costs already incurred and more importantly to the cash flow impact due to potential refunds. As a result, the annual earnings resulting from the new rates often appeared unrelated to current events due to the time delay between the original filing and the final regulatory decision. It was this type of financial uncertainty that had led Gardiner Symonds to pursue diversification back in the 1950s.

The uncertainties normally related to a single rate case were radically compounded during the 1970s. The rate cases being filed almost annually combined with delays in final regulatory approval for each case resulted in multiple rate cases pancaked on top of each other. At one time, the Rate Department had as many as five outstanding rate cases all pending decisions from the regulatory officials. Hanging in the balance was often hundreds of millions of dollars potentially refundable to customers. In fact, over $660 million in refunds was ordered during the 1976-79 period. The outstanding work of the Rate, Legal and Accounting Departments in the regulatory area allowed the Company to not only maintain but improve its financial position during the 1970s.

Conclusion of the 1970s

The overall Company operating and financial effectiveness and efficiency during the 1970s is illustrated by the $2.2 billion in net operating income contributed to Tenneco Inc. during the 1970 through 1979 period. Operating income grew from $121 million in 1970 to $279 million in 1979 while capital expenditures averaged over $89 million per year during the period. It was only through the cooperative efforts of all the departments of the Company that such excellent financial results could be secured while working to overcome supply shortages.

As the 1970s came to a close, it appeared the position of TGT was beginning to improve over the gas shortages experienced earlier in the decade. Gas reserves dedicated to TGT pipelines and deliveries to customers were both increasing due to available supply. While the Algerian LNG import contract had been rejected by the FERC, cold war politics had forced cancellation of the North Star Project and governmental decisions had forced abandonment of the Alaskan Gas Project, efforts were continuing on the other supplemental projects because long-term gas supplies were still deemed inadequate for the country. It appeared there was a light at the end of the dark ten-year supply tunnel, but whether this was the headlight of an oncoming freight train would be later determined in the 1980s.

The 1970s will be remembered by TGT employees, the pipeline industry and the American people as one of the more puzzling and frustrating times in U.S. energy history. The energy crisis that began in the early 1970s threatened to stop America in its tracks. A nation that had fueled its prosperity through cheap and efficient energy sources suddenly found itself facing a shortage of gas and oil. TGT and Tenneco Inc. made major decisions and committed significant capital to confront the current energy challenges and prevent their re-occurrence in the future. These actions unleashed an enormous global search for oil and gas and for any other energy form that could be transported to the U.S. and utilized in the TGT system. Domestic synthetic natural gas was also pursued through coal gasification and every effort was made to contract and connect any natural gas available to the U.S. interstate market. Federal government actions through regulatory and other decisions had both positive and negative impact on supply acquisition but the recognition of the need for more realistic gas prices was a major benefit. The overall result of all these efforts was that by the beginning of the 1980s both the Company's and the nation's supply of natural gas was once again sufficient to supply the current market demand. The goal remained to ensure that pipeline curtailment of supply to customers would become a relic of the past. All of these actions demonstrated that when the nation faced a crisis, the Company and its people would respond. Just as TGT had done during World War II, the Company responded to changes and rose to the occasion during the 1970s. The people at TGT had every reason to be proud of their response to these challenges. Unfortunately, the ominous clouds of economic recession moving across the country began to trigger potential storm warnings that promised to again test the character and capabilities of the people.

Since the first pipeline in 1944 TGT defined the art and mechanics of gas and oil transfer.

TGT EIGHTIES & BEYOND

More Years of Challenge and Change

The 1980s ushered in yet another new era for both TGT and the nation. A severe economic recession plagued the country. Fair or not, President Carter became the brunt of much criticism and scorn. He presided over an energy crisis and one of the worst economies since the Great Depression. Inflation remained in double digits, unemployment soared and interest rates hovered around 20%. Despite the nation's economic trauma, TGT opened the new decade in a position of relative strength. The energy crisis of the 1970s that had heavily affected the Company was rapidly disappearing into the history books and a new era of deregulation loomed. If any company was in a position to deal with the changes that the eighties might bring, it was TGT. Despite curtailments and downturns in the economy, TGT had met the challenges of the 1970s and had the benefits of being a part of an immensely successful parent corporation, Tenneco Inc. Both TGT and the parent had continued to grow throughout the preceding decade, surviving the energy crisis with few scars.

The primary objectives or focal points remained in place when entering the new decade. They were to secure long-term, non-traditional sources of supply, expand domestic supplies through pipeline expansions and innovative contracting and increase the import of pipeline gas from Canada and Mexico. But above all, the Company must ensure an efficient, safe and profitable delivery system regardless of the source or location of the supply.

Beginning in 1980, TGT still consisted of four primary entities: Tennessee Gas Pipeline Company, Midwestern Gas Transmission Company, East Tennessee Natural Gas Company and the intrastate, Channel Industries Gas Company. The four companies had a total of 16,638 miles of pipeline in service with 1.5 million horsepower of compression. Nearly 3231 employees operated and maintained a system that delivered 1.87 trillion cubic feet of gas in 1980. At the top of the corporate pyramid was Jack Ray who was ably assisted by an executive corps of experienced and seasoned natural gas professionals. Together they would have to meet the challenges of the new decade and carry on the Company tradition of growth and confidence. The obstacles would be formidable but the battle was joined.

The decade got off to a good start for TGT with regard to its facilities in the Gulf of Mexico area. The FERC approved the construction of facilities in the Sabine Pass. What became known as the Sabine Pass 18 Project consisted of a $117 million investment in both onshore and offshore facilities in the Gulf of Mexico. TGP was a partner in the project which included an expansion of the existing TGP system and its partners' onshore facilities. The new offshore line allowed the Company to bring 353 MMCF of natural gas per day onshore and into TGP's existing lines. While the Sabine Pass project was progressing, additional work in the Mississippi Delta area off Southeast Louisiana in South Pass 77 was completed, adding 200 MMCF per day to TGT's total system.

1980 TENNESSEE GAS TRANSMISSION CORPORATE STRUCTURE

President – Jack H. Ray

Executive Vice President	Senior Vice President	Vice President
J. S. Brogdon, Jr.	J. M. Johnson	L. F. Cadenhead
E. Wayne Hopkins	John M. Robertson, Jr.	E. H. Muse
J. L. Parrish, Jr.		Jerry F. Shivers
Robert C. Thomas		

Tennessee Gas Pipeline	Midwest Gas Transmission	East Tennessee Natural Gas	Channel Industries
President	President	President	President
Harry Long	John Robertson, Jr.	Tom Bell	Tom Ashton

Vice President
E. U. Cochrane   Charles A. Falkenhagen
Howard Gray   Don Weikman
William Such   Roger Stark
W. M. Rogers   George White

Division Managers	Division Superintendents	General Superintendent	General Superintendent
A – Dick Scroggins	VP & General Manager – Ned Thomas	Ben Simpson	Carson Dabbs – Pipeline
B – Hugh Fisher	General Superintendent – C. A. Cassity		
C – Otis Korn	Northern – Warren Henderson		
D – Tom Perry	Southern – C.E. Robideaux		
E – Dick Hines			
F – Sam Baugh			
G – Frank Ballard			

With additional gas supply coming on stream in late 1979 and 1980, TGP was able in 1981 to expand pipeline facilities in New York and New England to deliver an additional 74 MMCF per day of firm transportation and an additional 66 MMCF per day on best efforts basis. Pipeline construction included adding main line loops along TGP's 200-system's 24-inch pipeline in several New York and Massachusetts locations. This was the first mainline expansion in New England since the original 24-inch pipeline was placed in service in 1951. Construction of the new pipeline loops were completed and placed in

R. C. "BOB" THOMAS

Bob Thomas graduated from the University of Oklahoma with a B. S. degree in geological engineering in 1951. He served as an Air Force Sabre jet pilot during the Korean War and afterwards returned to OU for an advanced degree. A professor convinced him to go into industry while the hiring demand was great. Thomas was interviewed in 1956 by Tennessee Gas and about 17 other companies. He received job offers from all interviews, but took a job with TGT upon the recommendation of a classmate. Bob began as a junior engineer in Midland, Texas in 1956 and progressed upwards through several positions and numerous moves. In 1970, he was elected Vice President of Tenneco Oil's Canadian subsidiary. The following year he assumed responsibility for TGT's involvement in Canadian Arctic Islands exploration. He moved to Houston and headed up TGT's newly created International Energy Contracts Department in 1973.

His tenure at Tennessee Gas was marked by some of the most fundamental changes in the interstate pipeline business. The Arab oil embargo of 1973 had the effect of creating an unprecedented demand for natural gas. Thomas was in the midst of the fray with an array of unconventional projects like LNG from several international sources, synthetic gas from coal and hydrocarbon liquids and other supplemental supplies. Meanwhile, he worked his way up the ladder and was named President of TGT in 1983. The 1980s proved to be the most traumatic period yet in the gas business. Bob was at the helm of TGT when deregulation occurred in 1984. This was followed by a prolonged period when TGT attempted to negotiate their way out of long term gas purchase agreements with producers when FERC deregulated the market prices, but not the supply contracts pipelines had with producers. Faced with the possibility of bankruptcy, TGT was forced to make temporary changes in gas purchase contracts. Some producers agreed to negotiate settlements while others litigated and won substantial awards in the courts.

Thomas moved up to Chairman and CEO of Tenneco Gas in June 1990 and was replaced by President Steve Chesebro in 1994, who also held the title of Chief Operating Officer. In late 1991, the top management of the parent company, Tenneco Inc., changed suddenly. At first, the new management team was very supportive, but after more changes, it reflected a much lower level of interest in the energy business.

Bob Thomas was very active in gas industry affairs; holding officer and/or director positions in the Interstate Natural Gas Association of America, the Gas Research Institute, the American Gas Association and the Institute of Gas Technology.

service on time in spite of a very harsh winter environment. Pipeline expansion in New York and New England continued in 1982.

Development of mineral-rich southwestern region of the United States continued unabated in 1981. The Company's goal of tapping into Arkoma Basin gas supplies also became a reality in 1981 following receipt of FERC approval. As a 25% partner in Ozark Gas Transmission Company, TGT took part in the construction of a 265-mile line extending from Pittsburgh County, Oklahoma to White Oak, Arkansas. The system became operational in March 1982. Meanwhile, completion of the Bear Creek Storage Project in Northern Louisiana provided the Company with an additional 32 billion cubic feet of storage and added 450 MMCF of peak-day capacity to TGT's system. Its strategic location facilitated the Company's expansion of both offshore and onshore work in the region.

The Company also continued to search North America for additional gas supplies. Gas contracts offices were opened in Denver, Midland and Jackson, Mississippi to access the developing areas of the Anadarko basin, Western Overthrust belt and the Appalachian basin. A Canadian office was opened in order to handle the growing activity north of the border. A contract negotiated with ProGas of Canada for 60 MMCFD received regulatory approval and gas began to flow. Mexican gas also added to the Company's available deliverability with over 112 MMCF flowing daily in 1980 and 1981. All of this expanded activity resulted in the Company contracting for over one trillion cubic feet (TCF) of gas in 1981.

Considering the customer and governmental pressures for additional supply in the previous decade, the beginning of the 1980s was beginning to look much better for TGT and the pipeline industry at least in comparison to the 1970s. New reserves were available although at a rapidly escalating price and customers were receiving all the supplies they were requesting. Considering their past experience with curtailment, it was not surprising that TGT's customers continued to project the need for increasing future supply and deliverability. The Company felt reasonably comfortable about supply because new Canadian and Mexican imports were flowing and the Department of Energy had just approved a $2 billion loan guarantee for the Great Plains Gasification Associates Project (GPGA). TGT's net operating income was continuing to grow as was the net income of Tenneco Inc.

The Gas Bubble and Take-or-Pay

Unfortunately, the existing financial storm clouds were continuing to grow and would soon explode upon the scene impacting the country, the energy industry, TGT and parent, Tenneco Inc. Wellhead gas prices that had been about $0.18 per MCF in 1972 had escalated to over $2.45 per MCF in 1982 and consumers were clamoring for reduced costs because of the recession. These and other factors resulted in total U.S. gas consumption dropping from about 22 TCF per year in 1972 to slightly over 18 TCF in 1982 or a reduction of some 18%. This was a punishing blow that would soon be felt by the entire natural gas industry.

WELLHEAD OIL AND GAS PRICES, 1971-1983

Year	Gas (Dollars per MCF)	Oil* (Dollars per Barrel)
1971	0.18	3.60
1972	0.19	3.60
1973	0.22	4.75
1974	0.30	9.35
1975	0.44	12.21
1976	0.58	12.23
1977	0.79	14.22
1978	0.91	14.55
1979	1.18	25.08
1980	1.59	37.96
1981	1.98	36.08
1982	2.46	33.65
1983	2.59	30.30

* Stripper well crude oil price, 1971-1975   West Texas Intermediate crude oil price, 1976-1983
Source: US Energy Information Administration, Tim McMahon

By 1982, it had become glaringly obvious that the energy crisis had not only faded, but had ushered in regulation that no longer fit the times. A prime example was certain features of the Natural Gas Policy Act. This piece of legislation had been passed during the energy crisis to stimulate exploration through higher rates in the price of gas. When passed, it was generally heralded as one of the most significant and sorely needed pieces of legislation in the history of the natural gas industry. It was what Gardiner Symonds and others had been hoping for since the late 1940s. But by 1982, events had far outpaced governmental actions and the NGPA became a bit outdated and actually began to hurt the natural gas industry. Maintaining high fixed rates on natural gas at the wellhead during a period of plentiful supplies of both gas and oil was simply counter-productive. As a result of the declining price of oil on the world market, many industries turned to that fuel and moved away from natural gas. Mostly as a result of this Act, actual shipments of gas declined by 7% while net income increased by 26%. While this higher income was due to rate case timing and was good news in the short run, the impact of a declining sales and delivery rate would prove devastating in the coming years.

The rules promulgated by the NGPA put heavy pressure on what had been a mutually dependent, if sometimes contentious, relationship among all parties throughout the natural gas chain. In the early days of building the interstate natural gas transmission system, regulatory approval and financial support for a new pipeline required both the assurance of a long-term market and an equally assured long-term supply. To balance these requirements, pipeline sales contracts included a requirement that the customer purchase a minimum quantity of gas over a specific time period or make payment in lieu of taking the volumes below the minimum. This requirement was termed a "minimum bill." In return, pipelines entered into long-term supply contracts with producers requiring minimum purchase levels or a payment in lieu of not taking the gas below the minimum volumes. This was the "take-or-pay"

SAFETY FIRST

From the 1950s to the end of its life, TGT maintained a strong focus on safety in the workplace. Each quarter, safety statistics were published in the Company's "The Line" magazine. Particular attention was given to the field locations where pipeline and compressor work required the use of heavy equipment. Locations that passed safety milestones such as 5, 10, 15, 20, 25 or 30 years without a lost time accident or stations that achieved 500,000, one million or two million hours worked without lost time were honored by the Company. Achieving these major milestones in safety were celebrated with dinners, awards and many pictures taken of the event and the recipients. Safety ranked very high in the Company culture and as a result numerous safety awards were received from the American Gas Association and other pipeline industry groups.

TGT CULTURE
Employee Center

Tennessee Gas constructed a four story public parking garage in June, 1956 which was named Ten Ten Garage, because of its location at 1010 Travis Street. It was later connected to both TGT's Commerce Building and the 24-story Bank of the Southwest Building by Houston's first air conditioned tunnel. Ten Ten Garage provided valet parking only, fueling on the street level and minor auto maintenance and car washing in the basement level. Its second level basement was designated parking for the TGT auto fleet where officers and department heads parked their company vehicles. The Normandie Club was located in the first basement and was accessible only from the street level by stairwell. It was the favorite "watering hole" for many TGT executives who enjoyed two martini lunches and after hour refreshments at a time when Texas required private club membership for "liquor by the drink" sales.

Ten Ten Travis added two floors to the garage in 1962, expanded the street level commercial space to accommodate more retail and restaurant tenants and added the 450-seat public Normandie Cafeteria in the basement along with a new tunnel entry to the refurbished Normandie Restaurant and Club. All of these eateries opened in mid-January 1963. In addition, a future air conditioned tunnel connection to the soon to be opened Tennessee Building was constructed. A large emergency generator was installed in the garage and a heliport was also added on the roof.

In early 1982 another major renovation occurred to the Ten Ten Travis Garage when a two-level Employee Center was constructed which occupied approximately 100,000 square feet atop the

obligation and combined with the minimum bill provided a certain level of financial assurance for producers, pipelines and consumers. Unfortunately, the minimum bill requirement was eliminated and only take-or-pay remained as an obligation under the NGPA.

As the impact of higher gas prices began to disturb the marketplace, major pipeline customers were demanding the ability to access "spot gas" at prices below their long-term contracts with pipelines. In a policy shift by the FERC, pipelines were encouraged to form Special Marketing Programs (SMP) where regulators would issue blanket certificates allowing them to buy, transport and sell spot gas to their customers. This suddenly placed pipelines in pricing competition with themselves.

As the market share for natural gas began to decline, the effects of the "take-or-pay" clauses in producer contracts began to be felt by the Company. The NGPA of 1978 had validated the obligation of transmission companies to pay a certain price for gas whether or not it could be sold to distributor customers. This legislation was aimed at increasing revenues for producers to use in additional exploration for natural gas. While that may have been appropriate while gas was in short supply, it certainly was not going to work during a glut. Intensifying the problem were two other factors. First, fuel-use legislation passed along with the NGPA prevented industrial customers from using natural gas under boilers even when abundant supplies were available. Gas was deemed by the government to be too valuable to use in such a fashion. Secondly, although transmission companies were forced to take gas they might not need or be able to sell, the NGPA and later regulatory actions did not obligate pipeline customers to honor minimum bills when they reduced purchases from their pipeline suppliers. In effect, transmission companies were getting squeezed from both sides and TGT found the situation untenable. The Company recognized that unless immediate action was taken, the pipeline industry would be severely damaged and some pipelines would likely be forced into bankruptcy.

These new regulatory problems could not have come at a worse time. Several factors exacerbated the problem caused by the legislation. First, the continuing major recession caused many plants to close down, thereby reducing overall demand for gas. Second, the effect of several years of conservation efforts was now being felt. Third, the winter of 1982 was one of the warmest in the nation's history reducing demand for supply. Fourth, a world-wide oil glut had brought down the price of oil, seducing former users of gas to switch fuel sources. Fifth, for the first time natural gas had become more expensive than No. 6 high sulfur fuel oil. Finally, a notable but little appreciated change had been occurring over the past decade in the U.S. economy. Whereas the United States had long been an industrialized nation, the late 1970s and 1980s increasingly witnessed a transition from an industrialized base economy to that of a service and white collar based economy. The strength of multinational firms had become very apparent. Many U.S. industries moved operations abroad, mostly to Latin America and other less developed nations in order to take advantage of tax breaks, low business costs, and lower wages. Given this reality, TGT needed once again to prepare for the changes ahead due to a changing market unlikely to gain stability for many years.

By the end of 1982 and continuing through the first quarter of 1983, TGT's gas deliveries had continued to decline. Many of the earlier LNG projects had been abandoned due to governmental decisions and the remaining active ones were being deferred due to the probability of the delivered product being priced out of the market. A series of Management changes were made beginning in May, 1983. Jack Ray moved to Tenneco Inc. as Senior Vice President responsible for International Development and Bob Thomas was named President of TGT. Shortly thereafter, Cliff Rackley replaced Thomas as Board Chairman of Great Plains Gasification Associates which at that time was the largest, active, engineering and construction project in the U.S.

Recognizing that natural gas was losing market share to other fuels because of its higher cost, TGP had begun negotiations with some of their larger producers in November 1982, with only limited success. In-depth studies by TGP of current and projected market conditions found that its customers would continue to lose both industrial and residential/commercial markets unless the gas price was made more competitive. With over 1400 contracts with almost 2200 producers, individual contractual negotiations with each producer was impossible within any reasonable time frame and immediate action was required to rescue the gas market. Whatever strategy was utilized to reduce cost needed to apply to all producers in as equitable a manner as possible and had to become effective very quickly.

The Emergency Gas Purchase Policy

After extensive review and study, the Company instituted the Emergency Gas Purchase Policy (EGPP) on May 1, 1983 as a first step in response to the pricing problems brought about through the NGPA. The goal of the EGPP was to provide competitive, market-based rates for customers in order to regain some of the market that was continuing to be lost to oil. The key action within the policy was to regain control over the type of gas being tendered to the Company by producers. When volumes were requested by Pipelines, producers were very logically tendering as much as possible of the most expensive "new" gas rather than the lower priced "old" gas as the prices were designated by the NGPA. It was TGT's goal to adjust that by requiring a blending of old and new gas thereby providing a market clearing price of gas to customers. As explained by Bob Thomas, "We found we had little control over the quantity of different pricing categories of gas received at the producing end of our pipeline and this was adversely affecting sales at the consuming end." The EGPP sought to solve these problems by instituting a four-part plan. First,

Garage. It included a modern employee cafeteria and dining rooms, an expanded education center and a private, fully-equipped exercise facility. Two garden terraces, with live trees, landscaping and water features provided a relaxed atmosphere to enhance the dining experience in both the cafeteria and upper-level executive dining room. The new Employee Center contained a full service employee health facility with a 1/5 mile banked, enclosed jogging track around its perimeter on the eighth floor and several custom designed meeting rooms equipped with the latest audio-visual teaching aids. Access to the exercise facility was limited to those employees that passed a free annual physical exam by the Company doctor who maintained offices in the Tenneco Building. Tenneco's Employee Center indoor exercise facility provided work-out clothing, separate men's and women's exercise rooms and separate shower and locker facilities. Upon commencement of this renovation, the Normandie Cafeteria and the Normandie Restaurant and Club were closed permanently along with several street-level commercial shops.

In mid-1984 Addison-Wesley Publishing Company released a book, The 100 Best Companies To Work For in America, *which spotlights companies that employees say are a great place to work--and Tenneco Inc. was one of them. Tenneco drew the highest praise in the book for its Employee Center, with "a block-long indoor patio garden with live trees and one of the best health and fitness Facilities in Corporate America." The book also gave Tenneco high marks for its large fleet of 12-passenger commuter vans, subsidized monthly bus pass program, for Tennwood and for its employee's extensive involvement in community affairs.*

EXCO GATHERING AND STATE GAS PIPELINE

In 1982 it was decided that TGT should expand in the unregulated pipeline business as the returns on investment looked significantly higher.

In a cautious manner to "test the waters," a small experimental unregulated pipeline company was formed. The company was named Exco Gathering Company which I assume came from experimental gathering company. The word gathering was used as most unregulated companies were gas gathering companies. Edward J. Holm was hired to lead this endeavor. Jay was an excellent choice as he had experience in both the business and technical side of pipelines. Ruth Guarino was soon added as a secretary and Bob Otjen came from TGP District 555 to be the construction superintendent. Shortly after that, Tom Stubblefield was hired to be the sales and gas contracts person. Those job titles were really only for reference purposes as each of us found ourselves doing activities that were way outside of our "areas." That is one of the reasons that we were successful as we could maintain a very lean organization and still get the required work completed.

We found very quickly that we could compete in the faster running and more cost conscious unregulated market. Projects were won and built in New Mexico, West Virginia, Texas, Louisiana, Minnesota and other locations. In some cases we even competed with TGP.

The name, Exco Gathering, was changed about a year after the company was started. It was explained that we had a complaint from Exxon saying our name was too close to their name but they would not sue us if we changed it. So, the name was changed to State Gas Pipeline.

TGP decided that it was necessary to determine the volume of each category of gas that it purchased for shipment through the lines. As Thomas explained, "We generally received the volumes of gas we wanted, but not the appropriate mix." This new policy allowed the Company to control the volume received from each vintage. The producer would then know how much of what vintage was wanted. The intent was to establish a bias toward lower-cost gas to reduce the price to the consumer thereby reducing the loss of markets to oil. Second, EGPP capped the price at $3.40 per MMBTU where a market-out clause existed in a contract. As TGT Vice President Tom Matthews noted, "Market-out… stipulate that if the current price paid to producers is too high for us to market the gas, we have the right to nominate a new price at which we can sell it. The producer then has the option to accept our offer or see if he can get a better deal somewhere else." Third, in contracts that do not contain market-out features, EGPP capped the price to be paid for gas at 110% of the price of No. 2 fuel oil. This was obviously designed to keep gas competitive with fuel oil in the market. Finally, the Company agreed to meet take-or-pay obligations if producers agreed to the new "take" level and the blended price approach. This action arose out of the reality that in many cases pipelines could not sell the volumes at prices that producers were tendering and did not have the capability to store the gas if accepted. Many pipelines were simply refusing the gas and trying to re-negotiate contracts with producers. As Thomas observed, "Most pipelines aren't paying any take-or-pay. They are either trying to re-negotiate (which we tried unsuccessfully) or, like us, claiming economic force majeure" (an act of God, beyond our control).

With pipelines and storage facilities filled to capacity and consumer demand down, it was physically and economically impossible to accept the gas at prices that producers were tendering to pipeline companies. Thus "new" take levels needed to be agreed upon very quickly. One way of showing the EGPP worked as designed is the fact that TGP reduced its weighted average purchase price of gas from $3.26 per MCF to $2.85 per MCF from the May 1 enactment of the policy to the end of December that year. This had a major impact on the competition among alternate fuels in the Company's major market areas. Since it was believed that the pricing and volume imbalance would be relatively short lived, the EGPP was only to be in effect through 1985 unless sooner terminated.

The EGPP had a major impact on TGT's future. In the short term it sent out a message to all concerned that the NGPA was not workable and had to be changed to alleviate a growing crisis in the natural gas industry. More importantly, it put natural gas producers on alert that the Company could and would no longer sit idly by while choices made by regulators and producers determined the economic futures of gas pipeline companies. In the long term, the EGPP helped to correct the deficiencies in the NGPA of 1978, the most important being the legislation's unresponsiveness to market conditions. Finally, it can well be argued that the EGPP saved the Company, and perhaps the pipeline industry from eventual economic ruin. It was simply self destructive to sit by while the market was being lost to fuel oil due to the high prices of gas. To make gas once again competitive, it was necessary to increase the blending of plentiful "old" reserves with the "new" higher priced gas. EGPP did just that.

Implementing EGPP did not come without significant liabilities. The dollars paid by the Company in contract re-negotiations, take-or-pay payments and litigation settlements were huge but only one of the negatives. It was also uncertain at the time whether customers who benefitted from lower gas prices and market recovery would share in these costs. Another major impact was the major commitment of time by a large number of employees at all levels over a number of years in resolving the contract issues with producers. Probably the one that hurt the most was the belief by some in the producer community that this was blatant contract abrogation, that they had been treated unfairly and Tenneco's sister company, Tenneco Oil Exploration and Production, had not been subjected to the same EGPP restrictions. These views, although untrue, affected industry relationships for several years. In reality, the FERC had been carefully reviewing TGP and all interstate pipelines very closely for many years concerning their relationships with both producers and intrastate pipeline affiliates. Since TOC was TGP's largest single supplier providing 25% of their gas supply, the reduction in TOC revenue was also having an adverse effect on them and their parent. The mid-1980s was a very difficult period requiring tough decisions but outstanding work by employees in all areas ultimately led to problem resolutions. By 1989, however, settlements with most producers had been completed and the Company had restored its gas market and returned to prosperity.

More Regulation - FERC Order 380

With action taken to resolve one-half of the take-or-pay problem and a beginning recovery in the nation-wide recession, TGT was poised for its next challenge: responding to FERC Order 380, issued in July 1984. This order constituted the second half of the take-or-pay issue. In effect, Order 380 greatly increased the business risks of pipeline companies because it still did not support the contract obligations of distribution companies to pay a minimum bill for gas not taken below specified minimum levels but continued to obligate pipelines to serve local distributors up to full contract entitlements when requested. Moreover, this order threw pipeline company markets further into disarray by allowing customers to change suppliers at any time. In some ways this problem presented more difficulties than dealing with take-or-pay with producing companies because in the case of the latter, gas could simply be refused if the pipeline system was full. Furthermore, with existing surplus supply, the customer was almost always in a better bargaining position than

The success of Exco Gathering/State Gas Pipeline lead the corporation to expand the concept and we became the model and basis for Tenngasco Corporation. In 1984 Tenngasco was established and Jay Holm went into the regulated side of the business, Ruth Guarino retired, Tom Subblefield went into Tenngasco as a gas contracts person and Bob Otjen went to Tenngasco as Chief Engineer.

In the two plus years of its existence, this upstart little company made a difference in the way some pipeline business was done, added to Tenneco's bottom line and formed a model for Tenneco's unregulated business. We also had a great time making this happen.

- Bob Otjen

In those early formative years the original Houston Office employee group was somewhat younger than the field employees who had a higher percentage of married individuals in their ranks. This demographic created a demand for after-hours recreation among the Houston employee group. The earliest recorded Houston employee recreation function was the creation of an 8-team bowling league in September 1945, just a month after the end of WW II. The TGT Houston Employees Club was formed in October of the following year to handle all recreational activities except the annual Company Birthday Party on October 31st. Club membership required a $1 initiation fee with monthly dues of 25 cents to support its activities. The Club began with 205 members.

In mid-June 1952 some 1400 Houston employees attended a largest-ever Company picnic at a new 350 acre recreation area about 5 miles north of Hockley, Texas. It was then a partially wooded tract with two lakes, facilities for picnicking and boating and it included a softball diamond and a comfort station. Like previous picnics, this one featured a softball game between the "Executives" versus the "Regulars". In a short ceremony toward the end of the day's festivities President Gardiner Symonds officially turned over the area to the TGT Houston Employees Club. It became "Tennwood" as a result of an employee naming contest the following month. Tennwood was developed into an elite golf club and expanded over the years to meet the recreational demands of a growing workforce. It eventually included two 18 hole golf courses with a Club house, golf cart facilities and pro shop, tennis

the seller, especially when competition in the marketplace was present. And, this was certainly the case in dealing with the minimum bill with customers.

Pipeline Cost Management Program

The tariff or cost of gas service charged to customers for the volumes they requested, consisted of the actual cost of gas purchased from producers plus the cost of transporting the gas to the customer receipt point. While the EGPP had made a major move toward making the consumers' gas price competitive, a similar move had to be made to assure an equally competitive transportation charge. The ability of distribution company customers to switch suppliers under FERC Order 380 made it clear that, given a competitive producer price, the pipeline with the lowest transportation cost would be the winner. Since all of the Company's customers had access to the actual pipeline costs reflected in FERC rate cases, evaluating and reducing costs was a necessity. The fundamental objective of the Company to ensure a safe, efficient and profitable delivery system took center stage.

To meet this challenge, the Company initiated a cost-management program in 1984 aimed at evaluating and reducing all expenses. Since employee salaries and benefits were a big part of operating costs, personnel would be significantly affected. The results were that for the first time in TGT's 40-year history, workers had to be laid off. This was an extremely traumatic event for all employees since TGT was as much a family as it was a company. Many employees were offered early retirement and some were terminated, not because of performance or ability, but because certain jobs or services could no longer be justified if the Company were to remain viable. In reality, these actions were requirements rather than options. Reductions in force were felt at all levels of the Company and the actions taken reflected one of the darkest moments to that date in the history of the Company. The overall impact of the actions combined with the resiliency of the employees resulted in deliveries increasing by 24% by the end of 1984.

Another cost-saving device employed was the new computer system that TGT installed in 1984. The "TGT Information Center" was the product of brainstorming by leaders in the accounting, budget, rate, and other departments who met several times in an effort to upgrade the existing computer system. The Information Center was a vast improvement over the older system because it enabled more user-friendly programs. This made information available quicker, more accurately, and to more users. Moreover, it reduced the demand for programmers, eliminated redundancy, and coordinated and connected existing computer systems.

Not to be outdone, pipeline operations began to reduce construction costs by ditching the long held policy of contracting out construction work in favor of using Company employees on construction projects. By doing so, the Company not only saved a significant amount of money but also upgraded the skills of its present workforce. New work was carried out under the subsidiary Tennessee Gas and Construction Company.

Management and employees alike welcomed the opportunity to take on new tasks. George Benoit, TGP manager of construction, noted that "The significant point is that we would have spent that money on employees' salaries had they stayed at home on their regular duties, and paid contractors to do the construction. What we've done is keep ourselves from spending twice the money." Workers, too, liked the new challenges. As Richard Lyons, TGP pipeline engineer, noted while working on a job in Texas. "The unique thing about this year is the magnitude of the jobs we've undertaken…In some cases we worked under the worst conditions imaginable. We had never replaced nine miles of 26" line like we did in District 106 this year, or installed 36 miles of 36" as we did in District 25." His sentiments were echoed by Buddy Secor, Division A engineer, who also gained valuable new experience, as dirty as it might be. According to Secor, "The District 25 job, near Conroe, Texas, presented the worst working conditions I've ever seen for laying pipeline. We had torrential rains at the beginning of the job, and it never did dry up, except on the surface…Half the time you were stuck in the mud from the waist down, and choking in dust from the waist up." Some were more enthusiastic than others. For instance, Jay Petty, senior repairman for Midwestern Gas Transmission Company in Paris, Illinois noted, "I really enjoyed myself…The people from TGP made us feel very welcome, and they were very professional. There is no doubt in my mind that this Company could tackle any construction project it puts its mind or its muscle to…I've got almost 17 years with the Company and I have to say my experience in construction this year was by far my greatest accomplishment." By the end of 1984 the Company had logged nearly one-half million work-hours in construction.

The use of company employees on construction projects continued into 1985. One of the more important jobs performed was the improvement program in New England, called the "Annual Volumetric Limitations" project. Given improving market conditions in the Northeast, the program aimed to increase and improve service to New England and extend supply lines to potential new markets, enabling the Company to increase sales and provide additional capacity for interruptible sales. Company employees were recruited from TGT divisions all over the country to take part in this project. In the process of carrying out their duties, many of these employees were amazed by the vastness of pipeline construction work. Attaining rights-of-ways, clearing the right-of-way, and working closely with persons in the community was new to many employees. Some were surprised to find the human dimensions to the work, especially convincing landowners to permit work to be performed on their property. Others were surprised by the fact that not only did the Company rip up people's property, but more often than not, after repairing it had made significant improvements prior to finishing up the job. The New

courts, a large swimming pool, dining room and large meeting rooms, an oil and gas industry museum, a manager's residence and two additional fishing lakes. J. Curtis Lloyd was the first Tennwood Manager and golf pro. Curt became TGT's Director of Administration later in his career.

Meanwhile, the Employees Club continued to sponsor offshore fishing trips, travel events, golf tournaments, fashion shows, the annual Company BBQ, a July 4th picnic complete with a professional fireworks display, the Christmas Dance and many other recreational activities over the years. In the late 1950s the Houston Employees Club membership morphed into membership in Tennwood.

An underground dispatch center was built on the grounds in 1963 and TGT's Gas Control Department moved to Tennwood while the remainder of the Company moved into the new Tennessee Building. The new dispatch center was housed in a secure bunker which provided communications and emergency living quarters for dispatchers operating TGT's pipelines during the "Cold War."

By 1980, it was the most prestigious employee country club in the Houston area. Tennwood could accommodate several thousand employees and their families at the Annual Picnic. Members could reserve the various picnic areas at other times for family outings or for larger groups such as family reunions. Even the charcoal and starter fluid was furnished for the barbeque pits at each picnic site. Tennwood membership was available to Houston employees who paid a modest monthly fee. Upon retirement, Houston area Tennwood members were awarded "Tennwood Gold Cards" which entitled them and their spouse to free access to all facilities and free green fees on the golf courses.

Part of the route of the New York-New England expansion was across land owned by the State of Massachusetts in the Berkshire Mountains. Permits for crossing State-owned land required the State Legislature to pass a resolution allowing construction. The necessary permits were not obtained until late fall of 1981 resulting in winter construction. During construction, temperatures reached lows of minus 10 degrees. Hydrostatic testing of the new line was very difficult due to the freezing temperatures. While de-watering the pipeline after testing, the water spray turned to snow and the last of the water exiting the pipe was a solid plug of ice.

The pipeline contractor used dynamite to blast ditches for the new pipe. During one blast epi-sode, a huge boulder landed on the existing 24-inch pipeline causing a rupture. The pipe which served Boston was shut in for repairs. A TGP interconnect with another pipeline company could not be used due to PCB contamination in the other pipeline. However, by using TGP's 300-line system, TGP was able to make deliveries to Boston until the ruptured line could be repaired. Pipelining is full of unexpected happenings.

- Gilmer Abel

England project was successful in adding compressor horsepower to Stations 321, 313, 319, 267, and constructing new stations in Libertyville, New Jersey and Wyalusing, Pennsylvania, plus laying additional pipeline.

The Expansion of Marketing Programs

Gas deliveries were up in 1984 but the industry still remained in transi-tion and demand failed to increase enough to substantially diminish the ex-cess deliverability existing since the beginning of the 1980s. The Border Gas Group, Inc., of which TGT was a partner, announced jointly with Pemex that natural gas imports from Mexico would be temporarily suspended effective November 1, 1984. In addition to reducing deliverability from all possible sources, new marketing strategies were employed by the Company to increase sales and expand markets. The first of these was TGT's Marketing Assistance Program (MAP). Initiated in 1984, this program featured shared-cost adver-tising and gas appliance rebates to help TGT customers increase sales. That same year, TGT implemented the Flexible Industrial Rate Program by which the Company worked closely with distributors serving the industrial sector. The focus was put on designing rates to compete with other fuel sources. Fi-nally, TGT instituted the Builder Incentive Program which aimed at provid-ing incentives for contractors and others by subsidizing gas piping and vent-ing installation.

Regulatory officials had always voiced concern about TGT having own-ership of both interstate and intrastate pipelines and particularly its relation-ship with TOC. Every effort was made by the Company to maintain a "Chi-nese Wall" of separation between the regulated and non-regulated entities. In anticipation of the forthcoming deregulation of many categories of gas on January 1, 1985, Tenngasco Corporation was created in April, 1984. It was formed as a separate organization reporting directly to Tenneco Inc. While operating as a unit separate from both TGT and Tenneco Oil Exploration and Production, the three organizations worked as closely together as regulations would permit. Jerry McLeod was hired as president of the new corporation and a staff of 215 people was quickly assembled.

The new unit was established to enter and become a major player in the new natural gas spot market and to operate TGT's existing 784-mile pipeline network not regulated by the federal government. Tenngasco planned to grow through acquisitions and shortly after its creation, Tenngasco purchased Cre-ole Gas Pipeline Corporation which operated a 42-mile pipeline near New Orleans thereby providing access to an active gas supply and marketing area. By the end of 1984, Tenngasco was responsible for the operations of eight different intrastate companies including pipelines, gathering systems, sales and supply operations. They were also responsible for all spot gas sales for Tenneco including the TENNEFLEX program which was designed to move shut-in gas from the Gulf of Mexico into the spot market. This program had actually been initiated by Tenneco Oil Exploration and Production and it was the first producer-initiated effort to help deflate the existing gas "bubble."

In late 1984, Tenngasco established the concept of a spot price for gas established by geographic location. They initiated a formal posted price program for gas delivered to a specific major pipeline interconnection in Louisiana and an additional one in Texas. Each month Tenngasco would announce a purchase price for gas at each of these locations and their purchasing group would buy supplies from producers and aggregators at these two pricing points. While the volumes weren't initially that large, the program became widely recognized as the price setting indicator for these two areas. This Tenngasco Exchange pricing concept was utilized years later when the Henry Hub became the recognized trading point for both physical supplies of natural gas and futures contracts in south Louisiana.

1985 was a fruitful year for Tenngasco and they proved to be a major benefit to Tenneco. Not only did they double their net income in the first year, they also acquired two natural gas systems in Louisiana. Louisiana Intrastate Gas Corporation and Mid-Louisiana Gas Company operated 2740 miles of intrastate and interstate pipelines, interests in five gas processing plants and gas producing properties in Northeastern Louisiana. Tenngasco's activity continued into 1986 when they increased their transportation volume from 900 MMCFD to 1.5 billion cubic feet per day. With continued federal regulatory uncertainty expected, the spot market was initially very attractive to producers seeking to market their gas.

Industry Restructuring - FERC Order 436

1985 was another frustrating year for TGT with regulated gas deliveries down another 15% from the previous year and operating income declining 8%. Decreased demand due to warm winters and intense competition from other companies and fuels were resulting in lower delivery levels. Amidst these difficulties, the FERC issued Order 436 which was a watershed set of regulations designed to fundamentally restructure the interstate natural gas industry. The primary intent was to provide open access on interstate pipelines for transportation by third parties on a first-come first-serve basis.

This Order did give pipeline companies the choice to remain as wholesalers or open their systems to third parties. A pipeline company that chose to become a transporter was required to allow its customers having long-term contracts to decrease their contract purchase entitlements by 100% over five years. To the dismay of companies like TGT, the order still did not deal with the take-or-pay contracts between pipelines and producers. Again, the pipeline industry was caught in the middle of a regulatory maze. Other sections of Order 436 sought to phase in block billing (a way of allocating high-cost and low-cost gas), provided for accelerated certification procedures, and re-affirmed the FERC's position of remaining out of the conflict between produc-

for wall mounting or coffee table viewing. The selection of awards broadened over the years to include tie tacs, cuff links, rings, watches, belt buckles, crystal sets and a large variety of items appropriate for female employees. When the Company's logo changed in subsequent years, the awards were modified to reflect the attractive new logos.

As the years passed the "Original 22" dwindled to twelve at the 20 year mark and to seven (above) at 25 years. President Dick Freeman was included in the seven, after having had a break in service due to medical reasons. Marcella Shaw and Kenny Bradbury were the two remaining survivors receiving their 35 year awards in 1978, while Bradbury was the "last man standing" when he retired in November, 1986 after almost 43 years of service. Kenny was part of the group which comprised one of the largest Retirement Awards Dinners in Houston when 52 recipients and their spouses were honored at the event.

While the tremendous reduction in Tenneco Energy's workforce was occurring during the 1980s, the proud "family" culture crafted by Gardiner Symonds was slowly changing. Even El Paso Energy recognized the value of company loyalty and continued the Service Awards Program after El Paso's purchase of Tenneco Energy in December 1996.

ers and pipelines regarding take-or-pay. The Company's first inclination was to not seek a blanket transportation certificate. The rationale was that since transportation services were likely to displace sales, thereby substantially increasing take-or-pay costs, it might not be in the Company's best interest to seek a transportation certificate. Even before Order 436, TGT was already an interstate transporter of gas for third parties. After further evaluation, however, the decision was made to open the TGP system in December, 1986, as per the "Open Access" order. As a result, the volume of gas flowing through the system began increasing after that date. Since Order 436 also allowed customers to unilaterally reduce their pipeline purchase entitlements, seven of TGT's 103 customers chose to do so. Following TGP's lead, East Tennessee Natural Gas and Midwestern Gas Transmission opened their Pipelines to third-party transportation a few years later. The impact of Order 436 increased market competition with a significant reduction in the margins that could be earned in the unregulated and spot gas markets. This served notice that additional organizational restructuring would soon be required.

Contract Reformation Group

During the process of making the decision on open access, the Company recognized that FERC Order 436 would require the evaluation of every gas purchase contract to determine the remaining recoverable reserves and the estimated deliverability by NGPA pricing vintage over the remaining term of the contract. To accomplish this, a Contract Reformation Group was established and was led by personnel from TGP's Supply Department and shored up with others from Tenneco Oil with experience in contract negotiations. Members of the group included Dan Carter, Jim Gotcher, Larry Edwards, Ron Barnes, Dan Bullion, Mark Colrick and Ron Kothe. Over the next three years, this group was responsible for the renegotiation of some 3000 purchase contracts. The fact that these negotiations would be dovetailed with ongoing EGPP discussions added to their complexity. Needless to say, constant support of this group was required from the Reserves, Contract Administration, Legal and Accounting Departments. The objective of the negotiations was to achieve a contract buyout at a reduced, marketable price, ensure the gas remained dedicated to the Company and to improve business relationships with the producer. Due to the efforts of all the people involved, the objective was achieved.

Now that gas flowing through the TGP system had multiple owners, multiple delivery points and ever changing delivery requirements, a method to accommodate rapid changes had to be developed. A task group of Company employees developed a computerized program and system that allowed customers to conduct business with the Company electronically. This program, promoted as "TENN-SPEED," gave customers direct access to Tenneco's central computer in Houston and initially allowed a transportation request to be processed within 48 hours. TGP's utilization of this system contributed greatly to the Company's emergence as one of the major open access carriers in the nation.

Tenneco Inc. Financial Problems

Near the end of 1985, it became obvious that major storms were still ahead. TGP was still clearing up significant take-or-pay problems, the impact of Order 436 would need to be addressed and the Company's future net operating income would be impacted. The regulatory arena was still in turmoil due to Order 436 being faced with a court challenge because it had not addressed the pipeline/producer take-or-pay problems. In addition to pipeline Company issues, Tenneco Oil Company was also being affected by lower oil and gas prices. Since these two companies were the major income contributors to Tenneco Inc., this created major headwinds for the corporation and its net income fell rapidly. Their 1984 performance was a precursor of what would transpire in the next few years. In 1985, Tenneco Inc. net income dropped by $459 million leaving a net income of only $172 million. The following year was worse, ushering in a loss of $39 million. The year 1987 offered little reprieve as Tenneco Inc.'s net loss increased to $218 million. To get back to profitability Tenneco had to make some major changes.

In the process of regaining its forward momentum, Tenneco Inc. found it necessary to divest itself of selected companies and make several other cutbacks. In 1986, a wage and hiring freeze was ordered and additional cuts in capital and operating expenditures were also made. These measures were necessary due to the effect of the recession on the energy businesses, the almost 50% reduction in oil prices from the previous year and major losses in the construction and farm equipment business. Reductions in net operating income by Tenneco's integrated oil companies and natural gas pipelines were significant factors since these reductions could not be offset by income from other Tenneco Divisions.

TGT joined the other Tenneco divisions in the 1986 wage and hiring freeze as well as continuing its significant work force reduction effort which had begun in 1984. These changes, plus cuts in capital and operating expenditures and termination of all activities deemed non-essential to current pipeline needs were necessary to advance the Company's goal of becoming the lowest-cost transporter of natural gas in its market area. Consolidation of operations were enacted where they could be implemented without endangering safety or service to customers. In 1987, Tenngasco was consolidated into TGT and the resulting entity was re-named Tenneco Gas Pipeline Group. At that point, Tennessee Gas Transmission ceased to exist from a management standpoint.

INDUSTRY AFFAIRS

TGT had always been supportive of industry associations that worked to improve pipeline safety, fund research to encourage gas usage and efficiency and to carry pipeline industry positions to the elected and regulatory personnel. Joe Parrish held leadership positions in the New England Gas Association and the Southern Gas Association and other company personnel participated in the technical committees within these organizations. Jim Brogdon served on the American Gas Association (AGA) Board. Bob Thomas served terms as chairman of the Gas Research Institute (GRI) and the Interstate Natural Gas Association of America (INGAA) in addition to board membership in AGA and the Institute of Gas Technology (IGT). Both Thomas and Chesebro' later served as members of the National Petroleum Council (NPC) but at different times. Numerous other TGT executives, professional and technical people devoted time to improving the industry through cooperative effort. This type of extra effort was another aspect of the Company culture and it proved to be beneficial during the turbulent times of the late 1980s and early 1990s.

Since all pipeline marketing and transportation activities still required separation between the federally regulated and the non-regulated or State regulated areas, this reorganization was primarily for the purpose of consolidating and maintaining efficient overall management. Tenneco Gas Pipeline Group placed all transportation activities under Tenneco Gas Transportation Company headed by J. R. McLeod and all Marketing operations under Tenneco Gas Marketing Company headed by L. G. Garberding. All Pipeline operations reported to Executive Vice President Tom Matthews. Continuing regulatory change would require additional modifications of the organizational structure over the next few years.

Despite all these cost reduction efforts, the Pipeline Group's net operating income fell to $112 million in 1987, a reduction of 72% below 1986 and the lowest since 1967. On the positive side, Tennessee Gas Pipeline's operations as an "Open Access" pipeline were very successful with more than 1700 requests received for transportation service. The ability to process so many requests was due to the implementation of the TENN-SPEED program. The overall result was a 10% increase in TGP total deliveries in 1987. In December, 1987, the sale of the capital stock of Tenneco subsidiary, Mid-Louisiana Gas Company, was completed. Included in the sale was natural gas producing properties in the Monroe Gas Field in northeastern Louisiana, 450 miles of gas gathering lines in the Monroe field, 417 miles of gas pipelines in Louisiana and Mississippi and other related pipeline assets.

While the actions related to asset sales, staff reductions and cost controls were being taken, the federal regulatory pot had continued to bubble. The court review found that Order 436 had not addressed the pipeline/producer take-or-pay problems and was remanded back to the regulators. As a result, FERC issued Order 500 in 1987 which allowed the crediting of transportation volumes against pipeline take-or-pay exposure. This permitted the equitable sharing of some take-or-pay costs incurred by the pipelines with the transportation customers. While this was of some benefit, it was not a satisfactory solution. The real impact of Order 500, when combined with Order 436, was that it marked the beginning of the end for the regulated pipeline sales function which had been the primary business of the Company from its founding nor was the regulatory agency finished issuing orders affecting the Company and its organization. FERC Order 497 created additional communication barriers between the federally regulated business of the Company and its various non-regulated activities. As a result, Tenneco Gas Marketing Company once again realigned its organization by creating a Market Affiliate which was responsible for marketing, supply, transportation and exchange and volume coordination for the Texas and Louisiana intrastate business. The new affiliate was also responsible for the non-jurisdictional interstate marketing. Organizational restructuring continued to occur frequently as the Company adjusted to dynamic regulatory and market changes.

As the Pipeline Group was dealing with open access, cost reductions and regulatory change, Tenneco Inc. was continuing with their asset divestiture in an attempt to regain financial footing. It was essential that Tenneco quickly raise cash to pay down debt and avoid defaulting on bonds. A plan was presented to Tenneco Inc. Management and Board that proposed the sale of some TOC assets plus some non-energy related subsidiaries to raise the necessary funds. This would have resulted in a surviving, energy-dominant company. Needless to say, this proposal was strongly favored by the Pipeline Group management. Unfortunately, this proposal was rejected.

What followed was a major announcement of the sale of Tenneco Oil Company on May 25, 1988. Like the first reduction in force by the Pipeline beginning in 1984, this also hit the Pipeline employees hard. The Oil Company had been created by TGT and had been a member of the Tenneco family for almost 50 years. Apart from the shock of the $7.6 billion sale of a sister company, Tenneco Oil had been supplying about 25% of the Pipelines' gas supply and these contracts were now in jeopardy. Steve Chesebro', who was just in the process of being transferred from TOC to the Pipeline, was immediately charged by Tenneco Inc. Chairman Jim Ketelsen to coordinate the sale of Tenneco Oil. Key to the sale of the domestic gas properties, at least in the view of the Pipeline Group, was assurance that the gas contracts originally executed with TOC would remain valid when transferred with the properties. After significant negotiation, this was accomplished. There were a few of the smaller assets of Tenneco Oil that were not sold and were transferred to the Pipeline Group. Since the Group now had assets other than Pipelines, the Tenneco Gas Pipeline Group was re-named Tenneco Gas effective February 15, 1989. At that point, the storied name of Tennessee Gas Transmission Company was completely dropped from the employees' lexicon.

All in all, the time period 1983-1989 was branded indelibly on the hearts and minds of Tenneco people. Their confidence had been shaken and the mutually supportive culture tested. The key to current survival and future success would be the ability of the employees to look past the recent difficulties and rededicate their energies to preparing for the next challenges which were surely to come.

New Projects

It didn't take long for employees to prove they were ready to respond to the dramatic changes that had already taken place. Even as the Company was being buffeted by regulatory and organizational decisions, they were already looking to the future. While other companies were cutting back drastically on operations and cancelling major projects, the Company and its people were planning for the next decade and beyond. Now that the concern about gas supply had virtually disappeared, the Company began to look for new market

CONSTRUCTION OF THE KERN RIVER LINE

The actual construction of the pipeline proved to be the most exciting aspect of the project. Our pipe was manufactured at three U.S. facilities located in Florida, California and Pennsylvania. The first challenge we faced was maintaining our pipe order and our place in line during this excessive development period. Many midnight meetings were held at the manufacturing plants to maintain the required production schedule.

A key accomplishment in material management was the work our people did in assuring timely delivery of the pipe, and the herculean job of getting the pipe over and down the mountains. We did not have time to set up storage yards, as we were constructing as the pipe was being delivered. Pipe from three plants across the country was brought by rail onto sidings closest to construction locations across the seven pipeline spreads on a "real time" basis. The pipe was immediately loaded on trucks and delivered straight to the ROW for welding. The grades in the Wasatch section in Utah were so steep that all equipment had to be anchored from the top of ridges, tied to winches and slowly released downward. The pipe had to be helicoptered in and set on top of the ridges and winched down on side-booms. Welding was extremely difficult on such steep slopes, and the construction crew had to be anchored with ropes.

A particularly challenging construction issue occurred when a small seam lamination in some joints of pipe was found during fabrication inspection. An intensive review of the seams were made, the affected segments identified, and the search for the joints began. Although the joints were numbered, some had been buried on a spread that had not indicated the individual joint locations. To locate and replace these specific joints, we built a motorized sled with an oxygen supply to carry a man through the buried pipe a mile at a time. Distance had to be accurately tracked on the sled so the exact pipe location could be determined and communication with the "pipe traveler" had to be maintained at all times. Holes were cut in the line each mile for ingress and egress. Once located, the joint was then uncovered and repaired. The list of volunteers to take a sled ride through a 36-inch, buried pipeline was probably not very long.

- Jay Holm

opportunities. The search would be built on the foundation of long-standing employee expertise in designing, building and operating pipelines. The first order of business would be to follow through on several construction projects that had originated earlier in the 1980s.

Kern River

The Kern River pipeline project was first announced in 1985 but the actual history of the project dates back to 1984 or more likely to 1967. That was the year that Tenneco Inc. acquired approximately one million acres of land, much of it in California, in the acquisition of the Kern County Land Company. In December, 1984, Joe Foster called Ewell Muse, Tenneco Inc.'s Vice-President of Corporate Planning, into his office. On his desk, Foster had a map of the Western United States. Pointing to an area in Southwestern Wyoming, he said "there is a lot of natural gas in this area with no market." He then pointed to an area North of Bakersfield, CA and said "there is a demand for large quantities of gas here for steam flood operations." Foster then said "Ewell, go build a pipeline to connect these two areas." Muse found that certain oil companies were indeed willing to commit hundreds of millions of cubic feet of gas per day to the project if the gas were shipped to a viable market. On the other end, the oil companies in California looked upon the availability of gas

In the Wasatch mountains of Utah pipeline construction crews faced elevations of 8,600 feet.

as a way to increase oil production while simultaneously meeting increasingly stringent clean air standards.

By early January, 1985, the project, named Kern River, was under way with plans for the route, engineering, financial, marketing and environmental studies being pursued. Ewell Muse was moved to TGT to head the Kern River effort. Regulatory agency planning was also very important because the Company recognized that both pipeline competition and environmental opposition would become fierce. By early spring, The Williams Company approached the Company and proposed joining the project rather than considering a separate competing project. The two companies agreed and The Kern River Gas Transmission Company (KRGT) was born and structured as a Texas General Partnership responsible for building the pipeline. The two partners were a good fit with The Williams Company providing access to Canadian gas supply in British Columbia through their Northwest Pipeline Company and TGT providing access to potential gas reserves in the Rocky Mountain area and to potential customers in Kern County, California through Tenneco's oil interests in that area.

The Kern River Partners filed an application with the FERC in 1985 to construct the new Pipeline from Opal, Wyoming to Bakersfield, California. This immediately brought forth opposition from the Coastal Corporation's competing WyCal project, El Paso's Mojave Pipeline, the existing California interstate pipelines, The California Public Utility Commission and environmental groups scattered from Wyoming to California. Since Kern River would become the first interstate pipeline to be built within California, it was reviewed with apprehension by the State Regulator and the existing intrastate pipelines who currently had total control of gas transportation within California. Despite filing in 1985, hearings before the FERC in Washington, D.C. didn't take place until 1987. As these hearings were dragging on into 1988, KRGT personnel were working to secure private and public pipeline right-of-way (ROW) for pipeline construction. In addition, the Marketing team was working on both supply and sales contracts. After four years of regulatory delay, KRGT and Mojave Pipeline agreed to a jointly owned pipeline from Daggett, California, the Southern terminus of Kern River, into the Bakersfield area. The FERC then issued certificates in January, 1990, to construct the 685-mile Kern River Pipeline and the 221-mile Mojave common facilities into Bakersfield. Jay Holm was named President of Kern River and construction was soon begun.

The magnitude of the Kern River pipeline can only be appreciated by looking back at the accomplishments that led to its completion. The total length of 906 miles made it the largest single Tenneco pipeline project since the original 1265¬-mile pipeline built during the 1940's. It was also the largest U.S. pipeline built in the last 20 years. The Kern River Marketing team, composed of representatives from both partners, negotiated 15-year firm

THE DESERT TORTOISE

Perhaps the most interesting construction requirement involved the Desert Tortoise, an endangered and yet prolific animal in the desert we had to cross. To assure protection of the turtle, every worker and every person who set foot on the right-of-way (ROW) had to have formal training on the care and safety of the Desert Tortoise. Everyone learned very interesting tortoise facts. For example, one could not touch the tortoise because it recycled its urine during extremely dry periods and if it was touched improperly would lose its urine and not survive. If a Desert Tortoise ventured on the ROW, all work stopped and an environmental inspector was summoned to remove the tortoise before work could resume. We were given explicit "take" limits as well, but of course every tortoise found along every public road in the vicinity of the pipeline was counted whether it had to do with Kern River or anyone else driving the public roads, such as the dirt bike enthusiasts. In the end, the desert compressor station was designed with 12-inch high tortoise fences and tortoise guards were installed beside the cattle guards.

- Jay Holm

TGT CULTURE
Community Affairs

When Jim Ketelsen was replaced as Chairman and Chief Executive Officer in late 1991 by Michael Walsh, Tenneco had become a well-known entity in the Houston business and social community. By then, Tenneco had sponsored the high-profile Houston/Tenneco Marathon for 13 years, was sponsoring a laundry list of educational, community improvement and arts projects and was providing free office space in its 50%-owned 1100 Milam Building for five non-profit organizations. Both Jim Ketelsen and Gordon Bonfield were well-known names in Houston community and civic affairs while Jo Ann Swinney was the behind-the-scenes coordinator of Tenneco sponsored programs.

From a very modest start in 1946 when Personnel Manager Curtis Smith headed up the local Community Chest, Tenneco had truly become a leading corporate community benefactor. Tenneco and its Board of Directors believed they had a corporate social responsibility; first to its employees, second to its shareholders and finally to the communities in which the Company operated. Tenneco left a big imprint on the Houston scene before its new management departed for Greenwich, Connecticut in 1995. Today, if you mention Tenneco, the most common response is "Whatever happened to Tenneco?"

Founder Gardiner Symonds was never a publically-known figure in Houston. Some have suggested he had mixed emotions about community involvement, since several politiciansand the Governor had opposed the original TGT pipeline to West Virginia. The Tenneco Foundation and its Matching Gifts Program was

transportation agreements with Rocky Mountain producers and ultimate users for over 500 MMCF per day which was the required threshold level to allow construction. This was quickly expanded to the 700 MMCFD per day pipeline capacity. In addition to evaluating the original route, the engineering team also evaluated over 400 miles of alternative routing together with the related compressor station locations. These studies were done prior to the completion of the FERC's environmental impact studies in which the California State Land Commission jointly participated. Several of these alternative routings were later required to be followed due to environmental or geotechnical conditions. One alternate was the routing of the pipeline to the North of South Lake City rather than to the South. Unfortunately, the Northern route had steep mountain slopes requiring pipe stringing by helicopter and heavy equipment being tied down as they worked through the mountains. Another alternative was the dictated pipeline rerouting around North Las Vegas. This route passed through a master-planned, upscale community, requiring several miles of some 25'-40' burial depth for the pipeline.

Construction of the Kern River pipeline proved to be a tremendous challenge from beginning to the end. Physical challenges from crossing mountain passes at elevations of up to 8600 feet with 45 degree steep slope conditions to extreme Mojave desert conditions having temperatures up to 120 degrees. To ensure environmental protection, some 200 biologists, archaeologists and paleontologists were hired during construction to protect endangered species of plants and wildlife and to preserve fossils and artifacts in or near the construction areas. As an example, the endangered desert tortoise sometimes slowed construction traffic to a crawl and a 15 MPH speed limit was imposed at all times on the desert pipeline right-of-way and all roads used by construction crews.

Despite the challenges, construction took less than one year and the final weld was made in snow covered Wasatch Mountains in December, 1991. Kern River was the first interstate gas pipeline to be totally computer automated. Their Real-time, Automated Pipeline Integrated Data System (RAPIDS) enabled customers to send gas demand requests from their own computer directly into the Kern River system. Jay Holm, Kern River President said in summary, "We took hold of a once-in-a-lifetime opportunity, started a brand new company and built an idea into a reality." Kern River was a prime signal that Tenneco Gas, the last remaining energy company within Tenneco, was poised for another period of strong growth.

Additional New Markets

While work was being done to get approval to build the Kern River Pipeline to the West Coast, Tenneco Gas also expanded its market in the Southeast by building a new line to service Atlanta, Georgia. The project was initiated by East Tennessee Natural Gas in 1986 when a petition was placed before the FPC to construct a facility to expand its system into Georgia and provide Atlanta Gas Light Company with up to 50 MMCF of natural gas per day. Much of the gas would be transported through a pipeline to be built by East Tennessee. Unusually quick approval was granted by the FERC and the line was built during 1987. Gas began flowing to Atlanta Gas Light Company, the largest natural gas distribution company in the Southeast, in December, 1987.

With the growing market for natural gas in New England, Tenneco Gas focused its concerns on making improvements in its Northeast operations. In 1986, TGP gained FERC approval to establish Interim Natural Gas Service (INGS) to sell additional natural gas to existing customers in the Northeast. During this period, an application was also filed with the FERC to bring additional natural gas from Canada to markets in the Northeast. By 1987, TGP had a number of proposals before the FERC to assure service to the Northeast by constructing facilities that could transport gas from both Canadian and U.S. reserves. With natural gas quickly becoming the fuel of choice in the late 1980s, Tenneco Gas pushed ahead by announcing plans that would increase its volume of natural gas transported to the Northeast by 700 MMCFD in the coming years. The most important project in this regard was the Iroquois Gas Transmission System. Approved by the FERC in 1990, this $500-million system was designed to transport Canadian natural gas to customers in New York, Connecticut, and New Jersey. Moreover, the line was designed to deliver gas at the interconnection with Tennessee Gas in New York and Connecticut for utility and cogeneration plants in New England.

Expansion also took place in the Company's Midwestern markets. In December 1988, Tenneco Gas opened its Minnesota Intrastate Transmission System (MITS) to service. This system consisted of a 31-mile intrastate pipeline capable of delivering more than 140 MMCF per day to Minneapolis. The line linked Minnesota's largest gas distributor, Minnegasco, to Midwestern Gas Transmission's Northern interstate transportation network (later renamed Viking Gas Transmission) and increased Tenneco Gas' market in the State.

An Environmental Challenge

One of the foremost environmental challenges ever faced by Tenneco Gas reared its head in 1988. Concern about the industrial use of polychlorinated biphenyls (PCB) hit a fever pitch in the 1980s largely related to the alleged dumping of wastes containing PCB's in the Hudson River in New York by some industrial companies. In December, 1988 the Company announced its intention to clean up any PCB contamination at compressor stations along the Tennessee Gas Pipeline system. The contamination that had been detected had occurred well before the Environmental Protection Agency (EPA) banned the manufacture of PCB's in the late 1970s and began regulating the use of products containing the chemicals. The Company had never used lubricating oils containing PCBs in its natural gas compressors so PCB's had not entered Tenneco's pipelines. The Company did use a product named Pydraul

established in 1959 to match employee gifts to colleges and universities. Symonds quietly commenced making substantial contributions to various charitable programs from the Tenneco Foundation in the early 1960s through Asa Blankenship in Houston National Bank's Trust Department.

Symond's successor, Dick Freeman, was a very active supporter of the Houston Livestock Show and Rodeo and spectators would always see numerous Case tractors and farm equipment working at the event. Freeman served as President of the Houston Livestock Show and Rodeo and was instrumental in gaining tax exempt status for the organization which greatly enhanced their ability to increase money awarded for scholarships. He often rode in the rodeo's "Grand Entry" on horses from his ranch near Brenham, Texas. Freeman supported the National Jewish Hospital in Denver, Up With People, various livestock programs at Texas A & M University, a family-named scholarship at Blinn College in Brenham and the "100 Club" in Houston.

Employees continued to volunteer for many charitable causes over the years. In 1966, TGT President Harold Burrow was appointed by the U. S. Secretary of Treasury Henry H. Fowler to head up the Houston area U. S. Savings Bonds silver anniversary drive. In addition, TOC President Wilton Scott served as Chairman of the 1966 Junior Achievement of Houston (JA) fund drive which involved some 119 JA companies. He was assisted in this effort by several TGT, Tennessee Life, Houston National Bank and Tenneco Oil Company JA volunteers. Scott was also active in numerous oil industry trade associations and continued many of these activities when he became CEO.

As the company grew and

employee involvement in the community expanded, Tenneco formed the Department of Community/Consumer Affairs in late 1974 headed up by Bruce Conway. Jo Ann Swinney was reassigned to Conway to handle Community Affairs. The new department was also responsible for Office Space Design and for Policy and Procedures. Swinney designed the programs that enabled Tenneco to actively support education, health and human services, civic and social activities and the arts and in 1979, formed the Tenneco Volunteer Program. In 1980, Swinney was named Director of Community Affairs and became the first female department head at Tenneco.

Meanwhile, Jim Ketelsen replaced Scott as Tenneco CEO in late 1978 and became the first person with a manufacturing background to head the Company. He believed a corporation should assist a community in providing a safe and healthy environment, that it be a good citizen along with its employees and that it should actively participate and sponsor a wide variety of educational and community activities. Ketelsen recognized that Tenneco could not match the dollars that Shell and Exxon devoted to community/partnership affairs, but its funding could be leveraged with employee volunteers and in-kind contributions to achieve the same result. For example, when the Van Pool program was discontinued, Tenneco Gas donated the fleet to a number of non-profit organizations. Similarly, a warehouse full of furniture was donated to worthy non-profits after TOC was sold in 1988.

The Tenneco Board approved the annual company-wide contributions budget and about 50% was typically devoted to education. Much of the national education

on a limited basis in small air compressors and it contained PCB's. Purchase of that product had been discontinued in the early 1970s.

A sampling program initiated by the Company found low-level contamination primarily confined to small drainage ponds on the Company's own property at compressor sites in 16 states. It was later determined that excessive rainfall in selected areas had caused the ponds to overflow and allowed PCB contaminated rain water to flow off the Company property. Since the measurement of PCB's was in terms of parts per billion, a very small amount could affect all of the overflow area. Tenneco Gas took a proactive approach in facing the cleanup challenge and worked with six different EPA offices as well as the appropriate governing bodies in each of the affected areas. Because each of the various agencies involved had unique requirements, cleanup costs varied by site and by State.

Tenneco Gas initially announced its intention to spend $20-30 million over the several years to clean up the contamination. Because the various regulatory requirements became even more stringent over time, it is likely that the ultimate cost was significantly higher despite the extremely small area involved. In addition to the dollars involved, the staff time dedicated to the cleanup was substantial over the next several years.

Conclusion of the 1980s

The decade of the 1980s had presented striking challenges to Tenneco Gas. The Company had overcome the majority of their take-or-pay and open access dilemmas, resisted one of the deeper recessions of modern times, persisted in the face of rapidly changing oil and gas prices and still emerged from the decade in a strong position to make a mark in the 1990s and into the next century. Certainly, the going was rough. The downsizing of staff was still continuing and there were continuing re-organizations, including the merger of Tennessee Gas Transmission Company with Tenngasco to form The Tennessee Gas Pipeline Group in 1987 and the re-alignment following the sale of Tenneco Oil Company in 1988 that resulted in the new company name of Tenneco Gas. But the Company had remained strong, regained its momentum in late 1988, and looked to the future.

By the end of 1989, the Tenneco Gas net operating income had increased to $325 million, an increase of $211 million or 185% over the $114 million earned in 1988. Tenneco Gas had regained its position as the largest provider of income to Tenneco Inc. The employees had every right to be proud of the recovery because it was only through their actions in the face of adversity that allowed it to happen.

The 1990s - The Company

Entering into 1990, Tenneco Gas was organized into an operations function headed by Executive Vice President C. M. Rampacek and a marketing function led by Executive Vice President S. D. Chesebro'. Regulatory require-ments, combined with the necessity for continuing cost and service improve-ments, required clear separation between the two functions. Both functions were supported by the legal, financial, administrative and strategic planning groups within Tenneco Gas. All of the federally regulated pipelines including Tennessee Gas Pipeline, East Tennessee Natural Gas, Midwestern Gas Trans-mission and Viking Gas Transmission (originally the Northern system of Mid-western Gas Transmission) were managed from within the operations function.

The Company operated 17,938 miles of pipeline utilizing over 1.6 mil-

1990 TENNECO GAS CORPORATE STRUCTURE

Chairman & CEO – Bob Thomas

Gov. Relations	Strategic Planning	President & COO	Legal	Major Projects	KernRiver
Vice President	Vice President	Steve Chesebro'	SVP & GC	Sr. VP	President
Jim Keys	Rebecca McDonald		Vince Ewelll	Ewell Muse	Jay Holm
				Vice President	
				Gary Cheatham	

President & Chief Operating Officer
Steve Chesebro'

Administration	Operations	Marketing	Financial & Info Services
Sr. Vice President	Executive Vice President	Senior Vice President	Senior Vice President
Dave Gosselin	Charlie Rampacek	Joe Ramsey	Al Williams

Vice President	Vice President
Gilmer Abel Dan Carter	Byron Kelley
Dave Ellis Mike Falco	Tom Norris
John Hibbs Dave McNiel	Dick Snyder
ETNG President, Tom Bell	Tenngasco President, Jim Bujnoch

Division Managers
Texas Operatios – Mike McGonagill
TGPL Division B – Frank Ballard
TGPL Division C – Dave Mills
TGPL Division D – Frank Koslos
TGPL Division E – Windy Loyall
TGPL Division F – Bob Hall
MGT/Viking Gas – Dennie Dixon

lion compressor horsepower. 1989 gross volumes delivered to 27 States had totaled over 2.5 trillion cubic feet of gas or approximately 17% of the total interstate natural gas consumed in the United States. With the future actions already planned, all of these numbers were scheduled to increase. By the end of 1990, Tenneco Gas net operating income had increased to $340 million or a 5% increase over 1989. Unfortunately, this increasing income stream was not matched at the Tenneco Inc. level by other operating Divisions and declining corporate net income was beginning to raise concern.

The retirement of Company veterans in the mid to late 1980s combined with continuing cost reduction programs had led to major changes in leader-ship at departmental and officer level of the Company. Gone were such leaders as Joe Parrish, Harry Long, Jim Brogdon, Jolly Johnson and John Robertson to name only a few. Fortunately, the bench strength of the remaining Tenneco Gas staff proved to be more than capable of stepping up to the challenge. The magnitude of the overall management change throughout the Company can only be appreciated by a retrospective view over the years. In general, the World War II veterans that had continued to build the Company on the foun-dation laid by the original founders were being replaced by a younger gen-

support was linked to recruiting, research and nation-wide naming rights opportunities.

Tenneco provided funding for "Communities in Schools" (CIS), a nation-wide dropout prevention program, for Texas Southern University's "Excellence in Education" program and held a high level State-wide confer-ence titled "Building Excellence through Partnerships in Educa-tion." In addition, much of its local educational funding was directed at underserved populations in the pre-K through 16 age range.

Funding health and human services was also a major empha-sis. Tenneco employees were gener-ous contributors to United Way, which consistently had a successful track record for efficient funding of local programs. The Company supported and funded numerous health institutions such as Texas Heart Institute, M. D. Anderson Cancer Center and the UT Health Science Center.

Tenneco was at the table to create Central Houston and the Downtown Houston Manage-ment District, in addition to funding Tranquility Park, Buffalo Bayou Transformation and HPD's Mounted Police, all designed to revitalize a deteriorating inner city. Various major arts perfor-mances were underwritten and funding was made available for school children to attend or for the art organization to conduct classes at the school level.

The highest profile project for Tenneco was the Houston/ Tenneco Marathon. The first Houston Marathon was run in 1972 with 113 runners, about 200 spectators and 40 volunteers. By late 1978 the race promoters had exhausted all local sponsors and had no prospects for funding. The race director, George Kleeman, was lamenting his dilemma after a morning run with a friend when a fellow runner overheard him and said "I think I might be able to help." The runner was Dean Maddox, Treasurer of Tenneco Oil Company. His efforts were successful and Tenneco's sponsorship of the Houston/Tenneco Marathon began with a handshake agreement between Maddox and Jim Ketelsen. When marathon board member Tom McBrayer was measuring the course, he was stopped by the Houston Police and told he couldn't shut down Allen Parkway for the marathon. Tenneco's Director of Security, former HPD Chief "Pappy" Bond, not only got approval for the course, but a police escort for measuring the course.

In later years several hundred Tenneco volunteers helped on race day when the marathon had become a city-wide festival with almost 4,000 finishers. Tenneco's sponsorship of the marathon ended after 18 years when the sale of Tenneco Energy to El Paso Energy Corporation occurred in 1996.

Tenneco's most highly acclaimed program of corporate social responsibility was the Jeff Davis Educational Collaborative. In early 1981 Gordon Bonfield and Jo Swinney created a business/school partnership with Jeff Davis High School involving Tenneco volunteers in a release-time mentor/tutor program. Jeff Davis was near Tenneco's downtown headquarters and had the worst dropout record in the Houston Independent School District (HISD). It also had the lowest academic performance of any HISD school, the poorest attendance rate and was a dumping ground for incompetent teachers. Jeff Davis had no library and no cafeteria. Students had to use the Carnegie Public Library across the street and the nearby Marshall Middle School cafeteria. Jeff Davis was literally left "to die on the vine." Jeff Davis represents one more instance where Ten-

eration steeped in dealing with a rapidly changing regulatory environment and a constant cost management requirement. They proved fully capable of continuing the growth of the Company.

In June, 1990, Bob Thomas was named Chairman and Chief Executive Officer of Tenneco Gas and Steve Chesebro' was named President with the additional title of Chief Operating Officer. The purpose of the restructuring was to prepare for the upcoming retirement of Thomas and to ensure top level attention to the two primary tasks essential to the long term future of the Company. The first task was to remain the premier designer, builder and operator of pipelines in the world and that was the objective of the Chief Operating Officer. This tied directly to the focus of being the most efficient, safe and profitable pipeline that had been pursued by the Company from its founding. The second task to be undertaken by the CEO was to fully develop and implement Company strategies for expansion and growth opportunities without regard to where in the world they might be located. This utilized the 47 years of knowledge gained in designing and building pipelines in the U.S., Canada and Mexico and in the experience gained in searching the world for gas supplies in the 1970s and early 1980s. While the internal organization of the Company would be subject to continuing change throughout the 1990s because of regulatory and market changes, pursuit of these two primary tasks would remain paramount. The earlier focus on securing global supply was abandoned due to available supply in North America and the mandated change in the role of the regulated pipeline from being a merchant supplier of natural gas to that of being primarily a transporter of gas for others.

Projects

After the planning and preparatory work done in the 1980s, the 1990s would see a great many projects moving to completion. After six years in pursuit of all the necessary permits and contracts, construction of the Kern River pipeline began in early 1991 and was completed in December of that year. Initial deliveries began shortly thereafter.

About the time that Kern River received FERC approval in January, 1990, representatives of Amoco Canada Petroleum Ltd., Petro-Canada, Shell Canada Ltd. and Montana Power Company came to visit in Houston. Their purpose was to invite Tenneco Gas to join them as a 50% partner and operator of a gas pipeline they had named Altamont.

The plan was to build a $580-million gas pipeline starting on the Canadian border at Port of Wildhorse, Montana, and extending south to connect with Kern River at its northern terminus located at Opal, Wyoming. Kern River would then transport the gas to Daggett, California, with the ultimate destination being Bakersfield, California. The Canadian producers reasoned that with Tenneco as operator of Altamont, combined with its ownership in

Kern River would make the project more attractive to the California regulators. Applications were filed with the National Energy Board (NEB) of Canada for a certificate to build the Canadian facilities and for a certificate to export the gas to the U.S. An application was also filed with Federal regulators in the U.S. for a certificate to construct the U.S. facilities.

After the applications were filed, Ewell Muse was assigned the task of securing all the necessary approvals. With his five years of effort on behalf of Kern River, he was well acquainted with the challenges. A talented team within Tenneco Gas engineering, environmental, legal and other supporting groups was assembled and began pipeline design, regulatory proceedings and the securing of binding transportation agreements. These activities continued for about five years but ultimately had to be abandoned. By the time the FERC certificate approving construction was granted, the project was terminated because it was unable to compete in the California market which had been saturated with Canadian production moved through a Pacific Gas Transmission project completed earlier. Canadian producers were also becoming attracted to the new markets opening in the Midwest which made new access to California of lesser significance.

As a post script to the project, Altamont sold their technical data which included the surveyed route, all environmental impact studies and data and the right to construct a pipeline 25 feet off the center line of the Altamont route to Home Oil Company for $8 million. The Express Pipeline was built on this route to deliver Canadian crude oil into the Platt Pipeline near Casper, Wyoming. This was a forerunner of many later pipeline projects to move expanding Canadian oil sands production into the U.S.

A New Business

When Tenneco Oil Company was sold in 1988, some relatively minor assets had been retained and were transferred to Tenneco Gas for utilization or disposal. One of the facilities that remained was a methanol plant located near the Houston ship channel. The U.S. Government had previously promulgated rules requiring the addition of Methyl Tertiary Butyl Ether (MTBE) into motor gasoline to benefit air quality. Backed by the strategy of pursuing new and profitable endeavors, Tenneco Gas elected in 1990 to begin conversion of the methanol plant into a facility producing MTBE to capitalize on this growing market. Conceptually, this conversion was to be the first step toward becoming a major force in the world-wide manufacture of MTBE if the market continued to develop. Unfortunately, by mid-1991, Tenneco Inc. had once again begun to face major financial problems which put pressure on capital funding for completion of the project. Following a full project review with Tenneco Inc., the partially finished MTBE plant was put up for sale to raise capital for the parent organization. After an auction, the plant was sold to Enron in December 1991 for $632 million. It became clear to Tenneco Gas

neco never walked away from a challenge, whether it be a business or a community issue. Tenneco and the University of Houston Downtown (UHD) expanded the Collaborative to establish a guaranteed scholarship program for any student graduating with a 2.5 GPA and having completed a UHD summer prep seminar. The expanded program involved additional partners: CIS, The Metropolitan Organization, UHD and HISD. Tenneco created a later incentive if a student completed the first two years of college and declared "Education" as a major. Tenneco continued to fund Scholarships through 2006 and then closed the Tenneco Foundation with remaining funds going to UHD and the University of St. Thomas for Jeff Davis students majoring in Education. Today, Jeff Davis High School is a "state of the art" facility with changes led primarily by alumni like Congressman Gene Green, Felix Fraga and a host of others.

The secret to Tenneco's success in Community Affairs was due to its employee volunteers who exemplified the "spirit of Tenneco." Even during the period when the Oil Company was being sold, TOC volunteers continued to work on various projects. Tenneco also had an agreement with The American Red Cross to respond immediately to any national disaster with employee volunteers. The Reagan Administration recognized Tenneco with the first large company "Presidential Voluntary Action Award" in 1982. It signified that the Tenneco "family of companies" within this unique conglomerate were united in their community service and educational reform efforts nation-wide.

that the income needs of Tenneco Inc. would require additional divestitures in the coming years. Despite this realization, the strategy of Tenneco Gas was to continue the growth of the Company.

The Northeast

The Northeastern region of the country had long been a very important service area for Tenneco Gas. TGT and Texas Eastern Transmission Company had fought major battles in the 1940's and early 1950s to serve New England. The significance of the Northeast combined with the search for new markets led the Company to commit in the late 1980s to major pipeline expansion in this region and several applications had been filed with regulatory officials. With natural gas no longer excluded from use in power generation installations, new opportunities were beginning to appear in high-load-factor markets. One of the earlier projects approved for construction was the Northeastern Expansion Project (NOREX) which consisted of 54.5 miles of new and looped pipeline plus related compressor and meter modifications. This $50 million project was completed in December, 1990. Service was also commenced to the Ocean States Power Project, a combined cycle, two-unit plant which was the first major Independent Power Project (IPP) in New England.

The major addition to the Northeastern pipeline network was authorized in 1990 when the FERC and the Canadian NEB approved the building of the Iroquois Gas Transmission System utilizing the import of Canadian gas. Tenneco Gas, together with its partners, began construction of this 378-mile pipeline which would receive gas at the Canadian-New York State border and deliver 576 MMCFD to customers in New York, Connecticut and New Jersey. In addition, this $597 million project was designed to also deliver gas at interconnections with Tennessee Gas Pipeline in New York and Connecticut for re-delivery to utility and cogeneration plants in New England. To facilitate this re-delivery, TGP installed over 100 miles of mainline looping and lateral lines during the following year.

Tenneco Gas believed that passage of the Clean Air Act would result in increased interest in and demand for natural gas. Opportunities in new downstream markets would surely develop and Tenneco Gas wanted to be first in line. To capture opportunities like the Ocean State Power Project, the Company started developing two additional key sites for power generation at State Line Power in Ringwood, New Jersey and County Line Power in Richfield, New York. Tenneco Gas also took an equity interest in the Masspower Project

STEPHEN D. CHESEBRO'

Stephen D. Chesebro' (shown above with his security detail in Columbia) attended Colorado School of Mines on a partial athletic scholarship, playing both baseball and football. He graduated in 1964 with a petroleum engineering degree and was hired by Tenneco Oil for a position in Oklahoma City, but before his first day on the job, Dan Johnson moved him to Casper, Wyoming. Though he was late for work that first day, he was dispatched to Gillette to log a well and didn't get back to Casper until about 2 A. M. Steve spent two and one-half years in Casper, 4 months in Houston investigating computer usage for engineers, another two and one-half years in Lafayette and back to Houston to work in Joe Foster's Economic Planning and Analysis Group. He continued to be moved around to give him a wide variety of experience in the business; including the purchase of LaTerre in 1969, the 1970 offshore GOM lease sale, a role in devising nodal completions on offshore platforms and other educational assignments. Steve was named to head up Tenneco Inc.'s Long Range Planning in 1979, a position which put him at the epicenter of the Tenneco conglomerate. He was elected Vice President in 1980.

In early 1988, the Tenneco Inc. Board decided to sell both divisions of Tenneco Oil and Steve Chesebro' was selected to manage the sale. He

near Springfield, Massachusetts which was its first cogeneration project. This project, using gas delivered through TGP, would generate steam and up to 240 megawatts of electricity when completed. The Company also became an equity participant in the Concord Energy Project in Concord, New Hampshire which was being designed to generate 56 megawatts of electricity.

Additional Pipeline Expansion

As active as Tenneco Gas was in the Northeast, it was only a part of the tremendous effort to locate and serve new markets. Although the Company had been buffeted by the sale of Tenneco Oil Company and was facing continued cost reductions and a constantly unfolding regulatory scene, the entrepreneurial and energetic spirit of the people had not been damaged. They remained convinced they could successfully compete not only in North America but any place in the world that required project and pipelining skills.

Domestic pipeline expansion continued in order to become more efficient and serve more markets. The Ozark Gas Transmission System was expanded by adding compression and 92 miles of additional pipeline to connect with the Arkla AC line and the TGP 100 and 800 lines allowing Arkoma basin gas to be moved to the Midwest and Northeast markets. The Company was also making plans to file for a major gas gathering system in the Mobile Bay area located in offshore Alabama State waters. This system would have the capacity to move an additional 1.2 BCF per day into the interstate pipeline system.

A New Chairman and CEO

The early 1990s were extremely active years for Tenneco Gas in building new pipelines and entering into new markets. The 1991 net operating income, aided by a gain from the sale of the MTBE plant, totaled $561 million which was a 65% increase over 1990 and an all time high for Tenneco Gas at least in nominal dollars. Unfortunately, Tenneco Inc. was suffering a major net income loss of $732 million and in September, 1991, a new President was brought in with Jim Ketelsen moving to Chairman. Michael H. Walsh came from Union Pacific and initially indicated to Tenneco Gas that it would probably not remain as part of the Tenneco Inc. conglomerate over the long term. The financial uncertainty created by Federal regulations and requirements were apparently the basis for this view. However, the continuing economic strength of Tenneco Gas soon changed Walsh's view and he quickly indicated the Company would remain a core holding of Tenneco Inc. The Company remained the leading net operating income provider for the parent company over the remainder of its existence.

Walsh made major changes in the corporate direction of Tenneco during the last quarter of 1991 and during 1992. Various Company units across the corporate spectrum were sold to raise capital and reduce debt. A concen-

knew it was an unpopular job and, just as he predicted, the process got ugly. Bids were opened in New York City on September 29, where his target was to get $5 billion for the assets. Within one week of negotiations with bidders, he had 14 contracts in place to sell the two companies for $7.3 billion. This sale changed Tenneco to a manufacturing company with a pipeline subsidiary.

Steve was named Executive Vice President of Tenneco Gas in 1988. When Bob Thomas retired in February, 1994, Chesebro' became CEO and shepherded the company through an extremely difficult time, ending with its eventual sale to El Paso Energy in December, 1996. Steve had previously managed the sale of the methanol plant to Enron for $632 million and was also compelled to sell Tenneco's 50% interest in Kern River Gas Transmission Company, two of Tenneco Gas' most profitable holdings. He led Tenneco Gas into the international arena with several successful projects in South America, Australia and Asia. Under his watch, Tenneco Gas became the first ISO 9001 pipeline and he continued pressing toward his goal of maintaining Tenneco Gas as a premier pipeline to its many customers until the end. Unfortunately, the new Tenneco Inc. management, which had already relocated to Greenwich, Connecticut, "did not understand the energy business" and wanted to sell Tenneco Gas as soon as practical.

PIPELINING IS NEVER EASY

There are always a multitude of expected and unexpected problems encountered while building a new pipeline. Whether it is in the swamps of Louisiana, the mountains of Utah, the deserts of Nevada or across the Andes mountains between Argentina and Chile. Building the South West Queensland Pipeline (SWQP) in Australia was no different.

To begin the story, construction start was delayed on the SWQP while Tenneco struggled to reach an agreement on cultural heritage participation by the six aboriginal tribes along the pipeline route. While the Queensland government was obligated to provide an unencumbered right-of-way, Tenneco had the responsibility to involve the tribes in protecting their cultural heritage and any artifacts found during construction. The Goolburri Aboriginal Corporation Land Council, an umbrella organization sanctioned to represent the six tribes, negotiated with Tenneco for proper aboriginal representation during construction. A precedent-setting Cultural Heritage Management Plan (CHMP) was devised which permitted aboriginal observers to witness all excavations during construction and collect artifacts when found. A full time Phd archaeologist was employed to instruct the aboriginal representatives in what to expect and how to identify the most likely places to recover artifacts. The large majority of artifacts were found on or in stream banks where professional recovery protocols were employed. Tenneco's archaeologist catalogued the artifacts and at the end of the project offered them to the Queensland Museum collection.

Four aboriginal researchers from each tribe were selected to

trated focus on cost reductions and efficiency improvement was initiated in the form of a Total Quality Management (TQM) program pursued by all Tenneco companies. While Tenneco Gas had been involved in major cost reduction programs since 1984, there were still further improvements to be made. Unfortunately, Walsh was soon diagnosed with brain cancer and his aggressive leadership was lost. While Walsh was receiving major cancer treatments, Dana Mead acted as Tenneco Inc.'s top official. Mead had been hired as Tenneco Inc. President in April, 1992 after Walsh had been named Chairman and CEO replacing Ketelsen. Mead became Chairman when Walsh died in 1994. The changes that Walsh had initiated enabled Tenneco Inc. to drastically reduce losses in 1992 and return to profitability in 1993.

More New Business

Activity continued at a high level for Tenneco Gas in 1992. Some $251 million was invested in pipeline expansion, new marketing opportunities, efficiency and safety improvements. EnTrade Corporation, a Louisville, Kentucky-based marketing company was acquired to expand and enhance marketing capability. EnTrade had sales of 242 BCF of gas in 1992 and fit nicely in the Company's expansion plans. Tenneco Ventures was also formed in 1992 to attract funds for financing oil and gas development. The strategy was to raise money from outside investors to be used in supporting drilling by producers thereby creating new reserves which could be marketed, transported and partially owned by Tenneco Gas. Many of the major companies had abandoned the onshore Gulf Coast area and Ventures intended to revitalize development drilling by smaller independent companies. The key was to ensure low development costs by careful evaluation of producers and properties and by Venture maintaining low operating costs. The fact that all of the parties involved had the opportunity for profitability made this a very successful program and $72 million was committed to the fund in the first year. The program required repeated explanations to Tenneco Inc. management that the Company was simply securing outside capital to be used in expanding marketing and transportation opportunities rather than attempting to re-create a new Tenneco Oil Company like the one sold in 1988. Tenneco Ventures was an innovative response to changing industry conditions and was a win-win for all participants in the program.

The Regulators Strike Again

After the Natural Gas Policy Act (NGPA) was promulgated in 1978, the Federal Energy Regulatory Commission (FERC) had issued four major orders over the following 14 years and each had required Tenneco Gas and the industry to make changes in their organizational structures and methods of operation. Unfortunately, the FERC had not totally completed their industry restructuring and in April, 1992, Order 636 was issued. This order mandated completion of the "unbundling" of the traditional natural gas pipeline merchant business. Pipelines were to become non-discriminatory, open access transportation providers or contract carriers. While the regulators believed this Order would allow competition in the marketplace to govern how pipelines functioned, they unfortunately continued to specify how the companies would be structured and what their roles would be in the future natural gas industry. The Order mandated all pipelines to restructure their services in preparation for the winter of 1993-94. Tenneco Gas employees were once again subjected to major organizational changes in order to comply with the new regulations and once again to compete in a totally restructured marketplace. The innovative marketing of both sales and transportation would be essential to the future of the Company. The entire gas pipeline industry would need to develop new standards for operating in a changed world.

International Looks Attractive

The increasing complexity of the U.S. gas industry made the Company strategy of investigating international pipelining opportunities more attractive. Of particular interest was the high growth, non-regulated business in the Southern Cone of South America. In 1993, Tenneco Gas commenced its South American expansion with two large international gas pipeline projects. These were the Argentina to Chile project (Gasoducto Transandino) and the Bolivia to Brazil project. These projects fit the basic strength of Tenneco Gas as the premier designer, builder and operator of natural gas pipelines.

These two projects also led the way for a period of intense energy integration through the building of natural gas pipelines in the Southern Cone of South America. They would connect large gas reserves in Argentina and Bolivia with hungry gas markets in Chile and Brazil. Large investments would be made to transport, distribute and consume this newly available energy which would result in a changed energy matrix within the region and provide customers and consumers with clear economic and environmental benefits. It was a golden era for regional gas integration in the Southern Cone.

In October 1993, Tenneco was selected to be a 25% shareholder and technical operator of the $850 million, 1200 kilometer, 24"-28" diameter Trans-Andean project that would connect the gas reserves in the Neuquen basin, Argentina, to markets in central Chile. The partners in the Gasoducto Transandino project included the international companies Enersis/Chilectra, YPF, Astra, Bridas, Pluspetrol and San Jorge. Tenneco was primarily responsible for the engineering and design, the route selection, environmental studies, gas marketing, and financing for the pipeline. These activities continued through 1996, when Tenneco's participation in the pipeline came to an end due to a merger with El Paso Energy in December, 1996. Work continued to progress on the project after the merger and construction along the modified pipeline route, which runs from Neuquen, Argentina, to Concepcion, Chile,

observe construction and collect artifacts in their respective tribal "country." A typical two-man crew followed the clearing and grade operations while the other two researchers witnessed ditching and other excavation activities. As clearing and grade progressed into another tribal "country" the two front-end researchers were demobilized and replaced by two representatives from the newly encountered "country" such that no researcher was ever permitted to observe activities other than those in his "country." The selection and duration of the work by the observers was controlled by tribal politics. It was hot work in the outback during the summer months and many tribal members were not accustomed to maintaining regular hours on a job.

While the CHMP was a first in Australia and established unique guidelines for Aboriginal participation in a project, it provided opportunities for the three Aboriginal blockades to halt pipeline construction for varying periods of time. The first blockade by the Mandanjanji tribe occurred during the first weekend of construction involving "clearing and grade." After a brief delay, Tenneco agreed to mobilize all four of the observers, even though the second team had no excavation activities to monitor.

The second blockade occurred when the Gunggari tribe blocked "clearing and grade" activities by parking an old Mercedes Benz bus across the right-of-way at an unpaved road which marked the previously agreed upon eastern boundary of their "country." They were very agitated by the western neighboring tribe's new boundary claim which resulted in the Gunggari "country" being much smaller than the previously agreed upon area filed with the Goolburri Land Council. Tenneco negotiated with the Gunggari for about two days and the blockade was lifted, based upon a commitment to get the two parties together to resolve the boundary issue. Representatives from both the Gunggari and Bidjarra tribes came into Brisbane the following week at the State's expense to commence negotiations, but while the Bidjarra enjoyed an expense paid trip to Brisbane, they refused to attend the meeting.

The Gunggari re-established a more permanent blockade at the Maranoa River located about 19 Km west of their first blockade a week earlier. As construction progressed to that point, Tenneco moved the entire crew some 108 Km around the disputed Gunggari/Bidjarra "country" and resumed their work in the originally defined Bidjarra "country." The Gunggari filed a huge Native Title Claim with the authorities which overlapped tribal areas on all sides and also filed a lawsuit to stop the pipeline construction. Their attempts to halt construction failed when Tenneco effectively defended its right to build the pipeline.

"We didn't want to stop the pipeline," Gunggari Elder Angus Smith said. "We have no problem with Tenneco. They have been really good, but it was the only way we could get to those other fellas" (The Bidgarra).

Construction progressed rapidly on the 16" diameter pipeline with a target of about 5-1/2 Km of line completed each day. Tenneco encountered only one strike which was caused by "bull dust" which is a finely powdered red sand about the consistency of talcum powder. It was virtually impossible to control by sprinkling, since the working side of the pipeline was also the main road used by all equipment. The "bull dust" strike created an abbreviated work cycle. A few days after the workers had departed on the unplanned break,

began in June 1997. The pipeline was put into service in December, 1999.

In 1994, Petrobras (the Brazilian National Oil Company) embarked on a series of road shows to choose private equity partners for a Bolivia to Brazil gas pipeline project. Petrobras needed partners because it was not in a position to fund the project alone. In August, 1994, Tenneco was selected together with British Gas and BHP (the BTB consortium) to be a 29% shareholder in the $1.6 billion, 2600 kilometer and 32"-20" diameter pipeline that would connect the gas reserves of Santa Cruz, Bolivia, to markets in Central and Southern Brazil (Sao Paulo and Porto Alegre). Other partners in the project were Petrobras and YPFB. Tenneco acted primarily as the technical director responsible for route and engineering design, gas marketing, environmental studies and financing. Tenneco continued to lead the operations until December, 1996 when El Paso assumed control. Work continued on the project with construction beginning in July, 1997, and the pipeline was put into service in July, 1999.

Back in the U.S.

Meanwhile, back on the domestic front, Viking Gas Transmission was sold as was the Dean pipeline to provide additional funding for Tenneco Inc. In compliance with FERC Order 636, the Company had unbundled transportation from its other services in 1993. As expected, regulated gas sales dropped but non-regulated sales more than made up for the loss. During the year, gross volumes delivered increased to 3.3 TCF or 13% more than in 1992 and transportation volumes were 72% of the total. In reviewing the annual results, not only had employees overcome dramatic changes in the regulatory regime but had managed to increase net operating income to $411 million, a 14% increase over 1992. Truly an outstanding effort in the face of intense competition and regulatory trauma.

Not all changes in early 1994 came as a surprise. As had been planned, Bob Thomas retired at the end of February and Steve Chesebro' was named President and CEO of Tenneco Gas. This brought about several changes in responsibilities among the officer corps. Also, in February, Dana Mead was named Chairman of Tenneco Inc.

1994 saw a continuation of the previous activity in the non-regulated arena. In fact, 43% of the Company's 1994 capital budget was utilized in non-regulated businesses. Tenneco Ventures acquired $67 million of Gulf Coast producing properties and secured commitments of an additional $100 million for its second investment fund. A new business unit named Tenneco Energy Resources Corporation (TERC) was formed and entered into the gas processing business by acquiring interests in two operating plants and initiating construction on a third. Tenneco Gas moved to expand its power generation business by agreeing to acquire ARK Energy, Inc. for about $60 million. Because ARK Energy already held interests in two operational plants together with a number of others proposed for development, the Tenneco Gas plan of becoming a major player in the generation of electric power would be greatly accelerated.

The expansion of domestic pipelines was not neglected by the attention to non-regulated opportunities. A proposal was made to build the 350-mile Mid-Atlantic pipeline from West Virginia to Pennsylvania. In the Gulf of Mexico, Tenneco Gas received FERC approval to build their Mobile Bay Gathering System. To preclude Tenneco competition in the area, the Dauphin Island Gathering Partners (DIGP) proposed that the Company join them in their existing facility rather than constructing a new system. As a result, Tenneco Gas became a 50% partner in DIGP. Another new offshore facility constructed was the Viosca Knoll Gathering System. Tenneco Gas and Leviathon partnered to build a 95-mile, $63 million pipeline from the Tennessee Gas Pipeline location at South Pass 55 to the Viosca Knoll area at Main Pass 252. This deep water header system was designed to deliver up to 550 MMCFD to TGP.

More International

While Tenneco Gas activities were moving ahead in the Southern Cone of South America, another international bridgehead was being established in Australia. By 1994, Australia had already commenced privatizing its state-owned electric utilities and many observers, including Tenneco Gas, felt that divestiture of State-owned gas pipelines would soon follow. Tenneco already had a presence in Australia with both Monroe and Walker having profitable business and manufacturing operations enjoying good reputations.

rain commenced to fall in varying amounts along the job site, breaking a severe drought but delaying construction. Areas to the east recorded some 39 inches of rainfall over the first weekend, resulting in the rainstorm being named "The Big Wet."

While construction was proceeding over several months to its westernmost point, Tenneco and the State negotiated a settlement with Gunggari and Bidjarra for joint construction monitoring in the contested area, permitting the construction workforce to return to the 108 Km "skip" and fill in the gap some six months later. The Tenneco team completed construction of this outback pipeline on time and under budget. The commissioning of the new pipeline was held on the date of the Tenneco Energy sale to El Paso.

- Gary Cheatham

Trains were used to transport 450 miles of pipe to construction sites in southeast Queensland.

GARY CHEATHAM

Gary Cheatham--- was recruited on the University of Texas campus for Tennessee Gas Pipeline's 1961 Gas Cadet program. After a 24-month training program Cheatham worked in several field operating assignments and Gas Sales before joining TGT's International Energy Contracts group in 1974. He was Vice President of the Tenneco Synfuels team which became the lead partner in the Great Plains Coal Gasification Associates project. Later, he served as President of Midwestern Gas in 1987 and 1988, Vice President of Tennessee Gas Pipeline, Kern River Corporation and the Altamont project prior to being transferred to Australia in 1995 to build a 756km gas pipeline in the outback. When Tenneco Energy was sold in 1996, El Paso's affiliate retained Cheatham with a two year contract to operate the new South West Queensland pipeline and to grow their businesses in Australia. In 1997, he moved to Perth and directed the technical team which acquired the A$2.4 billion DBNGP pipeline in Western Australia. Gary managed the DBNGP Integration Team before his retirement and return to the US in late 1998.

Tenneco Gas International sent a three-man team to Australia to investigate energy business opportunities. Its team was headed by Hugh James, seasoned international business developer, with Bob Otjen, an experienced pipeliner and an acquisition attorney, Brad Lingo, as the supporting cast. Both Otjen and Lingo were long-time Tenneco employees, while Hugh James was a new hire.

They set up an office in Brisbane and soon began discussions with government officials about constructing a 756 Km. gas pipeline in Southwest Queensland to connect the Ballera gas field to the growing markets on the East coast. A pipeline from Wallumbilla to Brisbane already existed and its sources of gas production were in steep decline. In August, 1994, Tenneco Gas Australia (TGA) was named preferred developer of the South West Queensland Pipeline (SWQP) over 21 other bidders. Tenneco immediately mobilized talent from its Houston and field offices to ensure the SWQP was constructed timely and within budget. Tenneco engineers Tom Ribble, Dan Tennison and Mike Dubravek were involved in the early conceptual planning of the pipeline while TGP Vice President Gary Cheatham was transferred to Brisbane to apply his construction project management and pipeline operating skills to the SWQP. Just prior to start of construction, Tenneco veteran Jim Convery was brought in to be Chief Inspector.

Pipeline construction in Australia eventually linked the Ballera gas fields to coastal markets.

As part of a re-deployment strategy, a 20% interest in the recently created Tenneco Energy Resources Company (TERC) was sold to Ruhrgas AG, Germany's largest natural gas company. Tenneco Inc. was interested in monetizing some of the value of TERC and Tenneco Gas wanted to secure a potential partner for future European pipeline and downstream marketing ventures. Ruhrgas wanted to gain knowledge about how the U.S. gas market was responding to major regulatory and financial changes because it was felt that Europe would later follow a similar path. It was a beneficial arrangement for both companies. Working together, Tenneco Gas and Ruhrgas reviewed additional U.S. opportunities and began to identify joint development opportunities in Europe.

By the end of 1994, the future was looking good for Tenneco Gas. U.S. natural gas consumption had grown to 20.8 TCF and 16% of that volume was handled by the Company. Opportunities in non-regulated businesses, both domestic and international, were being captured and the organization was adjusting to management and regulatory changes. Tenneco Gas was again the leader in providing net operating income to Tenneco Inc. Unfortunately, this was not sufficient to prevent the continuing erosion of net income in the parent company. Efforts to dispose of the construction and farm equipment company continued at an intense level.

The Strategy

Tenneco Gas continued its focus on non-regulated and international businesses in 1995. The primary strategy was to utilize pipeline expertise to expand into related downstream opportunities. Ewell Muse had been assigned responsibility for the Latin American endeavors while Hugh James headed Tenneco Gas Australia Pty Ltd. Mike Ronca continued to grow Tenneco Ventures and it was gaining working interests in domestic oil and gas properties. Success in these and other non-jurisdictional projects were essential to the future of Tenneco Gas.

With construction planning under way on the South West Queensland Pipeline, Tenneco Gas moved to expand their operations in Australia. In July, 1995, Tenneco completed the acquisition of the Pipelines Authority of South Australia (PASA) which included the 781 Km. Moomba to Adelaide gas pipeline system and the 70 Km. Katnook Pipeline. In addition, PASA operated the Moomba to Port Bonython liquids pipeline and the 231 Km. Riverland Gas Pipeline. PASA was a well managed gas pipeline with fully automated gas turbine powered compressor stations and two maintenance depots. Tenneco had been the successful bidder amongst several prospective buyers. The PASA workforce quickly adopted the Tenneco safety programs and set about the process of qualifying for ISO 9001 Certification, since they often provided "stopple" and other repair and maintenance services for Aussy pipelines. PASA employees had also provided inspection services during the South West Queensland Pipeline construction.

In other Southeast Asian activities, Tenneco Gas designed an offshore pipeline in Taiwan to move gas from an LNG receiving terminal in Koushung on the South part of the island to a power plant to be built on the North coast. By proposing the laying of the pipeline offshore, the cost of an onshore pipeline was reduced by 75%. However, in their final decision, the Taiwanese government elected to build the pipeline themselves utilizing the Tenneco design. In Indonesia, Tenneco Energy developed a

OPPORTUNITIES IN CHINA

In 1995, Tenneco Energy pursued an equity investment in the proposed 1000-Km natural gas pipeline from gas fields in the Shaanxi province to Beijing. The pipeline would supply natural gas to Shaanxi, Hebei and Tianjin and alleviate pollution in Beijing in order that the city could host the upcoming Asian games. The local gas distribution company was a partner and Chinese state banks and Tenneco were to provide $450 million financing. The Chinese were unfamiliar with the structure of the modern gas industry and the necessity for commercial gas contracts which would be the underpinning for the financing. Construction delays would be an unknown – the Chinese would use more manpower if they were behind schedule and ordered countless shovels to be prepared! Although they eventually decided to own and operate the pipeline themselves, they acknowledged the expertise of Tenneco and awarded the company an extensive construction advisory contract for the project.

- Kay McKeough

GAS INDUSTRY STANDARDS BOARD

Tenneco Gas had the lead hand in creating what many would call an institution and a public-private partnership with the Federal Energy Regulatory Commission, the Department of Energy, the Department of Commerce, the National Association of Regulatory Utility Commissioners and many others. This partnership, originally named the Gas Industry Standards Board, has provided the industry a collective voice in the implementation of policy through standards in support of a well-functioning market. We would not have this organization today without the leadership of Tenneco Gas and that of Steve Chesebro', our first Chairman. We have now been operating for almost 20 years and have expanded the organization to also cover standards related to the electric industry. To reflect this expansion, the name of the organization was changed to the North American Energy Standards Board. The decision by Tenneco Gas to support the creation of the organization that became GISB/NAESB demonstrated a willingness to take on a role of industry stewardship with an eye to the future and the courage to work for long term achievements.

- Rae McQuade,
President, North American
Energy Standards Board

natural gas field and built a pipeline to feed a Tenneco electric power plant that was later operated by El Paso.

On the domestic front, unbundling of pipeline services required by FERC Order 636 had created the need for rapidly improved customer services in terms of real time ordering, delivering and billing for natural gas. To assure that customer needs would be met, major organizational changes were instituted. The intent was to provide a single point contact within the Company for each customer to handle all orders, answer all questions and resolve all problems. This also required substantial upgrading of computerized programs.

At the request of Tenneco Inc., the Kern River pipeline was sold during 1995 after a little over three years of operation. This was related to the need for Corporate capital rather than the performance of the jointly owned facility. The gain from the sale was recorded in the year-end 1995 books.

The Move to Greenwich

In September, 1995, it was announced that the Tenneco Management Headquarters would be moved from Houston to Greenwich, Connecticut. While this only involved the relocation of about 30 members of the senior management, the remaining staff would move to a new Tenneco Management Center annex housed in the new Tenneco Business Services headquarters in the Woodlands, Texas. The reason given for the relocation was that Tenneco had evolved from being a predominantly domestic energy company into a diversified industrial corporation eagerly searching for growth around the world. It was believed that the management and information processes used by Tenneco Inc. were such that it could lead its operating companies from any location in the world.

While Tenneco Gas would remain in Houston, the relocation of corporate Tenneco management was another unexpected shock to both Tenneco Gas employees and the City of Houston. While there are certain advantages to being separated geographically from ones parent, the move seemed to indicate that the Company's energy heritage and success was soon to be relegated to history.

Despite this dramatic and surprising turn of events, Tenneco Gas continued to pursue its strategic plan. Because Tenneco Ventures was being successful in adding oil assets to its portfolio and with success in the cogeneration and power generation fields, Tenneco Gas changed its corporate name from Tenneco Gas to Tenneco Energy in November to reflect these expanded energy assets. In addition, Steve Chesebro' was promoted to Chairman and CEO of Tenneco Energy and Edward J. Casey, Jr. joined the Company as President and Chief Operating Officer. At the end of 1995, Tenneco Energy was operating over 19,000 miles of pipeline in the U.S. handling over 16% of the natural gas consumed annually in the U.S. and providing service to markets in 16 States. Tenneco Energy provided a net operating income of $269 million to its corporate parent in 1995. It was a good year for Tenneco Energy if not a great one financially. Progress had been made both domestically and internationally and the strategic plan being pursued held promise for the future. Despite these and past achievements, concern was continuing to grow within Tenneco Energy about its future relationship with the corporate parent. There was a realization that the corporate office had developed a distaste for the energy business which had been pursued by Tenneco Energy and its predecessors since the beginning in 1943. In the face of this obstacle, Tenneco Energy and its employees adopted the approach of pursuing their strategic plan and continuing to strive for excellence while letting results speak for themselves. From its beginning, Tennessee Gas Transmission and successors Tenneco Gas and Tenneco Energy had overcome major obstacles and successfully adapted to significant change. 1996 would be met with the same determination

Tenneco Energy put forward three key messages for 1996 to all employees. First, customer service would be given the most important priority. The importance of customer service was reflected in the Company's vision statement committing Tenneco Energy to becoming a world-class company through customer satisfaction, employee excellence and financial strength. The second key message was to continue striving to achieve operating cost leadership. This had been an ongoing goal of the Company from its founding. Thirdly, Tenneco Energy would build a global presence in the international gas industry.

A major announcement concerning the future of Tenneco Energy was not long in coming. On March 21, 1996, a press conference was held in Houston where Tenneco announced its intention to sell, merge or spin-off Tenneco Energy. A data room was soon opened for companies interested in bidding for the Company. Other than staffing the data room, Tenneco Energy executives and employees were neither consulted nor involved in the planning, bidding or sale process. Tenneco Energy officials did investigate the possibility of separating the Company from Tenneco and creating a stand-alone entity but this effort failed due to timing, tax and other issues. Tenneco Corporate distributed guidelines to interested parties for submitting formal bids for Tenneco Energy on May 29. On May 23, Steve Chesebro' and Ed Casey praised the efforts of Tenneco Energy employees who participated in data room presentations. "It was a difficult task for employees because of the loyalty they feel to Tenneco Energy and our heritage" said Chesebro', "but these individuals did an outstanding job of representing us in a highly professional manner." It is interesting to note that even at this date, Tenneco Energy was still reviewing potential investments in a domestic intrastate pipeline, two expansions to existing interstate pipelines and potential acquisition of a 50% interest in a power generation plant in Hungary.

On June 19, 1996, El Paso Energy agreed to acquire Tenneco Energy. The remainder of the year was spent concluding all the legal, regulatory and financial documentation and the executed contracts were delivered on December 12, 1996.

MUFFLERS & TRASH BAGS

In the twilight of Tenneco Energy in 1996, there were lots of farewell parties but one in particular stands out to me as epitomizing Tenneco Pride. I went to many of these parties and tributes but no one had yet gotten it reduced in a retirement speech. Looking back, I still feel that way. No one had been able to capture that spirit until Ewell Muse spoke at his retirement party at the Cadillac Bar (maybe it was the margaritas talking) but I doubt it. What he said was how all of us felt but just couldn't string the words together. Certainly, not as well as Ewell did.

Ewell took the microphone and those assembled fell quiet (as quiet as can be expected after a few). Ewell went through the niceties, mentioning people he had worked with over the years. He wished all well and finished up with his plans for the future. "I intend to play a lot of golf, travel and enjoy my grandkids, but when they ask me "grandpa what did you do for a living, I'm sure as hell not going to tell them that I worked for a company that made mufflers and trash bags." The room erupted!!!

- Dick Snyder

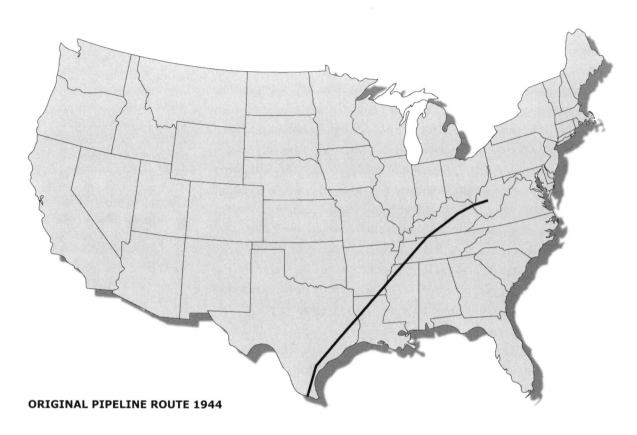

ORIGINAL PIPELINE ROUTE 1944

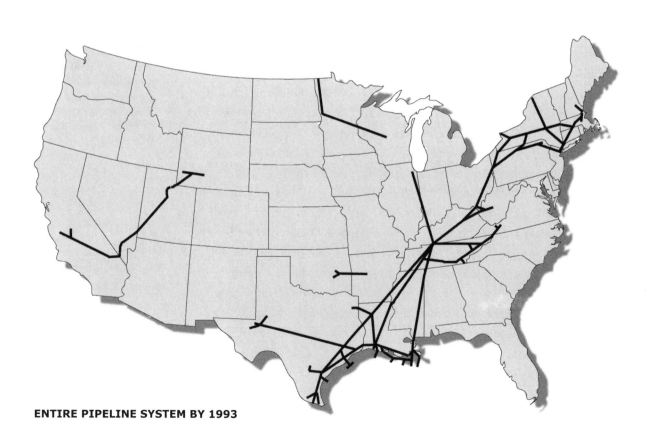

ENTIRE PIPELINE SYSTEM BY 1993

The Rest of the Story

The story of the Tenneco Energy Companies came to an end in 1996 with the sale of Tenneco Energy but what is the "rest of the story" behind the headlines? That the Companies "built from scratch" were sold for scratch might be a short but factual epitaph but that is neither our story nor the end of the story. Numerous case studies and financial articles have pointed out errors they feel were made by Tenneco along the way, but that is their story and not ours.

The heart of the rest of our story is found by looking back at what was built by the people in Tenneco. These accomplishments did not disappear when the name of the owners changed because most of the projects and facilities that were conceived, designed and built under the Tenneco umbrella are still providing critical energy supply today and continuing to yield a suitable return for their current owners. Neither did the story of the Tenneco people end with the sale of the Companies, although it still evokes some sadness among them when they contemplate what might have been.

As the sales were made, the Tenneco people responded to change as they always had and continued their individual stories of success in future endeavors. The list of Tenneco people continuing their industry leadership beyond the sales in 1988 and finally in 1996 is longer than our capacity to print but is well known and respected within energy circles.

Every Tenneco employee can look back with pride on what was accomplished in 53 years beginning in 1943, because each has been an integral part of this story.

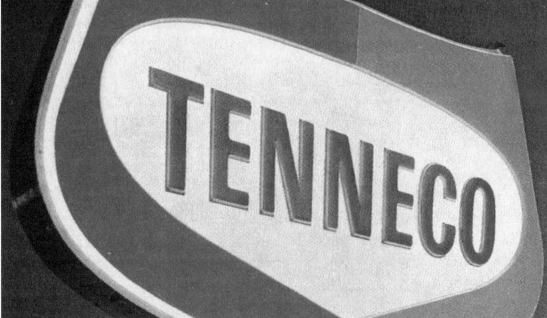

II

TENNECO OIL PROCESSING & MARKETING

1955 ~ 1988

By Cliff Rackley

Chalmette was the larger of Bay's two refineries, and became a strategic purchase for TGT.

P&M TOUGH COMPETITORS

High Value Assets

Tenneco entered Refining and Marketing in a cautious way. Entry was considered reasonable as the company produced about the same volume of oil as the capacity of purchased refining. They were short of marketing volume and were exposed to excess price volatility of sales in the cargo market. The company hired many people with extraordinary talents to achieve their goal to grow and become a recognized competitor. Efforts were persistent on all fronts. They learned how to refine the oil for the best profit and compete nose to nose against the largest and shrewdest of marketers. They took risk and won. They accumulated many high value physical assets. The asset that made it an extra valuable and a unique franchise was the assembly of highly skilled workers honed by competition and tied to one another by their respect for each other's skill. They built the company into a profitable and valuable entity. Using these skills they also broadened the scope of the enterprise.

This is the condensed story from the viewpoint of several individuals and was assembled by Cliff Rackley. If we could include the stories of many other participants we would be able to present a more complete history of the various functions labeled Processing and Marketing, and its derivative units. I give special thanks to the other providers of materials used in this company history.

I. Refining

When Tennessee Gas Transmission (TGT), the parent company, bought Bay Petroleum Corporation in 1955, a new chapter was written in the company's history. The pipeline company acquired two refineries, one in Chalmette, Louisiana, a suburb of New Orleans, and another in Denver, Colorado, along with a small number of retail outlets around Denver. With this purchase, an integrated oil company was born.

Bay Petroleum was acquired by TGT primarily for its oil and gas production properties. The refineries and marketing came with it. Although some of the board members urged Gardiner Symonds to sell the refining and marketing and stay out of that business, Symonds wanted to keep and expand it into a major oil company. He persisted and after about a year the decision was made by the board to keep it, believing that the refining and marketing would raise the public image of the enterprise. One of Symonds first steps was to hire a skilled team of refining engineers from the large oil companies to bring modern scientific management systems to their new enterprise. He began with employing George Meason with sixteen years of refining experience at Exxon.

But the company had bought more than just a refining business. It had bought a piece of history as well. The Chalmette refinery was located in the area where the Battle of New Orleans was fought in the War of 1812 and adjacent to a grove of oak trees where English General Packenham was killed by Americans. It had been an industrial site since before 1900. In fact, remnants of an old cotton warehouse still existed in the tank farm area, and the riverfront contained old wharf pilings and a railroad embankment for the shipping of cotton.

The first refinery itself was constructed about the time of World War I

The Chalmette Refinery in 1955 when it was purchased by TGT.

**TENETS OF REFINING
DEVELOPMENT,
CHALMETTE 1957-62**

1. The refinery has to make a profit; otherwise there is no incentive for Tenneco to keep it and the staff who is working there.

2. A small, 25,000 b/d, refinery has the same basic technical problems as those ten times larger such as Mobil and Exxon. We must apply past experience on simple problems utilizing our backgrounds and not rework all the technology.

3. The process engineers must mentally take the refinery apart on paper and reassemble the pieces to produce optimum results.

4. We must apply the scarce engineering time of the onsite engineers to the high value problems.

5. Focus on getting optimum yields and quality from the catalytic cracking and reforming units for making higher value products.

6. Apply advanced refinery management practices to as many aspect of the business as appropriate

and was known as the Chalmette Petroleum Corporation. In the early 1930s, the plant was bought and rebuilt by the D'Antonio and Vaccaro Interests, which owned control of the Standard Fruit and Steamship Company. The group had acquired the Chalmette refinery to insure a steady supply of fuel for their ships.

By 1944, Bay Petroleum Corporation had purchased the Chalmette refinery. The new owner, C.U. Bay, also owned the Bay Surgical Dressing Company, which had a patent on the Band-Aid™. At the time Mr. Bay bought the refinery, the capacity at Chalmette was about 7,500 barrels of crude oil per day, and the Denver plant was running about half of that.

When TGT acquired the refineries in June of 1955, Bay Petroleum had increased the Chalmette capacity up to about 18,000 barrels a day. They were dependent upon running only local premium grade crude oil delivered by barge or truck. Under the market conditions they were making marginally acceptable quality products and were marginally profitable although they had only 140 employees. The refinery's physical facilities, aside from the FCC unit, were in working condition but were old with much corrosion and other physical signs of age. Never-the-less the company embodied a going business of processing crude oil into salable products and a weak customer base. This franchise was of value to an enterprise with an ambition to grow which would have been costly to create from scratch.

Almost immediately, the company set about to meet competitive product quality with a million-dollar expansion of both refineries. The company's first addition at the Chalmette plant was a catalytic reformer unit, which was needed to improve the octane rating of the company's gasoline, thus assisting them in making the high octane gasoline demanded by the new autos of the time.

The Bay refinery at Denver had first been built to supply local demand. Competitors, during those earlier years, had to ship their gasoline by tank car or truck and Bay's refinery thus enjoyed about a three cent per gallon transportation advantage. In the 1950s a gasoline pipeline was built to Denver and Bay's transportation advantage had been lost. This had marginalized the economics of the refinery.

1956

After TGT's decision to keep the refineries, some staff was added; Rudy Dean was President of Bay Petroleum, George Mason Vice President of Refining, Amos Pollard Chalmette refinery manager and Dick Rankin Denver refinery manager. Joining the group as chief process engineer at Chalmette was Cliff Rackley. Shelby Gibbs joined as chief process engineer at Denver and Owen McBride as chief refining engineer, Houston.

By late 1956, the capacity at the Chalmette refinery had been increased to 24,000 barrels per day through improved utilization and optimization of the cracking facilities and a few hardware improvements. In early 1957 Symonds made a brief visit to the Chalmette refinery. Discussions centered on improvements made to date, the strategic advantage of its location as a refinery, the economic potential by expansion, and the limitations to growth due to the land and space impediments. Symonds appeared to be an enthusiastic supporter of the business and was not discouraged by the high cost of land for expansion.

All aspects of the conversation were encouraging. He left the Chalmette staff feeling they should present sound recommendations for expansions for board review. He also shared with employees his philosophy about earnings. Symonds advocated improving earnings and sharing it between the shareholders, employees and public interest. This attitude of generosity, when it comes to the employees and general public interest, was important guidance for the staff in future developments of the refinery.

The Chalmette refinery would be more profitable at higher through-puts, so planning for expansion was started in 1958. Due to the weak economy Symonds deferred the expenditures until 1959. Engineering and construction commenced by Bechtel and Procon and by mid-1960 a significant modernization program of the refinery was completed. The program included a new crude oil two-stage distillation unit, a new gas plant, a propylene-butylene

Al Caldwell

Amos Pollard

Joe Wink, Lewis Owens & Chuck Kilgore, 1965

Richard Rankin

Alkylation unit, a completely rebuilt, in an expanded format, Fluid catalytic cracking unit, the associated boiler, tankage and other offsite facilities. Upon completion, refinery capacity was now up to 45,000 barrels per day.

1961

The demand for benzene and xylenes for making nylon, styrene and other products was strong and growing. The refinery's capabilities were extended into the petrochemical field as well. Soon, Tenneco was supplying industrial customers with products such as benzene, toluene, ethyl-benzene, orthoxylene and heavier aromatic solvents.

Charles Rampacek

TGT/Tenneco had developed a reputation of acquiring businesses. Inquiries were received at various times regarding Tenneco's interest in acquiring additional refineries: two independent refineries on the Houston Ship Channel and one at Corpus Christi. After careful evaluation, these inquiries of interest were spurned since the operations were less efficient than Chalmette. In addition, Tenneco did not have enough crude oil production to supply them, nor markets for their products; therefore the risks of ownership were elevated.

1967

At this point Tenneco had been in the refining and marketing business for twelve years. The refining sector had consistently made a sound profit. Businesses often have to make their profit on the manufacturing sector although the marketing sector must maintain a satisfactory return. It was Tenneco's strategy to rely heavily on the manufacturing sector to assure that the combined refining and marketing group as a whole was profitable.

In 1967, the refinery added more new units, thereby producing more aromatics as well as increasing capacity for gasoline and fuel oils. This expansion included a hydrocracking unit, hydrogen plant, another gasoline reformer, a delayed coking unit and a crude processing plant to bring capacity of the refinery to almost 80,000 barrels per day. Ray Dudley was vice president of refining, Owen McBride chief engineer, Chuck Kilgore refinery manager, Louis Owen chief process engineer and Joe Wink chief project engineer during this expansion.

The federal government had in place a program to allocate importation of low cost ($2.00/barrel or less)($13/bbl in 2010 dollars) foreign crude oil among all refiners with special quotas for small refiners. This placed Tenneco, who was not classed as a "small refiner," at an economic disadvantage in owning the small refinery at Denver. Furthermore, the long-term competitiveness of it looked very doubtful. It appeared more profitable to sell it to someone who qualified as a "small refiner." Thus in 1969 a decision was made to sell the refinery and most of the marketing around Denver that it supplied. A small independent company bought the refinery and enjoyed the foreign oil import quota while Fina bought the marketing component.

The foreign import program had some holes in it. Two refining companies had created foreign trade zones for refining foreign oil wherein the products from refining qualified as exempt from the import regulations. Tenneco petitioned the government for the rights to set up such a foreign trade zone on an island at Savannah, Georgia about 1969. This would be a complex political situation. Gardner Symonds counseled to seek the assistance of lobbyist Tommy "the Cork" Corcoran. Corcoran, former Chief of Staff to President Franklin Roosevelt, then aided in arranging political support from the adjacent states. Tenneco appeared to have 100% sup-

Joe Wink, a LSU engineering graduate, with five years engineering experience at Mobil's Beaumont refinery, among a staff of 100 professional associates, had this to say about his experience. "My Tenneco story begins with a conversation with Cliff Rackley, engineering manager at their Houston office, who was looking for an experienced mechanical engineer for their Chalmette refinery. I was offered the position, accepted it and moved to New Orleans. In retrospect, it was a most fortunate decision. After college, military service and five years with Mobil's refinery, I was ready for a change. Tenneco allowed the younger group of professional engineers' great latitude in decision making regarding the company staff and plant operations. When I think back, we were probably one of the younger groups of professional staff in most refineries. Tenneco believed in hiring young people and providing them with opportunities for advancement. Because of that experience, I was able to start, after ten years at Tenneco, my own refinery professional consulting engineering firm, Wink Engineering, one of the largest privately held in Louisiana."

port from the Georgia and South Carolina congressional contingents but Herman Talmadge Georgia's Senator who supported the project, privately advised that President Lyndon Johnson controlled such favors. Hearings were held at Savannah and several competing oil companies fiercely opposed it. More importantly, the Independent Oil Producers Association, a heavy-weight Johnson political supporter, opposed it. The Administrative Judge pigeon-holed the hearing results and Tenneco eventually accepted the denial of the petition.

1972

Large autos were popular and gasoline demand was growing. About 1972, Tenneco obtained an option on 800 acres of land for a large new refinery on the west side of the Mississippi River between Norco and Baton Rouge, Louisiana. The only options available for crude oil supply were from OPEC countries. Due to the unstable international situation in 1973 this strategy was abandoned.

Then the 1973 Arab embargo of oil to the US caused the refinery to lose some of its domestic crude oil supplies, as there was an overall oil shortage. The Oil Import Quota policy was abolished. The output of the refinery dropped by about 15,000 barrels per day for over a year due to the shortage of crude oil available to the refinery. Some heavier Nigerian, non-Arab oil became available. At that point, the plant was updated to better handle the heavier types of crude and returned to full operations.

Expanding Chalmette was always constrained by inadequate land for the required storage tanks since it was bounded between the Mississippi River, Kaiser Aluminum's plant, a main boulevard and an Exxon petroleum terminal. The company had acquired all the land they could from adjacent sources. Exxon was not interested in selling their property to accommodate a competitor. Bill Heck, chief engineer at Chalmette, determined that a sizeable piece of land east of Exxon could be obtained and could be used for a crude oil terminal. Then they could pipeline the crude oil to the refinery, thus overcoming the big obstacle. This opened the prospect of a major expansion of the existing Chalmette refinery and planning of this large expansion began.

1976

In 1976 there was a flash fire in a refining distillation tower under repair and several contract workers were killed. Local publicity was not favorable and the morale of the work force deteriorated. During the next two years, two lengthy union strikes occurred along with some industry-wide strikes.

As the planners plotted strategy for the needed expansion, Jim Ketelsen, Tenneco's CEO, pointed out to Rackley, then President of Tenneco Oil, that they would have to get their labor relations in good shape and repair local public relations before making the major investments in the new facilities.

SUPERIOR TRAINING

I spent the vast majority of my 20 year TOC career at the Chalmette Refinery, with a 3+ year assignment in the Houston Office in Ray Dudley's Refining Planning group from 1973-1977. I started working for Neil McLauren in the Planning Group. I retired in 2000 in the position of Refinery Manager of the then Mobil Chalmette Refinery with the Exxon - Mobil merger.

What I remember and appreciated most about Tenneco was the supervisor and management training that we received throughout our careers. The investment in the employees and the foresight to develop future leaders was a win-win for both the company and the employees. We were challenged and given responsibility beyond our years of experience, but tempered with the oversight of mentors that would keep us from going into the ditch.

The number of Chalmette Refinery employees that went on to leadership positions with other energy companies after TOC was dismantled is testament to the training, mentoring and responsibility we, as young professionals, were given. I lost contact with most, but I know at least four or possibly five became Refinery Managers, and at least two became senior executives with other energy companies. This is quite a record for a single, medium-sized refinery oil company.

- Don Michael

Hugh Adams, Bill Heck, Sam Neff and Clark Johnson, 1981

To regain their local image, a public relations office was set up to define and engage the company in civic involvement. They purchased land from the railroad company that was occupied by the historical Packenham Oaks. They also engaged an expert to devise a program to save the deteriorating trees and set up a trust fund, administered by a local ladies association, to oversee future care of this historic site. They bought property and set up a ball park for the community. The public relations office began feeding the local media with newsworthy tidbits. Other such programs were undertaken and favorable publicity resulted. In the area of labor relations, there was a change of leadership within the union. The President of Tenneco Oil was invited to speak before the Greater New Orleans Chamber of Commerce. Afterward the company felt the local and employee relations were good. The marketing programs had succeeded which necessitated the purchase of some 20,000 to 30,000 barrels/day of gasoline from others. Refinery expansion was needed to supply the products to meet sales opportunities.

1981-82

The Chalmette Heavy Oil Processing Project (called CHOPP) was a strategic plan to refine low priced heavy, high-sulfur, foreign crude oils. The business plan focused on up-grading low market-value oil fractions to higher value products. There was less competition for purchasing certain oils that were difficult to refine, so there was reasonable assurance of low cost and a continuing supply. These low cost oils would be the most profitable under a wide range of world supply situations. The project encompassed new world-class fluid cracking, coking, alkylation and hydro-treating that would allow production of 80,000 barrels per day of gasoline and 40,000 barrels per day of jet and distillate fuels plus 7,000 barrels per day of aromatic petrochemicals. Facilities included the afore-mentioned down-river crude oil terminal, additional products pipeline facilities and a coke ship-loading facility.

Key strategy on crude supply presented to the board according to H. L. Britton's report stated: In comparison to the Middle East, the Caribbean is politically stable. Long-term crude oil contracts are available at official government selling prices and logistics are simpler because of the distances involved. Heavy Caribbean crude oils do have significant quality disadvantages since high metal levels (nickel and vanadium) cause operating problems with catalytic processes.

In Mexico, Tenneco has an established position. Although Pemex will not commit new crude oil until after the end of the present administration in 1982, reserves have been growing each year and directionally towards more of the heavy crude oils.

The Venezuelans are willing to commit to long-term contracts for heavy crude oils. The country needs oil revenues and must develop their heavy crude oil as their light crude oil production declines. There are significant untapped reserves of heavy crude oil from both conventional reserves and the Orinico tar belt.

The board then approved the $500 million dollar refinery expansion that would allow it to process at least 120,000 barrels per day of crude including a substantial share of the lowest price crude oil available from either Latin America or the Middle East. This assured Tenneco flexibility in

Chalmette Refinery after implementation of $500 million expansion program.

CHALMETTE REFINERY
1959-1979

From "Testament of Chuck Kilgore"

The Refinery Superintendent, Amos Pollard, was in overall charge of the refinery, except Engineering, but including Employee and Public Relations. He reported to George Meason in the Houston office who was vice president of Refining at that time. The refinery's supervisory staff consisted of a Maintenance Superintendent, Eddie Falgout, Chief Chemist, Ray Hanle, Operating Superintendent, "Salty Iglehart and Chief Clerk, Roblee Bernard.

Engineering was primarily responsible for design and construction of new facilities and reported directly to the Chief Engineer E.O. McBride, in the Houston office. This group was headed up by Cliff Rackley who was then Senior Engineer. He had a staff of four or five young Chemical Engineers, all recent college graduates and two Mechanical Engineers of varying experience who worked closely with the contractors in the field.

At the time I was hired by George Meason to head up Operations, Tenneco had embarked on what was the first phase of a modernization of the refinery's operating units. Engineering was complete and construction had begun on a new 45,000 b/d crude unit to replace the existing crude unit, vis-breaker, and a c3-c4 alkylation unit for production of high octane gasoline. The Fluid cracking unit was being expanded. A new maintenance building with space for shops, warehouse, locker and shower rooms, a large meeting room and additional office space was included in the project.

As the new units came on

obtaining a supply. The project plans were announced in 1981 at a time of high unemployment in the New Orleans area. The news was well received in the community. These investments virtually doubled the economic value of the Chalmette refinery. The facility was completed in 1984 and on a test run processed 157,000 barrels per day of lighter crude oil. The profit margin per barrel of crude oil processed increased as expected. Bill Heck was Project Executive of the team, which included Dick Mains, Jim Autry and Jack Cohn. Al Caldwell was refinery General Manager and Jerry Singletary General Superintendent.

Mobil Oil (now Exxon-Mobil) purchased the refinery in the oil company 1988 asset sale. Private reports indicated they believed it was perhaps their most profitable refinery. Afterward PDVSA, a Venezuelan National firm purchased half interest in this industrial complex because it will process their dirtiest, low-value oil. As of this writing it is operated as "Chalmette Refining Company" and reports a crude oil refining capacity of 192,000 barrels per day.

This industrial complex and its large tank farms, are visible on Google, Chalmette, LA. satellite view, see site at the Mississippi River and Paris Road

An evening shot of the Chalmette Refinery at full operation.

II. The Distribution System

As a key marketing strategy, Bay Petroleum under Rudy Dean, then president, acquired a number of marine and pipeline terminals through purchases in the late 1950s because competitors were not willing to allow Tenneco easy access to market in their territory. These acquisitions began with the 1956 purchase of Citizens Oil for the southeast, and the 1958 acquisition of Hartol Petroleum for the Northeast. The company then constructed some additional terminals on the Colonel Pipeline and elsewhere to bring coverage of the Southeastern and Northeastern states.

With these valuable assets in hand, the company could offer other companies transportation savings by exchanging products. With Tenneco's own terminals and the exchange arrangements, the company was then able to make direct and exchange deliveries reaching a wide marketing area while keeping distribution costs down. These exchange arrangements allowed low-cost deliveries from perhaps twice as many locations. Harry Horsh and Mike Falco were key persons in getting these exchange arrangements made. Later they led the effort to build the Collins Pipeline, a key connec-

stream engineering was already underway on the next step that would put Tenneco in the petro-chemical business. Cliff Rackley transferred to the Houston office and was replaced by Ray Dudley. This was the beginning an almost continuous series of projects that extended over the 20 years I spent at the refinery (largely as Refinery Manager) and extended into and beyond the four I spent in Houston prior to my retirement. The result was a thoroughly modern, efficient and technically sound, integrated refinery and petro-chemical complex that Mobil Oil Company acquired when Tenneco Oil Company was broken-up and sold piecemeal.

In the 1960s and 1970s both process and project engineers were in high demand. In addition to an excellent benefits package Tenneco could offer an opportunity to be in on the ground floor of a rapidly growing company with opportunities for rapid advancement and challenging work, often above the employee's experience level. Tenneco assigned responsibility for meaningful work to their young engineers earlier in their careers than any of my previous employers. We did not hesitate to discuss the value of these incentives to prospective engineers; whether they were being offered employment as new college graduates or came to us with industrial experience.

Prior to being hired by Tenneco, I had worked for two oil companies. I learned a lot from that experience. I have never regretted my decision to go to work for Tenneco. On the whole it was a challenging and gratifying experience. I worked with and for good people and for a good company. I am indebted to those who gave me the chance.

-C.H. (Chuck) Kilgore

**WHOLESALE MARKETING. &
DISTRIBUTION EXECUTIVES**

Norman Faulkner

Ron Moist

Shelby Gibbs

Mike Falco

tion between the Chalmette refinery and the vast Colonel Pipeline running from Houston to New Jersey. The area, pipeline tributary to the Chalmette refinery plus the exchange arrangements, then defined the company's prime marketing territory. This was an extensive system for the amount of product thus the cost was still greater than competitive rates.

III. Petroleum Product Marketing

The acquisition of Bay Petroleum included staffs of marketers for the products from the Denver refinery. They were headed by Vice President Leo Leobo. The Wholesale department handled the sales to distributors while a Retail Marketing group handled Bay's owned stations. At Chalmette, a national sales group handled cargo, barge and distributors sales. There were no owned stations.

The acquisition of Citizens Oil brought with it some important wholesale customers for the Chalmette refinery as they had four terminals in Georgia and Florida, and had been a Bay customer for years.

The biggest single jump in the company's marketing assets came in 1958, when Hartol Petroleum Corporation was acquired. The Hartol acquisition substantially expanded the company's presence in the East Coast market area. Hartol was the largest independent wholesale marketer of gasoline, kerosene and home heating oils on the Eastern Seaboard. Founded in 1923 in New Jersey, Hartol and its subsidiaries, including Atlantic Coast Terminals, owned and operated deep-water cargo terminals in Newark, Boston and Baltimore. The company, headquartered in New York, supplied refined products at wholesale to more than 1500 independent jobbers and distributors through 16 terminals in a trade territory extending from Maine to North Carolina. Its operations also involved barge and pipeline terminals in New Jersey, Pennsylvania and New York. Tenneco added facilities for the throughput of pipeline products which added further capacity. These were located in Virginia, North Carolina, New York and Pennsylvania.

Wholesale Marketing

Much of Tenneco's competition, the "Big 7 major oil companies" often called the "Seven Sisters" had ample low-cost crude oil and were the primary competitors in the wholesale markets. A newcomer such as Tenneco could get independent marketers as customers who often had been spurned by these older companies, sometime for poor operations or credit issues. Tenneco moved into wholesale marketing with liberal credit policy but at a cost for both credit losses and competitive pricing. This gave them a checkered start. The company had to write off as bad debt an amount equal to about 6% of Tenneco Inc.'s profit for the year 1963. As management throttled the credit to bring it under control, it put a burden on the Wholesale Marketing staff. They then focused on helping these marginal customers manage their finances and other business while the customers who were the greatest credit risks were phased out.

At the time larger more powerful cars were becoming popular and people were driving more which drove gasoline consumption up. Tenneco's sales went up with demand. With an excellent collection of distribution terminals, the Wholesale staff strategy evolved into being price competitive and a reliable supplier. As Tenneco tightened its management of sales pricing and expense management, weak managers were weeded out. The wholesalers worked their management problems. With this simple, solid system they thrived and grew into a profitable business. At this point Tenneco Wholesale Marketing's profits were satisfactory. This was a key turning point in the oil marketing. Norman Faulkner, Bob Skidmore, Ron Moist and Bob Baney were key leaders in transforming the wholesale marketing.

Retail Marketing

Retailing gasoline at the time was dog-eat-dog competitive business. Stations sit on a street along by or across the street from a competitor station that eyes every action taken and tries to woo the customer away. They put out their price signs or other ads on the street and match or undercut each other every day or even more often.

Tenneco had a checkered history in retail marketing. They started with a few stations around Denver that came with the Bay Petroleum acquisition. They were a private brand marketer who retailed gasoline at a couple of cents per gallon below the big oil companies. The first addition was the Red Dot Oil Co. in Denver, which Tenneco bought in 1956. Red Dot had been a gasoline distributor to 60 of Bay's service stations. Bay Petroleum had no distributor or retail marketing around the Chalmette refinery. Then, in 1957, the properties of the Georgia and Florida-based Citizens Oil Co. were acquired, with 75 service stations in the southeast. The stations were operated under the Speed and Citizens brands. (The Speed chain was a very efficient, low- cost marketer selling gasoline at a discount to the major oil company stations, a typical private brand operation. Their stations often had only gravel driveways and lacked overhead cover. The attendant collected cash and made change on the driveway. They had a good sales volume and were making money for the owner)

Tenneco's expansion continued and the Gulf Coast Oil Co. a private brand marketer of New Orleans was purchased, bringing in 41 service stations in Louisiana, Mississippi and Alabama. In 1959, Crown Petroleum Corp., a long-time retail marketer in Connecticut and Massachusetts, was acquired. The retail ranks grew again in 1961 when Tenneco purchased the successful Direct Oil Corp. headquartered in Nashville. They too were an independent gasoline marketer having about 75 stations with an efficient operating system. They were a profitable operation. Jim Jeannette was the strong operations leader of this business.

Symonds had said he wanted to build a major oil company. The staff, including recommendations from the Madison Ave. ad Agency, interpreted

A UNIQUE CULTURE

Norm Faulkner recalls: The culture of Tenneco Oil Company was unique in our habits, skills, desires and success oriented.
- Work ethic of employees
- All levels of management working together
- Upper management allowing freedom to lower management
- Promotions from within rather than going outside of the company
- Communications between various departments

Examples- Monthly meetings - Refining-supply – Transportation - Sales and Legal, if necessary.

Refining had been downgrading Kerosene to #2 oil resulted in the start of sales of Jet fuel. The helicopters at Lafayette, supporting rigs in the Gulf, were the first commercial customer followed by Eastern Airlines, the first airline customer.

At the time the refinery was upgraded from 75,000 to 135,000 b/d, one of our intermediate concerns was the sale of the volume of gasoline that resulted from the upgrade. We were able to get commitments from at least five or six larger jobbers on the east coast that were also accessible to the Colonial Pipeline. The result of the effort of refining, supply and transportation, wholesale sales and legal was successful.

There were many more such examples of various departments working together to accomplish our goals.

It was pleasure to recall this period of my life with Tenneco.
- Norm Faulkner

that to mean they should have highly visible service stations that looked like and functioned just as the major oil companies' outlets. It would need a brand name and a public image like them. The old-line oil companies generally used red, white and blue colors and had advertised them so much that the public associated a red, white and blue sign with oil companies. The advertising agencies came up with the Tenneco name and a red white and blue shield for the logo in 1960. The Tenneco name was then applied to the holding company for all its unregulated businesses.

Leo Leobo, VP-Marketing 1960

Tenneco Branded Retail Marketing

With recommendations of the advertising agency Tenneco plunged into branded marketing offering motorists' full, crisp service at the pump; credit cards were issued to more than 80,000 customers; gasoline was priced with the major oil companies and widely advertised. Marketing strategists produced a new T-shaped service station design for new installations. The wash and lubrication areas were located behind the sales office, with tires, batteries and accessories situated along the station's front. Customers were provided a lounge to avoid congestion at the pumps and to make the stations more inviting. Many were constructed in Houston. Along with the T-shaped stations, the strategists called for auto maintenance programs for Tenneco credit card holders. This consisted of service contracts under which consumers would pay a few dollars each month to receive routine lube jobs, oil and filter changes, tire rotations, wheel packing and other maintenance work.

In the 1930's Texaco had introduced a retail station design with two gas pumps, a canopy and two auto service bays that dealers usually used for auto repairs. They had solicited good dealers, trained and uniformed them. Other companies had followed suit with their minor adaptations. The "two bay" design had been the industry standard since that time. Texaco had built up a network of 40,000 stations throughout the USA, issued millions of Texaco credit cards across the nation, and employed a heavy national advertising program. They were formidable competitors for all gasoline marketers.

During the early 1960s, the customer was king in retail marketing. "Fill 'er up!" For years, those words conveyed the essence of gasoline retail marketing. Crisp service, provided by courteous attendants in equally crisp uniforms, was the yardstick customers could use to measure a "gas station's" quality. An attendant's ability to fill up the tank, wash the windshield, check the oil and give the correct change – while smiling sincerely – was graded each time a customer drove up to a pump. The smiling, full-service attendant era was but one of many marketing strategies employed by an industry that bloomed with America's love affair with the automobile, and swung with the nation's economic dictates.

The retailing companies Tenneco had acquired had been "private brand" or discount marketers selling at a couple of cents a gallon less than the major oil company stations. Tenneco's plunge into retail marketing with its new logo, credit cards, advertising and higher price was not a success. They lost the majority of customers they previously had as a private brand because the customers could no longer save the few cents. Now Tenneco was trying to woo the customers away from the major companies. Success was slow and they began some price discounting to compete with the independent oil stations. The major competition countered Tenneco's aggressive program by cutting prices also. Leading major companies began pricing gasoline as if "Tenneco offered credit cards and did widespread advertising" they would be classed as a major oil company competitor and not be allowed to price below the prevailing major oil company prices. They would counter at any location by pricing the same as Tenneco. This strategy would force Tenneco to compete on the major's terms where they would win. By 1962 Tenneco was building 100 new retail stations per year in the Southeastern states according to the plan. The new Tenneco retail stations built within a couple of blocks of competing major oil company new stations selling at the same price, were selling only forty percent of the volume of their competitors. Tenneco's franchised independent dealers at these stations could not pay their cost and often abandoned the franchise whereupon Tenneco's supervisor hired salaried attendants to keep the unit open. Tenneco was losing substantial money trying to look like the "big 7" major oil companies.

Tenneco's marketing operation, a conglomerate of small companies that had been acquired and reorganized under the Tenneco brand along with the new stations, were losing more money than the refinery was making. This impacted total company earnings. Gardiner Symonds, with Wilton Scott, the newly appointed president of Tenneco Oil, reviewed the financial results and called for a halt to the financial losses being incurred. They asked for a review of marketing strategy. Gardiner Symonds' initial directions to build a major oil company no doubt indicated he wanted to achieve an image of other big

REFINING & MARKETING
EXECUTIVES

A Ray Dudley

Lee W Marshall

Paul Sullivan

Dewey Mark

135

oil companies and was willing to pay a price. However his behavior would indicate he was not willing to pay "this price". The company was competing with the "big 7" oil companies who had access to large volumes of cheap foreign oil and were using their dominant marketing position to sell this oil. Even after the heavy advertising and distribution of credit cards in the marketing areas, the process of collecting a group of small private brand marketers, dressing them up, staffing them with independent dealers and increasing the price of gasoline was a financial disaster.

Scott reorganized Refining and Marketing and named Meason as Senior Vice President while Rackley was assigned as V. P. Economic Analysis. (Both were engineers who focused on the forces in play and numbers. Meason specifically assigned Rackley the duty of hiring and developing a cadre of high competence and well educated persons capable of being developed into business managers and to initiate a development program for all promotable employees in his respective groups.)

After the budgets reflecting big losses in distribution and marketing for the coming year were received by Scott, he called upon the economic analysts for a new plan for the year 1963 that would reduce the marketing losses in half. The planning group developed a plan and budget with significant operational changes and presented it to him that he accepted.

Culture of P&M Planning and Analysis

Scott, then the new president of Tenneco Oil, demanded a major reduction in operating losses from the marketing division. The Refining division was making a good profit but Marketing was losing more than Refining made. The Planning &Analysis (P&A) team of Refining and Marketing organized in late 1962, under Rackley, included Shelby Gibbs, H L Britton, Tom McIntosh and Eugene Anderson. All of these were engineers with some having an MBA. They first focused on operating cost improvements of product transportation, terminaling and retail marketing. They used the "cold-fresh-definitive view" with engineering and modern business class numerical analysis. Philosophically there was no justification for keeping Refining and Marketing in Tenneco unless it was profitable. It was not a profit contributor to any other function in the company.

Scott believed in decentralized management and this was put into effect. Many strict control measures around the decentralized divisions were adopted. This organizations model requires higher qualified managers for the outlying units than centralized organization. The deficiencies became apparent. There were many operations involved and first priority was to attack the units not involving marketing skills. Bob Brown was attacking the marketing activities. When his attempts failed Planning and Analysis addressed those.

The basic culture of the group was to apply the cold fresh view of each unit and evaluate alternative systems. A system was devised to estimate the

"The bottom line to me is that Tenneco Oil was always on the leading edge of using new technology to produce its products. They always ensured employees were highly trained, were able to represent the company well in public settings and of developing young employees into industry leaders. Those of us who were part of this company were extremely lucky. We would not have been given such great opportunity, support and responsibility in any other company. "
- Bill Cowser, a Project Engineer

true marginal and total overhead costs. Then the team would lay out options for management consideration. The cold-fresh-definitive view bypassed historical personal relations of the individuals who may have been involved.

By the end of 1964 Refining and Marketing as a whole was not losing money and by the end of 1965 Marketing was not losing money while Refining was making the expected return on investment.

The exercises challenged the group to use their studies on business modeling and financial analysis. The team began scrutinizing every function in Marketing and Supply to get costs down. They began modifying strategy and restructuring for efficiency. Working within Meason's leadership, the 1,200 person Marketing and Distribution function of 1962 was reduced to a 600-person operation by 1964 year end at which point the losses by Marketing were neutralized. Other Economic Analysis team members included Shelby Gibbs, Eugene Anderson, H. L. Britton and Tom McIntosh. This complete restructuring was a turning point. After the earnings improvements were made the individuals moved on to higher levels of management either in the company and/or new employment.

Direct Oil's success at running an efficient, limited service, low-price operation (a typical private brand style) was an indelible reference as they searched for profitable marketing business models. However, it did not fit the desired visual image of the Tenneco corporate enterprise. Direct Oil's operations were profitable and their model and marketing brand were kept intact and separate.

Getting retail marketing profitable was of strategic importance because when they could retail gasoline profitably they could also demand a better price from its wholesale customers. And if they could not, it would be more difficult to negotiate adequate wholesale prices.

Bob Brown, a creative marketer, was brought into the company in 1962 to work on variations of retail gasoline marketing in an effort to compete in this very difficult market. They needed a format of marketing that would survive the fierce competition and present an image as a respectable oil company. The chief competitors had large volumes of low-cost foreign crude oil they were trying to distribute. While Tenneco could wholesale its gasoline, it was only marginally profitable and that did not solve the problem of the losses being incurred in retail marketing. Small scale experimenting was easy. Many things were tried in retail marketing. Much was learned. Many experiments failed but some were discovered to have potential.

For example in 1962, under Meason and Brown's leadership, Tenneco implemented an experimental marketing endeavor called the Top Ten Program. Cut-rate gas, along with household goods, novelty items and general merchandise became the staples of the station/stores. This triggered many gasoline price wars.

Retired Senior Vice President of Marketing, Harry Daniel recalls: "In the

A GREAT PLACE TO WORK

I agree with my associate's assessment that the old Tenneco was a great company that fulfilled its obligations to the shareholders, while being a great place to work, with great people, and a true, family atmosphere. Even Tennwood" fit appropriately into the total picture". My loyalty to this entity (non-existent, except in our minds and hearts) still exists and I wish it well.

I recall that when an issue came up about safety at the refinery, and someone pointed out the cost, the executive, in response, made the point that "there is no contradiction between safety and profitability, we can and will do both." I always appreciate that story as well as the philosophy it stood for.

I also believe that the company's efforts in the environmental area (even complying with some regulations they felt went too far) are one of the reasons we have such a good environment to combine with our prosperity.

- Richard J. Lorenz, Attorney at Law

SOME ACHIEVEMENTS MADE WITH THE "COLD-FRESH-DEFINITIVE VIEW"

Terminaling cost was reduced by about 60%.

Trucking cost reduced by about 40%. Retail stations determined to have inadequate potential were decommissioned and the real estate put up for sale.

Some salaried service stations operations were changed to commissioned agency arrangement. Total employment in marketing was reduced by about 600 employees.

With the addition of a market-research teammate who created a marketing model, the team was able to more accurately compute the business volume of proposed station locations.

Performances of the newly acquired locations were materially improved. In the case of the "C" store locations success was about 98%.

A fundamental belief I learned at Tenneco that served me well. "Engineers do not lie. Engineers solve problems. It is illogical to lie, because you cannot solve problems by lying about the data."

- Clark Johnson

Top Ten program, we sold gas as-low-as 23 cents a gallon (versus a normal of 35 cents) and tried all kinds of promotional giveaways like trading stamps. We sold everything from hula-hoops to brooms and records. Problem was, we just couldn't do that and charge the same price for gasoline as the other oil companies. Our profit margin was too low. Those were hectic days, but we learned a lot about gasoline marketing (and customer response), which paid good dividends later on."

Birth of the Convenience Store

The company experimented with many types of gasoline and merchandise marketing. Eventually the Top Ten program was discarded and replaced with a whole new strategy. Many families were adding a second car to the household, thus wives were becoming a significant factor in gasoline purchases. The company wanted to appeal to their taste. They had to gain their acceptability. The combination of an air-conditioned, spic-and-span convenience food store with gasoline marketing, without stacks of tires and auto repair services, placed in residentially convenient locations, proved to be well-received by customers and profitable to Tenneco. Care was taken to insure demand for gasoline was adequate to allow Tenneco an ample share of business. This concept, with a full line of beverages and convenience foods, with a mini-supermarket environment was a pioneer in the gasoline retail marketing trade. It broke the oil company adage "you cannot sell groceries with gasoline." Among the many merchandising trials this model was demonstrated in New Orleans after a new unit was built in a suburban area with a high residence count, where traffic was confined by canals such that the specific community to serve was clearly defined.

This convenience store brought in a good gasoline trade. This business model, with adaptations for different locations, was then used throughout Tenneco Retail areas for its new locations although it did not apply to locations without adequate residential backup. These units could be branded "Tenneco" with full pride. As Tenneco's success was noted by the competition, many other companies cloned the model. Slowly this convenience-food-store /gasoline combination became the model for a number of oil companies. Petroleum journals began referring to them as "C" stores. By the mid-to-late 1960s Tenneco had set a new standard for gasoline marketing. As Tenneco Retail expanded with its new strategy they built business volume with a bag of traffic building tricks they had learned. Team leaders included: Lee Marshall, Paul Sullivan, Bennett Shotwell, Harry Daniel, Jim Sadler, John Robinson, Gil Walker, Ken Catmull and Hugh Taylor under the leadership of Cliff Rackley.

Development of Retail Marketing Cultures

Times like this set the stage for Tenneco to differentiate and crystallize cultures. Although there was a hustle by marketers to join the new food store marketing program, it was not large enough and some were left to carry on the traditional programs. These high energy guys would not be stopped. Many schemes were tried by various managers and progress was most often matched by our competitors leaving Tenneco with little progress. One supervisor, Bennett Shotwell seemed to be able to consistently get older established stations to make higher sales than other supervisors. One station on "heavy traffic" Clebourne Ave of New Orleans was an example. When he was asked how he improved performance where many previous managers failed, he said the unit had sales of 35,000 gallons a month when first assigned to him and his station manager said that was about the limit for it. Whereupon he shopped station manager candidates until he found one who believed he could small talk to customers and get the sales up to 40,000 g/mo. The new man was engaged and truly he worked until he got it to 40,000 g/mo. Upon urging for higher sales he claimed 40,000 was about the maximum potential whereupon Bennett shopped for a manager who thought the potential was 45,000 g/mo. The new manager continued pressing customer's attention tactics until he achieved sales of the new level. The story continues until Bennett's manager was achieving 55,000 g/mo.

Bennett was a fierce competitor whether marketing gasoline or playing tennis. He succeeded where others failed. In the course of changing marketing Bennett developed other supervisors who were willing to press station manager changes until satisfactory results could be obtained. The continuation of the process resulted in a cadre of a new culture of high energy marketers.

Tenneco led the industry is marketing with convenience food stores with gasoline. As the convenience food-gasoline marketing program progressed marketing procedures and financial controls were significant problems. Harry Daniels succeeded as manager of a group of these stores. Store manager candidates needed different training and skills. Harry succeeded where others had failed in developing a cadre of winning managers. They set up a training school for candidates. They discovered hiring candidates who had worked at the competing oil company locations were less successful than new hires into

"Tenneco was a great company. The practice there was to be professional, to treat everyone with respect, to expect the best, and to reward results. There was very little back-stabbing and back office politics, because simply the executives did not do that, and did not appreciate that behavior.

One of my favorite Tenneco stories involves a Houston executive. I was Manager of Marketing Planning & Analysis at the same time that Jason was manager of the refining planning group. Both he and I were scheduled to give presentations to the corporate office about our 5-year plans. We were both practicing our presentations before a Houston Executive in the conference room one day. Lee Marshall, Ray Dudley, HL Britton, and several others were present. Jason went first and was completely butchering his presentation. He could not stay on focus, and strayed off to all sorts of unimportant side things. The executive probably stopped him 15 times during his presentation to get him back on track. . The room was tense. Everyone was quiet, observing the carnage. Jason finally finished.

The Executive turned to me, and said "OK, you're up." I knew I had to break the tension, give a small bit of relief to everyone there, so that I could actually give my presentation. So, I quickly said "No way. I saw what you did to the last guy. I'm not getting up there." Everyone, including Lee, looked at me like I was completely crazy. He was about to say something when I said "OK, just kidding, everybody. My turn" and I got up to make my presentation. Everyone then had a good laugh, I gave my presentation with no significant comments, and all was well. Later that day, Lee told me "Johnson, I really thought you had gone bonkers, but that did work out well."

- Clark Johnson

TENNECO'S PRINCIPLES OF PERSONAL ACCOUNTABILITY

My first promotion provided reinforcement of the management principles of personal accountability learned in my first P&M assignment plus an additional guiding principle of P&M management. The promotion had me working for Paul Sullivan. At the time the presidents of our non-Tenneco branded subsidiary companies reported to Paul. The respective leaders were Harry Daniel, Gill Walker, Fred Holder, Bob Sudderth, George DaVita, Jack Chambers, Maarten Dekker and Hank Boxley.

The guiding principle under which I operated was to respect the autonomy of the management of these companies. I was not to act as an overseer of these employees. They must be allowed to lead their organizations in the manner they saw fit. P&M senior management recognized that there was no one management style that fit all organizations or managers. Also if the leaders of these companies were to be held accountable for the performance of their operation, they must be free to lead those organizations, limited only by Tenneco's overall policies of integrity and corporate ethics and policy. Thus I was instructed that my role as an internal consultant to these men must be one where they, and not my boss, sought my assistance. If I could help and they wanted my participation, that help was readily available to them, but, if in their judgment I had nothing to contribute, it was not my job to meddle in their affairs. In other words I was a utility infielder to be used when asked but was not to force my way into a company and was never to compromise their ability to lead their organization.

This principle of P&M management, which allowed managers a great deal of autonomy in ac-

the business since Tenneco's culture conflicted with the previous training. The success of the program speaks for the cultures they developed.

The tasks demanded many skills but the selection of durable candidates, providing clear objectives, and demanding financial performance were key cultures. It was noted that many former winning athletes did well in the programs.

Self-Service Gasoline Marketing

A few entrepreneurs were experimenting with self-service gasoline in the suburbs of Denver. Most were failures but a couple was modestly successful. This model appeared to have potential for Tenneco since it was vastly different from the dealer operated stations of our big competitors and Tenneco had a large number of dealer stations that were losing money. At the budget meeting the key phrase presented in favor of Tenneco authorizing funds to experiment with this was "If we can get just five percent of drivers to serve themselves we should be able to get enough business to make the self-service units more profitable than our older conventional retail outlets." The key counter by an executive was "Nobody is going to fill his own tank for just two cents a gallon discount." But the Tenneco executive approved the funds for the experiment. The staff had concerns about men wanting their windshield washed and women may want a disposable glove to handle the gas hose or want to be shown how to fill their tank. At the first locations the customers just filled their tank paid and drove off like they were in a hurry. The concerns were irrelevant. They just wanted to gas up and go.

The test proved quite successful. The self-service concept when combined with the food store proved to be a profitable system that allowed them to take business away from our old established competitors because Tenneco had the most labor efficient program and could still offer customers a discount. The times had come for a change as auto manufactures began providing windshield washers on cars. They were also providing autos requiring less maintenance. Full station service had less customer appeal. These programs when finely tuned were sufficiently effective in that a new Tenneco self-service food store could often cause a neighboring major oil company, dealer-operated station to close for loss of business.

These programs earned a good profit and defined the retail marketing business model. While it was successful in marketing, that did not mean we could cause major oil companies to cease competing. If we took too much business they retaliated with price cutting. Tenneco also initiated a program for licensing its self-service program trademarked "U-fill-em" to other existing convenience store operators. Wide self-service was limited because customer dispensing gasoline into a vehicle was prohibited in many states and localities as a safety matter. Tenneco pursued this extensively and obtained legislative changes in 22 states to allow customers to dispense gasoline into their own autos. Roy Pesson was the company's leader in this activity. Independent marketers quickly adopted this model. The major companies reluctantly experimented. Exxon, who had dominated the Baton Rouge market in the shadow of their huge refinery there, noticed an impact on their sales and one of their executives looked at one of Tenneco's self-service licensee's operation. The executive was quoted in an industry journal as saying "I was appalled to see a Cadillac owner filling up his own car at a self-serve outlet." The impact on their sales volume forced them to experiment and ultimately to make the big change. However, their business model was based upon their franchise dealer operated stations, which were resistant to make an effective change. Tenneco's food store and self-service models were true pioneers and brought about a complete revolution in gasoline marketing in the entire country.

Tenneco's system of retailing for "new outlets" was different from other oil companies. These new selective outlets were salary operated. As such they were labor, capital and management intensive. They were, at first, designed and best suited for metropolitan, suburban areas with extensive residential backup. Neighborhood customers were targeted in contrast to busy street drivers. Some employees did not adapt to the complexity of the program and left. The survivors were a unique culture of successful marketers i.e., tough competitors. Tenneco's retail promotions and training program kept the culture unique. Unfortunately as others noted Tenneco's success the competitors tried to clone the operations and hired many of Tenneco's experienced managers to operate their business. Tenneco's leadership and marketing culture embodied high personal character. The distinction was noted when several ex-Tenneco employees asked to return because they preferred Tenneco's culture.

complishing company objectives, prevailed throughout the company, resulted in a motivated work force, was effective in providing meaningful work, and also resulted in creating a fun place to work. With time I came to recognize the considerable efforts of P&M's president, Cliff Rackley, in reinforcing this principal within P&M while assuring that this principle was also respected by Tenneco Inc., the holding company, in its relations with P&M.

In future jobs of increasing management responsibility I always saw that my primary function as a manager was to set goals, provide needed resources to accomplish those goals to those reporting to me, while defending them from incursions into their areas of accountability in order to let them proceed as they judged fit.

- By Dan Carter

General Market Developments
1979 and 1980

After Tenneco sold its Denver Refinery in 1969 it also sold 132 outlets operating under Tenneco and subsidiary brands in a 10 state region tributary to it. Gasoline marketing competition in the area was fiercely competitive particularly for a new brand as Tenneco. The company could then place further emphasis on its Tenneco branded stations in other areas during the early 1970s.

In 1984 the company acquired 55 additional stations in Alabama, Florida and Texas. By 1987 the refinery expansion was compete and the marketing system was functioning well. The refinery averaged 140,000 BPD for the year, refined product sales were 177,000 BPD and NGL added 47,000 BPD for a total of 224,000 BPD.

Turmoil in the Middle East and the Arab embargo against oil sales to the US in 1973 caused a crisis for oil supply and the Tenneco refinery's supply was cut about 30%. Tenneco had to have an adequate supply or have customer's homes run out of fuel and have to reject gasoline customers, which had been costly to attract. The government invoked gasoline allocations and price controls. The company chased crude oil supply around the globe. Price controls and quotas of gasoline supply put a temporary halt to its retail marketing expansions as Tenneco was directed by government agency orders to divert a share of its traditional supply to certain independent jobbers. This tended to dull the great momentum of the unique retail marketing team of Tenneco. The company made a good profit during this period however complying with the government price-control regulations was a gigantic task. A committee made up of officers, Ralph Maynard for legal, Shelby Gibbs for operations and Charles Dodd for finance was assigned this difficult obligation.

By the late 1970s, Tenneco's retail marketing network included about 500 company-owned, salary-operated outlets in the US, which sold products under the Tenneco, Direct, and Red Diamond brand names. All of the brands were well accepted by its customers and the culture of the labor intensive operating staffs dictated keeping the brands separate. Tenneco had such an unfavorable experience when they re-branded retail operations, the advantage to doing so on the remainder was not obvious.

1980

In the early 1980s, convenience store competition began to heat up, with over half of all merchandise sales dependent on just four items: cigarettes, soft drinks, beer and milk. Tenneco held its market lead through grand openings, sales contests and incentive programs, food stores, self-service, price wars when necessary and by being flexible enough to adapt to the preference of local customers.

Tenneco had accumulated a group of bright marketers who had developed a leading marketing format. The retailing profits surged ahead as long as they kept new ideas coming with a distinct customer appeal or economic advantage. Competitors can copy a marketing style and they did. The marketer who has this leading edge makes more money. As Tenneco tried to apply their technologies to mass expansion such as buying out a company and convert the units to Tenneco stores they discovered that they would have to completely destroy the image of the takeover stations and rebuild in the Tenneco image because Tenneco's marketing style targets a select customer group.

A leader of the companies that challenged Tenneco in 1960 to not discount gasoline while offering credit cards and advertising was the slowest of all companies to adapt to the new standard of gasoline marketing. A note appeared in an industry journal in the early 1980s that the company was losing four cents a gallon nation-wide on their retail gasoline marketing. Evidently the new competition forced many marginal dealers to close. They soon reorganized and switched some of their marketing to the new format utilizing both convenience food and self-service.

At the same time, Tenneco retail focused on remodeling stations, demolishing and rebuilding some, giving outside and inside facelifts to others.

Meanwhile, each location site came under close scrutiny, and those that didn't show high volume and profit potential were closed and sold. In 1983, Tenneco retail had slimmed to a nucleus of about 450 locations with high sales volumes, a level that continued into the late 1980s.

Operating two businesses is labor intensive. Tenneco created the "Island Marketer" design for combined food-store and gasoline marketing using a long canopy with the food store as an island between the gasoline islands. This design allowed as few as one attendant at a time to operate the entire business. It was first used by Tenneco at Gulfport, Mississippi. The island marketer design, with bold lettering and simple, clean lines became the new Tenneco standard in 1984. The new look incorporated multi-product dispensers at the pump that featured advanced electronics to help control and track inventory. Inside the stores, new snack centers, coolers and enticing merchandise displays were installed to stimulate add-on purchased. The layout design became popular with other marketers. It was popular since three persons-per-week could operate it compared to twelve-per-week for a full service gasoline and food store.

While Tenneco pioneered the concept of marketing high volume gasoline with convenience food, much of the industry had caught up with the concept. No oil company had excess low-cost crude oil to try to sell. In 1987, rising wholesale prices squeezed retail margins as retail tightened its belt to perform in a highly competitive marketplace. Competitors were closing their low-performing service stations. Nationwide the number of gasoline retail outlets was declining. Like many other industries, retail determined that it was time to get back to basics: service and pricing, with few frills attached. The tactic worked. The industry enjoyed more favorable profit margins in 1987-88, and retail was poised to take advantage of that. Profitability increased.

The marketing business was sold along with the remainder of Tenneco Oil in 1988. After more than three decades in the business, Tenneco retail marketing could take satisfaction in its performance. Its history is a mixture of sound analyses and innovation, hoopla and lively hustle, strategic positioning and competitive pricing.

Development of Management Philosophy

Leadership of a large enrollment of employees begs for a positive statement of management philosophy. Tenneco Oil Company's was widely distributed in 1975. It had been developed over a number of years and came about generally as follows: Gardiner Symonds vision was to build, in his words, "a major oil company." He wanted a company that looked like, performed and carried the respect in the financial world of the big oil companies. A New York advertising firm was engaged to lay out a program to create this public image. The Tenneco name referenced the relation to the parent Tennessee Gas Transmission but the name and logo

RETAIL MARKETING

Harry Daniels

Tom Davis

Neil McLauren

Clark Johnson

(red, white and blue) was by design, noticeably similar to the major oil
companies. A significant part of the image had to be conveyed to the public through the retail gasoline marketing and a wide advertising program.
The identification program was initiated about 1961. Numerous segments
of the oil business, both P&M and E&P, had been acquired and held in
various corporate entities under the general leadership of Ralph Graham
and these were collected into the new Tenneco Oil Company.

Characteristic of Symonds management of acquisitions, he had taken
significant risks in the acquisitions of the sundry parts, he had allowed the
managers wide latitude to operate and now the time came to try to manage
it into a viable well-run business. Some units were not as profitable as projected and numerous missteps had been made. The unit was losing money to
the extent it depressed the parent company earnings for 1962 and Symonds
ordered change.

Wilton Scott, then a vice president of exploration, was chosen as President of Tenneco Oil in 1962 and directed to get the business unit profitable.
Scott had definite ideas about organization structure and went about decen-
tralizing operations. This was a major change from the previously used management style. This reflected Scott's view of placing the decision making as
close as possible to the commercial operations. This organization shifts much
of the responsibility to the local manager. Decentralized management became
a core element in the culture for the operating staff. This change seemed small
but it was accompanied with a strong reliance on the local managers for financial performance.

Scott, as he visited the various offices, emphasized the fact that the assigned
role of business was to make a profit. Substantial reorganizations were undertaken to align actions to our goals. Many skilled persons were transferred to
get definitive oriented managers in place who Scott believed could increase efficiency and carry out company goals. He set out his goals and allowed the new
managers latitude to exercise their judgment. He rewarded the successful managers. In employee affairs he consistently emphasized fair treatment and fair
reward for the workers. During the course of Scott's direct leadership of Tenneco Oil Company a distinct culture began to develop. It continued to develop
during Meason's, Rackley's and Foster's leadership.

The company experienced several years of hard-knocks as it assimilated
the acquired units and their staffs. These hard-knocks brought about a series of practical managerial philosophies. These also contributed to creating a
"culture" that most employees felt were unique to Tenneco.

Events of 1975, as "gasoline allocations and price freeze" brought to light
the need to distribute the written business philosophy to retail outlets as well
as all operating units. A copy of the Tenneco Oil Company Management Philosophy is shown that was distributed to all company business offices as a
placard for display.

Management Philosophy

THE ASSIGNED ROLE OF BUSINESS IS TO MAKE A PROFIT

We, as employees, are obligated to the stockholders whose capital has created our jobs. Therefore, we will strive to . . .

- Provide a reasonable return on investment,

- Generate and fully utilize opportunities for continuing profitable growth, and

- Protect the property our stockholders have entrusted to us.

Tenneco Oil Company has been given the responsibility by Tenneco Inc. to discover, acquire, develop, produce and/or market hydrocarbon resources.

Our objective is to optimize net return in a manner consistent with the corporate objectives of Tenneco Inc. and with a view toward the long term growth and viability of the company.

We shall pursue these objectives within the framework of, and in harmony with, certain basic and guiding principles which include:

RESPECT FOR ALL EMPLOYEES

We will respect the rights and dignity of each individual. We will . . .

- Provide, whenever possible opportunity for employees to grow personally and professionally and to contribute their talents in order to obtain that growth,

- Pay our employees fairly and recognize, encourage and promote productive employees who contribute fully to the success of our Company,

- Maintain an open door, two-way policy of communication to provide an opportunity for all employees to make positive suggestions or to voice their concerns without fear of reprisal,

- Actively develop individuals in order to provide the opportunity for promotion within our organization.

SERVICE TO OUR CUSTOMERS

We are dedicated to providing our customers with outstanding service and quality products, consistent with their needs. We will . . .

- Be constantly alert to both the present and future needs and desires of our customers and respect their opinions,

- Offer assistance in helping them obtain their raw material needs in a competent, efficient manner,

- Seek to keep our customers more than just satisfied by offering competitive prices, superior service and market intelligence.

FAIRNESS TO SUPPLIERS AND PARTNERS

We will deal fairly and impartially with suppliers of goods and services and with our partners in business ventures. We will . . .

- Select suppliers according to the quality of their product or service, their reliability and competitiveness of price,

- Provide each qualified supplier equal opportunity to compete for the sale of quality products to the Company, and,

Wilton E Scott

Geroge H Meason

Cliff W Rackley

Ralph S. Cunningham

STAFF LEADERSHIP

H L Britton - Planning

Ralph Maynard - Legal

Jack Kelly - Employment

Charles Dodd – Financial

- Communicate effectively with our partners, treat them fairly and ensure that our mutual interests are recognized and honored.

CONSISTENT AND RESPONSIBLE LEADERSHIP

Our present and future success is dependent on informed, intelligent and aggressive management. We will . . .

- Provide an organizational structure which will allow clear understanding of responsibilities and authority,

- In a timely fashion proceed to business decisions utilizing the best information and the most suitable technology available,

- Clearly state our near and long term objectives while providing the opportunity to our employees, at all levels, to contribute to the attainment of these objectives,

- Encourage creativity and innovation while permitting variations in management style.

GOOD CORPORATE CITIZENSHIP

We will, as a good corporate citizen, conduct our business lawfully, ethically and in a socially responsible manner.

EXCELLENCE AS A WAY OF LIFE

We want Tenneco to be known for excellence; therefore, we believe that every task in every part of our business should be performed in a superior manner and to the best of our ability. Nothing will deter our pursuit of excellence.

BEING A TOUGH COMPETITOR

We will use our full energy to utilize the synergism from various parts to create an organization known to others as a tough, successful competitor.

* * * * *

This history contains many elements of the "Tenneco Culture" that evolved in this era as described by various employees and writers. The company operated as one consolidated unit utilizing common staff functions until late 1978 at which time E&P and P&M were separated. Executive skill sets were very different and separation provided flexibility. The Management Philosophy continued to promote this culture.

IV. Autonomous Subsidiaries

The Autonomous Subsidiary group management was established to manage and control smaller business at less overhead type costs, utilizing a separate decentralized policy program. They overlooked the private brand marketing that did not fit the Tenneco Retail marketing format. The Autonomous Subsidiary divisions usually were highly localized, labor intensive units not compatible with Tenneco's branded operation nor the Houston salary, benefits and purchasing system. They had to compete in the local labor markets and sell our products in the local markets.

Mitchell-Supreme of Newark, NJ, led by George De Vita and TLC of Hartford, CT, were home heating oil retail sellers marketing in the local counties.

Blue Flame Gas of Bluffton, IN, led by Dick Schaffer, distributed propane fuel in the agricultural districts of Indiana, Ohio and Michigan.

Direct Oil of Nashville, TN and Red Diamond were private brand marketers of gasoline. Direct Oil marketed through more than 125 stations in TN, GA, FL & NC. Their business plan focused on sales in medium and small towns and tight controls of their stations. Red Diamond marketed in northwest SC. to a loyal clientele.

Tenneco expanded its operations to Europe when Globe, a gasoline marketer, was acquired in 1966 after a petrochemical sale contract went bad. This activity was not contributory to the US operation and ultimately sold to recover its investment. These companies grew profitably both internally and with occasional small acquisitions.

Culture of Autonomous Subsidiaries

Tenneco Inc.'s corporate overhead had to be divided among all divisions if services were provided. Six of P&M's subsidiaries did not use the parent's services and were called Autonomous Subsidiaries. All of these units had large employments of low wage people paid competitively with some benefits but not the usual Tenneco benefit package. The petroleum product marketers were required to purchase their products from the company at the price they would have to pay others. They were managed by an independent board of directors according to separate Policy and Procedures. Management bonuses were based upon the local unit profits after allowance for amount of capital employed.

Each company was acquired from an independent businessman and continued to be operated as such. The employee groups were like family. Their business was efficient before they were bought and they continued to use the systems they were accustomed.

If the usual corporate overhead computed by the "Massachusetts Formula" were applied to these, their return on investment would be reduced to half of what they made when operating as an autonomous unit.

Each company employed unique systems that made them equal or more efficient than their competitors. They marketed Tenneco products under their private brands and made more profit generally than if branded Tenneco because the big competing oil companies gave them more slack than Tenneco. Tenneco's Marketing was struggling for its existence against the giant oil companies and each of these contributed effectively.

Gebr. Broere of Holland was acquired in 1968. This was a strategic change to Tenneco's business plans and was considered with caution. Broere was accidentally discovered and viewed as a money making business opportunity. The operating functions were not strange to Tenneco. The Broere operation was largely a chemical shipping and terminaling operation. They had developed a group of well-located terminals to serve the European chemical industry.

SUBSIDIARY COMPANIES

Jim Jennette – Direct Oil

Dave Delling – Tenneco Minerals

Russel Bowers – Petro Tex

John Macon – Marlin Drilling

GAS PROCESSING

Ed Causey – Plants

Elton Shearer – LPG Marketing

Guy Southerland – Plants

Carol Belton – Petro-Chem Mkt.

In fact, Tenneco was shipping aromatic petrochemicals through them. They had a Dutch flag fleet of coastal ships, river barges and trucks designed to properly handle even the most hazardous chemicals. They offered customers a complete marketing service of storage, distribution and billing their authorized customer. Broere had earned an excellent reputation with giant chemical companies of Europe.

Broere had developed their systems to empty completely with the intention of handling dangerous chemicals. Customers had developed complete confidence in Broere to "deliver every liter of chemical given them to handle". Broere was staffed with employees who followed handling requirements militantly.

We would come to learn that the key person successors in Broere were excellent executives who always exceeded our expectations. Martin Dekker was a key leader during the early years of Tenneco's affiliation. Their business model differed from conventional European shippers because they enjoyed a significant back-haul business. This business was profitable, was serving the fast growing petrochemical businesses and they grew rapidly into a substantial chemical handling entity.

Fortunately a key competitor operating a fleet of ships with stainless steel lined tanks (usable for food grade products as salad oils and wine) agreed to be bought by Broere at a favorable price because they were only marginally profitable to the seller. When Broere's operating systems were applied they became profitable. This was a major uplift for Broere making it clearly the dominate entity in the business in Europe. In the request for approval Chairman Broere pleaded "This is not a normal purchase of ships; we are buying out an important competitor."

This business had an excellent franchise and continued profitable with a strong cash flow. Later Tenneco established a Tenneco Europe headquarters office in Holland to utilize the earnings of Broere to shelter losses of other Tenneco units in Europe. By the mid 1980s Tenneco rejected an $80 million offer to buy the unit from us because of our inability to replace the earnings with the cash. We felt it was worth $120 million. The company had paid only $11 million for it in 1968 and had made regular capital improvements to fill growth opportunities.

V. Gas Processing for LPG Extraction

The year 1953 marked Tenneco's entry into the gas processing business. It is an activity to capture the ethane, propane, isobutane, normal butane and some light gasoline from the raw natural gas streams. These are called LPG or liquefied petroleum gases for simplicity. With Tenneco's Coast Company beginning to buy and develop oil and gas producing properties, company management decided that gas processing was a necessary area of operations in which to be involved. A year earlier, TGT had purchased several small oil companies in an attempt to build up its newly established oil venture. Two of those companies were Del Rey Petroleum Corporation and Sterling Oil Company. All oil and gas properties were combined into one firm called the Tennessee Production Company to provide company name identification. The principal business of this company was a gas processing plant located near Eagle Lake, Texas. Known as the Chesterville Plant, it has been expanded and modified several times and was a valuable profit center for the owner.

In 1954, the first company-built natural gas processing plant came on stream near Agua Dulce, Texas. This plant, staffed originally with only three people in 1953, ultimately became the point of origin for the products pipeline, which was built to furnish feedstock for the La Porte Fractionating Plant in 1956. Seven more plants were added in the ensuing years, when the com-

At a meeting of accountants in 1965 (left to right) Leroy Capps, Tom Bartlett, Claude Richardson, Charlie Carpenter and Jim Farmer discuss wholesale pricing.

pany successively built the Pearce Plant in Rockport, Texas (1959); the Leobo Plant in Palacios, Texas (1961); the Stephens Plant in Haynesville, Louisiana (1968); the Ames Plant in Ames Oklahoma (1971); and the Gallegos Canyon Plant in Bloomfield, New Mexico (1977). The O. W. Ward Plant at McAllen, Texas came to Tenneco with the Delhi-Taylor purchase in 1964. Ken Pierce and Ed Causey were the principal drivers of these activities.

Operating in conjunction with the La Porte Plant was Tenneco's underground storage facility at Mt. Belvieu, where the company stored propane, natural gasoline, normal butane and isobutane in large underground salt cavities. Product was retained there until needed by the company's retail and wholesale customers on the Gulf Coast or other areas of the country. Tenneco had 11 wells developed in the Mt. Belvieu area, allowing the company to store a total of over nine million barrels of natural gas liquids, thus eliminating the need to build much more expensive conventional steel storage facilities. Products were marketed wholesale by Elton Shearer and Jim Jolly.

In 1963 the wholesale market value of propane dropped down to natural gas fuel value, storage tanks became full and many plants stopped extracting propane. During this period Tenneco was seeking alternate

**A Tribute To
WILTON E. SCOTT**

*Geologist, Univ. of Texas 1936 CEO &
Chairman of Tenneco Inc. 7/1974 to
7/1978 - President TOC 1962 to 1970*

*Wilton Scott, addressed as Scott
or Scottie by friends and acquaintances, worked at Buffalo Oil before
being named president of Tenneco
Oil (TOC) about 1962. He had been
hired as president of Tenneco Oil
Company after the company had
gone through a few years of assimi-
lation of several small acquired companies. Scott was an astute judge of
people and embraced sound leadership policies upon which managers
could rely. He was very conscious of
good treatment of company employees and compensated the successful managers well. His leadership,
good humor and generosity were
welcomed and admired.*

*Scott was not organization sensi-
tive; he would directly phone an
employee, who could get an immediate problem solved. He was what the
writer calls a "Three day Executive."
If his request of was not fulfilled in
three days, the staff member might
as well forget it because Scott would
be off on another high-priority task.
Scott had a great sense of humor
and enjoyed playing gin rummy. On
one trip from Houston to Calgary in
a prop plane he drew this writer as
partner. Scott razzed me on every
play I made. That trip was mentally
the longest plane trip ever. Others
who have accompanied him on plane
trips report the same good-natured
banter that made trips very long and
memorable but not boring.*

*The culture of company leadership
starts at a high level. Scott reported
that he became too busy to get his
annual physical exam one early year
of employment with Tenneco. When*

markets for its propane. Roger Isch, founder and major stockholder of Blue Flame Gas, contacted Tenneco about the financial entanglement of his company. He was seeking someone to buy out an unfriendly major stockholder. Blue Flame had a good retail business in Indiana, Ohio and Michigan and they were using a good business model. Tenneco acquired the major stockholder's interest and later the remainder of the stock. Blue Flame was a good sales outlet for Tenneco propane. It thrived under Tenneco and grew into a very good operation. A bonus for Tenneco was lease rights to a propane underground storage cavern in Ohio. This was connected to the Texas Eastern pipeline from Houston. It served as a new wholesale propane delivery point for the company's Houston marketing group. Blue Flame was a good fit with Tenneco.

Blimp-like natural gas storage tanks at the San Juan Gas Plant in Farmington, New Mexico.

Tenneco also had invested in 25 gas plants that are operated by other companies. Three of these were extremely large and are located in Louisiana. One plant is the Blue Water Gas Processing Plant near Egan, Louisiana, which came on stream in 1978 and increased Tenneco's ability to process natural gas liquids by almost 30 percent.

In 1985 and 1986 the company participated with a 50% interest in the construction of the largest gas-processing plant in the country, located in the San Juan Basin. It also constructed five smaller plants in Louisiana.

Times have not always been easy or profitable for Tenneco's gas processing business or, for that matter, for the entire industry. A shortage of natural gas, along with government pricing regulations, has caused supply and demand for natural gas liquids to fluctuate widely in the operating years. The Natural Gas Policy Act of 1978 began allowing supply and demand to stabilize as prices of natural gas and natural gas liquids reach alternate fuel BTU values. For Tenneco, this has meant constantly searching for ways to maximize profits in an uncertain climate.

Although the times have changes, Tenneco's philosophy of being alert to every possible business opportunity in the gas processing business has remained unchanged. That philosophy has meant growth for Gas Processing: seven natural gas processing plants, one underground storage terminal, two truck terminals and 134 employees.

The Marlin 17 crew logged an industry saftey record of 500 days without a lost-time accident.

I. Marlin Drilling Company

Marlin Drilling was created to support Tenneco's effort to explore for oil in the Gulf of Mexico. There was heavy demand for offshore rigs and some concern existed that Tenneco may not be able to lease rigs timely to complete its offshore drilling obligations. Schacht McCollum, managing the offshore operations requested the company to acquire some fee owned rigs. George Grafton, with extensive drilling rig experience joined the company and began constructions of drilling equipment starting with shallow water barge rigs followed by jack-up rigs. It was started in the early 1960s. Marlin jack-up rig #3

the time came for his next annual physical his senior officer told him to get two exams.

Scott's style of leadership was distinctive. His concern for employee health was genuine. On one occasion he offered Meason and his wife a few days in the Bahamas if he would stop smoking. For others he simply kept no ash trays in his office. Smokers who came to his office would have to abstain or put their ashes in the cuff of their pants. Perhaps that is when the writer stopped smoking.

Scott was a large man with a deep, powerful voice. When he called by phone, it was his style to boldly announce to the secretary only the name of the person he wanted on the phone. Some newcomer secretaries answering the phone were scared by the tone of his voice and were afraid to ask his name. All the others already knew. In private, secretaries most often referred to him as the "Bear", for example saying only: "The Bear is on the phone".

Scott had spent eight very productive years as president of the oil company and afterward provided senior counsel. He knew the industry well, sought many acquisition candidates and pursued foreign exploration, all of which contributed to its growth. By the time of his retirement in 1978, he was considered by most employees to have been the prime builder of Tenneco Oil Co. He had endeared himself to them and it was most appropriate that TOC employees honor him with a retirement party. The writer reserved the petroleum Club facilities, proposed the party plan to him and asked him for a list of persons he and wife, Loridene, would like to have attend. Most thought he would wish to invite a number the leaders of the oil industry with whom he had associated. After consideration with Loridene he asked that the attendance be limited to employees and their spouses, but he also ask we included on the invitation list a number of former employees – people who had worked in the trenches for the company for extensive periods but had since found growth opportunities elsewhere. The party of 275 filled the club ball room. The inclusion of former employees added an unexpected note of gaiety as many old good friends were able to revisit.

One of Scott's favorite expressions was "by-damn". He, in a good sense of humor, always insisted he was right on every issue. For every question he had a positive answer. He never left one in doubt. Over the years he had not been right on every occasion. "By-damn, I am good" was adopted as the theme for "the roast" at the retirement party and 16 speakers presented humorous stories about such encounters with him. It was a special evening for him and all the employees who were saying good-bye to one of their company builders.

was completed in 1965, #4 in 1966, #6 in 1971, #7 semi-submersible in 1975 and jack-up #14 in 1980.

Marlin was a division of E&P at the beginning. As the supply and demand for rigs shifted they also began leasing rigs out to other companies to keep the rigs and crews employed. Geological information gained on drilling is the exclusive property of the oil company leasing the rig thus Marlin was kept at a distance to insulate the third party drilling information from Tenneco E&P.

A material advantage of Marlins ownership prevailed when technology or schedules were changing and Marlin could provide Tenneco immediate response to technology or rig availability. For example when the famous Youlumne oil field was discovered in California, land rigs with capability to drill to 12,000 feet depth were not immediately available on the West Coast so Marlin ordered 3 such rigs assembled and moved them there for Tenneco E&P to accelerate field development. A similar situation prevailed when the big discovery was made in Columbia and Marlin came to the rescue. E&P personnel claimed close relationship with Marlin staff and have expressed their feelings that coordination of complex situations was better than with leased third party rigs. Most of their work was in the Gulf of Mexico but on occasion they took jobs in Brazilian waters to keep rigs and crews busy.

VII. Synthetic Fuels
Synfuel Consolidation, 1983

The coal gasification, shale oil and tar sands projects were initiated in their respective Tenneco Divisions with healthy capital investment commitments. It was in 1983, after most of these were started that Jim Ketelsen, CEO, wanted them pulled together. They were heavy in research, engineering, construction and likely would be joint ventures with extensive negotiations for finance. He brought his observations to Rackley, that inflation was rampant and that the businesses with older, fixed-assets, that were expensive to replace, were the businesses that were making good money in those inflationary times. It appeared to him that Tenneco's strategy should emphasize that the proper investments in these heavy industries would bring good profits in the future. Oil prices had jumped to $40/bbl. due to Middle East political shifts and had settled to about $34/bbl. (equal to $75/bbl. in 2010 $). The world markets seemed to believe that the price for energy would continue to rise. He outlined his strategy to make major capital commitments in synthetic fuel projects. Ketelsen wanted to consolidate all of the synthetic-fuel activities into one group and lead Tenneco to become a dominant force in the field. Tenneco Synfuels Company was formed as a new Tenneco Inc. division under Rackley.

Government involvement started when the US Department of Energy (DOE) was authorized to guarantee loans for energy projects. Later President Carter persuaded congress to appropriate funds to promote alternative energy sources to imported oil, thus the Synthetic Fuels Commission (SFC) was created.

VIII. Cathedral Bluffs Shale Oil Co

Frontier's men of western Colorado sometimes waked up to find the stones in their chimney were burning and this brought on the discovery of "the stone that burned" that came to be known as oil shale. The rock contains a rubbery substance known as kerogen. When heated to 900 degrees (F), kerogen decomposes and yields what has come to be called shale oil, a synthetic crude oil with properties resembling conventional petroleum.

In September 1979, Tenneco, in its broad goal of pursuing synthetic fuels, acquired half interest in an Occidental Petroleum project to recover shale oil from a 5000 acre federal lease located about 70 miles north of Grand Junction, Colorado. The tract is estimated to contain 3.7 billion barrels of shale oil with a recovery potential of 1.2 billion barrels. Occidental had developed what they called the modified "in-suti" process whereby oil is extracted by rubblizing an underground mine room and beginning a flame front downward. Neil McLauren and Bill Cowser led Tenneco's participation. It developed that, while innovative and interesting, initial capital costs would be difficult to recover. Unocal was developing their continuous retort of oil shale process. When combined with the "in-situ" process the economics improved. Unical agreed to license the process to us for use on the Cathedral Bluffs project.

The Synthetic Fuels Corporation, (SFC), created under the Carter administration to finance synthetic fuel development, was petitioned to provide a loan and price guarantee to support the project. They executed a letter of intent with the partners of Cathedral Bluffs to provide $2,190 million of loan and price guarantee for the project with certain caveats. This was during the "Cold War." The Dept. of Defense had concerns about the close relationship of Occidental with the Russian Government, our global enemy of the time. The SFC had inserted a condition that Occidental must divest ten percent of their interest to be allowed the SFC guarantee money. Occidental refused to comply and in the meantime the market price and price projections for oil decreased below $25/bbl. therefore Tenneco ceased funding development. The SFC guarantee letter expired. Later Occidental purchased Tenneco's interest in the project. The mine head frames stand nearly 300 feet high at the Piceance Creek, Colorado site as a monument to the effort. During this same period Exxon had massive projects underway to extract shale oil including a village built for workers at their remote location.

GEORGE H MEASON
b. Oct 1916, d. Jan 2003 Emp. 8/1956, Pres. TOC 1970-1974, Ex. VP Tenneco 1974-81

George was a native of Terrell and Dallas, TX. After attending the University of Texas where he obtained a B. Ch. Eng. he joined Exxon as a refinery process engineer at Ingleside, Texas. He married Martha Grissett and they had three children. He transferred to Exxon's Baytown refinery rounding out 16 years of engineering experience before joining Tenneco in August 1956 as Chief Engineer for Bay Petroleum.

George was the principle guide of professional engineering quality in the refining group. He was articulate and a perfectionist. He expected professionalism from those working for him. He was kind to others, a good listener and spoke in his mild manner.

He recruited Rackley from Mobil's refinery in September 1956 to be the senior engineer at the company's newly acquired refinery at Chalmette. LA (New Orleans). Both were skilled at certain process engineering technologies but not necessarily the same. They talked often exchanging ideas on solving the problems during which they developed extensive confidence in each other as to petroleum refining technology, approaches to problem solving and business ethics. Other engineers were recruited for staffing Denver and Houston. He instilled his professional engineering qualities in the group.

George was advanced to Sr VP for Refining and Marketing in 1963 in a challenging situation to help restore the marketing division to profitability after the initial business model was not as successful as desired. Marketers are of a different culture whereby different management styles are required and George made the transition. He was a friendly persuader but he could be an assertive persuader when the situation called for it. The transition was a two way street whereby he strengthened their cultures with more professionalism while becoming a marketer. His success was acknowledged when he was advanced to Executive Vice President for Refining and Marketing.

He gained the confidence of Tenneco's senior management and advanced to President of Tenneco Oil in 1970 succeeding Wilton Scott. In this capacity he learned the Exploration & Production side of the business and led it to higher earnings. He was elected Executive VP of Tenneco Inc. in 1974 where he maintained overview of the gas pipeline activities.

IX. Athabasca Tar Sands Project

In the early 1980s Suncor had their project operating in the Athabasca tar sands on a commercial basis utilizing open-pit mining of the oil sands with hot water extraction of the tars. The Canadian Government required that some exploration of processes be undertaken in order for Tenneco and its partner to keep the 49,000 acres of leases. At the time we felt that such a project as Suncor was low technical risk but premature as the economics were marginal at best. The Suncor type project would use the shallow sands. We began working on extracting oil from the deeper tar sands using a steam drive much like conventional oil secondary recovery. This was new technology in the tar sands field and considerable experimentation was necessary to solve the many problems that prevailed. It was a cost necessary to satisfy the Canadian government and allow us to keep the lease on the many barrels of heavy oil reserves until oil prices recovered and a Suncor type project using proven technology would be economical. This was occurring before horizontal drilling had been commercialized.

X. Tenneco Minerals

Tenneco's mineral activities started with the Kern County Land Co. acquisition. They had a dormant asbestos mining venture and had several mineral leases including colemanite, a mineral for producing borates, and trona for making soda ash.

The colemanite lease was developed in Death Valley California producing borates for the glass and fiberglass industries starting about 1973. Environmental groups protested the activity in Death Valley with nationwide videos and news stories. Tenneco sold the business to disassociate its name from the negative publicity.

Soda Ash

In conjunction with the petrochemical activities, Tom Stevenson, who had been marketing the potash from a New Mexico mine, pursued the trona leases. The leases involved 4500 acres near Green River, Wyoming. He evaluated the mining and market potential for commercial soda ash. He proposed Tenneco develop the Wyoming leases with a one million ton per year mine and soda ash plant. His vision was that Tenneco had a window of opportunity since a producer of soda ash in Ohio had to shut down a 600 thousand-ton/year plant due to environmental reasons. If we did not enter the market other Wyoming soda ash producers would expand to fill the demand, then it would be difficult to market the output at a later date. We set a target of 600 thousand ton/year of firm sales commitments from customers as a condition of interest. When this was achieved the project picked up speed. Stevenson hired Dave Delling a former soda ash mine and plant manager to be the project manager.

As plans for the mine and mill materialized, Rackley went to the owner of the Ohio plant, who also owned a 1.7 million ton/yr. Wyoming mine, and offered to sell to them Tenneco's trona leases and its plans for a one million ton/yr. facility. They declined Tenneco's offer but offered to sell their 1.7 million-ton/yr. mine and plant to Tenneco. We declined because we did not want their plant since they had the lowest productivity in the Wyoming trona basin and they had considerable problems with their union. They employed 1200 people. Delling's plans were to achieve one million ton/yr. with fewer than 400 employees. The Tenneco board approved the project and work commenced on the Green River, Wyoming facility in 1979. The project included housing for construction and operating employees to satisfy community needs. Over 9,000 acres of additional leases were obtained to provide reserves of over 100 years at the million tons/yr. rate. It covers a large area and a short line railroad is included to ship the two hundred rail cars/week of product to the major rail line.

Soda ash mine and mill in Green River, Wyoming.

The first commercial soda ash was produced May 9, 1982. The marketing group wormed their way into the market. They and the mine works achieved their one million ton/yr. of product sales and production, the design output, in 1987. Delling's mining plan using giant rotary continuous mining machines exceeded his efficiency estimate and facility employment was under 350 employees at design output. It is a world-class facility that was a true grass roots project. Antelope had to be shooed away when work began and they watched from a distance with their usual curious interest as it was built and operated. The group was elevated to Corporate Division status with Tom Stevenson as President first followed by Dave Delling..

XI. Gold and Silver Mining

Tenneco's entry was through Tenneco Exploration and Production's acquisition of Houston Oil and Minerals. They had a staff of about 40 geologists searching for precious metals in the USA, Alaska and Australia. They also

SUPPORT IN A TIME OF NEED

"I suppose most companies say that they care about their employees. But at Tenneco Oil Company (TOC), I saw that quality validated time and time again. I would like to cite just one example to illustrate.

After TOC joined Occidental Petroleum as a 50-50 partner in Cathedral Bluffs Shale Oil Company, an entity formed to ultimately produce shale oil in Western Colorado. I was assigned the task of assembling and then managing staffs in Houston and Grand Junction. Within a few months we had a Grand Junction office up and running, and about a year later Bill Couser was selected to head the office.

In the fall of 1982, the annual P&M management meeting was held in New Orleans, and as usual, started with cocktails and dinner on the first night. Soon after the event began, Bill approached me and said the wife of one our engineers in Grand Junction had died suddenly and that he was arranging to get back there as soon as possible. He then said he knew the funeral and burial would be in Houston and wondered if we could possibly get a company aircraft to fly the body and family there. I told him I would find Cliff Rackley and try to get approval. When I found Cliff he was having a discussion with George Meason. I described the situation to both of them and they immediately gave the go ahead. Then George said, "Hell if we can't use company planes for something like this then we might as well not have them."

For Cliff and George it was an easy decision, an employee was is need and the company could help.

- Neil McLaurin

CLIFF RACKLEY

b. 1923, Emp. 1956-1986

Cliff Rackley, an Air Force veteran of WWII, a Chemical engineer, married Sue Old and they had three daughters. He was employed by Mobil Oil for 7 years at their Beaumont Refinery before joining Tenneco as Senior Engineer at their Chalmette refinery. He led planning and executing the expansion of the Chalmette refinery during the late 1950s. When management acknowledged they had a problem in Marketing he was elevated to Vice President of Planning for Refining and Marketing. He led the team in de-centralizing and restructuring the entire petroleum marketing function. Then he and many others worked the problem of retail marketing that created the food store and self-service gasoline marketing systems. After serving as Sr. VP of Marketing he was elected Ex VP of Refining and Marketing, then President of Tenneco Oil 1974-78 and President of P&M 1978-82. After this he served as Chairman of Tenneco Oil and Sr. VP and Group Executive of Tenneco Inc. until 1986 and as Consultant until 1988. He also served on the Board of Directors of the API and on the National Advisory Board of Georgia Institute of Technology.

After Tenneco he was elected a director of Interhome Energy Inc. and Chairman and CEO of Texas Eastern Products Pipeline.

had several mines operating in Nevada. The operation was a financial success.

The enterprise, with its gold ore reserves, had a higher market value as a part of a gold mining company than as a part of a conglomerate company and thus it was sold in 1987 for financial benefit.

After the sale of the gold ore reserves the division re-entered precious metals exploration and developed two mines before it was sold in 1992

XII. Chemical Division Of Tenneco Oil

When Tenneco entered the aromatic petro-chemicals business in 1961, marketing of those products as well as LPG's was done under the direction of Dewey Mark. He did a great job in putting Tenneco's name before the chemical industry and even was named President of the NPRA Chemical Div., an organization of industry representatives. Later, Carol Belton headed Tenneco's petrochemical and LPG sales.

When Petro-Tex, a manufacturer of butadiene, was transferred into the group, Gordon Cain was the principal leader. Following him was Harry O'Connell and then Russell Bowers.

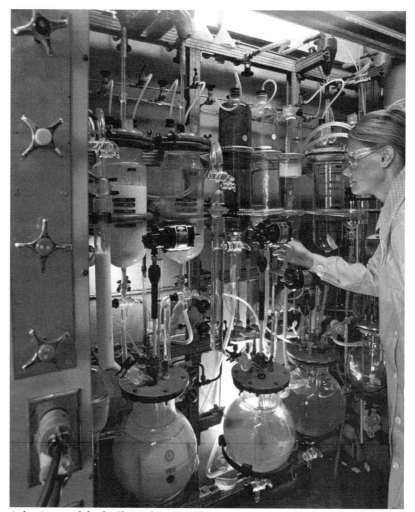

A chemist at work for the Chemical Division of Tenneco Oil.

Upon the dissolution of Tenneco Chemicals Co. the vinyl chloride, phthalic anhydride and methanol operations or joint venture interests, under the direction of Guy Disch, were transferred to Tenneco P&M. These facilities were built during the early popularity of vinyl chloride and before the product became a mass produced commodity. In the mid-1980s all of these functions were organized into the Chemical Division of Tenneco Oil and led by Russell Bowers. Petro-Tex and the vinyl-chloride related business were sold upon opportunity in the late 1980s.

XIII. Sale of Processing & Marketing

Tenneco Oil Company (integrated E&P plus P&M), in 1988 had a book asset value of $5,940 million . It had 951 million net equivalent barrels of oil and gas (salable) reserves (1987 yearend). It had earned cumulatively $5,020 million (operating income) over the prior ten years. It had good value and was marketable immediately. The employees had made it valuable. They had done a great job.

Due to severe financial problems of other Tenneco Inc. units, the parent company had depleted its financial reserves by 1988. The Board of Directors elected to raise cash late that year by selling the entire Tenneco Oil Company in segments to the highest bidders to avoid debt covenant default. The event is covered elsewhere in this book.

RALPH S. CUNNINGHAM

In 1980, Ralph S. Cunningham joined Tenneco Oil Processing and Marketing as Executive Vice President. Ralph received a B.S. in Chemical Engineering degree from Auburn University in 1962, a M.S. from Ohio State in 1964, and a Ph. D from Ohio State in 1966. He came to Tenneco following 14 years with Exxon. He managed Exxon's refinery at Benicia, California before coming to Houston to serve in Exxon's corporate planning group. He moved to Exxon's Baytown refinery in 1966 and, after several promotions, became refinery manager of Exxon's huge Benicia refinery in 1977.

In 1982 as Cliff Rackley assumed greater responsibilities for synthetic fuels and several other Tenneco Inc. subsidiaries, Ralph was named President of Tenneco Oil Processing & Marketing. After the sale of Tenneco Oil Processing & Marketing in 1988, Ralph served, successively, as CEO of Clark Oil, Texaco Chemical, Huntsman Corporation, and later, as CEO of Citgo. He continues to serve on several boards, including Tetra Technologies and Enterprise Products.

Ralph was instrumental in consolidating the vinyl chloride, phthalic anhydride, and methanol interests into Tenneco Oil Processing and Marketing, creating a Chemicals Division of Tenneco Oil P&M.

III

TENNECO OIL
EXPLORATION & PRODUCTION

1946 ~ 1988

By Harry Briscoe

Gauging an early gas well around 1951 at Hungerford Unit, the company's first gas field.

E&P FOUNDATIONS

Beginning at the End

On October 10, 1988, Wayne Nance, President of Tenneco Oil Exploration and Production Company, sat at his desk in Houston, shuffling papers and returning phone calls to a few close friends, but his heart was not in the work of the day. He was waiting to hear the results of the bids that would be disclosed shortly; bids that would identify the successful purchasers of the company he ran; bids that would define the end of his own life's work. Nance thought of the data rooms just closed that had revealed all the facts and details about the quality of the company's assets, and all of its secrets. He thought with pride of the exceptional work that employees throughout the company had done in preparing the company for sale and in continuing to operate the properties during the process. By drilling new prospects they had added value to the company in an effort to increase the value of the bids. He thought of the employees and his hopes for making them part of the deal, for making sure they had jobs. He felt helpless to do anything further. There was nothing to do but wait, and finally to think about the future. It had not even occurred to him to wonder about that. What to do? Take a year off? Look for another job? But again, his attention wandered. All he could imagine was the upcoming heartbreak that would mark the end for what had been such a special company.

Throughout the company, in all of its operating locations around the country and the world, 2112 TOE&P employees, and another 1500 in the subsidiaries, were planning their own futures, as best they could, and wondering in retrospect, "just what had happened". Those winning bidders would soon be known, and that would define the end for them as well, even if they did not lose their jobs. There was no doubt things were going to change. There was no place like Tenneco Oil. Multiple purchasers would soon claim their own respective geographic pieces of an exceptional and diverse inventory of assets, and that would be that.

Across the street in the Tenneco, Inc. headquarters building, Joe Foster was tying up the loose ends of his attempt to save parts of the company with a Leveraged Buy Out. Foster, with full approval of the parent company and the board of directors, had quickly assembled a team, made their own evaluations, and arranged financing to submit bids for key parts of the company. Foster knew that the difficult economics of the year would make winning a challenge, and probably a surprise. Although now a senior executive and Board member for the parent company Tenneco Inc., Foster had worked for Tenneco Oil during most of his 32-year career. His contributions to the growth and success of the company were inarguable, but like the rest of the employees, he was uncertain as to the future.

Steve Chesebro's days – and nights – during the summer of 1988 were full. Chesebro' was another career-long Tenneco Oil employee, 24-years' worth, but earlier in the year he had been moved to a new job as President of Tenneco Gas Marketing to further transition the dynamic gas business. Early in May, Tenneco Inc. CEO Jim Ketelsen tapped him to manage the sale of the company. He undertook this job with little choice and very mixed emotions, his strongest commitments being to the E&P employees. During a summer filled with requests from investment bankers, potential purchasers and prior colleagues he'd had precious little time for private thought to reconcile the two jobs - selling the company that had been responsible for his entire 24-year career - and managing what was to remain of Tenneco's energy business. The corporation had decided to keep the pipeline as it was a primary cash source, something the manufacturing interests sorely needed.

The employees themselves were tired. In predictable fashion they had taken up a considerable job for the year. It was not the one they had planned for 1988. Instead of looking for and producing oil and gas around the world, they instead were challenged with packaging, marketing and selling the company. They approached the challenge with the same zeal they'd used throughout their own careers. The actual summer of selling became one of the greatest projects of their careers. Budgets had been re-allocated, projects accelerated or re-directed, and priorities for everything changed. The urgency to the task was palpable and they had performed admirably, but now it was done. All was suddenly quiet, and it was time to think forward.

On October 11, 1988 the high bids were revealed. Considerable work of

**President Profile
H. GARDINER SYMONDS
1946-1950**

Gardiner Symonds was a geologist by training. He was born in Pittsburgh and educated at Stanford. He became the first president of TGT when it was formed in 1943. Symonds assumed the role of President of the 'first' Tenneco Oil in 1946 and served in that role until 1950. By all analyses he was the founder, the primary architect and the builder of what would become the Tenneco Inc. empire. During his career the corporation became the only industrial entity to attain more than $3 billion in assets within its initial 25 years of existence. He served as Chairman of Tenneco until his death in 1971.

You won't know the players without a program, so here's the list of name changes oveR the life of the company.

1943 - **Tennessee Gas and Transmission Co.** chartered.

1946 - Formed **The Coast Company** as a subsidiary of Tennessee Gas and Transmission Company

1947 - Parent dropped "and" from its name – **Tennessee Gas Transmission Company (TGT)**

1950 - Coast acquired by Sterling Oil & Refining Company, with Coast owning 40% of Sterling

1951 - TGT acquires 99.8% of Sterling; name changed to **Tennessee Production Company (TPC)**

1959 - **Tennessee Gas and Oil (TGO)** incorporated to replace Tennessee Production Company

1961 - Name changed to **Tenneco Oil Company (TOC)**, a subsidiary of **Tenneco Corporation**, which in turn was a subsidiary of TGT

1966 - **Tenneco Inc.** adopted as the name for the parent company, TGT and TOC as subsidiaries

1978 - **Tenneco Oil Exploration & Production (TOE&P)** and **Tenneco Oil Processing & Marketing (TOP&M)** formed as separate independent subsidiaries of Tenneco Inc.

closing and transition remained, but in fact, it was done. The fourteenth-largest oil company in the world, and an admired industry leader and competitor was soon to be – gone. Tenneco Oil, over 40 years in the making, was being sold, not because it had failed, but because it had been exceptionally successful… and because its parent company desperately needed the money. This is the story of how that company was built, and of its demise.

The Coast Company and Origins of TOE&P

The story of Tenneco Oil, Exploration and Production (TOE&P) is dynamic tale. That name alone, the name at the end, was just the "last" one. Tenneco Oil E&P evolved, in name and in form, over a period covering more than 40 years, from its founding in 1946 to its eventual sale in 1988. TOE&P had five different names during that history. Each new name along the way reflected the evolving personality of the company. Throughout its history, TOE&P was either a subsidiary of, or an affiliate of, other companies. Tennessee Gas Transmission (TGT) company was the parent of "Tenneco Oil" until 1966, so to that point in time the story of E&P was really the continuing story of TGT. Initially, the affiliated companies had complementary or related business strategies within the energy industry, and each benefited from synergies with the other.

Later, the corporation itself evolved into a complex conglomerate of disparate businesses, most of which had little in common with their siblings or with the original mission. The sometimes conflicting priorities amongst those many tentacles of Tenneco, Inc. figure prominently into the history of TOE&P. Tenneco Oil "E&P" was a major part of the Tenneco story.

From its own founding in 1943, the business of TGT was to construct pipelines and transport natural gas from fields in the south to market destinations in the mid- and north-eastern regions of the country. TGT grew at an impressive pace, and contracting for supplies of natural gas to keep the pipelines full was a major part of the business. The company eventually known as Tenneco Oil E&P evolved as an independent strategy within the Tennessee Gas and Transmission Company to help accomplish that need. The company that would become TOE&P came to be as the result of geologic curiosity.

* * * * *

Inside a pipeline company, the "reserves guy" was an important employee. Financing for new pipelines was always contingent upon having secure reserves to transport. In the fall of 1946, R. C. Graham, a petroleum engineer serving as Chief Geologist for Tennessee Gas (TGT), was evaluating a gas field southwest of Houston. Mr. Graham's job was to confirm the reserves that provided the supply to TGT pipelines, and to testify to the Federal Power Commission as to their extent. With this particular evaluation however, Graham's interest was focused not only to the producing wells, but also to some undeveloped property nearby. His analysis of the reservoir performance from the field led him to conclude the field held undeveloped potential. He was certain that adjacent un-leased acreage contained low-risk drilling opportunities that the company could develop for its own account.

Convinced by his sales pitch, TGT management agreed to take its first drilling lease, just west of the Hungerford Field in Wharton Co., TX. Since this strategy would mark TGT's first diversification beyond the regulated gas transmission business, TGT formed a new subsidiary. The Coast Company was chartered on September 19, 1946 with an initial capitalization of $100,000. The stated objective of the Coast Company was to discover and produce natural gas. Gardiner Symonds, President of TGT, assumed the same role and title with The Coast Company. R. C. Graham was named General Superintendent. Later that year the first well, the Hungerford Gas Unit #1 was spud, and the era of the Tenneco Oil Company had begun. Mr. Graham's intuitions proved correct as five of eight initial wells drilled at Hungerford during 1947 and 1948 were productive. The first three wells had initial flow rates of 85, 148, and 16 million cubic feet of gas per day (MMCFD), a successful, but hardly auspicious start.

Building By Buying

Since its own founding in 1943, Tennessee Gas had grown rapidly through internal expansion of the federally-regulated pipeline business. A desire to expand into non-regulated businesses to balance the portfolio was responsible for

**President Profile
R. G. RICE
1950-1954**

Rice, a native Texan and graduate of Baylor Law School, worked in the Land and Geological department at the Coast Company, joining TGT when it was formed in 1943. He was elected President of Sterling Oil & Refining when it acquired the Coast Company in 1950 and then became President of Tennessee Production Company when it was formed as the production arm for TGT 1951. He managed the early expansions into West Texas and New Mexico.

A Tennessee Production Company pumping unit in the Prentice Field in West Texas in 1952.

"*The* company (TOC) was so small at first, we really weren't conscious of it. It became much more recognizable in 1950 with the purchase of Sterling Oil."

*- Lurline Diener
Property Records Clerk*

163

**President Profile
RALPH C. GRAHAM
1955-1960**

Graham graduated from the Missouri School of Mines with a degree in Petroleum Engineering in 1931. He joined TGT in 1945 and served as chief geologist from 1945 to 1949. He was Senior VP of the Production Division from 1949 to 1954. From 1955 through 1960 he was President of the evolving E&P business, under a variety of company names, including the "first" Tenneco Oil Company in 1960. By the end of his career Tenneco had operations in 24 states, six foreign countries, and offshore Louisiana. He died in 1986.

a comment to a group of security analysts in New York, Gardiner Symonds predicted that "Tennessee Production Co. could be the gem of our subsidiary companies."

Mr. Symonds' principal strategy, that of growing by acquisition. Growth by new drilling on the acquired assets would prove to be a complementary effort. The plan with dual objectives would serve Tenneco Oil well for the next 40 years.

By 1949, the well count at Hungerford had grown to ten, and Coast opened a district office in Victoria, TX to manage the properties. The company began looking for properties to add to the portfolio. The first acquisition for The Coast Company came with the purchase of Portilla Drilling Co. for $1.5 million. Portilla owned 23 wells on 767 acres in the Heyser Field in Calhoun and Victoria Counties, Texas. Although the Portilla properties were a natural extension of the initial strategy of acquiring additional gas reserves in proximity to the TGT pipelines, the wells also included the company's first oil producers, and with those came the first departure from the focus on gas alone. Baby steps can lead to unexpected places. The E&P company owned over 1 billion net equivalent barrels (NEBs) of proven oil reserves when it was sold in 1988 (over 2 billion NEB including probable and possible reserves). No doubt few among Coast's initial 30 employees would imagine that their little company would eventually support a workforce of over 3500 good folks and their families.

Through a series of transactions during 1949 and 1950 TGT acquired a majority interest in Sterling Oil & Refining Co. The Sterling purchase added 145 wells on 62 productive leases holding reserves of 6.5 million barrels of oil (MMBO) and 114 billion cubic feet of gas (BCFG). As with Portilla, the Sterling purchase brought expansion. The new properties more than quadrupled Coast's well count and moved TGT (Coast) into areas that were no longer geographically tied to the TGT pipelines.

In 1949 TG&T sold the Coast Company to Sterling in exchange for 40 percent of Sterling's stock. Just weeks later, Sterling's employees moved to TGT's offices in the Commerce Building in downtown Houston. Then, almost exactly a year later, TGT acquired the remaining Sterling stock and made the company a subsidiary.

Why was the purchase handled in that manner? Harold Burrow, TGT purchasing agent at the time, (later President of TGT) speculates, "We probably didn't have the money to buy it outright. Sterling wanted new management, so we took over the management in '49, before we had the money to buy it."

The early years of Tenneco Oil were marked by a struggle to survive. Acquisitions, not exploration, drove the Coast Company's earliest activities. "Tenneco was built on purchases and acquisitions, starting with Sterling Oil," says B.E., "Des", Desadier, who joined the company as a junior draftsman about 18 months after its founding. Des retired as Chief Geological Engineer a year or so before the 1988 sale.

In 1951 The Coast Company was dissolved, replaced by a new entity named the Tennessee Production Co. (TPC), with R.G. Rice as its President. Rice had been Ralph Graham's supervisor at the time of the recommendation to take those first leases at Hungerford. In a comment to a group of security analysts in New York, Gardiner Symonds predicted that "Tennessee Production Co. could be the gem of our subsidiary companies." Most at TOE&P would agree that his prediction came true, and held through the sale of the company in 1988.

Acquisitions came quickly as TPC purchased the remaining interests in the Hungerford field from the Chicago Corporation in 1951, and bought independents Frankel & Frankel for $9 million and York & Harper, at a then-astounding price of $10.4 million; $21,000 per share, in 1952. These purchases included operations in south and west Texas, Louisiana, Mississippi, Arkansas and New Mexico. The gem of York & Harper was the Prentice Field in the Permian Basin of West Texas, a property that would still be going strong 35 years later when the company was sold. The "oil" company had grown to own 276 producing oil and gas wells, and 30,000 acres of non-producing leases. These leases became the target properties for the growing exploration effort.

By 1952, the still young subsidiary had grown to the point of needing independent financing, and 51% of TPC was sold in a public offering, with TGT retaining the balance. Also in 1952, the Del Ray Petroleum Co. acquisition brought another profit center to the portfolio with the company's first gas processing plant. M & M Production came next, and Reno Oil Co. was added in 1953, effectively doubling the size of the company's production base to about 5000 net equivalent barrels of oil per day (NEBOPD).

By year-end 1953, a district exploration office had been opened in Corpus Christi, and TGT valued its 48.7% of TPC at $10.7MM. With M&M and Reno, TPC had added properties in Texas, Oklahoma, New Mexico, Colorado, and the Appalachians. Extensive exploration acreage in the Rockies provided the seeds for TOE&P's long-time presence in that province. These deals also brought the first interests in Canada.

The company was restructured in 1954 to take advantage of a favorable court ruling that changed some tax and operating rules regarding regulated and non-regulated businesses. Tenneco Production Company was merged back into TGT as a subsidiary. The merger was a milestone of sorts for the company and allowed consolidation of assets and financial structure, a fact that would result in tax savings in the years ahead. Following the merger, the company owned 54,991 net producing acres, 242,873 net acres of yet unproven land, 858 net oil and gas wells, three major gas processing plants in Texas and minor interests in four others. Ralph Graham, the geologist responsible for the first wells at Hungerford, was named President of TPC.

Far West Oil Co., with properties in Wyoming, came next, acquired in early 1955 for $5 million. Far West brought the South Glenrock field in Wyoming producing 1600 BOPD. The field would contribute for many years. At year-end 1955 the company was producing 14,000 BOPD and 37MMCFD.

Gardiner Symonds, as CEO of TGT, continued to guide the overall effort, but by the mid-1950s saw the need to add additional high-level management. Among the first of these was a young geologist named Wilton E. Scott who came to TGT in 1955 from Buffalo Oil Company in Hobbs, NM. Scott went to work in Houston as manager of exploration for the company. Mr. Scott's Tenneco career included ten years as President of the E&P operation and seven more in the upper management of the parent Tenneco Inc. His impact on Tenneco E&P was substantial.

Turning Points

Tenneco Oil Company grew steadily over the years, but as with most successful ventures, there were several particularly significant individual events along the way. These were the "turning points" that altered the long-term direction or the fortunes of the company. Some of these significant events came in the form of acquisitions or major deals of one sort or another, others as specific discoveries, and still others as timely strategic decisions that affected the entire company. Throughout this story of TOE&P those events, happenings and decisions will be discussed more or less as they occurred. The first major Turning Point for the still-young company came nine years after the founding.

Bay Petroleum

The purchase of Bay Petroleum in 1955 was important for several reasons. The targets for the acquisition were primarily Bay's producing properties in the Rockies and the mid-Continent provinces. The purchase also brought TGT's first significant exposure outside the United States, with assets in Canada. But the "Turning Point" implication of Bay lay in its creation of Tenneco's first refining and marketing business units. CEO Symonds' long-range plan was to build the young company into a fully-integrated and competitive player in the oil and gas industry. The addition of refining and marketing to the Tenneco portfolio included the Chalmette refinery in Louisiana, a smaller refinery in Denver and marketing outlets in the Rockies. Those assets would initiate the growth of what would become Tenneco Oil Processing & Marketing (P&M) and allow the evolution into a fully-integrated oil and gas company to continue.

One of the first important projects that Wilton Scott was assigned was participation in the evaluation of Bay. He had worked on a similar mission in his prior employment and was familiar with the properties. Years later he recalled an interesting story regarding the project. Scott accompanied Gardiner Symonds on the trip to Denver to make the offer:

"Gardiner Symonds and I sat down at the table in a Denver hotel with the Bay people. I knew just about everyone there. One guy there had given me my first job as a young- buck geologist."

"Symonds told them, 'Gentlemen we're here to talk about buying Bay

Being of sound mind. At the time of the negotiations to purchase Bay Petroleum, C. U. Bay, the principal owner, had just undergone extensive brain surgery. In order to protect the Company from future charges by Bay's heirs that he was mentally incompetent at the time that the deal was negotiated, the Company brought in "a fleet of M.D.s" who had treated Bay both prior to and after his operation. They confirmed through affidavits that he was in a sound state of mind when the sale was made.

One of Bay Petroleum's "Red Dot" service stations purchased by the Tenneco Oil Compay in 1955.

Petroleum. We'll offer you $24 million.' They were stunned. Gardiner was that kind of a guy -- direct. Well, after a long silence, Bob Brothers, a fellow I knew, said, 'Mr. Symonds, we don't have the authority to even entertain an offer. We'll have to let you know.'"

"So Gardiner said, 'Well, when can we expect an answer?' Brothers said, 'How about after lunch?' So we went back to our hotel and waited by the phone." (former TOC President George Meason later commented that the Bay group had probably spent the lunch hour shaking hands with each other). "About 1:30, they called. They said Mr. Bay was not available -- we knew he was very ill -- and that they had spoken to Mrs. Bay. But they said that they had some more work to do before they could decide on our offer."

"Well, Gardiner knew they wanted to sell. It would just be a matter of time. So he told me 'You stay in Denver. I'm going back to Houston. We're going to buy it.' And we did, in June, 1955, for $24 million. And that put us into refining and marketing, and into the Rockies, the mid-Continent and Canada in a substantial way."

* * * * *

The acquisitions continued with Kirkpatrick Oil Company, Red Dot and Dixie in 1956. Negotiations to acquire Middle States Petroleum Corporation began in 1957. Middle States was the company's largest acquisition target to date with holdings of oil and gas reserves in seven southwestern states and Canada. Among the assets were 522 net producing wells, production facilities capable of producing 6,100 barrels of oil and 42 MMCF of natural gas per day, and more than 300,000 undeveloped acres. The deal was done in 1958.

Early Hiring

While the foundations of TGT and the original Coast Company lay in the Gulf Coast region, the acquisitions of the first half of the 1950s created activity for the company in many of the traditional oil and gas provinces of

"The company was not as specialized then as it is today. I was a petroleum engineer but I wore three hats and worked as a reservoir, drilling and production engineer."

- Bill Melnar (VP DGM, GCD)

O. W. "TINY " WARD

The York & Harper acquisition brought a young district production superintendent in West Texas. O. W. "Tiny" Ward would supervise the drilling of 26 successful wells in the Glorietta and Clearfork formations. Mr. Ward had a long and successful career managing Tenneco operations in many locales, and serving in numerous executive positions throughout the company locations, including his years in Canada and the Pacific Coast Division overseeing the development of the Kern County Land properties. He retired in September of 1976 as Senior Vice-President and General Manager of the Gulf Coast Division.

the United States. By 1956 the company was drilling hundreds of wells per year on their new properties. To manage the activity, offices were opened in Oklahoma City, Denver and Bellaire, Texas. TPC's production had jumped to 34,000 BOPD and natural gas deliveries were 91.5 MMCFD. Over the years, TOE&P's work would create offices throughout the world.

The rapid growth and expansion accelerated the need for new talent at all levels within the organization. From 1946 into the early 1950s the workforce and employee count grew somewhat more by opportunity than by design, depending on the locations of the acquired operations. Most of the work involved field operations, and many of the effective supervisors and managers of the early days came with backgrounds in operations. The need for specific talents, involving precise training and technical education, led the young company to consider selective recruitment of college graduates directly from their schools, in addition to adding talent from industry sources.

In 1956 the company employed its first college recruits, among them Bob Thomas from the University of Oklahoma (who would go on to become President, Chairman and CEO of Tenneco Gas), G P Walker III, Joe Abel and Richard Wheeler from the Colorado School of Mines. Joe Foster (who would go on to become Executive Vice-President of Tenneco Inc.) joined the company from the Texas A&M class of 1957. He was one of five college recruits in engineering that year. TGT accessed the colleges for numerous new recruits for accounting and administrative positions, as well as for the technical ones.

J. B. Foster on his TGT Interview

"I went to Texas A&M and got degrees in petroleum engineering and in business administration. I went to work right out of school for Tennessee Gas Transmission Company, but that was not by design. I had no plans to interview with TGT. I had my mind made up to go to work for Exxon (called Humble at the time). I had worked for them the two previous summers. I was over at the placement office to take care of a little bit of business. While I was waiting for my appointment the receptionist called me over and said, 'There are some guys from Tennessee Gas here. It's their first visit to A&M and nobody has interviewed with them all day. Would you mind talking to them?' Since the supply of magazines in the waiting area was pretty poor, I said, 'Sure.'

I did that, and was impressed enough to come back the next day in my suit and tie. I interviewed again, and they knocked my socks off. This was a growing, well-funded pipeline company just beginning to diversify into the oil and gas production business. Their Chief Engineer was only in his early 30's. The starting salary was not as high as Humble's, but they would assign me a company car, and they liked the fact that I was getting a business degree in addition to the engineering one. Humble had made it clear it was the engineer they were after. The TGT guys wound up convincing me that Humble was the second choice to Tennessee Gas.

Those early recruiters were John Fry from TGT Employee Relations, and Marshall Jeffers, himself a recently-hired engineer. Funny how little things sometimes make a big difference."

* * * * *

Jack Gregory (VP, DGM INT at sale) was another early college recruit, hired from Oklahoma University in 1957. Both Foster and Gregory started their Tenneco careers in Oklahoma City. (Foster noted that he was assigned to the "old hand" Dick Wheeler for training – a one-year veteran). Wayne Nance (President in 1987 and 1988) signed on in 1958, after six years with Amoco. Nance was assigned to the Odessa district field office in West Texas. Bob Taylor, (VP and GM, CGD) came in 1958 as did Bill Melnar (VP DGM, GCD at sale), from the University of Texas. Bill Medary joined the company as a geologist in West Texas and New Mexico and later moved to Lafayette as the offshore exploration manager. George H. Meason, whose career included service as president of Tenneco Oil from 1970-74, was hired in 1956.

Dr. Philip Oxley (President from 1981-1987) joined TPC in 1957 as District Geologist in New Orleans. None could imagine the impact he would have on the organization over the next 30 years. Dr. Oxley's name appears frequently throughout this text, and a more detailed profile and biography will appear later. Suffice it to say at this point, that "Dr. Phil" was one of the most genuine and beloved of all the Tenneco managers. He was also one of the most unique and one of the most talented. Oxley had an eclectic personality, skill set and personal manner that provided not only an exceptional contribution to the efforts of the business, but also projected a sense of trust, respect and comfort for and from the employees. He was a genuine gentleman.

In 1957 the company acquired its first interests in the Gulf of Mexico with the "Phillips Purchase." S.V. "Schacht" McCollum was recruited from Conoco to be the general manager of the new "Southeastern Division" with responsibility for Gulf Coast onshore and offshore operations. Jack Ray, a charismatic leader and one of the real pioneers of many of TOE&P's business practices and strategies, came from Magnolia to manage production and operations for the newly-formed Lafayette Offshore District. While "characters" abounded throughout Tenneco Oil E&P in those days, the ones leading the Southeastern Division were quite a crew. Jack Ray, was a great story teller who was profanely funny. Phil Oxley had a sarcasm which bit, because it was often so true. Bill Medary could doze off in a meeting, and awake to make a profound observation. Joe Foster, a young petroleum engineer who sat in many meetings with this group because he was doing lease sale economics, generally spoke only when spoken to, but listened well.

In retrospect, it seems remarkable that many of these early hires would stay with the company, indeed that they would run it at a point 30 years into the future. On the other hand, maybe that fact is simply demonstrative of the reality that Tenneco was a special place, even in those earliest days. In soliciting

DANIEL B. JOHNSON

In addition to property, the Reno acquisition brought a young engineer named Daniel B. Johnson to TPC. Johnson's Tenneco career would continue for 36 years, through the sale in 1988. Mr. Johnson would play a key role in many of Tenneco's most significant future activities and business practices. Dan served as Division Production Superintendent in Wichita Falls, Tx, Division Production Manager in both Oklahoma City and Denver, as VP Production for Tenneco Oil and Minerals in Calgary, as VP and General Manager for the Lafayette Offshore Division. In the offshore he was instrumental in lease sale bid determination, and in spearheading an effort by geological engineers in the production department to generate lower risk "exploitation" prospects in the Gulf of Mexico. He played a key role in establishing Operators Inc. as Tenneco Oil E&P's field operations unit, which resulted in significant production operating cost reductions. He subsequently became Senior Vice President in Houston for the Production and Operations side of Tenneco Oil E&P. Dan emphasized the need for reserve additions to exceed annual production, the need to hire top flight graduates directly from the colleges, and the importance of exploration and production working together at all levels of the organization. In short, Dan Johnson was intimately involved in nearly every significant program or policy that TOE&P developed. He was a trusted and quietly-effective mentor to many aspiring young supervisors and managers in their climb up the Tenneco Oil E&P ladder. Johnson is retired and lives on his ranch near Giddings, TX.

comments and stories for this book, "Hiring Well" was frequently referenced as a key factor responsible for the company's success. Certainly, the early management of the company did some very good hiring during the late 1950s.

Beyond the Borders

Although the "acquire-and-drill" strategy of the 1950s created a base for the young enterprise, the company always looked to expand its horizons. TPC began to investigate and invest in opportunities outside of North America in 1955 and from then through the mid-1960s Tenneco committed efforts to a variety of international venues. In the late 1950s TGT also took its first steps into the offshore province with pipeline operations there.

Early International Steps

In the mid-1950s Tennessee Gas began looking for oil beyond the boundaries of the United States. International properties were attractive since they were beyond the regulatory reach of the Federal Power Commission and TGT was still primarily a regulated business. Tennessee found itself owning producing properties in Canada following the Bay Petroleum acquisition in 1955 and the Mid-States purchase in 1958. In 1958, TGT established Tennessee

MRS, SYMONDS, "YOU CONTACT ME DIRECT"

"In 1958, Mr. and Mrs. Symonds visited the field camp in Yacuiba, Bolivia, Tenneco Oil and Gas' first international operations. My wife and I were the only U.S. family living in this small town with no electricity, running water, or paved streets. While Mr. Symonds toured the office and reviewed our activities, Mrs. Symonds hosted an afternoon tea at our home that included several Bolivian women who had given us a warm welcome to their small town. It was a wonderful lift to the spirits of a young couple so far from home, especially when Mrs. Symond's last words were, "If you need absolutely anything, you contact me direct, and I'll see that Daddy has it sent to you."

- R L Leggett (Admin, SAD)

Oil operations were extended into Canada in 1955; this was the Company's first well in Alberta.

Overseas Co. to own and direct business ventures outside of North America. The Canadian E&P operations resulted in an 11.5MMBOE field discovery in Alberta in 1957. This was in an area in which Tennessee Gas had operated the Midwestern pipeline project since 1955. In November of 1959, TGT built a gas processing plant to handle production from its Rosedale field in Alberta. Drilling was extended to British Columbia in 1962, with the completion of a well in the Wildmint Field. Tenneco E&P maintained activity in Canada through 1982 when all operations there were sold for $111MM.

In 1956, TGT, along with Union, Lion and Murphy Oil had formed a consortium called TULM to pursue opportunities in Venezuela, a country with a substantial oil reserve and a track record with major international companies. TGT ended up with a 15% interest in an operation near Lake Maracaibo. By the end of 1959 the concession was producing an impressive 5100 BOPD net to TGT's interest. As the production increased though, so did the government's demand for a higher and higher share of the spoils. Adjustments to the revenue-sharing agreements reduced the TGT share to the point the project could only be described as a modest economic success.

The TULM group took a position in Bolivia in 1957. This operation was troubled from the start, plagued by the problems of operating in a then-primitive country with little infrastructure or operational support. Logistical problems were compounded by a lack of significant discoveries. For six years the company tried to make something of its commitment to Bolivia but finally abandoned all of the operations there in 1962. A venture in Ecuador, commencing in 1958, included a "broken-down" refinery, 198 producing wells, and exploration acreage, but investments between 1958 and 1961 had not produced favorable economic returns and the company cut its losses with a sale of its position in 1962. A subsidiary in Colombia was formed in 1961. Initial wells were successful and production was established from the Dina Field, but political instability forced a sell-out in the late 1960s. Years later, through the acquisition of Houston Oil & Minerals, Tenneco Oil would return to Colombia, this time with a much more favorable outcome.

Tennessee's E&P efforts in South America also included a major venture in Argentina. In 1959, the TGT subsidiary, Tennessee Argentina, SA, partnered with the state-owned oil company Yacimientos Petroliferos Fiscales (YPF) on a 3.5 million acre concession in Tierra del Fuego, the remote island province at the southern tip of South America. By mid-1960 the partnership employed five hundred people and owned 44 producing wells, 27 of which had come by new drilling. Among the employees were geologist Rod Leland, an eventual manager in the Gulf of Mexico and other TOC International ventures, and Roy Patterson, who would have a long career as an administrative manager in many locales. At year-end 1960 the partnership in Argentina was profitably producing more than 20,000 barrels of oil per day from the La Sara field, and the future looked bright for TGT's foreign aspirations. Unfortunate-

NOT EXACTLY THE WELCOME WAGON

Tenneco established its first position in Nigeria in 1960 and quickly made several encouraging discoveries. In 1966 and 1967 however, political issues, resulting eventually in a civil war, hit home for Don Taylor (SVP at time of the sale in 1988) and his family in a big way. Discord between the Christian Igbo people from the south and the Muslim Hausa-Fulani in the north escalated quickly. The war became one of genocide with the Muslim Hausas attempting to cleanse the country of Igbos and Christians. Don and Barbara Taylor had a house outside Lagos, and as with many foreign assignments, were able to employ local residents as staff to help manage the home. The resident staff of employees who worked for the Taylors were southern Igbos. Rampaging groups of Hausas set about the countryside collecting all of the Igbos they could find, carting them off to prisons or murdering them outright. One night an overloaded pickup truck full of machine-gun toting Hausas swept onto the Taylor's property headed straight for the staff quarters. Their targets were the cook, Benjamin, and his brother Sam, who was actually a Tenneco employee, living with his brother in the staff quarters at Taylor's house. Taylor ran out of the house onto the roadway waving a handful of money hoping to buy the freedom of his employees. Rather than stop, the loaded pickup truck ran right at him. A soldier leaned over and whacked Don in the head with his rifle as the truck swerved by, knocking him into the roadside ditch. He watched helplessly as his terrified friends were carted off into the night. Don and Barbara feared the worst for their staff. Very shortly after that event Tenneco shut down their operations in Nigeria and transferred the Taylors, and also co-worker Gene Pollock and his wife Leslie, to the new office in Ventura, California. Some months after relocating, the Taylors received a letter from Benjamin. He and Sam had managed to talk their way out of execution but were still in prison in Nigeria. Don made contact with authorities and sent a sum of money to buy their freedom. Nigeria in the 1960's was not a comfortable place for a couple in their early-30's, with two children of their own.

ly, and probably because of the success, Tenneco would soon discover another risk to foreign operations when the Argentine government, in Nov. 1963, by presidential decree, decided to Nationalize the concession. After years of legal wrangling, TGT left Argentina in 1965 with $42.3MM in compensation – again, a mixed result to show for the efforts expended.

Foreign activities were not limited to the Americas. In 1957 TGT took positions in Spain and the Sahara Desert. In 1960 TGT established Tennessee Nigeria and obtained a prospecting license to nearly 1.3 million acres in that country's West African seacoast. By 1961 the Nigerian leasehold had grown to 2.24 million acres and the company had conducted extensive geological and geophysical surveys. Subsidiaries in Sierra Leone and Turkey were established in 1961 but operations ended in 1963. Exploration in Australia occurred in 1962, and during 1962 and 1963, Tenneco drilled three dry holes in Nigeria. In 1963 Sinclair International and Sunray DX bought in with a fifty-percent share in the Nigerian venture. Success finally came in 1965 and by 1966 the joint-venture owned 12 commercially successful wells. As in Argentina earlier, success in Nigeria though, would fall victim to political instability.

In summary, TGT's international expansions produced mixed results for the Company during the period from 1955 to 1965. Ironically, the Canadian properties that came first proved to be fairly successful and long-lived. Tenneco's most significant international success was to come years later.

Wading In – Early Steps Offshore

The state of Louisiana began leasing its offshore state waters shortly after World War II, and early activity there proved that the Gulf of Mexico contained large reserves of oil and gas. In 1957 Tennessee Production Company (TPC) undertook its first drilling in the Gulf of Mexico, with a "farm-in" (earned a partial working interest an operations by paying for a share of the owner's drilling costs) on a portion of South Timbalier Block 22. The well was not completed as a producer, but it did encounter sufficient hydrocarbons to hold the lease. There was a certain irony to this in that this marginal deposit adjoined the South Timbalier Block 21 field, owned by Gulf. Subsequent successful drilling on ST 22 led to TPC's first piece of a huge field. The South Timbalier 21/22 complex had produced over 325 million BOE, and was still cranking out 1000BOPD when the company was sold, thirty years later, and Tenneco's small original piece on the south-half of Block 22 was still contributing to that total.

At the same time, Tennessee Gas, having decided it was more tax-efficient and less risky to operate in the Gulf under the corporate umbrella, opened an offshore Louisiana exploration office in New Orleans. A staff was assembled, seismic data was acquired, and intensive geological and geophysical studies of the Outer Continental Shelf off Louisiana were commenced, initially out to a water depth of about 120'. Geology was favorable and TGT became one of the early operators in this nearly virgin territory. "Built from Scratch," certainly describes the early efforts in the Gulf of Mexico.

New district geologist Philip Oxley had been hired to help the company get into the new province. He must have done a good job. Oxley would retire in 1987, after serving his last seven years as President of Tenneco Oil E&P. As one of his retirement gifts he received a small bottle of oil from that original property at ST 22, oil from its 29 millionth barrel of production.

The big plunge into leasing property and drilling in the Gulf took place in 1959. The company acquired 29,400 acres in two state of Louisi-

Offshore operations commenced in the Gulf of Mexico off the coast of Louisiana in 1959.

"*We* had only one lease in the Gulf. I asked my boss where to start and he said, 'There's the whole Gulf of Mexico. You pick a place!' All we had were blank base maps."

- Harris Phillips (VP, DGM, MCD), geologist on his first assignment to New Orleans in 1959.)

ana lease sales and bought the properties from Phillips Petroleum. Six rigs were running at various times during the year, and every well found production. The "Phillips Purchase" became the basis for establishing an exploration and production office in Lafayette, and provided the base from which all future production in the Gulf would grow. Lafayette was selected as it was a good location from which to conduct operations from the Western Gulf, where most of TGT's pipelines were located. Lafayette became an early "center" for the company that would become Tenneco Oil and stories about "life in Lafayette" fill the scrapbooks and memory banks of many

TOE&P employees. It is unlikely that the famous "employee-oriented" culture would have developed as well in New Orleans.

Tenneco began hiring experienced offshore personnel from other oil companies and transferring some of its existing exploration and production people to Lafayette, or to New Orleans, where its exploration office was located.

Joe Foster was transferred to Lafayette, as a petroleum engineer with two years of experience, from Oklahoma City. He remembers being told by Chief Engineer Bob Stephens, "We are hiring people with experience in the Gulf to insure that we operate safely and competently, but we are also sending some younger guys down there to help them. You can learn from them about offshore operations and they can learn from you about how Tennessee does business." He also remembers thinking, " Fat chance of them learning from me!"

Jack H. Ray came from Magnolia to be District Production Superintendent. George Boudreaux came from Phillips to be District Engineer. Joe Stasney was hired from Richardson and Bass to be District Drilling Foreman. George P. Walker, a bright young Petroleum Engineer, came from Great Bend, KS. Lafayette became a desirable destination for young engineers in TOE&P. The work was challenging and rewarding, as well. Frank Poole and Scott Gregory, from Tennessee's onshore Gulf Coast division in Bellaire, became production foremen in the Lafayette Offshore District. This group was the beginning of Tennessee's presence in the Gulf as an operator. TOE&P would eventually become one of the "Top Five" operators in the GOM.

During 1959, Tennessee Gas and Oil drilled 11 wells in the Gulf of Mexico resulting in 28 individual completions, with no dry holes. Nowhere else in TGO were multiple completions so common, or success rates so high. Offshore Louisiana, with its multiple productive zones in most wells, became the arena for a rapidly-evolving technology to make safe multiple completions, and the leveraged economics that came with "cost of service" strategies became the operational drivers to accomplish this. Both Ray and Boudreaux had come from backgrounds where 'maximizing net present value' were the strategic drivers and the concept of "rate base" and "cost of service" accounting treatments were mysteries.

At the start of 1960, the Tennessee Gas and Oil inventory in the Gulf of Mexico consisted of: West Cameron 39 and 40, with three gas wells drilled by Phillips before the acreage was acquired by TGO; East Cameron 16, 17, and 24, four completed gas wells on 8,400 acres of leases taken at sales by TGO; Vermillion 77, with three multiple completion wells; Eugene Island 215, waiting to be drilled, and; South Timbalier 22 and 86, and the nearby Bay Marchand Block 5.

* * * * *

One of the last events of the 50's had involved yet another name change, and it was an appropriate one for what lay ahead. In 1959 Tennessee Gas and Oil (TGO) was incorporated to replace Tennessee Production Company. TGO was still a subsidiary of TGT and Ralph Graham remained as President. The decade closed with Tenneco owning over 2000 net wells, producing over 30,000 BOPD and 100MMCFD, and holding booked reserves of 265MMNEBs – and all this in addition to the fact that this had resulted in greater throughput for TGT's pipelines, and added supply to the pipeline and refining and marketing operations that had seen their own successes. Tenneco's first decade-plus had been furious. The groundwork laid during those early years set the stage for the next decade and beyond. The company had grown twentyfold in ten years and was positioned for an ambitious run into the 1960s. The 1960s would see equally spectacular, but in many ways different, types of progress.

From its founding in 1946 Tenneco Oil E&P grew steadily. By 1959 the operations had evolved to support the organizational structure that would serve it well for its remaining 30 years.

1959 TENNESSE GAS AND OIL CORPORATE STRUCTURE

Houston
President – Ralph Graham

SVP North America E&P Operations – Wilton Scott
SVP Tennessee Overseas Company – Sam Oliphant
VP Exploration, US and Canada – J. S. (Spence) Collins
VP Production, North America – A. R. West
Stuart King – Principal Assistant

Division Offices

General Manager	GCD (Houston) Exploration Manager	Production Manager
Roy Randerson	Don Gahagan	Albert Arnett
General Manager F. B. Stein	SED (Lafayette) Exploration Manager Phil Oxley	Production Manager Don DAmpf
General Manager Hal Craig	MCD (Okla City) Exploration Manager Jess Roach	Production Manager Dan B. Johnson
General Manager R. L. Sielaff	RMD (Denver) Exploration Manager Joe Wolfe	Production Manager R. M. Stephens
General Manager A. N. McDowell	SWD (Midland, TX) Exploration Manager W. C. Tillett	Production Manager J. P. Jacks
General Manager O. W. "Tiny" Ward	Canadian (Calgary) Exploration Manager Rex Byers	Production Manager Jack O'Brien

In addition to the Division Offices, in 1959 the company had operating district offices in Corpus Christi, Houston, Bellaire, Midland and Victoria, TX; Wichita and Great Bend, KS; New Orleans and Lafayette, LA; Jackson, MI; Durango, CO and Casper, WY.

Offshore oil storage emerged in the 1960s, with the "Unsinkable Molly Brown" the first of it's kind.

E&P TENNECO ADVANTAGE

Commitment to the Gulf of Mexico

The first three years in the Gulf of Mexico, 1957 through 1959, set the stage for the future. Significant events came quickly. Four of the most important "Turning Points" – things that truly shaped the future of the company - occurred in rapid succession in the early 1960s. Two of these were "events", and two were "strategies".

Throughout its entire history much of Tenneco's success in the Gulf of Mexico was attributed to its performance at lease sales. The Sale in 1960 was the company's first. The company's ability to bid aggressively at that and subsequent sales, and then to proceed aggressively with the development of the blocks won, can be attributed to a brilliant and unique strategy – "The Tenneco Advantage".

Built from Scratch

The quote on the opposite page, attributed to Wilton Scott, is an impressive statement, and it's true, but it deserves an explanation.

As mentioned, the early E&P ventures into the Gulf of Mexico were undertaken, at least in part, to support TGT's expansion of its own pipeline business. The Gulf was identified as a growing province with a bright future. It was also an arena that required a transportation network, thus yielding business opportunity from two different sources. TGT entered the GOM with the intention of becoming the dominant gas pipeline in the province. The purpose for the E&P effort was not only to earn a return on its investments, but also to help provide gas to keep the pipelines full. TGT made a visionary decision when it decided to create the "oil company" as a subsidiary, and then to make the move into the offshore, with its gulf-wide area pricing schedule. The synergy of the complementary functions of the pipeline and its exploration subsidiary provided a competitive advantage in and of itself, but in Tenneco's case, the ability to use piggy-backed financial leverage was critical.

Conventional wisdom of the day was that economic growth in the country would continue, that demand for natural gas would increase, that finding and development costs for new reserves would go up and that wellhead prices for both oil and natural gas would also increase. Given that scenario, Gardiner Symonds believed that TGT's earning and its stock price should and would increase over time, but that would be dependent on keeping the pipelines full, and expanding the network. Since, production of any given deposit of gas or oil is subject to decline as it is produced, TGT would need to aggressively and continually seek new gas supplies for the pipelines.

Utilizing the large amount of cash generated by the pipeline operations, the E&P company was able to behave as a much larger company than it actually was. In return, the pipeline - the parent, was able to use the intangible drilling costs (IDC's) from the drilling operations in its combined financials and that created important tax savings for the corporation. In addition, of course, the decision to enter the Gulf of Mexico, in and of itself, created an opportunity for continued expansion of the pipeline system – and of the "rate base".

The Tennessee Gas decision to expand exploration and production operations in the Gulf was heavily influenced by an expectation within the financial and regulatory groups in the company of obtaining "cost of service" treatment for investments in the Gulf. Basically, the concept involved "capitalizing" (for accounting purposes) all of the costs of leasing, drilling, completing, and equipping the wells in the area, and including those in the "cost of service" charged to Tennessee's customers. The total value of the assets involved represented the pipeline's costs of bringing the new gas supply to market.

The regulated pipeline businesses were allowed to recover capital and operating costs associated with their work within their supply areas, and also the opportunity to earn an allowable rate-of-return on those costs. The premise was that, since these costs were incurred by TGT in its search to add new gas supply for its customers, the capital costs of exploration, development, and production would be included in the "rate base", and used to determine its "cost of service" to the customers. The leases themselves were classified as ratable supplies of gas volume. For E&P, this accounting treatment of the capital investments related to the exploration for and production was a special means of leveraging their investments.

" • • •

Tenneco Oil was the largest oil company in the US 'built from scratch' in the last 20 years … and it was built from pipeline scratch!"

- W. E. Scott (CEO, Tenn Inc)

" • • •

Tenneco Oil was unique. It was a small company but had $3 billion of assets – TGT assets!"

- George Meason during his term as President of Tenneco Oil.

177

**President Profile
WILTON E. SCOTT
1961-1970**

Wilton Scott was a native Texan and 1936 graduate of the University of Texas. Mr. Scott joined the company in 1955 as Manager of Oil and Gas Exploration after tenures at Cities Service, Standard and Buffalo Oil Co. He was promoted to Vice President in 1955 and was named President in 1961. Mr. Scott was at the helm of the company through its most critical years and played a key role in many of the most-significant decisions that led to its success. He guided the company through four major acquisitions (and over 100 smaller ones) and a wide-ranging expansion of domestic and international interests. His tenure saw the growth of revenues from oil operations to exceed over $500 million annually. In 1970, Scott was promoted to Executive Vice President of Tenneco Inc. He served as Chairman and CEO of the parent from 1975 until his retirement in 1977. He remained on Tenneco's board until 1983. Wilton Scott died in 2005.

"West Cameron 180 was the crown jewel of the 1960 Sale, thanks to Harris Phillips and Phil Oxley!"

- J B Foster

At the operating level however, all drilling and productions decisions were made using the same economic criteria as in the other E&P divisions, and as used throughout the industry. But "the advantage" was nevertheless applicable here, as well. Since TGT was able to capitalize completion costs, they could afford to be less risk-averse with completion strategies and experiment with more aggressive techniques. The "advantage" allowed the company to maintain an aggressive drilling schedule, run extra-large casing strings and make multiple-zone completions (sometimes up to 9 in a single well). The inclusion of those costs in the TGT rate-base effectively increased the annual TGT cash flow, which in turn, created investment capital for the following year.

Although some of TGT's competition in the industry may have viewed the company's aggressive posture in the Gulf in line with Jack Ray's recollection above, the truth is that it was an incredibly insightful and effective business strategy, created by the unique pairing of sister companies working in both the E&P and pipeline businesses. Synergy among sibling companies at Tenneco would be applied in many forms over the years.

The "Tenneco Advantage" gave TGT a clear head-start on the rest of the field in the Gulf. The company used the advantage masterfully and established the company as a major force in the Gulf. Success at the 1960 and 1962 lease sales was a result of the bold and aggressive use of inter-company leverage and firmly established Tenneco's presence in the Gulf. That, in turn, provided the foundation for TOE&P's long-term strength there. From 1960 through 1968 hundreds of millions of dollars were invested in the Gulf using this synergy. The degree to which the "Tenneco Advantage" was employed in the early years clearly qualifies that strategy as a "Turning Point". It was responsible for Tenneco's ability to establish itself as an industry leader in the Gulf.

The 1960 Lease Sale
Adapted from E&P Update

Learning the ropes for lease sales began with the 1960 Sale. Preparations for this lease sale were intense, and success came in with the winning of six new tracts at the BLM (Bureau of Land Management within the Department of Interior, later replaced by the Minerals Management Service) auction. The bill for that first federal sale came to $16 million, a major share of corporate expenditures at the time.

It was a long and painful night of second-guessing back in September, 1960. The next day Tenneco Oil would bid in its first federal offshore lease sale. The company had identified its version of the grand prize as West Cameron, Block 180. Wilton Scott, then executive vice president in charge of exploration and production, "sweated that bid all night," as he lay awake in Houston, separated from his bidding team by 300 miles. "At 2 am Scott called us in New Orleans," remembered Phil Oxley, then offshore exploration manager. "He told us to cut the bid on WC 180 by $2 million." At 6 am, Scott called back. "He said he had the last minute spasms, and told us to 'do what we must' to get the block." Later, the team got together for pecan rolls and coffee in the Roosevelt Hotel café and "talked in whispers about what we would do" – they decided to split Scott's $2MM difference, and cut the bid by $1MM, but to add 'just a tad' for good measure. The resulting bid of $5,127,000 won the block -- by just $27,000 over the second highest offer!

The first well tapped a huge gas field that extended beneath five other blocks. By time of the sale in 1988, WC 180 had produced 1.1 trillion cubic feet of gas and still had enough reserves left to rank as E&P's 18th largest field. And Tenneco was lucky at that. The block had been previously held and the previous owner had drilled a dry hole just a thousand feet northeast of Tenneco's successful wildcat. "If they'd drilled a little farther north or south, they would have found the gas, and the block would have never been up for bid," Oxley explained.

That first sale in 1960 laid the foundation for E&P's long-time standing in the Gulf of Mexico. Eventual returns on the initial $16 million of bids at investment would amount to 'billions' over the years. In addition to West Cameron 180, Ship Shoal 169 and West Cameron 165 were other major finds from that sale. The discoveries from the 1960 sale would give E&P the courage to remain aggressive in the Gulf and the income to fuel growth throughout the company.

By the end of 1960, 30 wells had been drilled offshore. Twenty-five of those were productive, and the inventory of leases included over 30,000 acres. From 1959 through 1961, 51 of the 63 wells the company drilled in the Gulf of Mexico would be producers.

Scott Takes the Wheel

By year-end, 1960, company assets totaled 383 MMNEBs with a value just short of one-half billion dollars, but the company still struggled to make money. Significant capital had been deployed around the world, yet production and profitability lagged. CEO Symonds and the Board of Directors moved to address the issue in 1961. Wilton E. Scott was named President. His charge from Symonds was direct – "Make the company profitable!" Scott subsequently toured the company locations making a great speech which started and ended with the exhortation that "The assigned role of business in society is to make a profit!" Most of the folks in Tenneco Oil – both E&P and P&M – never forgot that mantra. Sadly, some in the eventual parent company never heard the speech.

Mr. Scott's first challenge was a formidable one. In 1961 the company faced a cash flow crisis. In a legal judgment, TGT had been ordered to refund $134MM to its customers, money it did not have on hand. At the same time, TGO was not yet making money at an acceptable level.

"I made a lot of tough decisions," said Scott in an interview years later. "We had to look at everything very carefully and I got the reputation of being a tough guy. I didn't enjoy that role, but I had to do it." Scott turned to a

"Wilton Scott was a key figure in the growth of Tenneco. He was a "sometimes-right, sometimes-wrong, never-in-doubt" manager. He demanded good work, made his positions clear, and earned the loyalty of those who worked for him. He was to Tenneco Oil what Gardner Symonds was to Tennessee Gas, an executive who secured good work and loyalty simply by his presence."
- *Joe B Foster*

"Wilton Scott was responsible for building the oil company!"
- *George Meason*

"Scott's coming to work for the company was the turning point. If you were ever asked to do a job for Scottie, you'd better do it right!"
- *Tom Spurlock*
(retired, Frontier Projects)

CATC (later CAGC) was a consortium of companies composed of Conoco, Atlantic, Tidewater (later Getty), and Cities Service. The group was one of TGT's major suppliers in the Gulf and Tennessee was by far CAGC's largest purchaser/transporter of natural gas. Gardiner Symonds had served on the Conoco board for a long time, and for quite a while CATC and TGT had a "special relationship". Not long after TGT began drilling in the Gulf, it became less special.

- J B Foster

young engineer named Cliff Rackley (President of TOC '74-'78, President of TOP&M '78-'86) who was working his way through processing and marketing. Rackley remembers, "Scott put me on a team to evaluate the P&M divisions that were losing money. When we got through, we cancelled all capital expenditures and made a budget and a plan that would work."

Wayne Nance and Jack Gregory recall the time as one of great anxiety. Young professionals from all of the operating districts were called into Houston for the first time in their careers. Presentations were made to Scott and even to Gardiner Symonds. Every project was reviewed in great detail and it was clear that choices would be made as to where the young company would focus its future efforts. The first "make-over" of Tenneco Oil would be the result, with substantial changes to all facets of the business.

Onshore, acquisitions continued in 1960 as Fifteen Oil Co. and Renwar Oil Corporation added 297 net oil and gas wells producing 4,400 BOPD and 29.4 MCFD of natural gas. The acreage count grew by 36,200 net producing and 382,600 undeveloped acres. The Slick Oil Co. was also purchased in 1960. With these purchases came two of TOE&P's best long-lived fields. The Charenton field in Louisiana and Slick Ranch in South Texas would both be major revenue generators for the Gulf Coast Division for many years.

In another direct example of the "Tenneco Advantage", the Ship Shoal 198/199 Field was purchased in 1961 by TGT for $54million from a consortium of Conoco, Atlantic, Tidewater, and Cities Service (CATC). The CATC group operated as a combine in the Gulf for many years. This purchase occurred at a time when producers were selling their gas for about 20 cents per mcf, under price controls of the Federal Power Commission (FPC). The in-place purchase allowed TGT to capitalize the acquisition cost and place it into the "rate base", earning its allowed return on the acquisition cost. It also gave Tennessee flexibility as to when to "take" the gas. Tenneco Oil E&P was compensated by TGT by payment of overhead and operating fees. The purchase included an estimated recoverable 16.2 million barrels of liquid hydrocarbons. This purchase brought in cash "up front" for the producers, which was a benefit to them. This field would still be producing 28 years later and would have provided over 120 million NEB's of product for the company. Given that the properties produced over seven times the amount originally estimated, the accounting advantage was of secondary importance.

A similar approach was used by TGT in the Bastian Bay field at the mouth of the Mississippi River delta with the acquisition of "in place reserves" there also. These acquisitions created controversy and legal issues with the FPC (FPC became the Federal Energy Regulatory Commission – the FERC - in 1977). Rather than having Tennessee (TGT) seek to include the costs of the acquisitions directly in its rate base or its cost of service, Tenneco found it better to have the E&P company (TGO by then) be the direct buyer of production or the lessor of prospective leases in Tennessee's supply area. It is fair to say that Tenneco Oil and Tennessee Gas, as well as their customers and shareholders, were significant beneficiaries of the aggressive efforts to expand gas supply in the Gulf of Mexico and its delta areas.

"Tenneco" Appears

On the corporate side of the business, the word "Tenneco" made its first appearance in 1961 when the company name was changed to Tenneco Oil Company (TOC), as a subsidiary of Tenneco Corporation, which in turn, was a subsidiary of the parent, Tenneco, Inc. Tennessee Gas was no longer the parent of Tenneco Oil. That was the result of a complex corporate re-structuring that had been implemented to provide separation between Tenneco's regulated (pipeline) and unregulated businesses. A combination of factors made the re-organization necessary; first, continued inquiries from the FPC questioned the comingling of unregulated and regulated assets, as a benefit to the unregulated side; and second, Tenneco Inc maintained a strong appetite for continued acquisitions of unregulated businesses.

Development of Lease Sale Bidding Process

Early drilling successes on the leases taken in the 1960 offshore lease sale set the stage for the growth in profitability that the company sorely needed. By 1962, 51 of the 63 offshore wells drilled by Tenneco were producers. That success also sent a clear signal that an aggressive strategy in the Gulf was well-justified. Any fair reading of the history of Tenneco Oil Company indicates that the Federal Lease sale in 1962 was another major milestone and turning point that would push the company forward.

In the March, 1962 Federal Lease Sale, TGO won over 116,000 acres of leases with winning bids totaling $43.3 million, a huge number for the company and the industry at the time. By 1967 ten new fields had been discovered on blocks acquired in '62, and the company would have doubled the size of its position in the Gulf. Notable discoveries from the "Class of '62" include SMI 66 (1TCF+), V245 (400+ BCF), SMI 78(400+BCF), and V250 (435+BCF). Over time, these leases would produce in excess of 300MMNEB.

Tenneco acquired some blockbuster fields with its purchases at the 1962 sale, making the sale itself a "turning point", but that success was the result of a very specific strategic plan. That strategy itself – the development of the lease sale bidding process – is also classified as a "turning point" in that it provided far-reaching and long-lasting effects on the company as a whole, well beyond the waters of the Gulf.

Success at the 1962 sale was the result of the specific process of evaluation and bid determination that was developed by Tenneco's early offshore pioneers. The decision to involve engineers and an engineering analysis along with the exploration professionals was the key. The strategy of employing

The 'Tenneco' name was created by a New York advertising agency for the holding company of the different energy divisions. Mr. Symonds' intent was that it would be a good name for a major oil company, suitable for retailing gasoline. Along with the new name came the familiar "Tenneco Shield" logo, originally in red, white and blue.

- C W Rackley (Ret, Pres TOP&M)

I was told by a TGP engineer named Tom Logston how Tenneco got its name. He said he was in Tennessee at a hospital and heard a nurse talking about a contest to rename Tennessee Gas Transmission. He claims he suggested the obvious name - Tenneco. The nurse submitted the name and won the contest.

- L Merriam (PE Consul MCD)

"As we look back, the 1962 sale was a legendary sale. It seemed pretty legendary to me at the time, simply because this was the first one that I had ever been to. I actually typed out many of the checks. We were afraid, for security reasons, that the amount of a deposit check, which is 20% of the bid, might be discovered by someone else. So, our landman, Mike Murphy, and I literally typed up the checks the night before. We put them in a large envelope and I put it under my mattress, between the mattress and the box springs. Since Mike was well known to the landmen of other bidders, he did not want to keep them in his room. He was afraid that someone from another bidder might get into his room and review those checks. Nobody with other companies had any idea who I was, so we assumed the completed checks would be fine in the engineer's room. That is how paranoid we were! But no competitor found the checks. We were high bidders on 26 blocks, (116,000 acres), nearly tripling our holdings in the Gulf in that sale."

J B Foster (EVP, Tenn Inc)

risk-adjusted economic models for bid determination would be a critical development in Tenneco's progress, and was clearly responsible for Tenneco's exceptional success at lease sales through the years, a notable "better than the competition" record.

The unique method of economic analysis developed for the sale proved its value throughout the business of TOE&P, and became a part of the basic fabric of the company, influencing not only the approach to prospect evaluation, but indeed to E&P's unique style of integrated "multi-discipline" teamwork. The office of Economic Planning and Analysis grew from lessons learned preparing for the sale. An argument can be made that the 1962 Lease Sale was the most-timely of all key events in the company's history. Preparation for the 1962 sale was a "buy one and get one free" effort as both our teamwork and our "Culture" which evolved over the years had their roots here.

Evolution of Economic Analysis and Integrated Teams in Tenneco Oil

By J. B. Foster

There were a number of "sponsors" of an integrated team concept for Tenneco Oil in the 1960s. Jack Ray, Bill Medary, Dan Johnson, S.V. McCollum, and Wilton Scott are names that come to mind.

The early leasing and acquisition activity led exploration and production to work together in the Gulf. Bill Medary, Division Exploration Superintendent, though a geologist by training, was open-minded to engineers participating in the evaluation of prospects. Even in 1959, Tennessee Gas's production business unit relied on the "numbers guys" for bid evaluations and, the engineers and operating people had to manage getting the wells drilled and the leases tested. The escalating costs of offshore leases, plus the very high cost of drilling the wildcats to test them, meant that, like it or not, engineers and explorationists were working with each other from early-on in the process. Opinions that were integrated with exploration information as well as projected production economics were crucial for the determination of bidding and drilling plans

For the early offshore sales, seismic and well log information from exploration was used to make reserve estimates while those from the production department made performance projections for each prospect. Bids were determined on a discounted cash flow basis, taking into account development costs and probability of success. Doing this work well turned out to be a true interdisciplinary exercise.

Whether Mr. Symonds or Mr. Scott, or the production and exploration managers, had designed it that way, Tenneco's entry into the Gulf of Mexico had prompted a bundling of the decision-making processes. However it might have been perceived onsite, a few people in Houston, chief among them Gardiner Symonds, viewed the project in Lafayette as being very much integrated. The combination of geology, geophysics, engineering and production, coupled with the development of a pipeline network, was intended to provide significant operating and financial synergy to the corporation.

To a degree, these concepts of synergy were already in play throughout the operations of Tennessee Gas. Within the pipeline operation itself, integration and cost-savings did not necessarily have a high priority. Building the rate base, and maintaining the mystery of cost of service parameters were higher on the priority list. Safety and appearance issues that enhanced the outside view of the pipeline were givens within the pipeline, as they were within E&P as well, but integration, per se, did not add so much value in the pipeline operation. In fact, it often created efficiencies which led to a reduction in the cost of service, lower transportation rates, and possibly, reduced profits, so to some degree, it was counter-productive to bottom-line results.

In its early days, with Mr. Symonds as the driver, Tennessee was very much an entrepreneurial organization, but integrated in its approach to business. Collaboration and sharing of information was emphasized where value could be added, where ambiguities existed, where multiple technologies were required, and where business risks and potential were high, but management was often perfectly content to take a "cookie cutter" approach where that made the most sense, such as within the pipeline and production operations.

The traditional oil company of those days was quite "silo-ed". Exploration, Production, Gas Processing, Transportation, Marketing, and Refining were each separate organizations or businesses, frequently working as separate profit centers, with totally independent staffing and management. Oil and gas were easy enough to find, or to purchase from independents, and each element of the business was on the look-out for assets that fit its own needs.

The "silos" may not have been most efficient, but the Humble's and Texaco's and Magnolia's were doing plenty well, thank you. "Teams", or integrated teams, were not necessary to insure success.

The senior management of Tenneco, led by Symonds and Scott, had this ability to integrate across disciplines, and they had a tendency to promote like-minded individuals. These tendencies resulted in a more conscious movement toward more integration of disciplines, beginning with the coordination of pipeline and production activities in the Gulf of Mexico. And, the offshore lease sales, with their huge up front exposures of capital, demanded a more thorough and better, integrated analysis. Starting "from scratch" had its advantages as no in-grained bureaucracy was present to prevent experimentation. The more such analysis we engaged in, the better success we had, the more management liked it, and the more satisfied were our employees.

I believe, as a young engineer who knew little about exploration, I was a mover of this effort. I asked questions of explorationists that had not been asked before. I made calculations which demonstrated that commonly accepted rules of thumb were not necessarily valid.

During this time, C. Jackson Grayson published his famous book, "Decisions Under Uncertainty: Drilling Decisions in the Oil and Gas Business". This resulted in a greatly-increased awareness of probability theory, and much greater use of it in the exploration and production side of the oil business. The application of these concepts changed Tenneco's way of evaluating and choosing its opportunities.

Once Tenneco Oil began using probability theory, or what we called "risk analysis", we discovered that this was not something an engineer running the numbers could do alone. Each prospect contained an entire list of "things that could go wrong", and we set about defining a whole series of probability assessments, with projected PS's (Probabilities of Success) for each of the components of a prospect, such as: Reliability of seismic data, Presence of a trap, Thickness of sand, Probabilities of oil vs. gas, Areal extent of reservoirs, Number of sands, Likelihood and extent of cost overruns.

The concept of "probability", of risk, did not come easy to many in the organization. For many, generally those with preconceived ideas about the success or failure of the venture, the Ps was either 1.0 or Zero – the project, as a whole, was either a success or a failure; the well will either be dry or it will be productive. The geologist or geophysicist is likely to say, "If we thought it was going to be dry, we would not have recommended it!" Those folks quickly learned that, under probability theory, this was not an acceptable answer. Although we always had a "success" case (a 100% positive outcome), we used the probability assessments to factor that down to what we called "expected value", or a "most likely" outcome.

"How can a well be 15% or 50% productive?", the geologist or engineer would ask. Then we'd ask for estimates of the best outcome (e.g. highest reserves we might expect), the worst outcome (the least reserves), and "most likely" outcome. This, of course, generated a wide range of potential outcomes, and made us realize that, in fact in real life, we experienced a wide range of outcomes on everything we do. It took a lot of time and effort to get a whole technical team (i.e. geologists, geological engineers, geophysicists, drilling engineers, reservoir engineers, and production engineers) to agree on these assessments. During all these early reviews in Lafayette, I was the note-taker, question-asker, and calculator of "expected values".

This type of analysis was first used in the 1962 Federal Offshore Lease sales. The sale results were excellent. The analysis models had been applied successfully and were then refined in succeeding years. Looking back, using probability theory for the 1962 lease sale in the Gulf of Mexico, may have been what first prompted an integrated look at the economics and project potential at the "working-hand" levels of the organization. Over the years, that concept became pervasive through everything we did, not only in the offshore, but throughout the company.

* * * * *

Continued success in subsequent sales, and elsewhere within the company, then led to the organization of an Economic Planning and Analysis (EP&A) group in Houston in 1968 with the objective of insuring that economic analysis methodology was generally the same throughout Tenneco Oil E&P, and that risk was quantified and discussed for all contemplated projects. Not surprisingly, Joe Foster was sent to Houston as the first manager of EP&A. Other technical people; the chief geologists, chief engineers, and chief geophysicists, had responsibility for technical quality control and consistency across all the divisions of North America. A matrix involving an integration of technical and economic analyses had been established as the basis for all TOE&P investments.

The 1962 lease sale provided an inventory of offshore acreage that took some time to evaluate. The company quickly expanded its presence in the Gulf of Mexico during the next few years as wildcats became discoveries and discoveries became major development projects. At the time of the sale in 1988, over 25 years after their purchase, eight fields from the '60 and '62 sales still ranked in the top 40 of all E&P production.

Stories from the Early Offshore

With its new assets TOE&P established an aggressive growth record in the Gulf during the decade of the 1960s. The inventory of good prospects was extensive, the activity testing them was furious – and it was successful. Along the way numerous projects would provide fodder for memories.

Eugene Island Block 215

In 1965, shortly after joining Tenneco in Lafayette, LA, Joe Foster asked Mickey Braden to study how to recover the remaining reserves from Eugene Island Blk 215. This was one of the "Phillips" properties and was characterized by numerous reservoirs, stacked vertically over several hundred feet. The A-Platform had been severely damaged by Hurricane Hilda in early October 1964. The cost of platform repairs was not supported by the value of the remaining reserves, but there was still much oil to be recovered. The platform was stable but weakened so that it could no longer support the weight of a drilling or work-over rig. Future work would be limited to a slick-line unit that could run wire-line tools inside the tubing. The challenge then, was to recomplete the wells to recover the remaining reserves using limited resources. Fortunately, the engineer who had designed the original development (one Joe Foster) had designed all the wells to accommodate multiple completions, some with 4 or 5 strings of tubing. Multiple completions were a common practice in the GOM offshore at that time as a way to offset the very low per well production allowables for oil wells as enforced by the State of Louisiana and the Feds as well. Regulations were later changed to allow only two production streams from a single well bore. However, with a multitude of tubing strings to choose from, the solution became viable by plugging off a zone when it was depleted and re-completing via wire line methods to a higher zone. Foster's fortuitous design allowed us to recover most of the remaining reserves over the next 15 years.

The Sleeping Turtle Line

Tenneco was always trying something new. In 1966 Bill Melnar was an engineer on a team charged with coming up with a way to reduce the costs of pipelining. The company established a "first" for the Gulf of Mexico by laying 34 miles of spooled continuous 6" pipeline to company production at Ship Shoal 176 and Eugene Island 215 in water depths of 100'. At the time it was the deepest water in which laying a spooled continuous line had been attempted. According to Melnar, "We went out on a limb recommending that to management. Fortunately it worked very well."

The Unsinkable Molly Brown

In 1967 the Offshore Division faced a problem in getting production to shore. Bill Melnar recalled the situation. "We had seven wells with 14 completions at Vermilion 245, located 70 miles offshore. We decided the best way to get the product to shore would be by barge. That meant we had to have some way to store the oil until it could be shipped. The conventional storage tank was a cylindrical or rectangular tank mounted on the production platform. This arrangement had two flaws. It took up platform space and had limited capacity. We had three criteria for a better system for the storage tank at Vermilion 245; We needed stability during hurricanes, ease off-loading into barges and, large capacity. We put the project up for bids, expecting that J. Ray McDermott would be the most-likely source for a solution."

Out of the blue, a young engineer with Chicago Bridge and Iron Company (CB&I) named Bob Chamberlain showed up in Joe Foster's office in Lafayette. Joe was the district engineer, and Bill Melnar was the person in Lafayette with engineering responsibility for VR 245 field. All three were brand new in their respective jobs.

Chicago Bridge and Iron Company proposed a unique two-tank design - one above the water and one below – with a 30,000 barrel capacity. The bottom tank sat on the ocean floor at 130'. It looked something like a doughnut with columns to support the top structure, itself a sphere that sat above the highest wave line. The bottom tank acted as an anchor for the structure, but had no conventional piles or stabilizers. When full, the top structure served as an anchor weight, keeping the bottom tank planted firmly in the ocean floor.

"The structure was dubbed the Unsinkable Molly Brown, when the 10-foot cans (legs) could not be driven more than five feet into the ocean floor. The design plans called for sinking the full 10 feet length of the supports. We tried several things to get it to sink further, but as far as I know it's still riding five feet high. This was a whole new concept in tank design, and we again went pretty far out on a limb with this proposal," recalled Melnar. "Fortunately, we had a turn-key bid for both construction and installation and it worked out just like we said it would, and it has weathered several tropical storms in the Gulf."

Adding Slots to a 6-Pile Platform

At South Timbalier Block 21, TOC discovered a nice field with multiple reservoirs. At that time (1966), the "standard" platform was a 4-pile McDermott design with six drilling slots. Full development would require more than six wells. The objective was to add drilling slots but avoid the cost of an extensive redesign or a second platform. It was not possible to decrease the surface spacing of the wells because the "wings" of the Christmas trees were too wide. A local fabricator came up with a "space saver" tree design with suitable pressure ratings but a much shorter wing span. By arranging these trees at 45-degree angles to the axis of the platform, the spacing for the well slots could be reduced from 9 ft to 6 ft, thus allowing more wells on the platform. Division management was satisfied with the proposal the platform was put into service with significant saving in construction costs. - M Braden (PM, Frontier)

Onshore During the 1960s

While headlines were being made in the Gulf of Mexico in the early 1960s, the onshore operations continued the "business as usual" plan of growing through acquisition and exploitation of acquired properties. Between 1960 and 1965 Tenneco Oil bought eighteen different companies with a wide variety of assets to complement the company's growing portfolio. In 1964 alone, acquisitions of proved reserves added 834 new wells. The Mayfair Minerals purchase brought more properties in south Texas, and the Wilcox Oil Co. deal added properties in the Texas panhandle, Kansas and Oklahoma. The prize among these represented yet another Turning Point for TOE&P.

Delhi-Taylor, 1964

The deal that brought Delhi-Taylor Corp. was important for several reasons. Delhi brought two of the most significant fields in the company's history and the manner of financing the purchase held nearly as much impact as the properties themselves. The San Juan Basin gas field in northwest New Mexico would become E&P's largest field, and remain so until the time of the sale. In the Texas Gulf Coast, the McAllen Ranch would influence activity in the Gulf Coast Division for years to come.

Wilton Scott recalls the transaction, "We bid $150MM in cash, most of it in the form of a production payment, but we still had to raise $10MM. Continental Oil approached us and offered to split the deal, so we did." In addition to relieving Tenneco of some significant cash requirements, the addition of Conoco allowed us to curry favor with one of Tennessee's biggest suppliers of natural gas.

LARRY OLIVER

In addition to the properties, the Delhi-Taylor acquisition brought some valuable talent as well. Larry Oliver came to Tenneco with that purchase and contributed substantially to the efforts of E&P throughout the following 24 years. Oliver served in a variety of the divisions and in a variety of roles throughout his career and was a key contributor to the development of many production and drilling practices that made the company a consistent leader in operational efficiency. He was promoted to Vice President of Production and also was President of Operators Inc. Following the sale of the company he continued to manage an "Operators' – type" organization on a contract basis for other companies.

C. E. "CHUCK" SHULTZ

Chuck Shultz graduated from the Colorado School of Mines in 1961 with a degree in Geological Engineering to work in Oklahoma City. The OKC office was the starting point for quite a number of E&P careers in those days as the acquisitions had brought baskets-full of properties. Shultz would find himself immediately in the field with a variety of challenging assignments. The challenges would serve him well in the future as during his career he took on a wide variety of tasks in all facets of the business. When the company was sold in 1988 Shultz was Senior Vice President in Houston with responsibility for the International fortunes of TOE&P but his path to that spot took him through many of the operating divisions and most of the activity and included extended stints in corporate planning at the parent Tenneco Inc. level. Chuck's contributions were numerous and his name will appear frequently in the narrative.

With a "down-payment" of only about 13% of the purchase price, the company acquired an asset that fueled onshore operations for years. From 1964 until the Sale in 1988 the Delhi-Taylor properties generated an immense amount of income for the company. In 1985, 20 years after the acquisition, a long-running litigation with El Paso over ownership of portions of the San Juan Basin properties was settled in TOE&P's favor. That event alone added 65MMNEB to TOE&P's books, worth perhaps $1.5 – 2 billion at the time. The production payment concept for Delhi-Taylor was an innovative approach to acquisition financing and an example of the non-traditional financing arrangements the company would use in years ahead. The long-term impact of the Delhi-Taylor purchase was measured in the billions of dollars. (Many of those same properties are "hot" again with the shale plays of the modern day.)

A Balance of Acquisition & Internal Prospecting

From its earliest days, TGT, and Tenneco Oil grew through the acquisition of carefully-selected existing companies. TOE&P's success though, came from more than purchased assets alone. Tenneco's prospecting skills were second to none and produced numerous notable discoveries. The balance between the two strategies served to mitigate the inherent risks of using one approach versus the other as myriad pitfalls exist in each. Much like an investment portfolio, the balance between acquisition and in-house prospecting was a competitive advantage for the company. Taking that logic a step further, one of the great talents among the technical professionals at the company was in finding unknown upside within the acquisitions themselves. TOE&P never purchased another company thinking to just "produce it out". All acquisitions were exploited thoroughly, and none escaped a thorough re-work by the combined teams of exploration and production staff. In many cases, significant production enhancements and substantial exploration discoveries were made on lands that came with the acquisitions; prospects that had not been part of the "sales package" at all.

* * * * *

By 1966 Tenneco was a changed company. Ten of the leases from the GOM 1962 sale had been proven productive and primary development there was proceeding rapidly. Exploitation of the properties that came with the onshore acquisitions was creating a steady base of revenue. The strategy of growth through drilling and by acquisition had built a formidable company. Year-end reserves in 1966 had reached 719 MMNEB, almost double the asset figure in 1960.

Tenneco Oil was entering a period of maturation – but not one of slowing down. Further expansion and success lay ahead, but likewise, so did change, this time in the form of new members to the corporate family.

Winds of Change – Tenneco Inc Appears

Meanwhile, back at the ranch …

For its first twenty-plus years, Tenneco Gas Transmission Company, the "parent" of Tenneco Oil, operated primarily within the energy industries. Oil and gas had provided the horsepower for the corporation, either through transport with the pipeline or production from E&P. With the purchases of Petro-Tex and Bay 1955, TGT had become a fully integrated oil operation. Those purchases added refining, retail marketing and chemical production to the mix. Even so, operations were still largely related to energy. In 1956 TGT pipeline deliveries exceeded 2 billion cubic feet per day for the first time, and company assets passed the $1 billion level. Six years later, in 1962, gas deliveries exceeded 1 Trillion cubic feet for the year and asset value exceeded $2 billion. By 1967 the asset value would pass $3 billion, making TGT the first company in history to reach that milestone within its first twenty-five years.

By any measure, the growth of TGT and its subsidiaries (Tenneco Oil, composed of E&P and P&M) had been an impressive success – as an energy company. This gave Gardiner Symonds, always the "deal guy", a license to deal. His eye was always out for opportunities in the non-energy sectors of business. TGT's first steps at diversification beyond energy occurred in the late 1950s, with forays into finance through insurance and later with banking interests in the Houston area, but these businesses were small in relation to the core. In 1965, success in the chemicals and petrochemical businesses led the company into plastics and paper with a number of acquisitions of small specialized firms. Those in turn, led to the company's first exposure to paperboard and packaging. The acquisition of the Packaging Corporation of America marked the first significant departure from energy into true manufacturing. Tenneco was no longer "just" a gas transmission company with related side interests, and diversification was no longer to be confined to targets related only to energy.

These acquisitions provided the basis for organizational change in 1966. On April 8, 1966 the stockholders approved a change in the name of the parent company from Tennessee Gas Transmission Company to Tenneco Inc.

The days of Tennessee Gas Transmission Company as the main operating and financial force inside the Company had passed. TGT became responsible simply for management of the gas pipeline business of Tenneco Inc. An era had come to an end. Mr. Symonds had often described the difficulties associated with businesses forced to operate in the regulated environment. Much of the diversification at Tenneco, initially within energy-related businesses, and then later to those outside that realm, was motivated by an interest to add non-regulated business strategies to the overall portfolio.

The new name provided a corporate identity that was distinct and not related to any specific product, whether it be gas, oil, chemicals, packaging or other manufactured or produced good or service. Indeed, The Company was a diversified and integrated business. It was not just a gas company!

TGT

"TENNECO is no longer wholly or even principally a natural gas pipeline firm, so our name (TGT) no longer fits us; We are, rather, a diversified major industrial company, based in natural resources."

- Gardiner Symonds

Changing the name also marked the end of the era in which oil and gas men dominated the management of the Company. The new era would see a rise to power of men who had come into the Company from outside the gas and pipeline industry.

**KERN COUNTY LAND
THE HISTORY**

The Kern County Land Company had its origins in the 19th century. Lloyd Tevis and Ben Ali Haggan were business partners who made their way to California in 1849 and 1850 hoping to cash in on the gold fever that was transforming the State. As it would turn out, they made their initial wealth by financing mining operations rather than by prospecting themselves. With their proceeds they invested widely in mining ventures in other states and other countries, and grew their business with diversification into transportation and shipping, and then into land acquisition. The partners acquired over half a million acres of the prime agricultural lands of the southern San Joaquin Valley to add to their 1.8 million acres of grazing fields throughout the western U.S. The Kern County Land Company was incorporated in 1890. Until the 1930's, the KCL businesses were primarily agricultural in nature, but in 1936 Shell Petroleum made a major discovery on KCL land and the company found itself at the center of a major oil boom. Through the 1950s KCL grew impressively with its mix of agricultural and energy assets. They expanded into real estate and manufacturing during the '50's by using the millions of dollars of oil and gas royalty income. Between 1957 and 1964 KCL expanded into the electronics, automotive, and agricultural equipment sectors.

Early oil wells in the Kern River Field in 1899. By 1903 over 800 wells had been dug in the area.

Kern County Land
The Good, The Bad, and the Ugly

Among the "Turning Points" that shaped the history of TOE&P, the 1967 acquisition of the Kern County Land Company in California ranks as one of the most significant. It can be argued that the KCL purchase did as much to change both Tenneco Oil and Tenneco Inc., in both positive and negative ways, as any other single event in the history of the company. Curiously, an acquisition targeted for its oil and gas potential would bring with it change in other ways – a metaphor of sorts of the entire history of the company. The acquisition of Kern County Land was pervasive.

The Kern County Land Company acquisition in 1967, at $432 million, was the largest single deal that Tenneco had made (perhaps $2.5-3 billion in today's terms). The story of this acquisition was a whirlwind of good management, good timing and good fortune. The centerpiece of KCL, at least from the Tenneco Oil perspective, was 406,000 acres of fee acreage (ownership of both the surface and the subsurface mineral rights) in the southern San Joaquin Valley of California. The KCL purchase made Tenneco a significant player in California. Existing KCL production of approximately 2000 BOPD would increase 10-fold within ten years as a result of major discoveries of the Yowlumne in 1974, and later of the Rio Viejo (1975) and Landslide (1985) fields, and double again by the time of the sale in 1988.

Tenneco had opened an office in Ventura, CA in 1964 to evaluate the California offshore arena but moved it to Bakersfield after the KCL purchase. Within just a few years, the Pacific Coast Division was a significant contributor to Tenneco Oil operations. The California properties would rank the PCD first or second in oil production and profitability throughout its entire history. Company-wide oil production jumped from 57,000 to 75,000 BOPD, and Tenneco jumped into the ranks of the nation's top dozen producing firms. At the time of the sale in 1988, oil companies still lined up to drill farm-out wells on the KCL fee land.

Although the fee lands were the target, the plums (pun intended) in the KCL acquisition were not limited to the oil and gas assets. Kern County Land Company, working off the exceptional base of its land ownership, had demonstrated an impressive growth of its own during its nearly 100 years of history. In addition to its oil and gas, KCL owned interests in agriculture, electronics and manufacturing. The southern San Joaquin Valley, with its year-round growing climate, was a breadbasket producing a wide variety of fruits, nuts and vegetables. Another KCL subsidiary, Walker Automotive put Tenneco into the automotive parts business.

Unfortunately, the KCL holdings also included a 54 percent interest in a farm equipment manufacturer, the J. I. Case, Co. For the next twenty years, the economic issues and management of Case would prove to be a challenge. In fact, directly and/or indirectly, the ownership of Case (which was later expanded to 100%) became the slow cancer that, some 20 years later, would kill the patient and bring an end to Tenneco Oil, and eventually, to Tenneco, Inc. (in any recognizable form). The move to add manufacturing businesses to the "Inc" corporate portfolio that began in 1965 with the Packaging Corp. purchase was solidified with KCL. Sometimes the box holding the Christmas presents has other surprises hidden among the wrappings. The good, the bad, and the ugly of the Kern County Land Company is well known and often studied throughout the world of business (see Dale Zand and analysis in "Epilogue" Chapter). The Kern County Land acquisition was clearly a "turning point" in the history of Tenneco Oil. The whole story deserves a good telling.

During its 75-year history, KCL had shown an impressive record of growth and expansion, but that record had put a bulls-eye on its back as a desirable acquisition. A hostile take-over attempt by Occidental Petroleum, and their legendary CEO Armand Hammer, was not a welcomed offer. KCL Chairman George Montgomery and Tenneco's Gardiner Symonds were acquainted through prior associations, (in fact, the story goes that the two were attending the same executive conference when the call about the Oxy offer came in). Montgomery immediately asked the Tenneco Chairman if he might be interested in being a more-friendly suitor. Tenneco jumped at the opportunity.

In 1967 Cliff Rackley (President of TOC from 1974 to 1978) had just moved from a job in Tenneco's corporate planning to a new position as Senior Vice President of Marketing for Tenneco Oil. Given his time in planning, he filled a second role as Mr. Scott's personal analyst for special projects. The story of his involvement in the rapid evaluation and purchase of KCL is an intriguing tale and demonstrates the aggressive nature of Tenneco, Inc. management, in particular Gardiner Symonds in "going after something", once they decided they wanted it. The story isfollows as Mr. Rackley wrote it – intriguing, indeed.

The KCL Acquisition - As Seen by One Who Was There
Extracted from My Life With Sue *by C. W. Rackley, 2009*

In May of that year (1967), at about 2:00 PM on a Thursday, I received a call from (CEO, Gardiner) Symonds, who was at the Greenbrier Hotel in West Virginia at a conference of corporate executives. He asked me to get Tenneco's valuation of the oil reserves of Kern County Land Company from our Exploration and Production department and to stand by for another call from him. About 4:00 PM he called back. After I reported the valuation of oil reserves he asked me to call the treasurer of Kern County Land and get the latest financial statements and valuations of the company by brokerage houses. The papers arrived the next day, Friday afternoon. Symonds called again and said we should look at an acquisition of the company. He had talked to (Wilton) Scott (then President of Tenneco Oil), who was in Central America and would be back Saturday, and instructed me to brief him Saturday afternoon. Symonds would return to Houston on Sunday and if the numbers looked OK, we would review those with him on the plane to San Francisco, leaving about 1:00 PM. I already knew Occidental Petroleum had acquired 10% of the KCL stock through a public tender offer and had made an offer for an additional 10% at $83.50 per share. I began my valuation. Proved oil reserves in the ground were generally selling at $1.00 per barrel. I looked up irrigated farm land to find the $1,000 per acre general number. West Texas barren land was offered for $15 per acre. KCL's properties were in large blocks in California, Arizona and New Mexico. The leased lands were sections intertwined in between the fee lands and I saw no marketable value. The livestock feeding operation made and lost money from year to year. The five-year average was small. I could value it at no more than the livestock inventory value.

J. I. Case was a traded security at $14 per share giving me a credible value for it, and Aikers Electronics was selling for $35 per share. Walker (Automotive) had good historical earnings and I put a P/E of 12 on it. This brought the total to $430 million. The company's earnings were not stellar because their exploration and production business was losing money and this was depressing the market price. My total company valuation was:

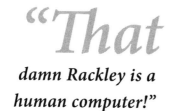

"That damn Rackley is a human computer!"

- W E Scott (CEO, Tenn Inc)

KCL HOLDINGS

Valuation based upon:	$ in millions
Oil reserves in the ground 150 million barrels. @ $1.00/bbl.	150 MM
Land, irrigated farm 110,000 acres @ $1,000/acre	110 MM
Land, ranch and not irrigated 1.5 million acres @ $15/acre	22 MM
Land leased from government 1.0 million acres @ $0	0 MM
Livestock feeding operation - Inventory value of $18.0 million	18 MM
J.I. Case Company, 54% 4.6 million shares @ $14	65 MM
Walker Mnfg. Co., 100% $4.1 million per year @ 12 P/E	50 MM
Aikers Electronics, 57% 1.0 million shares @ $35	35 MM
Liabilities	-20 MM
TOTAL	$430 MM

I walked through these numbers with Scott on Saturday afternoon. We boarded Symonds' company plane Sunday for San Francisco. David Packard, of the budding company Hewlett Packard, was aboard. After takeoff we closed off the back of the plane and briefed Symonds of the value and how I had arrived at the numbers. It looked to me that the acquisition would dilute Tenneco's earnings a little if we simply issued debt for the purchase and I showed this to him. With Occidental's offer on the table at $83.50 per share, I believed we would have to go to $90 per share. He fiddled with the numbers and said he wanted to consider offering the $430 million ($100/share) with a $4.50 per share Tenneco convertible-preferred stock for the company. All of this was done with us knowing very little of the quality and details behind the valuations. We all knew we needed more information.

Scott and I were staying at the Fairmont Hotel at the top of Knob Hill in San Francisco and Symonds was at an exclusive club across the street. We met the Chairman and President of KCL at 9:00 AM on Monday and by 9:15 Symonds had our offer of $430 million in convertible preferred stock on the table, subject to our review of financials and other key conditions. By 9:30 they had accepted it, subject to board and shareholder approval. Their board would meet the following Thursday (May 19, 1967) to consider it. I was sent to meet with the KCL Treasurer to get more details. Very early in those visits, I discovered Case had $100 million of notes outstanding, secured by inventory. When presented to Symonds, he said it was not a problem for Tenneco because we could disclose it as a footnote and not list it on our balance sheet (*Editor's Note – a liability amounting to 25% of the value of the acquisition was to be "off balance sheet," an ironic predecessor for a practice within J. I. Case for years to follow*).

For two days I dug out information and reported back to Symonds and Scott at his club. Lawyers and tax and finance staffers of Tenneco Inc. were summoned to San Francisco to study the deal and begin their analysis of issues that might derail the acquisition. One of our long-term lawyers commented that Kern County Land Company had more hard assets of value than any previous company Tenneco had acquired. Meanwhile Symonds was canvassing the Tenneco board members for their approval. Symonds contemplated a challenging counter-offer from Occidental and engaged a firm that specialized in proxy fights. On Thursday the board of KCL met and approved our offer, subject to approval by their investment banker. They came back and wanted the coupon of the convertible-preferred stock to be increased by ¼ percent making it a 4.75% per year dividend. Symonds accepted the higher coupon. We had a deal in the making and it was announced. This, only one week to the day after I had received the first phone call indicating I should begin a review.

J.I. Case's earnings had been erratic and I wanted more information. I visited the factory in Racine, Wisconsin to get a feel for their facilities. The Tenneco board meeting was set to meet shortly and Symonds asked me to make the presentation for the company to buy KCL. He had advised me that he had agreed we would not sell off the KCL company divisions, at least not right away. I hoped I would be looking at these directors in my future career so I was cau-

"In the plane (on the way to San Francisco) I told Gardner (Symonds) there was no way in God's Green Earth we could arrive at a value for that company. At 9:00 am on Monday we faced KCL's officers. By 9:15 our offer, concocted while on the plane, was on the table. The offer was a paper tender that amounted to their previous year's earnings in dividends."

- Wilton Scott
(CEO, Tenn Inc)

"I don't see how you can afford to do this."

KCL Chairman Montgomery when KCL accepted the offer of $100 per share ($432MM), less than a week after it had been made. In just a week, Tenneco had cinched its largest-ever acquisition.

"If it's a good deal, you have to act. Good deals don't wait."

Cliff Rackley
(Ret, Pres TOP&M)

tious about the claims. I felt I had to defend the value, but also to disclose the risks. As to the oil value, I used the $1 per barrel value placed by E&P. I discussed land value sources. When I commented on the cattle feeding operation, I advised that the earnings went up and down and if we had problems we could sell the animals to recover our investment and get out of the business. Since Walker had steady earnings I was comfortable. As to the electronics company, we should be able to sell the stock on the open market if necessary.

Symonds had said the KCL partners wanted no part of being a subsidiary of a big company and something would have to be worked out since the founders were the heart of the company. As to J.I. Case, I had to discuss the difficulties they had in previous years when they had some very poor earnings. KCL owned their stock because they considered themselves an agricultural company and they rescued them at a time of distress. I suggested we should be prepared for the possibility of a recurrence of poor earnings in the future, but if we valued it at stock market price and should be able to sell our shares at our cost if necessary. Due to the apparent need for some new equipment, I anticipated a need for capital. It might be necessary to buy out the minority stock for Case to get capital in the company or alternatively, to sell our shares. On this, Symonds gave me a little frown.

The board approved the purchase and the deal was closed on August 30, 1967. Occidental Petroleum did not contest our purchase. They had made a lot of money with the stock they had bought earlier. Tenneco and Occidental did engage in legal battles over whether OXY was an insider and therefore not entitled to our offer price but in the end OXY got the full price we offered. Two weeks after presentation to the board Dick Freeman, company President and adversary to Scott, sent an analyst to my office with his request for all of my information on the KCL transaction. I complied and returned to my business at hand.

Within six months, a fraud was discovered in the cattle feeding operations and it was liquidated. Also Symonds made a secondary offering (spinoff) of the electronics company stock and netted $70 million. These transactions recovered $90 million of our purchase cost. Within a few years a major oil discovery was made on the fee lands and Walker did well making catalytic converters. The University of California put a new campus at Bakersfield on land donated by KCL. KCL owned the land around it and recovered substantial capital from land development.

The KCL Acquisition

Observations from J. B. Foster, from an interview years later

The Kern County Land Company deal was a turning point deal for Tenneco. In addition to the 406,000 acres of fee land (surface and mineral ownership) in California, with significant oil and gas production (and exploration potential) the purchase also brought significant interests in J. I. Case, Watkins-Johnson (an electronics firm) and one or two other companies. It was the deal that really initiated the diversification of Tenneco away from energy.

After the acquisition, I was placed in a group called Value Analysis at the Tenneco Inc. level, and went to Bakersfield, not to assist in any way with the oil and gas operations, but to look for ways to enhance revenues from KCL's farming and real estate operations which it conducted on the surface of its fee lands.

The mineral interests in the fee lands were the crown jewel of the acquisition. They provided oil and gas royalties from other operators who leased the land. Unlike KCL, Tenneco Oil was an operator, and quickly ceased leasing to the Chevron's, Exxon's, and Oxy's, etc. of the world. We undertook to evaluate the entire holdings on our own, and to develop a complete engineering and geological understanding of the KCL properties, which came to be called Tenneco West. When Tenneco West became operator, its policy was to lease to a third party, or farm-out to another oil and gas operator, only if we had concluded we wanted to shed or share the risks of drilling. Even so, we always retained an interest of some sort…a royalty interest, an overriding royalty, and/or a healthy (direct or back-in) working interest. The industry deals made by Tenneco were constructed with much tougher terms than KCL had formerly received. As a result, the southern San Joaquin became a growth area for Tenneco Oil and the KCL deal came to be thought of as one of the most successful acquisitions that Tenneco Inc. or Tenneco Oil had ever made. We crowed about the KCL acquisition for years. I certainly did not make the deal, but did have a lot to do with making the deal work. It was a huge winner for Tenneco.

Ironically, it was this great acquisition of Kern County Land Company that led to the downfall and disappearance of Tenneco. As it turns out, when oilman Wilton Scott retired as CEO of Tenneco Inc. in 1977, he turned the reins of the company over to the then Chief Financial Officer, J. L. Ketelsen, who had come to Tenneco via the KCL acquisition. The J.I. Case component of KCL became a cancer which consumed cash unremittingly, but which remained a pet project of the new Chairman.

* * * * *

In the long run, the analysis of the Kern County Land acquisition is a very positive – a "good" - one, despite the "bad" and the "ugly" of KCL that is so often discussed in any story told about Tenneco. There is little argument that the corporate baggage that grew out of J. I. Case can be targeted as the item that led to the sale of TOE&P, and of course, J. I. Case came with KCL, but a great many very positive things came from the properties that were acquired. And those benefits were not limited to the energy side of the Tenneco Inc. family. For years the Tenneco efforts in California, both above ground and beneath the surface, flourished and added significant and continuing value to the corporation. For TOE&P the properties provided some of the very best prospecting and development projects in the company's portfolio.

The asset base represented by the KCL lands provided a forum from which other opportunities were exploited, and E&P developed a host of exciting and valuable long-term holdings there. Much of the effort in the San Joaquin Valley lent itself to the application of the unique management strategies and philosophies, and techniques developed in California made their way around the company. The KCL purchase provided the playing field that TOE&P needed in a new province, and the company managed it well. Certainly, there was much "good" that came with KCL.

A Culture Emerges

By the time of the sale of the company in 1988, the "Culture" within TOE&P had evolved to a high, unique and specific level. A diverse set of management and business practices defined the way business was done at Tenneco and were, in turn, responsible for the remarkable record of success. The "Culture" is most-often the item identified in any analysis that attempts to define what was "special" about TOE&P. In fact, a "culture" grows through a life of its own, integrating the "winning" strategies and ideas into the framework, while weeding out the ones that do not produce results, and the "culture" at TOE&P clearly evolved over time. The specific concepts that made TOE&P "special" will be discussed in detail in later chapters, but they had their beginnings in the 1960s.

The preparations for the early lease sale in 1962 laid the groundwork for the evolution of the effective manner in which Tenneco competed. Stated simply, Tenneco developed a method of economic evaluation and decision-making based on input from all technical disciplines and rigorous review of performance, risk and expected results. By 1968 the methods of analyses were being applied to projects beyond the Gulf of Mexico and, with favorable results, steps were taken to formalize the procedure throughout the company. The office of Economic Planning and Analysis was established to manage this task.

The Office of Economic Planning and Analysis (EP&A)

Business at Tenneco was managed locally through independent operating divisions. As the business grew, so did the number and diversity of projects under consideration at any one time. The need for a standard set of economic yard-sticks with analyses that could transcend the innate differences between and among the various provinces around the world was coordinated by the Economic Planning and Analysis (EP&A) office in Houston. The eventual spectacular success of TOE&P is largely credited to a working structure based on independent, de-centralized, autonomous divisions. It is something of an irony then, to learn that it was also dependent on a strongly centralized and coordinated program of economic analysis. EP&A was the analyst, the rule-maker and the referee. Autonomy was justified by results, and results were measured by the yardsticks developed at EP&A. In the early days, it became a sounding board for what would "fly" with management, and what would not. EP&A was the source for all methodologies by which economic valuations and projections were made. The goals and "driving goals" for the company came from EP&A as did the concept of "PVI" (present value as opposed to rate of return analysis) and the consistency of standards by which it was applied and measured.

Economic Planning and Analysis at TOE&P
Adapted from Joe Foster

The Economic Planning and Analysis group at TOE&P was formed at the beginning of 1968. It is unclear who in management actually took the lead in implementing the plan, but it is likely it was Wilton Scott, then President of Tenneco Oil.

Mr. Scott had observed good results achieved in Processing and Marketing through the work of a headquarters planning and analysis group headed by Cliff Rackley. Rackley was an excellent, profit-oriented manager, with good business acumen, and solid background as a refining engineer. He assembled a group of engineers to define and solve problems which seemed to be recurring at the Chalmette refinery and to analyze issues that developed as Tenneco struggled to compete against the larger major oil companies in carving out market share for refined products at the retail level.

From the mid-fifties the company had used a fairly rigorous evaluation process based upon discounted cash flow (DCF) rate-of-return which had been developed by and implemented by Richard Shoemaker, a petroleum engineer in the Calgary district, who had subsequently transferred to the Houston production department staff. DCF evaluations, and in many instances risk-adjusted valuations, were made for any significant production or development project. Tenneco Oil was very much attuned to "economic analysis", but historically, the planning and budgeting process looked only to the upcoming year, and it was created by analyzing the projected cash flow from the pipeline and its attendant need for tax deductions that would come from drilling. The company seldom looked back. The new group was asked to develop and implement several additional processes:

1. A "Review of Operating Results", to establish the historical results from geologically-defined project areas, as an aid in determining the areas of emphasis during the coming five years.

2. A consolidation of exploration and production budgets and plans by "project area". These analyses would be used for both planning purposes and to review and critique operating results by basin or by defined "project areas".

STEPHEN CHESEBRO'

A significant addition to the workforce came in 1964 when Steven D. Chesebro' brought his new degree in petroleum engineering from the Colorado School of Mines to apply to challenges at TOE&P. Over his 24-year career Chesebro' would be exposed to every element of the E&P challenge, and to quite a few beyond just that arena, with numerous assignments to special projects within Tenneco Inc. itself (including a couple he would likely have just as soon avoided). The Chesebro' family probably experienced as many job transfers and moves as any in the company. Chesebro's contributions to the growth and success of both TOE&P and TGT were considerable.

In fact, Steve Chesebro' was one of "the last men standing" with regard to the Energy Businesses of Tenneco. As described more thoroughly in the TGT section of the book (page 109), Chesebro' had been transferred into Tenneco Gas shortly before the sale of TOE&P in 1988. In 1994 he was promoted to CEO of the then consolidated Tenneco Energy and managed the remaining businesses until their final sale in 1996. Following his Tenneco career, Chesebro' went on to hold top executive positions at Pennzoil, PennzEnergy, Benton and Harvest Natural Resources, where he serves today as Chairman.

ROOR

"Our business-unit concept and degree of autonomy was far advanced for its time as were the business reporting measures. Few, if any companies, today have the detailed historical area and economic project analysis (the internal formal accounting practice to keep track of every working project) reporting system where we annually evaluated the economic and financial results of each of our major geologic investment areas. After the sale, I went to Gulf Canada, and I found an organization with top quartile-smarts, but no concept of the business or past results. It took five years to put in the Tenneco system and change the culture -- and this was within a major company."

"ROOR (Review of Operating Results) was not one of the favorite things for us to do each year, but in truth it was critical to our success. Practically all of the Tenneco managers who went on to careers in other companies installed something similar in their new spots. We lived and died by our area results and they had a big influence on determining the annual budgets."

- C E Shultz (SVP)

3. A five-year plan, in addition to the annual one-year budget.

4. A narrative description of and plan for the basins or areas to be explored and produced.

In addition, the group would be used to perform economic analysis of large or unique E&P deals or to make preliminary evaluations of acquisitions being considered by senior officers of TOC. It would also assist in providing whatever training was required to insure that the desired planning and analysis was being done at the operating levels (i.e. districts, at the time, and divisions). The group was also provided economic analyses of projects of particular interest to the senior officers of Tenneco Oil. EP&A also supplied information and analyses pertaining to Exploration and Production to the Tenneco Inc. corporate planning group.

* * * * *

Joe Foster was selected to head this new Exploration and Production group. Foster reported to S. V. McCollum, then executive vice president for the Exploration and Production side of Tenneco Oil. The founding members of the EP&A Group were all petroleum engineers. In addition to Foster, the group included Forrest E. (Eddie) Harrell, Jim Strother, and Mickey Braden. After the Kern County Land Company (KCL) acquisition in 1967, Jack Tindall, who had worked as a petroleum engineer for KCL, joined the group.

The EP&A group had two primary tasks. The first was to consolidate, analyze, and critique the five-year plans submitted from the divisions; and the second, to oversee the compilation and review of the annual "Review of Operating Results" (ROOR). This review was organized by "project area", normally a geologic basin or trend. It was a review of investment and results for exploration, development, and production activities - capital expenditures on one hand, and the reserve additions on the other. This allowed management to look at basin economics including the cost to find and develop reserves on an equivalent barrel of oil or cubic foot of gas basis. The ROOR was such a novel concept at the time that an entire accounting procedure needed to be designed to keep track of it.

In 1971, Joe Foster was promoted to become Manger of North American Exploration. He was succeeded at EP&A by Eddie Harrell, who remained until 1973, when he was hired away by Transocean. Steve Chesebro', who had just months earlier been transferred to Denver, was transferred again to head the Group. Mickey Braden, part of the original EP&A group, transferred back in to become Chief of EP&A in 1977 when Chesebro' was promoted to Lafayette. Barry Quackenbush followed Braden in 1978. The job as Chief of the Economic Planning and Analysis Group became a "stepping stone" position in Tenneco Oil Exploration and Production, and many of the company's leaders served time there. It was also a great "greenhouse" for growing and nurturing the capabilities of young engineers.

Ending the Decade – Late 1960s

The company history documents continued activity in International projects in the late 1960s. The list of projects is impressive, but unfocused, although the activity added to the learning curve for the company with regard to its foreign ventures.

TOE&P won its first license awards in the North Sea in 1967 with concessions in both the UK and Dutch sectors. In the UK, the company was eventually successful with the Heather discovery in 1973, on which E&P held a 31% interest with Unocal as the operator. The group had to wait until 1978 for production at Heather, but it turned into a profitable venture. A discovery was drilled on the Dutch blocks but was never developed. Exploration in 1968 included activity in Malagasy, offshore Saudi Arabia in the Red Sea, offshore Thailand and South Africa. The early properties owned in Colombia were sold in 1968. (Interestingly, a major acquisition fifteen years later would put Tenneco right back into the fray in this northern South American country, this time with spectacular results). Angola, the Dominican Republic, Greenland, Ethiopia and Indonesia all saw activity in 1969.

Long-term success in international venture involves being at the right place at the right time. Unfortunately, TOE&P was "ahead of its time" more than once. In 1969 in Thailand the company drilled a gas discovery estimated at 5 TCF but it was never developed for lack of market. Exxon is now developing the project, over 40 years later. The project in Indonesia was a joint venture with AGIP. The drilling produced a huge gas discovery – the only problem was that it was 75% CO_2, and would not burn. The company tried for several years to develop an LNG market but eventually dropped the concession. As in Thailand, Exxon is now developing that project.

"Exploration" moved forward in Nigeria, Australia, Labrador, Guyana, and Guatemala in 1966. Of those efforts an early discovery looked promising in Nigeria. Once again, international success seemed finally to be at hand, but again, unanticipated outside events changed the playing field. In 1967 a tribal Civil War plunged the nation into a chaotic and destructive period that would see the complete shut-down of production and operations. Tenneco abandoned the project, not to return until the mid-1970s.

Onshore, the district offices in Casper and Durango district offices were consolidated into the new Rocky Mountain Division in Denver in 1968. Altamont field was discovered there in 1969. The decade closed with year-end company reserves creeping close to another milestone - the one billion NEB level. Curiously, that number would stay fairly constant for most of the next fifteen years. Growth would become a greater challenge as some significant changes lay ahead for the industry as a whole in the years immediately ahead.

"*We* were in 'high cotton' in 1969 when we obtained a terminal hooked up to a GE time-share computer which allowed us to sort and assemble data much more effectively. We had one keyboard for a group of four engineers, with one assistant, in a tiny file room, but the work got done."

Mickey Braden
(Mgr Prod, Frontiers)

Taking the pulse of TOC delegates at a lease sale bid meeting in Lafayette in 1970.

E&P AT FULL SPEED

An Independent Identity

Through the 1960s, TOC evolved significantly from its initial founding, through periods of challenge and even survival, and then on through stabilization and notable growth. Maintaining the curve through the 1970s would prove to be a challenge, but a challenge met. Many significant events lay ahead for TOE&P during the 1970s.

The decade began with a change at the top. Wilton Scott was promoted into the upper management of Tenneco, Inc. George Meason, who had been EVP of Tenneco Oil Processing and Marketing, was named the third President of Tenneco Oil Company.

Back to the Gulf in a Big Way

The Lafayette office was a flurry of exploration and development activity during the 1960s. The "Tenneco Advantage" was applied skillfully and both TOE&P and TGT saw their fortunes grow through the synergy it provided. Tenneco, the "pipeline company with an exploration department", became a consistent competitor in the Gulf of Mexico. By 1970 the offshore prospects purchased at the 1960 and 1962 lease sales were nearing full development. It was time to re-stock the cupboard. The Federal Sale of 1970 was the first of the new "area-wide" lease sales. Prior to 1970, specific single blocks (usually 5000 acres) of interest to potential bidders were "nominated" by industry well before lease sale dates were set, and all of the companies working the Gulf evaluated the same group of tracts. Beginning in 1970, the government changed its policies and simply designated large contiguous areas in the Gulf as being available for bid. All blocks in the designated area that were not then under lease, were open for bids. These "area-wide" offerings created a "land rush" mentality among potential bidders, and the interest level was far greater than at previous sales, as each player pursued their own favorite prospects.

Given the new sale dynamics, the sale was highly anticipated, but it was only a guess as to "just what would happen." The result created some high drama. Tenneco was spectacularly successful, with winning bids on 14 tracts. The total expenditure for that single morning was an eye-popping $137MM! Unknown at the time to the majority of the ecstatic personnel who worked on the sale, was the fact that the allocated budget was in the $75-$90MM range! Fortunately, ten of those fourteen tracts would prove productive, and one held a portion of a 1.5TCF gas field, Eugene Island 330, discovered by Pennzoil/Pogo, but of course, that was not known to management at the time, and provided no comfort to the dilemma of the day – figuring out how to pay for the leases that had been bought. The stories of the '70 sale are numerous and fascinating. The sale of 1970 would prove to be yet another Turning Point for TOC.

**President Profile
GEORGE MEASON
1970-1974**

George Meason was a refinery engineer, a graduate of the University of Texas with a degree in Chemical Engineering. He had worked at Humble and came to TGT in 1956. He was elected President in 1970 and served through mid-1974 when he was promoted into Tenneco Inc. as Executive Vice President. Meason's tenure at E&P saw aggressive offshore drilling programs in both domestic and foreign waters and the extensive development of the Kern County Lands in California. Meason died in 2003.

Turning Point – The 1970 Lease Sale

Joe Foster - from an Interview for the Offshore History Museum

I was manager of the Economic Planning & Analysis group and was invited to sit in for the prospect reviews for the upcoming 1970 lease sale. The team that year included Bill Medary, VP of Exploration in Houston, and Lee Sargent and John Peterson, exploration and production managers, respectively, in Lafayette, both reporting to Dan Johnson, who was the division general manager. Phil Oxley, who had left the company some years before, was hired as a special consultant. We went to the 1970 sale all on our own; without partners. I had felt that this was going to be a very competitive sale as there had not been a sale offering as many blocks in a long time. I also thought we ought to take a lot of exposure authority. Historically, we and the industry in general had spent about one-third of the amount of money that was exposed. In other words, the winning bids were usually about one-third of the total of all bids that were made.

There was some debate about this within the company. We had a budget of $80 million – that's what we could afford to spend. I was pushing for an exposure target of $250 million. The president of the company, Wilton Scott, said we ought not figure on spending less than 50% of our exposure (so his target would have been about $160 million). In prior jobs, I had worked for Mr. Symonds, CEO of Tenneco, Inc. He called me in and asked what I thought. Fortunately, this was in a conference call and Mr. Scott was also present. I said, "I think we ought to go with an exposure of $250 million." So the next day Symonds called and said, "This is what we are going to do, Joe. I have talked to Scotty about it this morning and you've got your authority for $250 million." Well, to make a long story short, our winning bids totaled $137 million - on that $80 million budget - and on one block we left a $30 million over-bid on the table! And I was the 'numbers-guy' who had been responsible for justifying the bids!

Mr. Scott was mad as hell. Mr. Symonds was out of the country and he was going to be back in New York the next day. Scott called and said, "You and me are going to get on the plane and we are going to go tell Mr. Symonds what you have done!" I remember those words distinctly. It was a very long – and silent - plane ride to New York in a company plane. In New York we met with Mr. Symonds. We showed him a list of what the reserve exposure for the blocks we'd won and he said, "Well, that looks like a lot of good acreage." And then, "What are you most disappointed about, Joe?" I replied, "Well, I am most disappointed about Prospect 56 where we left $30 million on the table." And he said, "No, I did not mean that. I mean what are you most disappointed about not getting!?" That told me a lot about Mr. Symonds. He said, "Don't worry about it, Scotty. All these are good blocks, even where we left money on the table. We'll sell down if we need to, and keep a call on all the gas for TGT". He then said, "Joe, just go back and re-draw those maps and you can sell them to partners. That is your job. I want a limit of $80 million of expenditures." So that is what we did - and that's how we started working more often with partners.

It took about three weeks, but S. V. McCollum brought in Texaco, who had been totally shut out with their own bids, and they paid the other $57 million. Texaco insisted on operating at least half of the properties. So, for the first time, we had a partner in virtually all of our properties and an outside operator on a lot of those. Once you get in bed with somebody to the extent we had, you have obligations to work together on blocks around the ones owned jointly. We bid with Texaco for about five or six years after that. Over time, all of the guys that worked together initially got transferred to different places and we lost that relationship with Texaco, but that was the start of it. We bid with other partners most of the time thereafter.

The company also put together a consortium of 20 insurance companies to finance the rest of the commitment, and that in itself, created new partner-ships and leverage the company had not used in the past, relationships that would prove useful in the years ahead. In retrospect, the 1970 lease sale added tremendously to the company's reserves and to its long-term growth.

* * * * *

The stories that follow here are from several who were "in the trenches" for that 1970 sale. They add personal perspective to the process of preparation for that sale – and the outcome.

George Meason was an outstanding business-man. He did not have the broad experience or multitude of contacts on the upstream side of the oil business that Wilton Scott possessed, but it was good experience for all of us in E&P to report in to George. We really had to think through our recom-mendations and articulate them well as he was not as attuned to the nuances or vocabulary of our business as was Wilton Scott. During his term, Mr. Mason learned about exploration and produc-tion, and those of us from E&P learned a lot about how refinery econom-ics differed from E&P economics. George asked many questions which led to improvements in the E&P effort."

J B Foster (EVP Tenn Inc)

"I was the exploration manager for the offshore division for the 1970 sale. When we took the recommended bids to Houston and presented them to the Tenneco Inc Board of Directors, our proposed exposure was a staggering amount and there was total silence in the room after we finished. Gardner Symonds got up and walked around the room. He sat back down and said, 'Gentlemen, we have to back them.'"

- Lee Sargent (Expl Mgr, GOM)

"The offshore lease sale was held at the St. Charles Hotel in New Orleans, LA in early December 1970. As was division practice, all professional employees who worked on the sale preparation went to New Orleans for a night on the town at company expense and to attend the sale the next morning. We had a great time dining on Creole Cuisine and walking down Bourbon St. that evening—a nice reward for such a long, hard period of preparation. The next morning the crowd gathered in the packed hotel ballroom with both apprehension and anticipation rose. All the top company executives were there, Schacht McCollum, Bill Medary, Don Dampf, Lee Sargent, and a contingent from Houston. The sale began and we all began taking notes to document the tracts TOC had bid on. About halfway through the list of sale tracts, TOC had already won quite a few, and many of our most-favored tracts were still to come. Smiles spread among the employees—with one exception. I noticed Bill Medary as he left his seat and walked to the back of the room. He looked bad. I thought he might be feeling sick from too much partying the previous night. What I did not know at the time was that authorization had been granted for a total expenditure of about $80 million, and we had already spent the entire authorized amount by the mid-point of the sale. As the sale progressed, Tenneco's success continued and I noticed Medary getting paler by the moment. I learned later that he was afraid he would be fired for spending more than he was authorized. There were no cell phones back then so Bill could not call Houston for additional approval. Every time TOC won another tract his demeanor worsened. The final total of TOC winning bids was $137 million. The troops were elated. The Tenneco Tigers had arrived! We were now a significant player in the GOM. No more doom and gloom about the future.

Bill Medary did not lose his job. And Texaco agreed to buy into the entire TOC package. That was quite a change for the tiny upstart TOC to be in the driver's seat in negotiations with Texaco! Bill sent a letter to all Offshore Dist. employees thanking them for the work they had done in preparing for the sale including the statement "this is the best we have ever been prepared for an offshore sale". Medary was subsequently promoted to VP Exploration."

- Mickey Braden (Pr Mgr, Frontiers, Pet. Eng., GOM at the time)

"I will never forget having to explain to Scotty (Wilton Scott) what "Bright Spots" were and what caused them, and his question 'Have you ever

"**I encouraged** the bidding group to be bullish. They took me to heart. It was my first month as president, and they spent $137MM! We didn't have that kind of money. It was a crisis. Mr. Symonds told me not to worry and that the worst thing we could have done would have been not to buy anything."

George Meason,
President E&P at the time

"**If you want** to be aggressive in a sale, you go after more than you think you'll get. On average you buy 30 percent of what you go after. We exposed $251MM and thought we'd spend $75MM. Instead, our winning bids were $137MM. We were frozen solid for the next few days, waiting for the phone to ring. Eventually the calls came and we were able to bring in selected partners where we wanted to – folks who had been unsuccessful with their own bids."

Phil Oxley

done this before?'. I had to truthfully answer 'No, but I believe in them'. I guess we convinced him because as he left from the meeting he slapped me on the back and said 'I hope you are as smart as I think you are.'"

— *D G Westover, (Expl Mgr, MCD, Geoph, GOM at the time)*

"In the late 1960s and early '70's Tenneco's geophysicists were on the leading edge in applying "bright spot" technology to offshore prospecting. The early theory that seismic data, if properly analyzed, might suggest a direct indication of the presence of gas, was revolutionary. Over subsequent years these applications became quite sophisticated and complex and spread throughout the industry, but TOE&P was certainly among the earliest in applying it. To the best of my knowledge, only Tenneco and Pennzoil (POGO) bid real money on prospects based on applied seismic hydrocarbon indicators in the December, 1970 sale, and we were by far the big winners."

— *S D Chesebro' (Tenn Inc)*

"As things drilled out over the years, it became clear that we bought a lot of good things with the $137MM. On the block where we left $30 million on the table; it drilled out on the fourth attempt. We drilled three dry holes on it before we finally found where the pay was. So the prospect was hurting. The company was hurting. I was hurting! We were adding money to the $30 million left on the table.

That one was called "Prospect 56." Just after the sale I was named manager of exploration operations, and my boss, S. V. McCollum, presented custom-made tie tacks featuring the number 56 to members of the lease sale team. The pins were presented with a stern admonition to watch out for overbidding in the future, and to "Wear the damn thing every day until we make a discovery on Prospect 56." With the first three dry holes, the little gold-plated 56's were becoming millstones. When the next well was a discovery, the "56" pins became a badge of pride. Within a month all of the team members received a new tie tack, this time with a diamond in the center! I have my "56" to this day. That was East Cameron 280 and 281; two blocks I'll never forget!"

— *J B Foster (Tenn Inc)*

The 1970 lease sale was actually held on December 15 of that year. In January of 1971 several changes in company management structure were implemented. Joe Foster was promoted to Manager of Exploration for the Company, Phil Oxley was re-hired as Chief Geologist, and Bill Medary was promoted to Vice President of Exploration and Production for the company, with a focus on the new international projects. There were a lot of unique things about Tenneco, but one of the most forward-thinking was in the cross-training and cross-management within the various technical disciplines.

The inventory of quality prospects was restocked with the success of the

"*Our* heavy bidding scared the hell out of me, but I dearly love those bids now."

— Wilton Scott

1970 sale. The growth begun in the 1960s continued into the 1970s. The company retained its aggressive posture and between 1970 and 1974 invested $385 million on new leases in the Gulf of Mexico, an amount far larger than what might be expected from the 21st-largest oil company out there. Wilton Scott, Tenneco Inc. TOE&P discovered more oil than it produced in 1973, countering the norm in the industry.

In Lafayette, the growth driven by lease sale successes brought more and more eager young engineers and other professionals to do the work. Encouraged by management's aggressive support of technology these folks were constantly "pushing the envelope" for methods of improving their efficiencies. Mickey Braden provided a couple of stories that demonstrate just how far computers have come in the last 40 years.

Taking Computers into Your Own Hands
By M Braden

Combining reserve estimates, production forecasts, and capital and operating expenses into an economic analysis, and then applying risk factors for myriad scenarios to develop meaningful direction for company executives was a daunting task. Even with the new amazingly fast Wang calculators, the staff was hard pressed to get all the work for a lease sale done in time. The only computers available then were mainframes. Tenneco had one at the headquarters in Houston but there was no program available to do bid-analysis calculations. The mainframe was tended by a staff group of computer specialists, but I did not know the computer languages they used for programming and they did not understand our economic calculations. I had learned a computer language called "Basic" in college and decided to try that. The engineers got a program up and running, and were able to get all the bid analysis work done in time, but we earned the wrath of the Systems Dept. in Houston for consuming an alarming amount of computer resources.

In the "old" days the engineers needed to use logarithms to calculate exponential decline curves, and had to do all the calculations with slide rules or the few mechanical calculators available in the local offices. "Adding machines" could not do logarithmic calculations. The calculations were tedious, time consuming and prone to error. About that time the Wang Company had been marketing an electronic system for word processing (then known as typing) which involved a central electronic brain connected by cable to keyboard stations. Tenneco had acquired a system for the secretaries typing, and it was amazing how much it simplified the work. (The ubiquity of computers today makes it difficult to remember how different thing were before Bill Gates and Steve Jobs revolutionized our civilization). The Wang Co. also produced a calculator that worked much faster than the mechanical ones, and *it could also do logarithms!* The system was expensive, at about $10,000 for the central unit and six stations. At the time, oil brought about $2.50/bbl and we got $0.18/MCF gas prices, so

New lease acquisition was not the only activity in the Gulf in 1970. In early August Hurricane Celia, one of the most destructive storms to ever hit the Texas coast, caused damages estimated at $1.6 billion. Tenneco's office in Corpus Christi was destroyed by Celia.

EARLY COMPUTING

In those days, we communicated with the main-frame computer via teletype. The engineers would complete input sheets and Patsy Duhon, our secretary, would type the data into a machine cutting a narrow paper tape which later could be read by the teletype and sent to the computer input via telephone lines. Often these tapes would be yards long and coil up on the floor beneath the machine. Patsy wore spiked high-heels and more than once the tape curled around her shoes and ripped as she walked away, making the tape totally useless and requiring hours of repeated work.

that was a lot of money! We had to make several runs at Joe Stasney, our super-intendent, but he eventually relented, and we got the Wangs!

* * * * *

The early years of the decade of the '70's also featured a drive to maxi-mize financial returns. In the search for "efficiency" many new ideas were conceived and implemented throughout the company. Technical innova-tions at Tenneco in the Gulf of Mexico included 'outside the box' think-ing in the area of platform design, and again, identified E&P engineers as some of the best of the time.

Stretching The Platform

The goal for every offshore project is to build a structure that used the least amount of steel per producing well. An eight-pile platform was most often the correct economic choice for larger discoveries. Unfortunately, by the mid-1970s, the size of the 'average' discovery of the day was shrinking, but the industry continued to use eight pile platforms as it moved into deeper water.

Platform costs increase exponentially with water depth. Frequently, pros-pect economics would justify only a single eight-pile platform. A single plat-form would then require multiple well slots and room for associated equipment. In addition, the high cost of a platform rig often led to poor decisions regarding the number of wells drilled. The general philosophy was to drill as many as pos-sible while the rig was there in order to avoid having to bring a rig back to the platform in the future, and that sometimes led to unnecessary wells.

In contrast, Tenneco's use of the four-pile platform allowed the building of a smaller platform that could be linked to other small platforms on an "as needed" basis. It allowed much greater flexibility with the timing of critical decisions, and it saved considerable capital. Incremental decisions could be made as facts learned along the way dictated, as opposed to the need to know all the answers up front before a platform was built, as was the case with the industry standard at the time.

The stretch four-pile platform allowed expansion into deeper water. The costs required for a four pile platform still increased exponentially, but the base four-pile was less than half of the cost of an eight-pile. This allowed Ten-neco to bid on smaller prospects than anyone else in the industry. The four-piles could be built much more quickly, thereby allowing first production in eighteen months, rather than the more common three years. Accelerated cash flow meant bigger profits. The smaller platforms could be placed on small-er fields and allowed more efficient development. Cantilevered jack-up rigs could be mobilized easily and return to drill a few wells when data was avail-able to show new wells were justified.

The four-pile versus eight-pile project was developed in the early 1970s, before the 1972 lease sale. At the 1972 sale TOE&P was particularly successful in acquiring blocks in the near-300' water depth. Blocks like the East Camer-

"Among many others who worked on the four-pile "stretch" concept over the years, Fred Lentjes, Al Turner, Steve Mueller and Shorty Quibideaux were among the best platforms guys in the business."

S D Chesebro' (Tenn Inc)

on 271/272 complex, East Cameron 280-281, Ship Shoal 343 and the Eugene Island 330 complex were four-pile for Tenneco and eight-pile for everyone else. Some might call the use of the four-pile in this water depth as "stretch", but the true "stretch four-pile" occurred in the early eighties in +400' water depths with the early deep water production in Texas and then extending into offshore Louisiana. The concept proved to be a significant competitive advantage for TOE&P.

An interesting consequence of the development of the "stretched" four-pile model was that it allowed a "re-look" at operations in shallow water. The one-well caisson was "stretched" to become a caisson with up to four well-slots. This led to further economic advantages for Tenneco in redeveloping older fields or commercializing smaller shallow water discoveries. At about the same time Tenneco developed its first "subsea completion". The first Tenneco subsea tree was set in 200 feet of water in EI215 in the late 1970s.

International in the Early 1970s

For the first half of the decade of the 1970s, international exploration continued aggressively, but still without significant success. Exploration in Peru started in 1970, and an office was opened in Lima. An attractive 5000 BOPD offshore discovery justified excitement and investment. The company utilized a platform deck from the Gulf of Mexico and moved it through the Panama Canal while a jacket was being constructed on the beach in Peru. Once the platform was set, the early confirmation wells included four dry holes and the property was sold to Belco. It later became a centerpiece for the much smaller company. Also in 1970, prospecting spread to Iran (looking for sulfur), and to Spain as well. Drilling in the Arctic began in 1971 and continued there in one form or another for the next 16 years (see Frontier stories). Exploration in Gabon started in 1973 without significant success. Interestingly though, the acquisition of Houston Oil & Minerals in 1981 would bring eventual success from Gabon.

Another huge gas discovery came Tenneco's way in 1975 in waters offshore Trinidad. For years the company pursued various market options for the 2 TCF discovered there. Innovative (or 'wild') ideas included thoughts of building a pipeline across the entire Gulf of Mexico to the US. Thirty-five years later, EOG is now developing the reserve discovered there. Again, "Ahead of our time" might have been an understatement. The TGT section of the book includes a comprehensive discussion of the Trinidad/Tobago project.

Foreign duty could involve a wide variety of memorable experiences – from humorous to terrifying. An entire book could be compiled with a full range of exciting and interesting tales from those early "wild and wooly" years, as the following demonstrate. Unfortunately, until the early 1970s, the foreign ventures had produced more stories than profits. It was a tough business.

"*In* the summer of 1973, I came back to the office after a camping trip with the family and was handed a ticket to Houston with orders to see Schact McCollum. Eddie Harrell had resigned, so they put me into the EP&A job. All hell broke loose soon with the OPEC oil embargo and the first oil spike – the price jumped all the way up to around $9 per barrel."

S D Chesebro' (Tenn Inc)

The Russian Caper

Adapted from S D Chesebro' (Tenn Inc at Sale)

In the mid- to late-1960s the science of defining oil and gas generation (both volume, and type) began to spread in the domestic petroleum industry. This focus was important because the Gulf of Mexico was being opened to leasing out to the daunting water depth of 300 meters, areas with no well control and great uncertainties about productive potential. The first of the regional "area-wide" lease sale in the Gulf of Mexico was held in December, 1970, and subsequent sales would occur nearly every year thereafter. Information leaked from the research labs at Shell, Amoco, Exxon, Mobil, and parts of the service industry made it clear that progress was being made in this research, and hard knowledge would be a competitive advantage. During this same period, Tenneco was aggressively expanding internationally, as well as domestically. We were going to places where entire basins had yet to be explored. We needed all the technical tools available to reduce our risk.

In January, 1972 Tenneco sent a delegation as part of a group of partner companies to Moscow on a project called "North Star" to investigate bringing Russian gas to the U.S. in the form of LNG. The Tenneco delegation was led by Jack Ray (head of delegation), and included Harry Long (TGT), Bud Carey (Exploration research), Ewell Muse (TGT), and Steve Chesebro' (reservoir and economics). Things were progressing nicely until the Russians began to focus on those of us from Tenneco, due to Tenneco's involvement with Newport News Shipbuilding. For about four weeks, in and around Moscow, the Tenneco boys were under close surveillance. Rooms and belongings were searched at least once a day, and the "In-tourist Guides" were always close by.

However, on three different days Chesebro' and Carey talked the guides into visiting book stores under the pretext of looking for famous Russian authors. What they quickly discovered was that much of what the Russians knew about oil and gas source rocks was published. They found many graphs and tables with clear definition of what we were looking for.

During the month-long visit, the group dealt with approximately 25 "Ministries", including the Ministries of Exploration, Gas, Economics, Oil, Metallurgy, Economics, Geophysics, Drilling, Welding (Welding, because Tenneco had experience in Arctic welding)and on and on. Each Ministry was knowledgeable about their own silo, and the research and theoretical studies associated with their area was outstanding, but each knew nothing about the world outside their realm, and they did not care, or dare, to venture outside their sphere. There was nothing wrong with publishing everything they knew because only Russians had access to it. There weren't any Gringos around.

Translating as best they could, the 'investigators' studied at length to retain the information should the books be confiscated. They even entrusted one of the "Guides" to help translate some of the technical words. The guide was a nice lady, but got uncomfortable during the last week of the trip.

"The Russians knew we were after something, but the KGB had no clue what it was. They were sure we were spies of the highest order though. There were two of us in on this caper. The other gentleman was Dr, Bud Carey who headed up Tenneco's Exploration Research group. The monitoring and searches intensified, but The Russians could not find what we had, even though they reviewed the critical books several times." relates Chesebro'

"We left Moscow in February escorted by machine gun-toting guards. We were not sure whether we were going to the airport, or Lubyanka. At the airport the guards searched me and my suitcases for two hours, throwing the "useless" technical books aside while they cut open my luggage and inspected the Matrushka dolls. Obviously frustrated, they threw everything back into my luggage and escorted Bud and me to the waiting plane. We had flown in on Aeroflot, but left on JAL with real vegetables (and lots of champagne) for the first time in nearly a month."

Back home, Tom Spurlock in geological research completed the translations and Tenneco made some good, solid exploration decisions in the ensuing years by applying with confidence what other companies did not yet know, or were reluctant to integrate the knowledge into their exploration decision-making progress.

A Very Serious Matter
By Ken Watts (Mng. Dir, Norway)

The airport in Lagos, Nigeria was old, crowded, dusty and hot, and most flights from Europe arrived almost simultaneously in the evening. This guaranteed a major crowd of people pushing and shoving to get through the customs and immigration officials, who sat behind booths on one side of the hall. Everyone grumbled, but eventually the process worked and we could get through.

On one trip, Jack Edwards and I were traveling together. I got through without much hassle but Jack was caught in a long line. I saw Jack step up to an official, a handsome Nigerian dressed in the military green dress they always wore immaculately. The official thumbed through Jack's passport and the immunization records that were kept in the passports.

"Mr. Edwards," the official said, "it seems your cholera shot has expired". He handed the passport and shot record back to Jack, who looked at it and realized the official was right. "What can we do?", Jack asked the official. The official, pointing to a separate room across the immigration hall said , "You can go over there to that room, and I will call a doctor from Lagos to come administer the cholera shot you require. It will take approximately three hours".

Edwards calmly replied, "Is there anything else we could do?". "Perhaps," replied the official, whereupon Jack placed a $5 bill in the passport and asked him to look at the record again. The official calmly looked at the passport and the bill, and said to Jack, "Mr. Edwards, the problem is MUCH MORE SERIOUS THAN THAT." and passed the passport, with the $5 bill in it, back to Jack.

Jack found a $20 bill in his wallet, placed it in the passport and said, "Could you please check that date again", whereupon the official, seeing the $20, smiled, stamped the entry visa, and said "Pass On"!

You often encounter these sorts of shake-downs as you travel in the developing world, but seldom do you encounter one so skillfully played with a smile on his face and a friendly demeanor. I have gotten far more than $20 worth of pleasant memories of this encounter and the way Jack handled it.

* * * * *

Unfortunately, sometimes the news from the international venues had little to do with the discovery of oil and gas. Two of the most extreme stories from the years pursuing success in Africa, come from Ethiopia. Texaco was our partner there and the combine drilled a couple of discoveries but again, political unrest spelled the end to the venture.

Hijacked

On December 8, 1972, S.V. McCollum, Executive Vice President of Tenneco Oil, boarded an early-morning flight in Addis Ababa, Ethiopia. He was headed to Paris on the first leg of his trip home from a visit to company operations in the country. Hardly settled into his seat, McCollum found himself in the middle of a scene as bizarre as anything in a high-energy Hollywood production. In 1972 Ethiopia was experiencing the early elements of political unrest that would lead to a Civil War a year or two later. Shortly after take-off seven Ethiopian students, later identified as members of the Eritrean Islamic Jihad, stood up from their seats with guns drawn and announced "Hijack!" The plane also carried several armed Ethiopian air marshals, some of whom had been identified by the hijackers and were already held at gunpoint. As one hijacker made his way to the cockpit, a remaining marshal managed to engage him, and in short order a gun battle raged within the confines of the aircraft. An estimated 40 to 50 shots were fired during the next three minutes. Three of the seven hijackers were dispatched on the spot. But, one of the wounded pulled the pin on a hand grenade and tossed it onto the floor. The passenger nearest the grenade picked it up and threw it into the empty seat in front of him. Unfortunately, Mr. McCollum sat in the seat forward of that one, and when the hand-grenade exploded it tore through the back of his seat.

The Tenneco exec was gravely wounded by the shrapnel and had been hit by the gunfire as well. The hand grenade also blew a 15-inch hole in the side of plane and severed a number of the electrical and hydraulic cables that controlled the plane. The crew managed to regain control of the severely damaged aircraft, turn it around and return to Addis Ababa for an emergency landing. Later accounts would ascribe "heroic" actions to the crew for being able to land the plane without crashing. In all, six of the seven hijackers and one air marshal would die from their wounds. Eleven passengers were injured, McCollum among the worst. Mr. McCollum was airlifted to Greece for emergency

A young Houston trauma surgeon – the later infamous Dr. James "Red" Duke – was sent to accompany McCollum home. Dr. Duke was present as an intern to receive President J F Kennedy in Dallas when he was shot, and was the model for the "Buck James" television series.

treatment. When he had recovered well enough to travel, the company sent a specially-outfitted "hospital" plane to bring him back to the States.

Tenneco President at the time, George Meason, later remarked, "I don't think Schacht ever went back to Ethiopia." I suppose not!

Kidnapped

Unfortunately, Tenneco's problems in Ethiopia were not limited to this one spectacular event. By 1974, famine, economic problems associated with the Arab Oil Embargo of 1973, and general political unrest in Ethiopia had led to the outbreak of Civil War. Emperor Haile Selassie was under siege. The conflict would eventually bring an end to his long reign. The Eritrean Liberation Front (ELF), operating mostly in the remote north of the country, was the primary adversary of the government and was sponsored mainly from outside interests in neighboring Sudan and other countries. Tenneco was exploring concessions in Ethiopia in partnership with Texaco. In March of 1974 a party of five, including Tenneco employees Bill Cayce (later, the General Manager of the Rocky Mountain Division of TOE&P) and Cliff James, were doing field work by helicopter. The group had landed to inspect some outcrops in a remote area. Unfortunately, the noise of the helicopter had alerted an ELF force of 25 machine-gun toting soldiers who were operating in the area. The ELF apparently feared the helicopter was part of a government force searching for them and engaged the "invaders", disabling the helicopter in the process. Despite the mistaken identity, the ELF took the party of five into their custody. Although kidnapped, the Americans were treated relatively well and little true hostility was demonstrated towards them, but the six-month ordeal that followed was a nightmare nevertheless.

The rebels were poorly organized and had few resources. There was very little food for either rebel or hostage and they were always on the move. The party went from one hideout to another, always on foot and often moving at night through the remote desert. During the six months of their detention Cayce and James each lost about 40 pounds and suffered great physical decline. Tenneco management was of course anxious to secure the safe release of their employees, but the ELF was poorly organized and had little formal structure. One of the greatest challenges was in locating just exactly "who" to talk to, and "how" to negotiate the release with the several factions within the ELF. Finally, in September 1974, the captive group was taken to a spot on a large river. Their captors told them they'd been freed and instructed them to "walk downstream along the river. Your friends will be waiting for you." The Americans had no idea where they were or where they were headed. The "walk" turned out to be about twenty miles and it took them to the Sudanese border, where indeed friendly faces waited.

Tenneco Inc was able to negotiate an agreement for the release of the hostages in part by using its agricultural expertise. In return for helping negotiate their release, we put in a model farm in Sudan. Tenneco West provided farming expertise, and Case provided equipment. The project was in an area that had been farmed and irrigated for decades (if not centuries) and the soil was too salty and mineral rich to support good crops. We made some progress, but couldn't leach the minerals out of the soil.

- S D Chesebro' (Tenn Inc)

Fully committed in the Gulf and primed for rapid growth, Tenneco Oil was major offshore player.

E&P IN THE ARENA

The Offices of Tenneco Oil E&P

From the modest start in 1946, with just a few professionals doing the first drilling and production on the West Hungerford leases, the operations of Tenneco Oil Company grew to an eventual powerhouse with offices around the world. At the time of the sale in 1988, TOE&P had a workforce of 3573 employees (including subsidiaries) working in ten operating divisions in six American cities, and in 10 foreign countries. The corporate home office in Houston housed executive management and company-wide administrative functions.

By the early to mid-1970s the geographic distribution of the TOE&P offices, and its unique and successful practice of working through "independent operating divisions", had pretty much taken the shape it would hold through the remainder of its life as a company. Much of the credit for the long-term success of E&P's business is credited to the manner in which TOE&P managed its organization and work.

Offshore – The Backyard: Growth and Impact

By any account, the Gulf of Mexico became "Tenneco's backyard". From the days of its earliest ventures there, through its years of prodigious growth, and culminating with its eventual dominant position within the industry, the words "Tenneco Oil" and "The Gulf" were synonymous. The GOM produced a great number of the significant events, milestones and company turning points that shaped the company. Tenneco had established an operating office in Lafayette, LA with its first steps into the Gulf in the late 1950s. Early exploration was in New Orleans, but that effort was moved to Lafayette in the early 1960s following the first lease sale successes. At the sale in 1988 Tenneco was a major player in Lafayette with three operating divisions, the Eastern, Central and Western Gulf Divisions, and 412 employees in the workforce. In addition, Tenneco subsidiary Operator's Inc. had 645 employees in Lafayette and Houma, LA. At the time of the sale of the company in 1988, Tenneco was either the number 1 or 2 day-to-day producer of gas in the Gulf. TOE&P operated 435 of the 916 wells in which it owned interests on 230 platforms throughout the Gulf. Tenneco's proved reserves of 538 MMNEB in the Gulf of Mexico made it one of the top competitors in the Gulf. At the Sale of the company in 1988, Chevron purchased the Gulf of Mexico package for $2.6 billion.

Onshore – The Base: A Strategy of Exploitation

An old axiom in the oil business states, "A good place to look for oil and gas is in areas where it has already been found". The prolific onshore provinces of North America had been under development for many years before TOE&P first began its work in 1946. Although TGT's early acquisition strategy focused on specific properties along the routes of their pipelines, a purchase often brought properties beyond the target, and sometimes in areas completely outside their own area of service. In these mature provinces significant growth in Tenneco's operations came generally through the subsequent development of the acquired assets. Certainly, every onshore Tenneco office had an active exploration effort, and over the years most of the divisions produced several notable exploration discoveries, but the principal onshore US effort at Tenneco could generally be described as one of exploitation and extension, with true exploration developing as the divisions themselves matured. The onshore operations provided a dependable base of income, operations and opportunity as the generally long-lived assets were managed for maximum efficiency. The diverse set of properties with their many related technical challenges made the onshore offices a crucible for development of many of the company's most successful operating strategies – and people. For example, the signature asset represented by the multiple-discipline team concept was a product of the need for integration at all levels in the complex opportunity base of the onshore US.

As the company grew, small offices were located in a variety of cities and towns, mostly near the fields and operations themselves. Over the years, "district" offices were opened in many cities, including Calgary, Alberta; Midland, Wichita Falls, Bellaire and Corpus Christi, TX; Casper, WY; Durango, CO; Farmington, NM;, and Shreveport and Lafayette (onshore), LA. In 1971 and early 1972, E&P undertook a reorganization program and consolidated operations by closing the "districts". These changes led to the highly successful "Independent Division" concept. The Divisions became the basic business units and profit centers for TOE&P. At the time of the Sale in 1988, onshore offices were located in Bakersfield, CA – the Pacific Coast Division (PCD), Denver – the Rocky Mountain Division (RMD), San Antonio – the Southwestern Division (SWD), Oklahoma City – the Mid-Continent Division (MCD), and Houston – the Gulf Coast Division (GCD). In 1988 the company had interests in 20,800 onshore wells, operating 4221 of those. The onshore offices produced 46% of the company's oil and liquids and 35% of the gas.

Gulf Coast Division - Houston

The Gulf Coast Division (GCD) was the home of the oldest of the properties held in the TOE&P asset base. The GCD grew through acquisitions, extension and exploitation of the fields acquired and also through successful exploration both on and outside the purchased properties. The roots of the GCD are traced to the earliest days of the company when Tennessee Gas Transmission (TGT) moved into the coastal areas of Texas and Louisiana in 1946 to initiate gas operations. TGT's early drilling and property acquisitions in the Gulf Coast area, often along the TGT pipelines, formed the foundation for what later became Tenneco Oil Company.

The Gulf Coast Division covered the coastal states of Louisiana, Alabama, Mississippi and Florida as well as the southern portion of Arkansas and the south and northeast corners of Texas. (From 1981 – 1985 the Gulf Coast Division was subdivided to include a separate operation for the Texas Gulf Coast Division. Those two divisions were re-combined in 1986 after the economic downturn in the industry.)

Many of the early TGT acquisitions brought important properties to the GCD. Middle States Petroleum Company in 1958 provided the Bethany field and Old Lisbon Operating Committee in northern Louisiana. Another key property, the Charenton field in southern Louisiana, came with the company's acquisition of Fifteen Oil Company in 1960. That year Tenneco also acquired Slick Oil Company, bringing with it the Slick Estate and Slator Ranch properties in south Texas. The Delhi-Taylor purchase of 1964 added the McAllen Ranch, and the McAllen-Pharr and Talco properties in that region. With continued redevelopment and exploitation all of these properties were strong producers throughout the life of the company.

Tenneco's 1974 purchase of 184,000 acres of fee land in south Louisiana from LaTerre Company significantly improved the GCD acreage position and provided royalty and working interest in 20 oil and gas fields. In 1981 the GCD discovered the BCF Grand Bois field on LaTerre acreage. The 1983 Bold Forbes discovery came on non-producing acreage acquired from Delhi-Taylor.

The Gulf Coast Division was packaged with the Southwestern Division and sold to Fina for $600 million in the Sale of the Company in 1988.

A wildcat well being drilled just a stone's throw from the Pacific Coast Division's Bakersfield office.

Pacific Coast Division – Bakersfield, CA

The Pacific Coast Division in Bakersfield, CA was a prime example of taking full advantage of an opportunity when presented. California has always been regarded as a promised land of natural abundance. The state was a petroleum province for over 100 years before TOE&P entered the arena. Tenneco started its investigations there without any assets at all, and in fact, without much expectation of what it might become. In the mid-1960s the company established a small office in Ventura to work on upcoming offshore lease sales and investigate other opportunities.

The game – and the focus - changed totally in 1967 with the acquisition of Kern County Land Company. The office was moved from Ventura to Bakersfield in the Southern San Joaquin Valley to manage the vast fee acreage land position that came with the purchase.

The first, and crucial, ten years of the PCD were managed by O. W. "Tiny" Ward who had come to the company in 1951, with the York & Harper acquisition. Robert T. Bogan led the division following Ward's retirement in 1976 through the sale in 1988. The Pacific Coast Division was responsible for TOE&P's efforts in California, Washington and Oregon, both onshore and offshore, but the "home base" was right outside the office door in Bakersfield. Literally, working hands could, and often did, make a visit to a rig or field operation during their lunch hour.

Kern County CA is one of the geographically largest counties in the entire United States. It was also the largest oil producing county in the Lower 48. With the KCL acquisition and the subsequent exploitation and expansion of those assets Tenneco had become a major player in California. TOE&P engineers were able to establish a quick and significant increase in production and the exploration led to several new field discoveries including Yowlumne (Ten-

"I was given the assignment to make a study of California to determine its potential for Tenneco. The study lasted one year resulted in the decision to participate in the Ventura Basin Offshore sale. We opened an office in Ventura and with five other partners participated in the sale. Fortunately, we only purchased one lease."

- J Gregory (VP, DGM, Int.)

At the time of the sale in 1988 Tenneco's oldest producing well was located in the Midway-Sunset field in Kern County, CA. The Wilbert Oil Company, which Tenneco acquired, spudded the Wilber #2 on September 15, 1909. The 1400 foot well was completed one month later and at sale time was still producing 30 barrels of oil per day.

neco's largest domestic oil field), Rio Viejo (California's deepest production), and Landslide. In the 1980s profitability was enhanced with an aggressive waterflood at Yowlumne and thermal enhancement at the huge Kern River and Midway-Sunset fields. In the late 1980s the PCD was producing between 45,000 and 50,000BOPD making it the company's largest liquids contributor. An acquisition in 1985 added the 150MMBO Placerita Canyon field. With original reserves of nearly 1 BBO, Tenneco felt there was still a lot left and a major steam-flood was planned for the old giant. Peak enhanced production was scheduled for the mid-1990s, a time goal the company was unfortunately unable to witness, given the sale in 1988. The Pacific Coast Division was sold to ARCO for $ 670 million at the Sale.

Harry Briscoe started his Tenneco career in the Bakersfield office as a "junior geologist." He recalls a number of stories from the early years in the Pacific Coast Division.

BETTER TO NOT SPEAK AT ALL -Tenneco opened its first office in California to evaluate participation in anticipated offshore lease sales in the Federal waters of the Pacific. In 1969, the industry was rocked by its first major offshore oil spill with the infamous Santa Barbara blowout. Reaction to that event shut down nearly all offshore activity in California, a condition that has persisted for 40+ years since. Tenneco's office was in Bakersfield at the time of the blowout and, given that Tenneco was the largest oil company in town, a local TV reporter caught a young geologist for a quote. In responding to the question from the reporter, "We hear reports that seals have been killed by the oil spill, do you have a comment?" the eager young fellow (who shall remain nameless) was reported to have answered, "Yes, we understand that may be true, but from what we've seen, they are mostly the older seals!"

WORKING WITH OLD RECORDS - Among the records geologists and engineers use are the "Scout Reports" on each of the thousands of wells that have been drilled in any given area. "Scouts" were the ones who sought out both the mundane and the secret information about wells as they were drilled by the various operators. Which information to share was always a debate. Secrets on a given well were guarded closely and traded, frequently surreptitiously, from one company to the other. The books of records themselves were the primary library source for the working geologist as he built his interpretations.

As a rookie geologist I remember reading the report on a very old well – maybe 1924 or so - in the northern part of the San Joaquin basin. This "scout ticket" was hand-written as would be a note in a diary, well before the standard "form" was available for more organized data. It read something like this – "This well was drilled in Fresno County about 25 miles north of Kettleman Hills, by a big oak tree approximately 250 yards up Hogan's Creek from where it crosses the road to Coalinga. The well was drilled in 12 days to a total depth of 1400'. The cuttings showed mostly red, brown and blue sandstones and claystones. There was absolutely no showing of oil or gas or other minerals of interest … and it was Anderson's idea to drill here in the first place!"

Not much help in the prospecting of the area, but a sure sign not to hire Anderson!

FARM WORKERS COME CALLING - The Kern County Land Co. owned 100% fee (minerals and surface) acreage throughout the southern San Joaquin Valley. Heggblade-Marguleas-Tenneco, Inc (HMT) managed the surface and was one of the most active agricultural entities in the Valley. At that time the Oil Company occupied part of a large suburban office building on Stockdale Highway. We were in one end of the building and HMT occupied about four times as much space in the other end. We called them the "Fruits and Nuts Department". In 1973 the Great Valley of California saw the "organization" of the largely transient farm workers who came each year to harvest the crops. Tenneco, as a major employer of that labor force, became a prime target for Caesar Chavez and his legions of the United Farm Workers. I recall Mr. Chavez himself and a small group with picket signs banging on the window of my office, and yelling at me through the glass. I wondered just what a geologist might do to help their plight (the mob apparently did not realize they were at the wrong end of the building).

The employees did gain one huge benefit of this dispute. During that summer, the unions literally shut down the harvest in the fields. Each week a notice and a map would be posted on our bulletin boards directing us to any of several fields containing produce that would spoil on the ground. We were free to drive out and collect whatever we wanted. The "crop" at the "farmer's market" was different each week. We'd bring back trunk-loads of cantaloupes or onions, cabbages and cauliflowers, tomatoes or peppers, and the like. (Talk about the Tenneco Advantage!) We'd go back to our neighborhoods and share the booty with all of our friends. By "market time" the next week, the odor had usually subsided. We always wondered why they never let us into the almond orchards.

Rocky Mountain Division - Denver

Like most of the onshore divisions, the growth of the Rocky Mountain activities for TOE&P came through a combination of acquisition and discovery. Early TGT acquisitions had brought a number of properties in the Rocky Mountain province, including 131 wells in Wyoming's South Glenrock field, but the Bay Petroleum purchase in 1955 brought substantial assets and a division office was opened in Denver that year. The 1964 acquisition of Delhi-Taylor solidified TOE&P's long-term presence in the Rockies with the addition of the 23 TCF San Juan Basin field, E&P's largest field at the time of the sale (158MMNEB remaining reserves). District offices in Durango, CO and

In 1979, the RMD drilled 6 wildcat wells, and made 4 new discoveries with flow rates up to 3000BOPD. At one point, the division held over 1 million acres of leases and had 300,000 acres of fee land, much of it located in what is now North America's "hottest" play, the Bakken Shale.

"With nearly 2,300 wells in the San Juan Basin, the WRMD ranked as the largest operator of wells among the E&P Divisions

Bill Cayce - (DGM, WRMD)

"How this division could ever be considered 'fully-developed' is a mystery to me. They'll be finding things here for another hundred years."

Harris Phillips
(VP, DGM, MCD)

"While deep gas has been one main objective, there are a number of intermediate zones which don't have to be our primary objective - that can bail us out with an oil pay or with shallow gas. Obviously, 'serendipity' is high out here - good things can happen with multiple potential targets."

Jim Strother,

Casper, WY were closed in 1968 with all operations moved to Denver. The Four Eyes / Big Stick field complex was discovered in 1978, and by 1981 the division had grown to the point that two separate operating divisions were justified, the Eastern and Western Rocky Mountain Divisions, both in Denver. The settlement of the long legal battle over ownership interests in the San Juan Basin was settled in the company's favor in 1985 and in 1986 the two divisions were recombined into a single entity following the massive contraction in the industry. At the Sale, Amoco was the successful bidder for the RMD properties, with its $900 million bid.

Mid-Continent Division – Oklahoma City

Prior to 1955, Tenneco (TGT) activities in the mid-continent region of the country were operated out of a district office in Denver. The "Turning Point" acquisition of Bay Petroleum in 1955 was responsible for the creation of the Oklahoma City district office, still reporting to Denver. The Mid-States purchase in 1958 and Wilcox in 1964 added significant production and property. In 1974 the Oklahoma City district became the Mid-Continent Division with properties owned, at that time, in six states. Harris Phillips was transferred to Oklahoma City to lead the new division. The 1979 Ashland and Shenandoah deals added, among other things, the significant interests in the Hugoton gas field. Revenue in the Mid-continent division came from over 5500 total wells, over 950 being company-operated. The opportunity base in the mid-continent was diverse with production coming from wells as shallow as 1800' and as deep as 19,000'. Assets included a wide range of oil and gas fields and many secondary recovery projects. Over the years many of Tenneco's senior management 'cut their teeth' on the variety of assignments available in the MCD. The division was a steady, reliable and predictable contributor to the overall fortunes of TOE&P. The assets of the Mid-continent division were purchased by Mesa for $ 715 million, who targeted primarily the over 200 undrilled locations at Hugoton.

The Southwestern Division – San Antonio

The Permian Basin of West Texas and Southeast New Mexico is one of the most prolific oil and gas provinces in the world. Pay zones are present from every known type of reservoir rock and in every known type of trap. Proven production is present from depths ranging from less than 2000' to over 25000'. The basin is a virtual "kitchen" of hydrocarbon generating and trapping potential. In its 100+ year history the Permian Basin has been home to "booms and busts" in the truest definitions of the word. Midland/Odessa has been both a metropolis and a ghost town more often than any spot in the country. TOE&P had been in and out of the Permian on several occasions during its own history. In 1976 a small task force was sent to Midland to assess future opportunities and in 1978, the Southwestern Division was fortuitously established, just ahead of the huge boom of the late 1970s and early 1980s as gas and oil prices soared – in advance of the bust of the mid-1980s. Focusing on staff retention and quality of life objectives for a young staff, the new office was located in San Antonio, TX. Don Taylor was transferred from Bakersfield as the first General Manager for the SWD. The Division owned a broad variety of properties, ranging from advanced secondary recovery projects in some of the oldest fields in the basin, through conventional exploration and exploitation targets on "standard" projects, and on into plays for deep gas and rank wildcats that required advanced and innovative exploration, drilling and production technologies to define and develop.

The SWD was a smorgasbord of opportunity, and during its ten-year life span the SWD took full advantage of the spread on the table. At the sale, the SWD was combined with the Gulf Coast Division and purchased by Fina, who paid $ 600 million for the package.

International – Homerun Territory

Tenneco Oil E&P was built, literally, from the ground up, and in its early years was "made in America". Not long after its founding though, the young E&P company began its investigations of opportunities in foreign countries. Throughout its 40 years, E&P ventured onto every continent around the world and tested the offshore waters of several of them. While early international efforts provided a mixed bag of results, work in later years in the North Sea, Africa and South America was successful. At the Sale in 1988 the company had production in Colombia, the North Sea, Gabon, Tunisia and Nigeria with active exploration in 12 other countries. The company had interests in 327 international wells and operated 207 of those. Over 250 TOE&P employees worked in the international divisions in two Houston-based divisions with operating offices in Colombia, Norway, London, Gabon, Tunisia, Malaysia and Ecuador. At the time of the sale The South American Division was managed by Vice President and DGM Camilo Merendoni, who had come to E&P with the HO&M acquisition, and the International Division was run by VP and DGM Jack Gregory, a long-time TOC veteran. The international presence of Tenneco was clearly growing. Nearly half of the company's long-term oil reserves were located on international properties, and production had grown five-fold in 7 years. At the Sale in 1988 International properties accounted for $810MM of the $6.3B (13%) Tenneco Inc received.

Support for the technical exploration and production effort was provided at TOE&P by a diverse and competent group of administrative professionals located both within the divisions and in the Houston headquarters office. This largely silent and often overlooked group provided the same sort of exceptional effort that was characteristic of the entire E&P organization. The following article, adapted from an "E&P Update" profiles the group as it was late in the life of the company.

The Administrative Organization
Division and Headquarters

A primary management principle at Tenneco E&P held that the exploration and production technical professions needed to be free to perform their jobs without distractions and interruptions. For this reason tasks that were not directly related to exploration and production were assigned to administrative specialists, who were experts in their fields. Their contributions were essential in meeting financial obligations, legal compliance, regulatory requirements, recording of revenues and insuring that the organization's needs were being met; all of which were important to the success of the division and overall company. The division administrative staff was "The Glue" that held the organization together. Administrative professionals were located both in the divisions and in Houston. They worked for non-technical managers who reported to the local division general manager, or, in Houston, to their functional executive.

The initial development and structure of division administration came from the leadership of H. G. Irwin, administrative director. In the 1970s and early 80s, Irwin was instrumental in choosing which functions and activities would be handled at the division level, and which were best performed in the Houston headquarters. Irwin's input showed much insight at a critical point in time when many of E&P's most effective management philosophies were being implemented.

A motivator for the transformations H. G. Irwin imagined at E&P occurred in early 1982. Dan Johnson, senior vice president, stormed into Larry Augsburger's office questioning, "Why do we never know we have a problem in administration until the problem is completely around our neck"? He was referring to the company's sudden discovery of $50 million of unused pipe inventory scattered about in the various division locations. The division administrative organization was responsible for managing inventories at the division office level, and having this much investment lying idle was unacceptable. The obvious questions were; how could such an oversight occur, and how could it be avoided in the future?

Augsburger, VP of Administration, turned to Don Karrasch, director of administration in Houston, who had detailed knowledge of what went on in the division offices. After some considerable analysis during a joint meeting of the division administrative managers, the group moved to solve the current mess and prevent it from recurring. The problem affected all of them and they had a role in managing the seemingly small local issue, which had a big impact on the company as a whole. The managers developed a monitoring system to track inventories, create responsibilities and establish quantifiable indicators that would allow dynamic management.

Although the measurement system was designed to specifically address the problem raised by Dan Johnson in 1982, the concept became a key part of the administrative management process. Each month the performance of numerous key responsibilities were charted and presented to the administra-

LARRY AUGSBURGER

Larry Augsburger graduated from Lamar University in 1963 with a degree in business management. He was a four-year letterman on Lamar's basketball team and contributed to winning three conference championships. This experience taught Larry the importance of working together in achieving a common goal, which was demonstrated in his years with Tenneco. Joining the company in 1973 as an employee relations administrator, he advanced to supervisor, manager, director and eventually vice president over the next eight years. He attributes these advancements to lessons learned on the basketball court – work hard and know how to compete. In 1978 Augsburger was chosen to head-up Tenneco E&P's first employee relations department. In this role he assembled a cadre of top-notch professions, who supported the organization by hiring well, training well and seeking solutions which met the organization's needs and expectations.

tive manager, and distributed company-wide. Variances were identified and alerts were made where appropriate.

L. J. Olivier, administrative manager of the WGD Division, best described the measurement system as his assurance that there would be no surprises. Each morning he could advise his General Manager exactly where they stood, with certainty and without hesitation. This one project confirmed that the division administrative staffs could make a tangible bottom-line contribution to the performance of the division rather than to simply record and report of it.

* * * * *

The administrative organization had representatives in both the divisions and in the Houston headquarters. They provided service to the entire company and were assigned responsibilities were significant to the success of E&P.

Ed Milan, Sr. Vice President, headed up both Financial Controls and Information Systems Departments. At the time of the sale of the company in 1988, these groups included 325 accountants and computer systems professionals located in Houston, and another 110 located in the division offices.

The Financial Controls group provided strategic planning and direction through four major Houston-based financial groups -- Accounting, Special Finance/Treasury, Tax Planning and Auditing.

"In Financial Controls we had a job rotational program that developed a well-rounded, versatile staff. They were prepared for regulations and responsibilities ranging from multi-million dollar budgets to royalty payments. We found that a formal program best served all parties. A broad detailed, yet generalist knowledge was needed to meet the challenges of the future. " stated Stan Corbett, E&P Controller. And the employees liked the exposure gained through the rotation process. Keith Crews, senior accountant, International Division, added, "Financial Controls promoted continued career development through its rotation schedule. We like it."

The Accounting group recorded revenues, and made royalty payments, joint venture billings and accounts payable for all operating divisions. The group also handled the special reporting requirements of the SEC and various state regulatory authorities. They provided day-to-day information needed by the divisions in making informed decisions relative to active fields.

Special Finance/Treasury offered expertise including conventional and non-conventional financial structures, joint ventures, royalty trusts and partnerships. They coordinated the company's insurance and risk management programs. Treasury directed the company's cash management and collected all receivables and granted credits to joint interest holders. Payroll for all company employees was also handled there.

The Tax Planning department managed the company's federal, state and local income and production taxes. They performed tax compliance of existing and upcoming operating projects. They also recommended options on projects that would minimize overall tax liabilities.

ALL YOU HAVE TO DO IS ASK

The energy industry crash of the mid-1980s sent employees scrambling in all directions to find ways to save money and produce new revenue. Although most of the 'headlines' of the day involved the operating departments as they found ways to squeeze more production from older wells, or save on the costs associated with all new investments of capital, the administrative professionals took their own shot at the apple. In San Antonio, the Southwestern Division Administrative Manager, Joe Pesek, came up with a unique and simple idea. The company had been in and out of the Permian basin several times in the past. The division owned interests in thousands of different wells, many operated by others. Over the years ownerships changed hands frequently. Keeping track of just 'who owned what' at a given time was the job of the property records department, but given that the company had not had an active effort there, it was hard to be sure that the records were correct, especially for the outside-operated wells. Pesek's idea was simple. "Let's just write a letter to every single operator in the Basin and just tell them we are 'here'. Ask them to check their suspense accounts and ask them to see if they owe us or any of the companies we've acquired money". With only modest expectations, the letter was sent. Over the next several months the division received checks for over $350,000!

Auditing safeguarded the company's assets by ensuring that internal and external procedures and contracts were followed. The group traditionally recovered more than twice its annual operating costs through their audits.

Special Project Teams

Almost every time an acquisition, divestiture or special project of any nature came up, an administrative group was called into action to calculate the financial impact of the proposed transaction.

Stan Corbett, Controller gave the example of selling a property to illustrate the team concept. "In the past the company simply asked as high a price as possible. But in the post-80s boom era there were other considerations, such as the impact on income, and on the company's tax status to consider."

Lower oil and gas prices also left little room for error on projected income from acquisitions. And with "Successful Efforts Accounting," any loss on the sale of a property went immediately to the bottom line. So it was essential to thoroughly analyze the financial impact of a sale and acquisition. The company generated $25 million in cash from sales and trades in 1987, and spent nearly $30 million on acquisitions. "We didn't want to go out and make a bad deal due to a lack of knowledge," recalls Stan Corbett.

There was usually plenty of knowledge on reserves, production, future potential, and future cash flow. But translating that into a bottom-line impact on income was the function of the Financial Controls Department's two-person Special Projects Team. Teams were usually staffed with people borrowed from other financial departments. "It was imperative to allow our people to specialize in acquisition and disposition analysis for a year or two, so they could develop a high level of expertise," says Corbett.

In 1986 and 1987 the team was staff accountants Mickey Kinzer and Brian Donnelly. "They reviewed nearly every deal we made," says Corbett, "and unfortunately they had to kill some deals too."

Their job was to digest data produced by the Business Development Department, other Financial Controls groups and division staffs, and then determine a net present value on five-year and long-term bases for both E&P and Tenneco Inc. "This process was important because other companies could have put a value on a property that we couldn't justify after running the economics," says Bill Hunt, assistant controller. "Also, a lot of deals looked good until you threw in the tax impact."

Kinzer and Donnelly sat back-to-back in front of PC terminals, with a laser printer between them. "The paper was flying in here," said Kinzer. "The work was intense. There were nights and weekends at the office, but it was a good experience personally and professionally. I learned that I really liked the work," said Kinzer. Donnelly agreed, "I liked acquisition analysis. Things got intense, but that's just part of the job."

* * * * *

The Information Systems Department was headed up by Bob Foster, Systems General Manager. E&P's Systems group managed dozens of technical support and financial computer systems. At the sale, it was staffed by 188 employees located in Houston. Many of the managed systems were similar to standard systems at other oil companies, but there were others that were considered unique to Tenneco. They were such programs as Tenneco Oil Economic System (TOES), Risk Analysis System (RAS), Company-Owned Oil and Gas Reserves System (COOGRS), Land Information Management System (LANDS).

The I/S group managed a wide range of application systems that were developed for use exclusively in Tenneco's operating divisions. These included Tenneco In-Field Data Entry System (TIDES), which used personal computer software to capture daily production statistics at the source in the oil field, the Logarithm Versus Probability Plots (PROLOG), and approximately eight other such proprietary programs that addressed division level technical applications. "Our group managed the company's mainframe computers and oversaw the development of personal computer applications that would compare well with today's PC software," said Mike Grochett, Director of Division Systems.

The Legal Department in 1988 was headed by Glen E. Taylor, senior vice president and general counsel. The department consisted of a staff of 12 headquarters-based and 14 division- based attorneys and other specialists responsible for the company's legal affairs in such areas as environmental compliance, FERC activity, legislative issues, acquisitions and litigation. The department also included the corporate security function for operating divisions and headquarters. Its staff handled the legal work associated with extensive acquisitions and properties dispositions programs, the formation of royalty trusts and similar special finance programs. They also handled all legal matters relating to the sale and transport of natural gas. The group was knowledgeable of land transaction, establishing domestic and international legal entities, limited partnerships, drilling funds, SEC and other regulatory agency filings, tax law and contracts administration. There were three Associate General Counsels who gave leadership and direction to the Legal Department, Bob G. Lawrie, Phillis C. Rainey, and Laurent B. Webb. All were highly knowledgeable and well-respected in the organization.

Chuck Mills, director, Employee Relations, was responsible for a department of 24 ER professionals. Sixteen were located in the Houston office and eight were assigned in the divisions. The department was responsible for attracting, retaining and developing the company's workforce. It was also employee relations' assigned duty to serve as the employees' advocate and to represent employees' interest and point of view in matters relating to company-wide decisions and actions. A unique feature of this responsibility was that management fully supported this duty and sought out the department in making and announcing company-wide decisions relating to employees.

"The 1988 system applications offered by Information Systems were state of the art models that would rival most systems departments of the day. The technical applications provided were impressive and received well by the potential purchasers of Tenneco E&P"

Ben H. Grothues, Jr.
(Director, IS)

Successful staffing strategies were developed and implemented on an ongoing basis to support and enhance the feeder system for new employees. One of the more significant staffing efforts was the emphasis placed annually on college recruiting. This was the company's major source of young talented professions. Gilda Parker, employment manager; " I devoted most of my time to college recruitment. It is critical that we nurture E&P's image with university professors and placement office personnel. It pays off when we start counting our results at year end." And those results were mostly outstanding in recruiting top candidates from each of the universities we visit.

The employee relations department developed and administered compensation and benefit programs designed to attract and keep top-quality personnel. Annually detailed salary surveys were conducted to insure that Tenneco's compensation levels were comparable to or exceeded major competitors. Bill Bonnet, compensation manager, "Monitoring employee turnover rates and new hire acceptance rates were critical in maintaining a top workforce. We structured our compensation programs to insure that we remained competitive in the industry." Debbie Lewis worked closely with Bonnet in analyzing compensations data and implementing changes to insure that E&P remained competitive in the market place.

The company recognized that trained and updated skill levels were important in an employee's personal development. A training and development group supervised by Greg Nakanishi was actively involved in creating formal training programs that addressed professional development, interpersonal skills and supervisory skills. An added duty of the training and development group related to organizational development. E&P had skilled professionals who served as facilitators for improved teamwork and as a resource for resolving internal conflicts.

Tenneco Oil E&P established an internal communications function in 1979. "It was an exciting place from which to observe the company, learn and contribute," said James Bartlett, communications manager. The department's job was to reinforce strategic messages, report news and publicize the achievements of employees. They produced publications, speeches and presentations, and coordinated with Tenneco Inc. public relations on other tasks. "E&P was known for great people, and some of them were in communications." Others present at the end were Gilles Rideau, Gaylynn Stockwell-Rouse and Mike Russell, while contributing earlier were Janice Aston, Pat Kubick, Richard Kolb and several more. (The many excellent publications produced by this department over the years were a critical resource in the creation of this book).

Oil and Gas Products was also a Houston-based department that worked closely with and provided direct value to the divisions. The department was a marketing organization designed to insure that the company received the best price for its liquids and natural gas production. Under

John Gray, who had come to Tenneco with the Houston Oil and Minerals acquisition, the group maintained a staff of 49 persons. They arranged for the sale and delivery of the company's liquids and natural gas production, as well as managing its oil trading activities. The group was both a profit center, delivering more than $1 million in annual NOI, and a center of advice and direction for the company and divisions on marketing strategies. The department was experienced in international marketing, negotiations, contract administration, spot sales, and applicable regulations and handled these matters for the benefit of Tenneco Oil Company.

Operators Inc

Consistent with the re-alignment of its offices in the early 1970s, primarily for purposes of management efficiency, the company took a hard look at its field operations. Tenneco E&P's asset base, both onshore and offshore, had expanded rapidly and the company found the daily issues associated with the management of the 'on-the-ground' activities occupying more and more valuable engineering time. In another innovative move, the company decided to take some of the more routine tasks off the table and let division engineering staffs focus more time to generating ideas, rather than on managing and administering operations. Operator's Inc. was established as a wholly-owned subsidiary. Since most of the field work was done by "field" or "blue-collar" specialists the structure as a subsidiary allowed the company to avoid issues associated with union-based organizations, something learned by watching challenges at TOP&M.

Operators Inc. was the field operations arm of the TOE&P Production Department. The field effort required to operate and maintain Tenneco's far-flung properties was massive and complex, both in terms of managing the process and in actually doing the work.

Training facility for Operators Inc. in Lafayette, Louisiana.

The volume of the logistical work alone that was done by Operators Inc would have required significant staff oversight if managed from the home-base in the division office. Since Operators' was a well-known entity, a part of the same company, rather than an independent outside contractor, Tenneco could operate its leases more efficiently, with greater continuity, and with less direct oversight. Operators Inc. had a great reputation as a place to work and was able to attract and hold good field personnel and then to manage them with Tenneco's own priorities, methodologies and expectations.

Operators Inc. was founded in 1972 to consolidate the various third party contractors serving Tenneco and to improve the quality of pumping services available to the Company. At the sale in 1988 it operated over 160 offshore platforms in the Gulf of Mexico and more than 6,800 onshore wells. The workforce of 1,018 was distributed among Tenneco Oil's domestic operating divisions, with 612 in Lafayette. Those employees supported drilling, production, construction and work over activities. All field offices, both offshore and onshore, employ specialists in lease operations, safety, roustabout work, compression, measurement, work over and construction. Operators, Inc. also operated a comprehensive training center in Lafayette. Implemented in 1979, the Operators, Inc. training program was designed to make field employees highly competent lease operators. The center was widely used by other companies and other nations, and was recognized by the U.S. Minerals Management Service and the American Petroleum Institute.

The decision to create Operators Inc. was just another example of innovative thought at Tenneco and it paid off handsomely in many ways over the years. Like many of the other innovations at TOE&P, SVP Dan Johnson played a lead role in the support and development of the division. Many production and drilling engineers, with their common "Type-A" personalities, who might have gotten caught up in the many minutia of managing such an effort, were free to use their talents to add value with new projects, rather than just manage it with the existing ones. At the time of the sale in 1988 Operators Inc. was a major company in and of itself. R. H. Boyd was the manager of Operator's Inc from shortly after its founding until 1979, when he retired. Larry Oliver took the position following Boyd and managed the company through the sale. Oliver founded and ran a similar business for several years after the sale of the company in 1988.

The range of daily tasks was myriad for the people doing the work in the field. Being a lease operator is a full eight-hour-a-day job. Gauging the tanks is the first step each day, followed by checking the oil level in the pumps, the chemicals treating the oil in the separator, changing the charts used to measure gas production from each well and picking up the run tickets left by purchasers. Production charts are used to figure daily production, and a weekly report is sent to Tenneco. Salt-water disposal and gas-injection management might also be on the list for a given field. In addition Operators was responsible for supervising maintenance on all the equipment, and in many cases, actually participating in completion and work-over operations.

Onshore, some Operators personnel drove 50 to 150 miles a day, checking on the fields in their area and trouble-shooting problems. All work was coordinated closely with the Tenneco engineers. When a new well was brought onto production, it resulted in the installation of new equipment, laying a pipeline, or re-configuring the field layout. Operators Inc. was responsible for seeing that everything is done right.

The job of Operators Inc was even more significant and challenging in the Gulf of Mexico. Operators' personnel worked on almost every company-operated platform in the Gulf, and given the size of Tenneco's asset base, the logistical effort was substantial. Like most rig employees, the men in the GOM worked seven days a week, twelve hours a day, and then were home for a week. The stakes were a lot higher than onshore. With the costs of the lease, the drilling and the platform, a given property could easily represent hundreds of millions of dollars of investment. On the positive side, the platform might produce oil and gas worth thousands of dollars each minute, so operating efficiency came with a big responsibility. Production was reported daily to the division office using a microwave computer system, which was quick, accurate and secure. Much of the daily work paralleled that done onshore, but the unique challenges of the water-based province required a much more sophisticated logistical effort.

To manage the massive operation in the Gulf, Operators Inc established a yard and office at Intracoastal City, south of Lafayette. The Intracoastal facility received all of the equipment that went offshore and made sure it was delivered when needed. No small task that, when you are talking about all that's involved in, say, setting an offshore platform. Operators Inc was also responsible for storing equipment until it was needed, keeping an inventory of what Tenneco owned where all of it was headed. Operators coordinated all of the boat-leasing and helicopter services to facilitate the movement of the equipment and personnel to the platforms. They stored and shipped all of the chemicals used offshore, and also handled more mundane things like laundry, first aid kits and trash bags - whatever was necessary to keep things running. A materials checker inventoried all materials delivered to the Intracoastal base, and a drilling dispatcher dispatched supplies to the drilling platforms. Dispatchers were responsible for knowing where all boats and helicopters were at all times. They also keep track of the weather, and advised vessels at sea of conditions.

For 1978 the Intracoastal base chartered 50 boats and 22 helicopters. Thirty-nine thousand people made 78,000 trips to the rigs. And roughly $120 million to $130 million worth of goods and services passed through the base.

Nodal Analysis became a revolutionary completion technique for getting the most out of a well.

E&P REACTING WITH RESOLVE

Early 1970s

The year 1972 started innocently enough with another creative financing effort as the company formed Tenneco Exploration, Ltd., a publicly-owned partnership to finance offshore lease acquisition. International operations received a big boost with the discovery of the Heather Field in the North Sea where TOE&P owned 31% interest in partnership with Conoco. Heather immediately became one of E&P's most significant foreign discoveries to date. Heather would see significant investment and development over the coming years, eventually reaching a reserve asset exceeding 1 BBO. Elsewhere in the world, Tenneco discovered gas in the Ogaden Desert of Ethiopia and began exploration drilling in Spain, Gabon, and Thailand's Gulf of Siam. Wildcats drilled in the British North Sea, the Indian Ocean offshore Malagasy, and the South China Sea near Indonesia kept the international engineers busy.

But, the biggest news for the early 1970s did not come from the operations or from the "field". An "era change" for Tenneco and for the entire energy industry was to appear courtesy of international politics and economies as two unrelated events combined to turn the world upside down. In the USA, the economy was growing rapidly but natural gas struggled. Under an outdated and tightly-regulated pricing structure, demand was quickly outstripping supply. TGT and Tenneco Oil were keenly aware of the disparity and made many suggestions to federal agencies that might head off an impending crisis, but changes were not forthcoming.

Although issues with natural gas were the primary concern of the domestic industry, 1973 brought the event that would over-shadow all others as the Arab oil embargo hit the United States with full force. Shortages of gasoline at the neighborhood fuel pump brought the energy world onto the doorstep of every home. The effects of the new issues related to oil and gas changed the face of E&P for many years to come.

Adjustments of strategies throughout the company produced timely results. Joe Foster, a petroleum engineer and business major, was promoted from his position as head of EP&A to become Vice President of North American Exploration in 1972. The significance of this move was substantial in its implications to TOE&P's long-term culture. The integrated, 'multi-discipline', economics-based method of analysis and decision-making had reached a telling point.

Much to the surprise of many on the exploration side who feared what an engineer might propose, Foster immediately increased the exploration budget, particularly for leasehold, but also implemented a new, "most likely outcome" threshold for the drilling of wildcat wells. Only prospects that delivered significant present-value profitability would be considered for drilling on a "100%" basis, and those had to stand on a "risk-adjusted" basis, rather than simply on their 'perceived' quality. The logic held that getting someone else in industry to provide the risk dollars for the wildcat while retaining participation in the development wells would yield better long-term financial results in the aggregate.

The onshore divisions of TOE&P adopted an aggressive farm-out strategy for the drilling of most of the higher-risk wildcat wells. This approach was perceived to be primarily an effort to leverage limited capital, but in truth it was the result of that internal "risk vs. results" study of the drilling efforts, growing from the early work of the EP&A department. The risk-adjusted results for the company in the years ahead were significantly improved due to the strategy. The first of the successes of the farm out program (with a little help from oil & gas prices) delivered one of the best fields the company had ever found.

One of the most spectacular examples of the new farm-out strategy came on a dusty hillside in California. The acquisition of Kern County Land Company in 1967 had provided an extensive base of mineral fee ownership in the southern San Joaquin Valley. An active exploration program began almost immediately. A long-running farm-out strategy – featuring very tough deal terms – was implemented shortly thereafter and proved to be an effective method for evaluation of the position. Tenneco put the prospects together and solicited industry partners for the drilling of the higher-risk wildcat wells, while main-

"Early in 1971, S. V. McCollum called me into his office. He was holding the reports we had prepared in EP&A summarizing our 'ex post facto' look at the company's surprisingly disappointing exploration efforts. He said, 'Since you're so damned smart, YOU go run Exploration!' So there I was, at age 36, an Aggie engineer, in charge of all the geologists, geophysicists, and landmen. The culture shock was palpable …. But we got through it … and it was fun."

J B Foster (EVP, Tenn Inc)

The Yom Kippur war of 1973 brought a powerful new economic weapon on the world's stage. When the Arab members of OPEC choked off oil exports to the United States and other nations that supported Israel, they created an economic crisis in the US, but they also lit a fire under the energy industry, and in so doing, touched off an historic energy boom.

The posted price for oil rose from $3.39 to over $11 per barrel within a very short period and OPEC learned that the world would indeed pay higher prices for that product. At the same time, in the US, the years of regulation of natural gas prices had created shortages of that product, and market realities were finally allowing some increases there. Gas that had brought only $0.23 per mcf in 1973 would average over ten times that amount less than ten years later. The stage was set and Tenneco Oil was well-prepared to participate.

- E&P Update

"In the early days, Wilton Scott and I went around and around debating the strategy of farming out wildcats on 100% fee land. He was against it. I held my ground and we got quite a few wells drilled that we would not have otherwise. One of them was at Yowlumne."

J B Foster (Tenn Inc)

taining 100% ownership in offset acreage for eventual development to the company's sole benefit. In 1974 the strategy created a "Turning Point" for the Pacific Coast Division and for the Company with the discovery of the Yowlumne Field. The field would eventually exceed 100MMB0 in size. The "farm-out" strategy would further prove itself in the years ahead as the "cost to find and develop" numbers proved the value of leveraging the up-front risk dollars.

Yowlumne, The White Wolf
Adapted from Wes Franklin

Through the purchase of Kern County Land Co. Tenneco owned 406,000 acres of mineral rights, most of it in the southern San Joaquin Basin. For the first six years of the new PCD, development activity was restricted to fields on the Bakersfield Arch and the Paloma field. No significant new reserve additions had been made, so in 1973 the company accelerated evaluation of the extensive mineral holdings south of the Arch by initiating an aggressive farm-out strategy. The first prospect selected was San Emidio Nose West. Don Sprouse was the geologic prospect originator; the Exploration Manager at the time was Don Taylor and Bob Taylor was the Production Manager.

The target for the wildcat was a stratigraphic trap for Stevens sands pinching out across a structural nose. Don Sprouse was given the "green flag" to let the local industry know we would entertain farm-in offers, and he dropped the word one evening at a meeting of the San Joaquin Geological Society. The next day, a team of Texaco geologists were waiting at the door when Tenneco opened for business. They accepted a farm-out deal to pay 100% of the cost of the test well to earn half-interest in the prospect, if they drilled to 22,000', the Eocene, or to basement…whichever, came first. Tenneco would retain the other 50% interest and also a 25% landowner's royalty by virtue of the fee acreage. These were exceptionally tough terms for a farm out at this point in time and reflect the value of owning prospective fee acreage.

The San Emidio #1 ran into trouble at approximately 14500' and had to be sidetracked. Pushing on to deeper intervals, the wildcat encountered numerous exciting shows, but then became stuck at 20,704' in "Temblor" Sands. The "fish" could not be freed, so casing was run and a much-anticipated testing phase was planned. Texaco sent numerous personnel from their office in Los Angeles for the anticipated significant discovery from the first zone. Unfortunately, the test was a dud - the gas was characteristic of high pressure-low volume "tight sands". As successive zones were tested, each interval gave back fewer hydrocarbons than expected and enthusiasm for a discovery diminished. The eighth production test targeted an interval of approximately 1000' and gave up the first encouraging indications of oil. A ninth zone tested the lower portion of the previous test interval, and a 10th production was set for the Upper Stevens sand zone at approximately 11,250'. The first production from the field occurred on January 23, 1974 with a rate of 428 BOPD, 261

Citrus groves adjacent to the Yowlumne Oil Filed – treasures of the San Joaquin Valley.

Don Sprouse referred to the productive Yowlumne sand as the "suitcase" sand, as by the time oil first surfaced, all the trailers on location were packed and ready to leave - the consensus by that time being that the well would be a dry hole. The Texaco geologist was asleep when fluid surfaced - no one expected it by then - and almost lost his job because he didn't catch early samples. The rotation of Texaco geologists would stay at my house because their company was too cheap to give them motel fare and not much to eat on. We'd play cards till 3:00 in the morning, they'd grab some sleep then head out to the rig.

- W E Franklin (geologist in the PCD when Yowlumne was discovered, General Manager, SWD at the sale)

MCFD, and 33BWPD. After 30 days, the well was flowing 800 BOPD with no water production. Tenneco had a significant exploratory discovery and took over as operator. The field was named Yowlumne, which means Wolf, or White Wolf, from the local Yokut Indians language. The name was picked by Don Taylor and long-time exploration consultant Ralph Brodek.

The size of the new field was not obvious, but it was a start. The Yowlumne team was established with geologist Wes Franklin, geophysicist Earl Jaynes and geological engineer Dave Pearcy. The Division Geologist was Jim Dorman, Division Geophysicist was Lane Howell, Frank Collins was the Division Geological Engineer, Dick Sloan was the Division Reservoir and Jim Nusbaum was the Division Landman.

Tenneco cored the "Yowlumne" sand on the confirmation well, the 45x-11. When the core came out dripping oil, a celebration erupted, but evaluation showed the sand was relatively tight. The well never made more than

50 BOPD, and soon the production dropped off to just a few barrels per day. Development proceeded in a northeasterly direction until the 7th well was drilled. That well, the 25-12, yielded a shocking result – a complete absence of the pay sand. After much head-scratching, the only conclusion was that the original prospect model for the trend of the sand was off by 90 degrees. The new paradigm would prove to be of monumental importance.

At this point, the field still looked modest in size. Existing well control was not encouraging, and it limited the direction for field development. It became very important to try and get information from the limited seismic data. Earl Jaynes, the geophysicist, recognized a subtle seismic signature (a "doublet" in the reflection profiles) where the sand was present. With some degree of skepticism, the company began to shoot additional 2-D seismic lines, and the doublet became the signature indicator for the sand channel.

Development proceeded and the field began to reveal its many secrets. Gulf joined Tenneco/Texaco with a producer on 160 acres they held. Getty drilled an offset well to 300' deeper than the main Yowlumne pay zone and discovered a new sand, which came in at 905 BOPD, 836 MCFD. Another new well found production from the shallower Etchegoin sands. A portion of the field was unitized for orderly development and over 100 "primary" producers were drilled. A second unit brought the drilling of numerous water injection wells. In September 1994, the 100th million barrel of oil was produced, and the field has made more than 110 million barrels to date. Other Tenneco geologists and G.E.'s involved in the development were Greg Kelleher, Ridge Dorsey, Randy Metz and John Whitworth. Randy Groves was the landman for the project. Buddy Watsky succeeded Barry Quackenbush as Division Reservoir Engineer. Ralph McPhetridge was Division Landman in the later years of Yowlumne and Brian Rehkopf managed much of the EOR in Unit B. In all sense of the word, Yowlumne was a significant discovery, a "Milestone" and a "Turning Point", and an outstanding example of the teamwork and culture at TOE&P.

Rio Viejo

By 1975, the company's understanding of the complicated geology had grown and confidence led to additional discoveries. New seismic led to the drilling of San Emidio Nose North prospect and the discovery of the Rio Viejo field, the deepest production in California at that time. Since logs indicated the productive sand lay in contact with, wet sands below, a single foot was perforated and gave up an estimated rate of 600 BOPD. An additional 5' of perforations were added and the well went on at 691 BOPD, 140 MCFD, 4 BWD. Twelve additional wells were subsequently drilled in the field and the field is estimated to have an ultimate recovery of 10 million barrels of oil. Eugenio Viloni, long-time Argentine geologist in the PCD, was given the honor of picking the name – Old River, for a small town nearby.

I was a rookie geologist in the Pacific Coast Division at the time of the discovery of Yowlumne Field on KCL fee lands. Exploration Manager Don Taylor came to me with a sample bottle of the oil from the test, rubbed a bit on my nose and said, "Smell this; this is what you are looking for!" He also spilled one small drop on my nice polyester tie and it spread to the point it could not be removed. I saved the tie for years and always thought of it as my "oil-finding" tie. I have a picture of the discovery well on my office wall to this day.

H J Briscoe (VP Expl)

Change at the Top

In 1974, George Mason was promoted into Tenneco Inc, and Cliff Rackley moved from his position as Executive Vice President of Processing and Marketing to become the fourth President of Tenneco Oil Company. Joe Foster was promoted to Sr. Vice President of Tenneco Oil and served as the primary 'strategy' officer during Rackley's term as President.

Culture Firmly Established

The mid-1970s at TEO&P marked a period of maturity for the company, not only in terms of size and presence, but also in terms of the strategic stability with which the company worked, across the board, in all arenas. The district offices had been consolidated into the divisions, the management structure had been 'flattened' and streamlined, and the culture of economic-based decision-making had come to maturity. The "independent division" working environment and the defined processes for budgeting and planning, and for expecting what would occur as a result of the planning, were all now firmly in place. Although the "culture" would continue to develop in years ahead, the framework on which it would grow was set.

A speech presented by Joe Foster, then Senior VP for Tenneco Oil, at an E&P manager's meeting in 1974 set the tone for the business approach that would prevail from then until the sale of the company in 1988. Certainly, the many exact outside events that would influence business decisions in the years ahead could not be specifically anticipated, but the strategic approach was designed to work in any business climate. The speech was essentially a re-statement of principles and priorities. Foster began with a quote that Wilton Scott had often used during his tenure running the oil company, "We must ensure that there is no lack of leadership!" At that, he defined leadership simply as being, on one hand, a clear definition of objectives and expectations, and on the other the provision of a plan and resources necessary to make those things happen. He set goals for growth at 5% over the rate of inflation and pointed out that the growth would be achieved from projects with high present-values. Capital expenditures for the upcoming years were predicted to be only 70-80% of annual cash flow. This new investment target reality reflected the increasing corporate appetite for investments outside the energy sectors, and the fact that Tenneco Oil had used "more than its share" of corporate resources in the past.

For the foreseeable future, the company would "go offshore for supply and go onshore for returns". Supplying gas to keep TGT pipelines full remained a priority. These things would require an increase in the application of leverage through farm outs and a strict adherence to $/bbl and $/mcf profitability targets. A continued priority would be given to getting and keeping a quality workforce. The approach would be inde-

President Profile
CLIFF W. RACKLEY
1974-1978

Cliff Rackley took charge of Tenneco Oil in July 1974. Rackley had served an extensive career in the parent company since coming to Tenneco in 1956. Rackley was a native of Georgia with an engineering degree from the Georgia Institute of Technology. He had served as a B-17 pilot in WWII. Mr. Rackley's term as president of Tenneco Oil included the dynamic times following the Arab Oil Embargo in 1973, during which the company earned record revenues. He was named President of Tenneco Oil P&M in 1978 and served in thatcapacity until 1986, two years before the sale. Rackley lives in Houston and was the primary author for the TOP&M section of this book. A more complete biography of Mr. Rackley can be found there.

LaTerre Company was family-owned and through the years many individuals had been issued units of stock. The ownership was fragmented, so descendants abounded at the closing party. Few had seen more than photographs of the swampland that was LaTerre, but they all knew what a royalty check was. One lady I was talking to was a schoolteacher. I knew what her share of the proceeds would be and commented, "You will walk away today a wealthy lady, and the checks will keep coming for years to come." She looked at me, looked at her daughter, and looked around the room, before responding, "Well, I certainly would not want anyone to know!" And she was quickly gone.

J B Foster (Tenn Inc)

pendent but integrated with budget control remaining in Houston and operational control – and accountability – being within the divisions. The speech was a clear definition of what was expected and how it was going to be achieved. Given the culture, structure and philosophies in place by that time, it is a certainty that the assembled managers felt the mission was ultimately achievable.

LaTerre

In 1974 the company also acquired the family-owned LaTerre Company for $193 million. This acquisition, though smaller in size, held many parallels to the Kern County Land purchase. LaTerre added 184,000 acres of 100% mineral fee ownership and held 18 oil and gas fields, mostly in the salt-water marshes of South Louisiana. The Gulf Coast Division would conduct effective exploration and development on the LaTerre properties for many years into the future.

Mid-1970s in the Gulf

The 1970s had become a period of exceptional growth throughout Tenneco. Many positive events occurred in all arenas. TOE&P's offshore activity in the early 1970s found it pushing the limits of conventional technology. The following stories describe some of the forward-looking projects in the Gulf of Mexico of those days, projects that resulted in spectacular positive results for the company.

Wayne Nance (President TOE&P at the Sale) was transferred to Lafayette as Production Manager in 1974. His tenure there included some of the most active and robust times for the company in the Gulf. "When I arrived in 1974, the division had 70 leases and 140 employees; when I left in 1982, we had 580 people! We actually had to move some folks into a converted Tenneco service station for a while to make room for everyone. " Nance's time in the GOM saw his own career progress through jobs of increasing responsibility and the activities offshore were growing as well.

One of Nance's first jobs was to over-see the installation of the (at the time) deepest-water platform installation in the GOM. The WC 643 lease had been purchased at the 1970 sale for $43MM. In just over two years' time the division drilled the discovery and delineation wells, designed and built the 8-pile, 24-slot platform, for installation in 375' water depth, 128 miles offshore. The work was a stretch for those days and reflected the degree to which the division was running 'on all cylinders'. The big platform had been built and was loaded onto a barge but the government had been slow in approving the installation location. Nance had to shepherd the process through the bureaucracy in just a couple of days. The WC 643 field was still producing in 2008, when it was shut in after being damaged by hurricane Ike.

An offshore drilling crew working in orchestrated harmony for a clean, efficient wellbore.

Drilling Records

A few years after it was set the WC 643 platform became the site for another record. The team identified a new prospect that would require a "long-
reach" and high-angle well to test from the platform. Although targeted for
an angle of about 76 degrees, the actual angle reached as high as 82 degrees
and in fact, exceeded horizontal for brief sections. This drilling required very
careful drilling with a full rotating drill string, (this was well before the days of
contemporary down-hole motors). Logging the hole required fashioning little
'wheels' for the logging tool and pumping the apparatus down the well bore
since gravity was of little help in the horizontal hole. The well was the highest-
angle well in the world at that time, and even Shell came to visit to see if they
could use some Tenneco practices in the North Sea. The well missed the initial

target and was then side-tracked to its eventual discovery. Following that, the engineers devised a ground-breaking method to complete the well. A second platform, WC 643-B, was set in 1978 as a result of the efforts. Tenneco was a pioneer with horizontal drilling technology, a common and very important technique in the industry today.

Getting More From Each Well – Nodal Analysis

By the mid 1970s Tenneco had become the largest natural gas producer in the Gulf, and operated more platforms and drilling rigs than any other operator. Maximizing flow rates and therefore cash flow were prime objectives. In mid-1977, under the leadership of Steve Chesebro', the technical teams began developing a revolutionary completion technology for gas wells that became an industry standard. The "Nodal Analysis" program evolved from engineering theory to practical application through a complex series of practices involving such things as perforation patterns, sand-sieve analyses, gravel-pack design, and flow-velocity calculations. By utilizing large-diameter stainless steel tubing, and a revolutionary surface processing equipment configuration, Tenneco gained a competitive advantage over its industry competitors that lasted for years. Not only did this technology allow natural gas reservoirs to be depleted in less time, but it reduced the number of producing wells required to deplete reservoirs. That in turn, allowed for smaller platforms and the saving of substantial capital. The high-rate completion technology was used at HI 281 to deplete a lease-line competitive reservoir with Exxon before they could get an 8-pile platform set on the neighboring blocks. Similarly, the technology drained Conoco at V240/241, Shell at HI 270, Aminoil at SMI 60, and Mobil at V 261 and EC 334 (*memory of block numbers and offset operators courtesy of S D Chesebro' who admits he might have missed a few*).

In 1973 Tenneco Oil Company - the entire company - made $100 million of annual net operating income for the first time. Only five years later, using the high-rate completion techniques, the Lafayette Offshore Division delivered over $100 million in the first twelve months of production from one platform, the 11-well facility on SMI 61-C. Although not labeled as a "turning point", the use of "high-rate single completions" was one of the most significant of all of the technologic developments in the Gulf of Mexico, and in fact, within the energy world.

Pushing the Envelope

This short story from Gary Mabie, Production Engineer for the GOM at the time, is an excellent example of several of the management principles and business practices at TOE&P as discussed in later sections – the support for justified risk-taking and independent work, the use of applied technology, and an attitude towards maximizing cash-flow and economic returns.

Tenneco leveraged its learning after completing the first well with 4½" production tubing in the US Gulf of Mexico. Two gas wells on the South Marsh Island Block 61 "C" Platform had high rate completions, each capable of more than 50 million cubic feet of natural gas production daily.

Before the end of the summer of 1978, eleven wells would regularly produce in excess of 350 million cubic feet of natural gas per day – enough to fuel the annual electricity generation requirement for more than 1.6 million households at the average energy consumption rate in the United States in 2010.

The development of Nodal analysis began through our association with one of our service contractors, Macco Gas Lift, and their sales engineer Joe Mach. Joe collaborated with Kermit Brown, a University of Texas professor in Petroleum Engineering, to put a series of engineering evaluations and equations together as a "system analysis" using reservoir inflow performance, tubular vertical velocity equations and surface facility design into a package they called Nodal Analysis. Joe called on Clyde Crouch and me and over several months convinced us that Macco had a predictable model to use for reservoir, well bore and facility designs.

Concurrent with this sales pitch, Tenneco had just evolved from our standard completion practice using "duals and triples" concurrently in a single well bore to the "high-rate single" design. We'd convinced management that multiple reservoirs in a well bore could be produced more quickly and at less cost (with fewer mechanical problems) by using the "high-rate singles". In the meantime, Tenneco had been attempting to unitize V 241 with Conoco in order to conserve capital in the depletion of a reservoir over our adjoining blocks.

We brought the first well on at 25MMCFD (the highest rate in the GOM at that time), ran a BHP (bottom hole pressure) build-up survey and determined that the well suffered severe skin damage. Using our new NODAL Analysis theory we recommended an acid job (on the already record high-rate well) and predicted production rates of 40MMCFD. At the time, Division Manager Wayne Nance knew little of the new program and essentially threw us out of his office as being "out of our minds". After several attempts, and much education of the NODAL principles, Wayne finally conceded to the acid job (with the caveat of my job being on the line with failure). After the acid job we got the well up to 42MMCFD.

Meanwhile, the offset operator flew over our platform and saw two flow lines and assumed we had a dual completion. The fact was that we needed dual flow lines on the tree to handle the high rates and keep the surface velocities down below the erosional velocity! By the time they drilled their dual well, we had depleted our share of the reserves and were well into theirs!

As a result, we standardized on the NODAL design for future completions and used it also in developing our SMI 61 compression design. Shortly afterwards, Macco was bought out by Schlumberger, and they turned around and wanted to charge us for the NODAL analysis we helped design. We went to USL (University of Southwestern Louisiana, in Lafayette) and had them design another NODAL package for Tenneco's exclusive use.

TOE&P was certainly at the fore-front of a new and valuable technology with this one.

- Gary Mabie (Prod Mgr, SAD)

"We pitched a unitization proposal at those guys that with compromise would give both companies a fair shake. Since Conoco's structural position was better than ours, we were soundly rebuffed. Gary and company meantime had the plan for high-rate completions in their hip pocket. The reservoir rock was great so we drilled our own well and completed it with a 4-1/2" high-rate single on a small four-pile platform. We put down a couple more wells about a 100 feet, or so, from the first one and cranked the platform on at about 100mmcfd. This was absolutely unheard of at that time. We drained them big-time. Their most down dip well was watered-out by the time they got their platform on production. They were quite angry, but we did give them the chance to unitize.

Ron Christie (EM, WGD)

Wayne Nance, TOC Division Production Manager, studies the blowout while operations supervisor Jim Martin shouts to describe the action over the piercing shriek of the escaping gas.

Blowout!

On March 24, 1976, Tenneco Oil Company experienced its first and only significant blowout in the Gulf of Mexico. A producing well on an unmanned satellite platform, the WC 165-#3 blew out from a downhole failure, causing significant damage to the platform surface equipment and later, creating a substantial sea-floor eruption of escaping gas. The event was quickly discovered by company personnel on a nearby facility. A well-rehearsed, but seldom needed, emergency action procedure – the Offshore Contingency Plan – was immediately set into motion. The plan, devised in 1970, involved a team of professionals from all of the various disciplines in the Lafayette office, headed by then Offshore Production Manager, Wayne Nance. The team quickly assessed the situation and within a short time concluded that a relief well was

A week after the blowout, gas began escaping from the well somewhere below the surface, creating the "boil" that would eventually sink the rig.

required to kill the down-hole flow. Within hours, the Marlin 6 jackup was on its way from a location off the Texas coast. During the six weeks required to drill the well, the platform was lost, sinking beneath the seabed, but the relief well was successful in killing the flow. Throughout the process neither injuries nor environmental damage occurred. The U S Coast Guard complimented the task force on its quick reaction and execution of its plan. By September the division had re-directed a platform that was under construction for another lease, installed it on the block, and was making preparations to re-drill the lost well – and recover the lost revenue. Advance training and planning had paid off, the Offshore Contingency Plan had proved itself a fast and effective remedy to offshore emergencies, and the company had another excellent example of teamwork and the cool-headed talent of its staff.

Sudden Showers

Tenneco leveraged its learning after completing the first well with 4½" production tubing in the US Gulf of Mexico. Two gas wells on the South Marsh Island Block 61 "C" Platform had high rate completions, each capable of more than 50 million cubic feet of natural gas production daily. Before the end of the summer of 1978, eleven wells would regularly produce in excess of 350 million cubic feet of natural gas per day – enough to fuel the annual electricity generation requirement for more than 1.6 million households at the average energy consumption rate in the United States in 2010.

Management in Lafayette sponsored an offshore tour to the facility for a number of employee's spouses. Clyde Crouch, one of three division production supervisors, lead a portion of the tour and wanted to demonstrate the fire protection or "deluge" system on the platform. The design was another 'first' for Tenneco, warranted by the substantial investment and exposure the platform represented. When activated, the system created a dense mist of ocean water and air, cutting off the oxygen supply to an ignition source and cooling in the event of a fire. The misting produced a water-cloud so dense it could drown a man in the middle of it.

After assembling the wives on the lower deck near the control panel and proudly explaining its operation, Clyde pressed the "test" button. The deluge system performed exactly as designed. It cut off the air to the well bay and deluged not only the well bay with a cloud of mist billowing out from the nozzles, but also the spouses, who had been unfortunately positioned downwind. Nothing like a little extra humidity to do wonders for the wives' hair styles … and clothes…

- Terry W. Rathert (Mgr. EP&A)

Worth The Chance

One of E&P's nicest discoveries came about through some aggressive risk-taking and reliance on new technologies. The Ship Shoal 182 prospect was drilled in 1976 or 1977 (*if recollection serves Tony Brown right*). Here, the pros-

President Profile
JOE B. FOSTER
1978-1981

Joe Foster became the first President of Tenneco E&P, as a stand-alone company, following the establishment of separate companies for E&P and P&M in October, 1978. Foster is a native Texan and 1956 graduate of Texas A&M University, with degrees in petroleum engineering and business. He joined Tenneco that year in Oklahoma City. Under Foster's presidency, TOE&P made seven major acquisitions and pushed drilling programs to new records in all arenas. The concept of a "Driving Goal" was established and Foster's tenure initiated the unprecedented six-year run of replacing production with new reserve discoveries. The distinctive cultures and management philosophies that Foster had worked on for so many years, and that personified E&P's success, were solidified within this time. Foster's contributions to Tenneco were re-directed in 1981 when he was promoted to Executive Vice President of Tenneco, Inc. corporate office where he would have overall responsibility for Tenneco Oil E&P, Tenneco Oil P&M, TGT, and Tenneco Inc. corporate planning until the Sale in 1988.

pect was set up by a single well with modest shows, but it was enhanced by an emerging geophysical concept. The prospect showed an amplitude anomaly, not an unheard of technology at the time, but one still not fully understood. In the years that followed these seismic characteristics, or "bright spots" as they came to be known, became one of the most important prospecting tools in the business. Tenneco was on the leading end of their development. The well to test the prospect was drilled with an old jackup rig in the 60' water depth, but a storm hit and slid the rig a bit and stuck the drill pipe. There was no alternative but to run an incomplete set of logs through pipe. The logs were encouraging but not conclusive. Management confidence in the logs and amplitude was high enough however to set a platform from which the confirmation wells defined one of the company's best fields – eventually to produce over 20,000 BOPD.

- Tony Brown (Prod Mgr, WGD)

1976

Driven by the price increases for oil and gas, and the resultant world-wide economic restructuring of the energy industry in the wake of the OPEC embargo of 1973, the last half of the 1970s saw the company take a second look at some of the older onshore provinces. The Permian Basin in West Texas and New Mexico was targeted as one that had potential for expansion. A small task force of seven technical people was sent to Midland, TX in 1976 to open a project office with the objective of determining if the company should re-establish operations in the Permian Basin.

Also in 1976, seven leases were acquired in Baltimore Canyon for $33MM. This move was a bold step for the Frontier Projects office to secure a ground-floor position in the search for gas off the Atlantic Coast. A scant year later a federal judge would cancel these leases out of hand. Offshore in 1976, Tenneco installed its first subsea completion and replaced the WC 165 platform that had been destroyed in a blowout.

Getting International Right

Tenneco made its first forays into International arenas in 1955. The onset of the third decade of E&P exploration around the world brought with it a re-evaluation of the program itself. Although some of the recent discoveries were encouraging, the overall effort lacked focus and economic returns were below expectations. A news item from a 1977 issue of the company press included a headline - "International strategy revised to focus on West Africa, South America, North Sea, Far East following 22 years of mixed results in 32 nations." By 1988 Tenneco's positions in three of those four target areas - the North Sea, West Africa, and Colombia – had become significant within the company. At the time of the sale, International was poised for a bright future, but that was the result of a targeted effort beginning in the mid-1970s.

DIMENSIONS OF THE ENERGY CRISIS A TENNECO VIEW

The energy crisis of the 1970s came as no surprise to Tenneco executives. Many had seen it coming for years. …… Government regulation and lack of insight into the nature of the energy industries had played a large part in creating the energy crisis. …. The problems of government regulation had been delineated clearly by Gardiner Symonds and others in the Company for several years. While that message had fallen on deaf ears in Washington for decades, it suddenly began to resonate in the minds of many Congressmen and members of the Executive branch. (Extensive discussion of these times can be read in the TGT section.)

"Tenneco Core Research" The History Company", 1993

The Heather Platform, a Tenneco joint interest in the United Kingdom sector of the North Sea

The Heather Field was TOE&P's first significant discovery in the UK Sector of the North Sea. The block was acquired in 1972 and the discovery well was completed late in 1973, followed by delineation wells throughout 1974. It took over 3 years to build and install the platform and production commenced in 1978.

The success in the UK North Sea pushed the company north and an office was established in Stavanger, Norway. The first license awards in the Norwegian sector of the North Sea were awarded in 1979. The Norwegian holdings would become a center-piece for Tenneco at both the E&P and the parent-company levels, and as such, will be covered in detail following shortly.

Sometimes It Takes A While - Production from the Heather field was initiated in October of 1978 into a new pipeline that had been laid to tie the field to the nearest terminal in the Shetland Islands, 85 miles away. Since the pipeline was new – and empty - it took nearly two months for the first oil to reach the sales point.

A Company of Our Own - 1978

By 1978 the businesses of exploration and production, and that of processing and marketing, had each grown substantially. Although still sisters within a single company, the two had been running independently for some time. The day-to-day differences in all phases of their respective business functions were significant, and combined financial reporting did not reflect a truly accurate picture of either. Market prices for oil and gas had increased materially. E&P income of $293 million represented nearly 80% of the combined TOC, and was the major contribution for the entire corporation in 1977. TOE&P was growing rapidly, and managing the two entities under a single umbrella was no longer efficient.

In response, in 1978, Tenneco Oil E&P (TOE&P) and Tenneco Oil Processing & Marketing (TOP&M) became separate operating companies. Joe Foster was named the first President of the independent Tenneco Oil Exploration and Production, and Cliff Rackley moved from E&P to run Tenneco Oil

DRIVING GOALS

"When I joined TOC in Lafayette we had four company level goals that guided the day-to-day actions of the organization. One of these four goals was called the 'Driving Goal' (reserve replacement at the time) which was the overriding goal that drove the company strategy and subsequent actions for that planning period. The other three were qualifying goals (production growth, profitability and return on investment) which were used to maintain a healthy balance between growth and operational efficiencies and to make sure we didn't become too singularly focused on just the driving goal. During my 12 years with Tenneco the driving goal changed a couple of times to keep the company aligned as the environment we were operating in changed and we needed to focus our efforts toward a specific growth or profitability metric. In the 25 years since Tenneco was sold, I have continued to use this same planning philosophy in my various capacities at four different companies. The fundamentals of this philosophy are as valid today as they were 36 years ago. This was one of many tools I took from my Tenneco experience that have become a foundational piece of my E&P business acumen. Lessons such as this one have been shared by the many employees of Tenneco now throughout the industry, and are today more broadly used than any of us will ever know."

Jeff Sherrick (EP&A Sr. Analyst)

Processing and Marketing. The two new entities were independent subsidiaries of Tenneco Inc., now just cogs in a very large, and still growing, corporate machine. Such would be the case for ten more years. But there was little time to reflect or to project. A "boom" was on.

The 1978 lease sale in the Gulf of Mexico was another big one for the company, at least in terms of expenditures. Sabine Pass Blocks 13 was purchased for $93.89 million, one of TOE&P's highest bids for a single block. The company wasted no time in testing its purchase, and by Spring of 1981 the first platform was ready for installation. Sabine 13 joined Sabine 11 and Sabine 18, bought in 1979 for $54.4million and $74.4Million, respectively. Tenneco populated the shallow waters of Sabine Pass with eight platforms by 1982.

To address opportunity in the Permian Basin, the operating boundaries of Mid-Continent and Rocky Mountain Divisions were adjusted to create the Southwestern Division. In a move designed to focus on employee quality of life and staff retention the project office in Midland was moved and the new division was opened in August of 1978 in San Antonio, TX.

Also in 1978, E&P continued its efforts to explore off the Atlantic Coast with the purchase of eight more tracts in the SE Georgia Embayment.

Internationally, 1978 saw first production began from the Heather field in the North Sea and also in Nigeria.

The year 1978 was the first of a continuous run of eight years in which a special new objective was achieved. In 1977 E&P had established the objective of full replacement of production with new reserves as a company priority. R/P > 1 became the driving goal for the company, and Tenneco's performance in reaching the goal was unparalleled within the industry. The concept was simple; if you find more oil and gas each year than you sell, you'll never go out of business – at least that was the concept. Achieving the goal was not as simple. In 1976, for example, the company had produced 80,000BOPD and 1.2BCFD. With an average 12% per year decline rate, replacing that production meant that new reserves capable of producing 10,000BOPD would be necessary – just to stay "flat". The bigger the company got, the more difficult it became to grow. It was requiring capital of $160 - $200 million per year to stay flat. It was remarkable that TOE&P managed to achieve this new "driving goal" for eight consecutive years, a record unmatched by anyone else in the industry. The eventual "bust" of the business in 1985 and 1986 would end the run.

1979

Over the life of the company, each of the operating divisions would produce significant new field discoveries (in some cases, several such). That fact is another record of accomplishment that was rarely matched within the E&P industry. The Rocky Mountain Division made headlines in 1979 with the discovery of the Four Eyes – Big Stick field in North Dakota.

Drilling in the Four Eyes / Big Stick field in Williston Basin could be very challenging in winter.

Four Eyes / Big Stick

The Williston Basin in North Dakota produced a flurry of activity and discovery for the Rocky Mountain Division in the late 1970s and early 1980s. The Four Eyes / Big Stick complex of fields was located by employing a determined long-term effort to piece together a complex set of puzzle pieces. The reward was the most significant discovery in the division's history. The Billings Nose, a pronounced regional geologic feature, had been the site of considerable drilling through the years, yielding a mixture of success and failure.

Each of the wells however, added to the complex puzzle, and the RMD initiated a regional play around the complex feature. An aggressive leasing program and the UV acquisition in 1978 created a dominant land position for the division. In 1977 and 1978 they set about drilling and farming-out a number of wildcats, targeting the Mississippian, Devonian and Ordovician targets at depths reaching 15,000'. As with many onshore plays during that time, improvements in seismic data collection and interpretation aided the effort, but the area shed its secrets slowly. It all paid off in 1979 when, of the six wildcats drilled, four were discoveries. The initial discovery well was the BN #1-29 in 1978 with gas in the Red River formation and oil in the Duperow and Mission Canyon zones. The Four Eyes / Big Stick

NOT WHAT THEY EXPECTED

I was on my very first field-training assignment, sitting a rig for a month of extremely slow drilling. After months in the "Montana Outback" on the Gasho #1-23 we finally got near our drill stem test point. The test itself drug on but finally, before quitting time back in the office we had the dismal results. We had been up since three in the morning and were feeling a little punchy by the time we called in. Rob Christensen got on the phone and said to our manager, Tom Hemborg; "Tom, I have some good news for you and some bad news for you." Tom got excited. "Oh great, give me the good news first!" Rob said, "We didn't burn down the rig." "What do you mean?" Tom demanded. Rob followed up with, "Well, that's the bad news -- we couldn't have if we wanted to."

Betty Ann Clark, (Geol., RMD)

complex of fields was a series of separate but related discoveries with pay from several different formations. The fields became some of the most prolific in the trend, with some wells testing up to 3000BOPD. The RMD drilled 41 wells in the new field in 1979. In 1980 80% of the division's exploration budget and 40% of its production investments were targeting the remote and sometimes hostile landscape. By mid-year 1980 the division had 25 wells producing over 20,000BOPD. In 1981 the developments on the Billings Nose made Tenneco one of the most active drillers in the region and the leading oil producer in North Dakota.

Recollections from Jack Gregory, who was Division General Manager in the ERMD when Big Stick field was discovered: "The Big Stick discovery came as a pleasant surprise. We'd had leases over some Ordovician structures in this part of the Williston Basin for quite a while but it had not been a priority play. One afternoon Lou Parrish and I were sitting in his office discussing our exploration plans and I suggested we go ahead and drill a wildcat. The Ordovician structure looked good and we had identified up-hole potential in both the Devonian and Mississippian. The discovery well was drilled and had pay in all three zones. The wildcat paid out in just 28 days."

A significant contribution to the efficient development of field came through good teamwork provided by the gas marketing department. In North Dakota regulations prevented the flaring of gas during production and although mainly an oil-field, the new wells had plenty of associated gas. A market had to be found for the gas and a gas processing plant was needed. During the negotiations, the wells continued to drill and the capacity of the required plant continued to grow with the success of each new well. What was originally designed to handle 5MMCFD was expanded three different times during the negotiations to an eventual 25MMCFD capacity. The Four Eyes / Big Stick field was really a complex of fields on the Billings Nose. Dave Ellis in the Gas Contracts department was instrumental over the next year-and-a-half in keeping the field – and the cash flow – online by continually finding new markets for the associated gas. Tenneco held a major part of the 50 MMBO+ of eventual reserves.

(In an interesting footnote – much of Tenneco's former acreage in the Williston Basin has taken on an entirely new significance with the emergence of the Bakken shale-oil play in 2010 – another 'what could have/ should have been' story. Alums remember dealing with stuck-pipe issues in drilling through the Bakken in the days before its potential was recognized. A former Tenneco geologist, Richard Findley is credited by industry press as having been the individual responsible for discovering the first Bakken field.)

Williston Dangers

Challenging conditions in the Williston Basin winters were commonplace. Harold Korell, Division Production Manager at the time tells a story of the completion of the discovery well for the Four Eyes / Big Stick field. "It was most severe from the weather standpoint. We had winds of 70 to 80 miles per hour, with a wind chill factor of 70 degrees below zero that day in March." It had been snowing since early morning when it was decided to close the rig down early that afternoon. The drilling crew and roustabouts left, The Tenneco people stayed behind to talk about the operation. They departed about 4 p.m. and soon began hitting snow-banks. Suddenly they came across the rig truck. It had slid off the road and was disabled. The drilling crew piled into the two Tenneco cars and the tiny caravan set out. There were seventeen people. Meanwhile, the snow and wind had picked up, blowing about 60 miles per hour. The snow was drifting so badly that someone had to walk in front of the cars looking for the road. About eight o'clock they realized they weren't going to be able to get back. Their Citizens Band radio was broken (there were no cell phones back then), so they sat out the night in the cars. To compound the situation, one of the car doors was frozen open from being constantly opened and closed to let the scouts in and out. Around seven a.m., one of the cars ran out of gas. Help arrived only after a trainee managed to fix the CB radio. "That was the closest call we've had," says Korell. "Two of the guys almost froze. The snow was so bad it took us ten days to get back to the rig."

Other people went through as interesting, if not as dangerous, incidents during the completion of the BN #1-29. Paul Doyle, project production engineer, was forced to take shelter with a farm family. That night, when the temperature reached sub-zero, he was rousted out of bed and put to work helping herd the cattle into the barn to keep them warm. "The funny thing was," he says, "they asked me for room and board when I left."

Onshore Acquisitions

Acquisitions for the onshore divisions continued in 1978 and 1979 with Hanagan Petroleum in the SWD, UV Industries with properties for the SWD and fee acreage in the RMD, and Palmer Petroleum in the RMD. The prizes though, Shenandoah Oil Corporation and Ashland Oil, were pursued almost simultaneously during late 1978 and early 1979. When they finally came together they essentially doubled the size of the Mid-Continent division in terms of wells, operations, and reserves. The new properties held long-lived reserves with an estimated 15 to 20 years of production life. In addition, the MCD gained 350,000 acres of undeveloped leases. The new assets included 1850 gross wells, 555 of which were company-operated. The purchase included six enhanced oil recovery projects, among them the South Graham Deese and Southeast Vasser waterfloods. Ashland included major operations in the Hugoton Field in the Oklahoma panhandle and Southeast Kansas. Hugoton would represent a core piece of the division value at the time of the sale in 1988. The division estimated they would double the production from the acquired properties within a year.

The 1970s had been a decade of diverse growth and change. The changing of the calendar to a new decade did little to slow the machine.

By the 1980s TOE&P's evolving technological expertise enabled it to operate in the most hostile of environments, such as Alaska's Beaufort Sea.

E&P DECADE OF EXTREMES THE EIGHTIES

Riding the Wave

Tenneco Oil roared into the decade of the 1980s riding the wave of recent discoveries. In the Rockies, the Four Eyes / Big Stick discovery developed quickly with 25 wells completed and production reaching over 15,000 BOPD by the end of 1980. The Frontier Projects office acquired 15 leases on the Georges Bank offshore New England. At the Nov. 1980 MMS sale, the WGOM Division acquired 7 tracts for $80 Million. The first year of the new decade was a harbinger – the ride ahead was to be a wild one indeed.

In the first of several such moves over the next several years, the company addressed its growth in headcount by dividing its highly-successful Gulf of Mexico operation into three separate operating divisions. Through the 1970s and into the early '80's, TOE&P had focused intently on expanding its unique "culture". There was no doubt that adherence to a set of management philosophies was adding value to the company. One of the tenants of those philosophies was the concept of small operating units, with the value-creators being close to the decision-makers. With its prodigious success at buying leases and finding new fields, the Gulf of Mexico staff had grown to nearly 400 employees. The number was straining the efficiencies and accountability of the preferred smaller organization. The re-alignment of the divisions would create a significant number of operational issues, but the benefits were anticipated to outweigh the burdens, and in September the Eastern, Central, and Western Gulf of Mexico Divisions were created, with Chuck Shultz, Jack Gregory and Don Myers as the new General Managers.

In April of 1981 Joe Foster was called into higher service as Executive Vice President of Tenneco Inc., in charge of all the Tenneco energy businesses, and Dr. Phil Oxley was named President of TOE&P.

Significant markers for 1981 included new records for production, drilling activity and acreage under ownership and lease. An all-time high daily gas production rate of 1.222BCFD was set, largely on the backs of high-rate wells in the Gulf of Mexico, flow rates that were made possible by industry-leading high-rate completion techniques developed by TOE&P engineers.

Nineteen eighty-one also brought the next big "Turning Point" for TOE&P. The deal turned that year proved to be another home-run for the company, but that was not at all certain until several years after the purchase. The purchase proved that Tenneco's talented workforce, when served lemons, could make lemonade quite well, thank you.

The Saga of Houston Oil & Minerals Treasures in the Basement

A game-changing acquisition came Tenneco Oil's way in 1981 with the purchase of Houston Oil and Minerals Company for $680MM. The HO&M deal added acreage in six countries and an "advertised" 136MMNEB of new reserves. As it would turn out, the most significant of the new assets were in Colombia with the wholly-owned subsidiary, Houston Oil Colombiana (HO-COL). At year-end 1981, HOCOL properties were contributing 29,000BOPD, but the international properties were not perceived to be the centerpiece of the sale when it was purchased.

HO&M was a darling of the E&P industry in the late 1970s. The company was founded by Joe Walter, staffed by aggressive and successful explorationists. The company had been highly successful in the shallow offshore bay waters and with state leases in Texas. Industry had found several interesting shallow Miocene oil fields in these areas, but HO&M discoveries had opened a brand new deeper Frio play. The Point Bolivar North field, discovered in 1975 in Galveston Bay, was a prime example. In addition to top personnel, HO&M had a technical advantage. At this time major oil companies had nearly abandoned onshore and shallow state water exploration due to the rapid turnover of smaller leases, and perceived smaller rewards. In addition to focusing on a relatively unexplored area, HO&M had developed a technological advantage with seismic geophones that enabled significantly improved imaging through bays, marshes, over dikes, and on dry land. This technique resulted in the delineation of some ten Frio fields that made HO&M highly successful, and valuable.

With this success, came challenges. While several companies had tried to acquire HO&M over time (including Tenneco), the principals, Joe Walter,

**President Profile
DR. PHIL OXLEY
1981-1987**

Phil Oxley came to Tenneco from academia. Born in New York and educated in Ohio, his resume' was not typical of those in the energy business. Oxley was Chairman of the geology department at Hamilton College in 1957 when the company hired him to move to New Orleans as the first district geologist for the offshore. He left the company for a while in the 1960s but was seen as such a valuable resource that Wilton Scott hired him back as a consultant for the 1970 Offshore lease sale. Following that sale he rose through the exploration and upper management ranks. He directed the successful expansion of exploration efforts around the world. As President, he presided over the both the best of times and the worst of times with the drilling and income boom of the early 1980s, followed by the "bust" of '85 and '86. Oxley was instrumental in re-shaping the company after the downturn. He was named Chairman of Tenneco Europe following his retirement from TOE&P in 1987. Dr. Oxley died in 1998.

"Phil Oxley had an intuitive feel for exploration, as well as for the business. That ability was instrumental in our development of the Gulf of Mexico. Phil was one of the few people I've ever met whose right-brain and left-brain would work so well together."

Joe Foster (Tenn Inc)

chairman and a geologist by training, and Fox Benton, president , encouraged by their technical staff, persisted in believing that HO&M would be as successful in other areas as they had been in South Texas. As a result, it diversified into gold mining and embarked on an aggressive frontier and worldwide exploration growth initiative on a go-it-alone basis. A prime example was in the first U.S. east coast offshore lease sale in Baltimore Canyon, where HO&M successfully bid by itself, and did not join others in risk-sharing. The results were not positive. As capital expenditures increased, dry holes mounted and production decline set in on its producing properties, cash flow became a serious problem for HO&M. In the late 1970s HO&M issued a relatively new financial instrument, the Houston Oil Royalty Trust. Individual investors and institutions purchased "units" which provided them with a share of operating profit from proven reserves, and in some cases, profits from the exploitation of undeveloped reserves, plus an over-ride on selected exploration properties. This would have been good for early cash flow had the up-front proceeds from the sale of units been invested more effectively but, unfortunately, that was not the case with HO&M.

Toward the end of 1980 cash flow, or more correctly, the lack of it, became critical at Houston Oil. For the first time in the history of the company they solicited bids for a sale or merger of their company. Contact was made between Fox Benton (President of HO&M) and Jim Ketelsen, CEO of Tenneco Inc. Ketelsen was interested. TOE&P was seeking to jump-start an onshore Gulf Coast Texas exploration and production effort, and was therefore seriously interested in the HO&M opportunity at the Tenneco Oil Company level. Given the reputation of HO&M on Wall Street, Tenneco Inc. eyed the potential purchase as an opportunity to boost the corporate profile and stock price.

This resulted in an evaluation process that was not only more hurried than usual, but also undertaken under the premise that there was more competition for these assets than, in fact, turned out to be the case. Unfortunately, numerous negotiations with HO&M took place at the Tenneco Inc. level, and the reserve assets of HO&M received less than the "normal" due diligence from the technical staff at TOE&P.

With the anticipated value of HO&M perceived to exceed a billion dollars, it was evident that Tenneco would have to again come up with some innovative way of financing the acquisition. The idea evolved to issue a new (additional) royalty trust, the Houston Oil Royalty Trust, to finance the majority of the purchase price, with a lesser amount coming from internal sources. Since several of HO&M's properties were already dedicated to the existing royalty trust, new properties would have to be included in the new royalty trust to provide the necessary cash flow. The two new HO&M properties with the greatest potential were Cavallo and Galveston Island 391 Fields. These recent discoveries were only partially developed and consisted of both proven and probable, but undeveloped reserves. The TOE&P technical team began an evaluation of HO&M's properties, and concluded it was unlikely that all the proved, probable, and possible reserves existed, on a risk-adjusted basis.

Over a weekend, Jim Ketelsen, Joe Foster, and Dean Maddox (TOE&P CFO) met with Joe Walter, Paul Degenhart (HO&M CFO) and Fox Benton (HO&M president, and a financial officer by training). The group had arrived at an agreement that was signed, sealed, and delivered late on a Sunday night. Under the terms of the agreement, HO&M would issue the new royalty trust using their reserve estimates, contemporaneous with closing the transaction, thereby reducing the equity required. Tenneco Inc. would issue $500 million in common stock to cover its equity, and Tenneco Oil Co. would retain all of HO&M's debt.

By then, the investment banking firm of Morgan, Stanley, & Co. had become involved on behalf of Tenneco Inc. It would require months to conclude the sale of HO&M and the issuance of the royalty trust due to, among other things, obtaining HOM shareholder approval.

The rest of the deal provided that TOE&P would immediately farm-in essentially all of HO&M's prospects on a leveraged basis. The leverage was required so that HO&M had enough cash to meet payroll and pay bills prior to closing. The farm-in arrangement was also meant to start the evaluation of probable and possible reserves, not only to the benefit of the royalty trust, but to the benefit of TOE&P also.

The Seagull pipeline and processing plant (mainly servicing Cavallo Field) were excluded from the weekend sale package. Later this entity became Seagull Energy, which subsequently merged with Ocean Energy. Seagull would have been an excellent fit for Tenneco's Intrastate Pipeline system, as well as providing modern processing capabilities, had it been included in the deal.

The deal closed, with the issuance of the Houston Oil Royalty Trust on April 24, 1981. Also announced was the fact that HO&M would be a stand-alone division of Tenneco Inc., not of TOE&P. This arrangement was tax driven, but not organizationally efficient. Steve Chesebro', an E&P "lifer" serving at the time as VP of Corporate Planning and Development for Tenneco Inc, was called back into TOE&P to manage HO&M. It was a challenge, to say the least.

The early repercussions of the hurried transaction were not positive. Operational details prescribed by the agreement exacerbated the problems.

During the four months prior to closing, TOC was funding all of HO&M, including a weak, technically inferior inventory of exploratory prospects. As an example, a wildcat in the Marfa basin of far West Texas was one of their best.

In addition, during that period of time neither TOE&P nor even Chesebro', HO&M's officer-in-charge, had any control or authority over prospect evaluation, drilling decisions, or worse yet, personnel. In much of the domestic organization, absenteeism increased, short work days became the norm, and resumes were openly distributed. Notable exceptions were in the international and the marketing group where professionalism reigned due to internal

"1981 - the year was a wild one for me, beginning in January with the announcement that I would lead an 'independent' oil company within an oil company. By October it was clear that the plane would not work and HO&M was assimilated into the TOE&P organization. A few exploration staff from HO&M made the full transition, as did a few more operations and staff personnel. Ultimately, TOE&P added reserves, mostly from international operations in Tunisia, Gabon, and Colombia. Both Royalty Trusts were ultimately extinguished, and I made my way back to where I belonged, to Tenneco Oil Company."

S D Chesebro', (Tenneco Energy)

CREATIVE FINANCE

Tenneco's growth from the outset was a result of taking advantage of opportunities, or by creating them in the financial arena. Over the years TOE&P implemented innovative financing solutions to provide leverage the outcome of a planned event. On several occasions these creative financings produced exceptional results. The Delhi-Taylor acquisition was financed with an "ABC payment" (deferred payments over time). TOE&P used an innovative debt structure to purchase La Terre despite not having the highest cash bid, and Occidental's higher bid for Kern County Land Company was bested by utilizing Preferred Stock with a high coupon. The LaTerre Company was privately-held by a diverse family of heirs. Tenneco structured a unique family annuity with a coupon to accommodate their needs. The creation of the Houston Oil Royalty Trust and an unusual farm-in arrangement allowed the company to buy HO&M. The Tenneco Offshore and Tenneco Offshore II limited partnerships with insurance companies funded several GOM lease sales at levels greater than possible without them and, in 1988, the signing of a $250 million dollar agreement with a consortium of Japanese companies to finance future GOM lease sales would have had a similar effect in future years. In later years, Dean Maddox, CFO, working with the finance people at Tenneco Inc., was the master of creative finance at Tenneco.

management leadership. Interestingly, the leaders of these groups at HO&M, Will Frank and Camilo Merendoni in International, and John Gray in Oil & Gas Marketing would become exceptionally dedicated and valuable employees at TOE&P. Both of those groups, and these individuals, ultimately played extremely important roles in TOE&P in future years.

A very successful, proven, and accomplished exploration organization in TOE&P felt insulted that such a high price would be paid for HO&M with lesser prospects. Additionally, due to the farm-in agreement to keep HO&M afloat, E&P prospects were not being adequately funded, while lesser HO&M opportunities were drilled. The strained atmosphere between Tenneco Oil personnel and many from HO&M, all created early on by the agreement, never recovered.

TOE&P would ultimately be saddled with the new royalty trust. Even though it was issued by HO&M, TOE&P became the owner of the deal at closing. Tenneco's technical experts were correct in their fears as the Cavallo and Galveston Island 391 Fields would not prove to be as successful as advertised. The respective E&P divisions suffered burdens to their own internal financial positions by having to absorb the write-downs associated with the negative reserve revisions.

Using their own reserve estimates, not Tenneco's, HO&M had projected operating profits from the first year of the Houston Oil Royalty Trust adequate to provide $6.00 per unit to the unit holders. An outcry from the investors arose when first year distributions were only $1.60 per unit. Lawsuits ensued, and Tenneco was left to defend against them.

The HO&M acquisition was dysfunctional from day one. The deal talk originated between Tenneco Inc, CEO Ketelsen, and Benton, HO&M president, both of whom were financial people. Joe Foster, an engineer by training, and president of Tenneco Oil E&P was communicating with Joe Walter, a geologist by training, and CEO of HO&M. Investment bankers and lawyers then got involved. Multiple groups were communicating with each other. People from operations and people from finance often did not use the same terminology or have a consistent (even within the same company) understanding of the concept being discussed. The deal was influenced by a requirement that it close by year-end. The result was a deal with which management on the Tenneco side was unhappy, and with which the HOM exploration and production people (whom Tenneco had valued rather highly) were even more unhappy. It fell to Steve Chesebro' to sort it all out. He did a remarkable job. Chesebro' went on to continued success at Tenneco. This would not be the last time that fate would land him in a delicate position. In 1988 CEO Ketelsen tapped him to execute the sale of his "home" company. After the sale of TOE&P, he was President Tenneco Gas Marketing, and later headed Tennessee Gas Transmission Company (TGT) until its own divestiture in 1996. (see TGT section)

At the end of 1981, HO&M was operationally assimilated into the TOE&P

organization. A few exploration staff from HO&M made the full transition, while more operations and staff personnel made the switch. Both Royalty Trusts were ultimately extinguished.

As bad as the story to this point sounds, HO&M's international operations turned out to be the bright spot of the acquisition, and in the long run the acquisition was an economic success. Developments in Tunisia and Gabon were profitable, and the San Francisco Discovery in Colombia was one of Tenneco's largest, as the production in the country grew to over 40,000 barrels of oil per day. At the 1988 sale of Tenneco's E&P assets, the Colombian properties were sold to Shell for $552million. Tunisia and Gabon were included in a package purchased by British Gas for $195 million, and accounted for a majority of that value. Additional value for HO&M properties was included in Fina's $606 million bid for the package including its Gulf Coast and Southwestern Divisions. About 30% of this value would have come from the former HO&M properties. Thus, the proceeds from former HO&M properties in the 1988 sale of Tenneco Oil E&P are estimated at about $750 million. This would be in addition to cash generated by the properties from 1981 through 1987 while they were part of Tenneco. The application of TOE&P's talent and organization to the challenges of the deal turned up substantial treasures among the acquired assets.

* * * * *

Elsewhere in 1981, the Gulf of Mexico saw a record of its own when first production at Sabine Pass 13 was initiated only 2½ years after the lease was purchased. The Grand Bois field was discovered by the Gulf Coast Division on the LaTerre properties.

Following on the success of the re-alignment of the offshore divisions in Lafayette in 1980, the company took a look at a similar issue in Denver. Expansion of activities in the San Juan and Williston Basins in the Rockies led to the creation of two operating divisions in Denver, the Eastern and Western, with Mike Lacey and Jack Edwards as the new general managers. The HO&M acquisition, Grand Bois discovery and increased activity in the Gulf Coast led to the creation of the Texas Gulf Coast division, as a "carve-out" from parts of the Gulf Coast Division. Jim Cravens, from HO&M, was named to head the Texas Gulf Coast Division and Bill Melnar continued as DGM of the GCD.

JM North and Non-Conventional Thought

Another element of the culture was the development of the unique "multi-discipline" prospecting team. The early 1980s saw several good paydays as a result of that concept.

One of the best examples of everything that was representative of the effective culture at TOE&P was the work that led to the discovery of the JM North field in the Southwestern Division. At the time, in 1981, the SWD was something of a crucible for the development and implementation of the multi-discipline team concept. Dan Johnson, the Senior VP in Houston to

A VISIT TO A TRUCK STOP

The rancher who owned the surface above the JM and JM North field was Tom Mitchell. After the Shell discovery the royalties had allowed him to build a big truck stop on I-10 near Ozona. He had also developed a partnership and gotten into Indy car racing. Loren Leiker and Tommy Wells were returning to San Antonio with the logs from the Tenneco discovery well and decided to stop by and inform Mitchell of the good news. They found him on his back working on something under one of his race cars. He rolled out to hear the good news and said, "Well that's great to hear. Now maybe I can buy some new tires for this thing!"

ANOTHER EXAMPLE

According to Dan Johnson, the G T Hall well in West Texas was, "the most challenging onshore well drilled in the company in 1987." This well was another in the mold of JM North, starting with nothing but a concept, and then crafting a plan that ended up with a success right in the middle of 'someone else's' field. Every discipline in the company was represented on the 12-man team - geology, geophysics, reservoir, production and drilling engineering, land, legal and administration – and all played crucial roles in getting the concept drilled – and in booking over 2 million NEBs as the prize for the two-years of work that was required.

whom the SWD reported, was a strong supporter of integrated teams, and he encouraged pushing the boundaries of the concept. Both the opportunity base of the Permian Basin and likewise the asset base owned by the division, were diverse and prime candidates for "prospecting by team".

One prospecting philosophy utilized within the SWD involved sending young professionals from all disciplines back to take new looks at the largest fields in the basin, with general instructions to largely ignore "conventional wisdom"… and the published maps. Many of these old fields were huge, they'd been on production for decades, and everyone "knew" what they looked like. A second element of the study involved integrating the knowledge from the new interpretations of the fields into a regional framework, rather than seeing them only as unique features. Since the fields were old, every element of technical expertise had been involved in their development and all of the technical disciplines would have a role to play in the review. In addition, technology in all areas had evolved greatly since the fields were discovered. The plan was that modern methods and teamwork would uncover new opportunity. Geologists, geophysicists, reservoir, production and drilling engineers, and even landmen and lawyers played critical roles in these projects.

The Val Verde basin in West Texas held a number of very large gas fields with spectacularly high production from the Ellenberger formation. Some individual wells had produced over 100 BCF during their lives. (The huge (11 TCF) Gomez Ellenberger field in Pecos County had numerous individual wells with such 100+BCF reserves.) The northern border of the Val Verde basin was bordered by a well-known and fairly sharply-defined regional fault. Several of the giant fields lay right against that border fault.

The JM Field was discovered by Shell in the 1960s and had produced over 600 BCFG. The contour map of the structure was "obvious", and every published map in the industry showed essentially the same "bulls-eye" contours. One of the Val Verde team geologists was Loren Leiker (later to retire as the No. 2 man at EOG). He had thrown out the conventional model of the boundary fault on the north edge of the basin and instead proposed a "wrench" model that proposed a much more complex structural system than was normally depicted. Seismic data offered some encouragement through "creative interpretations" but not enough to confirm the new concepts. All things came together though at JM. An interpretation of the field's production, done by PE Mark Hoffmann and GE Jim Henley, indicated that historical production figures, when compared against well pressures and the structure maps, revealed an anomalous pattern. It looked as though the field should contain more reserves than it had given up. Hoffmann, Henley, Leiker and geophysicist Tommy Wells worked together to produce a joint map that embraced all the concepts, but existing seismic was not adequate to confirm a new interpretation of the field. A prospect to extend the field was suggested but impossible to confirm with existing seismic.

The terrain of the area is characterized by a flat-topped limestone mesas cut by multiple deep valleys. Laying out a seismic pattern and then acquiring decent data ranged from challenging to hopeless. Working with the ranchers in the area Wells devised a unique plan to run his vibrator trucks along the mesas and ridges, but then, rather than place the recording phones along the same lines, to place them in the bottoms of the valleys. By doing this he could "undershoot" the mesas and hopefully acquire better data in the needed spots. To complicate matters, the existing field was served by a gas processing plant and the noise from the compressors and other equipment would degrade the quality of any seismic obtained. Through some forgotten enterprise the team persuaded the rancher to get the plant to shut down for a day. And that day just happened to be the day that Wells had his crew in the field. The "undershoot" worked and the new data confirmed a new prospect adjacent to the field.

Shell owned the entire field, and the leases were held by production, except for two small slivers of land on the north edge. By the historical interpretation of the field, these properties were off- structure, and were leased by Shell but not "held by production". But with the new fault interpretation, now confirmed by the new seismic, an entire new fault block was possible. The land department, headed by Mike Hinze, and team-member Steve Wentworth, went to work and "top-leased" the lands, from the same rancher with whom the geophysicists had been working. When the expiration date arrived and Shell set out to re-new it, they received a big surprise. The land department "gerrymandered" two 640 Ac spacing units and filed a "Rule 31" exception with the Texas Railroad Commission to allow Tenneco to drill on the lands, at locations immediately offsetting Shell's wells. Shell objected but the team prevailed at the hearing. Tenneco SWD ended up drilling two wells and discovered the "JM North" Field. Shell objected to the proximity of the new wells to their own, but the new seismic and Hoffman's pressure analyses and testimony from GE Mike Steppe convinced the Commission that Tenneco had a new field. Over the next several years the two wells produced major revenue right from under Shell's nose, and at prices substantially higher than for the old field. The two wells were higher than any in the 20-year old JM field, and had reserves estimated at 60 BCFG. The project demonstrated for all that new interpretations in old areas can produce surprise results. The JM wells were included in the company's employee-owned "drilling fund" so the principals – and all of the employees who participated – had a direct benefit from them.

The integrated exploration/exploitation philosophy was pursued by the SWD, and other divisions within TOE&P, with continued success at multiple locations around old fields. In fact, Fina, the purchaser of the SWD assets, continued the exercise (under the direction of Wes Franklin, TOC DGM who was retained by Fina after the sale). The integrated approach produced many successes throughout the industry in years to come as "ex-Tenneco's" in their "later lives" applied what they had learned at E&P.

HARRY BRISCOE

Harry Briscoe joined Tenneco in 1972 as a Junior Geologist after graduation from the Colorado School of Mines. In 1974 he was transferred to Lafayette, LA for a look at the offshore game, and then in 1976 was sent to Midland, TX as part of a small feasibility team looking to re-energize Tenneco's efforts in the Permian Basin. In 1978 the Southwestern Division was created in San Antonio and Briscoe made the move as Division Geologist, was named Exploration Manager in 1980 and Division General Manager in 1982. In 1986 he was transferred to Houston and was named Vice President of Exploration in 1987. Briscoe is particularly proud of his work helping to develop and implement the Multi-Discipline Integrated Team approach to exploration and exploitation. He was an instructor for the company's Exploration and Prospecting School and served on the company's Industry Speaker's Bureau.

"We are very proud of the Piñón Field because of the way we discovered it. Reports from a geologist we turned loose led the division into the field - just one more example of our coming in and, through some hard work, turning around someone else's failure! The management style in the division had something to do with it also. Don Taylor, and his boss in Houston, Dan Johnson, were both huge advocates of giving employees as much freedom as they can handle to operate creatively and aggressively in their search for oil and gas."

H J Briscoe

"It took some aggressive management to get us involved in the Marathon Overthrust to begin with, but it took a total team effort to bring it to fruition."

Doug Keen, Div GE at the time, (Mgr,IEPS at sale)

A Southwestern Division prospect review session that led to the discovery of the Piñón Field.

The Piñón Field – A Frontier Discovery

At a Budget Tour reception shortly after Joe Foster had been promoted to Vice President of Exploration of TOE&P, a young geologist asked him a question; "Why don't we drill more truly exploratory wells? I think we should step out into the frontiers more often. In order to get the big prize, we need to be the first one's into some of these areas." Foster's reply was revealing, "When I read the history of the country, I find the very first explorers – the Mountain Men – who ventured into new territory were often the ones who got shot by the Indians. The settlers who came along in the second wave were generally the ones who reaped the rewards of a new territory."

The geography of most of the divisions included some areas with long-range potential, but they were areas in which wells drilled would surely be labeled as "rank wildcats". The Permian Basin contains several of those areas. Even today, but certainly in 1981, the basin held plenty of room for new frontiers. The Southwestern Division chased and found one of those giants in the Pinon' Field. Although E&P did not get "shot by the Indians", unlocking the secrets of the new trend was challenging, and the big rewards from Tenneco's work accrued mostly to the settlers that followed. The story is intriguing nonetheless.

The Southwestern Division had a "frontiers" group assigned to evaluate the fringe areas of the Permian Basin. Geologist Jan Vargo and Geophysicists Tommy Wells were the principal technical staff assigned to the project, but numerous others including Mike Anderson, Tom Bowman, Watt Wardlaw, Jim Fallon and Loren Leiker. The landman was Steve King. In the late 1970s several discoveries had been made around the United States from "Overthrust" plays (a general term for a number of complex geologic structures involving "plate margins"). A "hot" overthrust play had developed in the western Rockies, the Basin and Range province, and recent discoveries in southeast Oklahoma and Arkansas fueled the interest. The southern margin of the Permian Basin is home to the Ouachita/Marathon Overthrust. It lies in a very remote and somewhat hostile portion of south Texas, characterized by large land ownerships, a few cattle, and not much else. Over the years the Marathons had seen few wells and no significant production.

In 1981, the Houston Natural Gas Company (HNG) controlled a 45,000 acre block on a farm-out from Conoco. The underlying leases had expired and the acreage was being held only by performance under a continuous drilling clause. HNG had drilled several wells with minor shows but no real success and were losing interest in continued drilling. The Tenneco Marathon team made a quick evaluation. The lease would expire if a well was not spud in short order. The team and Don Taylor, General Manager of the SWD at the time, were intrigued by the amount of acreage on the interesting trend that could be earned with a relatively inexpensive well and a decision was made to pursue the deal. The seismic in the area was terrible, but Tenneco quickly picked a location and managed to get the well drilled before the leases expired. The JA Gray #4-1 was a dry hole, but it did offer some encouragement and its drilling bought another few months of time. The team set about picking a location for a second well. Geophysicist Tommy Wells picks up the story from there:

"I was sitting in my office puzzling over some of the new seismic. The new data was terrible, but that was the norm for the area. There were few obvious reflections on the sections. Don Taylor walked in to see the seismic (Taylor was likely to show up anywhere at any time and was always 'prospecting'). As I pinned the sections on the wall, I could see the disappointment on his face. I quickly pointed out that if he would squint his eyes and look at the data "sideways" (obliquely – a geophysicist's trick move), and use a little imagination(see Taylor story in "Budget" section), he could see a very faint reflection that might represent the top of a thrust sheet. I had drawn a time-structure map of the weak reflection that placed the structure in a poor position nearly off Tenneco's lease. Don hadn't said a word during my presentation, and after a bit, he stood up and walked to the office door. At this moment I did not know what to expect from him. Much to my shock and surprise, he turned around and said, "Call the drilling department and give them your location. This is where we're going to drill next."

The JA Green #4-2 field was drilled to keep the lease block alive. Before reaching its intended depth the well encountered an over-pressured zone, most-likely representing the top of a thrust sheet – a wedge of sediments jammed into the surrounding rocks of the basin. The well kicked strongly and blew the entire drill string out of the hole. For four days, the Red Adair folks battled a controlled blow-out, flaring an estimated 40MMCFD from two separate relief lines. Drilled to its ultimate depth, the #4-2 became the dis-

DON TAYLOR
Explorationist
The early years of the South-western Division were led by Don S. Taylor as General Manager of the new group. Taylor's personality was a perfect fit for the assemblage of predominantly young professionals who made up the original staff in San Antonio. Taylor was a geologist by training and had cut his own teeth on assignments in Corpus Christi, Houston, Nigeria and Bakersfield where he directed the highly successful exploration program on the KCL fee lands, leading to the discovery of Yowlumne. Taylor was an explorer of the first degree with an infectious and animated enthusiasm for the job, the division, the people, and for Tenneco. Matching his own physical presence, he lived his life in a big – and successful – way. Taylor was transferred to Houston as Senior Vice President in 1982 and spent his time until the sale as the Houston executive with responsibility for the Gulf of Mexico, and for the technical elements of exploration worldwide. An entire book could be filled with Don Taylor stories.

covery well for the Pinon' field. Eventually this well and several offsets would produce nearly 100 BCF for the division, and the overthrust play would be a "net positive" investment for the company, but that's hardly the whole story.

Once controlled, the discovery well was drilled deeper in an attempt to test the full potential. Multiple productive zones were encountered but presented a very confused picture. At various times, the well produced oil, condensate, wet gas, dry gas and CO_2 on several tests with multiple products from a single set of perforations. It was the first (perhaps still only) time that anyone could recall a single well bore that contained so many diverse products. The production itself defined the complicated geology. Many wells were required before the picture was understood. Since the field was remote, no pipelines or markets were close, and the high CO_2 content strained the economics. The SWD continued the exploration of the Marathon overthrust and took leases on several large ranches in the area. By the sale in 1988, TOE&P owned over 65,000 acres and had drilled 8 or 9 successful wells at Pinon, but the strained logistics, economics and the complex picture made for slow progress.

Following the 1988 sale, Fina (with Tenneco-ex Wes Franklin as GM), the purchaser of the SWD and GCD, drilled another 8 or 10 wells at Pinon' but still struggled with the economics.

The punch line, however, is impressive. Subsequent owners have continued to develop the trend. Riata, a local independent and Sand Ridge now have more than 850 wells producing along extensions of that first discovery. Some reserve estimates exceed 5 TCF for the trend, and 500 BCF for Pinon' itself. It's a substantial resource for the "settlers", although the pioneers got their pay-day as well. And the countryside is still mostly mesquite, wild pigs and cactus. By the way, Tenneco's first well, the J A Gray #4-1 is the only dry hole in the complex.

Riding a Tiger - 1978 to 1980

In response to the natural gas shortages of the early 1970s, and the economic pressures created by the Arab oil embargo of 1973, natural gas pricing was de-regulated – in phases. These changes had significant impact on business at TOE&P, but also at the pipeline. (The TGT portions of the book contain detailed discussions of the events). From the E&P perspective, many new categories of gas pricing had been created, with incentives offered for drilling to specific targets.

The late 1970s and early 1980s included a full-on effort to drill gas wells. Capital budgets were increased throughout the company. Both the industry and Tenneco responded aggressively, and both were very successful in finding new gas reserves. Unregulated prices for "deep" gas spurred a rush to the drilling of ultra-deep wells, mainly in the old onshore provinces where the potentially productive geologic section extended beyond the then-current reach of drilling technology. The Mid-continent, Southwestern and Gulf Coast divisions responded with a flurry of ultra-deep prospects. Many wells were drilled

"At one point in 1981 or 1982, I think TOC had 22 rigs running in the Southwestern Division and over half of them were drilling prospects with targets below 17,000' in the Delaware and Val Verde basins. The drilling was difficult and dangerous and we seemed to be trying to control 'kicks' and near blow-outs on a regular basis. We never lost a well, but we had plenty of excitement in those days. We also found a lot of gas!
- H J Briscoe
(DGM SWD at the time)

to target depths between 18,000' and 25,000' in those wild days. The prospects generally had huge reserve potential. Industry found a few such giants during those days but on balance, the overall economics of the deep-drilling boom were only marginally supported by the real value of the gas found. In 1979, the Penn Square Bank in Oklahoma City failed in a spectacular fashion as a result of aggressive lending to support deep drilling that did not produce results.

The frantic drilling of the time produced an all-out "Boom". The company grew more quickly than at any time in its history and in 1982 the total TOE&P workforce peaked at its all-time high of 3005 employees. With the addition of the 1208 at Operator's Inc. the total count reached 4213. With the rising prices, revenue also hit an all-time high in 1982 at $1.071 Billion, and that was from the TOE&P effort alone. Record high deliveries and the attendant record incomes created pressures on the company and each individual division to maintain that performance. Someone inside the company at the time made the observation, "He who rides a tiger cannot afford to dismount – lest the steed consume the rider!" During the late 1970s and early 1980s, TOE&P surely had a tiger by the tail.

Fortunately, some of the International ventures were reaching fruition, and they provided timely contributions to the revenue needs. Production at Heather in the UK Sector of the North Sea began in 1978. By 1982, it had reached 30,000 BOPD. Peak production at Heather exceeded 41000BOPD and by 1983 the field had produced over 42MMBO of the estimated 90–100MMBO reserve.

Mustang Island A-31

The Mustang Island A-31 Field in the Western Gulf of Mexico, discovered in 1982, was another in the long line of significant discoveries that TOE&P would hang in its trophy case, and one that came at a good time.

In the 1980s the average new gas field found in the Gulf of Mexico had average reserves in the 30–50 BCFG range. In 1982 TOE&P's Western Gulf Division discovered the Mustang Island A-31 field with estimates ten times that large. At that size the new field would rank as the sixth-largest company field in the Gulf of Mexico and the largest addition to the "top 10" within a decade. The discovery was the result of years of geologic work and confidence in a model that convinced the division to drill in an area where "everyone knew" no reservoir sands were present. At least a dozen explorationists and that many more production personnel worked on the project over the years. The Mustang Island field was the first on an entirely new trend in the Western Gulf and was large enough to convince TGT that a regional pipeline should be built into the area. When fully developed, production was estimated to reach 180MMCFGD. The mid-1980s were tight times for capital budgets and personnel from every department pulled together to drill and develop the field efficiently and at costs significantly below normal estimates. Drilling costs

NEIGHBORS BY ACCIDENT

In an unusual coincidence, two of the principals behind the Pinon' discovery, Tommy Wells and Jan Vargo, each ended up buying retirement property near Klamath Falls, OR, only about 30 miles apart, totally unbeknownst to each other.

THE PROMISE OF SADLER CREEK

The mid-continent division was a leader during the early 1980s in deep drilling with several wildcats pushing targets nearing 30,000'. The Sadler Creek, King #1-2 was a well that was carried on company drilling reports for nearly two years. The King well was spud in June of 1981 with a target depth of 25,200'. The well would take 500 days to reach 20,800'. Several pay zones were encountered in shallower secondary objectives while the deep Hunton target was being drilled. The shallow field was actually being developed before the well reached its ultimate total depth.

THE "BOOM"

Rising energy prices made E&P a star within the corporation. Income for TOE&P alone jumped from $42MM in 1973 to $414MM in 1978, and then on to over $1B per year in the early 1980s. Capital expenditures soared to cover a record number of wells – 503 – drilled in 1981. As the boom grew, the company feverishly generated new prospects, drilled new targets, expanded their operations and frantically developed their fields, E&P hired enough new faces to see its workforce grow by 20-30 percent each year! Success brought challenges, though. Employee turnover reached 25% in some technical disciplines, as head-hunters tantalized people with "deals of a lifetime."

In 1979 the stakes went even higher when the Iranian Revolution sent oil prices to over $40 per barrel and unregulated deep gas was bringing $8-$9 per mcf. Oil prices for years ahead were predicted to top $70 and budgets were revised upwards several times per year. By mid-1981 though, demand for oil began to wane. The "official" end to the boom came at midnight on December 31, 1981. The US rig count stood at an all-time high of 4530 (that number remains an all-time high, counts approaching 2000 are rare) but on January 1, 1982 new tax laws went into effect that no longer provided advantaged treatment for investments in drilling. At about the same time, the frenzied drilling of the prior decade had succeeded in the discovery of significant new gas reserves for the country. Demand and prices began a precipitous decline. The "gas bubble" had arrived and within months the market was flooded, creating huge new issues for pipelines and utilities. Within just a few years, the rig count had fallen to 600.

Adapted from E&P Update

The stretch four-pile platform at Mustang Island A-31 field.

were cut in half from the first to the third wells, a "stretch" four-pile platform was fabricated to save nearly 50% over the cost of a normal platform for such a field, 3-D seismic and early reservoir analysis led to a pattern allowing the field to be developed with only 15 wells, and coordination with TGT allowed a "just in time" schedule to put the field on production as soon as the pipeline was available. The new field was the first discovery in an entirely new regional trend so the company had a head start on the competition for the future. All in all, the Mustang Island A-31 field discovery was an excellent example of the types of things TOE&P did well to maximize "net present value".

With its billion-plus dollar contribution in 1982, Tenneco Oil became the largest contributor to Tenneco Inc's annual net income. But, as is so often the case within the energy industry, the pendulum swings are extreme, and often sudden. Despite the record growth and success, 1982 was actually one of severe contrasts. Several negative influences had quietly crept into play – influences that would last for years, and by some analysis, influences that would lay the groundwork for the eventual sale of the company.

Even OPEC acknowledged the market weakness and in 1983 made its' first-ever price cut, dropping their price from $34 to $29 per barrel. The boom ended quickly. The energy industry was still profitable but had to re-learn words such as "efficiency" and "cost effectiveness". Letting go was sudden. The sentiment of the times was captured on a popular bumper sticker of the times – "Lord, give me just one more boom. I promise not to screw this one up!"

Busts Follow Booms
The Gas Bubble Takes Over

The aggressive drilling enjoyed by Tenneco, and by industry in general, during the late 1970s and early 1980s was so successful that by mid-1982 a substantial oversupply of natural gas had emerged in the USA. Concurrently, the sudden slow-down of an overheated national economy reduced industrial demand. Supply and demand curves diverged suddenly and radically. The infamous "gas bubble" had arrived. US gas production capacity exceeded demand by as much as 3-4 TCF per year. Prices fell, and with them net income. It was a crisis of no small magnitude, and the challenges of managing it were substantial. Almost as suddenly as budgets had been expanded to encourage exploration and development, they were then reduced to cut drilling of all but the most essential wells. Gas production was curtailed, or shut-in altogether. Challenging times had arrived quickly and with them the pressures to manage costs and budgets suddenly became the issues of the day. Slamming on the brakes is hardly an adequate description.

Within Tenneco the "gas bubble" had the greatest impact on TGT as it found itself saddled with "take or pay" gas contracts that, unless re-negotiated, could potentially take the company under. The company had no choice but to abrogate many of its contracts, generally invoking the "force majeure" clauses contained therein. This language is present in many contracts and frees both parties from liability or obligation when an extraordinary event or circumstance beyond the control of the parties occurs. As one might expect, there was considerable discussion regarding the application of that clause in this instance. Joe Foster, who was head of all Tenneco Inc energy business at that time, was assigned an unpleasant and difficult task; that of re-negotiating contracts and defending the company in the many lawsuits filed against it. He found himself in the uncomfortable position of negotiating with people in the producing companies who had been our operating partners in the E&P business. Steve Chesebro' was transferred from E&P into the corporate planning office to help identify and manage the relationships between TGT and TOE&P.

TOE&P reacted quickly to the crisis, and in short order re-aligned its

"Being owned by Tenneco Inc. and affiliated with TGT created some restrictions on TOE&P, a challenge that its competitors did not face. That pushed E&P and TGT into doing some things that were imposed rather than bargained-for. A huge oversupply of gas had been created in the Gulf of Mexico, and TGT was not able to take it all. Tenneco Oil E&P was an industry leader in creating the "spot" market for gas – a piece of extremely innovative thinking from our marketing people, Rene' Alanis and Jack Dutton among them."

- J B Foster (Tenn Inc)

strategies to reflect the economic realities of the day. A first step in 1982 saw the sale of all the Canadian production for $111MM. That move was only a preview of the belt-tightening that would follow.

As the industry struggled with the distressed gas market in the US, Tenneco raced to create innovative solutions. No doubt the company's long history with its sister affiliate at TGT provided an advantage in both knowledge and experience. TOE&P needed to find or create more markets, more places to sell its gas. TGT however, needed wellhead prices that would support profitability in its own business.

Tenneco companies pioneered the spot sales market for natural gas through its TENNEFLEX program and the eventual independent (Inc) subsidiary, Tenngasco. TENNEFLEX gained regulatory approval to enable E&P to sell GOM production directly into a spot market, and Tenngasco allowed TGT to buy gas on the open market to keep its pipelines full. In 1983 the spot market contributed an additional 48BCF of gas sales generating $149MM in revenue that would not have been realized otherwise.

The downturn quickly changed thinking and action throughout the company. 'Getting more with less' became a by-line. Every division went back to the drawing board to figure out innovative methods of keeping economic performance up in the face of falling prices and restricted budgets. The tough times produced some of E&P's best work.

There's Always Something Left Behind

The Old Lisbon Operators Committee (OLOC) field was a 9,600-acre waterflood unit in north Louisiana. Production began there in 1936, recovering more than 11 million barrels of oil. Waterflood operations began in 1951, adding an additional 4.5 million barrels. But, by 1978, OLOC was again on its last legs, producing just 250 barrels of oil a day from 23 wells. In 1982 Gulf Coast Division engineers took another look and concluded an additional eight million barrels of oil remained to be recovered from the reservoir. They devised a unique a polymer-augmented tertiary recovery plan.

Division Petroleum Engineer Doug Gundy recalled, "We implemented a polymer-enhanced waterflood to plug off the most permeable streaks so water could sweep out some of the remaining oil. It gave us a more uniform injection and significantly increased production."

The polymer-augmented program improved OLOC's production to about 900 barrels of oil a day from 48 producing wells, represented 17 percent of the GCD's annual oil production, and netted $2.25 million a year.

1984 Brings Grace Blanche Discovery in GCD
Adapted from E&P Update

No E&P discovery better exemplified teamwork than the 1984 find of the Grace Blanche field in Jefferson Co., TX. "Effective teamwork by

TENNGASCO

"The Tenngasco division of Tenneco was established in 1984 to market TOE&P's natural gas production on interstate pipelines, and to identify and reach non-regulated markets directly. The marketing effort achieved a level of success that required supplemental natural gas supplies in excess of those available from TOE&P. In response, Tenngasco established a new natural gas purchase program entitled Tenngasco Exchange. This was the first time that a gas marketer used a "posted price" approach to acquire natural gas supplies. That practice was eventually terminated when it was perceived that the posted prices were driving prices down rather than reflecting market conditions. The Tenngasco Exchange was one of many innovations that are a part of the Tenneco legacy. The natural gas market of today had its beginnings in the Tenneco energy group."

- *Mike Rosinski (Mgr, Tenngasco)*

all disciplines of the division was instrumental in the discovery," reported Billy Hargett, exploration manager at the time. This discovery was made in the heart of a prolific oil and gas province and a combination of regional geology, modern geophysical technology, and "out of the box" thought combined to make the find in an area that was presumed to have been fully tested. The division farmed out three prior prospects in order to build the information set necessary to test the model. Once the wildcat was drilled, the production department applied drilling innovations to reduce the cost of the well and a combine of petroleum, production and geological engineers provided crucial analysis to demonstrate the well was testing a significant reservoir. "Reservoir evaluation is complex in the Yegua," reported Gary Mabie, production manager. "Efficient development will be a team effort in planning, drilling, completing and producing the development wells. Innovation and the application of new technology will be crucial." Team members included Bill Owens, Claude Watts, Bob Lemmon, Larry Meadows, and Mike Rankin.

One More Barrel per Day
Adapted from Spring, 1984 Prolog

When tough times hit the oil patch in the early 1980s, every division was challenged to "make more with less". In the onshore divisions, where 'exploitation' was already the order of the day, the challenges were amplified. Many of the wells from these old fields produced at steady but low rates and squeezing more from them would be a chore.

But in 1983 Mid Continent Division General Manager Harris Phillips challenged the division to an aggressive goal. "With close to 1,600 wells producing 27,000-plus equivalent barrels of oil and gas a day, we realized that just one more barrel per day would be significant, especially when you're not putting a drilling bit in the ground to produce it."

MCD Production Manager Ad Wilkinson said the division's 19 production engineers were eager to accept this new challenge. "The division has a lot of old producing wells that average about five barrels of oil a day." Harold Altendorf, MCD production consultant, commented, "While that isn't much of a rate, these wells are pure profit for us because they've paid for themselves long ago. Adding revenue with little investment makes sense all day long."

Wilkinson adds, "There are several ways to increase production from older wells. Some of these include reducing production down-time through routine equipment maintenance, expediting repairs when equipment fails, studying the economics of each well and efficiently scheduling work overs and maintenance."

To achieve their goal for 1983, production engineers had to find 585,000 new barrels of oil or gas equivalent from their base of producing wells. At year-end, they had recovered an impressive 550,000NEBs. The program generated 16 percent of the division's total production for the year.

"At a TOE&P management meeting at Columbia Lakes in either the fall of 1982 or the spring of 1983 an outside speaker spoke of the need for producers to become active in the Federal regulatory arena with respect to natural gas. At the time over half of the TOE&P natural gas deliverability in the Gulf of Mexico was shut in. Subsequently, the FERC gave Tenneco the first producer authorization to sell natural gas directly in the interstate market. This was just another example of TOE&P's leadership position in the Industry."

- Jack Dutton
(EVP, Tenneco Gas Marketing)

Strategies that produced these results came from a variety of unlikely sources. Rather than starting with the wells themselves, the engineers reviewed their own structure and daily activity. "Traditionally," Wilkinson explained, "MCD production engineers had been overloaded with paperwork which, while necessary, detracted from key projects, so the first change was to reorganize the department, passing many of these functions to the clerical and administrative staffs, allowing engineers more time to concentrate on engineering. This is where they can best produce revenue."

Rodney Myers, MCD production engineering supervisor, credits this change with giving production engineers time to better evaluate the needs of each well. Analyzing pumping unit efficiencies and fluid levels provided more incremental success. "It takes a lot of little pieces to make the total picture. Since we don't have 30 or so wells that will carry the whole division, we need 300 to 400 wells like these to help us achieve our goal!'

The organizational structure of the 175 Operators Inc. employees was realigned into a departmental ladder, with more clearly defined reporting relationships. The new arrangement enhanced communication and operating efficiency at both ends of the spectrum. "We used to have some wells off production for embarrassing lengths of time before the information got to the production engineers. Now, we catch problems quickly and correct them in a few days instead of weeks."

"Lots of small pieces add up to some impressive totals, and that creates good business practices for the future." (By 1984, the "One More Barrel" program had added 794,000 BO to annual division production).

Modeling Well Fractures

A 1984 E&P Update article highlighted some innovative technology and teamwork in the Mid-Continent division, and sheds some light on a 30-year old "new" issue – "Fracking"

An integrated team was formed in the MCD to improve the performance of fractured wells using new computer technology. Fracturing has been around a long time (this, in 1984). Over the years, rough guidelines evolved for how much liquid should be pumped, optimum pressures, and amounts of proppant - the sand-like material also pumped into the formation to prop open the fissure from which the increased production would flow. Too little, and it would close. Too much, and the proppant itself would seal off the fissure.

"In the past the industry depended on vendors to recommend procedures that worked," said Pat Drennon, project drilling engineer. "Then in 1984 a computer software program became available. It enabled engineers to model each fracture and test alternatives." The team re-evaluated a number of older frac-jobs. "We started looking for 'problem' wells, and then realized they didn't have to be problem wells. Even old fractures we thought were performing well turned out to be candidates for re-fracturing," said John Roffers, senior petroleum engineer.

"Re-fracturing old wells opened up a new frontier in our gas fields"

Doug Gundy,
MCD prod manager

The new models called for twice as much proppant as had been used in the past. "We'd take a laptop computer (a rarity in 1984) to the wellsite and track actual fracture performance - the volumes that are going down the well bore, and the pressure response," said Roffers. "The on-site engineering enabled us to modify our design during the fracture." The fine-tuning could greatly improve the fracture and thus the well's economics. Flow rates from many of the old wells were increased by factors of two or three.

"The models told us that a quarter of re-stimulated wells will flow at more than their original rates," explained John Van Fleet, senior project geologist and team leader. "These re-stimulation programs are also low-risk, because we already know the gas is there. We added reserves at a cost as low as $1.50 per net equivalent barrel. E&P had dozens of wells that are candidates for re-fracturing."

The infusion of technology and teamwork led the team to reflect-on the past. "In the early '80s we thought we were doing a wonderful job with fractures," said Drennon. "But some wells fell off fast, and acted like they weren't fractured at all. We didn't know why."

"The geologists would say the engineers ruined the well," laughed the late Jerry Upp, then geological engineering consultant and the fourth team member. "The engineers would say the geology was no good" countered Drennon.

Van Fleet and Upp agreed, "With more cross-training and teamwork, it's amazing how we all fit together! No one person or discipline could handle the knowledge we have available through today's technology, We all got an oil-business education."

LOU PARISH
A Pioneer

Lou Parish was another in the line of TOE&P's "founding fathers", or at least a member of the first generation following those fathers. At the end of his career (he retired in 1987) he was regarded by all in the company as the "consummate" oil-man. His own career began as a "scout", taking daily reports in the field, until he could prove himself and secure a job as a landman. He was also a self-taught geologist, knowing that he needed to be able to understand all elements of a prospect if he wanted to be a successful deal-maker. Through hard work, study and commitment he became one of the best. At his retirement he was Senior Vice President in Houston, responsible for the combined Rocky Mountain Divisions. Tenneco 'acquired' Parish with the Bay Acquisition in 1955 and served in a variety of locations during his career. Mr. Parish died in 1987. Joe Foster described him as, "a straight-shooter, a hard and tireless worker who cared immensely about doing a good job."

Teamwork and Technology
The Regional Drilling Group in the GOM
Adapted from E&P Update, May, 1984

The boom-times of the late 1970s and early 1980s created something of a "people crunch". In the Gulf of Mexico more and more wells were being drilled and younger and younger engineers were sent onto the rigs and platforms to manage the operations. This provided good hands-on experience, but also a risk of exposure to problems the young engineers had not encountered. Technology allowed the creation of the "Real Time Drilling Center" - something of a "Mission Control" inside the main office building back in Lafayette. Satellite transmissions from the rigs to the office allowed more experienced engineers in the office to monitor the wells being drilled in real time by looking at the same data that the engineers on the rigs were seeing. With the resources in the office onshore, the ground-based staff was able to provide support, "run the numbers", research information, and the like and provide help back to the rigs, making the operations both more efficient and likely safer. Bob Bowie was a primary champion behind the development of the center. A "best practices" manual was developed from this work to reduce drilling trouble costs.

The eight-person Offshore Regional Drilling Group in Lafayette was created to develop and utilize advanced technology to reduce drilling expenses and improve productivity. Comprised of seven drilling engineers and one geological engineer, the group offered a variety of technical services. All members of the team had operational field experience, in addition to expertise in computer programming, geo-chemistry, physics, rock mechanics and well design.

"Each individual had a niche," said Bill Kortlang, senior project drilling engineer who headed the group. "For example, Charlie Palmer and Oscar Bernard specialize in operational technical studies. Harvey Goodman was involved in petro-geophysical research. Rick Graff manned the real-time data center, while Ted Allen and Sonny Stelly were our self-taught computer gurus. Allen Gault, a rock-mechanics expert, selected the most effective drill bits."

"Computers convert electronic impulses from more than 20 gauges and sensors on the rig floor into usable data," explained Rick Graff. "Nearly every aspect of drilling activity was recorded."

As a result drilling operations could be monitored for potential problems at the drill site and in the office as well. The system also created another data base to assist the engineers when planning future drilling projects. One of the group's most notable achievements in 1987 was the computerization of daily drilling and completion reports.

Reaction to the new system was so favorable that the group hoped to eventually modify the program for company-wide use. (This of course, was written in 1987 – just before the decision to sell the company, so wider applications of the system never had time to develop).

* * * * *

Curtailed budgets slowed operations in gas-prone project areas, but that did not translate to shutting down the company. It did, however, change the focus to liquids. In Colombia's Llano Basin and Magdalena Valley, the two main provinces acquired in the Houston Oil and Minerals acquisition, production increased to 30,500BOPD. In the Gulf of Mexico, the company remained active at the leasing tables, adding 48 new leases in the GOM in 1983 and 1984, and an additional 7 in Alaska. Oil was discovered offshore Gabon. The change in focus from gas to liquids produced record oil and liquids deliveries in 1984.

Company President Phil Oxley noted the achievements of the year in a letter to all employees, "Each E&P division searched for more ways to control costs and improve productivity. We increased deliveries by developing new markets through special and spot sales programs. Innovative financing methods, farm outs and leveraging agreements maximized domestic drilling prospects. We learned to do more with less. The divisions drilled more wells, increased deliveries and added more reserves with less money. New technologies were implemented to enhance production and for the seventh consecutive year, we replaced our production with new reserves. We are proud of our efforts and our employees deserve congratulations for jobs well done."

Strategic irony.
Although the Yowlumne field had been discovered using the risk-balancing farmout strategy, the PCD chased the follow-up fields primarily with 100%-funded wildcats. After the five dry holes, they went back to the drawing board, and the prior strategy. The farm-out to Channel Industries that discovered Landslide, provides yet another irony. Channel was a subsidiary of TGT, charged with locating gas supplies for pipeline interests in the area.

1985 – Positive Results in Difficult Times

Despite continuing economic challenges, the activities of 1985 produced numerous significant accomplishments, providing a testament to the employees and the managerial philosophies that had been developed in the years prior. The workforce and the asset base were both in good condition, and the former managed the latter to make the year a good one.

A major and long-running litigation with El Paso Corp. concerning ownership of certain properties in the San Juan Basin was settled in Tenneco's favor. This decision added an immediate 65MMNEB of reserves to the company balance sheet, a "reserve add" that was almost as large as any of the largest fields the company had ever discovered and qualifies the event as a 'turning point' in the company history (detailed following). In Colombia, a complete overhaul of the exploration of the HOM (HOCOL) properties that had started after the acquisition in 1981 paid off in a major way with the discovery of the huge (152 MMBO) San Francisco field in the Magdalena Valley. In California, continued exploration of the KCL properties produced the discovery at the Landslide field and the company's highest onshore flow rate at 2000 BOPD. The Pacific Coast Division also acquired the huge old Placerita field north of Los Angeles.

Landslide

Playing off of the Yowlumne field, prospects both updip and downdip of the field were tested, but the Stevens channels proved elusive, and over the years five dry holes were drilled chasing them. A downdip well, the 27-29, was sidetracked and re-drilled a number of times, and eventually yielded a 700'-thick "sand-pile", but still with only marginal potential. Two more unsuccessful wells followed. Deciding it was again time to spread the risk, TOE&P farmed out the next well to Channel Exploration who drilled the San Emidio 63x-30. The discovery came in at 2,064 BOPD from a depth of 12,500', and was deemed the Landslide Field. Fifteen wells were drilled in the field, six of which for water injection. Reserves for Landslide were about 20MMBO. Tenneco personnel involved with the Landslide discovery were Mike Navolio, Barclay Collins, and James Caballero. Don Sprouse named this one.

Placerita

TOE&P bought the very old, "heavy-oil" oil field in a rugged canyon not far north of Los Angeles in 1985. The project was planned as a steam-flood with cogeneration of direct power. At this time the federal government had forced the utilities to purchase electricity from independent power generators at 'avoided cost' (the utilities' cost to put new supply on line otherwise). The economics for a project like this did were not based as much on the value of the oil recovered, but rather on the sales of power generated from the cogeneration. Tenneco was the leader in California with projects like this, having installed smaller cogeneration units at a number of its other heavy-oil, steam-flood projects. Due to

EL PASO SETTLEMENT

Like so many complex projects within the realm of TOEP's activities over the years, the settlement of the El Paso litigation involved talents from throughout the organization. The following quotes from various contributors make the point.

"When the controversy first began, I was division general manager for the Rocky Mountain Division. When I transferred back to Houston in my present position in 1982, the Rocky Mountain Divisions were one of my primary responsibilities. I was one of the five or six individuals in the company who followed this thing from beginning to end. Much credit has to be given to Vernon Turner, who retired as our general counsel in 1983. It was he who spearheaded the project and without his efforts there would be no settlement agreement. Tenneco took the initiative on the suit and the other leaseholders followed. I don't think anyone thought it would go on as long as it did.

The company will book substantial reserves because of the settlement. That will lower our DD&A cost because the reserves are added without a capital investment. In addition, the development potential of the properties is excellent. The natural gas processing plant offers Tenneco Oil P&M some exciting opportunities. The settlement is a boost not only for E&P but for all of Tenneco."
-L L Parish, Senior Vice President

"In 1952, I was an attorney for Southern Union Gas Company, the former parent company of Delhi-Taylor. Both companies used the same law firm In Dallas. When the first lease sale agreement between Delhi and El Paso was signed, a friend with the law firm thought I might find it interesting and sent it to me. I never dreamed as I read the document how much it would later Impact my career. Seven years later, I joined DeIhi-Taylor. In 1961, that company began to think seriously about renegotiating the overriding royalties, and we exhaustingly researched the matter. It was a briefing for the same kind of case Tenneco would get involved in almost 12 years later.

As early as 1964 when I came on board for Tenneco, Vernon Turner and I discussed the possibility of such a suit, and in the late 1960s, we actually began preparations for such a case. We felt that it was only a matter of time before the jurisdictional issue was raised. So, in reality, this case has spanned more than 15 years, 12 of it spent in the courtroom. From a legal standpoint, the case was fascinating. I'm convinced that the reason we came out on top was that Tenneco was better prepared. We never turned our case completely over to our outside counsel. Our legal staff always worked closely with them, offering support and advice with Vernon Turner directing the effort. We also made a special effort to educate them about the oil and gas industry. That made a real difference."

"The settlement was just that - a true settlement. There were concessions made on both sides. Full credit must be given to outside counsel, Baker & Botts of Washington, D.C., Vernon Turner and Lou Parish. They made a success of the lawsuit and settlement."

Millard Carr – Sr. Division Attorney, WRMD

"I became involved in the suit soon after I joined the company in 1975. An engineer with operations expertise was needed to assist outside legal counsel with interpretation of the data that was being gathered during the remedy proceedings ordered by the FERC.

the revenue generated by selling electricity at 'avoided cost', E&P was one of the few producers able to continue steam injection at the heavy oil projects when prices fell. This produced favorable economics in its own right, but also allowed the company to maintain the steam envelope on the heavy oil sands. Had this not been the case, the reservoirs would have cooled down and required total re-heating when prices rose, and that would have cost a lot.

The Deepest Well

In the Gulf of Mexico TOE&P stayed on the leading edge of prospect concepts and drilling technologies. The Eastern Gulf of Mexico was the Frontier area for the explorers in Lafayette. The company "went deep" in 1985 by drilling a well in the Eastern Gulf of Mexico, the Viosca Knoll 117-#1, that was targeted to be the deepest well ever drilled in the Gulf of Mexico. Located in 115' water depth in Mobile Bay, and with an objective in the Jurassic Norphlet formation, the well was planned for a total depth of 24,500'. The cost was estimated at approximately $12-million.

Reserves at the Courthouse
The El Paso Natural Gas Settlement

A major and long-running litigation with El Paso Corp. concerning ownership of certain properties in the San Juan Basin was settled in Tenneco's favor in 1985. This story demonstrates the value added to company coffers through teamwork, skill and persistence.

Although not exactly an acquisition, the impact of the settlement of a legal dispute had the same impact and surely qualifies as a "turning point" milestone in the history of TOE&P. This agreement, over ownership of gas in the San Juan Basin of northeast New Mexico, ended a 12-year legal battle between operating partners Tenneco and Conoco, and the defendant El Paso Corporation. The final approval by the Federal Energy Regulatory Commission (FERC) in September of 1985, gave outright ownership to Tenneco and Conoco and added 68 million NEBs of reserves to TOE&P's books, an amount equal to half the company's drilling reserve additions for the prior year, and nearly as large as any onshore field the company had ever discovered by drilling. The settlement changed the fortunes, and the operations, of the Western Rocky Mountain Division for years.

The 1985 settlement of a 12-year legal dispute between Tenneco, its partner Conoco, and EI Paso Natural Gas Company involving overriding royalty interests on oil and gas leases in New Mexico was a "classic" case; the type that sets legal precedents. The battle involved some of the most complex litigation ever heard by the courts, the resolution of which brought a new era of development to the San Juan Basin.

The San Juan Basin gas was first discovered in 1911. During the 1920s and 1930s several large gas accumulations were found, but because of the Depression and restricted gas markets, many gas wells were plugged and abandoned, and only a shallow gas field was developed for service in New Mexico. In the 1940s substantial commercial gas production was finally established, and the San Juan Basin grew to become one of the largest gas-fields in the nation, with over 30 trillion cubic feet of recoverable reserves.

In the late 1940s EI Paso Natural Gas Company first proposed building an interstate natural gas pipeline to serve the rapidly-growing markets in southern California. In order to ensure a large and consistent supply of gas for its pipeline El Paso created unique lease/sale agreements with the operators in the Basin and was assigned direct working interest ownership in the properties. El Paso assumed responsibility for developing and operating the leases, and the current leaseholders received monthly royalty checks with no obligation to drill wells or perform other work on the properties. Royalties were paid on gross income from production, with the price to be re-determined every five years. The first override was five cents per thousand cubic feet. Leaseholders also retained a right to one-third of the condensate and liquids extracted from the gas stream by EI Paso. The first company to sign such an agreement was Delhi-Taylor Oil Company, one of the principal property owners in the basin. Delhi-Taylor committed nearly 150,000 acres of leases. Development of that acreage as well as other areas of the San Juan Basin was greatly accelerated when EI Paso began transporting natural gas to California in 1951.

In 1964, TOE&P, with Conoco as its equal partner, purchased the properties of Delhi-Taylor Oil Co. – including its gas lease sale agreements with EI Paso Natural Gas and its other San Juan Basin properties. (The Delhi-Taylor acquisition has itself been identified as a "turning point" for the company – a double-dip on this one). As a result of the $150 million acquisition, Tenneco initiated a massive development drilling program in the area and also collected royalties on acreage covered by the EI Paso agreements. The basin became an important reserve and income base for the company.

The gas lease sale agreements, now between Tenneco, Conoco and El Paso, continued without question until 1973, when, in response to significant increases in gas prices, Tenneco and Conoco, and other operators in the area sought increases in the royalty payments.

In response to that demand, EI Paso filed a lawsuit and a complaint with the Federal Power Commission (the forerunner to the Federal Energy Regulatory Commission) asserting that the gas lease sale agreement transactions were, in effect, price-regulated sales of natural gas under the jurisdiction of the Natural Gas Act.

A complex series of suits, counter-suits, rulings, judgments, and appeals between 1974 and 1985 finally found Tenneco, Conoco and El Paso at a negotiating table to work out a settlement agreement. That process itself was complex, but in April of 1985, a settlement composed of 16 different documents was filed with FERC and in June, an approval order was issued.

I considered my involvement in the litigation a tremendous opportunity for me - one that is not over with yet. The settlement of the suit is just the beginning for those of us in the Western Rocky Mountain Division. I put a lot of time on the project, but I was exposed to some areas of the business I might not have ever seen. It was a tremendous learning experience."

Bob Gibb
petroleum engineering
supervisor, Western Rocky
Mountain Division

"I was the numbers man for E&P. During the negotiations, I translated how the different proposals would affect the company from a financial and production standpoint. From my economic analysis, we could quantify the impact of various considerations. There was always a great deal of uncertainty by both sides surrounding the litigation. It was not an open or shut case. The outcome depended on the court's interpretation."

The settlement virtually re-organized the entire focus of the Western Rocky Mountain Division. In anticipation of a settlement, division personnel began developing exploration and production strategies for the lease agreement acreage.

Rene Alanis – Manager of
Planning and Evaluation, Oil and
Gas Contracts

"The settlement agreement has put us in a very enviable position. Taking over operations on so many wells at one time is a real challenge, but one with immediate rewards. In the first two days alone we were able to increase production by 30 million cubic feet of gas per day - and that's only the beginning."

Bill Cayce - Division
General Manager.

"Some 95 percent of the division's production and income comes from the San Juan Basin. This settlement gives us numerous opportunities to expand our production base through workovers, recompletions and development drilling. The division began a development program on the lease agreement properties that could result in the drilling of another 1,000 to 1,100 new wells."

Harry Hufft - Division Production Manager

"It's a production engineer's dream. We've been making plans and waiting to take over those leases for almost a year. It's been like children waiting for a candy store to open. Production can be increased on almost every well. The potential of these properties is just overwhelming."

Doyle headed the four-man task force that was organized by the division after the settlement was submitted to the FERC for approval. Their job was to plan development strategies for the properties. Less than 24 hours after the transfer of operatorship was made, they were already implementing those plans. Improved production techniques on one well alone resulted in a production increase of 7.5 million cubic feet of gas and 1,100 barrels of oil a day. Recompletion efforts on two other wells increased combined production from 14 to 511 thousand cubic feet of gas a day.

Not all of the excitement was focused on the producing wells. Due to the then-existing "gas bubble" and tightly-held ownership in the San Juan Basin there had been scant exploration in the area. The expanded ownership put Tenneco's geological engineers to work looking for expansion opportunities, and another task force set about developing a history on the some 16,000 wells drilled within

El Paso reassigned the leases to Tenneco and Conoco, and the overriding royalty interests were terminated. With the end of the litigation, TOE&P doubled its operations in the San Juan Basin as the two E&P companies became working interest owners of the leases, assuming interests on 2575 well completions. Tenneco took over operations on 1375 wells that were producing 180 million cubic feet of gas per day. All of the gas from these leases would now be sold to El Paso through conventional sales agreements, a huge win for the producers.

The pair also began construction of a $60 million state-of-the-art gas processing plant capable of handling 500 million cubic feet of natural gas each day. The plant, operated by Conoco with Tenneco's half-interest residing with TOP&M, became the largest per-day producer of raw natural gas liquids in the United States.

For E&P the approval of the settlement agreement meant it could now concentrate its efforts in the San Juan Basin on what it did best, finding and producing gas and oil. Little did they realize that work would be for the benefit of new owners (Amoco in this case, now gone themselves), only 3 years in the future.

International in High Gear

Re-focusing the TOE&P International efforts in the late 1970s began to reap dividends, and the timing was good. During the last five years of the company's existence, International operations provided many of the highlights for the company. International projects are necessarily long-term in nature, and frequently involve partners. Once commitments are made and investments are begun, it is often difficult to re-direct budgets, regardless of the outside economic conditions. Fortunately, much of the "risk" portion of E&P's major foreign ventures had occurred in prior years, and success was welcome news for the company.

HOCOL – and Colombia

The Houston Oil & Minerals acquisition had provided yet another jewel, in Colombia. In truth, though, it was not just a jewel or even an entire necklace, it was a vault full of precious gems.

Immediately following the acquisition of Houston Oil & Minerals in 1981, TOE&P teams set to work evaluating the international holdings. Although the acquisition had been made largely for properties in the Gulf of Mexico, the international assets were deemed "promising". The Tenneco teams quickly identified a number of attractive targets and began a systematic exploitation of them. Production from the Llanos and Magdalena basins in Colombia commenced in 1983 and ramped up quickly as numerous wildcat discoveries followed in turn. The giant San Francisco field was discovered in 1985 and became the largest onshore field in the TOE&P portfolio. The South American Division was created in 1986 to manage the explosive growth and potential there. Between 1982 and 1988,

HOCOL (the TOE&P subsidiary operating in Colombia) found 26 new fields in Colombia. Tenneco, through HOCOL, employed 450 people in Colombia, all but one Colombian citizens. At the time of the sale, HOCOL was producing 38,000 BOPD, making it the largest outside producing company in the country (second behind the state-owned Ecopetrol). Projections from the new fields indicated production rates would double by 1991. San Francisco and Colombia became a model of the Tenneco brand of integrated teamwork and at the time of the sale were among the true highlights of the company portfolio.

The Discovery of a Giant - San Francisco Colombia
Adapted from E&P Prolog, 1986

The largest single oil field discovered in TOE&P's 42-year history was the "giant" (an oil-industry term indicating reserves exceeding 100MMBO) San Francisco Field in Colombia, South America. The discovery of the San Francisco field was the result of an integrated search that teamed individuals from multiple disciplines in the search for oil, and a culmination of their dreams.

For Kim Butler, the dream appeared after he spent nine months walking the rugged mountains west of Neiva, Colombia, carrying a compass and mapping surface geology. For geophysicist Dave Wiman, the dream was realized 17 years after he argued in favor of drilling a large surface anticline, only to see his employer at the time decide otherwise. For Jim Dorman (exploration consultant) and Art Thompson (exploration manager), the discovery of the San Francisco oilfield in March of 1985 was the culmination of an integrated effort that teamed geology, geophysics and other disciplines in the search for oil. For Will Frank and Camillo Merendoni, the discovery rewarded years of good relations with the Colombian government, as well as an outstanding track record of exploration and production.

San Francisco field was the largest oilfield ever discovered by Tenneco - 78 million barrels of oil recoverable through primary production. With a waterflood, the recoverable reserves could more than double, and it's possible that the final figure could exceed 200 million barrels. Tenneco's net was 40 percent.

The San Francisco oil lies in two lens-shaped zones only 2,000 to 3,000 feet below the surface. Wells can be completed in two short weeks, and they initially produce at rates of 200 to 1,000 barrels per day.

"This field will contribute nearly a billion dollars in net operating income to E&P over the next 20 years," said Will Frank, vice president and general manager of the International Division.

The cash flow began in 1985 at $12 million, reached $41 million in 1986, and was projected to climb to $100 million per year. The field was also of great benefit to the Colombian economy. When E&P's annual income reached $100 million annually, Ecopetrol, Colombia's state oil company would see its own revenues exceed $150 million.

the San Juan Basin, accumulating information on wells that were drilled more than 30 years prior.
Paul Doyle - Western Rocky Mountain Division production engineer,

"So far, we have proposed nearly 400 locations for drilling, concentrated in the Pictured Cliffs, Chacra, Dakota and Mesa Verde formations. Of these, some 90 will be dual completions, and we've only started to work. There is still a volume of information to gather and review. We have years of work ahead of us as we lay the groundwork for our future in the San Juan Basin."

Howard Musgrove - Geological Engineering Manager

TOE&P's largest single oil field discovery ever was the San Francisco Field in Columbia.

Thirty-two wells – all successes – were drilled in 1985, with 24 planned for 1986. The massive surface (6700 acres, more than 10 square miles) anti-cline had never been drilled until Tenneco spudded the # 1 wildcat. "All the companies working in the area recognized the anticline," said Frank, "but the geologic question was whether it was closed (trapped) on the south."

Dave Wiman had worked Colombia before, in the mid-1960s with an-other domestic oil company. "We mapped the area and recognized the surface anticline, but needed confirmation of the south closure. We had a seismic program underway that was stopped for a lack of funds. Of course, the remaining line to be shot was on the south end of the anticline. Because we didn't have seismic data confirming closure, the company dropped the acreage without drilling," recalls Wiman. And so did a Colombian firm a few years later.

Fifteen years later Wiman joined Tenneco, to work the same area of Colombia. Tenneco had become re-involved in Colombia as a result of the Houston Oil and Minerals acquisition. HO&M had hired Kim Butler, a geology PhD candidate at the University of South Carolina, to study the area's geology.

He and another student stayed in a hotel in Neiva and drove out to the rugged areas surrounding the town every day for nine months. They trekked up mountain slopes and through heavy brush, lugging charts and observing surface rock outcrops, recording the results notebooks. Carrying a compass, Butler took bearings and paced out the dimensions of surface features, "seat-of-the- pants, old-time geology," as one Tenneco production engineer put it. Butler's PhD dissertation was on the geology of the area.

Meanwhile, in 1983 Tenneco learned that the exploratory concession granted to a Colombian company was expiring. Tenneco applied for the acreage, and the other company requested a renewal. In a critical presentation in 1984 Ecopetrol's board members visited Tenneco's producing fields in the area. Will Frank and Camilo Merendoni, general manager of HOCOL, Tenneco's Colombian subsidiary, pointed out that the Palermo area containing the San Francisco anticline would complement the company's existing operations. The following week the board awarded the contract to HOCOL.

"Camilo and Art Thompson are principally responsible for us acquiring the contract," said Frank. "They and the entire Colombian staff have represented us very well."

With the prospect now in Tenneco's inventory, the full range of exploration tools was brought to bear. Seismic analysis, aerial photography, satellite photography, gravity/magnetic surveys, and geochemistry were applied to the task of confirming the prospect.

"The seismic lines analyzed by Glen Smith and Monty Hogue (senior staff geophysicists) confirmed a south closure, just as Wiman and Butler had foreseen," said Dorman.

There was more encouraging news, 12 miles to the northeast. The Hato Nuevo wildcat drilled by Tenneco in 1984 found significant oil production in the Caballos formation, confirming the reservoir's potential. The risk was growing smaller and the task of convincing management that the prospect was viable fell to Dorman. He succeeded. The wildcat drilled in March of 1985 found two oil-bearing Caballos zones, each ranging from 100 to 150 feet in thickness. The well tested at 500 barrels of 28 degree API gravity oil per day. A second well drilled a half-mile away confirmed the discovery. They came in exactly as mapped.

"HOCOL was so special that even years later when Ecopetrol finally managed to buy it back, they kept it separate in the hopes that Ecopetrol would become more like HOCOL than the other way around."

Mike Morgan
(GE, SAD-Colombia)

HOME TEAM

"Following the establishment of the Houston office for HOCOL, a young Colombian geo-tech was sent to Houston for a two-week visit. Geophysicist Raul Sarmiento impressed the staff with his talent and knowledge of the Llanos basin, and with his "ball of fire" attitude – to the point that the Houston staff never let him go home. He stayed and enjoyed an excellent run as an "oil-finder" for the Colombian Division. My recollection is that we found a few more fields in the upper and middle Magdalena basins in those final years, and another half dozen or so of those smaller fields in the Llanos."

Loren Leiker
(Division Geologist, SAD)

RISKS ON THE JOB

As was the case in a number of Tenneco's foreign operations through the years, the activity in Colombia brought certain perils.

In November 1984, the Nevado del Ruiz volcano erupted in the Andes mountains of Colombia. The mud avalanche that followed severed the Ecopetrol pipeline serving HOCOL's upper Magdalena valley and destroyed the native city of Armero, killing an estimated 25,000 residents. HOCOL immediately moved equipment and personnel to the area to assist in recovery. A Tenneco corporate aircraft was used to transport medical supplies and other relief assistance. HOCOL's operations were about 100 miles from the site of the eruption so no company personnel were in danger. The severed pipeline cut off production from about 150 company wells, including those in the San Francisco field. HOCOL personnel, working with Texaco and Ecopetrol repaired the pipeline quickly.

HOSTAGE IN COLUMBIA

During the late 1980s Colombia was a violent country, with drug cartels and other political factions battling each other and the government for control and for money. Tenneco's presence had grown quickly in the country through HOCOL. Many of the foreign companies with operations in certain parts of the country battled sabotage and other forms of violence as part of their daily operation. At least one Tenneco employee experienced this violence first-hand.

On August 16, 1985, Assistant Operations Manager, Mike Stewart (Division Production Manager in the Southwestern Division at the time of the sale), made his way downstairs from his Bogota hotel room for the short trip with his

"I was sitting on the edge of my chair," recalled Butler.

"It was vindication," said Wiman.

"It's what this business is all about," offered Dorman.

Successive wells continued to find oil. The oilfield measures seven miles north-to-south, and four miles east-to-west, more than twice the size of the surface feature. Furthermore, the San Francisco Field proved a concept. Since the discovery Tenneco found the Caballos productive in another, smaller field. It may well be found elsewhere. The finds could open the entire Upper Magdalena Valley area for Caballos exploration. (Prophetic words in 1986 as subsequent work in 1987 and 1988 led to nearly 20 more new fields in the Upper Magdalena and Llanos basins).

There were plenty of other places to look. Tenneco held interests in 2.5 million acres in Colombia, one of the world's hottest exploratory areas.

A Production Challenge

The discovery of the San Francisco Field brought the International Division's production department a big, though welcome, challenge - get oil from a rugged, remote area to market as soon as possible.

The field is a giant surface anticline, expressed as a mountain 1,200 feet above the floor of the Magdalena River valley, a formidable obstacle. Within nine months HOCOL, Tenneco's Colombian subsidiary, had mobilized a battalion of 25 bulldozers to cut roads and clear drilling pads, contracted for rigs, drilled 32 wells and laid countless miles of pipelines. The payoff was production of 10,000BOPD for the first year, with higher production possible if a pipeline serving the area had capacity to take the flow.

"The discovery well was producing five days after it was completed," said Camillo Merendoni, general manager of Tenneco's 420-person Colombian operation.

"The people in our Bogota and Neiva offices did an outstanding job of getting this field onstream. To get that first well producing they had to lay 11 miles of flowline over mountains, valleys and rivers, all of it a fairly remote area. "

Another 24 wells were budgeted for 1986. "Our productive capacity could be 16 to 22,000 barrels per day by the end of the year," said Buddy Watsky, technical manager for Colombia. "Ultimately, the field could produce over 50,000 barrels per day at its peak." The best wells in the field are capable of producing over a thousand barrels per day via pumping units.

"The field hasn't produced a lot of surprises to date," said Watsky, "other than many of the wells coming in higher than expected. So the top of the structure is broader than we thought at first, which means it may hold more oil than we originally thought. This thing is a monster. It's not the kind of thing you get a chance to develop every day."

With production at over 30,000 BOPD and no pipeline, HOCOL relied on a fleet of 1,600 trucks.

The Rolling Pipeline

Following its exceptional string of wildcat discoveries Tenneco (HO-COL) needed a pipeline to transport the production to the coast. Building the line would take most of two years, and while the line was being built, capital investment would still be required to drill development wells, but cash flow would not be generated to pay for it. The innovative solution to the problem came with wheels on it. For several years, a fleet of up to 1600 trucks carried the majority of HOCOL's 30,000+BOPD production up to 1000km to the coast or to refineries. The daily spectacle along the mountain roads was truly a rolling pipeline. The present value of the accelerated cash flow was significant and yet another indication of the innovative solutions we'd come to expect from Tenneco engineers.

Post Script in South America

The Colombian properties, including the San Francisco Field, and all of the prior and subsequent discoveries there, were sold to Shell, for about $500 million. At last review, the properties held 230 MMBO proved, probable and possible reserves, with that many more of potential from the exploration discoveries. Just before the sale was announced the company approved a new pipeline system for the entire Magdalena Valley to service all of the recent discoveries. The 480-mile long pipeline had an estimated cost of $550 million and was scheduled for completion in 1990.

The concentration on opportunities in South America expanded to Ecuador. In May of 1987 company press carried news of a $30MM exploration program for the Eastern lowlands – "the Oriente'" - of the equatorial country. An office, staffed by both US ex-Pats and Ecuadorian nationals was opened in Quito. The venture became the 13th active international project.

security guard who would drive him to the HOCOL office. Halfway through the 15-minute trip, Stewart's car was hit from behind by another vehicle. Immediately, six armed men surrounded the car. Three of the gunmen took Stewart at gunpoint and shoved him to the floor of a waiting car. The other three took the driver. Stewart had been kidnapped, in full daylight and right off a busy street in the capital city. He was handcuffed and held in the back room of a non-descript house for five months while the company negotiated a release.

On December 21, 1985 his captors abruptly wakened Stewart, gave him a scissors and razor and told him to clean himself up. He was blindfolded, taken on a twenty-minute drive across the city and dropped off on a unknown street corner. His captors gave him 800 pesos for a taxi and told him to make his way to room 961 in a certain Bogota hotel. Waiting in the room was Will Frank, Tenneco's Vice President the International Division. "The best-looking sight I'd ever seen!", according to Stewart.

Mike was finally home for Christmas with his family (photo below), 128 days later than planned. Steve Chesebro' reports that the FBI wanted to take over the case but the company resisted that intrusion which likely would have exacerbated the resolution.

PRESIDENT BONGO AND FAMILY VISIT HOUSTON

In 1987 President Omar Bongo of Gabon brought a contingent of family and government officials to Houston to meet Tenneco management and celebrate the discovery of oil on Tenneco leases in his country. The country owned a single 747 jet that was used commercially twice a week for trips to and from Paris. The President and his contingent used the plane to come to Houston, then sent it home loaded with a brand new J I Case tractor (a gift from Tenneco) so that it could perform its commercial duties, returning the next day to take them home. E&P President Wayne Nance met President Bongo at the airport (above), and a large security detail arranged numerous automobiles for the escorted trip through rush-hour Houston traffic, much to the chagrin of the normal commuters. The handlers also presented the travelers with a large black bag full of cash. During the visit to Houston the Gabonese group embarked on several major shopping expeditions and at one point managed a private after-hours session at Neiman-Marcus. Apparently jewelry, appliances, a piano and at least one automobile were among the acquisitions. A gala dinner was held that evening, but since most of the Gabonese spoke only French, the discussions as to the locations of the best deals around town were limited.

Two barges, carrying five platform jackets, under tow from Louisianna to Gabon, Africa.

Gabon, West Africa

In 1984 Tenneco made two significant oil discoveries offshore The Republic of Gabon in West Africa. Tenneco had acquired the properties at leasing rounds one year after the acquisition of Houston Oil & Minerals on prospects that came with that company. By 1986 the discoveries had grown to three new fields with estimated potential of 50MMBO on licenses covering 250,000 acres. Five platforms were under construction and an Operator's Inc. operation in Gabon was planned. First production from Gabon began in September of 1987 with an anticipated rate of 15,000 BOPD. At the time of the Sale, Gabon properties were producing 5000BOPD from five platforms and exploration was active both onshore and offshore.

Norway

Tenneco's efforts in Norway during the final years were another outstanding success and demonstrated the value of being a part of the larger corporation. Much of Tenneco's success in acquiring blocks in the Norwegian sector came from the influence of the "Tenneco Model" – the practice of using business interests within the entire Tenneco Inc family in concert with one another to their joint benefit. Reminiscent of the "Tenneco Advantage" used in the early days of the Gulf of Mexico, the "Tenneco Model" gave E&P a significant competitive advantage in its competition within the industry. Previous sections have described in some detail the synergistic advantages that Tenneco employed between the parent pipeline TGT and the E&P effort, on both operational and financial levels. Although it can be rightly argued that TOE&P's eventual position as a subsidiary of a large conglomerate was the unfortunate circumstance that led to its demise, for most of its lifetime, synergies that existed within the corporation were used to mutual advantage. The "Tenneco Model" was used effectively in a number of deals around the world.

Ken Watts, TOE&P's Managing Director of Norway, provided a comprehensive review of one of E&P's most exciting projects. Watts credits the assistance of Tenneco-Exes' Lindy Looger, C P Chiang, David Griffiths and Olav Heigre of STATOIL with this essay.

The History of Tenneco Oil Company in Norway
Ken Watts – Mng. Dir. Norway

In the fall of 1976, TOE&P assembled a team to assess our interest level and capabilities to pursue a license application effort for an anticipated (Fourth) Norwegian License Round. Many of the major discoveries in the United Kingdom (UK) sector of the North Sea straddled the international boundary with Norway, the most notable of which was the 3.5 Billion barrel Statfjord field, reserves that get anyone's attention. An internal study in 1977 ranked Norway number 1 on Tenneco's worldwide list for potential consistent with the company's long-range plan. A preliminary visit to Norway confirmed that the Norwegian government was going to issue a set of evaluation criteria that were very favorable for Tenneco.

Due to the potential size and scope of the projects in the North Sea, the Norwegian government required license-holders to hold substantial financial capability. Tenneco Inc. as one of the largest companies in the United States, certainly fulfilled this requirement. A second requirement was the need to have technical and operating expertise that could be brought to bear on the projects on the Norwegian shelf. Tenneco E&P's operating experience in the Gulf of Mexico, coupled with the North Sea experience gained from the Heather Field development in the UK, and our history of global exploration and production was directly applicable to the challenges in Norway.

The government required each applicant submit a detailed geological and geophysical review of each block in a company's application. These proposals required a recommended work program and a technical evaluation for each

CHRISTMAS SHOPPING

As had been the case in other countries, genuine risks sometimes come with international assignments. Tenneco's office in southeast London was a choice assignment in the company, at least most of the time.

This story really does define the "being in the wrong place at the wrong time" quote. Tenneco geologist, Mark McDonald, had been transferred from the international office in Tunisia to the North Sea office in London on Dec. 9, 1983. Only eight days later, on Dec. 17, he was critically injured in the famous "Harrod's" street-bombing. McDonald was Christmas shopping in front of the iconic London department store when a car bomb exploded. Six people, including three police officers who were responding to a phoned-in bomb threat, were killed and nearly 100 were injured. Later the Irish Republican Army (IRA) would claim responsibility for the bombing, although they suggested that attacks on civilians were not their intent. McDonald received shrapnel wounds in his thigh, shoulder, arm and hand and would spend several weeks in the hospital before returning to his work at Tenneco. As a partial accommodation for his ordeal

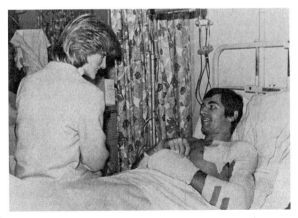

McDonald received bedside visits from Prime Minister Margaret Thatcher, and Princess Diana and Prince Charles.

"Of all the companies present on the Norwegian shelf, Tenneco is among the top five or six competing for the best acreage. It is my duty to communicate this fact to you because it isn't earned by plain chance—it is a matter of qualification—and Tenneco has earned it".

Arild Roedland, Deputy Minister of Energy of Norway

"In 1998, I took one of the candidates for President of Russia out to Heidrun to show him our (Conoco, since it was our engineering project and included the Conoco TLP design) capabilities and what can be done with large projects. I have to tell you, flying out to that platform and seeing it on-location was the fulfillment of a decades-long dream...and Statoil executives at that time told me that Heidrun (which was turned over for Statoil operation at first oil) was the number one platform in their entire company...."

"But, nothing will ever replace the thrill of that helicopter circling the platform before we landed...not many people ever get the chance to envision an idea, implement it, have it be a huge success, and then get to go back and see it....That sight made it all worth it... Just wish that Tenneco had been the beneficiary.....but I guess that is another story for another time."

"I recall an early exploratory trip offshore to Statfjord, we came out of the facilities and looked into the distance, and there was a rainbow. If you look today at the maps of the fields and the infrastructure that has been built over the ensuing decades, it does prove the old adage. There actually IS a pot of gold at the end of a rainbow...and in this case, it was Norway."

Ken Watts, Managing Director, Norway

prospect on any sought-after block. The application also required an indication of the amount of "carried interest" for the state that would be considered by the company.

Finally, the Norwegian government required that applicants should establish efforts to cooperate with Norwegian industry. This last criterion was perfectly suited to the strength and diversity of Tenneco Inc. We strongly felt this would allow us to establish Tenneco Oil as a preferred partner for Norway.

The Tenneco Model - TOE&P quickly enlisted the assistance of the various divisions in Tenneco Inc to document potential business opportunities that held true economic viability and could be developed for mutual benefit with Norwegian industry.

Virtually every Tenneco Inc. division contributed to this coordinated effort. Proposals ranged from marketing efforts by Tenneco West to joint ventures with Packaging Corporation of America for research into the production of improved spruce seedlings. TOE&P formed a joint venture with Wilh. Willhemsen A/S to establish Argosy Offshore to operate a fleet of offshore work boats in the US Gulf of Mexico (see story following).

Tennessee Gas Transmission, with its expertise in offshore pipeline construction and operations, and its experience with major operating equipment was instrumental in this effort. TGT provided strong support for technical efforts concerning pipeline installation and operation to both the Norwegian Petroleum Directorate (equivalent to U.S. MMS), and to STATOIL, the Norwegian state oil company. Further, TGT worked with a premier Norwegian firm, Kongsberg, to evaluate and utilize the new Kongsberg KG-3 turbine for production of steam and power in TGT operations.

Tenneco Oil P&M assisted significantly through their Dutch chemical tanker company, Gebr. Broere , and quickly contracted for three chemical tankers from two Norwegian shipyards. Albright & Wilson, the P&M subsidiary headquartered in London, contracted with a Norwegian shipping company to transport phosphate from Morocco to the UK.

Walker Norway, the Tenneco Automotive subsidiary, targeted construction of a 90,000 exhaust-system plant for Haldan, Norway. This plant was constructed in 1982 and employed 100 skilled workers producing a full line of exhaust products for the European market.

At the community level, Tenneco assumed the chairmanship of the Stavanger-Houston Sister City organization, supported the engineering school at Trondheim University by hosting their students in the US, and elected a prominent Norwegian businessman to Tenneco's European Advisory Council.

These efforts combined the financial strength of Tenneco Inc. and the technical capability of Tenneco Oil to enable TOE&P to not only satisfy all of the criteria established by the Norwegian government, but to lead the industry in the overall effort. The Norwegian government began to refer to these efforts as "The Tenneco Model", as they strongly wished to leverage their offshore resources to help further the industrial and knowledge base of their country.

When the Fourth License Round was awarded in 1979, Tenneco was granted a 25% interest in Block 30/2 in the Norwegian North Sea. This award validated our approach to the license application process. The industrial cooperation efforts continued as a key part of our applications throughout our participation in later license rounds.

Recognizing the key role that STATOIL, the state oil company of Norway, would play in the developments on the Norwegian shelf and beyond, Tenneco established a strong program of cooperation with their company. Ranging from a series of Executive meetings through to the assignment of key Tenneco reservoir engineering staff to work within STATOIL, our objective was to demonstrate our culture, technical and management philosophy, and capabilities. Our hopes were that, as STATOIL matured as a company and sought growth both inside and outside Norway, Tenneco would be considered among their preferred global partners.

Tenneco Oil E&P used this focused strategy to review, assess and select the blocks which were offered in each of the license rounds up to the 12th License Round that was finalized in summer 1988. We applied for a total of 22 licenses in rounds 4-11, and were successful in obtaining an interest in 10 of these licenses covering 12 blocks - a success rate of 46%.

As of the date of the sale in 1988, E&P had participated in 14 wildcat wells on our licenses, with a total of 5 discoveries. Delineation drilling on several of these discoveries yielded a success rate of 77%. The discoveries included Tenneco's largest international field, Heidrun, in 1985. Heidrun was declared commercial in 1986. A huge platform was being constructed by the operator Conoco for first production targeted for 1995.

As of June, 1988 the proved and probable net reserves discovered in Norway net to the company were calculated at 321MMBOE. Tenneco had invested a total of $131 million in Norway, resulting in a "finding cost" of $0.56 per barrel for proven and probable reserves. The estimated development cost forecasts for these fields, would raise the total cost to find and develop to $3.96 per barrel.

Epilogue Norway

The sale of Tenneco Oil was announced only weeks before the planned announcement of the license awards for the 12th License Round. We had applied for four blocks in that round, including the industry consensus "top block" of 35/9.

When news of the planned sale reached Oslo, the Ministry advised us that they could not continue with their planned award to Tenneco. In a subsequent trip to Oslo by our Executive Management, the Ministry explained that Tenneco had been selected to receive the highest award in the consensus "top" block in that round, but they could no longer continue with their plans to award this block to Tenneco since the sale would convey "the" prized license award to the unknown purchaser without Ministry input and control.

The "top block" of the 12th License Round, 35/9, and the adjacent 35/6 block, were awarded in the summer 1988. Subsequent drilling discovered the Gjoa Field with an estimated 1.2TCFG and an oil reservoir of 66 million barrels recoverable reserves. The Gjoa field unit came on-stream in November 2010, and is operated by Gaz de France with a 30% interest. We believe this was the interest that was planned for Tenneco.

All five of the earlier discoveries made on the Tenneco interest blocks are currently (2013) on production. Best estimates at this writing include the following:

Heidrun Field was placed on production in October, 1995 with initial reserve estimates of 757MMBO, later revised upward to 1.12 BBO and 1.6 TCF of gas.

Production of Smoerbukk began in October 2010 as a part of the AAsgard unit. TOE&P estimated reserves for this field at 529MMBO and 3.2 TCFG (gross, proved and probable).

Smoerbukk South also began production in October 2010. Initial estimates of the reserves of Smoerbukk South were 224 MMBO and 709 BCFG (gross, proved plus probable).

Huldra Field, with proven reserves of 31 MMBO and 585 BCFG, was developed utilizing a steel wellhead jacket in 360 feet of water.

Wildcat drilling in late 1988 resulted in a discovery called Oseberg South with original gross reserves at 358 MMBO 512 BCFG. Production from Oseberg South began in November 2006. In November 2011, approval was granted for a sub-sea template development of the 30/9-22 Sterjne discovery.

Summary

From the earliest inception of the idea of participating in Norway's license rounds until the sale of the company in December of 1988, a period of only 12 years, Tenneco Oil E&P achieved a success rate in acquisition of acreage, and oil and gas discoveries that was the envy of our competitors. We were a growing part of the Norwegian oil industry, with substantial reserves, developments in approval stage and in pre-production planning. Tenneco Oil Company had earned the respect of the industry, the government and our partners through our performance, and enjoyed the reputation of a preferred partner in Norway with STATOIL, our peer companies and the government of Norway.

Through our cooperative efforts with STATOIL, the government, and other industries we had positioned the company for long term growth on the prolific Norwegian shelf. We can only speculate on the amount of participation that we would have attained in the subsequent license rounds and ensuing potential developments, however our track record would indicate significant success was highly probable.

Argosy Offshore, Ltd.

The "Tenneco Model" was used effectively in a number of deals around the world for a long period of time to the mutual advantage among the subsidiaries. Among them was the formation of Argosy Offshore, Ltd. in the Gulf of Mexico. In 1983 Tenneco created a joint-venture with a Norwegian company (Wilh. Wilhemsen) to own and manage a fleet of oil field service boats in the Gulf of Mexico. Argosy Offshore, Ltd. operated about 20 boats from ports in Sabine Pass, TX and Intracoastal City, LA to supply about 35% of the company supply needs. Fred Lentjes, long-time GOM engineer, was General Manager of Argosy. Tenneco Inc. had partnered with Norwegian interests on other non-energy deals in Norway and no doubt the favorable relationships between the company and the country allowed TOE&P a favored position within the Norwegian sector of the North Sea. Shortly after the creation of Argosy, TOE&P was awarded an interest in three Norwegian North Sea blocks, which would hold the 1.2BBO Heidrun field. Said Tom Spurlock, International Exploration Manager, "Tenneco Inc.'s international development department, headed by Jack Ray (formerly TOE&P production manager), played a critical role in meshing manufacturing and shipping interests in Norway with E&P's interest in these licenses. The multi-industry approach is a major criterion by which Norway judges lease applications."

"The Argosy venture exemplified the type of industrial efforts that Tenneco was pursuing with the Norwegians. It was a sound business move. Wilhelmsen had extensive experience in North Sea operations and wanted to establish a presence in the Gulf of Mexico, the largest market in the world for this type of service. E&P, on the other hand, was striving to provide our offshore divisions with superior service. The venture strengthened our ability to meet that goal. I believe the formation of Argosy was the turning point in our relationship with the Norwegian government."

S D Chesebro' – SVP of International at the time.

An Argosy oil service boat off a platform in the Gulf during heavy seas.

Frontiers – Searching for Elephants

Through the 1970s and 1980s Tenneco explored a number of areas of North America that were totally "exploratory" in nature - areas with oil and gas potential but without an existing production (and income) base. These projects were managed by the Frontier Projects office in Houston rather than by the Operating Divisions themselves in order to not distort division budgets and disrupt operations with these high risk and more expensive investments. Prospects in the frontiers were always "company makers" in size, and as part of a balanced risk portfolio, tracking an "elephant" from time to time was part of the strategy. Wilton Scott, Tenneco Oil's leader for many years and a geologist by training, was an "elephant-hunter" at heart. He and Phil Oxley, who also had an eye for the big prize, were effective sponsors of the "Frontiers" effort.

Stories follow describing several of the most significant wildcats that were drilled over those years. The advanced technologic capabilities developed and utilized during that time demonstrated that Tenneco could operate anywhere. Each of the prospects pursued there involved "company-maker" potential, but by the time of the sale in 1988, those "frontier" efforts had still not found the elephant. In 1987, the Frontiers department was merged into the International Division.

The Phoenix and Aurora Adventures in Alaska

In 1982 the Frontiers group invested $19 million to acquire its first leases in the Beaufort Sea, offshore northwestern Alaska, and commenced an aggressive and innovative approach to testing them in hopes of finding the next Prudhoe Bay. The first wildcat was drilled in early 1983 on the Cross Island prospect.

Drilling a wildcat well inside the Arctic Circle required equipment and technology that was not simply "off the shelf". For up to 10 months of the year this portion of the Beaufort is frozen solid and conditions prevent the use of conventional offshore drilling equipment. For The Cross Island well, Tenneco used the then-standard procedure for Arctic drilling by constructing an expensive "ice island" upon which a drilling rig would work for the duration of the well. The Cross Island well was not productive, but results of the drilling set up another prospect.

Seven additional leases were acquired in 1984 on a prospect named Phoenix (as in rising from the ashes). To reduce costs, the company set about figuring out a way to avoiding the ice island approach. Working jointly with Sohio, who also had leases in the area, the partners secured a contract for the "SSDC" (Single Steel Drilling Caisson), owned by Canadian Marine Corporation (CanMar) and Reading and Bates. The partnership between Tenneco and the CanMar/RB crew would make Arctic history. The SSDC was a tanker that had been modified for arctic drilling. It somewhat resembled a drill ship like

VERNON BOLLETER

For much of its existence, the Frontier Projects group was headed by Vernon Bolleter, an explorationist with a 30+ year career at Tenneco. He served as Chief Geologist before taking over at Frontiers, and in 1980 was promoted to Vice President Exploration. During his time in Frontiers TOE&P acquired significant acreage off the East Coast of the United States where the Baltimore Canyon and Georges Bank Embayments were both target areas. The company bid aggressively in several lease sales in both areas and drilled several significant tests in these areas. In fact, TOE&P discovered a potentially commercial gas field and also found the first oil on the Atlantic OCS. Governmental approvals to develop the fields were continually denied and even to date (in 2013), no development has occurred in either of these provinces. During Bolleter's tenure Frontier Projects acquired significant blocks in the Beaufort Sea of Alaska, battled icebergs off Labrador and negotiated a 1MM acre concession in the Bahamas, all of which were sites of true "frontier" wildcats.

those used in the Gulf of Mexico or other offshore areas around the world. Since a traditional drill-ship could not operate safely here -- it likely would have been pushed off location by the shifting pack-ice during the winter -- the partnership contracted a shipyard in Japan to construct a unique companion vessel, a piece that was called "the MAT".

The Mat was a massive, 35,000 ton, flat-topped barge, equipped with chambers that were flooded to cause the Mat to partially or fully sink. The unique design of these two pieces of equipment allowed them to float and move separately, but then be merged together for the drilling operation. The project of positioning the two huge structures was an engineering marvel in its own right. The move had to be executed during a very brief open water window during August and September by a flotilla of tug-boats and support vessels secured from remote locations in Alaska and Canada. The Mat was towed into position over the drill-site. It was then partially flooded and sunk below the surface of the water, but not to the level of the seafloor. The entire surface of the Mat was covered with a foot-thick layer of a special high-density foam material – an area larger than two football fields in size. The SSDC was then guided precisely into place over the partially-submerged barge and the barge was re-floated to "mate" with the bottom of the SSDC, the field of foam making full contact with the bottom of the SSDC. The merged unit was then again flooded and sank fully to rest on the seafloor. The large area of direct contact between the foam and the base of the SSDC, fortified by the substantial weight of the SSDC, provided a "friction lock" that prevented any movement of the unit which might be caused by shifting ice floes during the drilling season. Calculations indicated that the seafloor itself would shear before the bond between the SSDC and the Mat would fail. The Mat was essentially a reusable island.

During the winter of 1985-86, the Phoenix well was drilled with the SSDC. The billion barrel potential for the prospect was as great as for any that was ever drilled by the company. Anticipation within the management in Houston was extreme, as was security regarding the daily information from the well. A huge discovery would not only have a transformative effect on the company's future. The target formation, the Triassic Ivishak, was penetrated and the daily mud-log described promising oil shows. Most of the target zone was cored and the cores were shipped immediately to Houston to the old geology research lab on Rice Boulevard. Initially, many thought we had hit the big time, but when logs were run at total depth of 9866', they transmitted instead the awful news that the formation was non-productive. Subsequent evaluation indicated that we had been "just a few million years too late". The Ivishak was present, but had been truncated by an unconformity and the massive amount of oil that was present at one time had been flushed out by later waters. Our trap had been breached. The shows we had seen were from residual oil.

But the story was not yet finished.

"I recall visiting the lab with Dan Johnson, Sr. VP, and going over the entire core. We smelled the pungent odor of crude oil as we walked through the door of the building and throughout the halls as we made our way to the back room. When we picked up a piece of the core, our fingers became wet with crude. The cardboard boxes in which the cores were shipped and stored were saturated with live oil. The hundreds of feet of potential pay sand in the core before us were as good-looking as any we had ever seen. How could this not be a major discovery? The water saturation measurements were conclusive. Dan remarked, "It looks like the core from a West Texas water-flood – after the water has been swept through." Close ….. but, no cigar; Phoenix remained in the ashes."

H J Briscoe (VP, Expl)

One big refrigerator.
During a visit to the SSDC and Mat in 1897, we actually went below decks of the SSDC, and then through another door into the Mat itself. We stood "on the sea floor", separated only by the hull of the Mat. The walls of the vessels were coated with ice like the inside of an old freezer, indicating the level on the outside to which the solid pack ice prevailed.

H J Briscoe (VP, Expl)

The massive undertaking that resulted in the use of the SSDC and Mat required a two-year commitment. Under the terms of the contract, Tenneco had agreed to take the unit for Phoenix during the first year, and Sohio was to pick up the second year of the contract for a nearby project where they held leases. Each company held a minimum commitment of around $26 million for their drilling season. Several months after the Phoenix well was abandoned, with the rig still frozen in place by the pack ice, Sohio decided not to drill their intended prospect, preferring to pay the substantial financial commitment to CanMar and Reading & Bates, rather than the greater expense of drilling a well. That decision allowed Tenneco an opportunity.

The modified SSDC oil tanker for drilling is joined to the mat which grounds it to the sea floor.

In 1986, hopes were high that portions of the Arctic National Wildlife Refuge (ANWR) would soon be opened for leasing. (Interestingly, 25 years later the industry is still waiting). The ANWR area lay about 150 miles east of the Phoenix location and a smattering of leases had been awarded in shallow waters close to shore, adjacent to the refuge. At that time (and still today) only one well had ever been drilled on ANWR lands – the Chevron KIC #1 on a very small native-owned property within the refuge. Information about the $50MM Chevron well was one of the most tightly-held secrets in all of the oil business. Beyond its TD of 15,193', few even at Chevron, and no one beyond, knew what information the well contained. That proprietary data gave Chevron a huge advantage in any potential lease sale that might have followed. When Dan Johnson, SVP in Houston, learned of Sohio's decision to pass on their year with the SSDC and Mat, he went to the land department in Frontier Projects with an idea.

Frontier Projects negotiated a farmout from ARCO on a 40-acre lease that was four miles offshore and only 6 ½ miles from Chevron's secret well. Johnson conceived the idea of utilizing the Sohio commitment to the SSDC and Mat to fund the drilling of a COST (Continental Offshore Stratigraphic Test) well. The well would be drilled simply for the purpose of gaining information about the geologic section and conditions (source, seal and reservoir rocks) present. He rightly presumed that E&P could attract a consortium of other companies who would be eager to take a small share of this well in order to gain competitive information for themselves, and effectively neutralize Chevron's proprietary advantage. The open-sea window was fast approaching and managing the relocation of the SSDC and Mat within this very short time frame required a substantial amount of planning and execution. The team had barely two months to negotiate a deal with as many companies as it could attract.

Sohio was, of course, interested in reducing the money they would owe CanMar. TOE&P's team began a solicitation of companies within the industry who might have an interest in eventually pursuing acreage in ANWR. That group included almost everyone of any size at all, except for Chevron. The simple proposal was to use the Sohio commitment as a foundation for funding the well, and then bring as many players as possible to the party with each sharing equally the balance of the cost of a well. The data from the well would be shared equally by the participants. Nine companies expressed interest in participating.

Negotiations with that many partners in a short amount of time were challenging to say the least, but an acceptable deal was reached at the "11th hour".

Using ice-breakers to beat the freeze-up, the SSDC and Mat were moved onto location and later that year drilled the Aurora well. Tenneco was the operator. Amerada-Hess, Amoco, Exxon, Marathon, Mobil, Petrofina, Phillips, Shell, and Unocal ended up paying equal shares towards the drilling of the well. Tenneco had negotiated a "carried" (free) share for itself and ARCO (by farmout of the lease) also got copies of the data. With twelve new companies now having details of the geology, the playing field for some future ANWR sale had been substantially leveled.

The well reached a total depth of approximately 16,500'. The logs and data were locked up quickly with few inside Tenneco knowing the secrets, and today, twenty-five years later, the hoped-for sale in ANWR has still never materialized. The Aurora well cost about $79MM. The negotiated agreement provided something around $5 MM as the per-participant share of the cost, and Sohio paid something in excess of $20MM, a "sav-

IT'S COLD UP HERE!

Tenneco opened a project office in Anchorage to manage the activities of the Beaufort Sea projects. Chief Drilling Engineer Frank Heinike managed the office with an all-star team of others sent from other divisions on an "as needed" basis. During the drilling of the Phoenix and Aurora wells, on-site drilling personnel were borrowed from other locations to handle the job. One Sr. Drilling Engineer, originally from West Texas, but then a long-time GOM driller from Lafayette, was sent north for his two-week turn. Our man arrived at Deadhorse near Prudhome Bay, wearing his South Louisiana golf jacket. As the door to the plane opened and he was hit was a 20-mile per hour wind carrying a temperature of about -10°, he's said to have commented. "Damn, if it's this cold here, it must be really bad in Amarillo!"

DEALING WITH SPECIAL PROBLEMS

The adventures in the Arctic brought several new experiences to TOE&P. The company established an office in Anchorage with a half-dozen employees. One of the engineers in Anchorage, Brady McConaty, relays a story of his first visit with the Eskimo "chief executive" for the tribes of the area – the head of the North Slope Borough. Brady was working out the approvals for the various operations we'd be doing in the province when the Chief suggested we employ "many of his people" to assist with the work. Brady agreed that such was probably a good idea and asked, "How many?" "All of them!" came the reply.

ings" for them. Through the tough negotiations E&P actually made a cash "profit" of between $5 and $10MM by putting the project together, and of course received the data "for free".

In a cruel irony for Chevron, they, a few years later, acquired Sohio, the company whose dilemma lead the industry to the data that compromised their own position.

In something of a similar irony, Tenneco won multiple awards from the MMS for safe and innovative operations in the hostile environments during the 1987 and early 1988 seasons. The SSDC and Mat appeared on the cover of the Oil & Gas Journal and inside National Geographic – the year the company was sold.

A Visit to Kaktovik

By H J Briscoe (VP, Expl)

In late 1986, after a visit to the SSDC drilling Aurora, we set down at Kaktovik, the only settlement within this part of northeastern Alaska. As a Native People, the Inupiat Eskimos here have authority to take a Bowhead whale each summer season. Dan Johnson had agreed to give them an update on the well and allay their fears that the noise from a drilling rig might scare the whales during their summertime migration. A crowd was assembling for this "town-hall" meeting, waiting for us to arrive. We stepped into a scene right out of National Geographic. The full-length seal coats with the fur-wrapped face-hoods worn by most everyone were "the real thing", as were the knee-high boots. Large fur-lined mittens hung from the coat-sleeves, connected through the coat with the "idiot-strings". One young woman wore a seal coat with beautifully detailed embroidery and carried a papoose board onto which was tightly wrapped a tiny baby, also completely outfitted in seal and fur. The only "modern" pieces of clothing were the "gimme" baseball caps that some of the men wore beneath their hoods. (Ironically, one of those caps was from John Deere).

The elders of the village are known as "captains" and manage the kayak-based hunt for a whale in a completely traditional manner. Issac, the eldest of the five whaling captains took charge of the meeting and welcomed us to their village. Dan did an excellent job of explaining the rig operations, assured the residents that only one well would be drilled, and explained that the rig would be moved away during the open water season of the summer, well in advance of their whale-hunting season. Issac asked if it would be all right for him to ride his snowmobile out to the rig so he could inspect it more closely. Dan advised against it saying that ice movement around the fixed rig could create unpredictably thin areas that might not be safe. One of the younger captains quipped, "That's OK, Issac's on thin ice around here most of the time!" The crowd got a good laugh and the meeting ended with Issac inviting us outside to the hillside where the frozen carcass of last-year's Bowhead harvest was buried – a perpetual meat locker - where we could carve off a nice piece and

---

E&P's "FIRSTS" & ENVIRONMENTAL AWARDS

In 1984 established the **Mitigation Banking Program**

Was the first major corporation to receive the **National Wildlife Foundation's Conservation Award**

Was the first to receive the **CARE Award** from the MMS for the Gulf of Mexico

Received the **Conservation Service Award** from the US Department of Interior

Received **Certificates of Appreciation** from the US Department of Commerce

Received the **Outstanding Industry Conservation Award** from the National Institute for Urban Wildlife

Was the only US oil company to receive the **Order of Merit from the World SafetyOrganization**

Was the first to receive the **SAFE Award** from the MMS (Minerals Management Service), for its operations in the Gulf of Mexico (won 6 such awards)

In 1986 won the **MMS Safety Award** for Excellence for work in the Beaufort Sea

**LEROY SEVIN
THE OTTER WHISPERER**

Tenneco acquired LaTerre, in the permanent marshes southwest of New Orleans, in 1974. With the acquisition came significant oil and gas production, and equally significant exploratory potential (one of Tenneco's largest fields – Grand Bois – was discovered on La Terre in 1981.) Beyond those tangible assets though, Tenneco found itself the owner of a unique environmental challenge – and opportunity. Through the years the company focused substantial effort to the management and protection of the marsh environment, and won numerous awards from the MMS, the Department of Interior, and the National Wildlife Federation. In most acquisitions, the selling company has a cadre of quality people who have worked with the properties for years, and Tenneco always tried to maximize the benefit of this resource, as well as that of the hard assets themselves.

In the case of LaTerre we gained introduction to not only a group of oil and gas professionals but also a group of folks who knew and loved the marshlands as well, and who provided very valuable input as to how we should best manage it. One employee of LaTerre was an old Cajun named LeRoy Sevin. Among the elements of "his marsh" were the rare and special Otters that lived there.

share some muktuk. The contrast between the cultures of that day could not have been more stark – the absolute latest in mechanical technology in the form of the SSDC and our well, against the barely-past-primitive subsistence culture of Kaktovik. And both groups, those from each of those cultures, could not have seemed more happy with their lot.

The Bahamas Well

In 1986 and 1987 the Frontiers Project group undertook the drilling of a well on a concession on the Bahamas platform. The drillsite location, only about 20 miles from Cuban territorial waters, evidently did not sit well with the neighbors (or perhaps it just provided a good excuse for a joy ride). The rig was visited from time to time by a pair of Russian MIG jets that would buzz the location in a menacing fashion. The water over the carbonate bank was crystal clear. The crew could easily see the sea-floor from the deck of the rig. One day a hand reported a strange sight. Across the seafloor marched parade of spiny lobsters. The lobsters were walking across the seafloor, clearly on their way to "somewhere" (something they apparently do almost every year). The rig was set up right in their path, or perhaps the vibrations the rig created while drilling attracted them. The invasion continued for some extended time. Never ones to miss an opportunity, the chef sent down a couple of divers for several days in a row and all dined very well for a short while.

Safety and Environmental Commitment

An extension of TOE&P's "Guiding Principles" was the simple concept that the company tried always to, put simply, "Do the Right Thing". Working with a high commitment to integrity and ethics was pervasive in everything the company did. Examples are numerous and are presented throughout this volume to illustrate that principle in every phase of company business. Among those examples are the TOE&P efforts focusing attention to environmental considerations. This was a wise strategic philosophy in an industry often viewed with a critical eye. Our efforts did not go unrecognized and through the years the company received many awards for its environmental efforts.

Three major environmental programs, all initiated during the 1980s, garnered significant press coverage for the company. In 1982, TOE&P became the first company ever to donate an abandoned offshore platform for use as an artificial reef. The retired Ship Shoal 198-D platform was dismantled, transported several hundred miles by barge, and then sunk to the seafloor 22 miles south of Pensacola, Florida to enhance marine life and improve sport and commercial fishing. With this effort the company established the "Rigs to Reefs" program that became a model for the industry. In 1985 sections of two platforms from Ship Shoal 168 and Ship Shoal 191 were transported across the Gulf, around the Florida peninsula, and then sunk offshore between Fort Lauderdale and Miami. Although considerable additional cost was involved in these projects, the company felt the efforts were well justified. The "Tenneco Towers" re very popular diving and fishing spots to this day.

"We feel it is much more useful and environmentally desirable to give a platform a second life as an artificial reef, which benefits society in many ways, rather than removing it to the shore and scrapping it," said Dr. Phil Oxley, E&P President.

Over the years, TOE&P's environmental efforts earned recognition from two wildlife organizations – also not something one would suspect to see in today's press. In 1983, the company received the National Wildlife Federation's Corporate Conservation Award and also recognition as the Conservation Corporation of the Year by the Louisiana Wildlife Federation.

Calling Tenneco's effort "a model for all corporations," the national organization praised the company for, "innovative environmental thinking and action."

The award from Interior Secretary Donald P. Hodel read: "The successful use of these obsolete platforms to enhance marine life demonstrates that energy development and marine life need not be incompatible. In fact, they can be wholly complementary and mutually supportive."

In the marshlands of south Louisiana, on the extensive properties acquired in the purchase of LaTerre Corp., TOE&P created a marsh preservation and management program with the construction of 105 weirs and over 20 miles of levees to combat saltwater intrusion and marsh erosion that threatened fish and wildlife habitat. Those efforts led to the establishment of a mitigation banking program through which the marsh management investments created credits that were used to offset mitigation requirements associated with future projects in the province.

Additionally, the company funded a fisheries management study with the Terrebonne, LA Parish Police Jury to increase fisheries production in Lake Penchant, and E&P's sister company, Tenneco Oil Processing & Marketing, donated $25,000 to fund a grant to a Florida university to determine the ecological benefit of the south Florida reef.

Another Interior Secretary, William Clark, congratulated E&P for its "demonstrated concern for this nation's wildlife heritage, and for the world environment. Through this project, Tenneco is leading the way for other companies to follow in developing new approaches to wetlands conservation." Clark further expressed, "It is gratifying to see a private corporation acting to protect wildlife values, especially wetlands, while responding to increasing pressure to produce vital energy resources for our country,"

Beyond its forward-looking work with environmental projects, TOEP also earned numerous recognitions for its safety records, and its developments of industry safety standards in provinces ranging from the Gulf of Mexico to the frozen seas inside the Arctic Circle.

Sevin was in fact something of an "Otter Whisperer". He had actually developed a special relationship with them and a visit with Sevin about them was a treasure. His counsel on Otters was widely known throughout the academic world where he was recognized as an authority. He attended many conferences and made many presentations about these animals, with little formal training but a ton of local knowledge.

Adapted from Prolog Summer '83

Fish habitat. In an interesting sidebar to the Rigs to Reefs program – as this book is prepared (in 2013) the federal government has implemented new regulations requiring the timely removal of non-producing structures from the Gulf of Mexico. Numerous conservation organizations are urging a re-evaluation of the policy as the value of rigs – both active and abandoned – to the fisheries is extremely well-documented. Local editorials muse as to the degradation of the fishing if the oil industry platforms are removed from the Gulf.

People form the culture of any organization, and are the ultimate resource to great success.

E&P CULTURE
THE SECRET FORMULA

The Culture and Business Practices at E&P

Culture, def. - "the skills, art and talents, of a given people, in a given time"

Throughout the preparation of this book, one concept arose in most every discussion amongst the coauthors and contributors. "Our Culture" was the phrase most often used to describe what was "special" about Tenneco Oil, and as the single item that contributed most to our success. As the definition above illustrates, the word covers a broad field, but the people of TOE&P certainly were "a given people, during a given time", and certainly, they did have some "skills, arts and talents". Tenneco's "trade secrets", or "secret weapons", if you will, had more to do with intangible concepts than with tangible "things", more to do with "how" they worked than with "what" they owned. It was all a part of that "Culture", and it was all critical to success. This chapter will explore some of the specific practices at TOE&P that made it a special place.

During the process of selling the company in 1988, Tenneco's culture was often a topic of conversation and interest by prospective purchasers. That "our culture" was known outside the company is notable, and unique in its own right. The greatest benefit derived from the Culture was that it gave employees comfort, confidence and trust in their jobs. Employees knew what they could expect and what and whom they could depend upon.

The specifics of the TOE&P culture were numerous, distinctive and real to almost every member of the organization. Descriptions of the E&P culture included words such as fairness, respect, ethics, flexibility, cooperation, shared responsibility, collaboration and teamwork. Many employees recognized an entrepreneurial spirit that existed as a part of the company's culture. The employees participated in the decision-making process. They understood and accepted responsibility for the performance of their duties and were accountable for the outcome of their work. This created pride of ownership and reinforced the value systems that prevailed in the organization. In many cases employees worked on integrated teams, which were driven by professional competence, collaboration, cooperative efforts and respect for others. The "Culture" was a set of beliefs and convictions that directed how we worked. These were the guiding factors that created the company's reputation and success.

Tenneco was Guided by Enumerated Principles

Every Tenneco office had a prominently-displayed plaque stating Tenneco's core beliefs and the principles by which it was doing business. The statements on that plaque laid out the company's definition of ethics and integrity, and spelled out the manner in which they treated the employees, the business associates and the competitors. These values and beliefs were often referred to as E&P's Culture. Primary among these was the simple statement, "The assigned role of business is to make a profit." The principles were established early-on in the history of Tenneco Energy and prevailed throughout its existence. This list of driving principles is included in the P&M section of the book.

The Workforce

With the Tenneco Culture as the basis, the company developed an equally-distinctive set of organizational, management and business practices. TOE&P had many strengths; it did many things well. Broadly subdivided, the strengths of the organization – the "Culture" - can be understood by reviewing The Workforce and then The Management Practices the workforce used to accomplish its objectives.

Tenneco Hired Well

All that was accomplished over the many years of TOE&P was a product of the work of talented and dedicated employees. Tenneco's workforce was recognized throughout the industry for its technical competence, strength, and competitiveness. The employees of TOE&P were top-notch and well-trained. Recruiting and maintaining top talent was the starting point. Tenneco started with the best and then worked to make everyone better. Compensation and career-development programs provided motivation and the top leadership of the company was well-regarded. This section on "Workforce" will both de-

"(The company prospered through ....) a culture of fairness, high ethics, commitment to technology, and focus on success. It started at the top and filtered down to all levels. It was people working together to achieve greater success."
C E Shultz (Sr. Vice President)

"....... people being proud to be a part of open communication and personal relationships at all levels."
Camilo Merendoni (V.P. DGM, South America Division)

"(The Company was characterized by ....) a culture of intelligent people, self-motivated and with an entrepreneurial mind set. I felt a clear balance between supervision and independence."
David Balusek (Prod Eng, EGD)

"The culture was defined as highly competent professionals working together with ownership in what they were doing."
Dave Pearcy, (Geol Eng Cons, SWD)

"The culture was the sense of empowerment given to people. Employees had responsibility almost from the date hired. It didn't work that way with other companies."
Jack Forster, (Drlg Eng, SWD)

"Tenneco as a company, and all of the managers I worked for, valued the employees, as people, first. This resulted in a company that achieved extra-ordinary results. I have worked for a number of good companies, but none had the magic we lived at Tenneco."
Glen Adams, (Prod Eng, SWD)

"As a very young landman, I remember Harris Phillips at a meeting, talking about an ongoing negotiation, 'Guys, we treat our partners the way we want them to treat us. Anyone who does not follow that rule gets run off!' Deals come and go but what you remember the most are the standards by which we were measured."

Larry Brunsman, (Landman, MCD)

"Symonds, Scott and Meason showed that ethics, trustworthiness, and character lead to a corporate climate of respect for employees, business associates and customers."

Cliff Rackley, (President 1974-78)

"An early hallmark of Gardiner Symonds' management style was the directive to 'Pay attention to our people!' It was a fundamental element of the Tenneco Culture from 'Day One', and common to both TGT and Tenneco Oil. This attention carried over and expanded at E&P as we grew."

J B Foster (Tenn Inc)

"I remember a time when Steve Chesebro' and I were reviewing the final 'offer list' for a season's recruiting. Steve remarked that it was good thing that the company did not have such high standards back in 'our day' – neither of us would have made the cut!"

H J Briscoe
(VP Exploration)

scribe the general nature of the staff at TOE&P but further note a number of the specific manners in which the company "paid attention to the people". It's the workforce – and the way they were treated – that made the difference.

For over 30 of TOE&P's 42 years, college recruiting played a dominant role in the building of the staff. The company recruited at a limited number of institutions, and pursued only the top students. Personality and character traits as well as academics were important. TOE&P had a top reputation on each campus at which it recruited.

The Employees
Adapted from L. A. Augsburger (V P Administration)

Joe Foster often remarked that he was amazed how young people at Tenneco were able to contribute at a high level, when called upon to tackle a difficult challenge. They were young, smart and capable. Despite their general youth, they always seemed to show up at the top of the list when someone was needed to fill a critical job. But who were they and where did they come from?

Tenneco E&P was a tough and successful competitor in the oil-patch partly because it was a successful recruiter of top students from a select group of only fourteen leading college campuses. These schools were chosen based on their reputation, the quality of their graduates, the curriculum and standards of performance they required from their students. Recruiting on campus was the historical feeder system for top talent into the organization.

College recruiting was conducted annually and involved a coordinated effort among a broad network of line and staff personnel from operating divisions and headquarters. This process was effectively nurtured and administrated by the headquarters-based "Chiefs" from each of the technical disciplines and was supported by Employee Relations professionals. It required considerable time, attention and manpower, and was in fact, a near year-round project. Effective relationships were needed with key professors, counselors and placement office personnel on each college campus. Tenneco's people worked at it. Their strategy was to know the right people and to nurture that relationship to the point of trust and confidence. E&P developed a great college campus image and it worked to the company's benefit.

Success was often measured by how many of the top-four student graduates from each campus could be recruited. Tenneco achieved this goal more often than not. On several occasions, the company attracted the #1 candidate at a particular school. From 1984 through the company's date of sale the average GPA of Tenneco's recruits was above 3.5 on a 4.0 scale.

Tenneco also enjoyed considerable success in keeping its recruits onboard and available for long-term development. In the five years prior to the company's sale, the average annual turnover rate was only 3.5 percent. The company's structure, work climate and overall organization philosophy were important factors in keeping this number low.

The low rate of turnover enabled Tenneco's workforce to steadily increase its average experience level. The technical workforce at the time of the Sale, included 278 exploration and 493 production professionals, with an average experience level of 11 years. Yet the average age was only 35, making for a young and dynamic but experienced team of professionals.

Tenneco Trained Well

Training at Tenneco involved both on the job experience and inside the classroom experiences. New TOE&P employees were assigned projects that quickly exposed them to the nuts and bolts of the energy business. The process was largely one of learning by doing. Frequently, new hires from college were assigned a "mentor", and set to work on a project, and often that mentor had only a year or two more experience than the recruit.

Internal company training programs for employees included 39 courses in exploration, 72 in engineering, 32 in finance, systems and accounting and 23 in personal and professional development courses. In addition, most employees periodically attended courses outside the Tenneco offices and seminars offered by professional societies and academia. During the 5-year period prior to the company's sale, 1,100 employees had utilized the company's Educational Assistance program by attending college level courses on their own time.

Employees at Tenneco worked with their peers to find solutions to problems, rather than being referred to a prescribed manual for answers. Most major companies within the energy industry had very specific and very formal plans of instruction with "how we do it here" manuals dictating the elements of one's work. (At the extreme, Exxon and Shell both had internal "universities" that new hires attended for extended periods of time during their early years before ever actually going to work on projects.) Tenneco management was well aware of the pitfalls associated with this sort of "inside the box" practice and worked specifically to avoid it. Any mistakes that might have been made using an aggressive approach to business and field decisions were more than compensated for by the positive affect of the successes that came from innovative thought, and Tenneco working hands clearly developed a sense of contribution to the end result much more quickly than did their peers in larger organizations.

EVP Steve Chesebro' notes that his decision to join Tenneco rather than accept a competing offer from Shell simply because Tenneco would put him straight to work learning the business. At Shell he would have gone through a spelled-out 18-month training program before being actually put to work in the field. "At Tenneco, training was a 'hands-on' experience, complete with performance expectations!"

Rapid Career Development and Pay for Performance

Management at TOE&P believed that competent employees, armed with clear expectations and objectives, were capable of generating results with a

In the Pacific Coast Division one common job for newly-hired geologists and engineers was to come to the office early, pick up a company car from the pool, and then make a circuit through the active rigs near the office to retrieve a copy of the daily mud-log and quiz the onsite well-sitters to get important perspectives for the day. One day I was making daily rounds and stopped at a wildcat we were drilling in partnership with Mobil. Mobil had five young guys assigned to the well. They were all there as observers, to see what it was like "on the rig" and they were wide-eyed about their experience. They were all being watched-over and instructed in the "Mobil way" by a very senior well-site engineer. These guys were essentially living on the rig for the duration of the well, and other than seeing what was happening there on a day-to-day basis, they were not getting a particularly broad exposure to the business. I swung through, asked a few questions and picked up what we came for, then excused myself to head on out. One of the young Mobil geologists asked, "How many rigs have they let you visit?" My answer, "You mean today?" (This one was my fourth stop of the day, and it was not even 9 am).
W E Franklin (DGM, SWD)

"The theme of having a well-educated and trained staff was evident to me as I attended 17 weeks of schooling in the 17 years with Tenneco, in everything from formation evaluation to management training. My lack of understanding of the economics of drilling led me to take some night school courses. That led to an MBA that only cost me about $750, given the company's support. This served me well at Tenneco, but also in my subsequent careers in management consulting and printing business"
Doug Keen, Mgr. IEPS

A forced four. Raises and promotions for employees were determined with the annual merit budget process. The merit budget for the company required a "forced ranking", on a scale of 1 through 4, of all personnel in each technical discipline. Sometimes this process led to awkward situations. "Early in my career I was transferred into the EPA department. I was by far the youngest member of the department and I took that as a sign the company had confidence in my work.", says Steve Chesebro, one of TOEPs top executives during most of his career. "Imagine my surprise when my boss, Joe Foster, told me I was ranked as a "4". 'You're the youngest of the four guys I've got, and somebody has to be at the bottom,' is how Joe explained it to me!"

minimum of oversight. It is not surprising then, that the company's compensation system was based on the premise that employees should be paid based on performance and results achieved. Every year, each employee met with his supervisor to work out a "PP&E" (Performance Planning and Evaluation) form for the year ahead. At this meeting the two discussed and set the individual goals and objectives for the employee for the coming year and also identified areas in which performance could be improved or elements of training or exposure needed for growth. Subsequent meetings throughout the year assessed the progress of the plan.

As part of the salary-budgeting process, the performance of every employee was evaluated by management. These annual reviews involved personnel from division management, headquarters functional management, and senior management. The review process provided an effective check and balance system to insure equity in salary increases and development plans. It improved management's understanding of each employee's strengths and weaknesses, the potential for advancement and identified any development needs with regard to training or job exposure. A part of the "merit budget" analysis required a "forced ranking" of every employee, as compared to peers within his or her discipline, both within the division and on a larger scale throughout the company. The process provided direction for both the employee and allowed the company to maximize the utilization of the workforce.

The company employed a "Y-ladder" of progression through the ranks as vehicles for career development – a managerial and a technical option. Designed to provide "upside" opportunity for all staff, an employee could advance through company management or choose to stay within his or her own realm of technical preference and expertise. The dual-ladder career paths provided equal potential for compensation and recognition for good work and very senior positions were possible without the "requirement" of being involved in management.

At Tenneco, filling vacancies for management positions with talent from outside the company was rare. A strong preference was in place to develop talent and promote from within for crucial vacancies in both the technical and managerial arenas. This practice demonstrated a confidence in and a commitment to the company workforce. On many occasions, the company promoted employees into jobs perhaps a bit "before their time", rather than hire a more experienced, but unknown, candidate from outside the company. This unique element of Tenneco's culture was well-understood within the ranks and was respected and appreciated by the workforce.

The Drilling Fund

The company provided a unique manner of participation in the work the company did. In the 'boom days' of the 1970s and 1980s smaller companies used over-rides and direct participation options as incentives to lure professionals away from the larger companies. Tenneco established a "drilling fund" as an optional participation vehicle whereby employees could invest directly in prospects chosen from the company's annual drilling portfolio, and by so-doing buy themselves a 'piece of the action'. Local and Senior management gave particularly close scrutiny to the prospects that were selected for the Employees Drilling Fund. It was a unique element of the culture at TOE&P.

The Chief (Technical Specialist) Concept

The quality of the company's technical staff revolved around having the right individuals in the right jobs and then providing them with the technological tools and training they need to remain at the industry's cutting edge. While this was a managerial responsibility at most companies, Tenneco E&P created an additional resource to provide for technical development. At the Houston headquarters, qualified specialists in each technical discipline had company-wide responsibility for balancing the technical quality of the workforce throughout the divisions. These specialists, or "Chiefs" as they were called, provided valuable expertise to the line management of the company, but also served as personal representatives for all the employees within their own technical discipline. The Chiefs helped manage the training programs for technical personal development, the dissemination of new technology and the administration of capital budgets. Annually, during the salary budgeting process, the chiefs played a significant role in ensuring salaries within their technical discipline were equitable, and that high-performers were identified and nurtured within their own divisions.

While the "Chiefs" monitored the progression of and acted as "advocates" for all professionals within a given technical discipline, senior "Line" management provided operational coordination and direction for the company projects. In the Divisions and at the headquarters level Tenneco truly had a "matrix" management with top officers being responsible for both operational results within the divisions as a whole ("line" responsibilities), and career development for all employees within their own specific areas of expertise ("staff"). The overall annual company merit budget was a merged effort ranking both technical and managerial career paths together.

Tenneco Was Characterized by Great Leadership

Any reading of Tenneco's history quickly identifies an ample handful of key personalities whose talent and vision shaped the company. It is no surprise that such was the case from the outset. There is little debate regarding the effectiveness of the early business strategies and management philosophies employed at Tenneco, or that the early canvas was predominantly painted by Gardiner Symonds, the first president of "Tenneco Oil". Symonds' impact on the company prevailed for 26 years from the founding in 1943 until his death in 1969. Among Symonds'

"Another unique aspect of Tenneco management was the "dual ladder" of professional progression. This process allowed those who were excellent technical people with no particular interest in management, to be promoted to levels equal to their management counterparts."

Doug Keen (Mgr. IEPS)

"The dual ladder for professional progression at Tenneco, featuring parallel paths for technical and management promotions, differentiated us from others and allowed us to keep many good people during the boom-times when attrition was high.

We put top young hands into important positions early in their careers. The innovative approaches they came up with allowed us to compete with and end up ahead of the majors whose procedures were much more constrained."

C E Shultz (SVP)

"When considering leadership at Tenneco Oil, the first thought that comes to mind was the "tone at the top" – the character of the senior management team. After Joe (Foster) took effective control as the CEO in the mid-1970s, an evolution began that would produce the culture that would differentiate the company from the competition. With Joe's ascension, the corporate office was restructured to include Wayne (Nance), Phil (Oxley), Dan (Johnson), Larry (Augsburger), and Lou (Parrish). These were all individuals for whom you would, "go to war", and with whom you wanted an association for a lifetime. They established a culture of fairness, high ethics, commitment to technology, and a focus on success. What a place to work! And as word got around, Tenneco became a preferred place for both new college recruits and experienced staff, ultimately leading to our success. Also, the senior management was responsible for promoting from within based on performance and leadership skills. This commitment led to our Division management teams that were second to none. This was particularly visible in the Offshore Gulf of Mexico where we competed directly with the majors and not only held our own but flourished. These senior guys were a unique team whose talents flowed down through the ranks and taught the rest of us. There is no doubt in my mind that the culture changed permanently, and for the good, under the leadership of Joe Foster, Wayne Nance, Dan Johnson and others of that era. There is no substitute for good people."

C E Shultz (SVP)

considerable talents was the ability to identify leaders. The contributions of Wilton Scott, who came to Tenneco in its second decade, are undeniable. As the company grew and evolved, the task of managing it became more complex. By the late 1960s the growth of the company and the nature of the business challenges evolved further and the management practices that would take the company through the 1970s and 1980s began to take shape. Leadership remained the key.

The ranks of Tenneco's management during the '60s, '70s and '80s include an impressive list of individuals and a long record of personal contributions, in all of the operating divisions and locations. At the top of that list is one Joe B. Foster. Although the humble Mr. Foster objects to be "singled out", his continuity in key roles within the company and his influence are clear. None among the top management of Tenneco Oil would dispute the leadership role "Joe B." played throughout his career.

The history of Tenneco, a specifically of E&P, includes many examples of Joe Foster's work. Whether by design, or by trial and error, a system of "best practices" grew up at Tenneco. Essays is this volume describe the initial efforts at building a "system" for offshore lease sale preparation, for integrating economics and business principles into an effort otherwise dominated by technical input, and for innovations in the specific manner in which employees worked with each other – the development of our teamwork. Both management and working hands were encouraged to refine the details of those practices – the key elements that made our workforce effective. Joe Foster was a key and consistent voice in seeing that those principles were developed and applied.

Tenneco Planned for the Future

Tenneco E&P continuously worked to enhance the abilities of all of its employees. As part of this process, the company conducted an annual Executive Resource Review to identify the strengths of its current and prospective managers and to target possible development needs. The objective was to ensure key positions were filled by the most capable individuals and that strong replacements were being cultivated and were ready and waiting for duty. The review established development plans for the high-potential individuals for the coming years. In 1988, the executive resource program showed 44 candidates had been identified as key position replacements or as high potential employees on track for further development and exposure. There were also at least three replacement candidates identified for each key position in the company, a fact that illustrates the depth of E&P's management team, and speaks to the ability of TOE&P to fill its needs from internal candidates rather than with external talent searches.

There is no doubt that Tenneco's workforce was an able and formidable competitor within the industry. Following the sale of the company many of E&P's managers and supervisors became high-ranking executives or officials with many companies in the oil and gas industry. Many more Tenneco alumni who were not yet in management positions within E&P also went on to positions of top leadership within the industry. Beyond everything else, the quality of the people who represented TOE&P was exceptional.

Tenneco Valued Its Workforce Highly

The consistent degree to which TOE&P was able to create and maintain its workforce at exceptional levels was itself a primary management objective. From Gardiner Symonds' earliest directions to "pay attention to the people", the company was focused on challenging, motivating, nurturing, keeping and rewarding its personnel. Most companies have an "Employee Relations" department. At Tenneco, it was more of an "Employee Importance" department. The "added value" at TOE&P came from the employees. Concepts such as "Quality of Life", and a "Sense of Family" were not esoteric notions, they were integral elements of the Culture.

The Sense of "Family"

Whether it was a stated "Management Philosophy" or not, Tenneco and TOE&P promoted a sense of "family" amongst its employees. One could argue this was simply an outgrowth of all of the stated philosophies – as one follows another – but it's an inescapable fact that the majority of the employees at TOE&P felt as though they "belonged" there. It's one of the most common comments heard when discussing the times at Tenneco. The company created an atmosphere that was conducive to confidence and achievement. Among most, there was a significant element of pride was associated with being employed by TOC, pride that continues to this day, 25 years later.

The Climate Survey

At Tenneco Oil E&P employees were encouraged to share their points of view with management. A climate survey was used to anonymously gather information and communicate the evaluated results back to the organization. Every other year, employees were sent survey forms to gather opinions on a wide variety of issues, conditions and policies affecting their work. Results were compiled and analyzed by the survey designer, a management consulting firm, and returned to E&P for evaluation and interpretation.

TOE&P was not the only company to employ the "Climate Survey", but E&P was unique in that all employees participated in the process and all received feedback regarding the results and the corrective actions being taken. TOE&P's commitment to sharing the results with employees and engaging them in the development of solutions to problems was an exception.

After the survey results were shared and explained to employee groups, managers established teams to address issues for their particular area. Problems were defined and action plans developed in each department to resolve

"The quality of their personnel in key management and technical positions was exceptional. These people were capable of strategically looking ahead without losing touch with day-to-day operational realities. You always felt that if you were told to do something, the person passing out the orders had a well-founded knowledge and understanding of the task."

D Waddell,
(Dlrg. Eng.,SWD)

"We had superb top leadership. Joe Foster had the ability to operate at all levels of the organization. I am convinced that Joe's influence on the organization was one of the key reasons for the company's success."
L A Augsburger (VP, Admin)

"Tenneco Oil Company was a great place to work, especially under the leadership of Joe Foster, a great guy and a great manager. He pushed responsibility down to that everyone felt they were key people in the organization."
L L Sargent (Expl. Mgr.,ret)

"Over the 27 years I worked for Tenneco, each location where I served was a delightful experience because of the office staff and fellow employees. It was like an extended family."
H C Nichols (Admin, Ret. 2006)

"In 1957, while waiting for my initial interview with TGT, I read a copy of "The Line" magazine and was favorably impressed with what the company had to say about itself. Twenty-two years later I retired from Tenneco Oil Company. During all of those years, the company continued to project the image I envisioned during that first reading of their in-house magazine. The name "Tenneco" was respected in the business world and when I told people I worked there they seemed to display a greater regard for me. With its competitive salaries, superior employee benefits, and opportunity for growth and promotion, Tenneco was just what I was told it would be; a superior employer. Notwithstanding by disappointment with the demise of Tenneco, I shall always remember the Tenneco that invigorated me throughout my career there."

J A Hannah (Sr Div Attor, MCD)

"Tenneco Oil was a successful company because the employees were treated with respect by both other employees and management. With this cooperative effort, it gave each of us the incentive to make things work and we took pride in what we did. No idea was rejected or approved until it was thoroughly discussed weighing both the pros and cons. Management was not autocratic."

DIck Sloan (Prod Mgr, PCD, VP Gas Reserves @ TGT)

"Tenneco was class all the way. The quality of the people was 100% First Class. The company treated people properly and was respected for it."

Larry Brunsman (landman, MCD)

issues as they were identified. Survey results from E&P were compared with industry averages and with results from other divisions. The climate survey process required considerable effort, but it was appreciated as an effective tool by the work forces.

Quality of Life A Priority

"Quality of Life" issues were very important with Tenneco management. Tenneco Inc. was a leader in promoting employee health and wellness. The parent corporation made headlines in the business world in 1985 when they converted the top floor of the Tenneco parking garage in downtown Houston into an employee center that included a fully-equipped and managed exercise center, a cafeteria and wellness counseling as no-cost perks of employment. TOE&P picked up on that lead very quickly, and although the operating divisions did not have staff numbers that would justify the full-blown facility that was present in Houston, each established a facility that suited the local office and health and fitness were encouraged for all.

Exercise facility at the Southwestern Division in San Antonio.

Offices were managed with the specific objective of maintaining a high level of employee morale. The company supported a significant array of employee and community activities. Athletic teams, cultural events, annual picnics and numerous charitable organizations all enjoyed company support and employees were urged to participate with their co-workers in all manners of outside activity.

Monthly Birthday Luncheons were an important tradition designed to involve all employees in the conduct of the business, regardless of their job duty or responsibility. These luncheons were hosted by senior company management. With attendance at any given lunch limited to fifteen to twenty employees, participants could easily ask questions and share thoughts, ideas and suggestions with the host. The hosts discussed the progress of current business goals and performance. The lunch was both a business meeting and an informal gathering to discuss common concerns and opinions.

A New Division

Many "Quality of Life" considerations figured strongly in the establishment of the Southwestern Division. In 1976 a group of 7 geologists, geophysicists and engineers was sent to Midland to establish a "project" office. Assistant Chief Geologist H. Louis Lee was assigned to oversee the team. The mission of the project was to evaluate the opportunities of the Permian Basin and determine if a full division office might be justified for the province. By 1978 it was clear that Tenneco could compete and that the province held good potential.

Most were not surprised when, in early summer, the announcement was made that the Southwestern Division would be opened. Surprise turned to shock when it was revealed the office would be located in San Antonio! Those on the ground could not imagine anything so foolish as an office outside the center of activity, but the bright minds in Houston had thought through the decision carefully. The industry was in the midst of a big upswing and Tenneco, like most other majors, was suffering from attrition with local independents hiring our best and brightest away for apparently more personal potential in smaller shops. By moving to San Antonio, Tenneco accomplished a multitude of related objectives.

Although Midland was well-liked by the folks that lived and worked there, it was certainly not considered a garden spot among the US energy centers. San Antonio, on the other hand, was exceptionally attractive from the family and lifestyle perspectives, and it had just enough of an energy industry presence to allow continuity – even though everyone else there was working the Gulf Coast region, rather than the Permian Basin. San Antonio had a great and developing reputation as a city "on the move" in Texas, affordable housing and office space was available, and the general perception of the "lifestyle" was very good. Whereas many talented people within the company were probably hoping they'd not be noticed for potential transfer to Midland, they instead started volunteering for moves to the Alamo city. For years the company hired almost every college recruit it wanted from the University of Texas or Texas A&M.

The office opened with a team of very good talent in all disciplines and maintained that throughout its history. Everyone loved San Antonio and the satisfaction of the employees there clearly contributed to the success of the division. The fact that the company would consider "quality of life" issues, even if for admittedly strategic reasons, speaks well to both the priorities and the business acumen of the Houston management who made this unusual decision. The performance of that office during the deep gas boom of the late 1970s and early 1980s is a testament to the decision. In exchange for the location, Houston management made clear the fact that our business was 'on the ground' in West Texas and expected our employees to be there frequently.

"These gatherings (speaking of a quarterly luncheon of a group of Tenneco engineers) are also a manifestation of the Tenneco Oil culture as we knew it. The fact that 24 years after the sale of the Company, we still look forward to sharing brief moments together is an indication of the friendships we developed. That is a testament and tribute to who we were/are and what Tenneco Oil instilled in each of us. I recently read a novel where the author defined friendship as requiring respect and trust. I believe this is the basis that defines Tenneco Oil Company, a friendship built on respect and trust. At Tenneco Oil individuals were given respect and the trust to be the best that they could be. When an individual is given respect and trust, he/she dedicates completely to fulfill that trust."

Rene Alanis (Mgr, Planning, O&G Products)

"The old Lafayette office was a converted filling station that resembled a motel and many of us were on the first floor. During the 70's lease sales, the work was intense, yet in the late evening hours or on Saturdays, Dan (Johnson), or John Peterson, or Lee Sargent would tap on the window with a church key and a six pack and the team would a take break. Competitors wondered how so few could do so much; this was one of our quiet secrets. It wasn't work, it was family."

C E Shultz (SVP)

"The ten years I spent working at Tenneco (25 years ago) are the best years of my entire working career. Tenneco's managers valued employees as "people" first; allowed people to contribute and recognized them for doing it. The company achieved extra-ordinary results by treating people with respect."

Glen Adams (Prod Eng, SAD)

"I felt at home and I trusted the people who I worked for and who worked for me. I believe it always starts at the top, whether it be a company, a church or a family, attitudes begin at the top and that sense of trust and loyalty exuded from the president and filtered down. Thank you for the opportunity to express how much I loved this company and the time I spent there. As we go on with our careers we sometimes forget how blessed we were at a specific time in our career path and reflecting back has certainly refreshed my memory as to that time of blessing."

George Maher (Admin, SWD)

"Bob Douglass was operating a thermal project in S.E. Kansas and he wanted to save the company money. He rigged up an "A" frame to pull rods by hand! While I was in the Thermal Oil Recovery Research Division, I took home a piece of pipe that needed to have insulation baked on the inside so we could use it in a fireflood in Hondo, Texas. I had the insulation, coated the pipe on the inside and baked the insulation to the inside of the pipe in my gas fireplace. The employees at Tenneco Oil took pride in our work because we knew the company cared about us."

Dick Sloan (Prod Mgr, PCD, VP Gas Reserves @ TGT)

"Harry Victery (a 'legendary' landman at TOE&P) submitted an expense account for $25/day for meals in a small town in southeastern Oklahoma. When Bob Bogan saw his expense account he called Harry in and asked how in the world he could spend that much for meals. Harry replied 'Bob, I didn't eat breakfast'. Bogan signed the expense report."

C E Shultz (SVP)

Management Philosophies – The Drivers

Anyone wishing to discover the secrets to Tenneco's success can find many of the answers in this chapter. Taken together, this extensive collection of management philosophies and business practices could be the primer for "how to run an oil company". Many of these principles evolved over time and that the true secret to the success involves the synergy of all of these items, taken together. It goes without saying, of course, that the elements described in this chapter could not have been developed - or utilized - without the existence of the resource of the previous section – the Workforce was the key to everything. This though, is the chapter that really describes "how this machine operated."

Many specific management philosophies and business practices contributed to the repeatable success enjoyed by TOE&P over its years. The company worked much more as a coordinated group of independent oil companies, than as the mid-major that it was. In and of itself, that fact was probably the major key to its success. TOE&P had a unique structure of organization and management that was flat and de-centralized; it was driven by economic analysis and goal-based objectives; and employed a unique and effective teamwork structure to integrate its many parts and accomplish those goals. The application of useful technology, as opposed to the development of it, was a primary tenant. The company's business practices were just standard operating procedures to us while we worked, but the degree to which they were "special" became evident in the years after the sale.

It is significant that the Confidential Offering Memorandum, prepared to promote the sale of the company in 1988, dedicates significant space to a description of the "Organizational and Management Philosophies" as value-added elements potential buyers. The OM also specifically identified the "unique team structure" as an element of value. Both items are mentioned numerous times in this document and in the presentations offering the company. Normally, at the sale of a company, the offering document contains mostly "numbers", describing assets – just the cold, hard, facts, if you will. Company management at TOE&P believed these principles were important elements contributing to the success of the company.

De-Centralized Structure and Philosophy

At the time of the sale in 1988, TOE&P had eight domestic offices, each functioning as an independent operating division. There was also an International Division, headquartered in Houston, and a separate South America Division. Smaller international operating offices were located in Norway and Colombia, Great Britain, Tunisia, Malaysia, Ecuador and Gabon. Each division functioned like a small, independent oil company, operating within its given geographic arena. This unique structure provided autonomy and local decision-making, promoted responsibility and accountability, and was directed to clear goals and tangible results. The structure had developed over a period of years and was a model of stream-lined and efficient operations.

In the 1960s, TOE&P operated from the headquarters office in Houston and small district field offices near the properties. In the early 1970s the districts were merged with larger division offices in the metropolitan areas within the geographic provinces of interest. The new divisions were established with independent authority – and accountability. Small independent companies enjoy the advantages of rapid decision-making, flexibility in changing details of a program or plan, a high degree of individual responsibility and a direct physical presence in a given geographical region. Over time, the company expanded to 10 separate divisions, located in each of the operating provinces. The principle of operation was successful, and lent itself to the integrated team concept. The divisions developed a high level of expertise in their areas and competed effectively on a one-on-one basis with the local independents, and frankly, at a substantial advantage to the majors with their burdensome "home-office" bureaucracies and processes.

The division general manager (DGM) was the lead person in each division. Joe Foster was reported to have instructed new general managers with the following advice, "You are the king of the division, just don't act like it!" The DGMs were directly accountable for division profitability, for the division's technical expertise and for overall quality of results. In the Fall of each year an annual budget for the upcoming year was developed. That budget defined the anticipated capital investments and operating expenses, but it also projected how results would be measured, in terms of income and reserves discovered. The budget was developed in coordination with Houston headquarters through the office of EP&A, but once approved, each general manager was able to make operating decisions within the boundaries of their budgets. This provided each division the flexibility it needed to act quickly on business opportunities. The general manager had the flexibility and freedom to call for support and assistance from the home office, when needed or desired. The headquarters staff, including the chiefs from each of the technical disciplines, was available and ready to support the division's needs. It is frequently noted that the job of the Division General Manager was the best position within all of Tenneco.

The Concept of Small Work Groups for Efficiency

Ideally, division employment numbered from 150 to 200 employees. The desire for a "flat" organization, with a minimum level of bureaucracy, was paramount within the company. When a rising level of activity for a given region created a need for more employees, TOE&P's approach was to divide the group's geographic territory and create a distinct division for each area. This was done in 1980 with the split of the Offshore Region into three separate divisions, each small enough to concentrate its focus on a distinct area of

"In the Southwestern Division, we tried to have fun while we worked. We knew what our responsibilities were, what our deadlines were and what was expected of us. We kept all of this in perspective and tried to develop an atmosphere that was as pleasant as we could make it. We wanted to be one big happy family with everyone sharing in the success."

H J Briscoe (DGM, SWD, at the time)

The Company's basic organizational structure, beliefs and practices are the result of years of testing and improvement. They are specifically designed for Tenneco Oil and they work. They provide assurance that the Company and its operating divisions have been managed with the overriding goal of achieving quality.

Tenneco Oil Offering Memorandum

"The autonomy and focus provided by the Division structure encouraged independent decision-making and risk-taking. The commensurate responsibility for the results gained that went with the autonomy was a crucial element in Tenneco's success."

S D Chesebro' (Tenn Inc)

"We learned a lesson in Lafayette. We need to maintain an operating unit of a size that is manageable for the company and its employees. A person identifies with an organization that is built on a reasonable human scale. We want to push the level of decision making as close to the work in the field as possible.."

P Oxley (President, ret)

the Gulf of Mexico, while enabling the company's management philosophy to flourish. The new downsized divisions retained the benefits of a small group – ready access to management, and high individual visibility.

Dividing up the Gulf
Adapted from 1980 E&P Update

According to Wayne Nance, (at the time vice president and general manager of the Gulf of Mexico Region), says, "Management recognized the Lafayette Offshore Division had grown into a large operation and was experiencing the problems inherent in such a successful effort. There was a need to review the organization's structure and see how it could be modified to better reflect our management philosophies."

"We had reached a point," said Phil Oxley (Exec. Vice President at the time), "that made it difficult to manage the division's activity. The decision-making process was becoming cumbersome."

"There was a general feeling that the chain-of-command had become too long," said Nance. "We needed the idea- generators and the managers closer together."

Since the general manager has responsibility for the profit and loss statement, he needs to be involved in all the decisions regarding the operations of the division. As the Lafayette Offshore Division grew, this meant more and more work was being generated, requiring more and more decisions from the top.

"People in the organization were frustrated because they didn't know everybody in the division. We'd like to have it so that people know the general manager and know him well. This is what everyone is used to throughout E&P. We want all of our Divisions to be similar. Lafayette was growing so big that it was becoming unlike any of our other Divisions," said Oxley. "We decided to sub-divide the Gulf, balancing it according to income and activity level. We were to decide on the key structural elements of the divisions such as general manager, production manager, and staff, and finally we were to develop the people needed to fill the various slots."

"At one time our approach was to concentrate on the Central area of the Gulf," said Nance, "because of limited manpower and limited capital resources. We had the philosophy of evaluating only the top blocks offered in each sale. This will allow us the opportunity to broaden our target base. Two additional divisions will also mean more promotional opportunities, important when you consider the number of talented people working for Tenneco E&P. We promoted a large number of people when we reorganized."

The three new Divisions are all still housed in the same building in Lafayette, so there will be quite a bit of interaction between them.

"They'll be distinct entities," said Oxley, "but there will still be a co-operation across the lines."

* * * * *

In 1982, the Rocky Mountain Division had grown from 95 employees in 1975 to 260, so a similar re-organization was undertaken there.

Larry Augsburger, Vice President of Administration explained the decision to create two divisions in Denver. "One of our stated management objectives is to maintain a small-company atmosphere. One factor we really believe in is that employees don't like layers of bureaucracy between them and the decision- makers. That's why we try to limit the size of our divisions. We make certain the organization changes to accommodate our growth in a way that doesn't submerge individuals in large faceless groups."

Chuck Mills, manager of employee relations for the new regional group, "We split the division roughly in half. A lot of thought went into it. We wanted to keep people familiar with particular basins working on those basins, if we could. In cases where we needed someone to work a new area, we tried to match the talents of the person to the job."

The new Eastern Rocky Mountain Division was opened with Mike Lacey as general manager. His counterpart for the Western Rocky Mountain Division was Jack Edwards, vice president and general manager. Lou Parish was promoted to senior vice president of Tenneco Oil Exploration and Production, with responsibility for the new divisions.

Later, to adjust to the 1986 economic oil industry downturn, the two Rocky Mountain Divisions were re-combined as cost considerations became a driving force in decision-making. With the consolidations, division costs and employee headcounts were reduced and efficiencies were achieved, but the resulting overall headcount remained consistent with the small group philosophy.

Flat Organization with Minimum Levels of Management

Tenneco Oil believed that managerial structure itself should be in keeping with the small group concept. It was important that the individuals who had done the work had a voice in the decision-making process. Economic accountability for the performance of the division was viewed as a shared responsibility of management and employees at all levels. Within TOE&P there were only four levels of management between the individual technical contributor and the company president. This structure allowed open communication and gave the entire organization both involvement in the success of the business and accountability for performance. Managers knew their employees personally and were aware of their capabilities. Employees in turn knew what management expected and when those expectations were or were not met.

The senior management team in Houston was itself accountable for company-wide results; general management in the divisions was responsible for division performance; and individual members of the working team were accountable for results within their own defined areas. Even at the senior level there was a clear understanding of responsibility and accountability. There

"I am not aware of any other company in which there was an open and available, direct line of communication between employees and top management."

C W Nance (President)

"Few of us knew anything about the provinces in which we were going to work. We were very enthusiastic and optimistic, and by doing our homework, we came up with some significant and timely discoveries. While everyone else was concentrating on the same old areas, we were being aggressive and thinking creatively. There was a real advantage to seeing the project with an open mind! By going after certain areas that other companies had avoided, we came out with some early winners, particularly in the Delaware Basin."

Wes Franklin (EM, SWD at the time)

301

INDEPENDENCE AND INTELLIGENT RISK-TAKING ENCOURAGED

The flat organization and communications structure created a two-way street of confidence that management and employees had with regard to the work or of each other. This, in turn and by design, led to freedom and authority for decision-making being pushed down within of the organization. Many of the submittals for this project mention that fact as being unique to Tenneco. This practice was established in the earliest days of Tenneco and prevailed throughout.

"The reason E&P could out-recruit its competitors on college campus was that individual responsibility was offered to and demanded of our employees. The word was out!"

Jack Dutton (Exec V.P., Tenneco Gas Marketing)

"At Tenneco, innovation by the folks doing the work was encouraged, both in the field and in the office. Tenneco hands did not wait for good ideas to come from the top down. They tried things and when they worked well sent them up for dissemination elsewhere. Tenneco management was tolerant of youthful errors, as long as we learned something from the mistakes."

H J Briscoe (VP, Expl)

"Here you had to be careful what you recommended, because you'd be told to go ahead and do it! I recall a time early in my career when I had made some recommendation a week or so before. I was waiting for approval from my boss when he asked me why I hadn't already gotten it done. The power of our employees to decide and act on things, on their own, was a huge asset."

Wayne Nance, President

were no standing committees and no group decisions made. Senior management understood and supported individual accountability and responsibility. Saying, "It's not my job" was not an option (at any level) for pushing decisions elsewhere within the organization.

Informal and Interactive Management Style

In keeping with its de-centralized organizational structure, the company encouraged managers to be informal and highly visible. Any of the managers within any Tenneco division were likely to show up just about anywhere, at any time, and the workforce was very comfortable with the arrangement. It was called "Management by Walking Around" – MBWA – and was a concept well-known throughout the company. Through this practice, managers had an opportunity to understand the details and issues involved with specific projects and, if needed, the opportunity to offer suggestions. The employees who were working on a given project were the ones responsible for presenting it to senior management. If for some reason, a presentation to executive management in Houston (or in the division) was necessary, the "working hands" were usually the ones who made it. This practice provided employees an opportunity to communicate directly with any level in the organization, and this was truly a unique feature within the industry.

The informal atmosphere in each division was supported by purposely locating offices in suburban, rather than the downtown areas. The objective was to make the office environment comfortable and convenient.

Goal-Driven Results and Thorough Economic Analysis

At Tenneco, employees learned very early in their careers that their jobs were not limited to the application of their technical training and talent, but rather the use of those talents and abilities to achieve a business goal. Good geology, good engineering, good financial management or good "support" was not enough. Dedicating all of those things to the role of achieving business objectives was paramount. Tenneco's technical professionals did not "do" science, they "did" business. That said, those critical business decisions were most-often driven by a management schooled with technical backgrounds, rather than by abstract financial concepts. This concept is a critical point in understanding when analyzing why Tenneco was successful. With all due respect to the MBA's of the world, Tenneco (TOE&P, at least) had few of them in their top decision-making roles, at least few that carried only that moniker. There were a few who had achieved those credits, and applied them well to company benefit, but generally those credentials were earned and applied after a full understanding of the technical nature of exploring for and producing hydrocarbons, rather than as an admission ticket on Day One in the office. Tenneco was not run via a template for success that had been generated by academic statistical research or theoretical models about "what makes a company successful". At TOE&P business decisions were driven by technical management rather than by financial managers with "ratios", "portfolio theories", or other academic concepts.

The main goal of Tenneco E&P was to maximize profitability from its production. Investments were based on sound technical analysis, followed by detailed economic analysis. Management encouraged each person in the technical organization to take an economic and business approach to finding and developing oil and gas. The multi-disciplinary team was one example of this philosophy. Each team was responsible not only for the technical merits of its projects but for the profitability of the projects as well. With the switch to successful efforts accounting, technical personnel became increasingly aware of the financial implications of their operating decisions. This was why financial specialists were frequently assigned to technical teams.

EP&A was the coordinator and administrator of the goal-driven management of the company. The geography of each division was subdivided into trends, basins, fields, project areas or other manageable sub-units on the map. Each team, in each area, would create that annual budget for their specific area. It was the action plan of investments and expected results for the year ahead. The summation of the plans within a division constituted the plan for that division and that was submitted to Houston where the total of all the plans for the company became our corporate goal. Everyone knew their part – their expectation – and worked diligently through the year to achieve it. The respective plans (and sub-plans) were driven by specific economic analysis.

Annual Budget Process and Division Tour

From its founding in 1946 until the early 1970s, the annual capital and operating budgets for the "oil company" were determined largely as a measure of the projected cash flow, and the need for tax deductions, by the then parent company, TGT. To a degree, the annual business of TOE&P was captive to the priorities of TGT, and with good reason. The pipeline, being a regulated entity with an allowed rate of return, could predict its revenues fairly accurately as a measure of the gas volumes they would transport. In addition, they could write off many investments associated with finding new reserves, such as the drilling and construction costs involved in developing those reserves. Balancing these estimates would provide a good sense of the investment that was required for a given year, and TOE&P was the primary vehicle through which those investments were made. As de-regulation of gas prices found its way into the market place and as TOE&P developed assets well beyond the TGT service area, the company had to develop a more independent process for estimating its needs and its projected performance. Concurrently, the procedures of analysis coming from EP&A, developed initially as tools for offshore evaluations, were proving their worth and finding their way into everyday business in all of the operating areas.

"Tenneco trusted their young professionals. The key person on the Green Canyon 205 prospect was a young geophysicist from Stanford - Jim Whitworth- he had the prospect pegged. While we were drilling the objective section and had just penetrated a thin pay section he said to me, 'Wait, you ain't seen nothin' yet.' Within a few hundred feet, we drilled the best sandstone reservoir I have ever seen in terms of porosity, oil saturation, permeability, and thickness. He was right on the money. The company had no qualms about trusting a multi-million dollar project to a talented young professional."

Bill Van Wie (Expl Mgr, CGD)

"At Tenneco the reservoir engineers knew how to evaluate reserves, rather than just count them. It was second-nature to work with a mentality that looked all the way to the bottom line – to know the cash-flow impact of the assets. Beyond that, management in the Divisions and also in Houston had an understanding of, indeed an intimacy with, the assets we owned. Nothing was left for 'someone else' to know. Properties, wells, project areas and plays were understood for their worth."

T W Rathert (Manager, EP&A)

At Tenneco we had a "magic number" – the present-value-index - or "PVI". Every project had its own "PVI". Everyone on a team knew what "PVI" meant, and that guided their decisions.

"It was a simple concept - focus on creating value for each dollar invested (PVI). The focus at the top was always on the bottom line; the leaders of the organization understood the creation of value and that guided decision-making."

Harold Korell (VP Production)

"I'll bet there are few companies working even today at which not only the engineers, but also the geologists and geophysicists, even know what 'DD&A' is, let alone how it applies to profitability. It was part of the mix at E&P."

W E Franklin, (DGM SWD)

"Of special importance were the annual division budget reviews attended by Houston-level staff. You always left these with the feeling that some things may change, but with a belief that prudent actions were being taken, and that TOC's employees and financially successful future were always utmost in the managerial minds."

R Waddell (Drlg/Prod Eng, SWD)

By the mid-1970s, senior management ensured the company's orientation toward results by requiring thorough technical and economic analyses of all projects. The preparation of the annual budget for a division was the initial step in that process. The Five-Year-Plan was developed at this time as well. It forced a focus toward the longer-term prospects or opportunities for specific regions or nations.

Once proposed budgets had been submitted to Houston for consideration and approval, work began within each division for a major presentation to top company management at which many of the individual professionals within the division would defend their proposed projects. The "Budget Tour" became one of the most important events of the year.

In late January and February of each year, all senior and executive management from Houston visited each operating division to view presentations by the working level professionals and team members on proposed projects for the coming year. Divisions competed for capital dollars based on the geologic and economic quality of their proposals. The tour inspired the divisions to complete the details needed for project recommendations, and it tended to move projects forward toward a decision on funding or termination.

The annual budget tour was the driving event in motivating, planning and directing the company's internal business activities. Presentations of each significant exploratory drilling and development project within a Division proposal were prepared and delivered at this annual event. The budget tour set the operational calendar for the company and determined its strategic direction for the upcoming year by proposing the allocation of capital to the best projects. The tour served as a key link between senior management and employees at all levels.

The budget tour also reinforced the concept of an interactive management style. Few companies the size of Tenneco created an opportunity for the working employees to present and interact directly with the President and other officers.

This 'Tour' Is No Sight-Seeing Trip
Adapted from E&P Update, June 1980

Budget Tour - two words that rumble through the divisions between October, when managers begin working on capital and operations budgets and their earnings projections, and February, when the management team from Houston spends one intensive day in each division reviewing the proposed projects for the coming year. Two words that mean scrubbing the numbers until they shine like a new penny, burning the midnight oil (sometimes with the wick lit at both ends), and taking every project apart piece by piece to make sure that it's built on a sound foundation.

Tenneco Oil Exploration and Production's operating budget this year (written in 1980) will be over $800 million, or about 55 percent of Tenneco

It's a tough "audience" during Budget Tour, so you better do your homework in advance.

Inc's total budget. This money must be divided among the company's seven divisions and invested on each division's most worthy projects.

"Although it means a lot of work, " says Joe Foster, president, "I think most people in the divisions agree that it is extremely useful. When we go into a division, we look at the quality of each prospect. We have to know if the geology of the idea is sound, what the risks are, the potential, the economics, and whether this project leads us anywhere."

"To answer those questions, the people working on the projects really have to do their homework. And in the process they reach a better understanding of what they're doing and how it fits into the total picture."

Foster was the instigator of the first budget tour in 1969 when he was the manager of economic planning and analysis (EP&A). Having watched the company grow to own a great diversity in projects, Foster saw a need for more information about each division's projects to provide a solid basis for deciding in Houston how to allocate the available money.

Through the years, the meetings have grown shorter, the presentations more formal and rehearsed, and the maps more colorful. But the purposes of the tour are still the same.

"First," says Foster, "we meet the people who actually do the work, because we have them make the presentations and answer our questions. By the time these people have their prospects far enough along to answer questions, they have really done their homework. We want the people who actually do the work making the presentations for two reasons. One, the people who work on the project usually know more about it than anyone else, and two, it helps us know our people better. As far as I know, we're the only company to handle budget reviews in this manner."

"There's another advantage. We like to give our young professionals, just a year or two out of school, every opportunity to develop the skill they'll need to be successful employees and managers in the company. Making presentations to top management and defending their ideas is a part of this development."

The tours provide an opportunity for me Houston staff to meet all of the people in each division, including the staff and support personnel who might not have a chance to travel to the Houston office.

As a part of the tour, employees in each division are invited to an off-site reception and meeting with the Houston staff. At the meeting, members of the Houston staff are introduced and present an overview of the company. They also try to show how that particular division fits into the big picture and answer questions the division people might have about the company.

"The budget tour is good for the division in many ways," says Don Taylor, general manager of the Southwestern Division in San Antonio. "When we've successfully completed the presentations and have our budget, we have the rest of the year with our plans already made, our goals set, and the authority to go ahead. This consolidates our work and provides clear direction for what we need to be doing. The 'getting ready' for the Houston staff reinforces the teamwork concept because we use the collective minds of the people involved to solve the problem. And since the tour doesn't start until after the year-end figures are out, we have a way to measure our performance."

The divisions run all the numbers on all the leases they want budgeted for the year. In order to make their presentations, they have to compile the figures in a report and make view-graphs so the Houston team can see what is being discussed at a glance. Once the projects have been identified, the last two weeks are spent refining and polishing reports. "When we're in the final stages of preparing for the budget tour," says Taylor, "everybody in the division is in there pulling together. It makes us stronger as a division, and I think it makes us stronger as a company, too."

Overheard During Budget Tour

The Budget Tour and the budget "show" itself frequently provided fodder for stories that would last year-around. These stories are provided by a variety of contributors.

Technical Terminology - I was sitting at a conference table in the Southwestern Division listening to a young geologist describe his exploration project. My boss, Dan Johnson, was sitting beside me and next to him sat Larry Augsburger, the Vice President of Administration. The prospect being shown involved a stratigraphic trap and the geologist described the environment of deposition as a series of bifurcating stream channels. I over-heard Larry lean over to Dan and ask, "What does bifurcating mean?" Quietly, Dan answered, "That means it splits." Things were quiet for a moment while Larry digested that answer. He then replied, "Hmmmm,.....Why didn't he just say splits?"

Profound Statements - In another presentation Joe Foster asked a question about another stratigraphic prospect that was being shown. "Does this particular sand produce anywhere else on the structure? In other words, is the sand productive from other parts of this field, or just in this strat trap?" Without missing a beat (and without much thought), the Geological Engineer presenting quickly replied, "No production has yet been established in any well that does not contain the pay sand!" ……. Huh?? Following up, Joe asked, "What I was trying to determine is if this sand has any upside potential anywhere else in the field?" and apparently undeterred, the GE answered, "Oh no, not really, anything else you find from that sand is just gravy on the cake!" Mr. Foster dropped the subject (if Phil Oxley had been there the discussion might still be going on).

Lesson Learned - My first ever presentation to Houston management occurred after I had only been employed (as, in those days, a Junior Geologist) for about three months. My supervisors had mentored me thoroughly on exactly what to cover and exactly what to say, but I was still paniced at the prospect of presenting to top management. Joe Foster was Vice President of Exploration at that time and was the principal attendee at the meeting. I ran through the regional budget for the area I was working and said something to the effect of, "We intend to spend xxxx dollars on seismic, and yyyyy dollars on leases here next year." Very politely Joe interrupted my speech and said, "At Tenneco we prefer to use the word "invest", rather than 'spend'." During the rest of my career I never used the word spend again, and I remember suggesting the same narrative many, many times to the young folks under my own direction.

Just Use Your Imagination – At a budget presentation in Oklahoma City a young geophysicist showed some seismic records and pointed out some subtle detail on the squiggly records. Sr. VP Don Taylor commented that he wasn't quite sure he could see exactly what she was pointing at and the young lady quickly responded, "Oh yes,…. it's right here,…. if you'll just use 'your little imagination' ….." The room, led by Dr. Oxley, burst into laughter at the slight mis-speak. Never one to lose the opportunity of the moment, Oxley quickly noted …. "If there is one person in the room who would be described as having a 'little imagination' it would surely not be Taylor!"

An Innocent Question - In 1974, Cliff Rackley became President of Tenneco Oil. Mr. Rackley had a stellar career in corporate planning and in running and managing the "P&M" (Processing and Marketing) side of the energy business, but to that date, had little exposure to the "E&P" side. An entirely innocent question during one of his first E&P budget presentations provided a good chuckle for all – including Mr. Rackley – a story I've heard re-told many times over the years. It was standard practice during a budget show for the geological engineer doing the presentation to end with a summary slide for his given project, totaling up the planned budget for the year. The slide would

SAN JUAN BASIN
GAS MARKETING

From E&P Update

In late 1986 the Rocky Mountain Division faced a problem of enormous potential consequence. The outside marketing firm that handled all of the natural gas spot market sales in the San Juan Basin was disbanded. Tenneco, along with thousands of other working interest owners, was left without a way to sell its production. The RMD derived 85 percent of its gas production from the basin. With little time to prepare, E&P had to become a natural gas marketer on its own. The San Juan Basin Spot Sales Task Force was formed to save the day – and the revenue.

Implementing such a program raised a host of technical, legal, governmental and accounting questions. The Task Force was a special team with a twist – this one was involved employees from the non-technical disciplines. Rene Alanis, Oil and Gas Contracts planning and evaluation manager, was named chairman of the group. In addition to Alanis, the team included production engineer Pete Mueller, division chief accountant John Bowen and support personnel from the various disciplines. Attorney Phyllis Rainey was a critical player in dealing with the FERC and complicated regulatory issues.

Tenneco was one of the largest operators in the field with working interest in more than 2,500 wells. Most of those had co-owners who could also independently market their share of production. It was critical to devise a system that allowed each working interest owner to market independently, but did not violate governmental or legal restrictions. Success was also dependent upon gaining the cooperation of the local pipeline firm that gathered the gas.

After extensive study the task force recommended that Tenneco,

list the number of wells intended to be drilled, the capital and operating costs associated with the project, and the expected outcomes in terms of success, reserves added, and income generated. Since drilling even field development wells involves some risk of dry holes, the "most-likely" economic outcomes for the year's work would include both successful wells and a dry hole or two. That's what was reflected on the summary slide, accompanied by words to the effect of, – "We plan to drill six successful wells at a completed cost of $1MM each, and we will have one dry hole with a dry-hole cost of $750 thousand…". After seeing a series of these slides over the afternoon, Mr. Rackley finally asked, "Why are you guys planning to drill all the dry holes? You could save a lot of money if you just skipped those."

On Improvising - At one budget review in Denver the lights suddenly went out. Division Exploration Manager Rod Eichler was in the middle of his summary presentation, which of course, was highly dependent on 35mm (at the time) slides. He never missed a beat and delivered the final 10 minutes of his summary in the complete dark, telling us, completely from memory, just exactly what was on each of his slides.

Not so Good on His feet - On the other hand, I also recall a presentation from management to the Division at a reception following the Division presentation. CEO Ketelsen was presenting a summary of the parent company's activity when the slide projector over-heated and all of his slides melted on the screen as they were shown. Maybe the melt-down was a premonition.

Before Air Quality Standards – There was a time before the EPA (the one the Feds run) and OSHA had such an influence in the work place. Both Phil Oxley and Lou Parish were avid pipe smokers and thought nothing of lighting up and puffing merrily away throughout the duration of the show. We always wondered if they knew how many folks were leaving the room quickly because of the smoke rather than their fear of follow-up questions. Maybe that was the plan.

Teamwork – A Common Concept
Taken to An Elevated Level

It may seem intuitive that "working together" and "teamwork" are required concepts in any organization. Tenneco – at least TOE&P - used these basic precepts to its advantage throughout its history, but a strong case can be made that the company refined and fine-tuned the concept of "teamwork" to a level well beyond its competition at the time, and likely, beyond that which is done routinely even now, these 25 years later, by most in the industry. The conversations that led to this following narrative were more detailed than for any of the other elements of culture we consider important. The tentacles of the "team-concept" at TOE&P are long and intertwined. As this story took form, it became obvious that teamwork was likely "THE" element that made TOE&P successful.

Integrated Exploration and Production Team

The management philosophies at TOE&P provided the structure for decisions about where divisions were located, the size of staff and of the work groups, the role of the general manager, the desired management style, reporting structure and other personnel practices. Key among these was the role, purpose and function of the "integrated exploration and production team concept". At the time of the sale in 1988, that "integrated team" concept was a crucial element of the Culture of the company. Rod Eichler, Rocky Mountain Exploration Manager at the time of the sale, stated the E&P position well: "The exploration for and production of hydrocarbons is so complex that no one person or department could supply all of the information necessary to prove up a prospect. To be successful and earn a profit, we had to work together as a team, a team that includes all exploration and production disciplines." Eichler's statement references the key concepts that, by 1988, were the "order of the day" at TOE&P.

Of course, teamwork in and of itself was not a proprietary concept. What was unique at TOE&P was that the integration of the exploration and production disciplines started at the ground floor. Technical professionals participated in all stages of project development from start to finish, and this represented a fundamental difference between Tenneco and most major energy companies. In most companies, exploration and production data was merged at a supervisory or managerial level, and the decision-making process normally would not involve direct input from the technical professionals. Technical people did their technical job, be it geology, geophysics or reservoir engineering, etc., and managers merged the data and made the decisions. The approach at TOE&P provided a distinct competitive advantage.

Likewise, at Tenneco there was no "production line" approach with work passing from one specialist to the next. Members of Tenneco's working teams shared responsibility for exploration and production from a defined geographic area. Explorationists and engineers worked together from the inception of a project in order to gain a complete understanding of the subsurface environment, the prospects and potential drilling or production issues involved. Together, they achieved a better integration of ideas and solutions. Individual team members were also exposed to the different challenges faced by other technical disciplines, and continuing education programs often involved cross-training into "sister" techniques. They developed a broader understanding of all the oil-finding skills, rather than remaining narrow technical specialists. Throughout, a team's over-riding objective remained that economic understanding of the assigned project area, and a "business-driven" approach to working it.

Team leaders were usually senior professionals in their particular technical disciplines. Within the teams, they acted as facilitators, ensuring that consideration was given to all points of view. The leadership role often rotated

as agent, market its own gas and in addition provide marketing services to the basin's multiple producers. The task force was immediately on the road selling Tenneco's idea to the thousands of other San Juan basin working interest and royalty owners. The potential clients were varied from independent oil companies, to individual families, to a university in Texas. "A number of them had no idea what was involved in marketing their own gas," says Alanis. "They were eager to join us."

Back in the office the project created a mammoth record-keeping job. "Where there's a will, there's a way," said John Bowen, chief accountant, Rocky Mountain Accounting. "We worked with members of our E&P Systems Department, the Controller's Systems Coordination group, the Denver office, and our Division Orders department to set up 80,000 new master files. Over 80 new accounting programs were created. It was a monumental task - and we had less than 60 days to achieve it. This was probably the first time so many different departments had worked so closely together. We put in a lot of long hours together, and we developed an appreciation for each other's expertise."

A colder-than-normal California winter in early 1987 proved a timely assist to the project. The task force sold volumes of spot market gas to users in that state from the San Juan basin. Together they'd found a solution to E&P's marketing problem in time to take advantage of a market upturn. They could be justifiably proud as the SJB accounted for $65 million in revenue in 1987, much of which would have been lost without their effort.

"It was absolutely critical to our financial performance to keep gas flowing from the San Juan Basin," said Wayne Nance.

"Bill Medary, the original exploration manager who accepted Joe Foster, the engineer, into the 1960 and '62 lease sale analysis, and a geologist in his own training, was a key player in the development of the cross-discipline interaction within the company. Medary was one of the first who realized that although geology and exploration are objective sciences at their core, the application of the science to business results was a much more subjective exercise."

J B Foster (Tenn Inc)

"We spent a good deal of time trying to exactly 'why' and 'how' we did things like we did, it was always a question that involved input from all arenas – technical, economic and administrative. We were trying to produce better results."

S D Chesebro' (Tenn Inc)

"Dan Johnson, one of the earliest, strongest and most persistent of the proponents of integrated teams even hired a consultant, George Roberts, to facilitate teamwork and leadership development in the Offshore."

C E Shultz (SVP)

"We did a lot of innovative things, but probably the most important to me was the establishment of 'prospecting teams'. The implementation of teams manned with geologists, geophysicists, geological engineers, reservoir and production and drilling engineers was break-through technology. Al Stevens (Expl. Mgr., PCD) and I realized we were wasting money and not getting the best results with our 'old style' approach. Things changed quickly with our new teams."

Harold Korell (VP Prod, Prod Mgr, PCD, at the time)

from one discipline to another based on the status and progress of the project. The experience of team leadership created a high level of maturity, the ability to express their views, and the willingness to listen to others. It also enhanced their ability to assume greater responsibility at an earlier stage of their careers, all elements that led to well-rounded and capable leaders. Most importantly, it provided thoroughly-researched investment opportunities for the company.

Evolution of the Integrated Team at Tenneco
From Joe Foster

Like many of the elements of the culture at TOE&P, the unique brand of teamwork was a practice that evolved over time, but one that developed by design, rather than by accident. A considerable number of related and un-related events and circumstances aided the evolution. Surprisingly, the company's preparation for the 1962 offshore lease sale, as described in earlier sections of the book, probably provided the original impetus for the evolution. The "integrated" team concept started out as a reaction to a need - the need for objective, economics-based analysis being applied to the process of lease sale analysis and bidding strategy. Joe Foster, an engineer, was dispatched to Lafayette with orders to supply an overprint of economic logic to the heretofore "seat of the pants" approach to buying offshore leases. The results spoke for themselves. In the offshore, with its 5000 acre lease blocks, many leases contained both development and exploration potential. That reality further integrated the efforts of the exploration and production professionals.

In much of the onshore however, exploration and production activities were most often not geographically close to each other. Through the mid-1960s the work of the two departments often remained in separate buildings with little interaction between the two sets of workers. Wayne Nance and Jack Gregory were both hired in the late 1950s, and report separately that the first efforts at integrating them began about 1965. Nance recalls that in 1959, when he was sent to Hobbs, NM as district engineer, the exploration office was not even in the same town – it was in Roswell. He was later transferred to Casper, WY and by 1967 exploration and production were at least located in the same building. A year later, both functions reported to a single General Manager in the original Denver (Rocky Mountain) Division office.

In 1966, S. V. McCollum, who had been the general manager for the offshore, was transferred to Houston as head of Worldwide Exploration and Production. He immediately brought both Jack Ray and Bill Medary along to bring the new culture to the international efforts. Ray followed by enlisting Joe Foster to bring the same sort of economic discipline that had been implemented in the Gulf into those foreign arenas, and that move further evolved, in 1968, into the Economic Planning and Analysis Department (EP&A) in Houston to create a "standardization" of economic analysis throughout the company.

* * * * *

The prodigious growth of the company and an expanding complexity and diversity of the asset base made cross-discipline management an effective choice. Likewise, the "independent division" management model, discussed earlier, with its high degree of autonomy and annual performance expectations lent itself to "teamwork" within the office, and the commitment to the lean and flat structure and to personal empowerment with commensurate expectations and rewards, allowed the team concept to flourish and expand. Most of all though, it produced results, and that above all else cemented it presence as "the" method by which the company worked.

Early acceptance of the integrated team concept, based on the superior results that it produced, led to an integration of management as well. Perhaps the most dramatic illustration of that fact occurred in 1971 when Joe Foster, a Petroleum Engineer and Business graduate, was promoted to Vice President – of Exploration – for Tenneco Oil Company. Throughout the 42-year history of Tenneco Oil the various presidents, the top management throughout, and the Division General Managers all came from a variety of technical backgrounds. At different times during his career, Petroleum Engineer Chuck Shultz, served as both Production and Exploration Manager of the GCD. It was business.

With integrated teams and detailed economic analyses having proved themselves as strategies, the divisions and the individuals within them, were encouraged to experiment with even more nuance in their application. During the 1970s and through the 1980s TOE&P continued to push the concept. Geologists, geophysicists and engineers of all stripes worked together on practically all of the company's projects. An individual team was built with the staff best-suited to handle the specific project and supervision of the activities was passed to those best-suited to perform those tasks. Sometimes team leadership came from first-line managers and sometimes it came from the team members themselves, sometimes in a "rotating" fashion. Landmen, administrative professionals and even the division attorneys were added to the teams when the project was served by such structure. By contrast, many competing companies still housed exploration and production personnel in separate quarters, with "technical" work being done by the individual professional and then handed "upstairs" for review, approval and integration by subsequent layers of "upper management".

Cross- discipline work, and even cross-discipline technical training – sending geologists or engineers to geophysical schools, and vice versa – was encouraged. Through this process the team members developed an understanding of and even some basic facility with the technical tools of their colleagues. It is a safe bet there were few companies, at least at that time, at which you might find a drilling engineer consulting directly with a geophysicist, examining the seismic records themselves to develop an understanding of the conditions he'd encounter with the well he'd be responsible for drilling.

"We would never have developed the integrated team concept if we did not have the structure of the divisions, with the Division General Manager having local responsibility for intelligent risk-taking, and the commensurate benefits of success. Risk evaluation became critical. Doing it right involved all disciplines."

J B Foster (Tenn Inc)

"I remember my direct supervisor telling me a story from early in his own career. He had been a geologist with a major oil company. He once learned that his company was going to drill a well on a project he had generated by reading about it in the company newsletter. He'd done the initial work a year or more before, passed it on to his boss, and never heard of it again. I could not believe folks could work that way."

H J Briscoe (VP, Expl)

"In 1980 to better focus on the Gulf of Mexico, which was a major area of success and growth, Joe (Foster) et al decided to break the Offshore Division into three separate business units. One of their concerns was that the competition among the three would result in two ganging up on one and not necessarily acting in the best interest of the whole. Hence, Wayne (Nance – VP in charge of all of them at the time) told us if we made certain decisions that affected all three divisions, and that those decisions were not unanimous, then we had to consult him. In the four years I was there as General Manager, we didn't consult Wayne once. This is a tribute to Jack Gregory and Bob Taylor and I think speaks to the unique culture of the company."

C E Shultz (SVP)

During the 1970s and throughout the '80s, advances in technology began to impact all aspects of the oil and gas industry. Tenneco's management of technology is the subject of discussion in future sections, but suffice it to say here, that the cross-discipline team concept allowed Tenneco's professionals a much more complete understanding of the prospects they developed, in concert with their co-workers.

This is not to say the team structure was without challenges. Earlier sections have discussed the "matrix" management structure at TOE&P. Within a division, the first-line supervisors were responsible for the work of those within their own discipline – the Division Reservoir Engineer, for instance, was responsible for all of the Reservoir Engineers within the office (and likewise, the supervisors for all of the other disciplines, each responsible for their own). He reported to the Division Production Manager who in turn, answered to the Division General Manager, and each group had its own responsibilities, priorities and expectations. At the same time, the day-to-day work was done in those inter-discipline teams, and the direct "manager" for that group might well be a geologist or geophysicist from the Exploration Department. Within the Division it was a constant requirement to balance priorities and workloads. Those annual budget targets and performance expectations – those objectives – were the common thread that allowed all to work smoothly, but constant communication among all the forces was paramount. The division-based reporting structure for the company, with its innate integration of exploration and production functions, working through a single management provided the perfect vehicle for the concept.

At the Houston headquarters, the discipline "Chiefs" were each responsible for "their own" guys, but the Senior VP's to whom they (and the Division General Mangers) reported had "line" responsibility, and their progress was measured by their performance. The potential for territorial battles was certainly present but the "Culture" that had been established was such that problems hardly ever occurred. By the time of the sale, Tenneco had taken "teamwork" to levels not imagined within the industry.

In the late 1980s Harry Briscoe was sent from the Southwestern Division to the top Exploration staff job in Houston. Very shortly thereafter, Harold Korell was transferred from the Pacific Coast Division into the equivalent job in the Production Department. Each of these two had served directly under Dan Johnson who had encouraged them to aggressively experiment with and employ expanded examples of the integrated, multi-discipline team concept, which they each had done, and which in each case, had been successful. The company was preparing to push the practice to even greater levels of application on a company-wide basis and Briscoe and Korell were to implement the change – as a team.

Many of the managers and top hands working at Tenneco at the time of the sale in 1988 went on to successful careers in other companies after the sale (see After the Sale chapter). Almost without fail, they report that the "teamwork" at TOE&P was far advanced over that which they found in their new career locations, and that in fact, many of the concepts they'd learned at Tenneco found good application within their new assignments - in companies with whom they formerly competed. On the other hand, some alums report a great resistance among entrenched management in their new jobs, especially at the larger companies, to their proposals to push coordinated work and decision-making downward within the organization.

Applied Technology

Tenneco Oil E&P believed that the best use of modern technology was to see it developed as it was being applied on the job. This belief was a substantial departure from the industry-norm. During the 1970s and 1980s when technology was evolving in all disciplines at its most rapid rate, most of the larger companies wanted to develop "in-house" schemes for applying it, and then distribute the final products as proprietary systems. At Tenneco, the "Chiefs" and the headquarters research specialists in Houston monitored the current developments in exploration aids and in production mechanics, but immediately put the equipment and concepts into the divisions and encouraged them to develop the best applications for it. The Tenneco working hands generally received new innovations well in advance of their counter-parts in other companies.

This approach allowed innovation in the field by the workers themselves. Successes and failures were quickly shared among the divisions and preferred applications developed quickly. What few conflicts arose through an occasional lack of standardization between divisions was easily offset by the efficiencies gained by allowing the professionals to find their own best uses for it. During the sale process, potential bidders commented often on the degree to which our exploration or production systems were advanced beyond those in their offices, and the principal reason was always the same – they were waiting for the home-office to get finished "perfecting" it. In addition, the team-concept working arrangements, discussed at length elsewhere, allowed a free exchange of both exploration and production technology "across the aisle", to the benefit of both.

Exploration technology (remember, this was 1988) included:

The IEPS (Integrated Exploration and Production System)

GeoQuest and LandMark workstations

Early adoption and adaptation of "bright spot" geophysical technology in the GOM

A complete seismic data re-processing center, with sophisticated attribute analysis capabilities

3-D seismic applications as early as any of the competition.

A full geochemistry department, geological research library and formation evaluation capability

"One day after logging a Tenneco well in the Anadarko Basin, an Exxon engineer drove up and asked about why we were running tubing instead of casing. Joe Abel told him we are using some new, cost saving technology. He commented that that sounded like a unique idea and asked where we got the technology. We replied, 'from an Exxon paper presented by a headquarters scientist at the local engineering society meeting a few weeks ago.'"

Chuck Shultz (SVP)

Uhh, you don't understand. An E&P geophysicist was reviewing an off-shore prospect for one of Shell's data room visitors as they reviewed the company for purchase at the time of the sale. He was using one of Tenneco's exploration workstations. As he tweaked the picture for each screen shot, he'd use words to the effect of, "All you have to do is hit 'this' to enhance that view, or 'make this adjustment' to see that affect, etc." After a number of such references the Shell geophysicist interrupted saying, "Uhh, I don't think you understand – at Shell we can't do any of that."

A Full Remote-sensing department with Landsat, Seasat, Magsat, and Thermatic mapping

The production department technologies and systems included:

State-of-the-art drilling and completion capabilities – Deep wells, deep water, directional

Offshore platform design innovations

The Real-Time Drilling Data Center in Lafayette

The "Nodal Analysis" system for high-volume wells

Advanced and computerized field development and reservoir management systems

Enhanced Oil Recovery applications with specific experience in water and steam-floods,

Tenneco frequently sponsored project-oriented research at various off-site facilities and universities, but these sponsorships focused on finding to specific questions rather than general research and looked to solve problems rather than to invent something new. The TOE&P approach was much more one of "applied" rather than "pure" research. In later years, TOE&P actually suggested a series of "Capstone" classes at the Colorado School of Mines from which students studying in any of the several technical disciplines related to oil and gas, could receive training in the actual business, through integration with their peers in other disciplines. Tenneco was actually attempting to assist the development of the integrated team structure, and the sharing of technology, at the university level.

A Central Gulf Division team examining one of 7,000 potential tracts for a 1983 lease sale.

Explaining "How It Was Done"

The following article appeared in the Fall, 1983 issue of the Tenneco Oil Prolog magazine. It is presented here as a complete example of the Culture, the Workforce and the Management Philosophies used at TOE&P. This piece was written as a "news" piece to describe Tenneco's exceptional performance at lease sales in the Gulf of Mexico, but the explanation of that success is, in fact, a demonstration of the principles noted in this chapter of the book. Interestingly, these concepts are presented simply as the routine and normal way in which the company conducted its business, with no suggestion they did anything 'unusual'. Tenneco could – and did – compete with anyone in almost any arena, and with far fewer personnel and often with fewer resources. A very strong case can be made for "the way we worked" as being the secret weapon that made TOE&P successful. This example is from the Gulf of Mexico. A similar piece could have been written for most any of Tenneco's operating arenas.

Quality – The Key to Lease Sale Success
E&P Prolog - Fall '83

E&P's success at Gulf of Mexico lease sales commands respect throughout the oil and gas industry.

An article in a recent issue of the Oil & Gas Journal explored lease sale bidding trends in terms of overbids and underbids - how much higher were winning bids compared with the second highest bid, and how close was the second highest bid to the winning one.

In comparing 11 aggressive lease sale participants, the article singles out Tenneco as the bidding strategy leader because the company has averaged the smallest overbid and underbid percentages.

Quality is the key because E&P's prowess at federal lease sales is not measured in terms of quantity. The company's success is based neither on garnering the most tracts, nor on making the overall highest bid at any given sale. Rather, E&P's performance reflects the quality of both its technical information and the company's ability to apply that information to strategic bidding practices.

The obvious questions are: What makes E&P such a keen competitor? Why is E&P able to edge out larger oil companies who ostensibly could wield superior technical know-how and financial muscle?

Staffs in E&P's three Gulf of Mexico divisions respond to these questions by citing three main points;

First is the company's senior officers' style of management;

Second, the quality of the professional staff and, consequently, the technical data; and

Third, a teamwork approach to preparing for the lease sales.

"Our senior management is intimately involved in our lease sale preparations." says Jack Gregory, vice president and Eastern Gulf Division general manager, referring to the first point. "Unlike the procedures with many other companies, E&P's senior managers get first-hand information about the tracts they bid on."

The technical staffers most familiar with possible prospects present them to the senior officers through a series of technical meetings that start months before the lease sale date. Most other major companies transmit the information through hierarchical management layers, often involving both geographical and philosophical distances.

Staying close to technical information sources allows E&P's management to remain flexible on bidding decisions. "If new information comes in, our senior managers can change rapidly to a more appropriate direction," explains Ron Christie, Western Gulf division exploration manager. "Even though we've grown as a company, we've not lost our ability to stay flexible. Other companies are more rigid."

The exposure to last minute information, coupled with the expertise of E&P's senior management, all of whom are lease sale veterans, results in the company's extremely competitive bids.

"Upper management can read the climate of lease sales," remarks Bob Waldrup, production manager of the Eastern Gulf Division. "At the May sale, Tenneco educated the industry on where the gas market is going. We led the industry with insight."

The moment of truth arrives as successful bids are called out to over a hundred oil companies.

The quality of the people and the technical data are more assets to E&P's lease sale performance. "We have excellent technical people," Gregory states. "They work hard. They have a good attitude about getting involved and being dedicated. They put forth extra effort without having to be asked. Most companies work with similar data, but our people get out there and uncover prospects not recognized by other people."

Carlton Sheffield, exploration manager of the Central Gulf Division agrees. "We have fewer people than a lot of companies but lots of directed thought. We can match the huge oil companies every time with fewer people."

"We run light", Christie adds. "Our people aren't shielded by layers on layers of management. And there aren't many companies where you find people taking such personal pride in their efforts and results. Each staff person takes individual pride in his or her prospect, and this really comes through. It really shows."

The result is high-quality technical data. "I've never been intimidated by another company's data." says Wayne Dowdall, division geologist of the Eastern Gulf Division.

"Mac" McWilliams, exploration manager of the same division, explains why. "I think Tenneco's right there with the best of them because I believe we're better prepared in defining the prospect of a specific block and then translating that into future economics. We thoroughly define the drilling costs and the reserves. We do a good job of quantifying what a prospect's worth."

Christie sums up E&P's technical quality when he says, "Historically, Tenneco's strong suit is striving for technical excellence."

Waldrup echoes this assessment, "We get the best people and use data from the best sources. Also, Tenneco's organization is integrated."

"Unlike lots of other companies, our exploration and production staffs are both under one roof and report to one general manager," Gregory says, explaining E&P's teamwork approach. "This leads to cooperation. The result is we do a better job of estimating what's there."

"Our people are given continuous exposure to multiple disciplines." Sheffield says. "We've got to create, and this keeps that creativity going. That's very important."

Gregory points out, "We start our people off by cross-training them. For example, we have a six-month program where geologists and geophysicists get exposure to what the other is doing, both on the job and through schools. That's one reason why we have better explorationists. The program really pays off down the road - like at lease sales."

Christie summarizes E&P's strong points when he says, "E&P has darn good management. We also have a staff that puts in a good performance. Working lease sales can be very exciting and rewarding, but this type of gratification can only come from the kind of team commitment that everyone makes."

The Houston Post

© 1988, The Houston Post

Tenneco to get $7.3 billion for its oil, gas operations

By Sam Fletcher

POST ENERGY REPORTER

Tenneco Inc. said Monday it has agreed to sell substantially all of the oil and gas operations of its Tenneco Oil Co. subsidiary to various buyers for more than $7.3 billion.

Analysts indicated that was a

stock to boost its value.

Chevron Corp. was one of the biggest buyers Monday with an agreement to acquire Tenneco's petroleum reserves, production facilities and lease holdings in the

☐ Related story/D-1

Every major paper in the world carried the story; in Houston the news was a shocker.

E&P TO AN UNANTICIPATED END

A Tsunami of Bad News – With Casualties

Despite the downturn initiated by the gas bubble, the company had done a very good job in managing its business during the 1982 – 1985 timeframe. In fact, at year end 1985 TOE&P reserves finally topped the billion barrel mark at 1052MMNEB, and the driving goal of reserve replacement was once again attained. The workforce was doing everything that was asked of it, and doing it well.

Unfortunately, no amount of good work would be enough to stem what would lie ahead. Driving goals would change; the industry was about to face the worst. Not surprisingly, TOE&P anticipated the event and began planning for it in 1985. Yet the magnitude of the crisis would leave everyone staggering.

For the country, and for the energy industry, negative news from the economy dominated 1986. During that year oil prices fell 45% from $22.33 to $12.37 per barrel, and the gas bubble remained a persistent impediment to sales, with prices falling 31% from $2.48 to $1.71 per mcf. By early in the year it was clear that the financial results for the year would be dismal. The low prices, exacerbated even further by a required change in accounting methods (from full cost to successful efforts), caused E&P net income to fall by nearly 80%, from $738 Million in 1985 to $127 Million in 1986. The effect was overwhelming. Options were few. Capital budgets were cut drastically and Tenneco experienced the only across-the-board reduction in its workforce in its history. Staffing was reduced by 25% during the year, creating a painful and lasting challenge to the "family" culture and productive work environment that had been the focus of so much work to create. The Eastern and Western Rocky Mountain divisions were consolidated into a single entity, as were the Texas Gulf Coast and Gulf Coast divisions in Houston. The drastic reduction in drilling brought an end to the eight-year record of reserve replacement.

The Economic Downturn

Adapted from Larry Augsberger and Update

In October, 1985 a "task force" of E&P top management was assembled and charged with devising a plan for restructuring the company for continued profitability. The company's net operating income was down and overhead costs were up. E&P president Dr. Philip Oxley had concluded that drastic moves were needed if the company was to remain profitable. A radical alteration of priorities was required. Profitability, rather than reserve replacement, which had been the driving influence for in the past eight years, was to be the new focus of our business. Growth and long-term sustainability were put on hold in favor of short term economics. The company needed to be more efficient and would pursue only projects that would make money in the shrinking oil and gas economy.

In November, 1985, the task force conducted a division-by-division review, meeting with division management to re- evaluate its economic and geological potential, based on a new set of projected market conditions. Company resources – capital, technology and people – had to be allocated for maximum effectiveness. These evaluations identified projects in some geographical areas that were no longer economic. Four domestic divisions were downsized. The two Rocky Mountain Divisions were merged and the Texas Gulf Coast Division was combined with the Gulf Coast Division. The study also indicated that the company needed to shift increasingly toward international operations since they offered the greatest opportunity for large field discoveries.

In the midst of the study, economic conditions worsened. In early 1986 prices plummeted, wells were shut in, and in many cases properties were sold for whatever they would bring. The oil industry collapse was demonstrating the agony of a market in its fifth year of decline. From the peak of $40 a barrel in 1981, oil prices had slid to $26 by January 1985. They bumped back up to $31 by November, but that was the calm before the storm. With OPEC's December announcement they would no longer defend the price of oil, spot prices began a decline that did not stop until early April, when they fell below $10 a barrel. In addition, persistent natural gas oversupply worsened as a result of cheaper supplies of heating oil in the northeast. This sent gas prices

THE BUST – 1986

Adapted from Final E&P Update

People remember years by recalling events – storms, floods, or the big game. 1986 was the year of the bust, when oil prices crashed, wells were shut in and many then sold for whatever they would bring. The oil price collapse in early 1986 was actually the final agony of a market in its fifth year of decline. From a peak of $40 in 1981, world oil prices had slid back to $26 by January 1985. Without warning, OPEC announced in December, 1985 that it would no longer defend the price of oil, but rather increase production in order to regain a larger share of the world market. The impact was wrenching. Spot prices immediately started down and did not stop until early April l, 1986, when they fell below $10 per barrel for a few days. Meanwhile the persistent US natural gas oversupply, worsened by suddenly-cheaper supplies of competing fuel oil, sent gas prices through the floor. The spot price fell from over $2 per mcf in December of 1985 to $1.30 the following summer.

E&P's earnings plunged. Capital expenditures were slashed; a quarter of the workforce either retired, left, or was laid off, and everyone in the company suffered from a collective sense of shock.

From the best of all possible businesses five years before, the oil industry had become, in the perception of the financial community, one of the worst. E&P began to recover from the affects. The lack of drilling dollars meant more time could be spent high-grading exploration prospects. Meanwhile, producing costs were down as marginal properties were culled.

No one would regard the "Bust of '86" as good, but those in the oil patch surely remember it.

down sharply. The spot price fell from just over $2 per thousand cubic feet in late 1985 to $1.30 by summer of 1986. It was evident that major steps would be needed to adjust to the situation.

On Friday, March 14, 1986, TOE&P implemented the most difficult decision of all. The company laid-off 337 employees, approximately 12 percent of the total workforce. "This was the most painful action I've had to take," said Oxley. "If there had been any alternative, we would have taken it." This was the first workforce reduction in the company's history, and it took place in every company location – headquarters and the divisions. It was also the first significant move to be made among all competitors in the oil industry. It caught many by surprise, but soon thereafter it was followed by similar workforce reductions elsewhere within the oil industry. The workforce at TOE&P had been reduced to levels not seen since 1981.

In typical E&P fashion, the company implemented a number of plans and actions during the weeks that followed the workforce reduction. Meetings were conducted for laid-off employees to explain the details of their continued employee benefits and to provide outplacement seminars for instruction in interviewing, writing resumes, financial planning and even starting your own business. Most important, TOE&P ran ads in newspapers and professional journals seeking job leads. Nearly 200 companies responded with more than 300 openings in virtually all the job categories affected by the reduction. Job openings were posted at job placement centers and mailed to the laid-off employees.

"Our employees did a good job of reducing costs," said Wayne Nance, who was named president in February, 1987. "We cut direct operating and maintenance expenses by $43 million and annual overhead by over $65 million. When you compare those reductions to income, you realize that cost-cutting was critical." The company had weathered the storm and profitability was achieved from that period forward and until the business was sold.

The May 1986 issue of E&P Update was devoted almost entirely to the "new world" that the company was going to experience going forward. Interviews with President Philip Oxley and Executive Vice President Wayne Nance were titled "Here for the Long Term", and "E&P Prepares to Survive", respectively. Detailed articles on Exploration, Production, Financial, Systems, and Strategies were presented, and an article from outside company consultant, Daniel Yergin described "a good sweating" as the remedy. News reports followed with details of the workforce reduction, the combination of divisions and some executive retirements. A small column on the last page reported new discoveries on ten prospects. The August issue was devoted to "The Task Force – A New Way of Doing Business". Prophetic words for the reality two years hence.

Although challenges dominated the year, not all of the news in 1986 was negative. The reporting of 'anything else' in 1986 as a highlight seems a reach, but in truth, the strategies for turn-around were having an effect quickly. The outstanding success in Colombia continued. In the Rockies, following the El Paso settlement, the San Juan Gas Plant was completed and came online. This plant, co-owned with Conoco quickly became a consistent profit center, but work in the area was to be challenged as well. The RMD sprang into action to address an unanticipated threat, resulting in a significant economic benefit to the company and illustrating the cross-discipline teamwork within the organization by then.

1987 Recovery

The effects of the troubled economics of 1986 carried over into early 1987 as a collection of under-performing properties were sold for $254MM. At the same time, the wildcat discoveries were moving towards development in Colombia, first production was established in Gabon, and the huge Heidrun field in the Norwegian sector of the North Sea was declared commercial. Exploration results for the year just passed were exceptional with 136 MMNEBs discovered at a cost of only $1.03 per barrel. The Frontier Project drilled the exploratory well offshore on the Bahamas platform and the South Marsh Island 78 discovery (estimated now at about 300 BCF) highlighted GOM activity. In West Texas the SWD put an expanded drilling and waterflood program in place that would increase production by a factor of 10 within three years. And in the Gulf of Mexico, the company returned to the auction table winning 20 blocks, with 20 bids. In a clear demonstration of the company's ability the shift its emphasis, the changes from gas to liquids drilling focus that had been implemented two years prior produced all-time high liquid production of 147,852 BOPD. The painful actions of the prior two years were quickly showing results.

In 1987, Dr. Phil Oxley retired and Wayne Nance was named President of TOE&P.

By late 1987, virtually all of TOE&P's gas wells were flowing at full capacity, following a summer during which many were shut in for lack of customers. "We entered 1988 on a very good note," said Joe Foster in an interview. "E&P sells a billion cubic feet of gas per day, 40% of it on the spot market, so our bottom-line improves immediately. Our pipelines also benefited. We rode the gas roller coaster up in the 1970s, and suffered from the ride back down in the '80s. It looks like things may be evening out."

"We're encouraged by the market. The worst is behind us. Customers are locking in supplies for longer periods of time.", Steve Chesebro'(President of the newly-formed Tenneco Gas Marketing Company)

"Oil and gas products is selling a billion cubic feet of gas per day, and if we had more, we could sell that, too!", John Gray (VP Oil and Gas Marketing)

With the company transformed by the events of the prior few years, with the new plans and strategies firmly in place, and with results already beginning to show themselves, it was largely thought, and reported, that the worst

**President Profiles
WAYNE NANCE
1987-1988**

Wayne Nance is a native Texan, born in a small town near Waco. He graduated from the University of Texas with a degree in Petroleum Engineering in 1952 and joined Stanolind (Amoco) Oil. He came to Tenneco in 1958 and was assigned to the Odessa field office. He worked in a variety of the onshore offices through 1974 when he was transferred to Lafayette in 1974 as Offshore Production Manager. He continued his work in the offshore through 1982 when he was promoted to Executive Vice President in Houston, the position he held until Phil Oxley's retirement in 1987. Nance saw the whole gamut of conditions at Tenneco – the highs and the lows – and all of its provinces during his career. His job as President would have been to manage the recovery and transition to new heights. Unfortunately, Nance did not get the opportunity to do that. Following the sale in 1988 he worked as a consultant and served on several Boards. At this writing he lives in Palestine, TX.

A STACKED DECK, OR GOOD BUSINESS

Tenneco's trip to Japan and Taiwan produced a few memories for Harry Briscoe.

Once JAPEX made the commitment to negotiate a definitive agreement fot the GOM drilling program, they invoked a smart trick to work things to their advantage. They suggested that rather than impose upon us to send staff to Tokyo, they'd be happy to send a team to Houston, a team that could stay as long as necessary to get the work done. Being the typical multi-task oriented operation, we were only too happy to accept that offer. What we did not think about though, was that JAPEX effectively doubled the length of their day with such an arrangement. Each day the negotiating team would meet at 9:30 am. All of the Tenneco personnel would have gotten to the office early to get their "regular" work tended to before the negotiation would start, and then each day, after the 3 pm cutoff for that day's session, we'd return to our offices and stay late trying to digest the arguments of the day, or get back to the other things we'd neglected while in the negotiations. The Japanese team, on the other hand, would return to their hotel, where they would fax all of the documents and the negotiating points of the day back to the home office in Tokyo, where the sun was just coming up. In Tokyo, an entire second staff would comb through everything, run numbers, propose changes, prepare arguments, and provide documentation, which they would then fax back to their Houston team, just in time for them to be all fresh and ready for us the next morning. They were pretty efficient, but we don't think their use of overkill ended up with much in the way of a "victory" for them.

of times were past. Indeed, 1988 began on a strong note with aggressive plans and new developments at home and abroad. In another demonstration of "the Tenneco Model", the Japanese were brought into Tenneco's businesses.

1988 Japan Comes to the Gulf

One of the last major joint ventures undertaken by TOE&P was a deal signed on April 25, 1988, only one month before the sale of the company was announced. Within this agreement, JAPEX, one of Japan's leading oil and gas firms, committed $27MM to the drilling of nine wildcat prospects on Tenneco leases in the Gulf of Mexico. Separately, JNOC, another major Japanese entity, had agreed to a bidding partnership for future lease sales in the GOM, with potential expenditures in future years targeted at $250 million. In addition to the significance of these agreements themselves, the timing of the projects lends some insight as to why the internal decisions about the sale of the company came as such a surprise only a few months later.

For some time, Tenneco Inc. had desired to create a relationship with the Japanese business community. Tenneco saw Japan as a market for many of its diversified products, among them the farm and construction equipment manufactured by J. I. Case. In late 1986, and throughout 1987, the parent company pursued various potential entrée's into the Japanese markets. The "Tenneco Model", the process of using Tenneco's diverse business interests in varying industries for synergistic benefit to the individual Tenneco companies, had been successfully employed in a variety of different countries, and the hopes were that the same would apply with Japan. Tenneco Inc. approached TOE&P with the request to create a basket of properties that could be shown to Japan.

In January 1988 Bob Winckler, Vice President of Business Development for TOE&P and Harry Briscoe, Vice President of Exploration were dispatched to Tokyo with a slideshow describing a bundle of E&P's top offshore prospects. The E&P objective was to solicit needed drilling capital, leverage the GOM wildcat portfolio and budget, and spread the exploratory risk through the addition of an outside partner. After a series of presentations to several different Japanese companies, JAPEX was identified as the intended suitor (see sidebar for a perspective on the internal workings of Japanese industry). JAPEX quickly sent a contingent of professionals to Lafayette to review the prospects in more detail and to form an opinion as to the "appropriateness" of Tenneco as a partner. In late March, negotiations began in earnest and by the end of April, the deal was in place.

The deal called for JAPEX to pay 90% of the working interest cost in the nine wildcats, the drilling of which was slated to begin in June, 1988. JAPEX would earn a 45% working interest in the properties. Since Japan produced only about 10% of its national oil consumption, JAPEX was looking for ownership of liquid oil reserves which could then be traded for exportable crude oil from other Tenneco properties around the world.

The energy business in Japan at the time followed a formalized regime. JAPEX was representative of the Japanese energy business as a whole. The energy business was representative of general business as a whole, and Japanese business as a whole was representative of the country itself. In the late 1980s Japanese business made no agreements involving international companies without a thorough "vetting" of the company who might become long-term business partner. Throughout the process JAPEX requested as much detailed information about TOE&P and Tenneco Inc. as they did about the drilling prospects themselves.

Both TOE&P and JAPEX (and through JAPEX, Japan) seemed pleased with the deal, and congratulatory messages were shared all around. JAPEX even organized and transferred a contingent of its own employees to Lafayette so that they might monitor their interests (and learn as much as they could about the E&P business) during the drilling program. It is not an overstatement to say that JAPEX was as shocked as the Tenneco employees to learn, scarcely a month later, that TOE&P was to be sold.

Very shortly after that public announcement of the Sale was made, Winckler and Briscoe were summoned to Joe Foster's office on the 29th floor of the Tenneco building. A Mr. Ohmori, from Japex had traveled from Japan to personally deliver a message of displeasure to those who had been involved in selling the deal to JAPEX. Mr. Ohmori began his statement from memory, but part way through his comments, paused, and stated, "I apologize, but it is so important that I get my statement exactly correct, and I am not so sure with my English, that I must read it to you." With that, he reached inside his coat pocket and pulled out a page and a half of written statement. In carefully chosen, and very direct, words he expressed his displeasure with the announcement of the sale of the company. He felt that Tenneco had misled his company – and his country - about the solid reputation of our businesses. The Japanese review process had conducted extensive research about Tenneco Oil and about Tenneco Inc. and had concluded that we were reputable companies who would be good partners and would take good care of Japan's interests in the foreign venture. They were highly embarrassed by the announcement of the sale of TOE&P and since they had no idea who might be the new owners of the Tenneco offshore properties, they might or might not approve of them as partners for their own interests. The entire "dressing down" was short and to-the-point, probably taking less than 5 minutes, and no discussion followed, other than Mr. Foster apologizing to Mr. Ohmori for the circumstances. Mr. Ohmori was indignant that we proceeded with making the deal with Japex, assuming no doubt that we knew (which we didn't) the company was to be sold. He stopped short of suggesting a hari-kiri sword for any of the E&P crew, he likely would not have objected had it been offered.

THE "TENNECO WHAT" COMPANY

In preparing for the trip to Tokyo to present the GOM prospect package to the Japanese Oil Companies, it was decided that we should carry business cards in both English and in Japanese. We enlisted a local Houston company to prepare those for us, but when we received them, we of course were not capable of proof-reading them. In a short stroke of smarts, someone suggested that we check with Larry Augsburger to see if we had anyone on Houston staff that might be able to do that for us. Sure enough, Larry located a young Japanese intern in the administrative department who could read the cards. Our company was officially called – Tenneco Oil Exploration and Production Company – that's what we wanted to hear. The fellow showed up at the office, took a look at the new cards, got a wry grin on his face and said, "I think you need to go back to the drawing board with these. They say, Tenneco Explosion Company!" It's a good thing we checked, but in retrospect, they might have been more correct the way they were, given that the sale was announced very shortly after we used them.

Chevron was the successful purchaser of the GOM properties and we believe the drilling program went forward as planned. The results of those wells were not known at this writing, and likewise, whether or not we sold any tractors in Japan.

Moving into Deepwater – GC 205

By 1988 technology and economics were allowing the industry to move into ever-deeper waters in the Gulf of Mexico. For many years, the "shelf-edge", a severe change in the topography of the sea-floor beyond which water depths increased rapidly, was a barrier to exploration. Shell, Texaco and Mobil had made initial forays into these waters, generally greater than 600' in depth, but most of the industry had adopted a "wait and watch" posture for the new province. (Today, 25 years after the sale, the deep and ultra-deep waters of the Gulf are the primary source of exploration and production there.) Tenneco's first moves beyond the shelf edge came at the 1983 lease sale. Jack Gregory, Division General Manager for the GOM recalls the sale; "We almost did not acquire GC 205. Our team had identified some of bright spot anomalies in this area and they were discussed at our final bid committee, but we decided at the Bid Meeting to not pursue any of them. After the bid session was over and all had left, Dr. Oxley (President at the time) and I were reviewing our proposed bids and Phil agreed to submit a minimal bid on GC 205, which we did, and which we won." The GC 205 block was later farmed-out to Exxon who agreed to pay 100% of the cost of the wildcat well in order to earn a 1/3 interest in the project. The initial well was drilled in 1988, as the process of selling the company was moving forward. It was an extremely "tight" (confidential) hole, and of course, with Exxon as a partner, Tenneco was not at liberty to release the information about the well. On the other hand, the company was anxious to report any news to potential buyers that would increase the amount of their bids at the sale of the company. It became apparent that the GC 205 was probably going to be a significant discovery. Steve Chesebro', who was managing the sale for the benefit of Tenneco Inc., had to devise a process by which the potential bidders could be advised to the value, yet maintain the confidentiality. Chevron was the eventual successful purchaser of the Tenneco properties in the Gulf of Mexico and ended up developing GC 205 – renamed as the "Genesis" field – with an ultimate estimated potential of over 160MMBO. Total investment for the drilling and development of Genesis exceeded $800 million. At its peak, Genesis was producing 63,000BOPD.

Spring 1988

The early months of 1988 came and went quickly. During the last quarter of the 1987 new budgets and strategies had been established to effect a continued recovery from the downturn. Those projections were designed to put the company back where it needed to be. The company was once again selling all the gas it could produce and several new wildcat discoveries, both at home and abroad, were announced in the early months. In February the annual budget tour swept through the divisions on its usual schedule. The message from the divisions reflected a combination of continued diligence to cost control and financial awareness, but the attitude reflected optimism about the prospect and opportunity base, and an anticipation of good things to come. Despite continued low product prices, the corrective steps put into place over the last two-plus years allowed financial projections indicating the company would nearly double its net income for the year. A cautious enthusiasm prevailed.

On Wednesday May 25, 1988, the employees of Tenneco Oil Company (both E&P and P&M) arrived at their jobs to news as shocking as any they had ever heard. Company networks carried the stark announcement that company was to be sold. Despite the surprise and shock, the reaction of the Tenneco employees was notable, and reflected perfectly the professionalism and talent of the workforce.

The process of the actual Sale of TOE&P was the last great adventure for the company, and in typical form, it was done with excellence, style and class.

The Sale of the Company
The Last Great Success

The year 1987 ended on a positive note; positive, at least in comparison to the challenges of the preceding three. Net income for TOE&P had increased to $189MM, up by 50% over 1986, and the company had raised an additional $254MM with strategic divestment of properties. Liquids production reached an all-time high of nearly 150,000BPD and the Gulf of Mexico had a major new discovery at South Marsh Island Block 78. Five of the seven 1987 wildcats in Colombia were new field discoveries, production had begun in Gabon, and in the North Sea, the huge Heidrun field was declared commercial. Much work had been done to inventory and high-grade prospects and producing properties for future drilling, and the organization had recovered from the psychological blow of the reduction in workforce in 1986. The 1987 Tenneco Inc Annual Report was dominated by an extensive section on the energy businesses.

"…in addition, Tenneco Oil Exploration and Production, among the best in the business at replacing reserves through new discoveries, found significant new reserves concentrations (in several areas) … (and) increased operating income by 49% …" James L Ketelsen in Tenneco Inc., 1987 Annual Report

Reading through the highlights of the year, the improved statistics and the optimistic projections for the future, it looked as though the company's hard work during hard times had paid off. Despite continued restricted capital budgets, the company was looking forward to 1988, the year immediately ahead.

In retrospect, there might have been a cloud or two on the horizon, but it

"In May, 1988, my life changed dramatically. Jim Ketelsen called me to his office and told me two things: Tenneco Oil Company was going to be sold, and I was going to sell it. I asked the CEO that, since I'd spent all of my professional life trying to help build TOC into the successful company it was, why would I be the one to sell it? Ketelsen answered that if I didn't manage the sale, his financial group would do it. I knew that would be a disaster, especially for the employees."

"Tenneco Oil Company was sold for one reason. That was to save Tenneco Inc. from bankruptcy. The cause was not the energy businesses, but the manufacturing businesses, with one notable culprit. Tenneco Inc. had to have the money from the sale of TOC by the end of 1988, or it was in financial jeopardy. That meant that the sale process, beginning in May, had to be complete with money in the bank by the end of the year, or else Tenneco Inc.'s financials would be a disaster. For such a large transaction, or series of transactions, accomplishing this would be a challenge."

S D Chesebro' (Tenn Inc)

was not the nature of the company culture to dwell on future storms. When the downturn had started a few years before, then President Phil Oxley had written a memo to the employees titled, "Predicting rain does not count, building arks, does." Over the prior several years, the E&P machine had concentrated on the ark, and had launched it; but the cloud was still there, just out of sight, over the horizon. (What we did not know at the time was that we were building an ark for all of Tenneco Inc., and that we were not going to be invited aboard.)

The first hint of concern could have been found in the October, 1987 edition of E&P Update, but it was a small story, largely unnoticed by most. That issue carried this very short account of an organizational change: Tenneco Inc. is reorganizing its corporate structure *"...in response to a Financial Accounting Standards Board's proposed rule change. Under the new rule, after Dec. 15, 1988, Tenneco will have to include the debt of all majority-owned subsidiaries in its consolidated financial statements. Without the restructuring Tenneco will not be able to issue new debt because of restrictions in existing loan and bond covenants".* The profound nature of that report would be revealed in the months ahead.

Three months later, the January 1988 Tenneco Update featured a letter from Tenneco Inc. CEO, James Ketelsen, with the following quote: *"The worst is behind us in all three of Tenneco's major businesses."* Things sounded "fine". Elsewhere in the same issue, however, another article carried the statement: *"In order to continue borrowing .... all financial and operating subsidiaries must be consolidated onto a single balance sheet. Neither employees nor stockholders will be affected by the change."*

The last sentences in that statement would prove to be breath-taking in its inaccuracy (at least as far as the employees of Tenneco Oil E&P were concerned), and prophetic in the degree to which it negated the implication of the quote from the CEO. Tenneco Inc. held something in excess of $4 Billion in "off balance-sheet" financing, principally as support for the failing business at J. I. Case. This non-recognized obligation amounted to nearly half of the entire corporate debt. Simply put, the changed tax laws required an infusion of cash, lest the financials of the parent be radically and negatively impacted (some say bankrupted). Tenneco Inc. concluded that selling Tenneco Oil was the only viable option. Tenneco Oil was the only marketable asset within the corporation capable of bringing in that much cash, in that short a time. There was no alternative.

Still, none within the rank and file of TOE&P had any inkling of the news that would break within a few months. Taking Mr. Ketelsen at his word in January, even he did not expect the outcome that would ensue. Documents indicate the financial stability of Tenneco Inc. became an item of concern among the financial community and the Board of Directors early in 1988. In mid-April proposals were floated that would straighten out the balance sheet by selling Tenneco Oil Company. In a Confidential May 2,

1988 memo, Joe Foster, the senior energy executive in Tenneco Inc. and a member of the Board of Directors proposed a radical re-structuring of TOE&P involving the outright sale of a significant number of assets and a spin-off and re-financing of the remaining entity, but CEO Ketelsen and his financial advisors decided that a complete sale was the best option. The fateful Board meeting deciding the fate of Tenneco Oil was held in New York on May 24, and on May 25, 1988, the announcement was made that TOE&P and TOP&M would be offered for sale. (An account of the meeting is found in the "After the Sale" chapter.)

Reaction amongst the employees was one of utter disbelief. Reaction amongst the industry competition, the potential purchasers of the company, was one of equal surprise.

Since only a very few among the upper management, and essentially no one among the rank and file, of the company had any indication that the sale was in the works, very little planning had been done to actually facilitate the project. The process of marketing and selling the company became the sole focus of effort for nearly everyone in the company. What would follow during the next four months of 1988, in some unfortunate and twisted way, would become as good an example of teamwork and accomplishment as any during the company's entire history. The job of selling the company was executed under duress, but with phenomenal results. "One more time", Tenneco Oil delivered results beyond expectations.

TOE&P's normal senior staff meeting on Monday May 30, 1988, was attended by Ken Otto, the senior Human Resource executive of Tenneco Inc. It had been five agonizing days of speculation since the announcement of the sale, but few details about the plan had emerged. Otto announced that the sale would be an "asset-only" sale. He explained that certain benefits and protections would be offered E&P employees during and after the sale. He described a special compensation plan designed to provide an incentive for managers and key personnel who were directly involved in selling the company, based on the achievement of a sales price target for the company. The purpose was to retain critical staff during the sales process and to maximize the value received. The meeting was short and to the point. There was an offer to answer questions, but few were asked. As the meeting broke up, the E&P managers seemed to walk away in shock and disbelief.

Following the meeting, some E&P managers met in the halls, visiting in quiet whispers while shaking their heads. Others headed for their offices for a few solemn moments to reflect on what they just heard. Harold Korell, vice president of Production, Harry Briscoe, vice president of Exploration and Larry Augsburger, vice president of Administration met in an office on the opposite end of the building. "What about the employees?" Harold asked firmly. "They said this was going to be an asset-only sell. That means our employees could be left in the cold. This just can't

5/26/88 - The decision to sell Tenneco Oil is based on Tenneco Inc's corporate and financial needs. It does not reflect on E&P's performance, which is exceptional. E&P employees will not be forgotten. (reports of improvements to the benefits packages and outplacement services appeared in five subsequent newsletters). I will communicate with you frequently.

6/2/88 – Let's keep in mind why we are being sold. It's because together we created a company that is highly attractive. We can be proud of that, and pride should continue to be a part of our outlook.

6/16/88 – As usual you've turned in quality work, you've gone beyond the black-and-white request. Gathering the information (necessary to offer the company) brings into focus the capability of all of you as well as the quality of our reserves and exploration prospects.

7/28/88 – I hear good reports on how well our work in the data rooms has been received. One analyst called his boss after being in the data room for only a short time and said the quality of our work is "unbelievable."

(With regard to our ongoing exploration drilling) …… If this trend (of discovery) continues we may be reporting the best results in our history.

8/12/88 – Your work continues to stand out. One company's senior executive commented that his people reported to him that, "We wish we were organized like Tenneco, and had their team concept."

Our first-half net income was $179.5MM, up over 68% from last year,….. reflecting the hard work you've done in challenging times.

8/26/88 – These are exceptional achievements.

happen. We need to do something - like purchase the company ourselves".

Although that sounded a bit far-fetched at the time, it wasn't long before Joe Foster announced that CEO Ketelsen and the Board had given him authority to pursue a Leverage Buy-Out (LBO) transaction to acquire the E&P company. He was given the option to purchase individual E&P packages or possibly acquire the entire company. That announcement was well-received with in the E&P organization.

Tenneco Inc. chose Morgan Stanley to broker the sale of Tenneco Oil Company. Its duties included working with Tenneco in preparing an offering memorandum, advising E&P about data rooms and presentations, identifying and contacting potential purchasers and scheduling the evaluation sessions. Later, Morgan Stanley would assist Tenneco Inc. in reviewing the bids. Longtime TOE&P executive, Steve Chesebro', who had been transferred into a new position within Tenneco Inc earlier in the year, was appointed by Ketelsen to be the executive in charge of the sale.

Bob Winckler, E&P's vice president of Business Development was tapped as the coordinator of the sale for E&P and with working with Morgan Stanley to coordinate the sales process. Within 30 days they had prepared the Offering Memorandum containing 1,252 pages of text and hundreds of charts, tables and maps to be sent to prospective purchasers.

TOE&P was offered for sale in its entirety but, the company was so large and diverse it was feared only a limited field of bidders could pursue this option. Therefore, it was also offered as eight separate geographic units, as represented by the Operating Division boundaries. Packages were prepared for the Gulf of Mexico, Rocky Mountains, Mid-Continent, Pacific Coast, Gulf Coast/ Southwestern, Colombia, Norway, and Other International assets. Using valuation parameters acceptable for accounting purposes, the company's assets were valued at $4.3 billion as of December 31, 1987, comprised of nearly 1.2 billion net equivalent barrels (NEBS) of proved reserves, interests in 22,041 total wells (6,078 net), 2.1 million net acres of mineral or royalty land and 10.6 million net acres of leasehold. TOE&P employment was listed at 3,573 domestically-based or US expatriate employees, including 2,112 in E&P, 1,018 in Operators, Inc., and 443 in other subsidiaries. In addition there were 450 employees in Houston Oil of Colombia. The refining, processing and marketing businesses of TOP&M were packaged for sale at the same time, as a separate transaction.

Within a few days, Joe Foster contacted Larry Augsburger with questions regarding the adequacy and appropriateness of the Tenneco Inc. benefits and protections that were offered to the E&P employees. Foster wanted assurance that the employees were being treated fairly with regard to severance pay, retention bonuses, vesting of benefits, value incentive programs, and the like. A well-regarded management consulting firm was engaged and evaluated E&P's coverage, concluding that the package was fair, and in some areas, even a bit generous. However, since a sale of this magnitude had not occurred there was no direct analog, and since E&P was being offered as an asset-only sale, concerns regarding massive and sudden job losses prevailed. Discussions with Tenneco Inc. regarding the structure and detail of the employee protections continued, and during the summer several additional provisions were secured.

In September, prospective bidders were advised that Tenneco would look favorably upon purchasers who offered E&P employees continued employment and credit for their years of service with Tenneco in respect to their future benefits. All full time E&P operating division personnel, including Operators, Inc. employees, would be automatically transferred to the acquired division at the time of the sale, and Tenneco would encourage the purchaser to continue their employment. This was a major change in the structure of the offering and was not viewed favorably by the bidders.

Houston-based headquarters personnel would be eligible to join a Transition Organization to manage the ongoing headquarters functions after the closing date. These employees would be treated as full-time Tenneco Inc. personnel for a minimum of six months after the sale, with potential extensions of up to a year, depending on the specific job. While in the Transition Organization, employees would earn a retention bonus, for each three months of continuous service following the sale. In addition, employees would continue to participate in the benefit programs and accrue service for benefit purposes. These modifications took the pressure off employees and management as the closing dates approached.

Business did not shut down when the sale was announced; quite to the contrary, in fact. Within a week, E&P senior management had finalized plans for interim operations. The company's driving goal became "adding value". "Of course it was business as usual in the sense that adding value to the company wasn't a new strategy," said Harold Korell, vice president of Production, "but we were now more focused on confirming reserves and developing recent discoveries." Meetings were quickly called to re-focus the budgets in both Production and Exploration to accelerate projects that would produce short-term benefits and defer those that produced results years down the road. "Proved, developed reserves are the same as money in the bank, and brand new discoveries are the next best thing," said Harry Briscoe, vice president of Exploration. "For that reason we will take some of our better wildcat projects and get them drilled." As successes mounted, updates were added to data rooms so that potential buyers could assess these new reserves. In the August 26 E&P Update of Sale newsletter Wayne Nance reported that the company's "adding value" strategy was working. He stated that since July 1, exploratory drilling programs had initiated 55 wells. Of the 24 that had been completed to that date, 11 were new-field discoveries, accounting for an outstanding 46 percent success rate for the accelerated prospects. Those 11 new fields came on top of 12 discoveries that had been drilled during the first six months of 1988. The potential reserve additions for the discoveries were conservatively

> "*The* employees of TOE&P have done a tremendous job in this sale effort, both in compiling the data necessary for the Offering Memorandum and also with organizing the data rooms. It would have been nearly imposible to conduct this sale without their work."
>
> **Tom Hassen,**
> **(Morgan Stanley principal)**

> "The accomplishments of our employees in selling this company jump right off the page. Once again, our people have put forth a first-rate effort for the very reason that it is the only kind of job they know how to do!"
>
> **DS Taylor (SVP)**

**TENNECO OIL E&P
MANAGEMENT AT TIME
OF SALE 1988**

Houston

J B Foster
Executive Vice President, Tenneco Inc.

C W Nance
President

C E Shultz
SVP – International

D S Taylor
SVP - Offshore and Exploration

D B Johnson
SVP - Onshore and Production

Glenn Taylor
SVP, Legal

L A Augsburger
VP, Administration

Ed Milan
SVP, Chief Financial Officer

H M Korell
VP Production

Don Muncy
Chief Drilling Engineer

Scott Haire
Chief Reservoir Engineer

John Simon
Chief Production Engineer

Gary Rapp
Chief Geological Engineer

H J Briscoe
VP Exploration

Al Erxleben
Chief Geologist

Bob Williams
Chief Geophysicist/Geophysical Mgr.

Ned Snodgrass
Chief Landman

T Rathert
Director, EP&A

Larry Oliver
President, Operators Inc.

John Gray
VP, Oil & Gas Products

R H Winckler
VP, Business Development

S D Chesebro'
(to Tenn Inc., President, Tenneco Gas
Marketing in Jan '88)

estimated at more than one hundred million net equivalent barrels, with extremely low finding costs. This was exceptional achievement under a difficult situation, and truly a testament to the quality of the prospect inventory that the company had built over the prior years. (… if only there had been a chance to develop them!)

Dealing with rumors, frustrations and fears during the sale process was an issue for E&P management. The initial announcement of the sale of the company was completely unexpected. Providing timely and consistent factual information was crucial in addressing employee concerns and anxieties. On May 26, 1988, one day after the announcement of the sale, Wayne Nance, E&P president, issued the first of twenty newsletters. The "E&P Update of Sale" memos to all employees were informative, positive and supportive and addressed an array of topics ranging from employee benefits matters to data room updates and prospective buyers' reactions. The near-weekly reports included progress reports regarding exploration and production activities which were being conducted at a furious pace to add value to the sale. Nance also offered encouragements and sympathetic support to those employees stressed with the sale. He adopted the slogan "Don't Worry, Be Happy" from Bobby McFerrin's pop hit of the day. The new issues of the "Update" were eagerly anticipated and became a source of comfort during the process. In retrospect, these 20 memos are a touching testimonial to the employees and the management of TOEP and provide a tangible record of the mutual respect between the two critical elements of the company.

On July 25, thirty-eight E&P data rooms opened. These were located in each of the operating divisions and also within the Houston headquarters. Analysts from the first of more than 20 bidding companies entered and began the process of evaluating TOE&P. Copying documents consistently came up first as the main topic of the data room. Each division needed at least four copies of everything – one document for each of the 4 data rooms per division. Documentation was required for producing properties, wells and leases, contracts, environmental statements and legal papers.

In Lafayette four printers were at it seven days per week, and until 3:00 a.m. on many days, preparing their data room. At one point, Mike Collins, data room coordinator, reported, "We completely exhausted the total paper supply of the entire city!" A truck was dispatched from Dallas on an emergency run to Lafayette with reams of reinforcement. Collins stated, "We will be ready in time. "Just like McDonalds, we'll have our doors open, with biscuits ready."

Each visiting prospective buyer was greeted with an executive presentation that provided an over-view of the strengths and opportunities available in that division. Division personnel were accustomed to selling their prospects or programs through the presentation format, since that was what they did each year during the annual Budget Tour before senior management, so they made the presentations. They were good at it and everyone knew they would be forceful in enticing prospective buyers to strongly consider their division. It also gave E&P's well-known technical professionals an opportunity to be seen, which would work to their personal advantage. They were on display along with the company's other assets and technical competence and capabilities. Many felt the data-room presentations were the key in maximizing the sales price for each package.

In addition to the division presentations and data rooms, presentations were made in the headquarters office for the few suitors large enough to consider purchasing the entire company. Tenneco's senior management presented an overall company summary explaining strategy and philosophy, organization and structure, a production and exploration overview and financial results. Again, the purpose was to sell the company's assets for the maximum value possible, but on a total company basis. After one presentation one of the prospective buyers, and there were approximately 45 to 50 in attendance, openly stated that he was originally of the opinion that the way to buy Tenneco was as an individual package – but after seeing the presentation he was convinced best value would be achieved by buying the entire company. Everyone at Tenneco was excited to hear these remarks, even though, in the end, it didn't work out that way.

After a five-week-long run, on August 28, the data rooms were closed. More than 4,000 analysts – accountants, economists, engineers, geologists and lawyers representing dozens of companies -- had visited the 38 different data rooms. As an example of the work this entailed, the Gulf of Mexico region alone produced 20,000 copies for each visiting company -- a grand total of 300,000. The official closing did not mean that the data rooms were ready to be dismantled. Every room remained intact until after the September 30 bid date, and after the winning bidders were named, one data room in each division remained available for use by the purchaser, and another had it contents boxed as a legal record.

The Company at the Time of the Sale

"In my judgment, the company was operating at its peak levels when it was sold in 1988. We were a mature and able organization in all regards – our technical expertise, managerial philosophy and operational efficiency were all exceptional." - C. W. Nance (President)

Offshore – The Backyard

At the time of the sale of the company in 1988, Tenneco was the number 1 or number 2 daily producer of gas in the Gulf. The company operated 435 wells on 230 producing platforms, and owned working interests in 329 federal leases. In addition, the company owned interests in nearly 500 additional wells that were operated by our partners.

TOE&P had platforms as far as 120 miles from shore and was served

The Operating Divisions

Pacific Coast (Bakersfield, CA)
DGM VP, Bob Bogan
EM   Al Stevens
PM   Clyde Crouch
Admin Gary Johnson

Rocky Mountain (Denver, CO)
DGM Bill Cayce
EM   Rod Eichler
PM   Louis Jones
Admin Andy Moreland

Mid-Continent (Oklahoma City, OK)
DGM Mike Lacey
EM   Gene Westover
PM   Doug Gundy
Admin Larry Shaver

Southwestern (San Antonio, TX)
DGM Wes Franklin
EM   Steve Mueller
PM   Mike Stewart

Gulf Coast (Houston, TX)
DGM VP, Bill Melnar
EM   Bill Hargett
PM   Herb Newhouse
Admin Jack Williams

Eastern Gulf of Mexico (Lafayette, LA)
DGM VP, Ad Wilkinson
EM   Bill VanWie
PM   Bob Waldrup
Admin Ron Lege

Central Gulf of Mexico (Lafayette, LA)
DGM VP, Bob Taylor
EM   Carlton Sheffield
PM   Harry Hufft
Admin Steve Durio

Western Gulf of Mexico (Lafayette, LA)
DGM Bob Bowie
EM   Ron Christie
PM   Tony Brown
Admin L J Olivier

International (Houston, TX)
DGM VP, Jack Gregory
EM   Art Beall
PM   Gary Mabie
Admin Don Karrasch

Norway (Houston, TX)
Ken Watts, Managing Director Norway

South America (Houston, TX)
DGM VP, Camilo Merendoni
EM   Jim Dorman
PM   Buddy Watsky
Admin Roy Patterson

by an 1800-mile network of pipelines predominately operated by Tennessee Gas or Tenneco Oil. Over its last 5 years of existence, Tenneco Oil E&P had daily gas deliveries in excess of 700 million cubic feet of natural gas per day and oil and condensate production exceeding 30,000BPD. Eight major fields contributed over half the total Tenneco production from the Gulf. These fields include West Cameron 180, Vermilion 245, Vermilion 250, South Marsh Island 78, Ship Shoal 198, South Marsh Island 66, Ship Shoal 169, and Mustang Island A31. Five of the top ten TOE&P fields, and 17 of the top 40, were located in the Gulf of Mexico. The Gulf of Mexico produced 25% of the company's liquids and 65% of its gas. It held 25% of the company's remaining reserves. Tenneco's proved, probable and possible reserves in the Gulf of Mexico were listed at 538MMNEB.

In addition to the producing properties, significant untested potential remained in the Gulf of Mexico at the time of the 1988 sale. The data room presentation to potential bidders cited 3 dozen different drilling programs that would permit the buyers of these properties to boost deliverability by 450 million cubic feet per day at a capital cost of less than $250 million. From an exploration point of view, 100 offshore exploration prospects and leads were shown in the Tenneco offshore areas, which were listed as having 4.1 billion gross equivalent barrels of potential hydrocarbon reserves. This remaining potential was created by continuing technical work, despite the offshore capital budget having been reduced from $300 million in 1980 to the $30-$40 million per year from 1985-87, as more and more capital dollars were diverted away from the energy side of Tenneco to address the issues on the industrial side.

Block by block, layer by layer, Tenneco Oil built an exceptional record of discovery over a thirty year period in the Gulf of Mexico. These were the principal fields which provided the basis for its growth in production from the Gulf. Annual production had expanded from two million barrels of oil equivalent (BOE) in 1959 to over twenty million BOE in 1988, a compounded growth rate of 8.5% per year, while replacing an average 10% per year natural decline. (Reserve figures shown from MMS records and are field totals, all operators).

TENNECO'S TOP GULF OF MEXICO FIELDS

1960s	1970s	1980s
South Marsh Island 66 (1.2TCF)	Main Pass-311 (120BCF+105 MMBO)	Mustang Island A-31 (265 BCF)
Ship Shoal 198/176 (1.3TCF+65MMBO)	East Cameron 271 (1.3TCF+ 69MMBO)	Mustang Island 847 (22BCF)
Ship Shoal 169 (879BCF+167MMBO)	High Island 270 (163 BCF)	Eugene Island 172 (100BCF+10 MMBO)
Vermilion 245 (508 BCF+47MMBO)	South Marsh Island 60 (1.3 TCF)	Chandeleur 29 (145 BCF)
Vermilion 250 (509 BCF+14MMBO)	Vermilion 246 (see V 245)	South Timbalier 100 (100 BCF)
West Cameron 180 (1.84TCF+13MMBO)	Ship Shoal 183/170 (878 BCF)	Mobile 864 (176 BCF)
West Cameron 165 (324BCF)		Vermilion 131 (654 BCF)
South Timbalier 196 (367BCF+7MMBO)		Vermilion 252/273 (140 BCF+27MMBO)
South Timbalier 22 (422BCF+256MMBO)		
South Marsh Island 78/79 (366 BCF)		

Truly, the Gulf of Mexico was E&P's "backyard". Reports are that Chevron fared well over the years that followed with the prizes they obtained at the sale. The portfolio was a gem, or a series of gems, and more than anything stands as a tribute to the people who assembled it over the years.

Was "the sky's the limit" the future for Tenneco before the sale in 1988 - as some data suggests?

Onshore – The Base

At the time of the Sale in 1988, onshore offices were located in Bakersfield, Denver, San Antonio, Oklahoma City, and Houston. In 1988 the company had interests in 20,800 wells, operating 4221 of those. Oil flowed from Yowlumne and Landslide fields, and the steamfloods in the San Joaquin Valley, and from the major waterfloods in the Mid-Continent and Southwestern Divisions, and the Four Eyes / Big Stick field in the Rockies. Primary gas producers were the Rockies with the San Juan Basin, Hugoton in the Mid-Continent, and the historic old fields of the Gulf Coast. The onshore offices produced 46% of the company's oil and liquids and 35% of the gas, and held about 42% of the remaining reserves.

"We were at the crossroads of an unprecedented new era of international exploration at Tenneco. We had assembled an outstanding organization and we anticipate that future success will outstrip current income projections."

Art Beall, (Explor Mgr, International)

International - The Romance

In 1988, TOE&P was producing oil from Colombia, the U.K. sector of the North Sea, Nigeria, Gabon and Tunisia. Production was scheduled to commence in the Norwegian sector of the North Sea in the early 1990s. International production was at an all-time high from quality fields with substantial and sustainable quality. The ownership positions were in generally stable countries with strong contracts. The company held 3.8 million net acres in 56 different licenses in eleven countries. Thirty TOE&P employees were located in offices in five countries and the number of Operators Inc personnel in overseas assignments had reached 45.

In the early months of 1988 wildcat drilling in Colombia had discovered several new fields – 26, in total since 1981. In the North Sea, beyond the production at Heather in the U.K. and the development at Heidrun in Norway, TOE&P was drilling a wildcat 600 miles south of the North Pole on Spitzbergen Island. In a contrast of extremes, the company was also at work in the Sahara desert of Egypt and in the jungles of Ecuador, New Guinea and Malaysia where we were operator for an onshore and offshore concession awarded in early 1988. International operations produced 30% of the company liquids and held 30% of the remaining reserves. Projects already underway were scheduled to increase both figures in very short order. The plan ahead clearly saw international ventures playing a larger role in Tenneco's world.

* * * * *

Data rooms for the sale were opened on July 25, 1988; bids were due on September 30, 1988. The winners of the auction for the assets of the Company were announced on October 11, 1988. National newspapers carried various versions of the following story:

Oil Company Sells for $7.3 Billion

AP News Story

Tenneco Inc. will receive $6.4 billion in cash after taxes and other expenses from the $7.3 billion sale of Tenneco Oil Company. The company announced Oct. 11 that the business is being sold in segments to a number of purchasers. The transactions will be concluded in a series of closings beginning in December.

Proceeds from the sale will be used to retire a large portion of the company's outstanding debt, and, depending on market conditions, to repurchase shares of the company's common stock. "Our board is extremely pleased with the outcome of the sale," James Ketelsen, Tenneco Chairman and CEO said. "The level of bids testifies to our ability to build value for our shareholders, and with the prevailing climate of unsettled oil prices we believe that now is an excellent time to realize that value for our shareholders' benefit."

The offerings were divided along geographic and industry lines into eight packages of exploration and production operations and three packages of refining and marketing holdings.

In its announcement, Tenneco Inc reiterated its commitment to maintain its annual common stock dividend of $3.04 per share. The company also said it will keep its headquarters in Houston.

The sale leaves Tenneco active in six businesses with annual revenues of $12 billion, or 75 percent of existing revenues. Tenneco Gas (which was not sold) generates roughly 25 percent of those revenues.

* * * * *

In just a few short months, the event that no one had considered, nor could even imagine had gone from a bad dream to "*fait accompli*," Tenneco Oil Company, was gone. A cynical reaction found its way around the halls, and the industry – "They've sold the farm so they can buy another tractor!"

Personal Reactions

The sale effort involved a variety circumstances that demonstrated the "personal" side of TOE&P. And why not, as Don Taylor noted in his comment above, "…it's the only way we knew how to work." It's appropriate to include a few examples of those attitudes here – after all, it's just another instance of that special "culture" showing through.

"When I first heard of the announcement of the sale of Tenneco Oil Co, piecemeal, the wind went right out of all my sails. With my thirty-two years of service I had a large number of personal ego sails flying from the many functions I had served. …. I felt as if my ego ship was powered by a big sail for each. I felt I had some credits from my participation in the acquisition of Kern County Land as well as many other Exploration & Production deals that I supported (during the time I served) as President of the oil company. When I heard about the pending dismemberment of the oil company, it seemed to me that all of these organizations to which I had contributed, along with the culture I had imbedded, were collapsing without human reason."

Cliff Rackley (TOP&M Pres, ret)

"….after Tenneco Inc. elected to sell off Tenneco Oil Co., the resulting restructuring of the company (TGT) cannot be done without pain. For over 40 years, the Pipeline Division worked side by side with our sister company and the relationship has been mutually beneficial. We will feel the loss deeply."

Bob Thomas (President, TGP)

Two of the most poignant of these pieces are letters that came from Wayne Nance and Joe Foster, a while after the decision to sell had been announced, but before the results were known. They are exceptional, but not surprising.

Reflections on E&P

"As I read the Offering Memorandums for the total company and geo-

WHAT WAS SOLD

Tenneco Oil Company included domestic and international exploration and production operations, a state-at-the art refinery and a chain of retail outlets. In 1987 the company had total sales of $3.3 billion and operating income of $233 million before interest and federal income taxes. It also had proved liquid petroleum reserves of 407 million barrels and natural gas reserves of 2.95 trillion cubic feet. Some 9,700 employees were affected by the sale.

CHEVRON $2.6 BILLION

Offshore Gulf of Mexico Divisions – Oil and natural gas reserves producing 700 million cubic feet of gas and 40,000 barrels of oil daily; 600,000 undeveloped acres

AMOCO PRODUCTION $900 MILLION

Rocky Mountain Division New Mexico gas reserves producing 70 million cubic feet of gas and 11,000 barrels natural gas liquids per day; interest in 4,000 producing wells; 50 percent ownership in Blanco gas producing plant

MESA LIMITED, MLP $715 MILLION

Mid-Continent Division – Oil and gas reserves producing 5,100 barrels of oil and 110 million cubic feet of gas daily

ARCO $670-$700 MILLION

Pacific Coast Division – California oil and gas reserves producing 32,000 barrels of oil and 24 million cubic feet of gas daily; 500,000 undeveloped acres

AMERICAN PETROFINA $600 MILLION

Gulf Coast, Southwestern Divisions – Oil and natural gas reserves of 28.4 million barrels of oil and 437 billion cubic feet of gas

BRITISH GAS
$194.5 MILLION

International Division – Reserves of 47 million barrels of oil equivalent (30 percent gas) and approximately 1.6 trillion cubic feet of undiscovered gas from acreage in Ecuador, Egypt, Gabon, Malaysia, Nigeria, The Bahamas, Trinidad, Tunisia, United Kingdom

ROYAL DUTCH SHELL GROUP
$500 MILLION

South American Division – Oil and gas reserves in Colombia producing 60,000 barrels of oil per day

CONOCO
$115 MILLION

International Division – Interests in 10 Norwegian North Sea licenses with 125 million net barrels of oil equivalent reserves awaiting development

SEAGULL ENERGY
$16.4 MILLION

Houston Oil & Minerals Corp., Houston Oil Trust, Houston Oil Royalty Trust – Texas Gulf Coast oil and gas reserves of 43.3 billion cubic feet of gas and 3.1 million barrels of oil

MOBIL
$650 MILLION

Chalmette, Louisiana Refinery – Produces daily 80,000 barrels of gasoline and 60,000 barrels of distillate

F. PHILIP HANDY

Retail service stations, 450 outlets in 13 states in the southeastern and southwestern U.S.

graphic packages, I felt a sense of pride in being a part of this organization.

The history of this company is impressive, and I am proud of the accomplishments it has achieved. I am proud of the values by which the company operates. I am proud of the people and their tremendous contributions and loyalty.

This is the Tenneco Oil that's up for sale - not just the properties that we own. This is the heart of the company. As I thought about these things, it occurred to me that no one can take away our self-worth or the record that we have compiled. In my opinion, it is a record that has been unequaled. Never before has there been a company for sale with such quality. We have all accomplished this by bearing the heat of the day and overcoming many obstacles in putting together the asset base of this company. You have served long and hard in building this organization.

I have a feeling of sadness when I consider new ownership. Even though I know that the future can still be bright for each of us, I know that things won't be the same. But as I reflect upon the company, I ask: "Why wouldn't someone want to buy the entire company and keep this organization together?" Indeed, I hope someone will. At least eight companies are interested in purchasing the total entity. I believe they will see the value of the people and the organization - not just its physical assets.

We have many commitments that we must honor. We must do this while making presentations to potential purchasers. Many of you have already been working long hours, and I am sure there will be many long days before this process is finished. I have not heard any complaints about the work. This says a lot about the character of Tenneco employees. We don't complain about the way things are, but we certainly question why they're that way. This is the mind-set of successful people, and it is the heart of an outstanding company.

I have also observed that relatively few terminations have been reported. This may mean that everyone feels we are in this together. We built this company together, and we will see it to the end together. I don't know what the future holds for any of us, but I am optimistic that something good will come out of this.

I have enjoyed the many cartoons that have circulated in recent weeks. We still have our sense of humor, and I think this is very healthy. We must be able to laugh to relieve the stress and tension and maybe even sometimes to cry together.

As I think about what is happening, there are times that tears come to my eyes. I recognize that the next few months will come and go, and Tenneco Oil will be sold and ownership will pass to new hands. Our world will be changed, but it will not end.

I am convinced in my own mind that the purchasing company will need us. As I face this change. I have the confidence that no one can take away from us the feeling that we have for each other.

We are good and we have a right to be proud of our record. We can let it speak for itself."

- Wayne Nance

Alleluia Anyway

"Not long after the announcement of the sale of Tenneco Oil, I was driving along the freeway feeling dejected and frustrated when I came up behind a car with a bumper sticker which said "Alleluia Anyway!"

Alleluia Anyway! It perked me up. That's about as good a response to trouble and frustration and disappointments we don't understand as any I know. Once one of those events occurs, what really matters is not "Why?" or "Why me?" but "How shall I respond?"

I want to tell you how proud I am of the way Tenneco Oil E&P has responded to the shocking sale announcement; With professionalism; With pride in the job you have done; With unity and teamwork and realism and humor; With hard work, above and beyond the call of duty; With support for one another; With a focus on the future.

It has been an "Alleluia Anyway" kind of response. I appreciate it! I also appreciate the many expressions of support I have received from so many of you; Cards; Notes; Phone calls; Comments in elevators and hallways and on street corners; I needed them, and I am grateful for them. I have been working to secure financial backing to permit an "LBO" -leveraged buyout - bid for E&P. Management and employees would have an ownership position in the resulting company. If its bid is successful, it would permit us to retain much of the culture and character and spirit of Tenneco Oil E&P.

At the present time, it appears we will have the financial support to make a bid. There is no way we could have obtained this backing without the superb reputation and track record Tenneco Oil E&P has established. Virtually all the financial people I talked to were well aware of Tenneco Oil E&P's outstanding performance record.

Everyone I have talked to in E&P is supportive of this LBO effort and has been helpful wherever possible. I'd like to make sure you understand several points about the LBO group:

First, the bid is being encouraged by Tenneco Inc. and Morgan Stanley, its investment banker. In their view, another bid by a knowledgeable bidder works to increase the value of the asset sale to Tenneco. I have the expressed consent of Tenneco Inc. to form such a bidding group, to use designated E&P employees in the evaluation, and to involve selected members of management in the review process.

Second, the outside investors in the LBO group are to receive no data or information that other bidders do not receive. The presence of an LBO group should in no way inhibit the efforts of E&P management or employees to obtain maximum value for the properties. I expect, and expect each of you, to behave in an absolutely ethical manner about this.

Third, the LBO group, which will be using primarily borrowed money, will be competing with some of the richest companies in the world in the bid-

THE LBO PROJECT

Joe Foster, Executive Vice President of Tenneco Inc. at the time of the Sale of Tenneco Oil, and the officer responsible for all of the Tenneco energy subsidiaries, recalls his efforts to pursue an "LBO" (leveraged buy-out) to purchase some of the company.

At the time of the sale of Tenneco Oil, I was one of 5 members of Tenneco's corporate office. I had responsibility for Tenneco's energy operations. I was also on its board. I strongly opposed the sale of Tenneco Oil. The CEO of Tenneco Inc. (J L Ketelsen) was its former CFO. He controlled the board. I learned in this process what many before me have learned - that it is impossible for an inside director to win a board battle against a sitting chairman who has spent years currying favor with the outside directors.

When the vote to sell Tenneco Oil was concluded, with my vote being the only "No" vote, the board told me that, if I thought I could find the financial backing and put together a credible bid, they would allow me to create a team of Tenneco Oil Company people with which to do all the technical, analytical, and legal work, and the negotiating required to raise money from the outside to make a leveraged buyout bid for the properties being offered. Further, Tenneco would foot the bill for the evaluation costs of what we called the LBO Team. The people on this team who were doing this work were already on the Tenneco Oil payroll and many no longer had growth projects to deal with. They were willing to do this because the Company had obligated itself to keep all employees on the payroll until the company was sold. The people not on the LBO Team were on the "Sell" Team, preparing data rooms and making presentations for potential buyers, under the direction of Morgan

I was permitted to select the "LBO Team" from each of the E&P Divisions in Tenneco Oil. I was on my own to go outside to find people in the business world willing to commit equity capital -remember now, the cost of the evaluation was basically being borne by Tenneco - and others who would provide debt capital. At that time, "leveraged buy-outs" were in vogue, with debt to capitalization ratios up to 90%. Those were the kinds of firms – on both the debt and equity side – that were willing to work with me and my Tenneco team.

Tenneco sold its oil company for $7.3 billion in 8 different packages E&P packages. Our LBO effort bid on just 2 of those packages, but were not successful on either one. We simply could not raise enough equity capital to make competitive bids against companies like Chevron, Arco, Amoco, and the other big oil companies who were bidders.

To the disappointment of most, but realistically, to no one's surprise, both of the LBO bids failed.

ding process. But I believe our group has a fighting chance to make a winning bid. Obviously, our investors think so or they wouldn't be willing to bear the expense of making a bid. But competition will be intense! There is no assurance we will be a buyer.

Fourth, even if the LBO group makes a winning bid, it will not be "business as usual" for Tenneco Oil E&P. Costs will have to be cut. Properties must be disposed of. Organizations will be changed. We can retain much of the culture and character and spirit which have been responsible for our success. But things will not be the "same." That's just a fact of life.

Whether the LBO group or another group is the buyer, I am optimistic that the new owners will need most of our working level people. I would not advise jumping ship prematurely. In any event, I think the kind of people we have in E&P will not be out of work for very long. There are plenty of other companies out there who wish to "build on quality," and our people offer quality. Of that I am sure.

In the meantime, let's do our jobs. Let's continue to behave professionally. Let's sell hard and operate well. If or when we have to turn the key over to someone else, let's do it with our heads held high, with the sure knowledge that we are winners. Then, collectively or individually, let's as the Crystal Gayle song says, "Do it all over again."

Thank you for your efforts in building an absolutely outstanding oil company, and thank you for your mature and professional reaction to Tenneco Inc.'s surprising decision to sell it. I count myself fortunate to be "one of you."

- Joe Foster

After the Sale
This Ballgame Is Not Over

By year-end 1988, most of the purchasers of the Tenneco Oil assets had closed their transactions. Employees were hard-about adjusting to new jobs with new bosses, looking for the next step in the careers, or using the unexpected "opportunity" provided by the loss of their lives at Tenneco to decide on their best next direction. A great many of the employees at Houston headquarters were actually busy with their jobs on the "transition team". There was a lot more work involved in dismantling 42 years of history than some might have anticipated. There was little time, and frankly at that point, little interest, in reflecting on just what had happened or in projecting what might be ahead in the future. As things settled out for most, it became obvious just how "special" a place TOE&P had been. The years that followed would only amplify this conclusion. This chapter will explore a bit of what happened to Tenneco and its employees and properties after the sale. It will also include a bit of retrospective analysis to add clarity to the thinking that led to the decision to sell the company.

The Future

Adapted from the Final E&P Update – November 1988

"We entered the Sale not as a company that had run out of prospects, potential or vision … we were poised to enter the 1990s." Those words were spoken to visiting executives of prospective purchasers. Would this future have held?

Today, six months after the plan was submitted, the oil side of the price assumption looks shaky, but gas prices are near target. As prices go, so would E&P's income. The years ahead would have seen accelerated development of the new South Marsh Island 78 gas field in the Central Gulf Division, along with completion of several short-term gas development programs offshore. The Texas Offshore Pipeline System was scheduled to begin deliveries from the Western Gulf's Mustang Island A-31 field in 1989.

Onshore, the plan projected higher gas production from the San Juan Basin and Hugoton fields, and higher oil production from the Placerita field cogeneration project.

In the International sector, a new pipeline system in Colombia's Magdalena Valley would have greatly increased oil deliveries from that nation. Oil production was scheduled to being in 1990 from a floating rig in the Heidrun Field offshore Norway, with a massive concrete platform planned for installation in 1993.

Summing up impact of these projects, the company's liquids production was projected to reach record levels of nearly 157,000BPD in 1993, with gas deliveries remaining flat at about a billion cubic feet per day after a spike upward in the early 1990s.

Some of these events will still occur, some with E&P people working on them, but no one will ever know what else the E&P team might have achieved.

It Was A Tie

During the summer of 1988 exploration and exploitation projects were accelerated to provide add value to the company with new reserves and production. Green Canyon 205 was a very recent deep water discovery TOC operated jointly with Exxon. It was a dandy! Exxon would not give Tenneco permission to show the results to potential bidders because it was a tight hole. If it wasn't shown, it was highly likely the GOM value would be diminished. The two company's legal departments argued, but Exxon wouldn't budge. Tenneco Inc counsel Walter Sapp and Steve Chesebro', manager of the Sale for Tenneco Inc. discussed it at length. Chesebro' proposed showing the information if Tenneco would indemnify him. Sapp ruled that out but Chesebro' nevertheless showed logs, cores, tests, seismic, and maps to interested companies.

One of the more contentious issues with the sale of TOC was whether Tennessee Gas Pipeline would retain all, or a portion of the contractual rights,

ON WHAT MIGHT HAVE BEEN

"I can't help but wonder what the outcome might have been had TGT, Refining and Marketing, and E&P been spun off and allowed to compete on their own. Cliff (Rackley), Ralph (Cunningham) and Bob (Thomas) had established similar cultures and outstanding organizations at P&M and TGT. Combined, it could have been a great story. However, all we can do is speculate. My years in Tenneco Inc. corporate planning revealed a corporate culture far different than I had experienced at Tenneco Oil. I don't know how many times Joe (Foster) kept me from being hung, but it was several. The telling factor of events to come, was that of the top five active (Tenneco Inc.) executives, only one (Joe Foster) came from the energy companies. The handwriting was on the wall and we never had the chance to perform as stand-alone companies.

I have no doubt that TOE&P, had it survived would have continued to evolve and would have been right in the middle of all of the significant developments that have come along since the sale. Just look at where our people went and what they've done. 'We' were there, 'we' just weren't Tenneco, then.

We'd have been there with everything….. deepwater... shale ….whatever."

C E Shultz (Sr VP)

"We had Athabasca, Heidrun (1.5 Bbbl), San Francisco - We were in coal-bed methane before anyone – that's the precursor to all the shale plays – we just ran out of time."

S D Chesebro' (Tenn Inc)

NOTABLE SUCCESSFUL CAREERS AFTER TENNECO

Following the sale of TOE&P, the workforce found itself looking in all directions for jobs and careers. One of the topics of comment among many Tenneco alums in the years that followed the sale was the degree to which the "Tenneco Style" circulated throughout the entire energy industry. It was well known that E&P had a great workforce – that's reviewed extensively in the main narrative – but when you sit down and put a pencil to it, it's just short of astounding to see how many Tenneco alumni achieved exceptional success in their subsequent careers. Many succeeded in careers with the majors, the large independents, and the smaller public and private firms. It's an amazing list. Many of the Tenneco folks also went into business for themselves, frequently in small groups who had worked together in their "E&P" days. If one had the resources to track down all of the success stories it would likely be a book or two in and of itself.

In the years following the sale, numerous discussions among Tenneco management have included the observation that the sale may have created career upside for many of these folks. We had a flat and lean management structure at TOE&P, and in the long run, probably did not have enough top jobs available to cover the incredible number of talented people listed below. (A caveat to this list – It is certain that there are many folks out there who should be included on this list. The compilation following was built through inquiries to and responses from various Tenneco "ex'es", but we did not have a complete 'network' to access. Given the years since the sale, it was impossible to locate everyone. That is a great disappointment to the editors. Be assured that no

to dedicated gas contracts. Obviously, a major portion of TOC's production in the GOM and along the Gulf Coast was dedicated to TGP. Producers wanted absolute control of their production, and had spent a lot of time and effort to that end. Many potential bidders expressed their desire to have all the gas released from TGP contracts. TOC felt that releasing the gas from the contracts would fetch a higher price. TGP was going through the deregulation process, but still had merchant obligations, so they needed at least some remaining dedicated gas. So, Chesebro' included in the final bidding instructions that the base line was for the contracts to stay in place, but if a bidder wanted them released it would detract from their bid. The bidders were welcomed to quantify the value of releasing the gas contracts to them.

As it turned out, Shell and Chevron both bid $2.6 billion for the GOM properties. Shell said if TGP kept the contracts, their bid would be reduced by $275 million. Chevron said their bid was firm, but after one year all contracts would be reopened. In other words, TGP would lose the gas at that time. The bids were submitted on a Friday, and all winning, and second place bidders were to be in Houston on the following Monday to sign binding contracts. By Wednesday, discussions with Shell and Chevron regarding their "tie" bids made some progress, but nothing was finalized. That afternoon, the two company's presidents and natural gas managers were located on the 30th floor of the Tenneco Building. Shell got their first, so they were stationed in the board room. Chevron was next, so they got the luxury of the exercise room, weights and all. At that time, both companies were told that there was a tie, but the other bidder was not identified. Each was told that the first one to let the gas contracts remain with TGP would be the winner, immediately. After about two hours Chevron agreed, and you know the rest of the story. Shell did not believe there was another bidder, to their chagrin Friday when all the winners were announced after signing Sale/Purchase agreements. Fourteen agreements totaling $7.5 billion were negotiated and signed in five days. Tenneco received full value for the properties, as exhibited by the GOM price. In fact, the value received was more than Tenneco Inc. expected, or even hoped for.

"Pre-Sale" Options / "Post-Sale" Reflection

By Spring of 1988, Tenneco Inc. had concluded it had few viable options to its financial predicament, other than the sale of the energy companies. A look back indicates that was not necessarily the case. There are, however, several indications from prior (and subsequent) events that suggest the preference of the management of the company had turned from energy in favor of manufacturing as the pathway forward. Retrospect would suggest that was not wise. Some might call these following observations "Sour Grapes", but if so...

1) We're probably entitled to a few, and

2) These do provide some perspective, sour or not.

Get Another Opinion

An account from Chuck Shultz, lifelong TOE&P employee, on assignment in Tenneco Inc. corporate planning at the time -

"A Tenneco Inc. management meeting, held at TenneCott in September of 1987, featured a presentation to the upper management of the company by a consulting group that had been hired to evaluate "strategic options" for the corporation. The firm had done an extensive review of all of the business units within the conglomerate and reported that TOE&P and TGT were the biggest "winners" amongst the subsidiaries. The manufacturing businesses were identified as the "losers", and among those, J. I. Case was listed at the bottom. Following that presentation Tenneco Inc. management hired McKinsey and Co. for a "second opinion". After their analysis, McKinsey recommended selling the oil company. "

The CEO's Perspective

A paraphrased account of a speech given by Mr. Ketelsen in May 1987 (one year before the sale) demonstrates his thought process –

"Tenneco Inc. is comprised of approximately eight major subsidiaries. Basically though, we are three things – Energy, J. I. Case, and 'everything else'. Energy accounts for 51% of our assets and 49% of our income. J. I. Case has 19% of our assets and negative income (to say nothing of the debt). 'Everything else' makes up 31% of our assets and 51% of our income. We measure things by "return on net assets employed". Energy right now is not so good – we need an improvement in energy prices. If the future for Tenneco's energy operation is not inviting, then the future of the entire energy business is grim. "We view Case IH as a turnaround with potential for significant increases in NOI."

Foster Offers Alternatives

Joe Foster's own summary of the events of the Tenneco Inc Board Meeting at which the decision was made to sell Tenneco Oil Company –

At the May 24, 1988 Board Meeting of Tenneco Inc. at the Plaza Hotel in New York City, the Tenneco Inc Board of Directors listened politely as Joe Foster made a strong argument opposing the sale of Tenneco Oil Company and offering an alternate proposal.

Foster listed the following negatives of selling Tenneco Oil:

1. It does not make sense to sell a value-creating organization which represents 40% of the enterprise value of Tenneco Inc. Further, the oil company is a strong cash-generator and a recognized performance leader as compared to its peer companies in both the upstream and downstream oil and gas businesses.

2. It does not make sense to sell one of the earliest businesses of Tenneco, a core business which is profitable, which has significant upside, and offers numerous synergies with Tennessee Gas Transmission Company.

3. A sale of Tenneco Oil leaves Tenneco Inc. not only less profitable, but

slight is intended with the inclusion or exclusion of anyone listed below), but the list, incomplete as it may be, clearly makes the point that we had a great many special people at TOE&P).

Senior Management
Joe Foster, Executive Vice President of Tenneco Inc. – became Founder, President, Chairman and CEO, Newfield Exploration Co –ret. 2004 (see Newfield list below), Interim CEO – Baker-Hughes Corporation

Wayne Nance, President Tenneco Oil E&P - became Consultant, Director Cabot Oil & Gas, ret.

Steve Chesebro', Senior Vice President, TOE&P, prior to 1988; President, Tenneco Gas Marketing - became President and CEO post-sale, The "new" Tenneco Energy (TGP),TGP sold to El Paso in 1996, President and CEO, Director, Pennzoil/Pennz Energy, Chairman, Harvest Natural Resources

Chuck Shultz, Senior Vice President, TOE&P – became President and Chief Executive Officer, Gulf Canada Resources Limited, Chairman, Gulf Canadian Oil Sands Limited, Director, Enbridge Inc. & Enbridge Pipelines, Newfield Exploration Company, Co-Founder & Chairman, Matrix Solutions Inc., Founder, Chairman and Chief Executive Officer, Dauntless Energy Inc.

Don S. Taylor, Senior Vice President, TOE&P – became Executive Vice President Deep Tech International, CEO Tatham Offshore, (dec. 2006)

Harold Korell, Vice President Production - became Executive Vice President, McCormick Resources, Senior Vice President, American Exploration, Various executive positions, ending as CEO and Chairman, Southwestern Energy, ret. 2011, Chairman BOD, Southwestern Energy

Larry Augsburger, Vice President, Administration – became CEO, Owner, Samik Physical Therapy and Rehabilitation

Harry Briscoe, Vice President Exploration – became President and COO, Tatham Offshore, Exec. Vice President DeepTech International, ret. 2005

Alphabetical

Bill Albrecht, Project Petroleum Engineer, Southwestern Division – became President, OXY USA

Ron Barnes, TGP contracts at sale, long-time E&P Landman – became Executive Vice President, Oil and Gas Clearinghouse

Jack Bergeron, Project Petroleum Engineer, Southwestern Division – became Sr. Vice President, Southwestern Energy

Rick Bott, Exploration Geologist, International Division – became President and COO Continental Resources

Ron Christie, Exploration Manager, Western Gulf of Mexico – became President and COO, Cockrell Oil Corporation

Clyde Crouch, Production Manager Pacific Coast Division – became Senior Vice President, Hess Corporation

Phil deLozier, Senior Landman, Economic Planning & Analysis – became VP, Acquisitions and Development, Enervest Management Partners

Paul Doyle, Division Production Engineer, Gulf Coast Division – became Director, Production and Construction, Tana, LLC

Doug Eberts, Division Drilling Engineer, Pacific Coast Division – became President, Sierra Resources, Inc.

Rod Eichler, Exploration Manager, Rocky Mountain Division – became President and COO, Apache Corporation

Wes Franklin, General Manager, Southwestern Division - became General Manager North

less coherent, with no "theme". It becomes an amalgamation of a regulated pipeline company with a conglomeration of disparate companies ranging from ship building to packaging to automotive parts to farm equipment and insurance.

4. The sale of Tenneco Oil is likely financial overkill. Six billion dollars are not required to preserve corporate financial ratings or repair its balance sheet. This sale and its infusion of cash will not create the environment for cost reduction, or for streamlining and financial discipline in those business units which Tenneco will retain. Several of those divisions have no track record of financial discipline.

5. The sale does not address the looming near-term problems at Case IH. To the contrary, it enables the current dysfunction to continue. It provides the capability for further subsidies to Case. It erects no barriers to prohibit or inhibit them from poor business decisions and ignores the fact that the industry outlook for Case is poor.

6. The sale will be viewed with skepticism by the stock market. It will be construed as selling profitable assets in order to subsidize questionable ones. It is a strong deviation from our stated direction of capitalizing on our energy capability and taking advantage of what those of us in the energy sector see as a coming gas price play.

7. Tennessee Gas will lose its benefit of producer/pipeline integration. Tennessee Gas Transmission is a much stronger competitor and earnings producer as a result of its interplay on the supply side and in the gas market with Tenneco Oil E&P.

8. The energy business is a good, long-term business; better than the tractor business, the packaging business, the automotive parts business, the chemical business, and the insurance business or any combination of them. The integrated energy business offers exposure to long term price upside as well as to the upside potential of "company changing" discoveries. Evidence of this is that, both inside and outside Tenneco, our energy entities are highly valued.

9. Finally, apart from the "value" issues, the sale of Tenneco Oil presents significant questions of internal equity among business units and employees which will likely lead to ongoing negative culture and morale issues.

Foster made an alternate proposal for Tenneco Inc. to:

1. Sell $1.5 billion of energy assets and $1.5 billion of manufacturing assets, which would, in Foster's estimation, bring in cash (and rid the company of cash drain) sufficient to get the remaining cash drain from Case under control. These proceeds would come from Newport News, Albright and Wilson, and some smaller marginal businesses.

2. Announce its firm intent to sell 20% of Cash IH via an IPO as market conditions permit, so that both the "Street" and other units of Tenneco would have evidence that "changes were coming" at Case to make it a more competitive independent entity. These other units to be offered for sale would include Newport News Shipyards and Albright/Wilson Chemicals.

3. Announce and undertake a defined program to reduce Tenneco Inc corporate and business unit overhead and A&G expenses. Foster volunteered to seek $60 million of overhead cuts on the energy side of the business as part of a larger overhead reduction effort in Tenneco Inc.

Foster then listed the following advantages of the alternative proposal:

1. It would be a "crown jewel" strategy. It would allow Tenneco to retain assets and operations where it had established both leadership and upside.

2. It would continue Tenneco's integrated producer-pipeline strategy. It would not be a dramatic change in direction, but a clear re-structuring which would result in two well-defined business segments. The Energy segment, which would likely be valued on an asset basis and the Industrial segment, likely valued on an earnings basis.

3. This strategy would not only be more even handed internally, it would take the first step of insulating Case IH from the rest of Tenneco.

Joe B. Foster, Executive Vice President of Tenneco Inc.

Foster closed by illustrating that the financial parameters from this option looked reasonable. Sale of E&P properties with high depletion, depreciation, and amortization (DD&A) rates plus removal of North Sea capital requirements would improve both earnings and cash flow from energy operations. Further, from a debt service standpoint, better long term borrowing ratios would be achieved with retention of energy cash flow in Tenneco.

He then made the following recommendations:

1. Proceed with obtaining bids, in packages, for most U. S. onshore properties. However, the Pacific Coast Division, the Hugoton (Texas Panhandle) properties, and a few smaller selected onshore areas would not be offered for bid.

2. Seek bids for a package of high DD&A (e.g. high unit cost) properties in the Gulf of Mexico.

3. Begin negotiation of the sale of Norway properties to Total. Seek bids for U.K. properties.

4. Proceed with negotiations with Pemex on refinery joint venture. Talk again to Venezuela and other potential buyers.

5. Offer Newport News and A&W Chemicals for sale.

6. Develop a program for corporate-wide cost reduction program of A&G, general operating expense, and corporate overhead.

7. Develop a plan of reorganization to ultimately permit separation

America Exploration, American Petrofina

John Gray, Vice President, Oil and Gas Marketing – became President and COO, Leviathan Natural Gas Pipeline Partners, MLP

Jack Gregory, Vice President, International Division – became Director and General Manager, British Gas International

Bill Hargett, Exploration Manager, Gulf Coast Division – became President , North Central Oil, President, Amax Oil and Gas, President, Snyder Oil / Santa Fe Energy, President, Houston Exploration, later CEO/Chmn

Scott Heck, Senior Petroleum Engineer, Pacific Coast Division – became Senior Vice President, Hess Corporation

Tim Hildenbrand, Senior Geological Engineer, South America Division – became President – Zachry Exploration Co.

Mike Hinze, Division Landman / Project Leader – became Senior Vice President, Land, Sabine Oil and Gas

Harry Hufft, Production Manager, Central Gulf of Mexico – became President, Graham Royalty Ltd., Vice President Exploration & Production, Forcenergy Inc., Vice President New Resource Capture, Altura Energy, President & General Manager Mid Continent/Rockies, Oxy US, Vice President, Oxy USA

Louis Jones, Production Manager, Rocky Mountain Division - became   Vice President, Hess Corporation

Mike Lacey, Division General Manager Mid Continent Division – became Senior VP Exploration and Production, Devon Energy

Lance Lauk, Production Engineer, Mid Continent Division – became Senior Vice President, PDC

Loren Leiker, Division Geologist, South America – became Executive Vice President EOG Resources (ret. 2011)

Fred Lentjes, General Manager Argosy Offshore, LTD – became Vice President, Petro-Marine/BCI Engineering

Lindy Looger, Senior Project Petroleum Engineer, Norway – became President, EOG International

Gary Mabie, Production Manager, International Division – became President and COO, Milargo Exploration

Ron Manz, Senior Geophysical Specialist, South America Division – became Vice President International, Nexen Exploration

Bob McBride, Senior Project Production Engineer, International Division – became]Vice President Operations, American Exploration

Brady McConaty, Project Production Engineer, International Division – became President, Merrimac Oil & Gas, LLC

Camilo Merendoni, Vice President and General Manager, South America Division – became Vice President, South America, Shell, CEO, Bridas Energy, Argentina – sold to Amoco, CEO, Bridas Energy International, ret. 2002

Chuck Mills, Director, Employee Relations became Vice President, Employee Relations, Hunt Oil

Steve Mueller, Exploration Manager Southwestern Division – became CEO Southwestern Energy

Greg Nakanishi, Manager Organizational Development and Training – became Vice President, Human Resources, Baker Hughes Corp. (ret 2007)

Elliott Pew, Senior Exploration Geologist, Southwestern Division – became Senior Vice President Exploration, American Exploration Company, Vice President Exploration, Newfield Exploration Co., Co-Founder, Chief Operating Officer, Common Resources

of energy and industrial companies.

a. If required, begin proceedings at FERC to transfer pipeline assets.

b. Decide where Case IH fits best and finalize plans for Case IH IPO, which would result in it becoming a stand-alone entity.

c. Develop plans for 1988 and 1989 write-offs associated with restructuring.

d. Seek to complete $1 billion of energy asset sales by January 1, 1989.

e. Seek to complete $1 billion of industrial assets sales by January 1, 1989.

f. Complete all asset sales by July 1, 1989.

g. By January 1, 1990, have strategy for dealing with remaining ownership in Case IH completed and be prepared legally and tax wiser to separate Case IH from Tenneco.

Joe Fogg of Morgan Stanley then gave a presentation of the divestiture plan recommended by Morgan Stanley, Ketelsen, and his direct reports, including members of Tenneco Inc.'s corporate office, other than Foster. (Morgan Stanley represented Tenneco in the Sale and earned a substantial fee for doing so).

Foster's Personal Notes

Joe Foster's personal notes from 5/28/88 recall the Board meeting at which the vote to sell the company was taken:

On Tuesday, May 24th of this week, Tenneco's board voted to "offer for sale" Tenneco Oil Company. I voted against it, talked against it, and was very sad to see it happen.

We met in room 937 of the Plaza in New York, ostensibly to make it easy for our Director David Plastow to come from London, and to accommodate directors Sisco, Eichoff, and Harris. It was probably also better for the investment bankers, and to get out of Houston, away from the press and employees. Maybe also, it was to avoid the large portrait of Gardiner Symonds in the Houston board room that looked down over these deliberations.

The meeting began with an "executive session" between Jim Ketelsen and the outside directors which lasted over 1½ hours. I don't know what was said in there. Nobody volunteered anything, although I asked Peter Flawn what sort of commitment they got out of Jim on dealing with Case. He didn't remember the exact words and was vague about the commitment.

The meeting itself was pretty cut and dried. Joe Fogg from Morgan Stanley made his presentation.

I made mine. I genuinely believe I had credible numbers to demonstrate that we could get by comfortably during the next 2-3 years with low oil/gas prices, still "maintain our ratings," and retain the bulk of our oil and gas business. My two closers were;

1) "A good long term business, and an outstanding player within it do not add up to decision to exit."; and

2) "Leave the shareholders with the best of what they bought. Keep the crown-jewels, not the laggards."

The vote was taken. I was the only one to vote "No."

There were expressions of regret.

(Editor note – clearly Mr. Foster's alternative proposals would have had a significant affect on TOE&P, but likewise clearly, there were alternatives. See the Epilogue for an independent outside-generated analysis of the decision that was made, and the outcome of that decision year's later as it worked out for what remained of Tenneco Inc.)

Ketelsen Reports

The following are excerpts from Mr. Ketelsen's Letter to the Shareholders in the 1988 Tenneco Annual Report (issued in early 1989):

I am pleased to report that in 1988 Tenneco returned to profitability, took a series of major steps to enhance the value of your shares, and positioned the Company for much improved earnings performance in 1989 and beyond. The most significant event of the year was the $7.6 billion sale of Tenneco's oil and gas businesses, a difficult but necessary move that enabled us to unlock significant immediate value for shareholders and restore our flexibility to capitalize on growth opportunities in our remaining businesses.

The decision to discontinue any business is always difficult. This was particularly true with Tenneco Oil Company, which had been developed over the decades into an aggressive, fully-integrated operation with a remarkable record of success. In recent years, however, the steady decline in oil prices on the world market, combined with the high cost of replacing reserves, clouded the company's prospects for future profitability. Despite cost containment measures and other controls, it became clear that the oil division could not regain its former levels of profitability so long as prevailing oil and gas prices were inadequate to justify the required capital outlays. We simply were not satisfied to wait an indefinite period of time for that to happen. We also recognized that our properties and refining operations represented substantial value that was not being reflected in our stock price and which could best be unlocked by their sale. We believed that these assets could be sold at a premium to an industry hungry to improve its assets by acquiring proven reserves and modern refineries.

With proceeds from the sale, Tenneco purchased approximately 21 million shares of common stock at $50 per share and applied almost $5 billion to debt reduction. At current interest rates, this debt reduction would produce an estimated interest expense savings of $500 million.

Those who have been familiar with Tenneco over the years know of our commitment to leadership in all of the industries in which we participate. They also know that, with the sale of our oil businesses in 1988, we have moved from an energy-orientation to an industrial-orientation. Today, Tenneco is a diversified industrial company with interests in natural gas pipelines, farm and construction equipment, automotive parts, shipbuilding, packaging, chemicals and minerals.

Mike Rosinski, Manager, Tenngasco – became Chief Financial Officer, Santa Fe Energy Resources, Senior Vice President and Chief Operating Officer, Municipal Energy Resources Corporation, Executive Vice President and Chief Financial Officer, Rosetta Resources

Ken Roy, Senior Project Production Engineer, Pacific Coast Division – became Vice President, Baker Oil Tools, Vice President, Enron Oil & Gas

John Simon, Division Production Engineer, South America Division – became Senior Vice President, Hess Corporation

Jeff Sherrick, Senior Petroleum Engineering Specialist, Economic Planning & Analysis – became Senior Vice President, Bus. Development, Enron Oil & Gas, Chairman, CEO & President, Enron Global Exploration & Production, Senior Vice President, El Paso Production Company, Senior Vice President, Houston Exploration Company, Senior Vice President, Corporate Development, Southwestern Energy

Cathy Sliva, Senior Petroleum Engineer, Economic Planning & Analysis – became Founding Partner, Blue Rock Capital Ventures

Dan Tearpock, Project Geological Engineer, Central Gulf of Mexico – became President and founder – Subsurface Consultants, Inc.

Al Turner, Project Manager, International Division – became Senior Vice President, Operations, Triton Energy

Jeff Ventura, Project Petroleum Engineer, International – became President, Range Resources

Bill Van Wie, Exploration Manager, Eastern Gulf of Mexico – became Vice President, Exploration, Devon Petroleum Corp.

Matt Wurtzbacher, Petroleum Engineer, Central Gulf of Mexico – became President and COO, Caerus Oil and Gas, LLC

Newfield Exploration Company was founded after the Sale by Joe Foster. That company was initially staffed almost exclusively with Tenneco alumni, and over the years has enjoyed its own record of exceptional success (See Mr. Foster's book – "Something From Nothing"). The following Tenneco "Ex-es" have all held executive positions at Newfield. The company is still managed predominantly with a "Tenneco-inspired" core.

Joe Foster – Chmn, CEO, Founder
Lee Boothby – Chmn, President, CEO
George Dunn – Sr. VP Development
Sam Langford - VP Corp Development
Ron Lege - Controller
Jim Metcalf – VP Drilling
Gary Packer - EVP and COO
Elliott Pew – Executive VP Exploration (see above)
Terry Rathert – Executive Vice President and CFO
Dave Schaible - President, dec. 2007
Bill Schneider – Sr. VP Exploration
Mark Spicer - VP Information Technology
Mike Van Horn – VP Geoscience
Bob Waldrup – VP Production
Jim Zernell – VP Production

EVEN IN ARGENTINA
"There was a standing joke at Devon when we first met with a new company. My boss, Larry Nichols (Devon CEO) would always ask me who among the folks on the other side were the Tenneco people? My response was, "Oh this one, this one, this one and this one….there were always some. He was really shocked when we met with an Argentine company and I pointed out that Camilo Merendoni was indeed an ex, as well."
Mike Lacey (DGM, MCD)

Tenneco Gas remains one of the largest natural gas transportation systems in the United States with some 18,000 miles of pipeline. Its deliveries of natural gas were up by 9 percent in 1988.

(Editor note – although technically correct, the information reported above is misleading as to the reason driving the decision for the Sale – that being poor returns in recent years. It would have been impossible for improvements in the market to create the $5 Billion or so needed to pay down debt. The debt, in particular off balance sheet debt, was the immediate issue.)

Ketelsen Reflects

In 2005, seven years after the sale of Tenneco Oil, Mr. Ketelsen provided further insight as to the corporate thinking during the times that led up to – and after – the decision to sell.

"This sits as a backdrop to the period as we went into the 1980s. I think we went into almost what you call a "perfect storm" in terms of the fact that we had the deregulation of the pipeline business and all the contractual problems of getting out of long-term gas contracts. It costs us a lot of time and money. The drop in oil prices is the second thing. In '84, '85, '86, oil had hit $30 a barrel. Then it proceeded to go down and I think in '86 or '87 it was down to $12 a barrel. Natural gas mirrored it. It went up to I guess $3 and back down under a dollar or $1.20 or something."

James Ketelsen, Tenneco Inc. CEO

" …Of course, the investment community is beating on the door, "break it up, break it up", and I did not want to break it up. But the asset that we had to get us out of this thing had the most value out there, which was unrecognized in the Tenneco portfolio, if you are going to create value, the one asset we had to create value was with the oil company. The other companies in the business certainly had a higher price deck than we were looking at internally where the oil price was going to go. The other thing was that we had built up most of our production at a time when prices were quite good and therefore costs were quite high. And Joe Foster would say this, we had a lot of high cost properties and we don't have that reservoir from the 30's and 40's that an Exxon -Mobil or these other guys that had very cheap base, long term production to work with. So we were in a different position. I made the decision, with prompting from the financial community and our own financial department that we would sell the oil company. It was not a pleasant decision or one that I liked, but it looked like one thing we could do to keep Tenneco. Our debt had gone up, no question about that. It wasn't to the point where there was any kind of crisis, nor were rates changing that much, but it was out of line if you looked at capitalization. One of the things that hurt also, and it's a minor item to some extent, was accounting changed in that period. You had to present your finance companies consolidated with industrial companies. You used to be able to keep those totally separate and present a separate balance sheet and everything for the finance companies and insurance companies and things like that. The accounting rules changed and you had to put all that on your balance sheet. The debt didn't change any, but it made it look worse when you consolidate it. That hurt us in the eyes of the investment public."

"…You know it's a problem when you are in a business like that (J. I. Case), because it's not very salable. There isn't anybody that's going to buy the damn thing. So you've almost got to make it work. The write-off (of Case debt) would have been devastating to us. It would have exacerbated the debt load from the other businesses."

"…Well, I'll hand it to Scotty (Wilton E Scott), he didn't say anything. I know damn well he didn't like it, and I wouldn't have if I was him either. But that looked like the thing that we needed to do."

"I thought Joe Foster had done a fantastic job of building a company with terrific people. I thought it was a hell of a good business, but as I say, if you were going to try and not completely disassemble Tenneco, you had to sell something of value, not something that was overvalued on your books. You can't get out of the problem that way. I think I made one major mistake there in looking back at it now, as I think about it. And again, it was the investment bankers and everybody that were advising us to sell it. The reason for doing it was the debt load would allow us to get in better financial condition than we were in. But they said, the shareholders have got to get something out of this. Part of the money has to go to them with a share buyback ..... And we bought back a little over a billion dollars-worth of stock, I think, … in looking back, that was a major mistake. We should have just toughed it out."

"Joe Foster argued that we should sell the properties that were (marginal and)get out of (the) refining and marketing business, but hang on to some of our better lower cost production properties and keep a smaller staff of people in the oil company. I don't know whether a billion, three hundred million (the stock buy-back) would have been enough to have retained enough of management. But if it had been, that would have been the way to go, preferably. You know you always say, what if, what if. I don't know whether we had done it that way and not bought back any shares what would have happened to us. I just don't have any idea. I don't think it did anything for the shareholders, frankly at the time, there wasn't anybody that was willing to give us any kind of an opinion that we didn't have to do something like that. So we did it."

"#!*&,
they've sold the farm so they can buy another tractor."

Overheard on sale day

IV

POSTSCRIPT

EPILOGUE

What Happened to Tenneco?

Why would the parent company, Tenneco Inc., choose to sell Tenneco Oil Company, its largest earnings contributor? This was a common question when the sale was announced in 1988 and is still being asked today.

Dale E. Zand, a management consultant and Professor of Management, Emeritus, at the Stern School of Business, New York University chronicled a background study in 2009 of Tenneco and the issues it was forced to address leading up to Tenneco Oil Company's sale. His case study entitled "Managing Enterprise Risk: Why a Giant Failed" was published in Strategy & Leadership (Volume 37, issue 1) and can be found on the internet. Zand's study was based on extensive interviews of management, board members, and a review of documents and publications. He was also previously a management consultant to Tenneco Oil Company from 1981 through 1988.

The purpose of Zand's study was to document the dismantling of Tenneco because it failed to manage risk. Behind its actions of problematic acquisitions and questionable financial policies were underlying lessons that could serve as counsel for other companies. Our purpose here will be to document those actions and occurrences that lead to selling the Oil Company. The information herein only relates to our purpose, but full context of the case is available through the Strategy & Leadership publication.

Managing Enterprise Risk: Why a Giant Failed
Adapted from the Study by Dale E. Zand
Prof. of Management (emeritus), Stern School of Business
New York University (KMC 8-90)

When a large prosperous firm fails, it offers a uniquely valuable opportunity to study what can go wrong in the management of enterprise risk. The precipitous fall and dismantling of Tenneco Inc., once ranked eighteenth in the Fortune 500, illustrates how a company management accustomed to prosperity put an enterprise at risk by making problematic acquisitions and adopting questionable financial policies that became destructive when the firm experience volatile earning. But Tenneco's decline from a seemingly unassailable position also has a lot to do with the relationship between its CEO, senior managers, and the board. Tenneco needed prudent senior managers and a tough-minded board to rein in its overly optimistic, risk taking decisions. Too often, however, rather than rock the boat, managers and the board approved dubious ventures and choices.

Tenneco originated in the 1940s as a natural-gas-pipeline company – a federally chartered and regulated public utility. It then started an oil-exploration-and-production company, Tenneco Oil Company, and later acquired several unrelated businesses. In the early 1980s, Tenneco was a large, moderately diversified firm with 103,000 employees worldwide. With $15 billion revenues and $2 billion earnings in 1981, it ranked ahead of AT&T, Boeing and Dow Chemical in the Fortune 500.

By 1982 its two energy businesses, generated 76 percent of Tenneco's earnings. Tenneco Oil Company (TOC), a low-cost finder and producer of oil and gas, had become the firm's star performer and contributed 54 percent of earnings. The natural gas pipeline Tennessee Gas Transmission (TGT), one of the top three in the US, was a high-volume, low-cost system serving the burgeoning demand in the mid-Atlantic and northwest and contributed 22 percent of earnings.

A group of unrelated manufacturing, mineral mining, petrochemical, and insurance businesses contributed the remaining 24 percent of corporate earnings. The largest was J.I. Case, a manufacturer of agricultural and construction equipment. Other smaller divisions included Newport News Shipbuilding, a builder of naval vessels; Walker Automotive, a manufacturer of automotive equipment; and Packaging Corp. of America, a packaging manufacturer. This diversification, according to the CEO, smoothed Tenneco's earnings and balanced its investment program. Profitable businesses, he asserted, offset poor performers and funded investments that strengthened weak performer. In practice, this usually meant that the energy business supported the other businesses. The history of how Tenneco managed this diversification and the risks that arose from it provides insight into the corporation.

Years of prosperity instilled complacency and deference into the relationships executives and directors had with the CEO, J.L. Ketelsen. He was an articulate, astute, politically skilled executive who had led the firm through a decade of extraordinary growth. Under his guidance, Tenneco's revenues tripled to $15 billion, equity tripled to $5.5 billion, and earnings quadrupled. He had been CEO of J.I. Case, Tenneco's farm and construction implement business, before becoming CFO and then CEO of Tenneco. Many of the strategies he advocated – diversification, debt leveraging and strategic acquisitions – were based on reputable management theory and were, on their face, effective ways to grow the company. He was also Chairman of the Board of Directors, and he used this position to control the board's agenda and information and the nomination and retention of directors. In meetings, directors routinely expressed complete confidence in the CEO's judgment. They occasionally asked question for clarification, but there was an implicit understanding that any reservations they expressed were suggestions that the CEO could accept or reject.

Tenneco generated billions of dollars of "slack" during the height of its prosperity. "Slack" is a term for excess resources above those needed to operate efficiently. Financial slack consist of surplus cash flow, large cash reserves, unused bank credit, unused debt capacity, and the ability to sell additional equity.

TENNECO TODAY

From its roots in the energy business, the Tenneco empire grew over the years into one of the largest multi-faceted conglomerates in the world. Working principally through acquisitions, the Tenneco portfolio grew initially to include Tenneco Chemicals and the Packaging Corporation of America. Between September 1950 and March 1966, Tennessee Gas had acquired 22 companies.

In addition to oil and gas properties, the 1967 purchase of Kern County Land Company included agricultural interests, the J.I. Case manufacturer of farm and construction machinery, and Walker Manufacturing, which produced automotive exhaust systems.

In September 1968, Tenneco Virginia purchased the nation's largest privately-owned shipyard, the Newport News Shipbuilding

Slack seemed to increase Tenneco's management's complacency and inclination to take risks. Under pressure to invest in riskier projects to increase earnings, management assumed that slack, mainly generated by the energy business, would cushion failures. For example, Tenneco entered and exited the insurance business at a significant loss. Ultimately, management made several decisions that, combined with each other and with adverse external events, pushed the company to the brink of bankruptcy.

J.I Case, Tenneco's largest and most problematic manufacturing business, had, by 1983, grown to $1.8 billion in revenues with $2 billion in assets, mainly through acquisitions. But it had been losing money or breaking even for years.

J.I Case had a 10 percent market share, below average products, weak distribution, and high production costs. John Deere, the industry leader, had a 30 percent market share. It had the highest quality products and the strongest dealer network. Deere dominated the emerging large-machine segment with a 45 percent market share. International Harvester (IH) was second with a 20 percent market share. Farm equipment was a declining, low-profit industry with high excess capacity and dominated by Deere, an extremely strong competitor. The industry outlook was bleak. The top four companies had already lost $5 billion. Demand had dropped 60 percent as thousands of small farmers, hammered by low commodity prices, were going out of business. The surviving efficient, large farmers demanded fewer, more powerful, technically advanced machines requiring billions of dollars to develop. Capacity utilization was so low that Deere alone had enough unused capacity to fill the industry's entire demand.

Rational analysis would indicate that management should have downsized Case or exit the industry. Management understood this but was unwilling to absorb the financial loss of downsizing or selling at a distressed price. A more rational course would have been to follow Jack Welch's dictum: "If you don't have a competitive advantage, don't compete."

Management needs to be especially wary when opportunism and optimism override rational analysis. Merging the number two and three firms in an industry is a strategic management maneuver that has occasionally worked. But in this case, demand had fallen so low that even International Harvester (IH), the second ranking firm, was on the verge of bankruptcy. Counting on earnings from its energy business, Tenneco management concluded that acquiring IH would revive J.I Case. An energy executive opposed the decision, arguing that acquiring IH would be "doubling down" – that is, doubling the bet on a losing proposition – but he was overridden.

Management argued that the Case-IH combination would be a formidable competitor with a market share of 30 percent, high product quality, a strong distribution network, and reduced production costs. The CEO optimistically projected that farm-equipment demand had reached bottom and would shortly improve. He argued that Tenneco should acquire IH before someone else did. CEO and management's confident estimates persuaded the board, composed of four inside directors and seven independent directors, to approve the acquisition of IH, despite the misgivings of several directors. One of the concerned directors quipped sarcastically, "You don't mate two mutts to breed a greyhound." The acquisition was completed in early 1985 and the CEO predicted that by the end of 1985 the combined Case-IH would be operating efficiently and profitably.

Contrary to management's predictions, however, Case-IH did not achieve its projected synergies and it lost half a billion dollars in the three years following the IH acquisition. The reasons for the shortfalls were; First, the market synergies did not materialize. Deere moved aggressively and increased its market share to 40 percent. Case-IH combined captured only a 20 percent share, rather than the 30 percent share management estimated it would get when it justified acquiring IH.

Second, product synergy failed. Surveys showed that Case machines ranked among the lowest in reliability and buyers avoided Case-IH products that did not have Harvester engines. Case kept cutting prices but continued to lose market share.

Third, cost reduction synergies were slow to materialize. Combining Case and IH product lines, manufacturing facilities, R&D, warehouses, dealer networks, and accounting systems took longer and cost more than projected.

Fourth, the industry continued to be extremely unattractive. Demand fell another 40 percent in the three years after the IH acquisition

Tenneco's acquisition of IH in the hope of reviving Case was an irreversible decision. Case-IH became a millstone around Tenneco's neck that put the entire enterprise at risk.

Tenneco originated as a regulated utility, with long-term depreciating physical asset – the pipeline – and a monopoly position. Tenneco was guaranteed capital recovery and a return on capital by regulatory agencies, so high debt made sense at the time. However, management continued the high-debt policy as Tenneco expanded into the commodity-oil and cyclical-manufacturing businesses. Debt, which allowed interest to be charged off as an expense, lowered the overall cost of capital. With the goal of maximizing profits, management made debt a major component of Tenneco's capital structure, keeping it close to 50 percent of total capital.

By 1987, Tenneco's long- and short-term debt, including off-the-books debt, rose to $11.5 billion and its ratio of debt to total capital soared to 75 percent. There was $3 of debt for each $1 of equity for a D/E ratio of three. Unearned-dividend payouts had siphoned away equity, earnings continued to decline as the price of oil dropped, and mandated accounting changes would put off-the-books debt on to Tenneco's balance sheet within one year.

Tenneco had historically paid uninterrupted, generous dividends, thus

& Drydock Company which was engaged in the construction of nuclear-powered submarines and aircraft carriers.

Between 1968 and 1976, Tenneco acquired an additional 13 companies, including the British chemical company Albright & Wilson Ltd., and consolidated its ownership of J.I. Case. The automotive parts division added AB Starlawerken of Sweden in 1974, Monroe Auto Equipment in 1977, and Lydex, a Danish company, in 1978. Tenneco started to purchase insurance companies in 1978, including Philadelphia Life and Southwestern Life Insurance.

In 1984, the Tenneco Packaging Corporation of America acquired Ecko Housewares and Ecko Products, and in 1985, Tenneco purchased the farm machinery division of International Harvester, combining these operations with its Case subsidiary.

Significant divestitures began in 1986 and included the sale of all its precious metals operations, the agricultural operations of Tenneco West, Tenneco Oil Company, and the retail muffler shops of Tenneco Automotive. Throughout the later 1980s, and the 1990s sales and spin-offs were the primary strategies.

Today the company is a manufacturing-based business focusing primarily on 'clean-air' and 'clean-ride' products for the automotive and commercial vehicle market.

giving it stock and image of reliable, stability. The CEO and the board faced a critical dividend-policy decision, near the time of the IH acquisition, when Tenneco's net income fell to $460 million in 1983; continuing the generous dividend policy would consume the firm's net income. The CEO persuaded the board to maintain the dividend policy and increase the dividend rate. Doing so, management argued, would sustain investor confidence and signal an expected increase in earnings.

Contrary to the CEO's projections, however, future earnings did not cover dividends. Tenneco paid out unearned cumulative dividends of $1.8 billion for five years, decreasing equity by 30 percent. Then in 1987, an unanticipated crisis occurred when earnings fell $200 million short of covering interest charges of almost a billion dollars. Tenneco was about to default. In theory, diversification was supposed to prevent such an emergency but it didn't. In fact, all Tenneco's businesses declined together.

Tenneco's management underestimated the dangers of certain risk assumptions – that is, its dependence on volatile energy-business earnings. The key assumption was that energy earnings would prop up the enterprise by cushioning failed ventures such as the acquisition of International Harvester, offset manufacturing business losses, cover interest charges, and pay dividends. When energy earnings plummeted, management faced a financial meltdown. Tenneco Oil Company was a commodity business with earnings highly sensitive to oil and gas prices. In the early 1980s, with a price of $27/barrel for oil, TOC earned more than $1 billion. By the mid-1980s, prices declined to $22/bbl, a drop of 19 percent, and TOC's earnings dropped 55 percent to $453 million. Then oil prices plunged to $12/bbl and TOC's earnings practically vanished. If TOC had been a stand-alone enterprise, it very likely would have weathered the decline. But through acquisitions Tenneco had become a multi-business enterprise and now it had lost the energy business earnings that supported its multiple investment, debt, and dividend decisions.

Management had known for several years, from regulatory agency hearings and notices, that the pipeline would be deregulated beginning in 1985. Tennessee Gas Transmission's pipeline earnings would be vulnerable to market prices and competition, like any unregulated business. Deregulation changed the pipeline from a gas merchant to a common carrier. It now had to transport gas for anyone, instead of buying, selling, and transporting only its own gas. End users began buying low-price spot gas directly from producers and called on TGT only to transport the gas, and so the pipeline's earnings fell.

Worse, gas prices declined in tandem with oil prices and TGT faced a substantial take-or-pay liability of $2 billion. In settling its disputes with gas producers, TGT took a charge $600 million against earnings. The combination of deregulation and contractual liabilities caused TGT's earning to drop to $100 million, a decline of 75 percent.

Tenneco's management did not have a risk-crisis plan that would serve to deal with such a scenario of multiple calamities occurring simultaneously in all facets of the business. Therefore it was very painful and difficult to anticipate what would happen if it had to sell some or all of its most valuable assets to obtain the funds to reduce debt. Under the pressure of imminent bankruptcy, management evaluated five options for quickly reducing debt:

Sell the Case-IH farm-equipment business. Management rejected this option on the grounds that the sale would incur a loss of billions of dollars. It was also doubtful that a buyer could be found courageous enough to enter the depressed agricultural market. The CEO still insisted that demand would recover and Case-IH would be profitable.

Sell one or more of the non-core manufacturing businesses. Management concluded that selling shipbuilding, automotive, and packaging units would not reduce debt sufficiently to resolve the crisis.

Sell the TGT gas-pipeline business. This option was rejected because quick sale of the TGT pipeline business was not feasible. Before it could be sold, management would have to go through years of negotiation with hundreds of creditors to restructure and simplify it complex mountain of debt.

Spin off Tenneco Oil Company and sell 20 percent of its stock to the public. This option would have been attractive but the drop in oil prices had depressed the price of energy stock. Selling stock would get a fraction of TOC's value and would not sufficiently reduce Tenneco's debt.

Sell all the assets of Tenneco Oil Company. This was the option management advocated. Management divided TOC's oil and gas reserves, properties, and leases into several geographic packages and auctioned them to the highest bidders. After the auction, management shut down TOC, Tenneco's crown jewel, and discharged its workforce of several thousand.

The sale of TOC brought in $6.5 billion and relieved the debt crisis, for the time being. Management used $5 billion to reduce debt from $12 billion to $7 billion, which saved $500 million a year in interest. Management also paid its generous dividend of $450 million. The board agreed to pay the dividend to mollify institutional investors and corporate raiders threatening a takeover.

The corporation entered a paradoxical strategic twilight zone after selling TOC. Case-IH, formerly Tenneco's weakest, most problematic business, became its dominant business. Tenneco, once a vibrant energy company, had become a manufacturing company that incidentally owned a pipeline. Case-IH assets of $6 billion were twice those of the pipeline and larger than all Tenneco's other manufacturing businesses combined.

Risky decisions had changed Tenneco strategically and swept it into another industrial area. Management still faced the question of Case-IH's long-term viability. When, if ever, would Case-IH prosper without support from Tenneco's other businesses?

The board now felt obligated to rally around the CEO's efforts to make Tenneco a profitable manufacturing company. The CEO had argued that manufacturing was a cyclical business and it would take three to four years, a full business cycle, to reap benefits, but one had to prepare during the downturn for the upturn. The CEO was optimistic about the outlook for the farm-equipment business for 1988 and thereafter. Although Case-IH revenues were $4.5 billion in 1988, its loss of $142 million was still a drag on corporate earnings.

Tenneco was still vulnerable and now it had even less capacity to absorb a flawed decision or a recession. Long and short-term debt ballooned to $9.8 billion on a $3.4 billion of equity for a debt to total capital ratio of 74 percent and interest expense climbed to $1 billion by the end of 1990. Interest, taxes, and dividends consumed practically all of Tenneco's operating income.

The US economy contracted when Iraq invaded Kuwait and the US prepared for the Gulf War in 1990. Demand for agricultural equipment dropped, but Case kept shipping products, swamping dealers with a year's sales in inventory. Deere, on the other hand, cut production and entered 1991 with an inventory of only three months sales.

Tenneco's manufacturing businesses and pipeline were still carrying Case-IH. In 1990, they earned $1.2 billion on assets of #8.7 for a ROA of 13.8 percent whereas Case-IH earned $247 million on equal assets of $8.7 billion for an ROA of 2.8 percent. Cumulatively, despite management's best efforts over the prior four years, Case had lost $11 million. Case's weak competitive position had not changed. With one year's sales in inventory, Case would incur substantial losses in 1991 as it would have to cut prices drastically to clear those inventories.

Tenneco's CEO was replaced in 1991 after a disaffected subgroup of outside directors began private discussions. They had to persuade other directors who considered it extremely disloyal to meet with the CEO-Chairman. Finally, the board decided that it wanted a new, outside CEO unencumbered by past decisions or loyalty to any employees. A major stumbling block for directors was how to maintain effective management during the transition. The board, after difficult, confrontational negotiations, arranged a six-month transition period with the incumbent CEO. After this transition, the two succeeding CEOs spent the next ten years dismantling Tenneco. First, Case-IH was drastically downsized and spun off and, in the mid-1990s, the pipeline was merged into El Paso Natural Gas Company. The packaging business was spun off at the end of the 1990s. The dismantling process was completed by 2001 when its auto equipment company, the last remaining business, was renamed Tenneco Automotive Inc. and traded on the New York Stock Exchange in place of the once formidable Tenneco corporation.

FINAL WORD

To A Close – the Last Chapter

And so it was over. By the end of 1996, the last of the energy businesses at Tenneco had disappeared. In the years that followed, much would be written and discussed about the demise of these three great companies, Tennessee Gas and Tenneco Oil, both "E&P", and "P&M". Much of that writing would focus on the judgments that were made, the business decisions, that determined the ultimate fate of those three. Much debate would analyze the relative wisdom of those decisions. Plenty had been written about the demise. We did not think enough had been written about the details, the day to day hard work, wise decisions, and good fortune that brought the entities to the point of having such value.

This has been a long story. There was much to tell. The "committee" who brought it together hopes some good memories have been recalled by reading it. Maybe some – maybe many - other old stories have come to mind, and maybe some fond and comfortable smiles have found their way onto the reader's face have been the result. We hope so. That was part of the intent. But, there was a larger mission.

The truth is, that many of those working in the Tenneco Energy companies realized at the time, that they had signed on with a 'good bunch'. But for many, the true magnitude of that experience was not fully appreciated until years later. Subsequent jobs were compared to the days at Tenneco, often wishfully so. Those working at Tenneco were so busy doing a good job, that they hardly stopped to think about just 'where' we were or just 'what' we were creating. We really were so busy that we did not realize how unique it all was. We knew we had good people, but the degree to which the "Tenneco Crew" went forward and populated the energy industry in the years following the sales is truly astounding. The Energy Companies of Tenneco were special, exceptionally so. This book was an attempt to not only reinforce that point, but indeed to celebrate it! It was intended as a tribute to the many fine people who helped make it special.

Tennessee Gas, the original, lived a life of 53 years - from 1943 to 1996 – 66 years if you count the 13 or so before the founding during which it was trying to get off the ground. That's a period of time that might be compared to a person's lifetime, but one that for some reason was cut short. From birth, through growth, into maturity, and eventually towards wisdom, the metaphor can be drawn. The ending though, did not come with the grace of a comfortable old age with a decline to some fitting and calming conclusion. It was rather a sudden and drastic event, or series of events. It was a tragedy. So be it. It was a life well-lived, and one that left many legacies. Most of them have faces and names.

Harry J. Briscoe